LEARNING

A. Charles Catania

University of Maryland Baltimore County

LEARNING

Third Edition

Prentice Hall, Englewood Cliffs, New Jersey 07632

Library of Congress Cataloging-in-Publication Data
Catania, A. Charles
  Learning / A. Charles Catania.—3rd ed.
    p.   cm.
  Includes bibliographical references and index.
  ISBN 0-13-528662-X
    1. Learning, Psychology of.   2. Conditioned response.
  3. Psychology, Comparative.   I. Title.
  BF318.C37   1992
  153.1′5—dc20   91-26354
                                                       CIP

Editorial/production supervision, interior design,
  and page makeup: *June Sanns*
Acquisitions editor: *Susan Finnemore Brennan*
Copy editor: *Jim Tully*
Cover designer: *Barbara Singer*
Prepress buyer: *Kelly Behr*
Manufacturing buyer: *Mary Ann Gloriande*
Editorial assistant: *Jennie Katsaros*
Supplements editor: *Sharon Chambliss*

©1992 by Prentice-Hall, Inc.
A Simon & Schuster Company
Englewood Cliffs, New Jersey 07632

Printed in the United States of America

10 9 8 7 6 5 4 3 2 1

ISBN 0-13-528662-X

PRENTICE-HALL INTERNATIONAL (UK) LIMITED, *London*
PRENTICE-HALL OF AUSTRALIA PTY. LIMITED, *Sydney*
PRENTICE-HALL CANADA INC., *Toronto*
PRENTICE-HALL HISPANOAMERICANA, S.A., *Mexico*
PRENTICE-HALL OF INDIA PRIVATE LIMITED, *New Delhi*
PRENTICE-HALL OF JAPAN, INC., *Tokyo*
SIMON & SCHUSTER ASIA PTE. LTD., *Singapore*
EDITORA PRENTICE-HALL DO BRASIL LTDA., *Rio de Janeiro*

To Connie, to Bill, and to Ken

Contents

Preface

A little learning is a dang'rous thing;

Drink deep, or taste not....

—Alexander Pope

Learning is central to the problems of psychology. To ask what an organism can learn is to ask how much of what it does depends on its evolutionary history, and how much depends on what it has experienced during its own lifetime. Studies of learning have ranged from relatively simple animal procedures to the complexities of human language and problem solving. Research in these areas is so different and the literatures are so extensive that the temptation is great to restrict attention solely to issues of animal behavior and learning, or solely to issues of human learning and memory. Many texts in learning yield to this temptation. In turn, the study of learning has become more and more divided, with each approach developing its own languages and research methodologies.

In this book, part of my purpose has been to bring these literatures together and to explore some of the continuities between human learning and the learning of other organisms. Humans are undoubtedly unique, but they share an evolutionary heritage with other species. The properties of nonhuman learning are therefore likely to be relevant to learning in humans. If we only show that some types of human learning are not reducible to types of learning known to occur with other organisms, we have at least begun to define what is peculiarly human.

This book surveys the major areas in the psychology of learning from a consistent behavioral point of view. I will not attempt to outline the nature of a behavioral orientation here. That view has evolved considerably from its parochial origins and is better treated in the context of specific psychological issues (some will be taken up later in the text). I will only note that taking a behavioral position does not exclude aspects of human behaving such as thinking and feeling and imagining. For those who like to think in terms of scientific paradigms and paradigm shifts, this text illustrates a new behavioral paradigm that has emerged among behavior analysts over recent years; this paradigm encompasses all of the phenomena of behavior. Thus, topics often regarded as the province of contemporary cognitive psychology will be treated here along with those more traditionally regarded as behavioral.

In its overall structure, this book has three major parts (II through IV) framed by an introduction (I) and a conclusion (V).

Part II deals with behavior without learning, and does so in an evolutionary context. Part III (Chapters 4 through 10) covers learning without words; in so doing, it surveys basic topics in nonhuman behavior and learning. Part IV (Chapters 11 through 15) covers learning with words; in so doing, it examines human learning and memory. These parts are in some places fairly independent, but more often the concepts developed earlier are prerequisites for the treatment of more complex issues later. I have made a special effort to include examples of human behavior in discussing the relevance of nonhuman studies of learning, and to refer to appropriate concepts from nonhuman behavior in discussing human learning and memory. The choices were to some extent dictated by the logic of the subject matter and by the availability of appropriate cases in the relevant research literature.

Students often miss the use of human behavior to illustrate the significance of findings from nonhuman research. For example, one multiple-choice exam question I used for several semesters asked how many instances of human behavior were mentioned through Chapters 4 or 5 of the prior editions of this text (these corresponded to the present Chapters 5 or 6). The four choices were: (a) none; (b) fewer than 10; (c) about 20; (d) more than 40. By actual count, there were more than 50 human examples through those chapters of both the first and second editions of the text, but the modal answer was typically a or b; students who challenged d as the correct answer sometimes found it instructive to check the number of human examples for themselves.

Further information on students' responses to questions based on the text is available in a test-item file that includes a variety of multiple-choice and true-false items keyed to chapters; adopters can obtain copies of the *Instructor's Test-Item File* from the publisher. Another supplement to the text is a set of computer programs, *Behavior on a Disk,* including simulations of shaping and other behavioral processes, experiments in memory and verbal learning, and vocabulary review exercises. The programs are available in 3.5-inch and 5.25-inch disk formats for IBM and compatible computers, from CMS Software, P. O. Box 1514, Columbia, MD 21044-0514.

Like the previous editions, this third edition of *Learning* includes some etymological notes at the beginning of each chapter. These capsule word histories are important reminders of how easily our language changes. Consistencies in vocabulary are essential to technical treatments, but the language must also grow and adapt to new findings and new perspectives. We must use our language of behavior with care, but perhaps we will be less likely to become rigid about it if we know something of its origins.

This edition also adds a Glossary to provide a convenient summary of the major terminology of the field and a helpful organizer for study and review. The preparation of a Glossary forces an author to attend to potential contradictions and ambiguities in basic concepts, and it may serve that function for the reader as well. The Glossary includes an introduction with some comments on its scope and its special features. In the Reference section, entries are keyed to the pages on which they are cited in the text; they have been chosen as useful starting points for further research in learning as well as for documenting specific points.

To study learning, one should know what learning is. Chapter 1 begins with the problem of defining learning (but does not solve the problem). The remainder of the chapter is organizational, providing an outline of topics treated in detail in Chapters 3 through 9. Chapter 2, a new chapter, deals with selection as a core concept for what follows and provides some background on evolution. Chapter 3 examines the reflex and other relations generated when stimuli are presented to an organism. Other texts typically introduce conditioning at this point, but within the present organization that topic is more effectively deferred until later.

Chapters 4 and 5, on reinforcement and on aversive control, show how the consequences of responding can affect behavior. These topics raise the issue of classes of responses and classes of stimuli as behavioral units. They therefore lead to the concept of the operant in Chapter 6, and the concept of the discriminated operant in Chapter 7. Some implications of these concepts are illustrated in Chapter 8, which examines how complex behavior can be synthesized within the context of reinforcement schedules. Chapter 9 then takes up conditioning and shows it is related to processes discussed in earlier chapters. Chapter 10 on social learning, another new chapter, provides a transition to that eminently social outgrowth of human behavior—verbal behavior.

In its treatment of language, Chapter 11 introduces the complexities of human verbal behavior. Some features of behavioral and cognitive approaches are explicitly compared in Chapter 12, on psycholinguistics. These two chapters set the stage for an examination of verbal learning and transfer in Chapter 13, and of memory in Chapter 14. Cognition and problem solving, the focus of Chapter 15, present an opportunity for synthesis, because they bring together topics considered separately at various points throughout the text. The final chapter is an overview and an integration of some major issues in the psychology of learning.

In addition to the treatment of selection and social learning in the new chapters, many topics have been given expanded or revised coverage. A few of these are animal cognition; sequential responding; motor plans; cognitive maps; generalized imitation; optimal foraging; equivalence classes; discrimination of one's own behavior; autoclitic processes; rule-governed behavior; simulation; animal language; coding in memory; and metaphor and other phenomena of human language. Continuity between the nonhuman learning and conditioning chapters and the human learning and memory chapters has also been enhanced.

Throughout its history, the psychology of learning has been concerned with theories. Particular learning theories were developed, elaborated, and then displaced by others. Many remain with us, typically more restricted in their scope than when they were first introduced. Whatever their current status, the data that gave rise to these theories are still to be dealt with. For that reason, this text emphasizes research findings rather than learning theories. It is theoretical mainly in that it adheres to a consistent behavioral language and attempts a systematic organization that accommodates the various procedures and processes of learning. Although theory is not emphasized, I have tried to include enough information about experimental procedures, terminology, and data to provide an effective starting point for the student, instructor, or general reader who wishes to pursue particular theories. The emphasis of the book is not so much on the interpretation of particular findings as on the relations among the varied phenomena included within the psychology of learning. My intent has been to make this book, *Learning*, useful not only to those who are already behaviorally inclined, but also to those who are decidedly not of the behavioral persuasion.

This book has been an effort of some years. Its content grew over successive offerings of an introductory lecture course in the Psychology of Learning, first at the University College of Arts and Science of New York University and then at the University of Maryland Baltimore County. I am indebted to my students and colleagues at both campuses, and especially to Eliot H. Shimoff. As my teachers and my colleagues, numerous others contributed by their comments, discussions, and encouragement. As in the earlier editions, I name only a few, mainly because I can still identify particular contributions of each: Peter Balsam, David Carlson, William J. Catania, Leonard Cook, Willard F. Day, Israel Goldiamond, Lewis R. Gollub, Stevan Harnad, Eliot Hearst, Ralph F. Hefferline, Philip N. Hineline, Herbert M. Jenkins, Victor G. Laties, Byron A. Matthews, J. A. Nevin, Koichi Ono, Robert R. Provine, George S. Reynolds, Terje Sagvolden, B. F. Skinner, Deisy de Souza, William C. Stebbins, S. S. Stevens, Mark Sundberg, and Vicci Tucci. In such a listing, omissions are inevitable; fortunately, the contributions of many of the others are acknowledged by their inclusion among the references. I wish also to express my appreciation for the invaluable help of Madelon Kellough, Terri Harold, and Mary Johnston in preparation of the manuscript, of Jack Burton for encouragement, and of Susan Finnemore Brennan and June Sanns in guiding the book through its successive stages from conception to publication.

Above all, and as in past editions, one further acknowledgment remains. I owe more than I can say to Fred S. Keller and W. N. Schoenfeld. Their courses and their *Principles of Psychology* introduced me to the analysis of behavior. I hope that this book is true enough to their teaching and their writing that they will recognize something of themselves in its pages.

A. Charles Catania
Columbia, Maryland

LEARNING

PART I *Introduction*

CHAPTER 1
Learning and Behavior

The English word learning *probably comes from an Indo-European root,* leis-, *which meant a track or furrow. Before reaching its present form, it went through many changes:* læstan, leornian, lernen. *At various times in the evolution of our language it might have been understood as following a track, continuing, coming to know, or perhaps even getting into a rut. The verb* last, *to endure, came from the same root.*

The word behavior, *like* habit, inhibit, *and* ability, *is related to the Latin* habere, *to hold or have. The prefix* be- *became attached in such words as the Old English* behabban. *As a word for how one held oneself, it was closer to the sense of comportment or demeanor than to the more contemporary sense of activity, just as* habit *was once more commonly what was worn than what was habitually done.*

Suppose you had never seen or heard the word *phenomenon*. After noticing it in a few sentences, you might decide from its context that it means something like a thing that happens or an event worth noticing. At that point you could look it up in a dictionary, which might define it as an event that can be observed; a secondary entry might define it as a remarkable or unusual person or thing. The dictionary would probably show that the word is a singular noun and its plural is *phenomena*. Even after reading the definition, you might hardly ever use the word yourself. Still, you would have learned something about it that could be useful the next time you encounter it.

But what about the definition of the subject matter of this text? What is this phenomenon called *learning*? The word gives us no trouble in everyday conversation, but a dictionary definition that tells us it means getting to know something or gaining knowledge and skill is not very helpful. The word *learning* is much more familiar than *phenomenon* and yet it is much harder to define. We can usually say whether we have learned something and we can usually agree on what counts as learning. Even so, we run into problems when we try to frame a definition.

For example, a textbook might define learning as a relatively permanent change in behavior resulting from experience (cf. Kimble, 1961, pp. 1–13). But what is meant by "behavior" or by "experience," and

1

how permanent is "relatively permanent"? Staring at an eclipse of the sun is an experience, and if it damages your eyes it will certainly change your behavior. Yet if someone claimed that this damage was an example of learning we would probably disagree.

Section A   The Language of Learning and Behavior

This text is about learning, but from the outset we must face the fact that we will not be able to define it. There are no satisfactory definitions of learning. Even so, we can study it. We do so whenever we look at how organisms come to behave in new ways. In our study of learning, we will ask two types of questions: first, what is the nature of these events we call learning, and second, what is the best way to talk about them?

Consider words like *learning* or *knowledge*. They seem obvious and important. But often we fail to notice that they function in different ways in different contexts, and that can cause confusion. For example, sometimes we speak of learning about something; at other times we speak of learning how to do something. Someone who has learned how an automobile works may not know how to drive one; conversely, someone who has learned to drive a car may not be able to say how it works.

Some kinds of learning involve words; others involve deeds. Should we treat these two kinds of learning together or separately? Philosophers are concerned with this type of distinction when they debate the difference between "knowing how" and "knowing that" (e.g., Ryle, 1949). Psychologists sometimes make the distinction by speaking of *declarative knowledge* and *procedural knowledge*. The distinction is so fundamental that, as the table of contents shows, this book is divided into two major parts, one concerned with learning that does not involve words and the other with learning that does.

If *learning* could be defined in a sentence or two, we would have no problem. We would define the word and then discuss the conditions under which learning takes place, the kinds of things that are learned, the ways in which different instances of learning can be combined, the limitations of learning, and so on. But learning means different things at different times to different people.

Consider some examples. A pigeon discovers food in its travels, and returns to that place later when it is hungry. A child becomes able to read a story or to spell simple words. A dog is taught to sit or lie down on command. A patient who once had a bad experience in a dentist's office consistently feels uneasy in the waiting room. A young cat, after its early hunting expeditions, comes to avoid skunks and porcupines. A student, after reading a chapter in a mathematics textbook, finds a way to solve a problem that once was baffling. A shopper sees an announcement for a sale that has not yet begun, and several days later returns to the store to take advantage of the bargain prices. An author who encounters an unfamiliar word later uses it in a short story.

What do these examples have in common? They involve dogs and cats, children and adults, and we would probably agree that they are all instances of learning. But is it reasonable to group together a pigeon who learns a route to food and a student who discovers a solution to a mathematical problem?

Someone might suggest that we could resolve our problem of definition by adding that learning had to come about through some change in the brain. But do we ever look at an organism's brain to decide whether it has learned something? We all have learned to say when we or others have learned something, but how many of us have ever seen a brain do anything? Even if we could watch a brain do something, how would we know that what it was doing was learning?

This is not to say that learning has no physiological basis. It would be fascinating to know what physiological changes accompany learning. Yet we might have trouble figuring out what to look for in the nervous system if we cannot even say what learning is. In fact, we cannot have an adequate physiology of learning without an adequate understanding of the behavioral properties of learning. Those properties determine the sorts of things that neurophysiologists who are interested in learning must look for in the nervous system. That is why our main concern will be with the behavioral properties of learning rather than with its physiological basis.

The issues so far have hardly been about the facts of learning; they have been mainly about our language. Languages are changeable; their vocabularies reflect what is currently important to their speakers. One trouble is that the language that has evolved in our everyday interactions with others is not necessarily well suited for a language of learning (that is one reason for the etymologies, or word histories, included at the beginning of each chapter).

We are usually more interested in what other people know and in what they are likely to do than in how they came to be that way. For example, a parent might be concerned if a child consistently fights with other children instead of playing cooperatively. But once the child had learned to play cooperatively, the parent might not care whether the child came to be that way because of the natural rewards of cooperative play or because cooperative play was explicitly taught or because the fighting and other alternatives to play were punished.

Our language for describing what people do is useful. It is important to know what to expect of others. Thus, we describe people in terms of how they are likely to behave. We speak of each other as outgoing or reserved, easygoing or compulsive, trustworthy or unreliable. Describing people with words like *artistic, athletic, social, intellectual,* or *musical* specifies their preferred activities. This kind of vocabulary, however, is not suitable for discussing how particular interests or traits developed in an individual.

Consider another example. There is an important difference between lying and telling the truth. But if one child has learned to keep out of trouble by telling lies and another by telling the truth, we would not be surprised if the first child grows up to be less truthful than the second. Yet the behavior of each child is shaped by its consequences; each child behaves so as to keep out of trouble. This shaping of behavior should concern us, but our everyday vocabulary does not equip us well for discussing it.

Similar problems exist in fields other than psychology. When physicists look at events in the world, they do not find the everyday vocabulary adequate. They coin new terms or take over existing ones. The latter course can create difficulties. Words like *work, force,* and *energy,* for example, mean different things to physicists in their technical talk than they do to most other people in casual conversation. Fortunately for physicists, much of what they now study is far enough removed from our daily experience that we do not confuse their technical language with our ordinary discourse.

This is not so in psychology. We are all inescapably concerned with behavior. We speak of how people grow and change, we speculate about the reasons people have for doing things, and we ourselves learn new facts and acquire new skills. If we wish new ways of talking about these events, we must take care that the new language does not get confused with the old one. We all have spent most of our lives talking in certain ways about what we do, and these familiar ways of talking may interfere with any new ways of talking that we may try to establish. Some parts of this book will be concerned with establishing a behavioral language, and the language will not merely be a paraphrase of everyday usage; it will instead require some new ways of dealing with familiar phenomena or events.

THE WORLD AND THE LABORATORY

The problems of language are made even more difficult because we live in a complex world. The events that influence our behavior do not occur in isolation. Thus, to understand a situation we must strip away the unessential details and analyze it. To analyze something is simply to break it down into its component parts. For this purpose, we turn to the laboratory. We begin with the study of organisms simpler than ourselves, in simple environments. We must face the objection, of course, that a laboratory experiment is artificial and therefore may not be appropriate for establishing generalizations about learning outside of the laboratory. But we must start with simple events if we are to develop techniques and vocabularies with which to deal with complex ones.

The controlled laboratory environment enables us to look at one thing at a time.

We arrange circumstances so that we know what goes into an experimental situation; if we are careful, we can exclude the distractions that might otherwise obscure the processes we wish to study. The simplicity of our laboratory environment may also help us to see the varied features of learning more easily. We have to be able to identify events before we can study their properties. One place to start is to look at behavior that does not involve language, because it will probably be simpler than behavior that does involve language. The easiest way to do that is to look at the behavior of nonhuman organisms. What they tell us about behavior without words may later help us to appreciate what is special about behavior with words.

To illustrate the advantages of the laboratory, therefore, let us begin with the example of a pigeon that earns its food by pecking. The account is of interest because the outcome is not at all intuitively obvious. In itself, it is not a learning experiment, but it grew out of experiments on how organisms learn to order their behavior in time and its methodologies have proved useful in other studies.

Imagine a pigeon in an experimental chamber. The pigeon has been trained to earn food by pecking a key, a translucent disk recessed in the chamber wall (in recording pecks, this key operates much like a telegraph key). The key can be lit from behind to present visual stimuli to the pigeon. Currently the key is lit white. Our equipment is set so that every two-hundredth peck gives the pigeon brief access to food in a hopper below the key. We reached this point gradually, first by letting every peck produce food, and then only every fifth peck, and then only every tenth, and so on, until finally the pigeon was pecking 200 times for each food delivery.

In this situation, with only the food produced by pecking, the pigeon easily maintains an adequate daily ration. In fact, the pigeon eats its daily diet in as little as 4 or 5 minutes. If each food delivery lasts only 5 seconds (including the time to get from key to food hopper), the pigeon may be finished eating for the day after only 60 food deliveries. Even so, this pigeon must peck at least 12,000 times daily to earn this much food.

Technically, the requirement of 200 pecks per food delivery is called a fixed-ratio schedule of reinforcement: *fixed* because the required number is constant from one food delivery to the next, and *ratio* because the schedule specifies the ratio of pecks to food deliveries (in this case, 200 to 1). The pecks occur because they produce food; we therefore say they are *reinforced* by food. But we do not have to reinforce every peck to keep the pigeon pecking, and the schedule simply specifies how we choose the particular peck that will produce food. Reinforcement schedules will be considered in a later chapter, however, so let us return to the pigeon.

Food has just been presented, the hopper has moved out of the pigeon's reach, and the pigeon is standing before the white-lit key. Time passes, perhaps only 15 or 20 seconds or perhaps several minutes. Eventually the pigeon approaches the key and begins to peck. Within a few pecks, the pigeon is pecking as rapidly as 5 to 10 pecks per second and is not likely to pause as it completes its 200 pecks. The last of these pecks operates the food hopper. Because the pigeon pecks so rapidly, it may peck 2 or 3 times more before its stops and moves down to the hopper to eat. When the food is withdrawn, time again passes before the pigeon returns to the key and begins its next 200 pecks.

This is typical fixed-ratio performance: a pause after eating followed by rapid and uninterrupted pecking that ends with the next food delivery. The point is that this is easy to get the pigeon to do. Our pigeon will earn enough food daily to keep itself alive and healthy for an indefinite time (its life expectancy is roughly 15 years). If we kept it in its chamber 24 hours a day, we would not have to intervene except to provide water, clean the chamber, and keep the food hopper filled.

But pigeons cannot count very well, and we might wonder whether the pigeon is at a disadvantage each time it goes through its 200 pecks. Suppose we try to help it estimate how many pecks are left in the sequence by presenting different lights on the key depending on the number of pecks. Let us arrange that, after each food delivery, the key is blue until the pigeon has pecked 50 times. The fiftieth peck turns the key green. After 50 more pecks, the key turns yellow. Then, after 50 more, the key turns red. After 50 more pecks with the key now red, 200 pecks have accumulated and the last peck operates the food hopper. The pigeon eats, and the key is once again blue. The number of pecks required for food remains the same; only the lights on the key have changed. (The pigeon, by the way, can easily distinguish among these colors.)

With no distinctive stimuli, the pigeon worked well enough, earning an adequate daily ration. Have we helped the pigeon by providing the colors to tell it where it is in the sequence? The surprising effect of adding these stimuli is that the pigeon slows down. After food deliveries, when the key is blue, the pauses lengthen. When the pigeon finally begins to respond, the pecks that once came in rapid succession now occur sporadically. When the key turns green, after the fiftieth peck, the pigeon may even pause before starting the next 50-peck sequence. When the key had been always white, the pigeon did not pause after 50 pecks; the 200-peck sequence usually occurred without interruption. In green, another 50 pecks, and the key turns yellow. This time the pigeon is less likely to pause at all: 50 more pecks turn the key red, the pigeon now quickly completes the last 50 pecks, food is delivered and the pigeon eats. But then the key is blue again, and another long pause begins.

The added colors did not help. The pigeon takes much longer to earn each food delivery than it had when the key remained white. In fact, even though this pigeon had maintained an adequate diet at 200 pecks per food delivery when the key was always white, we would now be wise to watch it carefully to be sure its daily food intake does not decrease drastically. And this results not from any change in the pecks required for food but simply from a change in stimuli.

When we added the colors, we broke down the 200 pecks into four distinct units of 50 pecks each. We call these *chained* fixed-ratio schedules: the separate stimuli correspond to the links of the chain. But the chain does not hold the 200-peck sequence together more cohesively; instead, it breaks it up. When the key was always white, pecking at the start of the sequence was not so very different from pecking near the end, when a peck finally produced food. Once the stimuli were added, however, pecking in the presence of the early stimuli became less like pecking later. In blue, for example, pecks never produced food; at best they turned the key green, but pecks never produced food during this color either. With pecking reduced early in the chain, the time to complete each 200 pecks increased. In chained schedules, a stimulus supports less responding the further it is from the end of the sequence. Even severe deprivation of food is not sufficient to counteract this effect.

There are other ways to alter the pigeon's performance. For example, in-creasing the required pecks, to 300 or even 500 per food delivery, also slows down the pigeon, creating long pauses after reinforcement and frequent interruptions of pecking; this effect is called *ratio strain*. We could now go on to examine the phenomenon in more detail, separating those properties of the situation that mattered from those that did not. For the present purposes, however, the point is that the outcome is not obvious. It was discovered through an experimental analysis of behavior. It occurs with other organisms besides the pigeon, with different kinds of responses and different response requirements, and with different kinds and orderings of stimuli. Because it has substantial generality, we may wonder whether it is relevant to human behavior.

The things that people do, of course, depend on consequences more complex than food deliveries. Any account of human behavior must grapple with the fact that completing any sequential task, such as writing a paper, preparing a meal, or finishing a research project, is affected not only by its properties as a behavior sequence, but also by competing obligations and interests, delays between actions and outcomes, and any number of other factors. Nevertheless, so much of what we do involves sequential behavior that we must wonder whether we might sometimes operate under the strain of too many links in our chains. The ability to formulate and achieve long-range objectives is supposed to be a unique characteristic of the human species. But in the pigeon's behavior, adding even a single link to a chain can have devastating effects. Perhaps we ought not assume that human behavior is immune to such effects.

In any case, the example demonstrates that the laboratory may yield interesting phenomena even under relatively simple circumstances. The pigeon's chamber with its single key and its feeder may seem austere, and yet merely adding some colored lights produces effects with perhaps far-reaching implications. The controlled laboratory environment reveals properties of behavior to us that might otherwise have been hard to see, and it helps us to develop a language that is appropriate to this subject matter.

BEHAVIORAL AND COGNITIVE PSYCHOLOGIES

But what is our subject matter? Sometimes we speak about what people do; sometimes we speak about what they know. Even psychologists sometimes disagree on whether the subject matter of psychology is behavior or mind. On the one hand, what an organism does is the only thing accessible to us. There is nothing else for us to examine but behavior. A human in a learning experiment may describe thoughts or feelings, but these descriptions are still only behavior; verbal behavior may be special, but it is behavior nonetheless. No matter what the phenomena we study in psychology, our terminology and observations and theories must ultimately be derived from behavior, from what organisms do.

On the other hand, there is more to an organism than shows in its behavior. Two students may sit silently through a lecture, and yet it may be clear to the instructor that one is able to answer certain questions and solve certain problems while the other cannot. Although the students might be distinguished on the basis of past performances, it remains that they are not currently behaving differently. The difference is in what each potentially can do; we might say simply that one student knows more than the other. When we study this knowledge, it is tempting to say that we study the student's mind.

The debate between psychologists who call themselves behaviorists and those who call themselves mentalists or cognitivists has been long-standing. To some extent, it has been about appropriate ways of talking about psychological events. The behaviorist argues that, because behavior is all that is available to measure, the language of mental events misleads by calling attention away from this fundamental subject matter. The behaviorist is especially troubled when a mentalistic account is accepted as explanatory and therefore discourages further inquiry.

For example, we may sometimes say that an idea, a feeling, or a hunch led someone to do something. The behaviorist does not dispute the existence of ideas, feelings, and hunches, but rather criticizes their invocation as causes of behavior. It is too easy to be satisfied with an explanation in these terms; it is not enough to say that someone did something because of an idea, a feeling, or a hunch. Ideas, feelings, and hunches are about the world, and therefore must have their origins in our experiences with the world. We must look further, to these past experiences or, in other words, to past behavior, to account for what we do. If we are successful, we will at the same time have something to say about the origins of our ideas, feelings, and hunches. We will be able to say that these are names for certain things that happen to us when we deal with events in the world.

The cognitivist maintains that such a view is unnecessarily narrow. Processes must occur in our dealings with the world that are not observable in our behavior. When we try to recall a word that is "on the tip of our tongue" or try to solve a problem by "sleeping on it," things are happening that do not show directly in our behavior, and we may not even be able to report them. If we can find out something about such processes, it cannot help but be relevant to our study of learning.

The dispute between behaviorists and cognitivists involves ways of talking about behavior more often than it involves research findings. The difficulties persist because these two kinds of psychologists are usually interested in different types of questions. The behaviorist tends to deal with questions of function, and the cognitivist with questions of structure.

Suppose we are interested in teaching a child to read. On the one hand, we may become concerned with what we have to do to involve the child in reading. We worry about what will keep the child alert, what will make the child pay attention to the words presented, and what will help the child remember what the various words are. Will we be more successful if we reward the child for being correct or penalize the child for being wrong? When we arrange different consequences for different answers the child might give, we determine the functions of these various answers or, more precisely, the functional relations between behavior and its consequences.

On the other hand, no amount of concern with the effects of reward and punishment on the child's mastery of reading will tell us the most efficient way to present reading materials to the child. How is reading structured? What is the best way to order the materials? We might debate whether we should teach the child to read by starting with single letters, with syllables, or with whole words. When we present the materials to be learned in different orders, we are concerned with the effective structural relations within the subject matter. Are words unitary structures, or are they complex structures built up from simpler units, such as letters or syllables? Problems of structure are concerned with how behavior and the environment are organized.

Both problems are important. Any attempt to improve how children learn to read will be deficient if it ignores either of these concerns. Consider another example. Suppose we discovered that children who read from a text that is accompanied by pictures are more likely to attend to the pictures than the words. One of our problems would be functional and might lead us to ask whether we could improve the teaching of reading by putting words on one page and a relevant picture on the next. That might also help the teacher, who must judge whether a child has really read a word or has only guessed the word from the picture. We might even try to create a system of computer instruction in which the child gets to see the picture only as a consequence of correctly reading the words.

But another of our problems would be structural, because it would still be important to know which pictures should accompany which words and the order in which different reading materials should be presented. However good the computer-assisted instruction was in handling the relations among words and pictures and the child's responses, its effectiveness might well be undermined if we tried to teach difficult words before easy ones or irregular spellings before regular ones. A reading program to teach an alphabetic language such as English would probably be quite different from one to teach an ideographic language such as Chinese. Each program would have to take into account the structure of the spoken and written language being taught.

Historically, some of the controversies in psychology arose because those interested in functional problems tended to speak a behavioral language whereas those interested in structural problems tended to speak a mental or cognitive language. Behaviorists can study structural problems just as cognitivists can study functional ones. But the problems in which behaviorists and cognitivists were interested tended to be correlated with the words they used.

It is easy to see how this correlation may have come about. If one's experimental concern is functional, one studies the consequences of particular relations between specified environmental events and specified actions; these are conveniently expressed in the behavioral language of stimuli and responses. If one's experimental concern is structural, one studies the properties of particular capacities or abilities; these are conveniently expressed in the cognitive language of knowledge and mind. (A parallel distinction between structure and function, the separation of anatomy and physiology, occurred in the history of biology; see Catania, 1978, and Chapter 16 of this text.)

We need not be sidetracked by this controversy. We will consider both functional and structural problems in learning and will therefore examine both types of research. In either case, it will often be useful to describe situations in terms of *antecedents*, or the circumstances that set the occasion for behavior; the *behavior* that occurs in these circumstances; and the *consequences* of that behavior (these three terms are sometimes abbreviated as *ABC*). We can consider either *function*, the relations among the terms (e.g., given certain antecents, what consequences are produced by behavior) or *structure*, the properties of particular terms (e.g., what are the critical properties of certain antecedent conditions).

The orientation from which this text is written deals with both function and structure, and therefore encompasses both behavioral and cognitive concepts. These two psychological positions differ in their languages and in the research problems that they emphasize, but they have in common the reliance on experimental method, the anchoring of concepts to experimental manipulations and observations, and the assumption that our subject matter, however complex, is orderly and not capricious. Our concern is with what determines behavior. If we are worried about the misuse of our knowledge of behavior, we must recognize that we cannot eliminate a determinant of human behavior simply by choosing not to study it; in fact, we can best defend against the misuse of techniques for controlling human behavior if we understand how they work.

This does not imply that we expect to be able to interpret any instance of behavior. There are limits to what we can know. It is tempting to ask a psychologist to explain why someone behaved in a certain way, what led up to a certain incident, or how someone came to have certain interests, fears, or attachments. But the psychologist often has so little information available that only a plausible interpretation can be provided.

This situation does not differ except in degree from that in other sciences. Just as the principles of aerodynamics are not invalidated if we cannot account for every twist and turn in the path of a particular falling leaf, the principles of behavior are not invalidated if we cannot account for every detail of an organism's performance on a particular occasion. In our study of learning, it is important to recognize what remains out of our reach. In what follows, we will find that the most profitable course is one that stays close to the data; we will worry less about psychological theory than about properly describing our findings. For example, it will usually be more useful to describe what an organism has learned or remembered than to attempt to explain its learning or its memory.

ANTECEDENTS, BEHAVIOR, AND CONSEQUENCES

We turn now to behavior as a subject matter. The study of learning is about how behavior can be modified, so we must first consider what behavior is, how it can be investigated, and what vocabulary might best describe it. Behavior is no easier to define than learning. We may say glibly that behavior is anything an organism does. But this definition is too global. Should we count respiration or metabolism along with muscular movements and glandular secretions? We describe behavior with verbs: people walk, talk, think, do things. But although we may say that someone breathes, we are not likely to say that someone "heart-beats." We also distinguish between active and passive actions. People bleed when cut and fall when they lack support, but we may not wish to speak of such bleeding or falling as behavior.

Let us not try to resolve this problem. Our aim is to examine some properties of behavior. The phenomena of behavior are varied even though they sometimes share common names, so we shall probably do better by considering examples than by attempting definitions. We can deal with specific examples without much risk of misunderstanding. When we observe an organism, we see properties of its environment and properties of its behavior. We call these properties *stimuli* and *responses*, but neither a stimulus nor a response is of interest by itself (cf. Gibson, 1979). An experimental analysis determines what kinds of relations exist between stimuli and responses, and how these relations can come about. It must also consider broader contexts, the *situations* within which these relations between stimuli and responses are embedded.

For example, consider a food-deprived rat whose press on a lever immediately produces a small amount of food. It is one thing if the alternative, not pressing, is never followed by food; it is another if it is followed by a delayed but much larger quantity of food. In each case a response, the lever press, is followed by a stimulus, food. But the contexts are quite different. We would expect the rat to press the lever in the first case, but what about the second? If the rat did not press, we might be tempted to say it had exhibited self-control, forgoing the small amount of food it could have produced immediately for the larger amount it received later. We will discuss this type of situation in more detail in Chapter 8. For our present purposes, the point is that we must consider not only the moment-to-moment details of events but also their context over extended periods of time.

Now that we have considered the close relation between environment and behavior, let us illustrate it further by observing a human infant. We might like to begin by asking what the infant feels, but we would confront many complications if we did so. The infant is not yet verbal and so cannot tell us. Even if this were an older child who could tell us, we would have to wonder how the child learned the appropriate words and whether they would mean the same thing to us as to those in the culture that taught them to the child. When we get to language, in Chapter 11, we will examine the role it plays in molding our knowledge of ourselves and others, but it will not be helpful to us here.

We know the infant is active, learning from the environment and interacting with it. We can begin simply by observing. We watch for a time, and we notice movements of the hands or arms or legs. Perhaps at some point the infant begins to cry. If the crying stops without our intervention, the infant might sleep or might lie quietly with open eyes. If we look closely, we might see the infant's eyes moving, although it would be difficult to judge just what, if anything, the infant was looking at. We could begin to catalogue the various things that the infant did, and we might discover that particular movements usually occur in particular sequences. But if we only watched, we could not say much more than that certain movements occurred more or less often and more or less in a certain order.

We need not be restricted to watching. We might touch or rock the infant, move objects in or out of view, make sounds, or offer a nipple. We would expect the infant to respond to each event in a characteristic way. If a touch were to the infant's palm, for example, the infant would probably clench that fist, grasping the object that touched it. The vocabulary for these events is already familiar: we call the touch to the palm a *stimulus*, and the grasping a *response*.

In this case, we are not interested in the stimulus alone or in the response alone; we are interested in their relation to each other. We call this relation, the reliable production of a particular response by a particular stimulus, a *reflex*. We will consider reflexes in Chapter 3. The important point here is that the term *reflex* is simply a name for a behavioral relation: an observed correlation between a particular stimulus and a particular response (Skinner, 1931). It is neither a theory nor an explanation, and it is only one of many possible relations between behavior and environment.

Besides the production of grasping by a touch to the palm, we might wish to catalogue other examples of reflex relations: crying caused by a loud noise; sucking produced by a nipple in the mouth; blinking triggered by a flash of light. These are not the only kinds of relations possible, however. The environment acts on the infant when stimuli produce responses, but the infant can also act on the environment. Crying, for example, often brings attention from mother. Crying, then, is a response that can produce a consequence: the mother's presence. This relation involves stimuli and responses, but we cannot call it a reflex. For one thing, the stimuli and the responses do not occur in the appropriate order; more important, behavior had consequences.

The relations can become even more complicated. If the infant's eyes move while the lights are on, the eye movements change what the infant sees. Eye movements cannot have this effect when the lights are off. Thus, the infant may come to look about in the light but not in the dark. In the presence of one stimulus, the light, moving the eyes has consequences; it produces other stimuli, namely, new things seen. Eye movements cannot have this consequence in the dark. The relation involves three terms: a prior stimulus, the light; a response, eye movement, in the presence of this stimulus; and a consequence, what is newly seen given this response in the presence of this stimulus. This three-term relation, stimulus-response-consequence, is important because an organism's behavior depends both on the situations in which it finds itself and on the consequences of its responses in these situations; it is sometimes called a *three-term contingency*, and is another way of speaking of antecedents, behavior, and consequences.

An *antecedent* is simply something that comes before, and a *consequence* is simply what is caused by or what happens as a result of some event. Thus, everyday usage corresponds reasonably well to the technical senses of these terms in the analysis of behavior. It is important to note that consequences should not be identified with stimuli. Responses can have many types of consequences. They sometimes produce stimuli that would otherwise have been absent, but they can also prevent things from happening or change the consequences of other responses. For example, food produced by a response is both a stimulus and a consequence, but food that is presented independently of behavior is a stimulus only; shock that is prevented by a response is a stimulus, but the consequence of the response is the absence of shock, which is not a stimulus.

For *stimulus* and *response*, the relation between technical and everyday usages is not so simple. Stimuli are events in the world and responses are instances of behavior. The term *stimulus* is often restricted to specific physical events such as lights or sounds or touches. But organisms respond to varied features of the environment, including relations (e.g., to the left of, on top of), complex behavior (e.g., facial expressions, tones of voice), functional properties (e.g., edible, comfortable), and so on (cf. Gibson, 1979). We will often speak of such environmental features as stimuli, even though we may be unable to specify physical dimensions that characterize them.

The line between stimuli and responses is rarely ambiguous. Even so, special cases sometimes complicate our definitions. For example, what about stimuli that originate within the organism? Consider the difference between a loud noise and the pain of a toothache. Both are events in the world and each might function as an antecedent of behavior (the toothache might set the occasion for going to a dentist). They differ in that the noise is public and the toothache is private; in other words, the noise may be heard by more than one person whereas the toothache can be felt only by the person with the bad tooth. That would be a problem if we insisted that all stimuli had to be outside of the organism, but if

appropriate receptors exist we have no reason to exclude as stimuli the important parts of the world that are within the organism's skin.

As for the term *response*, everyday usage often implies that the response is to something (typically a stimulus). The term will not function that way here, however, because an account of what causes responses typically includes other factors (e.g., their past consequences, characteristics of the organism) along with the stimuli in the presence of which they occur. With these reservations noted, we now consider some other properties of stimuli and responses.

A stimulus is an event in the environment, but such events have varying degrees of complexity. In the example in which the infant's crying produced the mother's attention, we regarded the infant's mother as a stimulus. The infant's environment is certainly different when its mother is present than when she is absent. Yet what sort of stimulus is the mother? We do not know which aspects of her looks, her voice, or her touch are important to the infant early in life. We might wonder whether the infant would react to her any differently than usual if she approached wearing a surgical mask. Despite our ignorance with respect to these questions, we have no doubt that the mother is an important part of the infant's environment, and we may still find it useful to speak of the effects that she has as she comes and goes in the infant's world.

This example again illustrates the different problems of structure and function. When we try to analyze the visual, auditory, and tactile features of the mother that are important to the infant, we deal with the structure of this complex stimulus, the mother. We might ask how the infant learns to respond to a particular individual as mother despite changes in her dress or hair style, her facial expression or posture. But if we concentrate instead on how the mother interacts with the infant's responses, we are concerned with the functional significance of the mother in the infant's environment. For example, if an infant was crying, we might not care whether the infant recognized the mother by her face, her hair, or her voice as long as her presence made a difference; it would be enough to see that when she went to the infant the crying stopped.

Later, we will often be interested in simpler stimuli: lights, sounds, food in the mouth. But even with simpler stimuli we will have to distinguish between structural problems, as in analyzing stimulus properties, and functional problems, as in analyzing the interactions between stimuli and responses.

And what about responses? How shall we deal with them? In describing responses, we encounter at least two difficulties. The first is that behavior is not repeated exactly from one instance to the next. If the infant grasps an object on two different occasions, the grasping will not be the same each time. The difference may be small, in the force of the grasp, for example, or in the exact placement of the fingers. But if there is any difference at all, we must worry whether we should regard the two grasps as two instances of the same response or as two different responses. We must speak not of individual responses, but of classes of responses having common properties.

The second difficulty is that responses are sometimes adequately described in terms of movements, but at other times the description must include the environment in which the responses occur. For example, suppose we want to compare the infant's grasping of an object with clenching a fist. In terms of the muscles that move, grasp-ing an object with the right hand and clenching the right fist have more in common than grasping an object with the right hand and grasping an object with the left hand. Yet it may sometimes be more important to speak of the act of grasping an object, no matter which hand is used, than to speak of the movement of closing a particular hand.

An account of behavior must distinguish between *movements*, responses defined by their form or the musculature used, and *actions*, responses defined by their relations to the environment. We will find that actions are more important for our purposes. Consider how often we speak of doing things, going places, or manipulating objects, without regard to the particular manner of performing these actions.

Even in the absence of movement, we may sometimes conclude that behavior has occurred. For example, an infant will typically grasp an adult's fingers so tightly that the infant can be lifted into the air. Once lifted, the infant may not move while holding on and yet the very fact that the infant does not fall leads us to conclude that the grasping response continues. Similarly, if we see an adult standing still, our judgment that the adult is behaving stems partly from our knowing that the adult would fall down if unconscious or dead. It might be argued that the standing adult is in fact moving in small, unnoticed ways, but even if minor postural adjustments occur in standing still, we do not have to observe them to conclude that the adult is behaving. The critical feature of the infant's grasping and the adult's standing is simply that these responses have an effect; they determine whether or not the organism falls.

Thus, not all movements need be instances of behavior, and not all instances of behavior need be movements. We do many things that do not involve any obvious movement. For example, while listening to music we may shift our attention from one instrument to another. That shift of attention is behavior even though we do not measure it as movement. Many aspects of thinking, imagining, and dreaming need not involve movement, but each is something we do and therefore is a variety of behavior.

Whether behavior involves movement or not, it typically has consequences, and one of the most significant consequences of behavior is that it provides opportunities for other behavior. For instance, if a rat's lever press produces food, the food gives the rat an opportunity to eat. The significance of food as a stimulus is based on the rat's eating, its behavior with respect to that stimulus. As we will see again and again, we cannot characterize stimuli independently of an organism's behavior, nor can we characterize responses independently of an organism's environment.

One way to classify an organism's behavior is to rank responses according to the relative frequencies with which the organism engages in them. For example, if we gave a rat an opportunity to eat, to run in an exercise wheel, or to stand on an electrified grid, we might find that it runs a lot, eats occasionally, and hardly ever stands on the grid. Running, as the most likely or most probable behavior, comes first in this ranking, followed by eating, and finally standing on the grid. Such a ranking has been called a *response hierarchy* or a *behavior hierarchy* (cf. the habit family hierarchy of Hull, 1943). An equivalent way of describing the ranking is in the language of preference: We might say that the rat prefers running to eating and prefers either of these to standing on the grid.

Behavior hierarchies are changeable. For example, if we deprived the rat of food for a while and then gave it an opportunity to eat or to run, we might find that eating had become more probable than running or, in other words, that eating had moved up in the hierarchy relative to running. Furthermore, even responses that are not occurring at the moment can be ranked in behavior hierarchies. For example, while the rat is eating it is neither running nor standing on the electrified grid, but we could still find out about the ranking of those responses by picking up the rat and placing it in the wheel or on the grid. We might discover that it spends some time running in the wheel before returning to the food but that it leaves the grid immediately whenever we try to place it there. We might also find that when the rat is given an opportunity to move between the wheel and the grid it prefers the wheel. In these cases, we conclude that running in the wheel ranks above standing on the grid in the behavior hierarchy. To reach that conclusion, we had to consider when the rat terminated behavior as well as when it initiated it.

It is often convenient to speak of stimuli rather than of opportunities for responding. Thus, we might describe food as an *appetitive* stimulus and an electrified grid as an *aversive* stimulus, with stimuli that are neither appetitive nor aversive described as *neutral*. Unfortunately, we may be able to use such terms in a specific situation, but stimuli in general cannot be grouped into such a neat classification. Context makes too much of a difference, and so we cannot divide the environment into three simple classes of events called appetitive, neutral, and aversive. Instead, each stimulus must be evaluated relative to the others that are available, and its significance may change along with changes in the behavior hierarchy. For example, consider how food may change from an appetitive to an aversive stimulus over the course of an unusually large holiday dinner.

We have surveyed some general properties of stimuli and responses as they enter into the relations among antecedents, behavior, and consequences. With these preliminaries behind us, let us now examine some classic experiments and findings in the psychology of learning.

Section B   Basic Procedures and Findings

Procedures for the study of behavior are sometimes called experimental *operations*, and the changes in behavior they produce are sometimes called behavioral *processes*. We study the relation between environmental events and the organism's behavior by manipulating the environment and observing how this affects what the organism does. We operate on the organism's environment or, in other words, we perform experimental operations. In the analysis of behavior, operations are *what the experimenter does or arranges*, and processes are *the changes in behavior that result*. (A convenient analogy comes from medicine, where the surgical operation is what the doctor does to the patient and the processes that follow are the physiological effects of the operation, such as changes in circulation, respiration, and so on.) Particular learning procedures can be described in terms of these operations, taken either alone or in some combination.

The simplest operation, of course, is merely to *observe behavior*. The behavior that we observe tells us what an organism is capable of doing. But because we have no control over events when we only observe, we may be unable to draw conclusions about the causes of behavior. We therefore must intervene, and the simplest intervention is to *present stimuli*. A more complicated intervention is that of arranging the environment so that the organism's behavior has *consequences*. Once responses have consequences, they may occur more or less often, and therefore consequential operations lead to the processes sometimes called *reinforcement* and *punishment*. We have not exhausted the possibilities: We can arrange things so that stimuli *signal* events, such as the presentation of other stimuli or the opportunity to produce consequences. We then speak of *stimulus-control* operations; these operations can only occur in combination with one of the simpler operations, presenting stimuli or arranging consequences. Behavior may then depend on whether the signaling stimulus is present or absent. We must also consider the operations that can change the effects of the consequences of behavior, as when food becomes a more potent reinforcer after a period of food deprivation. Such operations are called *establishing operations*, in that they establish the conditions under which consequences may become effective as either reinforcers or punishers.

Thus, the basic operations that we will consider are: *observing an organism's behavior, presenting stimuli, arranging consequences for responses, signaling stimuli, signaling consequences,* and *establishing the effectiveness of consequences*. We now survey several classic experiments to illustrate these operations and to introduce some major researchers from the history of the psychology of learning.

THE OBSERVATION OF BEHAVIOR

What must we do to observe behavior? In the last section, we argued that interesting behavior depends on interesting environments. But what would happen if we tried to move in the other direction, avoiding the contamination of behavior by the environment? For example, imagine that we take a rat and fit it with goggles to exclude visual stimuli and with ear plugs to exclude sounds. We then remove odors with a ventilating system. Realizing that the rat can still touch things, including its own body, we arrange a suit of hollow tubes that holds the rat's legs so that tactile contact is reduced, at least for its paws. This still may not satisfy us, because the rat's weight produces pressures where the suit meets part of its body and thus allows it to orient spatially. The next step is to send the suited rat up to an orbiting space station, where gravity is eliminated. Yet after we had accomplished this much, what could we say about the rat's behavior? What might we observe the rat doing?

The rat example is hypothetical, but experiments on sensory deprivation have placed humans in environments that approximate the minimal stimulation we have imagined for the rat. The problem is that in such environments, for human as well as for rodent, there is not much to do; there is no place to go and no one to see or to speak to. Although humans in such environments report a range of activities during their waking time, from thinking to hallucinating, it is no surprise that they spend much of their time sleeping.

We must conclude that we were right in the first place. To observe interesting behavior, we must observe the organism in an interesting environment. Let us consider some examples. Early in the study of the psychology of learning, speculations about the nature of learning were often based upon anecdotal evidence derived from simple observation, as in the following:

> The way in which my dog learnt to lift the latch of the garden gate, and thus let himself out, affords a good example of intelligent behaviour. The iron gate outside my house is held to by a latch, but swings open by its own weight if the latch be lifted. Whenever he wanted to go out the fox terrier raised the latch with the back of his head, and thus released the gate, which swung open. Now the question in any such case is: How did he learn the trick? In this particular case the question can be answered, because he was carefully watched. When he was put outside the door, he naturally wanted to get out into the road, where there was much to tempt him—the chance of a run, other dogs to sniff at, possibly cats to be worried. He gazed eagerly out through the railings...and in due time chanced to gaze out under the latch, lifting it with his head. He withdrew his head and looked out elsewhere; but the gate had swung open.... After some ten or twelve experiences, in each of which the exit was more rapidly effected with less gazing out at wrong places, the fox terrier had learnt to go straight and without hesitation to the right spot. In this case the lifting of the latch was unquestionably hit upon by accident, and the trick was only rendered habitual by repeated association in the same situation of the chance act and the happy escape. Once firmly established, however, the behaviour remained constant throughout the remainder of the dog's life, some five or six years. (Morgan, 1920, p. 144)

Observing this behavior was perhaps a lucky accident, like the dog's lifting of the latch. More can be learned about learning by arranging the environments within which behavior is observed. One researcher who did so was Wolfgang Köhler, who studied the behavior of chimpanzees maintained from 1913 to 1917 at the Anthropoid Station on Tenerife, an island northwest of Africa (Köhler, 1927; chimpanzees are not native to Tenerife, and the station was probably a front for German espionage activity involving World War I naval operations: Ley, 1990). In some of Köhler's experiments, bananas or oranges were placed in visible but inaccessible locations, and the chimpanzees could use materials within the area as tools to obtain the fruit. The following describes the behavior of the male chimpanzee, Sultan:

> The six young animals of the station colony were enclosed in a room with perfectly smooth walls, whose roof—about two metres in height—they could not reach. A wooden box..., open on one side, was standing about in the middle of the room, the one open side vertical, and in plain sight. The objective was nailed to the roof in a corner, about two and a half metres distant from the box. All six apes vainly endeavored to reach the fruit by leaping up from the ground. Sultan soon relinquished this attempt, paced restlessly up and down, suddenly stood still in front of the box, seized it, tipped it hastily straight towards the objective, but began to climb upon it at a (horizontal) distance of half a metre, and springing upwards with all his force, tore down the banana. About five minutes had elapsed since the fastening of the fruit; from the momentary pause before the box to the first bite into the banana, only a few seconds had elapsed, a perfectly continuous action after the first hesitation. (Köhler, 1927, pp. 39–40)

In many instances, of course, chimpanzees made unsuccessful attempts to solve problems such as these; such attempts were aptly described as fruitless.

Köhler was concerned with the ways in which chimpanzees could respond to the relations among objects and events in the environment, and he discussed these and related observations in terms of the chimpanzee's intelligence and insight. His major contribution was in demonstrating what chimpanzees were capable of doing, and the readers of his time were impressed

by his descriptions of chimpanzee performance. The problem was that it was not possible to say from observation alone where the behavior came from. Was Sultan able to solve a particular problem because of some inherited cognitive disposition? Because the problem had features in common with some situation he had already encountered? Because he had seen chimpanzees whose behavior he was able to imitate? Or because of some combination of these and other factors?

The term *insight* seemed appropriate because of the suddenness with which a solution to a problem often emerged. Problem solving that seemed insightful led to further questions: whether learning took place abruptly or gradually, and whether this type of problem solving could be explicitly taught. Debates about how much nonhuman primates can learn continue to the present. But observation alone rarely identifies the sources of behavior and therefore rarely resolves such issues.

Köhler did more than simply observe behavior. He arranged environments within which to make his observations. Observation without intervention is difficult to achieve. To observe organisms successfully in the wild, one must know the possible effects of a human presence on their behavior, and even bringing an organism into captivity is itself an intervention. To study such effects, one must present appropriate stimuli. In any study of behavior, therefore, presenting stimuli is virtually inevitable.

THE PRESENTATION OF STIMULI

Köhler did in fact present stimuli, by arranging environments for the chimpanzees he observed. But let us now turn to a different set of examples, in which the role of stimuli is examined more directly. The following, by the ethologist Niko Tinbergen, describes the first feeding of the Herring Gull chick:

> Sometimes the parent stands up and looks down into the nest, and then we may see the first begging behavior of the young. They do not lose time in contemplating or studying the parent, whose head they see for the first time, but begin to peck at its bill-tip right away, with repeated, quick, and relatively well-aimed darts of their tiny bills. They usually spread their wings and utter a faint squeaking sound. The old bird cannot resist this, and if only the chicks persist it will feed them. First the parent stretches its neck, and soon a swelling appears at its base. It travels upward, causing the most appalling deformations and the most peculiar turnings and twistings of the neck. All at once the parent bends its head down and regurgitates an enormous lump of half-digested food. This is dropped, and a small piece is now picked up again and presented to the chicks. These redouble their efforts, and soon get hold of the food, whereupon the parent presents them with a new morsel. Now and then the chicks peck at the food on the ground, but more often they aim at the parent's bill, and although this aiming is not always correct, it rarely takes them more than three or four attempts until they score a hit. (Tinbergen, 1960, p. 178)

So far we have here only some observations of chick behavior. But they involve the effects of stimuli and therefore prompt some questions. What exactly are the critical features of these special stimuli presented by the parent gull? Are some more important than others? Are they the most effective ones possible?

Tinbergen set out to answer these questions by preparing stimuli that resembled the parent gull in various ways. He then measured the pecking generated when these stimuli were presented to recently hatched Herring Gull chicks. The Herring Gull parent has a white head and a yellow beak with a red patch near its tip. A beak with a black or a blue or a white patch produced less

pecking than one with a red patch, but a beak with a patch of any color produced more pecking than a beak without any patch at all. Compared to the red patch, the color of the beak and of the head were relatively unimportant in generating pecking. In fact, as long as the model had a beak with a red patch on it even the presence or absence of a head made little difference.

Tinbergen also varied the shape of the beak, as illustrated in Figure 1–1. Next to each stimulus, pecking is shown as a percentage of the number of pecks generated by the normal beak shape at the top. With the red patch and other color differences eliminated, changes in pecking depended solely on changes in shape. Most models

FIGURE 1–1 A series of models used to analyze the properties of the parent gull's beak that produce begging pecks in the hatchling Herring Gull. Pecks to each other model are expressed as a percentage of the reference level (100%) provided by pecks to the top model. (Adapted from Tinbergen & Perdeck, 1950, Figure 15.)

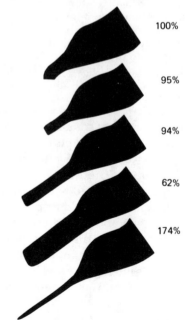

100%

95%

94%

62%

174%

produced less pecking than the one with the normal beak shape. The model with an elongated beak (see bottom shape in Figure 1–1) produced considerably more pecking than any of the others, including the one with the normal beak shape. Because of its effectiveness relative to the normal shape, Tinbergen called this model a *supernormal* stimulus, but he speculated that its shape might be more like what the chick first sees of its parent's beak, as it looks up from beneath the parent's head, than the profile view used for most of the other models.

Tinbergen also varied other properties of the Herring Gull beak, such as movement, slant, and height above the ground. His analysis enabled him to construct a truly supernormal stimulus, a red pencil-shaped rod with three narrow white bands that generated more pecking than an accurate three-dimensional model of a Herring Gull head. More important, he was able to specify those features of the parent's head that are important in generating pecks and to distinguish them from unimportant features. In other words, by presenting stimuli and observing their effects, Tinbergen was able to identify the critical *structure* of the stimuli that generate pecking in the hatchling Herring Gull.

Stimulus presentations are a common feature of research conducted by ethologists, whose concern is the evolution of species-specific behavior patterns in an organism's natural habitats. One effect of stimulus presentations, as we have just seen, is to produce responses. This process, an outcome of presenting stimuli, is called *elicitation*; the stimulus is said to elicit a response. In the language of ethology, the critical stimuli or stimulus features are called *releasers*, and the behavior they produce is called a *fixed action pattern*. But variations in vocabulary should not ob-

scure the simplicity of the basic operation of presenting stimuli.

The eliciting or releasing effects of stimuli can change over time. Data from the Laughing Gull chick provide an example. Feeding in the Laughing Gull chick differs in detail from that of the Herring Gull but includes the begging peck at the parent's beak followed by the parent's regurgitation of partly digested food that the chick then eats. The accuracy of the begging peck was tested by presenting beak models to chicks of various ages. Only about one-third of the pecks of newly hatched chicks struck the model, as opposed to more than three-quarters of the pecks of two-day-old chicks (Hailman, 1969). Did the improved accuracy depend on changes in coordination or visual experience or other factors? Some kinds of behavior might be built in ("prewired") whereas others might have to be learned. How do we tell which is which?

The consequences of accurately aimed pecks differ from those of poorly aimed pecks. In the Laughing Gull's natural habitat, a more accurately aimed peck is more likely to contact the parent's beak and therefore to be followed by the parent's regurgitation of food than a poorly aimed one. Because of their different consequences, we might expect accurately aimed pecks to increase relative to poorly aimed pecks. Hailman's observations in fact suggest that the chick's behavior is determined by such consequences:

If an inexperienced chick is too close to the target at first, its pecking thrust against the bill or model is so strong that the chick is thrown backward as much as an inch. If the chick starts out too far from the target, the pecking thrust misses and the chick falls forward as much as two inches. Older chicks rarely make such gross errors, suggesting that the experience of overshots and undershots has helped the chick learn to adjust its distance. (Hailman, 1969, p. 100)

To study such cases, it is not enough simply to present stimuli. A more complex operation must be arranged: Stimuli must be presented as consequences of the organism's behavior.

CONSEQUENTIAL OPERATIONS

Again we move to a new set of examples, this time from Edward L. Thorndike's research on animal intelligence (Thorndike, 1898). The critical difference between Thorndike's research and Köhler's was that Thorndike systematically observed changes in behavior over many repetitions of an organism's behavior in a given setting rather than looking only at single instances of a problem solution. The problems he studied did not lend themselves to the sudden or insightful solutions seen by Köhler, but they did show that responding in a given situation depends significantly on the consequences such responding has had in the past.

Thorndike described his experimental procedures in this way:

> I chose for my general method one which, simple as it is, possesses several other marked advantages besides those which accompany experiment of any sort. It was merely to put animals when hungry in enclosures from which they could escape by some simple act, such as pulling at a loop of cord, pressing a lever, or stepping on a platform.... The animal was put in the enclosure, food was left outside in sight, and his actions observed. Besides recording his general behavior, special notice was taken of how he succeeded in doing the necessary act (in case he did succeed), and a record was kept of the time that he was in the box before performing the successful pull, or clawing, or bite.... If, on the other hand, after a certain time the animal did not succeed, he was taken out, but *not fed*. (Thorndike, 1898, pp. 5–6)

One of Thorndike's problem-boxes is illustrated in Figure 1–2. In such devices, Thorndike studied cats, dogs, and chicks. He gave the following description as typical of the behavior of most cats:

> When put into the box the cat would show evident signs of discomfort and of an impulse to escape from confinement. It tries to squeeze through any opening; it claws and bites at the bars or wire; it thrusts its paws out through any opening and claws at everything it reaches; it continues its efforts when it strikes anything loose and shaky; it may claw at things within the box.... The cat that is clawing all over the box in her impulsive struggle will probably claw the string or loop or button so as to open the door. And gradually all the other non-successful impulses will be stamped out and the particular impulse leading to the successful act will be stamped in by the resulting pleasure, until, after many trials, the cat will, when put in the box, immediately claw the button or loop in a definite way. (Thorndike, 1898, p. 13)

FIGURE 1–2 A Thorndike problem-box (Thorndike, 1898, Figure 1). In most situations that Thorndike studied, the animal had only a single way to open the door. In the box shown, three different methods are illustrated: a treadle inside the box (A); a wire or string that can be reached from inside the box (B); and two outside latches that can be reached from within to free the door (C). The door (D) was usually counter-weighted so that it opened by itself once the animal made the appropriate response.

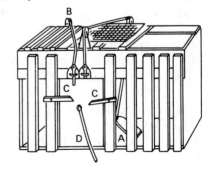

As a consequence of its responding, the cat escaped from confinement and also gained access to food. We may assume that both escaping and eating were important in making the successful response gradually dominate over other, unsuccessful ones. In either case, the procedure cannot be reduced simply to the presentation of stimuli. In getting out of the box, the cat encountered a new part of the environment. It was not merely presented to the cat; it became available as a consequence of what the cat did. The cat's behavior changed as a result of this consequential operation. Contemporary experiments, which often examine simpler responses in simpler situations, are similarly concerned with the relation between responses and their consequences.

We arrange consequences for responses by constructing environments. If we place food in the goalbox of a maze or runway, for example, we create an environment in which a consequence of a rat's movement from the startbox to the goalbox is the availability of food. After the rat has reached the food once, we can find out how this consequence of finding food affected its behavior by seeing what it does the next time we place it in the startbox.

The consequences that can be arranged in consequential operations can vary from events of obvious biological significance such as presenting food or water to relatively minor changes in things seen or heard or touched. But not all consequences involve the production of stimuli. Responses can alter stimuli, as when turning a dimmer switch changes the brightness of a lamp. Responses can remove stimuli, as when operating a switch turns off a light. Responses can prevent stimuli, as when unplugging a lamp before repairing it eliminates the possibility of an electric shock. Responses can even change the consequences of other responses, as when replacing a burned-out lightbulb makes the previously ineffective response of operating the light switch effective again.

Any type of consequence may affect behavior. Two classes of consequences are often distinguished on the basis of their effects on behavior: *reinforcing consequences* are those that increase or maintain responding, and *punishing consequences* are those that decrease or suppress it. (It is useful to have a term for arranging consequences that does not prejudge whether the consequences will be reinforcing or punishing. *Consequation* has been introduced for that purpose. For example, if we do not know whether gold stars will reinforce the classroom behavior of a kindergarten child, it would still be appropriate to speak of *consequating* the behavior with gold stars; e.g., Powers & Osborne, 1976).

STIMULUS-CONTROL OPERATIONS

We speak of stimulus control when a stimulus becomes effective as a signal. The presentation of stimuli and the arrangement of consequences seldom occur in isolation; they are often signaled by other events in the organism's world. A flash of lightning typically precedes a clap of thunder. A traffic light typically alerts drivers to the possible consequences of proceeding or stopping at an intersection. These two examples illustrate that the signaling or discriminative effects of stimuli may be combined either with stimulus presentations or with consequential operations. Both demonstrate the signaling or stimulus-control functions of stimuli even though, as we shall see, the properties of the two types of signaling can be very different.

Signaling Stimulus Presentations

Stimuli that signaled the presentation of other stimuli were the basis for Ivan P.

Pavlov's experiments on conditional or conditioned reflexes (Pavlov, 1927). Pavlov studied how stimuli could acquire signaling properties. He examined responses to stimuli such as food and then showed that these responses were sometimes produced by other stimuli that had reliably preceded the food. Pavlov spoke of the effects of food in a dog's mouth in terms of the alimentary reflex, the components of which included both the glandular response of salivating and motor responses such as chewing and swallowing. He concentrated on salivation in his studies because the technology available to him made salivating easier to measure than motor responses: By surgery, the duct of one of the dog's salivary glands was brought to the outside of the dog's cheek where it was connected to a fluid system that allowed drops of saliva produced by this gland to be counted.

For one dog, food presentations were consistently preceded by the sound of a metronome. Pavlov gave the following account of the conditions necessary to make a stimulus function as a signal:

> On several occasions this animal had been stimulated by the sound of the metronome and immediately presented with food—i.e., a stimulus which was neutral of itself had been superimposed upon the action of the inborn alimentary reflex. We observed that, after several repetitions of the combined stimulation, the sounds from the metronome had acquired the property of stimulating salivary secretion and of evoking the motor reactions characteristic of the alimentary reflex.... Hence a first and most essential requisite for the formation of a new conditioned reflex lies in a coincidence in time of the action of any previously neutral stimulus with some definite unconditioned stimulus. Further, it is not enough that there should be overlapping between the two stimuli; it is also and equally necessary that the conditioned stimulus should begin to operate before the unconditioned stimulus

comes into action. If this order is reversed, the unconditioned stimulus being applied first and the neutral stimulus second, the conditioned reflex cannot be established at all. (Pavlov, 1927, pp. 26–27)

Pavlov's conditioning experiments are effective demonstrations of how a stimulus-control or signaling operation can be superimposed on the simpler operation of stimulus presentation.

Signaling Consequences

Instead of signaling the presentation of stimuli, a stimulus may signal occasions on which responses will have consequences. The signaling of consequences played an important role in the history of the psychology of learning long before it began to be studied experimentally. For example, it was involved in the analysis of the case of Clever Hans, a horse that seemed to have been taught to solve problems in arithmetic (Pfungst, 1911). The horse apparently not only took addition and multiplication but also square roots in its stride.

> The visitor might walk about freely and if he wished, might closely approach the horse and its master, a man between sixty and seventy years of age. His white head was covered with a black slouch hat. To his left the stately animal, a Russian trotting horse, stood like a docile pupil, managed not by means of the whip, but by gentle encouragement and frequent reward of bread or carrots.... Our intelligent horse was unable to speak, to be sure. His chief mode of expression was tapping with his right forefoot. (Pfungst, 1911, pp. 18–19)

Clever Hans gave its answers by the number of times it tapped. Its performance was investigated by Oskar Pfungst, who discovered that the horse was responding to subtle cues provided by the behavior of its owner.

...we sought to discover by what movements the horse could be made to cease tapping. We discovered that upward movements served as signals for stopping. The raising of the head was most effective, though the raising of the eyebrows, or the dilation of the nostrils—as in a sneer—seemed also to be efficacious.... On the other hand, head movements to the right and to the left or forward and back...remained ineffective. We also found that all hand movements, including the "wonderfully effective thrust of the hand into the pocket filled with carrots," brought no response. (Pfungst, 1911, p. 63)

The owner had cooperated in the investigation and there was no evidence that he had been aware of the signals he had provided. Pfungst noted that

Hans's accomplishments are founded...upon a one-sided development of the power of perceiving the slightest movements of the questioner.... we are justified in concluding from the behavior of the horse, that the desire for food is the only effective spring to action.... The gradual formation of the associations mentioned above, between the perception of movement and the movements of the horse himself, is in all probability not to be regarded as a result of a training-process, but as an unintentional by-product of an unsuccessful attempt at real education. (Pfungst, 1911, pp. 240–241)

The case of Clever Hans is often cited when critics wonder whether experimenters have unwittingly provided cues to the organisms whose behavior they have been studying, and it demonstrates that even very subtle properties of stimuli can signal the consequences of responding. In this case, the owner's movements provided the stimuli in the presence of which the horse's taps were followed by food.

When such signaling effects began to be examined more systematically, they came to be called the *discriminative* functions of stimuli; they were different in many ways

from the kinds of signaling functions that had been studied by Pavlov. The research that most decisively established the distinction was conducted by B. F. Skinner, who arranged an environment in which a rat's lever-presses produced food when a light was on but not when it was off, as illustrated in the following passage.

[The apparatus] consists of a dark, well-ventilated, sound-proofed box...containing...a horizontal bar, made of heavy wire, which may be pressed downward approximately 1.5 cm. against a tension of 10 grams. As the lever moves downward, a mercury switch directly behind the wall is closed. We are concerned with the response of the rat in pressing this lever, which we may define as any movement by the rat which results in the closing of the switch. The switch operates a food-magazine, which discharges a pellet of food of standard size into the tray, where it is accessible to the rat. The connection between the lever and the magazine may be broken at will by the experimenter.... The only additional requirement for the investigation of a discrimination is an extra source of stimulating energy...a small (3 c.p.) electric bulb.... The experimenter controls the current to the light and the connection between the lever and the magazine in such a way that the response to the lever-plus-light is always followed by the discharge of a pellet of food into the tray, while the response to the lever alone is never so reinforced. The animal eventually learns to respond to the lever when the light is on but not to respond when the light is off. (Skinner, 1933, pp. 304–305)

In this example, the light signals the consequences of pressing the lever, and the rat comes to press the lever more often when the light is on than when it is off; we may say that the lever press is reinforced in the presence but not the absence of the light, and that the light is a *discriminative stimulus*.

The relations between a discriminative stimulus and the consequences of responding are elaborated in the following passage by Skinner (the term *operant* refers to a class of responses having particular consequences, and the term *reinforcement* refers to these consequences):

> ...the operant must *operate* upon nature to produce its reinforcement. Although the response is free to come out in a very large number of stimulating situations, it will be effective in producing a reinforcement only in a small part of them. The favorable situation is usually marked in some way, and the organism...comes to respond whenever a stimulus is present which has been present upon the occasion of a previous reinforcement and not to respond otherwise. The prior stimulus does not elicit the response; it merely sets the *occasion* upon which the response will be reinforced.... Three terms must therefore be considered: a prior discriminative stimulus (S^D), the response (R^0), and the reinforcing stimulus (S^1). Their relation may be stated as follows: only in the presence of S^D is R^0 followed by S^1. A convenient example is the elementary behavior of making contact with specific parts of the stimulating environment. A certain movement of my arm (R^0) is reinforced by tactual stimulation from a pencil lying on my desk (S^1). The movement is not always reinforced because the pencil is not always there. By virtue of the visual stimulation from the pencil (S^D) I make the required movement only when it will be reinforced. The part played by the visual stimulus is shown by considering the same case in a dark room. At one time I reach and touch a pencil, at another time I reach and do not.... In neither the light nor the dark does the pencil *elicit* my response (as a shock elicits flexion), but in the light it sets the occasion upon which a response will be reinforced. (Skinner, 1938, p. 178)

Skinner explored this three-term relation experimentally with lights as discriminative stimuli, the lever-presses of rats as responses, and food pellets as reinforcing consequences. His example of reaching for and touching objects in the seen environment illustrates the broad range of situations to which the concept of stimulus control applies.

The three-term relation, discriminative-stimulus—response—consequence, will be a recurrent theme. Each term is critical, because their combination distinguishes this case from other, simpler behavioral relations. In the Pavlovian situation, for example, in which a stimulus presentation is signaled, the organism's behavior has no effect on the sequence of events; no consequences are arranged for responses.

Consider the earlier examples. Our blinking or startling at the lightning flash will not prevent the subsequent clap of thunder. But if a traffic light is red as we approach an intersection, our stepping on the brakes is occasioned by this stimulus only because we have learned the potential consequences of doing or not doing so. Only the second of these two examples involves all of the terms of Skinner's three-term contingency. An important difference in vocabulary accompanies these distinctions. *When a stimulus is the primary cause of a response, we say that the stimulus elicits the response or that the response is elicited. But when a response occurs in the presence of a stimulus because the stimulus signals some consequence of responding, we say that the stimulus occasions the response and that the response is emitted.*

The development of stimulus control over consequential responding has been called discrimination learning. Early animal experiments often were concerned not so much with the nature of discrimination learning as with the sensory capacities of organisms. For example, rodent vision was studied by arranging two paths, only one of which led to food (Yerkes & Watson, 1911). At the point where a rat had to choose the left or right path, two stimuli were presented (e.g., a black card and a white card). The path to food varied from left to right but was always indicated by the same card (e.g., black). Once the rat learned to take the path indicated by the stimulus that was correlated with food, the limits of its vision could be studied by substituting other stimuli (e.g., light and dark gray cards) for the original pair. Such experiments were laborious; to demonstrate discrimination learning might take hundreds of trials, if the rat learned at all. Several problems existed in this type of study, not the least of which was ensuring that the rat looked at the stimuli when it reached the choice point.

Apparatus improved over time. Figure 1–3, for example, shows the jumping-stand developed by Karl S. Lashley (1930). Lashley described its advantages:

> ...it requires the animal to jump against the stimulus patterns from a distance, instead of to run past them.... I have usually trained the animals by placing the stand against the screen and allowing the animals to step through the open holes to the platform, then gradually withdrawing the stand until, in ten or fifteen trials, the distance of 25 cm. is reached. Cards are then placed in position and training in discrimination begun. (Lashley, 1930, pp. 454–457)

In Lashley's apparatus, rats typically learned to discriminate black from white with perfect accuracy within 4 or 5 trials, and even more difficult discriminations such as vertical versus horizontal could usually be mastered within less than 50 trials.

In these cases, discriminative stimuli still signal response consequences, but they are more complex than the example in which a rat's lever-presses produced food in the presence but not the absence of light. There, our concern was only with how often lever presses occurred when the light was on and when it was off. Consider the jumping-stand, however. It seems to involve only two responses and their re-

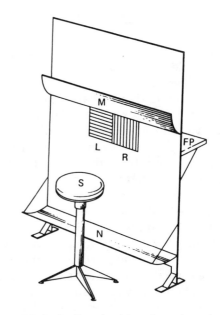

FIGURE 1–3 The Lashley jumping-stand (Lashley, 1930, Figure 1). A rat was trained to jump from the stand (S) to one of two doors (L and R). If it jumped to the correct door, the door gave way and the rat reached the food platform (FP). If the rat jumped to the incorrect door, the door remained fixed and the rat fell into the net below (N). The projecting metal sheet (M) prevented the rat from jumping too high. In the illustration, the right door (R) would be correct for a rat being trained to jump toward vertical lines.

spective consequences: jumping toward vertical and finding food, and jumping toward horizontal and landing in the net. But left and right are not irrelevant to the rat. The situation involves at least four responses, each with a particular consequence: jumping to vertical on the left, to vertical on the right, to horizontal on the left, and to horizontal on the right. Rats may be more likely to respond on the basis of position, left or right, than on the basis of stimulus cards. For example, if the first four trials of vertical-horizontal training were set up with vertical on the right, as in Figure 1–3, it would be no surprise if on the fifth trial, with vertical on the left for the first time, the rat jumped right, toward horizontal. Until the fifth trial, jumping to the right led to food just as well as jumping toward vertical.

The kind of discrimination in which a single stimulus is present or absent, as in the lever-pressing example, is called a *successive* or *go – no go* discrimination. That in which two or more stimuli are present at the same time and in which each is correlated with a different response, as in the jumping-stand example, is called a *simultaneous* discrimination. Both illustrate stimulus control superimposed on consequences of responding. The comparison between successive and simultaneous discriminations shows that stimulus control comes in varying degrees of complexity.

ESTABLISHING THE EFFECTIVENESS OF CONSEQUENCES

Some consequences of behavior are more important than others, and their effectiveness can vary over time. For example, water is likely to be an effective reinforcer if someone has been deprived of water for some time, but it is less likely to be so after a large quantity of water has been consumed. The things that can be done to change its effectiveness are called *establishing operations. Deprivation* and *satiation* are two examples, but they are not the only possibilities. For example, a mouthful of overly salted food may have the same effect as a period of water deprivation. Establishing operations change the effectiveness of consequences by changing the likelihood of behavior, as illustrated in the following passage from B. F. Skinner (1953).

...the probability of drinking becomes very high under severe water deprivation and very low under excessive satiation.... The biological significance of the change in

probability is obvious. Water is constantly being lost through excretion and evaporation, and an equal amount must be taken in to compensate for this loss. Under ordinary circumstances an organism drinks intermittently and maintains a fairly steady and presumably optimal state. When this interchange is disturbed—when the organism is deprived of the opportunity to drink—it is obviously important that drinking should be more likely to occur at the first opportunity. In the evolutionary sense this "explains" why water deprivation strengthens all conditioned and unconditioned behavior concerned with the intake of water. (Skinner, 1953, pp. 141–142)

Skinner spoke of such phenomena in terms of drives:

The term is simply a convenient way of referring to the effects of deprivation and satiation and of other operations which alter the probability of behavior in more or less the same way. It is convenient because it enables us to deal with many cases at once. There are many ways of changing the probability that an organism will eat; at the same time, a single kind of deprivation strengthens many kinds of behavior. (Skinner, 1953, p. 144)

Skinner also pointed out that the effects of establishing operations must not be equated with those of stimuli.

A common belief is that deprivation affects the organism by creating a stimulus. The classic example is hunger pangs. When an organism has been without food for a sufficient time, the contractions of the stomach stimulate it in a characteristic way. This stimulation is often identified with the hunger drive. But such stimulation is not closely correlated with the probability of eating. Hunger pangs are characteristic of only a small part of the range through which that probability varies continuously. We usually eat our meals without reaching the condition of deprivation in which pangs are felt, and we continue to eat long after the first few mouthfuls have stopped any pangs which may have occurred. (Skinner, 1953, pp. 144–145)

As Skinner's example indicates, the effects of discriminative stimuli and those of establishing operations must be distinguished. Consider another example (cf. Michael, 1982). You need to make a telephone call, and on locating a pay phone you look in your change purse or pocket for a coin. The pay phone is a discriminative stimulus in that it sets the occasion on which you can make your phone call. But with respect to the coin in the purse or pocket it is an establishing event: It makes the coin important. It is not a discriminative stimulus with respect to looking into the purse or pocket and finding a coin, because you would have found the coin by looking there whether or not you had seen the pay phone. In other words, the pay phone is not a stimulus in the presence of which you are more likely to find coins on your person. Instead, the pay phone has established the significance of the coin as a reinforcing consequence of checking purse or pocket.

Our treatment of establishing operations has been brief, because in themselves they do not provide examples of learning. As we shall see, however, they provide the contexts within which learning typically occurs, and it is therefore difficult to study learning without them.

OVERVIEW

The study of behavior is concerned with relations between environmental events, *stimuli*, and the organism's actions, *responses*. These relations can be examined by analyzing how changes in the environment produce changes in responding. A critical first step is *observation* of behavior, but it is typically not enough simply to watch an organism. To understand behavior we must intervene by changing the environment. We can describe environmental changes in terms of classes of experimental operations: *stimulus-presentations*, *consequential* operations, *stimulus-control* operations, and *establishing* operations. These are summarized in Table 1–1.

Aside from observation, presenting stimuli is the simplest operation. When we present stimuli, we can observe the responses produced. For example, we might make a rat salivate by presenting food. Stimulus presentations are relevant to learning because the responses produced by stimuli can vary depending upon the conditions under which stimuli are presented.

Sometimes the organism changes its environment: behavior can have consequences. Arranging the environment so that it is modified by the organism's responses is called a consequential operation. Consequences can include the presentation, removal, or prevention of stimuli, or more complex events such as changes in the consequences of other responses. For example, we could present food to a rat whenever it reared up on its hind legs, or electric shock whenever it moved to a certain floor area, or we could allow a lever press to produce food only if the rat had first pulled a chain. Some responses that have consequences may occur more often and others less often. If an organism responds more often because its response changed its environment, we say that the response was rewarded or *reinforced*; if an organism responds less often for the same reason, we say that the response was suppressed or *punished*.

We can signal either stimulus presentations or consequential operations by arranging them only when some stimulus is present. Organisms do not behave indiscriminately. They do some things in some circumstances and other things in other circumstances.

One stimulus can signal the imminent occurrence of another. For example, the

TABLE 1-1 Basic Behavioral Operations

OPERATION	DESCRIPTION	EXAMPLES	USAGE
Observation	No intervention.	We watch an animal behaving.	
Stimulus-presentation operation	Stimulus *A* is presented.	*Loud noise (A)* startles child. Doctor shines *light (A)* in patient's eye.	Stimulus *elicits* response; response *is elicited* by stimulus.
Consequential operation	Response *B* has consequence *C* (e.g., a stimulus is produced or terminated).	*Putting coin in vending machine (B)* produces *soft drink (C).* *Touching hot stove (B)* produces *burn (C).* *Light goes out (C)* when *switch is thrown (B).*	Response is *emitted.*
Stimulus-control operation			
Superimposed on stimulus presentation	Stimulus *D* signals presentation of stimulus *E.*	*Lightning (D)* precedes *thunder (E).*	Stimulus *elicits* response; response *is elicited* by stimulus.
Superimposed on consequences	Stimulus *F* signals that response *G* will have consequence *H.*	*Red traffic light (F)* signals that *driving through intersection (G)* may lead to *traffic ticket (H).* *Ringing telephone (F)* signals that *answering (G)* may provide *opportunity for conversation (H).*	Stimulus *occasions* response; response *is emitted* in presence of stimulus.
Establishing operation	Effectiveness of consequence *I* as a reinforcer or punisher is established.	*Food (I)* becomes an effective reinforcer after food deprivation. The presentation of shock makes *shock removal (I)* a reinforcer. When it is important to unlock a door, *the key to the door (I)* becomes a reinforcer.	An event is *established* as a reinforcer or punisher.

child may learn that the sound of a key in the door reliably precedes the return home of a working parent, or that a lightning flash is often followed by the sound of thunder. In these cases, stimulus control is superimposed upon stimulus presentations: The sound of the key signals the parent's appearance, and the lightning warns of thunder. On the other hand, a stimulus might signal the conditions under which a response has some consequence. For example, a child may learn that requests are more likely to be granted in the presence of either parent alone than in the presence of both parents together, or that misbehavior is more likely to be followed by a scolding in the presence of one parent than in the presence of the other. In these cases, stimulus control is superimposed upon a consequential operation: The presence of the parents signals various consequences of requests or of misbehavior.

The changes in behavior produced by stimulus-presentation operations or consequential operations may begin to occur only in the presence of the corresponding stimuli. When a stimulus signals that some event is about to occur or that an organism's behavior might have certain consequences, the organism may come to respond differently when the stimulus is present than when it is absent. This pro-

cess is called *discrimination*, and the organism's behavior is said to be *under the control* of the discriminative stimulus.

Finally, the significance of events as consequences of behavior can be altered by *establishing* operations, such as *deprivation* and *satiation*. These operations work by modifying the organism's opportunities to engage in different classes of behavior, and thereby change the effectiveness of events as reinforcers or punishers.

Behavior can be complicated. Different stimuli can have different effects on different responses, and different responses can have different consequences. Nevertheless, as we shall see, a variety of learning procedures can be treated as combinations of these basic types of experimental interventions: *stimulus presentations*; *consequential* operations, such as reinforcement and punishment, in which responses act on the environment; *stimulus-control* operations, in which these other operations are signaled by discriminative stimuli; and *establishing* operations, which alter the significance of the consequences of behavior. These operations will take us a long way, but later, especially when we consider the transition from learning without words to learning with words, we will find that they do not exhaust the possibilities.

PART II *Behavior Without Learning*

Evolution and Behavior

Evolution *and* revolution *are descendants of the Latin* volvere, *to roll; they differ in that* evolution *implies an unrolling or rolling out whereas* revolution *implies a rolling over or turning around.* Selection *can be traced to the Latin* legere, *originally to gather or to choose (cf. the etymology of* logos, *Chapter 11). The prefix,* se-, *adds the implication of a weeding out from a large number, as contrasted with the bringing together implied by* con-, *the root prefix for* collection.

Phylogeny *as evolutionary history and* ontogeny *as the life history of the individual organism share the Greek root* gen-, *in the sense of kind or sort (cf. the etymology of* generalization, *Chapter 7).* Phylo- *has a Greek root implying a tribe or clan or racial stock and* onto- *has one implying being or reality. In their combination with* gen-, *each implies origin: the origin of a biological phylum, or the origin of a living entity.*

Our planet is roughly 4.5 billion years old. That is a very long time. If you tried to count to a billion, you would take more than 30 years to finish even if you maintained a continuous pace of one count per second; if you took time out to sleep, of course, you would take much longer (the one-per-second estimate is very generous, it is easy to count quickly when numbers are small, but 9-digit numbers like 854,316,972 would be bound to slow you down, especially if you worried about losing count).

Life has existed on earth for most of that time (see Gould, 1989, for a detailed account). Chemical and fossil evidence indicates that it began within the first billion years. Over most of the next 3 billion years, it consisted of single-celled organisms. Multicellular organisms only appeared roughly 570 million years ago, in the geological period called the Cambrian. An explosion in the diversity of multicellular life occurred during the Cambrian period and was followed by a weeding out; the survivors provided the major groupings from which contemporary species evolved. One such grouping was the vertebrates. The evolution from amphibians to reptiles included many significant events, such as the colonization of land. The dinosaurs were a spectacular part of the story, but by 65 million years ago they were gone. Their passing allowed the evolution of large mammals and we humans eventually emerged from that line. All of us are descendants of a very long line of survivors.

These are merely a few of many facts about evolution. The fossil record is incomplete and there is much detail we do not know, but the evidence from biology and geology and other disciplines establishes evolution as something that happened. Theories of evolution are not about whether contemporary species are descended from the very different ancestors that we find in the geologic record. All theories of evolution take that for granted. They differ in what they say about the way evolution came about, and the theory that has been most successful in accommodating the facts of evolution is Charles Darwin's account of evolution in terms of natural selection.

Section A   The Nature of Evolution

Natural selection refers to Darwin's account of evolution in terms of the differential survival and reproduction of the members of a population; the environment selects the individuals who pass their characteristics on from one generation to the next and thereby shapes the characteristics of those in later populations (for discussions of the details of natural selection, see Dawkins, 1976, 1986). Evolution by natural selection requires variations within populations; these variations are the stuff upon which selection works.

Selection was well known even before Darwin, but it was the sort used by humans in horticulture and animal husbandry. People knew how to breed plants or livestock selectively for hardiness or yield or other characteristics. This selective breeding was called *artificial selection*, and it created new varieties of vegetables and flowers and so on. Workhorses were selected for strength and racehorses were selected for speed. One part of Darwin's insight was that a similar kind of selection occurred in nature, without human intervention; that was *natural selection*.

Darwin's main argument was first published in his book *On the Origin of Species* (Darwin, 1859). In some quarters it was warmly received but in others it was strongly resisted. The resistance grew, and by the end of the nineteenth century the belief was widespread that Darwinism was dead. It did not recover until well into the twentieth century. The half century or so that preceded that recovery has been called the eclipse of Darwinism (Bowler, 1983; cf. Catania, 1987).

The reason for the eclipse was not that evolution itself had been discredited but rather that other theories than Darwin's had become dominant. The main alternatives were *Lamarckism, orthogenesis,* and the combination of *Mendelian genetics* with *mutation theory.* Lamarckism was based on the work of an eighteenth-century French scientist who in his time had done much to make a case for the fact of evolution. Lamarck's theory was that characteristics acquired during an organism's lifetime could be passed on to its offspring, through changes in its own genetic material or germ plasm. One problem with this theory was why advantageous acquired characteristics should be any more likely to be passed on than disadvantageous ones such as injuries.

According to the theory of orthogenesis, evolution was directed by forces within organisms, without reference to the demands of the environment; it could be likened to a developmental unfolding. One manifestation of this unfolding was supposed to be the recapitulation of phylogeny by ontogeny. *Ontogeny* is the development of the individual organism and *phylogeny* is its evolutionary history. During ontogeny the embryo was thought to pass through stages corresponding to its phylogeny. This idea of recapitulation, however, has severe limitations and is no longer central to evolutionary theory (Gould, 1977).

The problem with Mendelian genetics was that by itself it provided no mechanism for variation. In strict Mendelian descent, dominant and recessive genes in one generation determined their proportions in the next. Without variation, there was nothing on which natural selection could work. To provide for the appearance of new forms, Mendelian accounts added mutation theory, which held that evolution proceeded through spontaneous and usually large genetic changes.

RECIPES AND BLUEPRINTS

In the nineteenth century, genes were theoretical entities. The techniques of cell biology had not yet reached the point at which genes had been located in actual cells. Nevertheless, all of these evolutionary theories assumed that hereditary material of some sort was passed on from one generation to the next and that evolution was determined by the properties of this material. A major flaw in some theories was the assumption that genetic material constituted a representation or copy of the organism. In the earliest versions of orthogenesis, called preformationist, the embryo was literally a homunculus, a tiny individual complete in all its parts; in later variations it took on ancestral forms, as ontogency was said to recapitulate phylogeny. As for Lamarckism, the transmission of acquired characteristics required that they be preserved in the germ plasm in some way, so the germ plasm had to contain some kind of plan of those parts of the organism that were to be altered in subsequent generations. In either case, the germ plasm could be regarded as a representation or copy of the organism.

A *recipe* is a sequence of procedures or instructions. It describes how to create a product, but it does not necessarily incorporate a description of the product (a recipe for a cake does not look like a cake). A recipe can be informative, but it is not likely to contain information about its origins, such as the number of tries it took to make it work. A *blueprint*, on the other hand, does not ordinarily say how to construct the structure that it shows. Like a recipe, it can be informative, but it too is likely to omit information about its origins, such as the order in which different parts were designed. A blueprint is a representation or copy but a recipe is not, and Lamarckism and the preformationist orthogenetic accounts treated genetic materials as blueprints rather than recipes.

A major achievement in contemporary biology was the reinterpretation of genetic material not as a blueprint for the organism's structure but rather as a recipe for its development (see Dawkins, 1986, Chapter 11, for an elaboration of the metaphors of blueprint and recipe). The modern formulation demanded rethinking of the sense in which genetic material can be said to contain information, whether about evolutionary history or about the structure of the organism (cf. Dawkins, 1982, Chapter 9). Genetic materials provide limited information about the past environments in which they have been selected because they do not include the genetic materials of all those other organisms that did not survive. And they provide limited information about the eventual structure of an organism because they are recipes for the production of proteins rather than blueprints for body parts. The implications were profound. One is that Lamarckism and at least some varieties of orthogenesis became untenable alternatives to Darwinian selection because their implicit copy theories were inconsistent with what had been learned about how the genetic material worked.

It is ironic that, along with Lamarckism and orthogenesis, Mendelian genetics had also been seen as a serious challenge to Darwinian selection. The integration of Mendelian genetics with Darwinian selection in the 1920s and 1930s, known as the modern synthesis, became the core of contemporary biology. Genetic experiments with fruit flies not only elaborated on genetic mechanisms but also brought mutations into the laboratory. With fruit flies, many generations could be studied within a relatively short time. The research gave evidence on natural rates of mutation and on the magnitude of mutation effects, which were relatively small in comparison to the changes that had been assumed in prior mutation theories. The combination of Mendelian genetics with the facts of mutation provided the variability needed for the workings of natural selection.

The Darwinian view had to face and overcome other hurdles besides the competing theories (cf. Mayr, 1982). Earlier we mentioned the incompleteness of the fossil record. Our understanding of prehistoric life depends on the accidental preservation of occasional members of earlier species, but the circumstances of their preservation and discovery inevitably leaves gaps. Furthermore, hard parts such as bones or shells are much more likely to be preserved than soft parts. Even if we find all of the parts intact, our information about how these creatures behaved is limited. We must often resort to indirect evidence (e.g., analogies with living species; fossil records of behavior such as fossil footprints).

The age of the earth had been another problem. That age has been revised vastly upward during this century, but in the nineteenth century the estimate was so short that it did not seem that there had been enough time for evolution to have come about through natural selection. The likelihood of improbable events when these events have many opportunities to occur over an extended period of time had also been misunderstood. For example, suppose that some organic molecule was a crucial prerequisite for life, that it occurred in nature only when lightning created it by passing through some mixture of the gases present in the early atmosphere of the earth, and that the odds of this happening were a million to one. The creation of that organic molecule might seem very much a long shot under those conditions. But assume now that there were many lightning storms during the early history of our planet, so that over a few million years those conditions were repeated many millions of times. Given these assumptions, it is a virtual certainty that the molecule would have been created not just once but many times, even though the particular moment of its creation would not have been predictable (cf. Dawkins, 1986; Gleick, 1987).

VARIATION AND SELECTION

Now let us consider an example of natural selection. We start with a population of prey animals (e.g., zebras) the members of which vary in the speed at which they can run; the reasons might include differences in anatomy such as bone length or muscle size, sensory differences that allow some to get off to a quicker start than others, and/or indirect factors that slow some down, such as susceptibility to disease. If these animals are preyed upon by predators, the ones most likely to be caught are the slowest ones, everything else being equal. The proviso that everything else must be equal is important; for example, an individual who is fast at the expense of requiring much more to eat might forage longer and thus run a higher risk of being seen by a predator during foraging. That higher risk might counterbalance its advantage in speed. But this does not negate our argument, because the members of the population will vary even after such factors are taken into account. We could then recast the argument in terms of the effects of these factors on the probability of being caught. For the present purposes, however, speed is a more convenient dimension.

At any time during its history, this prey population has some mean or average speed. Some members are above that mean and others are below it. The ones below are those most likely to be caught and so are less likely to pass their genes on to the next generation. The next generation will then include more descendants of those above the mean than of those below; in other words, it will include fewer of the previous slow and more of the previous fast runners. An implication is that the mean speed will be higher in this generation than it was in the last one. But the same kind of selection still operates on this generation: Again, the slowest ones are more likely to be caught than the fastest ones. Over many generations, therefore, the mean speed becomes faster and faster (a similar kind of selection will also operate on the speed of the predators, because the slowest of those will be less likely to catch their prey than the fastest).

The evolution of the horse provides striking evidence for this kind of selection (Simpson, 1951). Over the 50 million years or so since *eohippus*, the so-called dawn horse, the individuals in the populations from which modern horses are descended gradually increased in size. These size changes were accompanied by other changes, such as bone length, anatomy of the foot, and presumably also behavior: Eohippus was the ancestor of modern horses, but compared to them it was undoubtedly very slow.

Eohippus is extinct, and that fact is also relevant to our story. Many descendants of eohippus must have been the fastest of their kind in their time, but they are no longer around either. When selection operates on some relative property, such as speed relative to the mean for a population, the mean for the population changes. For example, after capture by predators has repeatedly selected faster escape in a population, few descendants of the originally slow runners will be left even if that slower running speed had provided a selective advantage at a much earlier time when it had been a very fast speed relative to the population mean. In other words, as eohippus demonstrates, we should not expect to find examples of ancestral forms within current populations. The mean running speed of horses has been moved so far by 50 million years of equine evolution that in its prime even the slowest contemporary horse would be able to outrun the vast majority of its ancestors.

According to these arguments the source of selection is in the environment (the environments of predators include their prey and the environments of prey include their predators). Selection creates the features of organisms, but selection is necessary to maintain them as well as to create them. For example, the ancestors of whales were once land mammals. After they moved back into the sea, the environmental contingencies that had made legs advantageous no longer maintained the selection of well-formed legs. Instead, selection began to favor limbs that were effective for movement through water. The legs of the ancestors of whales gradually disappeared; in a sense it is appropriate to say that the legs had extinguished or become extinct (Skinner, 1988, p. 73). Selection operates on species, but it does so by acting on particular organs and systems and body parts.

Consider another example. Environments that include tall trees with edible leaves are environments in which long necks may be advantageous, especially if shorter trees are scarce or if their leaves are often depleted by competitors. Giraffes arose through the natural selection of relatively long necks; such selection could not occur in environments that lacked tall trees (the tall trees set the occasion for the selection of long necks). But the selection also depended on what there was to start with. In one species variations among individuals might allow the selection of those with longer necks, but in another they might allow the selection of those who climb trees more efficiently. The environment selects from populations of organisms, but that selection can only operate on the range of variations available within those populations. Structural factors must be included among the constraints on possible variations. In the human species, for example, our four-limbed mammalian ancestry precludes the evolution of a pair of wings emerging from our shoulder blades.

The kind of phylogenic selection we have discussed so far involves gradual changes taking place over long periods of time (we will see later that it has much in common with a kind of selection that occurs within the lifetime of the individual organism; see Chapter 6 on shaping). Some controversies about evolution have been about whether evolution takes place gradually, as in the example of the horse, or in fits and starts (punctuated evolution or saltation). For example, the fossil record in-

cludes evidence of major changes in species over periods of time that are relatively short by evolutionary standards (e.g., the explosion of multicellular life in the Cambrian period or, at the end of the Cretaceous period, the extinction of the dinosaurs, perhaps as a result of the impact of a comet or some other planetary catastrophe, and the later proliferation of large mammals). Given the strong evidence for both kinds of evolutionary change, perhaps it is most reasonable to conclude that evolution can take place either way: Some features have been selected gradually and continuously relative to some population mean whereas others have been selected following punctuated events that produced massive environmental changes (perhaps including large-scale extinctions).

Natural selection along a single dimension such as running speed seems straightforward enough, but evolution involves more than changes along single dimensions. It results in organized complexity, such as the intricate structure of the human eye. Is it reasonable to believe that natural selection could have produced such organized complexity? Using an analogy from aeronautical design, Dawkins (1982) posed the problem this way:

> The designers of the first jet engine started with a clean drawing board. Imagine what they would have produced if they had been constrained to 'evolve' the first jet engine from an existing propeller engine, changing one component at a time, nut by nut, screw by screw, rivet by rivet. A jet engine so assembled would be a weird contraption indeed. It is hard to imagine that an aeroplane designed in that evolutionary way would ever get off the ground. Yet in order to complete the biological analogy we have to add yet another constraint. Not only must the end product get off the ground; so must every intermediate along the way, and each intermediate must be superior to its predecessor. (Dawkins, 1982, p. 38)

If the eye is a product of natural selection, it could not have emerged full blown. But what good is part of an eye? What selective advantage could it confer? The answer is that even 1 percent of an eye is a substantial advantage if all of one's contemporaries have even less. Any sensitivity to light is better than none; 2 percent is better than 1; 3 percent is better than 2, and so on. Dawkins here describes the advantages of a lensless eye over no eye at all:

> You can tell if you are about to walk into a wall or another person. If you were a wild creature, you could certainly use your lensless eye to detect the looming shape of a predator, and the direction from which it was approaching. In a primitive world where some creatures had no eyes at all and others had lensless eyes, the ones with lensless eyes would have all sorts of advantages.... each tiny improvement in sharpness of image, from swimming blur to perfect human vision, plausibly increases the organism's chances of surviving. (Dawkins, 1986, p. 81)

Once a complex system such as an eye has evolved in a given species, it becomes exceedingly unlikely that it will ever be displaced by another system that has the same function. For example, the 1 percent of seeing that might be an evolutionary precursor of a complete human eye provides considerably less of an advantage if the complete eye already exists than if the alternative is not seeing at all. Selection does not replace existing mechanisms with others that do the same job, so a third eye will never evolve in the middle of our foreheads.

What about other cases, such as animal mimicry? A stick insect may look so much like a stick that a bird that otherwise would have eaten it will pass it by. But how much good would it do to have merely a 5 percent resemblance to a stick? In response to this question, Dawkins (1986, pp. 83–84) points out that a 5 percent resemblance

may be just enough to make a difference in twilight or in fog or if the bird is far away. Once individuals in the population vary in their resemblance to sticks, natural selection based even on small differences may drive the population to more and more convincing mimicry.

Resemblance to sticks is an unusual property, and it is of course only one of many possible directions of selection. We have already noted that selection can operate on different features in different populations, and not every feature that seems adaptive is necessarily a product of natural selection. Darwin regarded natural selection as the most important mechanism of evolution, but he took pains to point out that natural selection was not the only possible one: "I am convinced that Natural Selection has been the main *but not exclusive* means of modification" (Darwin, 1859, p. 6; italics added). Selectionist accounts of the features of a population demand more than just a plausible story about how those features might be advantageous.

Some features might come about as incidental by-products of selection. Gould and Lewontin (1979) use the spandrels of San Marco as an analogy. San Marco is a cathedral in Venice with a dome that is supported by arches. Any two adjacent arches come together at the top of a common pillar, and in the construction of San Marco the tapering triangular space above the pillar and between the two arches was filled in and its surface was used for a mosaic. The space is called a *spandrel*:

> Each spandrel contains a design admirably fitted into its tapering space. An evangelist sits in the upper part flanked by the heavenly cities. Below, a man representing one of the four Biblical rivers (Tigris, Euphrates, Indus and Nile) pours water from a pitcher into the narrowing space between his feet. The design is so elaborate, harmonious and purposeful that we are tempted to view it as

the starting place of any analysis. (Gould & Lewontin, 1979, pp. 581–582)

The point is that the cathedral of San Marco was not built in order to create the spandrels. The spandrels were an inevitable but incidental architectural by-product of constructing a dome on top of rounded arches. Analogously, some features of contemporary populations may not be direct products of natural selection; instead, they may be incidental by-products of other unrelated features that have arisen through selection. When the source of an inherited feature is uncertain, the question is sometimes put in terms of the San Marco analogy: Is it a product of natural selection or is it a spandrel?

We have so far concentrated on properties of selection, but what can we now say about the evolution of behavior (cf. Skinner, 1984)? We have already noted that behavior has left only indirect evidence in the fossil record. It is reasonable to assume, however, that response systems evolved before sensory systems. For an organism that cannot do anything about what it sees, there is no advantage to seeing. Some organisms remained immobile but others began to twitch and squirm. Some organisms were passively moved by ocean currents and others anchored themselves to particular places. The organisms from which we are descended developed means to get from one place to another.

As motor systems developed, the advantages of responding differentially to environmental events were presumably the basis for the selection of sensory systems. Withdrawal upon being touched might be enough to avoid a predator and would certainly be more advantageous than withdrawing at random. Ingesting things on the basis of their chemical properties would certainly be more advantageous than ingesting things randomly. These properties of behavior are so important that it is hard to imagine a world in which all creatures lacked them. We may then recall that we should not expect to find examples of ancestral forms within current populations.

The most primitive patterns of movement were probably driven primarily by eliciting stimuli. For example, suppose bright light elicits random movement. An insect larva in the light starts moving and continues to do so until, by chance, it moves into darkness; once there it stops. We will not find many of these larvae in the light, but we may find large numbers in dark places (e.g., under the rotting bark of a fallen tree limb). Once we expose them to light, they all begin to move. But their behavior is not directed toward dark places; they get there by chance, some sooner than others, and they end up congregated there only because that is where they stop.

Orientation that occurs on such a basis is called a *kinesis*; it is distinguished from orientation that is directed toward or away from some stimulus, which is called a *taxis* (plural *taxes*; Fraenkel & Gunn, 1961). Examples of a wide range of possible taxes include movements toward light (positive phototaxis) and upward movement, away from gravity, as in climbing a tree (negative geotaxis). The details of these and other types of orientation vary (for example, in an organism with two eyes a phototaxis may come about because the organism consistently moves so as to equalize the amount of light received by each eye).

These examples, like reflex relations, share the property that each involves a fixed pattern of responding to environmental events. First there was movement; then the movement came under the control of stimuli. Such patterns were particularly advantageous in stable environments. For example, given a sharp stimulus to its paw, a dog flexes its leg, drawing its paw up toward its body. For an animal that walks on the ground, that response is advantageous: If the dog steps on a thorn, its flexion pulls its paw away from the thorn. The sloth, however, lives in a very different environment. It hangs from trees and its comparable reflex involves an extension rather than a flexion of its limb. If the sharp stimulus is a thorn, the hanging sloth that pulls its limb toward its body instead of extending it will only drive the thorn in deeper (cf. Hart, 1973, p. 176).

But not all environments are stable. It must have been a major evolutionary step when such patterns of behavior became modifiable or, in other words, when some organisms became able to learn. Learning may at first have been selected within restricted domains. For example, upon leaving its nest the digger wasp flies around it in ever-widening circles; its later return to the nest is based on landmarks, such as rocks or plants, that it had flown over before its departure (Tinbergen, 1972). Its capacity to learn landmarks is part of its phylogenic heritage and might be very specific to nest localization. With learning, behavior may change as a function of the environment within which it occurs, but the capacity to learn must itself have been selected (we will return to the topic of biological constraints on learning in Chapter 9).

KINDS OF SELECTION

Of the various kinds of learning that we will explore in the chapters that follow, one is the case in which responses are affected by their consequences. For example, if an organism is food-deprived and some response produces food, that response is likely to occur more often. We

have already discussed such cases as instances of reinforcement. Reinforcement can also occur in particular environments or settings, when we say that a situation sets the occasion on which responses are reinforced. These cases involve selection, but this kind of selection operates within the lifetime of the individual organism rather than over successive generations (it is ontogenic rather than phylogenic).

This kind of selection may be called *operant selection*; it involves *selection by consequences* (cf. Skinner, 1981). For the food-deprived organism, for example, responses that produce food continue to occur; other responses do not. Food is the consequence that selects some responses and not others. We could say that the responses that produce food survive and that the others extinguish. Parallels between these two varieties of selection, natural selection and the selection of behavior by its consequences, have been explored in considerable detail (e.g., Catania, 1978; Skinner, 1981; T. L. Smith, 1986); we will note some of them as we explore the phenomena of learning.

There is a third variety of selection that occurs when behavior can be passed on from one organism to another, as in imitation or, more important, in language. For example, what someone has said or written can survive the person's death if it is passed on to and repeated by others. The verbal behavior that has survived within and been shared among the members of a group is part of the culture of that group. We will give special attention to this kind of selection in the chapters on social learning and on verbal behavior (Chapters 10 and 11).

We have been considering issues of phylogeny and selection mainly in the context of the evolution of populations of organisms and their characteristic features. Behavior is one of those features, and it can change during ontogeny, the lifetime of the individual organism, as well as during phylogeny. We now turn briefly to the relation between the phylogeny of behavior and its ontogeny.

Section B Phylogeny, Ontogeny, and Behavior

Behavior is a joint function of phylogenic contingencies—those that operated in ancestral environments during the evolution of a species—and ontogenic contingencies—those that operated during interactions between an organism and its environment within its own lifetime (cf. Skinner, 1966). Ontogeny does not recapitulate phylogeny, so we cannot expect to trace the evolution of behavior by following the development of behavior in an individual (or vice versa). Whether in spite of these limitations or because of them, a recurrent issue has been the relative contributions of phylogeny and ontogeny to behavior: To what extent does behavior depend on evolutionary history and to what extent on learning? The issues have been framed in various terms: nature versus nurture, heredity versus environment, and so on.

The research of Spalding, a nineteenth-century British naturalist, provides an eloquent case for the role of phylogeny in behavior.

> ...we have only to look at the young of the lower animals to see that as a matter of fact they do not require to go through the process of learning the meaning of their sensations in relation to external things; that chickens, for example, run about, pick up crumbs, and follow the call of their mother *immediately* on leaving the shell.... I have observed and experimented on more than fifty chickens, taking them from under the hen while yet in the eggs. But of these, not one emerging from the shell was in a condition to manifest

an acquaintance with the qualities of the outer world. On leaving the shell they are wet and helpless.... (Spalding, 1873/1954, pp. 2–3)

Spalding noted that the chicks advanced rapidly. Within 4 or 5 hours of hatching they were pecking at objects and preening their wings. But he also recognized that a lot could be learned in 4 or 5 hours.

> To obviate this objection with respect to the eye, I had recourse to the following expedient. Taking eggs just when the little prisoners had begun to break their way out, I removed a piece of the shell, and before they had opened their eyes drew over their heads little hoods, which, being furnished with an elastic thread at the lower end, fitted close round their necks. (Spalding, 1873/1954, p. 3)

Spalding kept the chicks blind for one to three days and then removed their hoods.

> Almost invariably, they seemed a little stunned by the light, remained motionless for several minutes, and continued for some time less active than before they were unhooded. Their behaviour, however, was in every case conclusive against the theory that the perceptions of distance and direction by the eye are the result of experience, of associations formed in the history of each individual life. Often at the end of two minutes they followed with their eyes the movements of crawling insects, turning their heads with all the precision of an old fowl. (Spalding, 1873/1954, p. 3)

Our primary interest in this text is in behavior that is learned, but we must always entertain the possibility that the behavior we study has phylogenic sources. We can try to create arbitrary environments to minimize the role of phylogeny. For example, a standard pigeon chamber is an arbitrary environment, because natural environments do not include keys on which a pigeon's pecks produce food only when the key is lit. But arbitrary environments are not always arbitrary enough; they will not necessarily make the behavior that occurs in them arbitrary. Consider a pigeon's key pecks:

> Such responses are not wholly arbitrary. They are chosen because they can be easily executed, and because they can be repeated quickly and over long periods of time without fatigue. In such a bird as the pigeon, pecking has a certain genetic unity; it is a characteristic bit of behavior which appears with a well-defined topography. (Ferster & Skinner, 1957, p. 7)

Behavior may start very early in an organism's life, but that in itself is not evidence that its sources are phylogenic rather than ontogenic. Recall that Spalding had misgivings about how much a chick could learn within just a few hours after hatching. Creatures may be prepared by phylogeny to do the same sorts of things that their ancestors have done, but they also may be prepared to start in early to learn. Behavior begins in the embryo (e.g., Hall & Oppenheim, 1987). Both prenatally and postnatally some of that behavior is independent of sensory input and of consequences. Other behavior, perhaps even prenatally, is modifiable: Behavior changes even with the organism's earliest interactions with its environment (e.g., Johanson & Hall, 1979; Rudy, Vogt, & Hyson, 1984). By this point it should be evident that the answer to the question of whether behavior is a product of phylogeny or of ontogeny is that it is a product of both (to questions about the relative magnitudes of their contributions, of course, the answer is usually "It depends").

Before we turn to behavior that is learned, we must note the variety of behavior that is available before learning. Behavior that is not learned comes in many varieties (Gallistel, 1980; von Holst,

1939). Some types have characteristics of oscillators (e.g., the beating of the heart). Others have characteristics of servomechanisms (e.g, the maintenance of balance, during which small displacements produce compensating adjustments). Still others are produced in various ways by stimuli (e.g., as in reflex relations or as in kineses and taxes or as in the continuous change in pupil size with changes in light intensity). The various sources of behavior provide our *taxonomy*, our system for the classification of behavior. From this classification, respondents, operants, discriminated operants, equivalences, meanings, and rememberings are some of the classes that will be examined in the chapters to come.

SUMMARY

We began with a brief survey of the evolution of life on earth. Darwin's account of that evolution, natural selection, faced challenges from other approaches, such as orthogenesis and Lamarckism. It overcame those challenges when it was integrated with Mendelian genetics and mutation theory. The genetic material was more like a recipe than a blueprint for an organism. The cumulative changes produced by natural selection over time created organized complexity, but also often meant that ancestral forms did not survive in current populations. Some biological systems were shaped directly by selection and others were incidental byproducts (spandrels). The advent of learning was one important event in the evolution of behavior; it allowed for a second kind of selection, the selection of classes of behavior within an organism's lifetime, as when responding persists because it has certain consequences. The analysis of behavior must consider both its phylogenic and its ontogenic sources.

Elicited and Emitted Behavior

Stimulus *can be traced to an Indo-European root*
steig-, *to stick. The same root also generated* distinguish, instinct, *and, via* stylus, *a writing instrument,* style. *Through the Old French* estiquet, *to
impale and later to label, it also produced a modern
French word now related to behavior,* etiquette.
    The Indo-European root spend-, *to pour a liba-
tion or to make a treaty, led to the Greek* sponde, *a
drink-offering, and the Latin* spondere, *to promise. Through these words,* response, *originally an
undertaking in return, is linked to* spouse, spon-
sor, *and perhaps even* spontaneous. *The latter
relation is interesting because* response *now refers
to a unit of behavior that need not be produced by
a stimulus; responses may be elicited by stimuli but*

*they may also occur spontaneously, when they
are said to be emitted.*

The concept of the reflex has played an
important historical role in th psychology
of learning. In the context of the vocabulary of reflexes, the first section of this
chapter deals with some effects of presenting stimuli. It starts with some relatively
simple situations in which a stimulus produces or elicits a response, and it shows
that we cannot judge the effect of the stimulus if we do not also know about the
responding that occurs in its absence. The
concepts of probability and conditional
probability provide a means for coping
with this problem. These concepts play an
important part in the treatment of several
different phenomena throughout the text.
    After examining simple reflex relations in
terms of conditional probabilities, we deal
with some circumstances under which elicited behavior changes over successive stimulus presentations. These cases set the stage
for the second section of the chapter, which
explores the ways in which behavior can
emerge if it has not been produced by an
eliciting stimulus; such behavior is said to be
emitted. The chapter closes with a discussion
of how the behavioral significance of a stimulus may change over time; imprinting is an
example used to relate such effects to the
concept of drive or motivation.

Section A   The Reflex: Elicitation

A simple way to change an organism's behavior is to present a stimulus. For someone standing and talking, for example, a sudden loud noise will probably stop the talking and produce the change in posture called the startle reaction. This reliable relation between a stimulus and the change in behavior it produces has been called a *reflex*. The vocabulary of the reflex has a long and complex history (Fearing, 1930), extending from Descartes to its contemporary usage. René Descartes, a seventeenth-century philosopher, was familiar with hydraulic devices constructed to amuse visitors in the royal gardens of France. Stepping on a concealed trigger released a flow of water that made statues move. Descartes saw a similarity between such devices and behavior. According to Descartes, stimuli were comparable to the garden visitors who

> entering into one of the grottoes containing many fountains, themselves cause, without knowing it, the movements which they witness. For in entering they necessarily tread on certain tiles or plates, which are so disposed that if they approach a bathing Diana, they cause her to hide in the rosebushes, and if they try to follow her, they cause a Neptune to come forward to meet them threatening them with his trident. (Descartes, translated in Fearing, 1930, pp. 20–21)

Just as a step on the concealed plate triggers the movement of a statue, a stimulus triggers a response. For Descartes, the role of pipes and water in these statuary systems was played by nerves and animal spirits in living organisms.

For our purposes, the most important part of Descartes' concept of the reflex was that it captured the fact that behavior is sometimes caused by environmental events, as when you quickly withdraw your hand upon touching a flame. Eventually physiologists turned their attention to the mechanism of such behavioral relations and began to explore the components of the reflex arc, the path from the original sensory impact of the stimulus through the central nervous system and then back to the muscular or glandular system within which the response occurred. Analyses of the reflex became more and more sophisticated (e.g., Sherrington, 1906), and in the conditioned-reflex concepts of Pavlov (1927) and the related behaviorism of Watson (1919) the reflex was treated as the basic unit of behavior.

We noted two examples of reflexes above, in the startle reaction and in the withdrawal of a hand from a flame. Many others are familiar: the knee jerk produced by a tap on the patellar tendon; salivation caused by food in the mouth; the postural adjustments triggered by an abrupt loss of support. These examples have the common feature that some stimulus reliably produces some response, and this is what defines a reflex. In these circumstances, we say that the stimulus *elicits* the response, or that the response is *elicited* by the stimulus; the stimulus is an *eliciting* stimulus, and the response is an *elicited* response (we never use *elicited* the other way around, to refer to the effect of a response on the occurrence of a stimulus).

The reflex is neither stimulus nor response; it is the relation between them (Skinner, 1931). For example, we would not speak of a reflex if we set off a firecracker but observed no startle response; the noise alone is insufficient to justify using the term. Neither would we speak of a reflex if we observed a response without an identifiable stimulus; by itself, the startle reaction is not a reflex. And we should not confuse startle reactions produced by loud noise with those produced in other ways. Many reflexes have been named after their characteristic responses; the startle and patellar reflexes are examples. But it is useful to remember that these are *not* names for responses; for knee jerks without eliciting stimuli, the reflex terminology would be inappropriate.

For some cases that seem superficially to involve reflex relations, the language of the reflex may be misleading. For example, the production of pupillary constriction by bright light to the eye has usually been called the pupillary reflex, but this relation involves a response that adjusts continuously to stimulus levels: As brightness increases, the pupil constricts; as it decreases, the pupil dilates. In very bright light, the human pupil may become roughly one-twentieth its area when the eye is relaxed in total darkness. Here the language of the reflex diverts attention from the inverse functional relation between pupil size and brightness by focusing on only a particular change in pupil size taken from a continuous range of possibilities.

We also will not be concerned here with reflex coordinations among responses, as when, in limb flexion or extension, the contraction of a muscle is accompanied by the relaxation of the opposing one, or with other more complex coordinations (e.g., rhythmic coordinations in locomotion; Gallistel, 1980). Some examples will be treated in Chapter 6.

PROPERTIES OF ELICITED BEHAVIOR

Once we identify a reflex relation between some stimulus and some response, we can examine its properties (cf. the Laws of the Reflex; Skinner, 1938). Consider an eliciting stimulus such as an acid or sour-tasting solution on the tongue (e.g., vinegar) and an elicited response such as salivation.

Above some *threshold* value, acid on the tongue reliably elicits salivation, but a very low concentration or small quantity may not do so; when the magnitude of a stimulus is too small to elicit a response, the stimulus is said to be *below threshold.*

The threshold is not a fixed quantity; it is a statistical summary of our measurements. As we concentrate the solution or increase its quantity, we are more likely to produce salivation. At a given concentration, we can find out how many drops on the tongue will reliably elicit salivation; conversely, for a given number of drops, we can find out what concentration is required. Some concentrations and quantities will have only marginal effects, sometimes eliciting salivation and sometimes not.

Note that a stimulus does not itself have a threshold. Rather, threshold values are determined for particular features of stimuli, with other features held constant. For example, the threshold number of drops for eliciting salivation would typically be smaller given a strong than a weak acid solution; it would therefore not be meaningful to specify the threshold number of drops without also specifying acid concentration, or vice versa.

Some time must elapse between stimulus and response; this time period is called the response *latency.* In addition, the response must exist in some *magnitude* and have some *duration.* Because these properties often vary together, they have sometimes been given a common name, *reflex strength.* Thus, responding with long latency, small magnitude, and short duration corresponds to weak reflex strength, whereas responding with short latency, large magnitude, and long duration corresponds to strong reflex strength. (The rate at which the elicited response occurs is not relevant to reflex strength, because it is determined by the rate at which the eliciting stimulus is presented.)

Sechenov (1863), a Russian physiologist, noted that the organism's energy expenditure in many responses (e.g., sneezes and coughs) far exceeds the energy provided by the eliciting stimulus. The eliciting effect of a stimulus does not depend on a direct transfer of energy from the environment to the organism; rather, observed Sechenov, the stimulus should be regarded as a trigger, releasing energy that the organism already has available in muscles or glands or other structures. This view was, of course, consistent with Descartes's conception of the reflex.

Even though the eliciting stimulus is most accurately regarded as a trigger that releases energy already available in the organism, the magnitude of the eliciting stimulus may affect the elicited response. Response latency typically varies *inversely* with stimulus magnitude; in other words, response latency decreases as stimulus magnitude increases. And response magnitude and response duration typically vary *directly* with stimulus magnitude; in other words, these measures increase as stimulus magnitude increases. Saying that reflex strength increases with stimulus magnitude simply summarizes these relations.

Once it became common to speak of reflex relations in terms of strength rather than in terms of specific measures, it also became easier to regard the reflex relation as a fundamental unit of behavior: Reflexes began to be treated as the main building blocks from which more complex behavior was constructed. The concept of the reflex had a tempting simplicity, and as it came to be more widely accepted as a behavioral unit, it seemed reasonable to conclude that reflex relations might be a basis for understanding a variety of behav-

ioral processes. Some stimuli had been identified as causes of some responses, and the faulty assumption was made that for *every* response there must exist a corresponding eliciting stimulus.

Pavlov's conditioned-reflex system and Watson's behaviorism of the 1920s and 1930s grew out of such an assumption. With reflexes serving as units of behavior, complex behavior was treated as nothing more than the combination of such units. When a response occurred with no observed eliciting stimulus, stimuli with appropriate properties were hypothesized. In addition, the responses of one reflex were assumed to have stimulus properties that enabled them to elicit other responses in turn. Thus, behavior extending over long periods of time could be interpreted as a sequence or chain of reflexes, with each response functioning simultaneously as the elicited response of one reflex and the eliciting stimulus of the next. These reflex systems were elaborated in various and sometimes ingenious ways, but they no longer command major attention in the psychology of learning. The concept of the reflex has its place, but its scope is limited and it cannot stand alone.

ELICITING STIMULI AND RESPONSE PROBABILITIES

Of the possible relations between stimuli and responses, the reflex is only one relation among many. In a reflex, some stimulus reliably produces some response. But the stimulus of that reflex may affect other responses differently, and the response of that reflex may be affected differently by other stimuli. For any stimulus, its presentation may raise the likelihood of some responses, lower the likelihood of others, and have no effect on still others. For any response, its likelihood may be raised by some stimuli, be lowered by others, and be unaffected by still others.

Furthermore, simply noting that a response reliably follows a stimulus is not enough to justify the language of the reflex. We must also know how likely the response is without the stimulus. For example, if a rat in a running wheel spent much of its time running and ran when a noise was on as well as when it was off, we could not say that noise had elicited running just because we saw the rat run after we presented noise; it might have run anyway, even without the noise. To speak of reflex relations, we must know how likely the response is in the absence of the stimulus as well as in its presence.

Consider a dog scratching. If a cat approaches, the scratching stops as the dog growls and assumes an aggressive posture. If the cat leaves and then the dog's master enters, the dog barks and jumps and wags its tail. But if the master now scolds, the dog whines and drops its tail between its legs. We cannot even say whether the dog's responses to its master are strictly elicited or depend to some extent on the consequences of past responses in the master's presence.

The cat, the master, and the master's scolding each make some responses more likely and others less likely. Some of these responses might be observed from time to time even without these stimuli, and none necessarily occurs every time a particular stimulus is presented. In a reflex relation, a response that is infrequent in the absence of some stimulus occurs reliably when that stimulus is presented. This relation is only one among many possibilities. Barking, for example, is affected by several different stimuli, and we may be interested in stimuli that make it less likely as well as those that make it more likely.

Probabilities or Relative Frequencies

These relations among stimuli and responses can best be described quantitatively. We must introduce the concept of probability, or relative frequency, so that we can define the effects of stimuli on the basis of both the probability of a response when a stimulus is present and its probability when the stimulus is absent. A probability or relative frequency is a proportion or ratio: the number of times an event occurs compared with the number of times it could have occurred.

For example, in the Babinski reflex, a splaying or spreading of the toes is elicited by a light stroke across the bottom of an infant's foot. We calculate response probability by counting how many times a response is produced over some number of stimulations. In the newborn, the splaying of the toes may be produced by each of 20 touches to the foot; the proportion of responses is therefore 20 out of 20, or a probability of 1.0. The Babinski reflex ordinarily diminishes with age, so if we test again at a later date, only 6 out of 20 touches may produce a response; the probability is now 0.3. Eventually the reflex completely disappears: None of the 20 touches produces a response, and the probability has become 0.0.

In the mathematical notation for probabilities, these examples may be written respectively as:

$$p(R_1) = 1.0; p(R_2) = 0.3; \text{ and, } p(R_3) = 0.0.$$

Here, p stands for probability and the terms in parentheses are abbreviations for the events whose probabilities are specified (in this instance, R for responses, where the subscripts 1, 2, and 3 correspond to the three successive tests). These examples also illustrate that probabilities must fall in the range from 0.0, when the event never occurs, to 1.0, when the event always occurs.

Conditional Probabilities

The Babinski reflex is uncomplicated for our purposes, because the toe-splaying does not occur often without its eliciting stimulus. But what about the blinking elicited by a puff of air to the eye? If we study this reflex with an infant who already blinks once every second or two, how can we tell elicited blinks from those that would have occurred even without an air-puff (cf. Spence & Ross, 1959)? In fact, we may not be able to say whether any particular blink is elicited. We can assess the overall effect of the stimulus, however, by comparing the probability of a blink after an air-puff with the probability after no air-puff.

Our procedure is illustrated in Figure 3–1. We watch the eyelid and record

blinks within some time period after each stimulus, and we compare responding in those time periods with responding in equivalent time periods that do not follow a stimulus.

The probabilities in this example are expressed as:

$$p(R/S) = 1.0; \; p(R/\bar{S}) = 0.6.$$

In this notation, R is a response, S is a stimulus, and a bar over a symbol (as in $\bar{S}$) is a negative sign, equivalent to *not*. Thus, the first equation may be read as: probability of response given stimulus (blink given air-puff) is 1.0. The second may be read as: Probability of response given no stimulus (blink given no air-puff) is 0.6. This kind of probability, in which the probability of one event is specified in terms of the presence or absence of another event, is called a *conditional probability* (the terminology

FIGURE 3–1 Estimating eye-blink probability with and without eliciting puffs of air. Each solid vertical line represents a blink. In Line A, no air-puffs were presented. Dashed lines mark off five 1-second periods during which blinks were recorded; blinks occurred within three of these, and the probability of a blink without a stimulus is therefore 0.6. In Line B, arrows represent puffs of air to the eye. A blink occurred in each of the five 1-second periods that followed these stimuli. The probability of a blink given an air-puff is therefore 1.0. Only the first of the two blinks following stimulus X counted toward this probability; a time period is scored either as one with no blinks or as one with at least one blink, and probability is then calculated by dividing the time periods with at least one blink by the total time periods. The air-puff raised the probability of a blink from 0.6 to 1.0 (An actual experiment would use a much larger sample of observations to calculate probabilities).

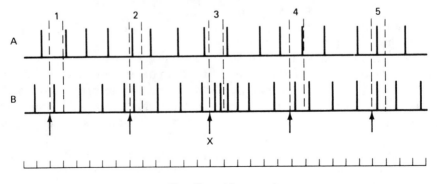

should not be confused with that of Pavlov's conditioned or conditional reflexes, even though both have the feature that one event is a condition for some other event). In other words, $p(A/B)$ can be read as: probability of A given B, or probability of A on the condition that B is present. Similarly, $p(X/\overline{Y})$ can be read as: probability of X given not-Y, or probability of X on the condition that Y is absent.

Later discussions will favor the language of probabilities over other ways of describing behavior. Saying that a stimulus caused a response is pretty much the same as saying that the stimulus elicited the response. Either usage can be applied to single instances of a reflex relation (as when this particular stimulus, M, is followed by this particular response, N). Similarly, saying that a stimulus increased response likelihood is pretty much the same as saying that it raised response probability. Either usage can be applied to average effects over many instances (as when stimulus O usually produces response P).

TYPES OF STIMULUS-RESPONSE RELATIONS

We have discussed cases involving one stimulus class and one response class. But behavior is usually more complicated: Environments include a variety of stimuli and organisms produce a variety of responses. For example, we might notice two kinds of chirps produced by a recently hatched duckling. Those produced when the mother duck is present are referred to as contentment calls; those when a strange bird appears are referred to as distress calls (e.g., Hoffman & Ratner, 1973). We could lower the likelihood of contentment calls and raise the likelihood of distress calls either by removing the mother duck or by presenting the strange bird. Our language must allow us to de-

scribe the effects of either stimulus on either response. We deal not with stimuli alone or with responses alone, but with stimulus-response relations.

Now we may summarize some of these relations in terms of conditional probabilities. For this purpose, we will use the coordinate system in Figure 3–2. The y-axis is a scale of response probability given that a stimulus has been presented; the x-axis is a scale of response probability given that the stimulus has not been presented (cf. *Coordinate* in the Glossary). In other words, any point on this graph represents two conditional probabilities: response probability given a stimulus, $p(R/S)$, and response probability given no stimulus, $p(R/\overline{S})$. For example, the point labeled A in Figure 3–2 represents a stimulus-response relation in which response probability is

FIGURE 3–2 Stimulus-response relations represented as response probabilities in the presence of a stimulus, $p(R/S)$, and in the absence of the stimulus, $p(R/\overline{S})$. Examples are shown in which a stimulus raises response probability (A), has no effect on response probability (B), or lowers response probability (C); the increase in response probability, called a reflex, in which the stimulus reliably produces or causes the response, is illustrated at D.

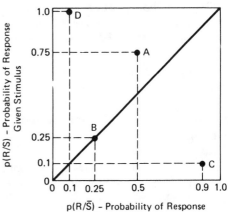

0.75 when the stimulus is presented and only 0.50 when it is not; in this instance, the stimulus raises the probability of the response.

The diagonal in Figure 3–2 is of particular interest. A response that occurs without being elicited by a stimulus is said to be *emitted*. The diagonal represents stimulus-response relations in which response probability is unaffected by or independent of the stimulus. Thus, at point *B* response probability is 0.25 whether or not the stimulus is presented. To say a response has been elicited we must know more than that it followed a stimulus. A response can just happen to follow a stimulus; we cannot say it was elicited unless we know that it was actually caused by the stimulus.

A third class of stimulus-response relations is illustrated by point *C* in Figure 3–2, for which a probability of 0.90 without the stimulus is reduced to 0.10 by the stimulus; in this instance, the stimulus reduces response probability. Such reductions of response probability by a stimulus are sometimes called *reflex inhibition.* For example, if a dog's tail-wagging stopped when a strange dog appeared, we could say that the strange dog inhibited tail-wagging.

Point *D* in Figure 3–2 represents a case in which a stimulus raises response probability from about 0.1 to about 1.0. This is the kind of stimulus-response relation we have called a reflex. The graph shows it as only one among a range of possibilities. Somewhere between the upper edge of the graph, where $p(R/S)$ is near 1.0, and the diagonal, where S has no effect on R, we must decide that the eliciting effect of the stimulus is no longer reliable enough to justify calling the relation a reflex. But where should that boundary be? Probably we would include cases in which $p(R/S)$ is just a little less than 1.0 (e.g., 0.95; maybe

even 0.90). But probably we would also exclude small effects of stimuli. For example, if a stimulus raised response probability from 0.25 to 0.35, would the stimulus-response relation qualify as a reflex? Almost certainly not.

All points above and to the left of the diagonal in Figure 3–2 represent cases in which a stimulus raises response probability, whereas those below and to the right of the diagonal represent cases in which a stimulus lowers it. Within those areas, any boundary we drew to mark off reflex relations would be arbitrary. This conclusion is important. We noted that some earlier behavioral systems, such as those of Watson and Pavlov, were based on the reflex as a fundamental unit of behavior. No doubt highly reliable reflex relations were easier to work with than other, less reliable stimulus-response relations. But if Figure 3–2 is appropriate for describing stimulus-response relations and if the reflex is only one special case among them, then any system of behavior built solely on the reflex as a behavioral unit is bound to be incomplete.

One property of behavior left out of early accounts was the emission of responses, the occurrence of responses without eliciting stimuli. Emitted responses were given such names as *instrumental* or *operant*, because they were studied in terms of how they were instrumental in changing the environment or how they operated on the environment. They derived their importance not from their relation to eliciting stimuli but from their consequences. By contrast, elicited responses were called *reflex* or *respondent*.

Once that distinction had been made, qualifications were added. In particular, it was argued that instrumental or operant behavior consisted of skeletal responses, such as movements of the limbs, whereas reflex or respondent behavior consisted of autonomic responses, such as glandular secretions. This distinction was also seen as paralleling the traditional one between voluntary and involuntary action. Such distinctions have since been seriously questioned. Skeletal responses can be elicited and autonomic responses can be emitted. It is important to maintain the distinction between elicited and emitted responding. But the same response may sometimes be elicited and sometimes emitted; thus we cannot classify responding effectively into these two categories on the basis of such physiological properties of behavior as the difference between skeletal and autonomic responses.

The graph in Figure 3–2 supports an earlier point. When we defined the reflex, we argued that the reflex is neither stimulus nor response but rather the relation between them. The graph represents stimulus-response relations; it cannot represent stimuli by themselves or responses by themselves. Thus, food as a stimulus does not have a location in the graph; its location depends on the response we measure. Similarly, a dog's tail-wagging as a response does not have a location in the graph; its location depends on the stimulus we present.

EFFECTS OF SUCCESSIVE ELICITATIONS

We have described some effects of stimulus presentations on behavior. A complication is that two different presentations of a single stimulus may have different effects. For example, you may startle much more to the first lightning flash in a thunderstorm than to later flashes. Furthermore, the effects of stimuli may depend on how quickly they follow each other. For example, if you are peeling onions, the tears elicited by the present onion may depend

on whether you began working on it immediately after finishing the last one or had just returned after taking a break. And in another effect, called *summation*, a stimulus that is below threshold in eliciting a response if presented once may become an effective elicitor if presented repeatedly at a sufficiently high rate. In other words, elicited responding often depends on the number of stimulations and on their spacing in time.

Habituation

The startle reaction is produced by an unexpected event such as a lightning flash or a sudden loud noise. Even without other events that signal it, a repeated loud noise usually produces successively smaller startle reactions, until eventually no startle at all follows the noise. Many stimuli elicit responses called orienting or observing responses; for example, a dog pricks up its ears in response to a novel sound or begins sniffing in response to an unusual odor. As these stimuli recur, the dog's responding decreases; it occurs with smaller magnitude and longer latency, perhaps until vanishing completely (we will see later, however, that orienting or observing responses may depend not only on eliciting stimuli but also on their consequences).

This reduction in responding with repeated stimuli has been given various names. For the present purposes, it will be called *habituation*. (Another possible term, *adaptation*, sometimes refers instead to changes in behavior in the continued presence of some stimulus or situation, as when an organism is said to adapt to a laboratory setting; some features of the vocabularies of habituation and related terms depend on whether changes in responding can be attributed to specific kind of changes in the nervous system; cf. Groves & Thompson, 1970).

Habituation is a characteristic of the elicited responding produced by a variety of stimuli. It has been studied with such diverse responses as the change in skin resistance produced by electric shock (the galvanic skin response, or GSR), distress calls of birds to the silhouette of a predator passing overhead, and contractions in earthworms produced by exposure to light, not to mention the startle reactions and orienting responses mentioned earlier (e.g., Ratner, 1970). It may also be an important component of the dynamics of emotion (Solomon & Corbit, 1974).

Potentiation

But stimuli sometimes have opposite effects. For example, electric shocks elicit squealing in rats; if several shocks are delivered, later presentations produce more responding than earlier ones (e.g., Badia, Suter, & Lewis, 1966). This effect has been called *potentiation* (another term sometimes used is *facilitation*; e.g., Wilson, 1959). Potentiation seems more characteristic of stimuli regarded as aversive or punishing than of stimuli regarded either as neutral or as appetitive or reinforcing.

Potentiation must not be confused with another phenomenon called *sensitization* (cf. Ison & Hoffman, 1983). In sensitization, the eliciting effects of one stimulus are enhanced as a result of presentations of some other stimulus; one stimulus amplifies the eliciting effect of another stimulus. For example, an electric shock may make it more likely that a later loud noise will produce a startle reaction; the shock is said to *sensitize* the organism to the noise.

The method of stimulus presentation can determine whether habituation or potentiation occurs. For example, Kimble and Ray (1965) studied a wiping reflex in the frog: A bristle touched to a frog's back elicits a movement over the back by the hind foot. In one group, successive touches were made to a specified region of the frog's back, but within this region the exact location of stimulation could vary from one touch to the next; in a second group, successive touches were made to precisely the same location on the frog's back each time. In both groups, 100 touches at 10-second intervals were delivered each day for 12 days. The groups began with roughly equal probabilities of elicited wiping movements, but this probability increased over days for the first group whereas it decreased for the second group. In other words, potentiation occurred when the location of the eliciting touch varied slightly from presentation to presentation, whereas habituation occurred when its location was constant (see also Hutchinson, Renfrew, & Young, 1971).

Effects of Time Since the Last Eliciting Stimulus

If the stimulus is absent for a while after habituation or potentiation, the probability that responding will be elicited returns to earlier values. For example, the startle reaction to loud noise may diminish or even disappear after several noises in succession, but it is likely to appear again in full strength if the noise later follows hours of silence. If elicited responding decreases over successive stimuli, it usually recovers to its earlier higher levels after the stimuli are discontinued. Conversely, if elicited responding increases over successive stimuli, it usually returns to its earlier lower levels after the stimuli are discontinued. Habituation and potentiation are not permanent, and the return to earlier levels takes place as time passes.

These relations are summarized in Figure 3–3. Each line shows hypothetical effects of 10 successive stimuli on response probability or reflex strength. The upper

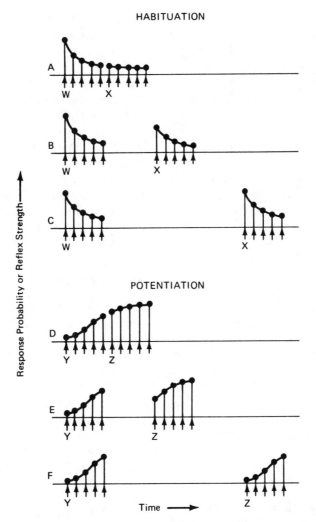

FIGURE 3–3 Temporal effects of eliciting stimuli. Arrows indicate stimuli; vertical lines indicate probabilities with which the stimuli elicit responses. Effects usually called *habituation* are illustrated in A, B, and C; probability decreases with successive stimuli. Effects sometimes called *potentiation* are illustrated in D, E, and F; probability increases with successive stimuli. In both cases, response probabilities return to earlier levels as the time since the last stimulus increases (Xs in A through C and Zs in D through F).

part of Figure 3–3 (A, B, and C) illustrates habituation; the lower part (D, E, and F) illustrates potentiation. In both cases, three examples are given that differ only in the time separating the first 5 stimuli from the second 5 stimuli. As this time lengthens (from A to C and from D to F), the respond-

ing produced by the second 5 stimuli becomes more like the responding produced by the first 5. In other words, responding returns to its earlier levels with the passage of time. For example, in A responding is elicited by the later stimulus x with a lower probability than by the first stimulus w. But when stimulus x is presented after successively longer periods without stimuli, as in *B* and *C*, the probability with which stimulus x elicits responding approaches that with which stimulus w elicited responding. Analogous relations exist for stimuli y and z in *D*, *E*, and *F*.

It seems reasonable that responding should recover from habituation and potentiation with time. If the decrease was irreversible, habituation could either occur only once in an organism's lifetime or else successive habituations would drive responding to lower and lower levels until it finally disappeared altogether. A parallel case for potentiation would similarly lead either to a single case of potentiation in the organism's lifetime or to continuing and unlimited increases in elicited responding. But such things can happen. For example, reactions of the immune system, which may be regarded as instances of elicited behavior, sometimes seem to show irreversible potentiation (e.g., for someone who has developed an allergic reaction to bee stings after having been stung several times, the reaction may diminish little if at all as time passes).

Section B   **From Elicited to Emitted Behavior**

We have seen that the reflex is just one of the many possible relations among stimuli and responses. Now we move on to examine how stimulus presentations can pattern the way in which responding is distributed over time. When stimuli occur repeatedly, they can produce temporal patterns of behavior (many effects are comparable to the way in which patterns of vibration, analogous to stimuli, produce resonances in various structures; cf. Hineline, 1981a).

Adjunctive, interim, and terminal behavior are the first topics examined in this

section. They are concerned with the order and temporal patterning of responses that occur when two or more different responses are generated by a stimulus. Other effects of repeated stimulus presentations are explored in a treatment of the law of exercise. Taken together, these topics identify possible sources of responding when responding is emitted rather than elicited. The chapter closes with a discussion of ways in which the behavioral significance of a stimulus may change over time; imprinting is an example used to relate such effects to the concept of drive or motivation.

ADJUNCTIVE BEHAVIOR

Presenting a stimulus may determine the sequence of responses that occurs over an extended time. For example, if we give a rat food it will eat. Once it has finished eating, it will then typically drink if water is available. This relation between eating and subsequent drinking is so strong that by delivering food in small amounts over an extended period we can make the rat drink several times its ordinary daily ration of water (Falk, 1971, 1977; cf. Wetherington, 1982). Falk named this increase in drinking *polydipsia*, and he called responding that depended in this way on other responding *adjunctive* behavior. Adjunctive behavior is behavior in which one response reliably accompanies some other response.

As one type of adjunctive behavior, polydipsia follows at least partly from the rat's normal feeding and drinking pattern. With food and water freely available, the rat ordinarily takes a few large meals daily and drinks after each meal. If we then force the rat to take many small meals by delivering food in many small portions at intervals of a few minutes, the rat still drinks after each meal but does not reduce the size of each drink enough to compensate for its more frequent drinking. Thus, a rat that went from five large to 50 small meals per day would now drink 10 times as often. If drinks after each of the 50 small meals were only half instead of a tenth the size of drinks taken after each of the five large meals, the rat would drink five times as much as before. Such increases in the rat's daily water intake are so reliable that polydipsia can be used to get rats to consume substances that they ordinarily reject (e.g., alcohol; Meisch & Thompson, 1971).

Adjunctive behavior can include many other responses besides eating and drink-ing. For example, if a running wheel is available to a rat instead of water, running in the wheel will follow eating in much the same way as drinking follows eating in polydipsia (Levitsky & Collier, 1968; see also Hutchinson, Renfrew, & Young, 1971).

INTERIM AND TERMINAL BEHAVIOR

The presentation of a stimulus may impose temporal structure on behavior in other ways. Figure 3–4 illustrates an experiment that examined patterns of behavior generated in pigeons by repeated

FIGURE 3–4 Probabilities of a pigeon's responses in successive seconds of a 12-second period between presentations of food. A sequential pattern is implied by the different times at which each response reaches maximum probability. Data are from the last 3 of 109 sessions of 64 food deliveries each. Orientation toward the feeder wall, not shown, increased over time in each 12-second period; low-frequency responses such as wing-flapping and preening are also omitted. (Adapted from Staddon & Simmelhag, 1971, Figure 1)

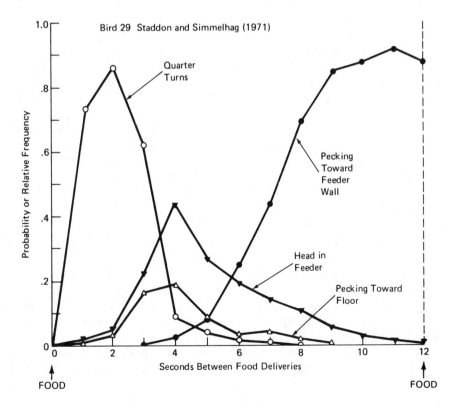

food presentations (Staddon & Simmelhag, 1971). Each pigeon was placed in a chamber on one wall of which was an opening to a feeder, a tray of grain ordinarily out of the pigeon's reach; food was presented by lighting the tray and lifting it to a position where the pigeon could eat from it. Figure 3–4 illustrates a pigeon's behavior during constant 12-second periods that separated successive 2-second food deliveries.

The experimenters observed the pigeon through a window in the chamber and scored responding in various categories. Some were movements, such as pecks directed toward the feeder wall or toward the floor; others were postures that could be maintained for some time, such as orientation toward the feeder wall. The categories were determined by watching many pigeons for an extended period.

Early in each 12-second interfood period, Bird 29 usually made quarter-turns, and then, but less frequently, put its head into the feeder opening or pecked toward the floor. Other pigeons showed patterns that included different responses, such as preening or pacing. These responses became less likely and pecking became the dominant or most likely response as the time of the next feeder operation approached. Staddon and Simmelhag called the varied responding early in each period *interim* behavior (in Figure 3–4, quarter-turns, head-in-feeder, and floor-directed pecks). The more consistent responding later in each period, which typically included some form of pecking, was called *terminal* behavior (in Figure 3-4, wall-directed pecks).

Staddon and Simmelhag's original purpose was to evaluate an earlier experiment on repeated food presentations by Skinner (1948). Skinner observed that pigeons tended to repeat responses that had preceded earlier food presentations and called this repetition an experimental *superstition.*

> The conditioning process is usually obvious. The bird happens to be executing some response as the hopper appears; as a result it tends to repeat this response. If the interval before the next presentation is not so great that extinction takes place, a second "contingency" is probable. This strengthens the response still further....The bird behaves as if there were a causal relation between its behavior and the presentation of food, although such a relation is lacking. (Skinner, 1948, pp. 168–171)

Skinner noted that the pigeon's responding often changed gradually as the procedure continued. The topography or form of responding did not seem forced in any particular direction. Instead, accidental relations developed between responding and food deliveries. Skinner referred to these gradual changes as *topographical drift.* A pigeon might respond temporarily as if its responses were producing food as a consequence, but its responding changed or drifted over the long run and no particular response could be identified consistently as superstitious behavior. Staddon and Simmelhag observed that, over longer periods of time with this procedure, pecking often dominates as the response just preceding food deliveries.

Superstition remains controversial, and we will return to it later. For the moment, our concern is with the temporal structure that repeated stimulus presentations impose on behavior. Responding early in interfood intervals—interim behavior—varied from one pigeon to another, whereas later responding—terminal behavior—was fairly constant across pigeons and usually included some form of pecking. Pecking is also the behavior occasioned by food presentations; the bird takes food into its mouth by pecking. At least in this case, terminal behavior seems to have something in common with the responses produced by stimulus presentations.

It would be convenient to conclude that repeated stimuli not only elicit responses but also produce terminal behavior closely related to the elicited responding. Unfortunately, behavior is not that simple. How or even whether the classes of behavior called adjunctive or interim and terminal or superstitious should be distinguished is not yet settled. The problem is that it is hard to show that sequences of behavior generated by successive stimuli are unaffected by their consequences, the discriminative effects of stimuli, and other variables (e.g., Reid & Staddon, 1982). We will return in Chapter 6 to the organization of behavior.

THE ROLE OF EXERCISE

"Practice makes perfect" is a familiar saying about the role of repetition in behavior. Before the effects of the consequences of responding were appreciated, it was believed that the mere repetition of responding, without regard to its consequences, was sufficient to maintain behavior. Consider the following from Sechenov.

...an infant is able to cough, sneeze and swallow immediately upon birth. The act of sucking also belongs to this category of complex movements....Indeed, everybody knows that a new-born child is able to suck....Moreover, it is a well-known fact that the activity of this complex mechanism in the infant is called forth by irritation of the lips; put, for example, your finger, or a candle, or a wooden stick between the child's lips, and it will begin to suck. Try to do the same with a child three months after it has been weaned, and it will no longer do so; however, the ability to produce sucking movements at will is retained by man for life. These are highly remarkable facts: on the one hand, they show that the con-

duction of sensation from the lips to the central nervous mechanisms which produce the sucking movements apparently ceases in the child after weaning; on the other hand, they indicate that the integrity of this conduction is maintained by the frequent repetition of the reflex. (Sechenov, 1863, pp. 28–29)

Sechenov here emphasizes the complexity of the sucking response, but more important is his observation on the role of repetition. Not only does repetition maintain the response, according to Sechenov, but the response also becomes independent of the effects of eliciting stimuli. In the infant, sucking is elicited by stimuli ("irritation of the lips"); later, these stimuli no longer elicit the response, but the organism through adulthood remains able to produce the response even in the absence of these stimuli (cf. Schoenfeld, 1966; Segal, 1972; see also Hall & Oppenheim, 1987, p. 113: "For most altricial species, the ability to suckle from the mother is reduced if suckling is not practiced....virtually all of the organized maternally oriented behavior of most infant animals can be shown to be heavily influenced by experienced events").

On the basis of such phenomena, we might say that the repeated elicitation of a response increases the likelihood that the response will be emitted. Early accounts of learning (e.g., Thorndike, 1921; cf. Verhave, 1967) treated effects of response repetition as basic components of learning, described in terms of laws of *exercise* or laws of *practice*. These laws were usually ambiguous on such questions as whether it mattered if the repeated response were elicited or emitted. In any case, they soon were overshadowed by other concerns. As the psychology of learning turned to other phenomena such as reinforcement and stimulus control, the possibility of a role for exercise or practice became neglected. The evidence is too scanty to allow firm conclusions about whether exercise or practice might be a basic component of learning. Nevertheless, some tantalizing data exist.

For example, Dill (1974) studied escape responses of a tropical fish, the zebra danio, from a stimulus designed to resemble the rapid approach of a larger predatory fish. As the stimulus loomed, the danio began to swim away from it (despite its aquatic medium, this swimming response of the fleeing fish can aptly be called a flight reaction). The latency with which swimming began (or the threshold for size or rate of growth of the stimulus) decreased with repeated exposures; this is equivalent to saying that the stimulus more and more strongly elicited the escape response. When tested after 10 days without further elicitations, the response had not returned to its earlier values. The change produced by the stimulus was not reversible (recall the discussion of potentiation; see also Chapter 5 on species-specific defense reactions).

But not all responses begin with elicitation. Some of the earliest responses in an organism's lifetime occur spontaneously, in the absence of identifiable eliciting stimuli. For example, inside its egg the embryo chick makes uncoordinated movements of its limbs and body. These movements may prevent the developing bones from becoming fixed in their sockets, or may modify the form of the growing bones and connective tissue. Later in the embryo's development, eliciting effects of stimuli appear, perhaps simply as the embryo's sensory apparatus matures. This progression from spontaneous responding to elicited responding may be summarized by saying of chick embryos that "they 'act' before they 'react'" (Provine, 1976, p. 210). Stimuli become more important later, as

when the chick's rotating movements in pecking its way out of its shell during hatching are affected by whether the chick continues to encounter intact portions of the shell.

Evidence suggests that pecking in the young chick depends not only on the conditions that elicited pecks and the consequences of earlier pecks but also on how much pecking the chick has already engaged in (Hogan, 1971). Once responding occurs, whatever its origin, it may have consequences, and the chick's survival may depend on whether those consequences in turn affect its behavior. Among gulls, for example, pecking at but missing the parent's beak has different consequences from striking the beak; only in the latter case is the parent gull likely to feed the chick. These differential consequences affect the accuracy of the chick's later pecking only as the response becomes independent of its eliciting stimuli. Once a response has been elicited by a stimulus, the response may become more likely even in the absence of the stimulus.

In experiments on salivation, dogs at first salivate only when food is presented, but after several food presentations they begin to salivate even when food is absent (e.g., Zener & McCurdy, 1939). Such responding, called *spontaneous* salivation, had been attributed to conditioning of the salivary response to features of the experimental setting. For example, it might be argued that the eliciting stimulus was a spot on the wall that the dog just happened to see when food deliveries began. No other eliciting stimuli were identifiable, so the only way to justify the inclusion of all salivary responses in a reflex relation was to assume that salivation could be elicited by such arbitrary features. Yet the problem of identifying a stimulus simply vanishes once we admit the possibility that responses can occur without eliciting stimuli; in fact, we cannot otherwise conceive of emitted responding at all. The concept of emitted responding will be essential to our treatment of consequential operations such as reinforcement and punishment.

Early behavior theories held that the simple repetition of behavior was important in its own right to the development and maintenance of that behavior. Consider the following from Sechenov: "If a child which has just learned to walk becomes ill and remains in bed for a long time, it forgets the previously acquired art of walking....This fact testifies once again to the great import for nervous activity of frequent repetition" (Sechenov, 1863, p. 29).

We can no longer be sure of the evidence upon which Sechenov based his conclusion (e.g., did he observe one child or many children?), but we can consider a contemporary example, in Zelazo, Zelazo, & Kolb (1972). This research involved the walking reflex, which appears in newborn infants and disappears at about 8 weeks (McGraw, 1945). The response of the walking reflex has much in common with the behavior that the child engages in later when learning to walk. Coordinated walking movements resembling those of an adult can be elicited by holding the infant under its arms with its feet touching a level surface. When parents exercised their infants' walking reflexes by holding them so as to elicit the walking response, the walking reflex was less likely to drop out and walking was initiated earlier on the average than in other groups of infants for whom walking was not exercised. Thus, exercise of this reflex during the first 8 weeks of life not only increased elicited responding that ordinarily decreases during this time period; it may have shortened the time to the later appearance of this response as a component of emitted behavior, walking.

But, as Zelazo, Zelazo, and Kolb recognized, walking movements produce other changes in the infant's world (visual, kinesthetic, or tactile) that might reinforce such responses. Even during the 8 weeks of exercise, walking was sometimes emitted rather than elicited, and more was going on than simple elicitation: "Walking...seemed to progress from a reflexive to an instrumental response. There is little doubt that learning occurred....Not only were there more responses...but they were better executed" (Zelazo, Zelazo, & Kolb, 1972, p. 315). The situation is further complicated as an example of elicitation by changes in the infants' weights and in the supporting capacities of their limbs over the time course of such studies (Thelen, Fisher, Ridley-Johnson, & Griffen, 1982).

We have speculated that after a response is produced by a stimulus it may become more likely even in the absence of the stimulus. In other words, eliciting a response may raise its probability of emission. This formulation differs from the classical laws of exercise or practice to which we have related it, and it depends only on the simple experimental operation of stimulus presentation. But we need not try to establish such laws. Some emitted responses may originate because they are first elicited whereas others may be emitted from the start. The issue, then, is not the universality of laws of exercise or such alternatives as spontaneous emission; rather, it is what the source of responding is in particular cases. We will treat other problems in behavior analysis in this way in later chapters. Instead of attempting to explain instances of behavior in terms of exhaustive formal laws, we will seek an appropriate *taxonomy* of behavior, a systematic classification of behavior in terms of its origins.

STIMULUS PRESENTATIONS
IN IMPRINTING

Up to this point, we have concentrated on how stimuli affect responding. Virtually all of the phenomena considered so far can be defined and described in terms of response probabilities: In a reflex relation, a stimulus raises the probability of a response to near 1.0; in reflex inhibition, a stimulus reduces the probability of a response; in habituation, response probability decreases over successive stimulus presentations; in adjunctive behavior, the elicitation of one response changes the probability of some other response; in the phenomenon of exercise, successive elicitation raises response probability in the absence of the stimulus. We now examine an outcome of stimulus presentations, *imprinting*, that must be discussed in terms other than the effects of the stimulus on response probability (cf. Lorenz, 1937; Hess, 1973). Imprinting includes some effects of stimulus presentation that provide a bridge to the treatment of response consequences in the next chapter.

When a duckling hatches, the first moving thing it is likely to see is its mother, and even on this first day of its life outside the egg the duckling will probably begin to stay close to her. But if the mother is gone and the duckling first sees something else in motion, such as a human, the duckling will behave toward this stimulus as it otherwise would have toward its mother. Such stimuli are said to be *imprinted*, or, in a figurative sense, stamped into the duckling.

Imprinting has been demonstrated in both laboratory and field with a variety of stimuli, ranging from real and model birds to electric trains (some stimuli, of course, work better than others). The development of imprinting is sometimes said to have a *critical period* of one or a few days: If imprinting does not occur during this critical period, it may not occur at all. One view (Hoffman & Ratner, 1973) suggests that this happens because fear of novel stimuli develops by the end of the critical period; as the birds get older, they make characteristic distress calls in the presence of and they move away from novel stimuli. Thus, older birds do not ordinarily stay near such stimuli long enough for imprinting to occur. This view implies that imprinting could occur at any time in the duck's life if this later effect of novel stimuli could be prevented or reversed (see also Hoffman & Solomon, 1974).

Whatever the basis for the critical period, the duckling begins to respond in significant ways to a stimulus, whether mother duck, human, or some arbitrary moving object, if the stimulus is introduced early enough in the duckling's life. One of these responses is following the imprinted stimulus as it moves; it has sometimes been said that the duckling's following is elicited by the imprinted stimulus, but it is misleading to speak of elicitation.

If the imprinted stimulus is the mother duck, the duckling follows her about and emits distress calls in her absence. But how does the imprinted stimulus produce following? When the duckling walks toward the mother, it finds itself closer to her; when it walks from her, it finds itself farther away. In other words, the natural consequence of walking in different directions is to change its distance from its mother. If closeness to the mother is important to the duckling, it is no surprise that it walks toward rather than away from her. It follows that if we change the duckling's world so that the mother's closeness requires some response other than walking, the walking should be replaced by that other response.

Such an experiment was designed by Peterson (1960). A dark compartment on one side of a window contained a moving imprinted stimulus. A duckling, on the other side of the window, was given a response that could light up the dark side. It did so even when the response was one incompatible with following, such as pecking at a disk on the wall or standing still on a platform near the window. In other words, the critical property of the imprinted stimulus was not that it could elicit particular responses, such as following or pecking or standing still, but rather that it had become important to the duckling and therefore could reinforce or increase the frequency of such responses as following or pecking or standing still. In the natural environment, the duckling's response of following ordinarily keeps it close to the imprinted stimulus (usually its mother), but a laboratory environment shows that ducklings can learn another response if it instead of following has this important consequence of keeping the imprinted stimulus close.

In imprinting, the initial presentations of the to-be-imprinted stimulus do not change response probabilities. Rather, they are establishing operations: They change the significance of the stimulus. The imprinted stimulus acquires its significance simply by being presented at a particular time in the duckling's life. It begins as a stimulus toward which the duckling is relatively indifferent but ends as a stimulus that functions as a reinforcer and therefore can shape the duckling's behavior toward it.

DRIVE AND THE SIGNIFICANCE OF STIMULI

There are other ways to change the significance of stimuli. Some were treated in Chapter 1, as examples of establishing operations. For example, if a rat was more likely to eat than to run in a running wheel, we would expect the rat to press a lever more often if its presses produced

food than if its presses produced only access to the wheel. While continuing to allow the rat free access to food, however, we could lock the wheel so that it could no longer rotate, thereby preventing the rat from running. After deprivation of wheel running, we might then find the rat more likely to run than to eat if the opportunity to run was available again, and more likely to press the lever if presses produced access to the wheel than if the presses produced food. In other words, by depriving the rat of one or another of these, we changed their relative significance; through the deprivation of one or the other, we were able to make running more likely than eating or eating more likely than running.

Changes in the significance of stimuli are the basic concern of the study of *drive* or *motivation* (e.g., Bolles, 1975). Stimuli may be made more or less reinforcing or more or less aversive, depending upon such factors as the time since their last presentation. Food, for example, becomes more reinforcing as time passes since the last opportunity to eat, and it may even become aversive after eating if an unusually large quantity is consumed.

The significance of stimuli can also be changed through means other than deprivation; for example, as we shall see in later chapters, conditioned reinforcers and conditioned aversive stimuli are stimuli that have acquired their reinforcing or aversive properties through their relation to other stimuli. (For a discussion of the interaction between motivation and habituation effects, see Solomon & Corbit, 1974).

Physiological studies of motivation are typically concerned with relations between organic factors and the significance of stimuli (e.g., effects of blood levels of glucose on behavior with respect to food, effects of hormonal levels on sexual behavior, etc.). Motivation or drive, therefore, is not a special force to be located somewhere within an organism; rather, it is a term applied to the many environmental and organic variables that make stimuli significant to an organism.

SUMMARY

We have concentrated on how stimuli affect responding. Many of the phenomena considered so far can be defined and described in terms of response probabilities: In a reflex relation, a stimulus raises response probability to near 1.0; in reflex inhibition, a stimulus reduces response probability; over successive stimulus presentations, the probability of elicited responding may decrease (habituation) or increase (potentiation); in adjunctive behavior, the elicitation of one response changes the probability of some other response; cyclic presentations of stimuli alter the probability of interim and terminal behavior; successive elicitations may raise response probability in the absence of the stimulus, as in the phenomenon of exercise. The example of imprinting involved additional effects of stimulus presentations, and set the stage for a discussion of drive.

We are now ready to move on to the consequential operations of reinforcement and punishment. When responding has consequences, the consequences also have their effects as stimuli. We will therefore find our understanding of the effects of presenting stimuli useful in dealing with the effects of consequences.

PART III *Learning Without Words*

CHAPTER **4**

Consequences of Responding: Reinforcement

The Indo-European root, sekw-, to follow, links
consequence *to sign and* designate *(from the
Latin* signum, *something that one follows) and*
to social *and* association *(from the Latin* so-
cius, *a companion or follower). It shares its
prefix,* con-, *with* conditioning, contingency,
and contiguity. Conditioning, *through the
Indo-European root* deik-, *to show or pronounce, has many relatives:* teach, *from the Old
English* taecan, *to show or instruct;* judgment,
from the Latin judex, *he who pronounces the
law; and* paradigm, *from the Greek* para, *beside, and* deiknunai, *to show.* Contingency,
from the Latin contingere, *to touch on all sides,
to happen, has varied meanings: a possibility; a*
*condition of being dependent on chance; some-
thing incidental to something else. Like* contact,
it combines the roots com- , *together, and* tan-
gere, *to touch.* Contiguity, *the condition of
touching or being in contact, has the same origins. Curiously,* contingency *and* contiguity
are usually contrasted in psychology: contingency, *in its technical use, stresses how the
likelihood of one event may be affected or caused
by other events, whereas* contiguity *simply implies the juxtaposition of events in space or time,
without regard to causation.*

The environment can do things to an organism, but the organism in turn can do
things to its environment. An organism's
behavior can have consequences. A rat in
a place without food may find food by
going somewhere else. The rat can change
its environment merely by moving from
one place to another. This consequence
may also change the rat's future behavior:
The rat may go to the same place later
when again deprived of food. An important property of behavior is that it can be
affected by its consequences.

Arranging consequences for behavior
is more than simply presenting stimuli.
The stimuli must occur in some relation to
behavior. The environment must be arranged so that the organism's responses
make something happen. Consequences
for behavior already exist in the natural
environment. Even before we intervene,

organisms change their environments by doing things or by going from one place to another. But we can better study how consequences affect behavior by arranging consequential operations in the laboratory. For example, we can build a maze so that a water-deprived rat will find water after making an appropriate sequence of turns, or we can build a chamber in which a food-deprived pigeon can produce food by pecking a key on the wall. Then we can see how water affects the turns the rat takes as it runs through the maze or how food affects the rate at which the pigeon pecks the key. In both cases, responses have consequences and the consequences affect future responding.

This chapter begins by exploring the historical development of experiments on the consequences of behavior. It then treats some properties of the contemporary concept of reinforcement: the significance of discontinuing reinforcement (extinction), the relativity of reinforcement, the kinds of consequences that can be reinforcing, and the range of responses that can be reinforced. The chapter concludes by showing that reinforcement is relevant not only to behavior maintained by physiologically significant consequences such as food and water, but also to such simple sensory-motor interactions as the visual consequences of eye movements.

Section A   Reinforcement and Extinction

Chapter 1 considered Thorndike's experiments with problem boxes from which animals could escape by operating a device that released the door. Typically, a food-deprived animal was placed inside the box with food available outside. In its varied activity, the animal sooner or later operated the device that released the door and was free to leave the box. With repetition it operated the device that opened the door more and more rapidly upon being placed in the box. The response was at first of low probability, but because it opened the door it became more and more probable.

Thorndike described how the consequences of responding affected later responding in terms of a principle he called the *Law of Effect*. The law went through many revisions, but its essence was that responses could be made more probable by some consequences and less probable by others. In language closer to Thorndike's, responses with satisfying effects were stamped in whereas those with annoying effects were stamped out. (The earliest version of Thorndike's law was called the *strong* Law of Effect. Later, he repudiated the second half of the law, leaving the increase in probability, or stamping in, but discarding the decrease in probability, or stamping out. What remained was then called the *weak* Law of Effect. This historical point will be relevant in Chapter 5, when we deal with punishment.)

Figure 4–1 illustrates data from an experiment with one of Thorndike's cats. To escape from this box, the cat had to pull a string that ran from a wire loop at the front of the box to a bolt that held the door. The first time in the box, the cat took 160 seconds to escape. This time decreased gradually and irregularly over successive trials until, during the last few trials, the cat was reliably escaping in less than 10 seconds. This process, the gradual decrease in the time taken to complete a task, came to be called trial-and-error learning (Köhler later contrasted this gradual change with the sudden or insightful solutions he observed with chimpanzees).

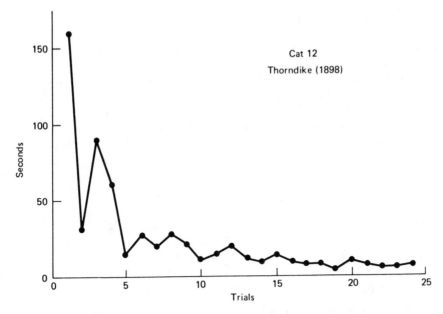

FIGURE 4-1   A learning curve. A cat's time to escape from a problem box as a function of trials. (From Thorndike, 1898, Figure 1)

MAZES AND LEARNING CURVES

In later years, trial-and-error learning was studied with many different organisms in many different types of situations. Experimenters believed that the intelligence of different species could be compared by seeing how rapidly learning went in problem-boxes, mazes, runways, and other apparatuses (e.g., Hilgard, 1951). Apparatus design began to be dictated by theoretical questions: whether learning took place in discrete steps, on an all-or-none basis, or instead occurred gradually and continuously; whether organisms learned movements (response learning) or properties of the environment (stimulus learning); whether the consequences of responding led directly to learning, or only made the organism perform so as to demonstrate what it had learned in other ways.

A common feature of these experiments was that responding became more probable when it had certain consequences. The change in probability was measured differently depending on the apparatus and the experimental aims. Graphs showing how behavior changed during an experiment were called *learning curves:* time to complete a response as a function of number of trials (e.g., Figure 4–1); the percentage of correct responses; the proportion of animals reaching some criterion of successful performance. Sometimes these measures were transformed to ease comparisons among them. When rats ran through a maze, for example, the time to run from startbox to goalbox ordinarily decreased whereas the percentage of correct turns and the proportion of rats making errorless runs increased. Converting the time to run through the maze to speed, defined as the reciprocal of the running time, made all three measures increase with learning. But the shapes of learning curves depended so much on the apparatuses used and the measures taken that the progress of learning was not describable in any unitary way.

The problem was that these experiments produced complicated performances. For example, measuring the time course over which a rat stopped entering blind alleys as it learned its way through a maze did not show how learning proceeded at a single choice point. This consideration led to the gradual simplification of mazes, as illustrated in Figure 4–2.

Diagram *A* in Figure 4–2 shows the plan of the earliest maze used to study animal learning (Small, 1899–1900). The maze was a six-by-eight-foot modification of the hedge maze at Hampton Court

in England. (Curiously, such mazes may also have provided the setting for the hydraulically operated statues that contributed to Descartes's concept of the reflex; cf. Chapter 3.) When a cage door at the start was lifted, rats could enter the maze; food was in the goal area at the center. With increasing experience in this maze they reached the goal area more rapidly and with fewer wrong turns along the way. But it was difficult to examine learning at any particular choice-point. The choice at point 1 in diagram A might be learned more quickly than that at point 7 either because of the early and late positions of these choice-points in the maze or because their floor plans differed; the choice at point 4 might be learned more

FIGURE 4–2 Stages in the evolution of mazes in studies of animal learning: *A.* the Hampton Court maze, as adapted by Small (1899–1900); *B.* a U-maze with six choice-points; *C.* the single-choice-point T-maze; and *D.* the runway or straight alley.

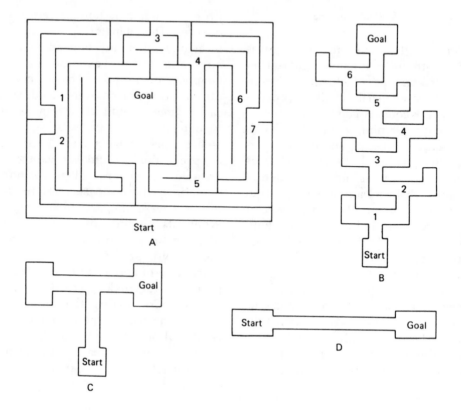

quickly than that at point 5 either because of the different ways in which point 4 could be approached (from 3 or from 5) or because of the fewer occasions on which point 5 would be encountered if the rat often went from point 3 to point 4 directly rather than by way of point 5.

Gradually, mazes evolved into more systematic forms, as in diagram *B* of Figure 4–2. In this maze, sometimes called a *U-maze* after the form of the successive units, choice-points were essentially the same as the rat approached each one; they differed only in their locations in the sequence and in whether left or right turns were correct. This kind of systematic arrangement made it easy to specify the correct sequence (in *B*, right-left-right-left-left-right) and to keep track of errors. Even here, however, possible position and sequence interactions complicate the analysis. For example, is the rat's choice of left at point 4 affected by the preceding right turn at point 3 or the following left turn at point 5; would it matter if the rat approached point 4 after coming back from the blind alley at point 3, having made an error there, instead of after a correct right turn at point 3; does it matter that point 4 is in the middle rather than near the beginning or end of the maze?

It was perhaps inevitable that the maze would be reduced to a single choice-point, as in the *T-maze* shown with a goalbox on the right in diagram *C* in Figure 4–2. Here, when the rat left the startbox it had only to make a single choice of right or left. But complications were still possible. For example, suppose one rat in its first trial in the T-maze turned right whereas a second rat turned left. Should the second one be allowed to retrace its steps after reaching the empty box at the end of the left arm? If instead it is returned to the startbox, should it be forced to the goalbox, by

blocking the left arm of the alley, to make sure its experience in the goalbox is comparable to the first rat's? The next logical step was to eliminate choice points completely, leaving nothing but a simple runway, as in diagram *D* in Figure 4–2. Now no errors were possible, and the measures of behavior were reduced simply to the speed with which the rat moved from startbox to goalbox.

There were other problems. Average measures of the performance of a group did not necessarily represent performances of the individuals in the group. Suppose that single rats running in a T-maze usually change abruptly from making frequent errors to making consistently correct turns, but this change occurs on different trials for different rats. In a large group of rats, 65 percent might make correct turns by the fifth trial, 72 percent by the sixth, 79 percent by the seventh, 83 percent by the eighth, and so on, until performance becomes stable at 98 to 100 percent by the twentieth trial. This group performance, giving the appearance of a gradual increase in correct turns, would completely obscure the abrupt change in performance by individual rats (cf. Sidman, 1952).

Even the simple runway was not an ultimate solution, because the speed of running down a straight alley was affected by many trivial factors. If trials began with the opening of a startbox door, speed depended on the direction the animal was facing when the door opened. It could also be affected by the experimenter's handling of the animal when moving it between trials from the goalbox to the startbox, or by odor trails left by other animals, and even by whether the room in the goalbox allowed a running animal to slow down without banging its head against the goalbox wall (cf. Killeen & Amsel, 1987).

With mazes or runways, the experimenter had to return the organism from goalbox to startbox to begin a new trial, and only recorded behavior indirectly by measuring time taken to get from startbox to goalbox. In such cases, the experimenter rather than the organism determined when behavior occurred, and the overall time measure did not specify what the organism did on each trial. Two experimental innovations helped to solve these problems: first, an apparatus designed so that the organism could repeatedly emit an easily specified response without the experimenter's intervention; second, a recording method based directly on the rate or frequency of responding rather than on indirect measures derived from complex response sequences or groups of organisms. Inspired partly by an interest in reducing the handling of the organism and thereby simplifying the experimenter's work, these were important features of a direction of research initiated by Skinner (1930, 1938, 1950; see especially Skinner, 1956, for a history of these developments).

EXPERIMENTAL CHAMBERS AND CUMULATIVE RECORDS

Figure 4–3 illustrates two representative apparatuses: a standard rat chamber with a single lever on the left and a three-key pigeon chamber on the right. They share response devices (the rat's lever and the pigeon's three keys), mechanisms for delivering reinforcers such as food or water (a pellet dispenser for the rat and a grain hopper for the pigeon), and stimulus sources (a speaker and a lamp for the rat and lamps or projectors behind each of the keys for the pigeon; the rat chamber sometimes also includes a grid floor for the delivery of electric shock).

In a typical arrangement with a rat, the rat is placed in the chamber when food-deprived. A lever protrudes from one wall. Near the lever is a food cup into which food pellets can be dispensed from a delivery system on the other side of the wall; each pellet delivery is usually accompanied by a distinctive sound. General illumination is provided by the houselight, and noise can be broadcast

FIGURE 4–3　A rat chamber (left) and a three-key pigeon chamber (right). The rat chamber includes a lever (*A*), a food cup and pellet delivery tube (*B*), a speaker (*C*), a lamp or houselight (*D*), and a grid floor through which shock can be delivered (*E*). The pigeon chamber includes three keys (*F, G, H*) and the opening to a food hopper (*I*). Lamps or projectors behind each key allow colors or patterns to be displayed on them.

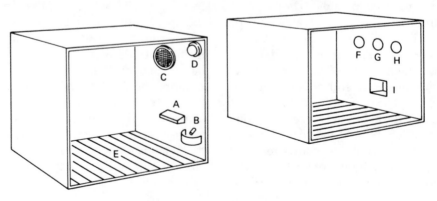

from the speaker to mask sounds from outside the chamber.

The first step is feeder training. Pellets are delivered into the food cup. Sooner or later, the rat finds and eats them. Once this happens, pellet deliveries continue until the rat comes quickly to the food cup from any chamber location upon each delivery; ten or twenty pellets are ordinarily sufficient. Once feeder training is completed, the apparatus is changed so that pellet deliveries depend upon lever-presses. Eventually the rat presses the lever, this lever-press produces a food pellet, and the food pellet occasions eating. The rat will then probably go back to the lever and press it again. (Alternatives to waiting for the lever-press are considered in Chapter 6.) The outcome of interest is the frequency with which the rat presses the lever. If this frequency increases, we call the food pellet a *reinforcer*. In the type of chamber shown in Figure 4–3, other kinds of reinforcers can be substituted. For example, the pellet dispenser could be replaced by a dipper that delivers small quantities of water or milk.

A pigeon chamber differs from one for rats in that keys substitute for levers and the feeder accommodates the pigeon's standard diet. A key is a piece of plastic mounted behind a round hole in the chamber wall. One of its components is a switch that electrically records the pigeon's pecks if they are forceful enough (keys are routinely sensitive to forces of less than 0.1 Newton, which is about 10 grams, or one-third of an ounce). The plastic is usually translucent, so that lamps or miniature projectors behind the key can project patterns or colors on it. The chamber in Figure 4–3 contains three keys, arranged horizontally about 23 centimeters (9 inches) above the chamber floor. Any particular experiment might use only one of these keys,

some combination of two, or all three. Keys are typically lit when they are in use.

The feeder opening is centered below the keys. When operated, the feeder brings a tray of pigeon food (mixed grain or commercially available pigeon pellets) within the pigeon's reach. Like the delivery of the rat's pellet, operation of the pigeon feeder is accompanied by characteristic sounds; it is also common practice to light the feeder and turn off all other chamber lights whenever the feeder is operated. The chamber typically includes other features, such as a houselight for dim general illumination, sources of masking noise or other auditory stimuli, ventilation and temperature control, and so on.

As with the rat, if the pecks on a key by a food-deprived pigeon produce food, the rate at which the pigeon pecks the key will ordinarily increase. In these apparatuses, the opportunity to eat is used to raise the probability of a response. A common property of these arrangements for a rat's lever-presses or a pigeon's key-pecks is that responses have consequences and these consequences change behavior. The rat and the pigeon are common laboratory organisms. They each have idiosyncratic species-specific behavior patterns that must be taken into account, and we must not assume that what we observe with rats or pigeons can be generalized to other organisms. Nevertheless, the diet, housing, susceptibility to disease, and other characteristics of these animals are reasonably well understood, and their size, relatively long life span, and economy make them particularly convenient. Thus, we will find that they have often served in experiments on the consequences of responding.

The responding in apparatuses like those in Figure 4–3 has sometimes been called *free-operant* responding: *free* because the organism is free to emit the response at any time rather than waiting for the experimenter (as when the rat in a goalbox must wait to be placed back in the startbox before it can run through a maze again); and *operant* because the response operates on the environment. Free-operant responding lends itself to a recording method, the cumulative record, that provides a detailed and convenient picture of how responding changes over time. In a cumulative recorder, illustrated in Figure 4–4, a roll of paper is threaded around a roller. A motor drives the roller at a constant speed, feeding out the paper. A pen or other writing device rests on the paper as it passes over the roller, and each response (e.g., a rat's lever-press or a pigeon's key-peck) moves the pen a small distance along the roller, at right angles to the movement of the paper. The resulting record therefore shows the total responses accumulated at any time during the session.

Examples of cumulative records are shown in Figure 4–5. Because the paper moves at a constant speed, the slope of the record is steeper the higher the rate of responding, as illustrated in records *A* and *B*. In the scale for Figure 4–5, the rate of responding is roughly 30 responses per minute for record *A* and 12 per minute for record *B*. Record *C* includes only a few responses; the horizontal portions indicate periods of time without responses (note that a cumulative record cannot have a negative slope, because the pen can record responses only by moving in one direction across the page).

FIGURE 4–4 Principal components of a cumulative recorder. The roller drives the paper at a constant speed, and each response moves the pen a fixed instance across the paper. The paper speed and the step-size for each response vary with the behavior under study. A common scale is about 1 centimeter per minute (about 2.5 minutes per inch) and 1100 responses across the width of the paper (about 200 responses per inch). At this scale, a slope of 45° represents a rate of about 40 responses per minute. When the pen moves to the top of the paper, it resets automatically to its starting position near the bottom.

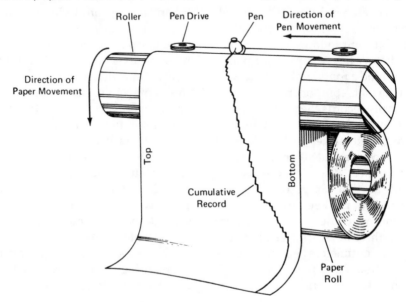

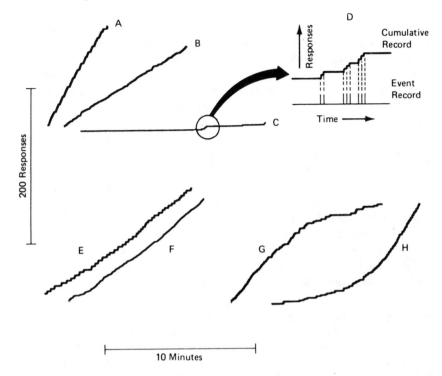

FIGURE 4–5 Some representative cumulative records. Records *A* and *B* differ mainly in rate of responding, which is higher in *A* than in *B*. Rate is zero throughout most of *C;* a segment of *C* with a few responses is magnified and shown in *D* in relation to an event record. Records *E* and *F* are roughly equal in rate but show different detailed patterns of responding: *E* is steplike, indicating periods of responding alternating with pauses, whereas the smoother-grained *F* indicates relatively steady responding. Records *G* and *H* show rates that change over time: response rate decreases in *G* (negative acceleration) whereas it increases in *H* (positive acceleration). In this figure, a slope of 45° represents about 20 responses per minute.

In record *D* in Figure 4–5, a small section of record *C* that includes a few responses is magnified and accompanies an event record on the same time scale. For each response in the event record, a small step occurs in the cumulative record; this property of cumulative records is not usually obvious because typical response and time scales are too small for such fine resolution of detail.

Nevertheless, different patterns of responding can be distinguished in cumulative records. For example, the response rates in *E* and *F* are roughly the same, but *E* is steplike whereas *F* is relatively smooth. This

means that *E* was produced by short high-rate bursts of responding (steep segments) separated by pauses (flat segments), whereas *F* was produced by responding that occurred at a much more uniform rate. This property is sometimes called *grain;* of the two cumulative records, *E* has the rougher grain and *F* has the smoother one.

Records *G* and *H* provide other examples of properties of behavior made visible in cumulative records. In *G*, the rate begins at roughly 25 responses per minute, but as time passes it gradually decreases; in record *H*, it changes in the opposite direction, increasing from a relatively low rate to roughly 30 responses per minute (records in which the slopes decrease over time are called *negatively accelerated*; those in which they increase are called *positively accelerated*).

Figure 4–6 shows additional features sometimes incorporated into cumulative records. Records *A* and *B* show how pen displacements can indicate other events besides responses. In these records, only some responses produced food, irregularly in *A* (as at *a*, *b*, and *c*), and regularly in *B* (as at *d* and *e*). The repeated concave pattern in *B*, as shown between *d* and *e*, is sometimes called *scalloping*. In *C*, responding that began at *f* and continued through

g was followed by food delivery, indicated by the pen displacement at *g*. The pen was then reset to *h* and the sequence repeated, as at *h* to *i* and so on. This type of record makes successive segments easy to compare (e.g., more responding occurred in the segment ending at *g* than in the one ending at *i*). Record *D* shows how sustained pen displacements can distinguish different conditions. For example, during a tone the pen may be in its normal position, as in segments *j*, *l*, and *n*, whereas in its absence the pen may be displaced downward, as in segments *k*, *m*, and *o*.

With this treatment of free-operant behavior and cumulative records, we have explored part of the technological devel-

FIGURE 4–6 Additional features of cumulative records. In *A* and *B*, pen displacements superimpose a record of other events, such as food deliveries, on cumulative responses (as at *a* through *e*). In *C*, pen resets simplify comparisons among successive segments of the record (*f* to *g*; *h* to *i*). In *D*, sustained pen displacements distinguish responding during a stimulus (at *j*, *l*, and *n*) and nonresponding in its absence (at *k*, *m*, and *o*). In this figure, a slope of 45° represents a rate of about 40 responses per minute (the scale differs from that in Figure 4–5).

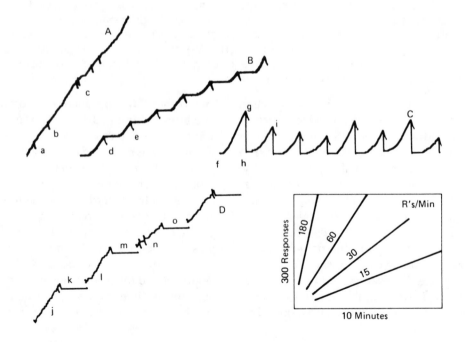

opment of the science of behavior. Before we can effectively consider the findings made available through such analyses, we must turn our attention to some aspects of the language of behavior.

REINFORCEMENT

Lever-pressing becomes more probable when a water-deprived rat's lever-presses produce water than when they do not. Key-pecking becomes more probable when a food-deprived pigeon's key-pecks produce food than when they do not. And

perhaps a child's crying becomes more probable when it produces the parent's attention than when it does not. These cases illustrate the principle of reinforcement: Responding increases when it produces reinforcers. The principle is simple, but as it evolved from Thorndike's initial versions of the Law of Effect to its contemporary status it carried problems of language and logic with it. Some properties of the contemporary vocabulary of reinforcement are summarized in Table 4–1.

The vocabulary of reinforcement includes the term *reinforcer* as stimulus and

TABLE 4–1 The Vocabulary of Reinforcement. This vocabulary[a] is appropriate if and only if three conditions exist: (1) a response produces consequences; (2) the response occurs more often than when it does not produce those consequences; and (3) the increased responding occurs *because* the response has those consequences.

TERM	RESTRICTIONS	EXAMPLES
reinforcer (noun)	A stimulus.	Food pellets were used as reinforcers for the rat's lever-presses.
reinforcing (adjective)	A property of a stimulus.	The reinforcing stimulus was produced more often than the other, nonreinforcing stimuli.
reinforcement (noun)	As an operation, the delivery of consequences when a response occurs.	The fixed-ratio schedule of reinforcement delivered food after every tenth key-peck.
	As a process, the increase in responding that results from the reinforcement operation.	The experiment with monkeys demonstrated reinforcement produced by social consequences.
to reinforce (verb)	As an operation, to deliver consequences when a response occurs; responses are reinforced and not organisms.	When a period of free play was used to reinforce the child's completion of school work, the child's grades improved.
	As a process, to increase responding through the reinforcement operation.	The experiment was designed to find out whether gold stars would reinforce cooperative play among first-graders.

[a]A parallel vocabulary is appropriate to punishment (including *punisher* as a stimulus and *punish* as a verb; cf. Chapter 5), with the difference that a punishing consequence makes responding occur less rather than more often.

the terms *reinforce* and *reinforcement* as either operation or process. For example, when a rat's lever-presses produce food pellets and lever-pressing increases, we may say that the pellets are reinforcers and that the lever-presses are reinforced with pellets. The response that increases must be the one that produced the consequences. For example, if a rat's lever-press produced shock and only the rat's jumping increased, it would be inappropriate to speak of either lever-pressing or jumping as reinforced.

Although a reinforcer is a type of stimulus, reinforcement is neither stimulus nor response. As an operation, reinforcement is presenting a reinforcer when a response occurs; it is carried out on responses, and so we speak of reinforcing responses rather than of reinforcing organisms. We may say that food reinforced a rat's lever-press or that a pigeon's key-peck was reinforced with water, but it is incorrect to say that food reinforced the rat or that the pigeon was reinforced for pecking or that a child was reinforced. The main reason for this restriction is illustrated in the last examples: When we speak of reinforcing organisms, it is all too easy to omit the response or the reinforcer or both. The restriction forces us to be explicit about what is reinforced by what. Nor must we omit the organism; we can always say whose response it was (e.g., the child's crying).

The term *reinforcement* has also often served as a name for a process, the increase in responding that follows from reinforcing consequences. This dual usage, as both operation and process, complicates the description of behavior but remains established in the psychological literature. For example, the statement that a response was reinforced can be interpreted in two ways: Either the response produced a reinforcer (operation) or responding increased

because it produced a reinforcer (process). This text favors the usage of reinforcement as an operation. The process can be described so easily in terms of changes in responding (i.e., responding increased) that substituting other terms for a direct description of what happens to responding seems hard to justify. Nevertheless, the process usage has so much precedent that it cannot be completely avoided. In addition, the overlap between operation and process vocabularies extends to a variety of other terms in learning (e.g., extinction, punishment, conditioning; cf. Ferster & Skinner, 1957).

The vocabulary of reinforcement leads to some logical difficulties even when restricted to operations. When a response becomes more likely because it has produced a stimulus, we say the response has been reinforced and we call the stimulus a reinforcer. If asked how we know that the stimulus was a reinforcer, we point to the increase in responding. If then asked why the increase occurred, we may say it did so because the response was reinforced. Soon we begin to repeat ourselves. Once we define a reinforcer by its effect on behavior, we create a problem of circular definition if we simultaneously define the effect by the reinforcing stimulus (Meehl, 1950).

One solution is to recognize that the term *reinforcement* is descriptive rather than explanatory. It names a relation between responses and the environment; it does not explain the relation. The relation includes at least three components. First, a response must have consequences. Second, it must increase in probability (i.e., it must become more probable than when it does not have these consequences). Third, the increase must occur *because* it has these consequences and not for some other reason. For example, if we knew only that responding had increased, it would not be appropriate to say that the response must have been reinforced; the response might have been elicited by a stimulus. It would not even be sufficient that the response was now producing some stimulus it had not been producing before. We would still have to know whether responding increased *because* the stimulus was its consequence.

Suppose a parent attends to an infant whenever the infant starts babbling, but suppose also that the infant is more likely to babble when the parent is present than when the parent is absent. The infant babbles and the parent comes, and now the infant's babbling increases. How do we decide whether the infant is babbling because babbling has been reinforced or simply because the parent is now present and makes babbling more likely? The behavior of parent and infant interacts: The parent's behavior may reinforce the infant's and the infant's behavior may reinforce the parent's. In working out these interactions, it is important to distinguish reinforcing effects of consequences from other effects (cf. Poulson, 1983, 1984).

Consider another and less pleasant example. Assume an abusive parent who gets annoyed whenever an infant cries and tries to suppress the cries with slaps. The infant cries and then gets slapped and this produces even more crying. In this instance, the consequence of crying is getting slapped and getting slapped produces more crying, but we would not want to say that the crying was reinforced by the slapping. Two of our criteria for reinforcement were satisfied, but the third was not. Crying did not increase because slapping was a consequence; the slapping would have brought on the crying even if the infant had not been crying when slapped. Whenever responses produce stimuli as consequences, the stimuli may have eliciting or other effects along with

or instead of their effects as consequences of responding. (Under these unhappy circumstances, by the way, the infant may learn eventually to suppress the crying; as we will see in Chapter 5, it would then be appropriate to say that the slapping punished the crying).

The vocabulary of reinforcement requires that responding has a consequence, that responding increases, and that the increase occurs because responding has its consequences and not for other reasons. Once these conditions are met, we may say that the response was reinforced and that the stimulus was a reinforcer. We may also assume that the stimulus will continue to be effective as a reinforcer in the future and that it will reinforce other responses in other situations.

Either assumption, however, may be incorrect. The effectiveness of reinforcers can change over time, and some stimuli may reinforce some responses but not others. For example, money is more likely than a smile to reinforce the services of a plumber or an electrician, but the opposite is likely to be the case if the behavior to be reinforced is a lover's embrace. Despite these reservations, the reinforcers used in many standard experimental situations (e.g., food with food-deprived organisms) are likely to reinforce a variety of responses; the experimenter who chooses a stimulus that will reinforce some responses but not others will sooner or later have to cope with the difference. There will be more about the relativity of reinforcement later in this chapter.

EXTINCTION

The consequences of many responses remain reasonably constant throughout life. For example, we usually hear our voices when we speak; we usually touch the objects that we reach for; we usually get from one floor to another when we climb a flight of stairs. But for other responses, consequences change. Responses reinforced during childhood may no longer be reinforced in adulthood. Educational systems often arrange consequences such as praise or grades for spelling or solving arithmetic problems or answering factual questions, but sooner or later these artificial consequences are discontinued (with the hope that other more natural consequences will maintain the responses when the student moves on to other settings). When a response is reinforced, it increases in probability. But the increase is not permanent: Responding decreases to its earlier levels when reinforcement is discontinued.

The operation of discontinuing reinforcement is called *extinction,* and when responding decreases to its earlier level as a result it is said to be *extinguished.* This return of responding to its level before reinforcement mainly demonstrates that the effects of reinforcement are temporary. Responding is maintained while reinforcement continues; it is no longer maintained when reinforcement stops. Thus, the decrease in responding during extinction is

not a special process requiring a separate treatment; rather, it is part of the process generated by reinforcement. The persistence of the effects of reinforcement is shown by how quickly responding decreases in extinction.

At one time, responding during extinction was a primary measure of reinforcement. *Resistance to extinction* was expressed as the time elapsed until responding dropped to some specified level. Two hypothetical records of extinction of a rat's lever-presses are shown in Figure 4–7. Response rate decreases over time in both (negative acceleration), but depending on the extinction criterion either might represent greater resistance to extinction. If the criterion is the time until 2 minutes go by without a response, then A shows greater resistance to extinction than B; A does not include two minutes without a response whereas such a period begins halfway through B. If instead the criterion is total responses emitted, then resistance to extinction is greater for B than for A. Resistance to extinction diminished in significance because its definition permitted such ambiguities. Nevertheless, extinction remains as a demonstra-

FIGURE 4–7 Two hypothetical cumulative records of extinction of a rat's lever-presses after food reinforcement. Either A or B might be said to demonstrate greater resistance to extinction, depending on whether it is measured in terms of the time taken until 2 minutes without a response or in terms of total responses during the extinction session.

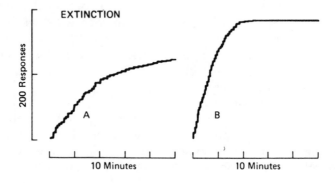

tion of the persisting effects of reinforcement; resistance to change (of which resistance to extinction is a special case) is an important property of behavior (cf. Nevin, 1974).

Extinction vs. Inhibition

If extinction did not occur, the effects of reinforcement would be permanent. Any response produced by reinforcement would last throughout an organism's life. Clearly that is not the case. For example, if you wear a watch you probably often turn your wrist to look at it; the consequence of looking is finding out the time. But if you stop wearing the watch for some reason, you will eventually stop looking; seeing a bare wrist is not an effective reinforcer.

The history of the concept of extinction, however, was not so simple. It came to be argued that extinction did not merely allow the passive decline of responding but rather somehow actively suppressed responding. Extinction was said to have *inhibitory* effects (in contrast to assumed *excitatory* effects of reinforcement). The view that some process actively reduces responding during extinction long dominated the alternative view that responding decreases during extinction because it is no longer maintained by reinforcement.

Thus, texts on learning tended to devote separate chapters to reinforcement and extinction rather than treating them as two aspects of the same phenomenon.

This treatment of extinction goes back to the inhibitory language established in the context of Pavlov's conditioning experiments (cf. Chapters 1 and 9; see also Skinner, 1938, pp. 96–102). Once that language was carried over to the language of consequences, it was retained because it seemed consistent with effects during extinction other than the decrease in responding that defined it.

Consider the phenomenon called *spontaneous recovery*. In a typical extinction session, responding begins at a relatively high rate that decreases as the session continues. But if the organism is then removed from the situation for a while, the rate at which it begins responding in the next extinction session is usually higher than the rate at the end of the last one. Some hypothetical cumulative records illustrating spontaneous recovery are shown in Figure 4–8. Responding at the start of a session is said to have recovered spontaneously from inhibition built up by the end of the last session; presumably this inhibition increases within sessions, when it actively suppresses responding, and dissipates between sessions.

FIGURE 4–8 Hypothetical cumulative records of spontaneous recovery in successive extinction sessions for a rat's lever-presses previously reinforced with food. Responding in session 2 begins at a rate higher than that at the end of session 1; similarly, responding in session 3 begins at a rate higher than that at the end of session 2.

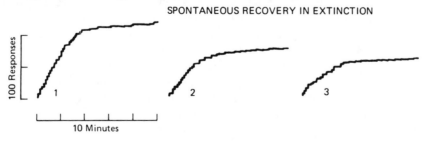

SPONTANEOUS RECOVERY IN EXTINCTION

Phenomena such as spontaneous recovery were taken to mean that responding that had been reduced by extinction was somehow "there all the time but inhibited." But accounts that assumed responding was actively suppressed in extinction were criticized on the grounds that they explained extinction in terms of unobservable events or processes (Reid, 1958). For example, when it was said that a response had been inhibited in extinction, the inhibited response could be measured but not any events or processes doing the inhibiting. Perhaps for this reason a variety of competing accounts of extinction were formulated in terms of such inferred processes as inhibition, frustration, interference, and fatigue (cf. Kimble, 1961). These accounts agreed that responding did not merely decline passively in extinction but rather was actively suppressed; they differed only in how they characterized the events that generated the inhibition.

Other accounts, however, did not assume suppressive or inhibitory processes in extinction. For example, one account of spontaneous recovery notes that the organism may respond differently to the experimental setting at the beginning of the session than later, perhaps because of lasting effects of handling and other pre-experimental conditions. Thus, the effects of extinction late in one session might not transfer to the different and perhaps novel conditions at the beginning of the next session. On this basis, Kendall (1965) reasoned that the usual pattern of response rates in extinction sessions should be reversible under proper conditions. An experiment with three pigeons first reinforced key-pecks in one-hour sessions. Then repeated one-minute sessions of extinction were arranged. The first long extinction session came only after responding had reliably decreased to zero in the brief sessions.

Within a few minutes, each pigeon began to respond. Until this session, responding had never been permitted to extinguish at times later than one minute into a session; responding occurred at these later times when the opportunity was finally available. In a sense, Kendall had demonstrated spontaneous recovery within a session rather than at the beginning of a session.

Another example of recovery of extinguished responding has been referred to as *regression* or *resurgence* (e.g., Epstein & Skinner, 1980; Keller & Schoenfeld, 1950, pp. 81–82). For example, suppose a rat's chain-pulls are extinguished and then lever-presses are reinforced. If later the lever-presses are extinguished the extinguished chain-pulls are likely to reappear. By analogy to clinical terminology, the phenomenon suggests a regression from current behavior (lever-presses) to the older and previously effective form (chain-pulls).

Response-Reinforcer Contingencies and Reinforcer Deliveries

Nevertheless, accounts of extinction remain controversial. This may be because discontinuing reinforcement has not one but two effects: Reinforcers are no longer delivered; in addition, the contingency between responses and reinforcers ends.

In this context, the term *contingency* simply describes the consequences of responding; it is defined as *the effect of a response on stimulus probability* (we will later consider other types of contingencies, such as stimulus-stimulus contingencies; cf. Chapter 9). For example, in a contingency in which a rat receives food if and only if it presses a lever, lever-pressing raises the probability of food from zero to 1.0 (no food if no lever-press and food if lever-press). In a contingency in which lever-presses do nothing, lever-pressing does not affect the probability of food (food is independent of lever-presses).

Contingencies expressed in terms of probability relations between responses and their consequences can be summarized in graphic form in much the same way as relations between stimuli and the responses they produce (Figure 3–2). The coordinate system is illustrated in Figure 4–9. The y-axis shows the probability of a stimulus given a response, or $p(S/R)$; the x-axis shows its probability given no response, or $p(S/\overline{R})$. Note that, relative to Figure 3–2, the S and R terms have been reversed. The earlier figure was concerned with effects of stimuli on responses; this one is concerned with effects of responses on stimuli.

FIGURE 4–9 Various response-stimulus contingencies represented in terms of stimulus probability given a response, $p(S/R)$, and stimulus probability given no response, $p(S/\overline{R})$. The graph includes reliable production of stimuli by responses (A), response-independent stimuli (B), extinction (C), prevention of stimuli by responses, as in avoidance (D: see Chapter 5), and intermittent production of stimuli, as in reinforcement schedules (E: see Chapter 8). Cf. Figure 3–2.

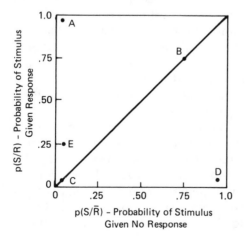

At A, the probability of the stimulus is high given a response, but is otherwise low, as when a rat's lever-presses produce food. At B, stimulus probability is independent of responses, as when food is delivered without regard to lever-presses. At C, stimulus probability is zero whether or not a response has occurred, as when food is discontinued in extinction. We will later consider other kinds of contingencies in other contexts. For example, cases in which responses reduce stimulus probability, as at D, illustrate avoidance and negative punishment (Chapter 5), and those in which responses produce a stimulus with a probability of less than 1.0, as at E, illustrate reinforcement schedules (Chapter 8).

Let us now compare procedures in terms of changes in contingencies and changes in stimuli. Consider first the food-deprived rat whose lever-presses are reinforced with food. Once every 10 or 15 seconds the rat presses the lever and eats the food delivered. If lever-pressing is then extinguished, lever-presses no longer produce food and the rat no longer eats. As a result, the rat presses the lever less often. This rat is now different in two ways: Not only have lever-presses stopped having their earlier consequences, but this rat is no longer eating.

Here is a different arrangement. The rat stays food-deprived, but when we stop reinforcing lever-presses we begin to deliver food automatically every 10 or 15 seconds. In this case, we change contingencies, just as in the last example: Lever-presses that once produced food now have no effect. But even though food is no longer a consequence of lever-presses, this rat gets food every 10 or 15 seconds and so still can eat. This rat too will press the lever less often; on the other hand, it will differ from the first rat in important ways.

These two procedures distinguish the effects of terminating a reinforcement contingency from those of terminating reinforcers. The standard extinction procedure terminates both a contingency and reinforcer deliveries; the last example shows, however, that the contingency can be terminated while reinforcer deliveries continue (e.g., Hart, Reynolds, Baer, Brawley, & Harris, 1968). In both cases, responding that had been reinforced decreases. But terminating reinforcers, which occurs only in the first procedure, affects a range of behavior broader than the reinforced response, and this effect is independent of whether the reinforcers depended on responses.

For example, if food is suddenly taken away from a food-deprived rat that has been eating, the rat becomes more active and perhaps urinates or defecates. If food was produced by lever-presses, the rat might bite the lever (Mowrer & Jones, 1943). If other organisms are in the chamber, the rat might attack them (Azrin, Hutchinson, & Hake, 1966). Once such aggressive responses become probable, the opportunity to engage in them may reinforce other responses (e.g., the organism might pull a chain if chain-pulls produce something it can sink its teeth into: Azrin, Hutchinson, & McLaughlin, 1965). These effects, though observed in extinction, are not direct results of terminating the reinforcement contingency. They occur not only during extinction but also after the termination of response-independent food deliveries; in both cases, a rat that has been eating stops receiving food. These side effects are usually superimposed upon the decrease in responding during extinction because the termination of reinforcers is necessarily part of extinction.

Behavioral operations often have more than one effect. A stimulus that is a reinforcer may affect other responses besides the one that it reinforces: It may elicit some responses and serve as a discriminative stimulus for still others. In the history of research on extinction, the various effects of terminating reinforcer deliveries may have contributed to its treatment in terms of inhibition. Yet the phenomena seen as indicating that extinction was more than the temporary effect of reinforcement were probably only side effects. Many of them could have been observed in situations that did not involve the consequences of responding (e.g., the aggressive responding generated by terminating reinforcer deliveries). To that extent they are peripheral to accounts of the effects of contingencies.

Extinction and Superstition

In extinction, changes in response-reinforcer contingencies are confounded with the termination of reinforcer deliveries, because the general effects of terminating reinforcer deliveries are superimposed on the more specific effects of terminating contingencies. Why then has extinction for so long been the primary basis for studying the effects of terminating contingencies? Part of the answer is that disconnecting the lever from the equipment that operates the feeder is more convenient than disconnecting the lever and at the same time substituting a clock that operates the feeder periodically. Yet it is unlikely that this change in apparatus alone discouraged further research. Rather, the difficulties rested with some additional properties of behavior.

As we saw in Chapter 3, the presentation of stimuli can have many effects. A stimulus presented independently of behavior may follow as well as be followed by responses. For example, suppose that the response-independent delivery of food occurs just after the rat has pressed the lever. What could distinguish this succession of lever-press and food from that in which the lever-press actually produces the food? Shouldn't this accidental succession of response and reinforcer affect the rat's future responding just as much as if it were the outcome of a reinforcement operation?

In Chapter 3 we discussed *superstition* (Skinner, 1948). Food was presented to a food-deprived pigeon at 15-second intervals, and responses that occurred just before food deliveries were likely to be repeated (and therefore followed closely by still more food deliveries). Through the accidental succession of responses and reinforcers, stereotyped patterns of responding tended to develop. The responses were different for different pigeons (variability), and they usually changed gradually in form over successive food deliveries (topographical drift). A response is not likely to be superstitiously maintained over extended periods of time through accidental correlations of responses and reinforcers, but the possible effects of such accidental correlations must be considered in any experiment involving response-independent reinforcer deliveries.

Maintenance of superstitious responding depends to some extent on the temporal spacing of reinforcer deliveries. In the optimal spacing, a response made more probable by one reinforcer is likely to occur again just before the next. Eliciting effects of the reinforcer might also contribute, because the reinforcer may directly generate responses between reinforcer deliveries (e.g., as when a pigeon's pecks are made more likely by presentations of grain; cf. Chapter 3; Staddon & Simmelhag, 1971).

Superstitious responding generated by an accidental succession of responses and reinforcers is a recurrent problem in behavior analysis, because such accidental sequences can occur whether reinforcers are independent of or consequences of responses. A serious difficulty created by the phenomenon of superstition is that it is too easily invoked to explain behavior not accounted for in other ways (cf. Guthrie & Horton, 1946; Moore & Stuttard, 1979). As a result, response-reinforcer contingencies are sometimes overlooked (see Parsons, 1974, 1978, for a human example).

For instance, if one response is followed by a different response that is reinforced, the reinforcer may affect both responses even though its delivery depended only on the second response. Even when a response does have consequences, properties unrelated to reinforcement may become stereotyped if they typically accompany reinforced responses (e.g., the bowler's gestures after releasing the ball may persist because of their close relation to earlier responses and to the impact of the ball; cf. Herrnstein, 1966). Furthermore, if reinforcement contingencies change so that features of responding that once were relevant become irrelevant, and if these old features are not incompatible with the new ones that have become relevant, they may persist simply because they continue to be followed by reinforcers (cf. Stokes & Balsam, 1991).

We now reconsider what happens when a reinforcement contingency is terminated while reinforcer deliveries continue. First, a rat's lever-presses are reinforced with food; then, when presses no longer produce food, food deliveries continue independently of behavior. For some time after this change in contingencies, lever-pressing continues, and thus many presses will be followed closely by food. Lever-pressing may decline slowly because the frequent incidental succession of responses and reinforcers counteracts the effects of terminating the reinforcement contingency. Eventually lever-pressing is replaced by other responses, but it would be difficult to argue that this decrease in pressing is simple. For this reason, arranging a transition from a reinforcement contingency to response-independent reinforcer deliveries may be a poor way to examine the effects of terminating reinforcement contingencies (Rescorla & Skucy, 1969; Boakes, 1973; see also Catania & Keller, 1981); we return to this issue in Chapter 8.

The most important property of extinction is its demonstration that reinforcement has temporary rather than permanent effects, but other events accompany extinction and can be superimposed on the decrease in responding it produces. It is difficult to conceive of reinforcement without extinction; the effects of extinction tell us that organisms are sensitive to the consequences of their behavior when these consequences stop as well as when they start.

Section B   **Reinforcers as Opportunities for Behavior**

The preceding discussion buttresses the logic of the vocabulary of reinforcement but does not tell us how to identify reinforcers independently of their effects. Without making a stimulus a consequence of responding we cannot say whether it will serve as a reinforcer. Even demonstrable reinforcers such as food can vary in effectiveness depending on deprivation. With food continuously available, a rat's lever-pressing might not be much affected by food as a consequence of lever-presses.

Reinforcers are inevitably oversimplified by treating them merely as stimuli. The presentation of any reinforcer involves a transition from one situation to another, and each situation may have complex properties that manifest themselves only over extended periods of time (cf. Baum, 1973). We will see that an important property of a reinforcing situation is the responding for which it sets an occasion.

Chapter 1 introduced establishing operations, the procedures that make events more or less effective as reinforcers, and Chapter 3 discussed some effects of establishing operations as examples of *motivation* or *drive* (we can now define these terms more precisely: When we study motivation or drive we are concerned with what makes consequences more or less effective as reinforcers or as punishers). Deprivation and satiation are not the only possible operations that can change the effectiveness of stimuli as reinforcers or punishers. This section considers some establishing operations and surveys the variety of events that may serve as reinforcers.

Reinforcers are sometimes distinguished on the basis of the types of operations that established them. For example, a *conditioned reinforcer* is one that has become effective by virtue of its relation to some other reinforcer (e.g., the light that comes on when a pigeon feeder is operated will eventually become a conditioned reinforcer because of its relation to the delivery of food); a reinforcer that does not depend on such a relation is called an *unconditioned reinforcer*. The establishing operation here is that of arranging the relation between the stimuli (e.g., setting up the feeder so that the light comes on whenever it delivers food). Many events that are regarded as unconditioned reinforcers have obvious biological significance (e.g., food, water, sexual contact; cf. Richter, 1927).

Reinforcers have also been distinguished on the basis of their relation to responses. An *intrinsic* reinforcer (sometimes also called an *automatic* reinforcer) is one that has a natural relation to the responses that produce it (as when a musician plays because of the music that the playing produces), whereas an *extrinsic* reinforcer (sometimes also called a *contrived* reinforcer) has an arbitrary relation to those responses (as when the musician plays for money). The term *extrinsic* has also been applied to stimuli presumed to function as reinforcers because their function has been instructed (as when a child is told that it is important to earn good grades); despite their label, such stimuli are often ineffective as reinforcers.

We have discussed various functions of stimuli (e.g., eliciting, discriminative, and reinforcing). The presentation of stimuli can also have establishing functions (cf. Michael, 1982). Consider some examples: Tasting unsalted soup does not make it more likely that salt will be passed when you ask for it; encountering a bad connection while making an electric repair does not make it more likely that you will locate your soldering iron when you look for it; arriving in front of a locked door does not make it more likely that you will find the key in your pocket. In each case something that had been neutral (the salt, the soldering iron, the key) has become reinforcing. (Such effects have sometimes been called *incentive* functions; the term *incentive*, however, has been applied both to the establishing and to the discriminative functions of stimuli; e.g., Bolles, 1975; Logan, 1960).

THE RELATIVITY OF REINFORCEMENT

Reinforcers exist in great variety. Some are consumed; others are not. Some appear effective on the organism's first experience with them; others acquire their reinforcing properties during the organism's lifetime.

No common physical properties allow us to identify reinforcers independently of their effects on behavior. It is tempting to equate reinforcers with events that colloquially are called rewards, but that would be a mistake. Reinforcers do not work because they make the organism "feel good" or because the organism "likes" them. Our everyday language does not capture their essential properties. Some events that superficially seem "rewarding" may not function as reinforcers; others that seem the opposite may have powerful reinforcing effects. For example, falling from high places or being violently twisted and shaken hardly seem like potential reinforcers, and yet they surely contribute to the reinforcing effects of roller coasters and other amusement-park rides.

Laughter seems like a reinforcing consequence for the telling of jokes. Suppose an instructor tells some jokes, the class laughs, and, as a result, the instructor tells jokes more often. We can say that the laughing has reinforced the telling of jokes, but we cannot say that in general laughter is a reinforcer. Suppose now the instructor puns, the class laughs, and, as a result, the instructor puns less often. We cannot say that the laughing has reinforced the punning; in fact, we should say that it punished the punning (cf. Chapter 5). Whether laughter was a reinforcer or a punisher depended on whether it was contingent on telling jokes or on punning. Actually, punning is more likely to be reinforced by groaning than by laughing. Suppose the instructor puns, the class groans, and, as a result, the instructor puns more often. Now we can say that the groaning has reinforced the punning. Depending on whether the consequences are laughter or groans, punning is either reinforced or punished (in fact, laughing at puns can be bad enough to make a groan man cry). The effectiveness of a reinforcer depends on its relation to the responses that produce it.

When a rat's lever-press produces food, the food gives the rat an opportunity to eat. If we make lever and food simultaneously available to the rat, the rat is more likely to eat than to press. This kind of observation led to the hypothesis that the probability of one response will increase if it provides an opportunity to engage in another response more probable than the first (Premack, 1959, 1971). In other words, if response *A* is more probable than response *B*, an opportunity to engage in *A* can be used to reinforce *B*. According to this account, food is an effective reinforcer for a food-deprived rat's lever-presses simply because eating is usually more probable than pressing.

Consider an experiment that reversed the reinforcing effects of two stimuli by varying the probabilities of the responses occasioned by each (Premack, 1962). A rat's running in a wheel was controlled by engaging or releasing a brake on the wheel. The rat's drinking was controlled by moving a drinking tube into or out of an opening in a stationary wall on one side of the wheel; licking was recorded with an electrical device called a drinkometer. As tested during brief periods when both responses were available, running became more probable than drinking when the wheel was locked with water freely available, but drinking became more probable than running when the drinking tube was removed with the wheel freely available. In each case, the opportunity to engage in the more probable response became an effective reinforcer of the less probable response. When running was more probable than drinking (after the wheel was locked), licking became more likely if it released the brake and allowed the rat to run than if it did not allow an opportunity to run. Con-

versely, when drinking was more probable than running (after the drinking tube was removed), running became more likely if it produced the drinking tube and allowed the rat to drink than if it did not allow an opportunity to drink.

This demonstration implies that reinforcers cannot be defined independently of the responses that they reinforce. In Premack's experiment, drinking reinforced running when drinking was more probable than running, but running reinforced drinking when the probabilities were reversed. According to this account, reinforcers are relative and not absolute. Their important properties are based on the responses for which they provide an opportunity.

This relativity had long been unrecognized. Most learning experiments restricted attention to responses with relatively low probability (e.g., a rat's lever-press) and to reinforcers that occasioned highly probable responses (e.g., food and eating). These cases were common and convenient but were special cases nonetheless. Few thought to ask, for example, whether situations might be arranged in which opportunities to press a lever or peck a key could be used to reinforce eating (cf. Neuringer, 1969; Sawisch & Denny, 1973). The example is not so far-fetched. The opportunity to eat a good meal can be an effective reinforcer, but consider how often children are persuaded to finish their dinners by making other activities depend on that eating. Eating can reinforce, as when a child's dessert depends on whether the child has completed homework, or it can be reinforced, as when the opportunity to watch television depends on whether the child has finished dinner.

The relativity of reinforcement can be illustrated further by expanding the previous experiment to three responses. Let us add a feeder to the running wheel and the drinking tube. By restricting access appropriately, we can establish eating as more probable than running and running in turn as more probable than drinking. In this case, running is reinforced by the opportunity to eat but the opportunity to run reinforces drinking; running can simultaneously reinforce and be reinforced. These relations are shown on the left in Figure 4–10. If water deprivation now makes drinking the most probable response, the reinforcement relations change, as shown on the right in Figure 4–10. In other words, by changing the relative probabilities of the three responses, we can make an opportunity to engage in any one an effective reinforcer with respect to either or both of the others.

In this view, deprivation makes reinforcers effective by restricting the opportunity to engage in some response and thus raising its probability (cf. Allison, Miller, & Wozny, 1979; Timberlake, 1980). The detailed operation of Premack's principle has engendered controversy, especially because its operation depends on how probabilities are calculated. Choice among simultaneously available responses may be a more satisfactory measure than the proportion of time occupied by each (cf. Dunham, 1977; Eisenberger, Karpman, & Trattner, 1967; Terhune, 1978). A further complication is that some responses are more likely than others to substitute for each other (Bernstein & Ebbesen, 1978; Rachlin & Burkhard, 1978). For example, deprivation of the opportunity to eat one food may not make the eating of that food effective as a reinforcer if another food is available, but it would do so if only water was available instead of the second food. In this case, eating one food and eating the other are substitutable responses, but eating and drinking are not.

We introduced reinforcers as types of stimuli, but we are now speaking of them in terms of responses. The treatment shifted because we found that an important property of a reinforcer is the responding that it occasions. Like the reflex, reinforcement is a relation; it includes responses, their consequences, and the change in behavior that follows. Reinforcement is not a theory or a hypothesis; it is simply a name for this relation.

FIGURE 4–10 Reinforcement relations given different response probabilities in a behavior hierarchy. When eating is most probable and drinking is least probable (left), an opportunity to eat reinforces running or drinking but an opportunity to run reinforces only drinking. At another time (right), when drinking is most probable and running is least probable, (e.g., after water deprivation), eating still reinforces running but both eating and running can now be reinforced by an opportunity to drink.

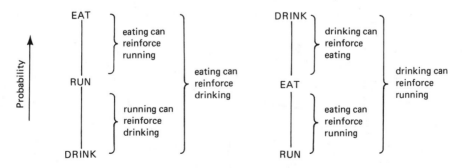

THE ACQUISITION OF BEHAVIOR

Let us return now to learning, by examining how an organism may acquire responses through reinforcement. Record *A* of Figure 4–11 shows a hypothetical cumulative record of a rat's very first session of reinforced lever-pressing. The first few responses are separated by long pauses. Within 5 minutes or so, the long pauses disappear and responding increases for the rest of the session. The acquisition of lever-pressing seems gradual. To repeat these observations, we extinguish lever-presses until responding decreases to previous levels and then conduct another session of reinforcement. Record *B* of Figure 4–11 shows what it might look like. Because of the prior extinction, there is no responding at first. When responding finally occurs and is reinforced, it immediately rises to a rate roughly equal to that at the end of the first reinforcement session. This time, acquisition of lever-pressing was abrupt rather than gradual. How shall we reconcile these two very different performances?

Sidman (1960) has discussed an alternative to the view that the initial learning produced an irreversible change.

The animal learned not only those responses that succeeded in depressing the lever but also learned to go to the tray, to pick up the small pellet, to bring it to its mouth, etc. And these responses were learned in their correct sequence, because their reinforcement was correlated with the appropriate stimuli both from the environment and from the preceding behavior. The tray approach, for example, could be reinforced only after the sound from the food magazine; reaching for the pellet could be reinforced only after the pellet had dropped into the tray, etc....What did we extinguish when we disconnected the feeding mechanism?...There is no magazine sound, no pellet sound, no visual pellet, no tactual pellet, etc. Tray-approach is still possible, but only in the absence of some of its controlling stimuli. The responses involved in picking up and ingesting the pellet can no longer occur in their originally learned context. While our extinction procedure may have returned the lever-pressing response to its preconditioning level, other components of the total learned sequence could not have undergone complete extinction. (Sidman, 1960, pp. 101–103)

From this analysis, Sidman summarized the reasons for the difference in acquisition in the two sessions: "When reinforcement was again introduced..., the animal did not have to relearn the whole sequence,

FIGURE 4–11 Hypothetical cumulative records of a rat's initial acquisition of lever-pressing during the first session with each response reinforced with food (*A*) and reacquisition of lever-pressing with reinforcement introduced again after a period of extinction (*B*).

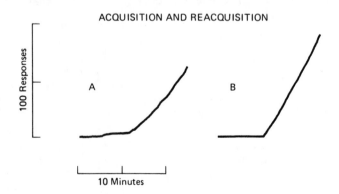

ACQUISITION AND REACQUISITION

100 Responses

A

B

10 Minutes

because the whole sequence had not been extinguished" (Sidman, 1960, p. 103).

Reinforcement, then, does not produce learning; it produces behavior. In looking to see whether a rat presses a lever when a reinforcement contingency operates and not otherwise, we are concerned with the extent to which the rat has learned the consequences of its lever-pressing. The consequences of responding are critical to learning not because learning follows from them but because *they are what is learned.* Contingencies involve the ways in which the environment is affected by behavior and are therefore important

features of the environment for organisms to learn.

Latent Learning

These issues were implicit in a controversy based upon a phenomenon called *latent learning* (Blodgett, 1929; Thistlethwaite, 1951). Consider the experiment illustrated in Figure 4–12 (Tolman & Honzik, 1930; see also Tolman, 1948). Food-deprived rats in each of three groups negotiated a maze. In one group, the rats found food in the goalbox of the maze, and over successive daily trials their entries into blind alleys gradually decreased. In a second group,

FIGURE 4–12 A latent-learning experiment. Rats were allowed one trial per day in a 14-choice-point maze. One group (filled squares) always found food in the goalbox and a second (unfilled triangles) never did. A third group found no food in the goalbox through day 10 (unfilled circles) but thereafter found food there (filled circles). This group, which had been performing like the second one, quickly became like the first one. They had been learning the maze all along, so food in the goalbox was necessary only to get them to demonstrate what they had already learned. (From Tolman & Honzik, 1930)

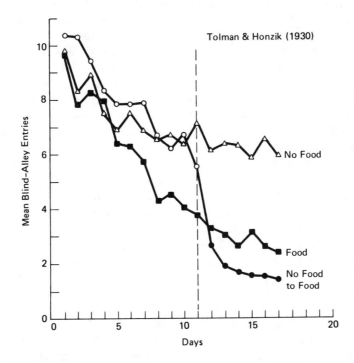

the rats found no food in the goalbox. Their entries into blind alleys decreased but remained substantially higher than those for the first group. In a third group, food was introduced in the goalbox only after 10 sessions. This group, which had been like the second group (no food), quickly became like the first group (food); the rats that previously negotiated the maze without food in the goalbox now began to run with as few entries into blind alleys as did the rats that had always found food there. Until food was introduced, the learning of the third group had been latent; what had been learned was demonstrated by introducing food.

The argument at first was that rats learned the maze equally well whether or not food was in the goalbox, and thus learning was not to be attributed to food reinforcers. The argument was then extended to reinforcers in general, and latent-learning experiments were said to have demonstrated that learning could occur without reinforcement. But soon came the counterargument that food in the goalbox is not the only possible reinforcer of a rat's maze-running. Its removal from the maze at the end of the run, its escape from the constrained spaces of blind alleys, or its return to a home cage where it is fed might all function as effective reinforcers. Experiments then varied the rat's handling at the end of the run, the width of the alleys it ran, and its home-cage feeding. Each time one experiment showed that some reinforcer could generate maze learning, some other experiment demonstrated latent learning in such a way that the reinforcer could not have been effective. And so it went.

Even in principle the argument could not have been resolved, and latent learning gradually faded away as a critical experimental issue. The reason was that a rat's negotiation of a maze inevitably involves the consequences of responding. At any choice-point, one turn is followed by an entry into a blind alley and the other by an opportunity to move farther through the maze; at the final choice-point, only one turn is followed by entry into the goalbox, whether or not the goalbox contains food. The rat's sniffing, touching, looking, and moving through the maze are consequential responses, even if this behavior is not as easily accessible to us as correct turns or entries into blind alleys. These consequences are what the rat learns. Whether to call them reinforcers is mostly a matter of preference, but the language of latent learning seems to have led to a blind alley.

Sensory-Motor Learning

The consequences considered thus far have mainly been major classes of stimuli, typically with biological significance for the organism's survival (e.g., food or water). But many presumably lesser consequences are important in day-to-day interactions with the environment. We open a book to read it. We listen to hear what someone says. We reach toward a nearby object to touch it. Each consequence may set the occasion for new responses. When we finish one page of the book, we may turn the page and read the next; when we have heard what has been said, we may ask a question or make a comment; when we touch the object, we may pick it up and do something with it. To the extent that each case involves behavior maintained by its consequences, each may be discussed in the vocabulary of reinforcement. Seeing reinforces looking; hearing reinforces listening; and touching reinforces reaching out.

The interaction of sensory processes with behavior has been a long-standing source of controversy in the psychology of learning. Theorists took sides in debates on whether learning was sensory or motor. Did organisms learn responses or did they learn relations among stimuli? Did they learn response-stimulus or stimulus-stimulus associations?

One issue is whether sensory processes should be treated as behavior. Doing so is consistent with the view that behavior must be dealt with in terms of relations among stimuli and responses rather than in terms of stimuli alone or responses alone. We cannot measure seeing and hearing as unambiguously as we can measure a rat's lever-presses or a pigeon's key-pecks, but they are behavior nonetheless. They depend not only on whether visual or auditory stimuli are present but also on what the organism does. Looking makes seeing more likely, and listening makes hearing more likely. The organism is not passive in its contact with its environment.

Sounds and lights and other basic events have sometimes been described as neutral relative to potentially strong reinforcers or punishers (e.g., food and shock). But the label *neutral,* though convenient, is a misnomer. Events that are consequences of behavior are unlikely to be truly neutral; it is unlikely that they will have absolutely no effect on behavior. Nevertheless, before the relativity of reinforcers was appreciated, reports of the reinforcing effects of stimuli such as lights and sounds were received with skepticism. Repeated demonstrations, however, led to the acceptance of the phenomenon called *sensory reinforcement* (Kish, 1966). For example, a rat's lever-pressing in darkness increased if the presses briefly turned on a light. Although the effect was small and transient, the light had served temporarily as a weak reinforcer. Phenomena like these soon came to be discussed in terms of *exploratory behavior* and curiosity, and experiments were extended to a variety of sensory consequences. For example, for a monkey alone in an enclosure, the opportunity to look at other monkeys outside

can be used to reinforce the operation of a switch (Butler, 1957).

In this research, responses chosen for ease of measurement were used to assess the effects of sensory consequences. But in any environment behavior inevitably has such consequences. The organism changes its environment simply by moving from one place to another; the things it sees and touches change as it moves, and spatial relations among the components of its environment are a fundamental part of what it learns (Gallistel, 1990).

An experiment by Held and Hein (1963) illustrates these relations between behavior and sensory consequences. Pairs of kittens were raised in darkness; their first visual experience was in the apparatus shown in Figure 4–13. Both kittens received the same kind of visual stimulation: Each wore a shield that prevented it from seeing its own feet and body; each was prevented from seeing the other by the wide central post; and each saw the same pattern of black and white vertical stripes uniformly covering the walls of the circular enclosure. A sort of miniature carousel linked them, but one kitten (A) moved actively whereas the other (P) was moved passively. The active kitten stood on the floor; the passive kitten stood inside a carrier suspended above the floor. As the active kitten walked around the post, the passive one in its carrier moved a corresponding distance on the other side. If the active kitten turned around in place to walk in the other direction, the pulley system turned the passive one's carrier so that it too turned to face the new direction.

The kittens were exposed to similar visual stimuli, but those for the active kitten were consequences of its own behavior whereas those for the passive kitten were not; they depended on the active kitten's movements rather than its own. The kittens were then both given standard tests of

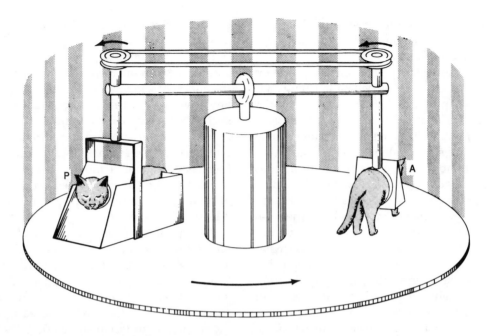

FIGURE 4–13 An apparatus for studying the relation between behavior and visual stimuli. Both the active kitten (A) and the passive one (P) are harnessed to a pulley system with its fulcrum at the central column. Kitten A stands on the floor whereas Kitten P rides in a carrier. As Kitten A moves about, the pulley system duplicates its changes in position for Kitten P (see arrows). (From Held & Hein, 1963, Figure 1)

visual-motor coordination, such as visual paw-placement (normal kittens who are held in the air a short distance away from a table edge or other horizontal surface extend their paws toward it). Even though their exposure to visual stimuli was equivalent, only the active kitten responded appropriately in these tests; the passive kitten became able to respond appropriately only later, after it was allowed to walk about freely in a lighted room.

This experiment has much in common with a classic one by Stratton (1897), who for 8 days wore prisms that inverted and reversed his visual fields. At first his world looked upside-down and backwards and his movements were not coordinated with his surroundings. For example, in walking he looked down to see where he was going, but with the inverting prisms he found that he was looking at the ceiling

instead of the floor. Similarly, he had difficulty in pointing at or reaching for objects, because things once seen below eye level were now seen above and things on the right were now seen on the left, and vice versa. As time passed, however, coordination improved and Stratton reported that the world no longer even looked so upside-down.

The consequences of behavior are again crucial. Looking and moving in the visual field have different consequences with and without inverting prisms, and adjustment to the prisms requires that the new consequences be learned. For example, seeing the floor as one walks is important, but when one begins wearing inverting prisms, seeing the floor, which was once a consequence of looking down, has now become a consequence of looking up (in these situations, of course, up and down can be defined either relative to the visual field or relative to the body; cf. Harris, 1965). Thus, if seeing the floor is a reinforcer while one is walking and one walks while wearing inverting prisms, seeing the floor will reinforce the response of looking up instead of the response of looking down.

With Held and Hein's kittens and with Stratton's inverted vision, we moved from the organism's locomotion to responses of smaller magnitude, such as eye movements. Even such small-scale responses can have profound consequences. If you notice something out of the corner of your eye, you are more likely to see it clearly if you look toward it than if you look away from it (except in dim light, when you see an object best by looking a little bit away from it). Suppose that, relative to a uniform visual field, seeing a contour such as the edge of an object is a reinforcing consequence for eye movement. We should expect eye movements to become coordinated with events in the visual field. Data from the eye movements of newborns are consistent with this view. For example, when shown a simple figure such as a triangle in a uniform visual field, infants tend to fixate more and more accurately on the edges and vertices of the triangle with continued visual experience (e.g., Salapatek & Kessen, 1966).

We have much to learn about how arbitrary such relations between responses and consequences can be (cf. Hein, Vital-Durand, Salinger, & Diamond, 1979). For example, suppose an optical system that projects visual stimuli in an infant's field of view is set up to alter the natural consequences of eye movement. It presents stimuli only when the infant is looking straight ahead. If a stimulus appears in the right visual field and the infant looks right, the stimulus disappears. But if the infant looks left, the stimulus moves left, to where the infant is now looking (and vice versa for stimuli appearing in the left visual field). In other words, this optical system creates a world in which the infant can fixate on an object only by looking away from it (cf. Schroeder & Holland, 1968). Consequences are part of the description of what is learned even with respect to our simplest interactions with events in the world.

SUMMARY

We began with a brief history of the Law of Effect: puzzle boxes, mazes, runways, and operant chambers. Out of these apparatuses and methods, the principle of reinforcement emerged as a descriptive term appropriate when responding increased because of its consequences. The effects of reinforcement are temporary, as demonstrated by extinction. When responses are reinforced, stimuli are necessarily presented; extinction is therefore complicated because it involves both terminating a contingency and terminating stimulus presentations. The contributions of contingencies and stimulus presentations can be disentangled by comparing behavior during reinforcement, extinction, and superstition procedures. The reinforcement relation is relative. A stimulus providing an opportunity to engage in one response can reinforce less probable responses, and reinforcement relations can be reversed by changing response probabilities through establishing operations such as deprivation. Phenomena such as latent learning and sensory-motor learning demonstrate that reinforcement is not an explanation of learning; rather, it is part of the description of what is learned. Organisms learn the consequences of their own behavior.

CHAPTER 5
Consequences of Responding: Aversive Control

Punishment and reinforcement have fairly straightforward histories. Punishment stems from the Latin poena, *pain or penalty, and* reinforcement *from the Latin* fortis, *strong, which is related to such structural words as* fort *and* burg.

    Escape, as ex-, *out of, plus* cappa, cape, *seems to be derived from the Old North French* escaper, *to take off one's cloak or, by extension, to free oneself from restraint. Avoidance shares its sense of getting out of as in making empty with several of its relatives:* vacant, evacuate, vanish, waste. Aversive *is derived from the Latin* a, *away, plus* vertere, *to turn. Vertere has*

a Germanic relative, the suffix -ward *or* -wards, *which has had senses of warding off, guarding, or regarding; the suffix appears in* reward, *an occasional synonym for* reinforcement.

So far we have emphasized a relation, *reinforcement,* in which the consequences of responding make responding more likely. There also exists a relation, *punishment,* in which the consequences of responding make responding less likely. Furthermore, a stimulus that reinforces when responding produces it may serve a different function when responding removes it: Its removal may punish responding. Inversely, a stimulus that punishes when responding produces it may reinforce when responding removes it. For example, money may reinforce behavior, as when a child is paid for completing a chore, but its removal may punish behavior, as when the child's allowance is cancelled because of a misdeed. Similarly, a painful burn may punish behavior, as when you learn not to touch a pan just taken from a hot oven, but its removal or prevention may reinforce behavior, as when you learn to treat a burn with appropriate medication or to put on a kitchen glove while handling things around a stove.

    Except for positive reinforcement (reinforcement by presenting a stimulus: Chapter 4), these relations are often grouped together as instances of *aversive control*. In other words, aversive control includes both *punishment* and *negative reinforcement* (reinforcement by removal or prevention of aversive stimuli). This chapter first treats punishment and then turns to negative reinforcement, in escape and avoidance procedures.

Section A   Punishment

As an operation, *punishment* is arranging a consequence of responding that makes responding less likely. The stimulus arranged as a consequence is called a *punisher*. For example, if a rat's lever-presses produce electric shock, the lever-press is said to be punished and the shock is said to be a punisher, because this operation reduces lever-pressing. In these respects, the vocabulary of punishment parallels the vocabulary of reinforcement (cf. Table 4–1).

Like *reinforcement*, the term *punishment* has been applied to both operations and processes. Thus, stating that a response was punished may mean either that the response produced a punisher or that responding decreased because it produced a punisher. As with reinforcement, preferred usage will be to restrict the term *punishment* to the vocabulary of operations and to describe the process directly in terms of changes in responding. Because usage varies, however, the alternative of punishment as process will occasionally be convenient.

The vocabulary of punishment also parallels that of reinforcement in the object of the operation: Responses, not organisms, are said to be punished. If a rat's lever-pressing produces shock and lever-pressing decreases, it is appropriate to say that the rat was shocked and that the lever-press was punished; it is *not* appropriate to say that the rat was punished. As with

reinforcement, this grammatical distinction encourages us to be precise when we observe and describe behavior. It also contrasts dramatically with everyday usage, in which the concern is more often with retribution than with producing a change in behavior.

Consider a child misbehaving. A parent calls the child and when the child comes administers a spanking. To say simply that the parent punished the child may be convenient, but this usage makes it too easy to omit the responses that might be affected. The immediate consequence of the child's misbehaving was that the parent called; the spanking occurred after the child obeyed the call. Although the child might misbehave less in the future because of the spanking, the spanking may also reduce the likelihood that the child will approach next time the parent calls. (But it would be inappropriate to recommend that the parent intent on spanking should go to the child rather than having the child come to the parent; too many better alternatives do not require spanking at all, such as reinforcing responses incompatible with the misbehavior.)

The point is not merely grammatical. We are more likely to notice what is happening if we state the punished response explicitly (spanking punished the child's approach) than if we settle for a less precise description (spanking punished the child). In endorsing the grammar of reinforcing responses and punishing responses, we need not prejudge how these operations affect behavior; we may assume that they can affect other responses besides those for which they are arranged (e.g., a spanking may elicit crying even though it does not depend on the crying). Working with a vocabulary of operations that unambiguously states the consequences of behavior helps us to describe such effects.

COMPARING REINFORCEMENT AND PUNISHMENT

The effect of punishment is simply the opposite of that of reinforcement. The relation between the two is illustrated in Figure 5–1, which presents hypothetical reinforcement and punishment data. The top graph shows changes in a rat's lever-pressing during food reinforcement and then during extinction. During *baseline*, when lever-pressing has no consequences, responding occurs infrequently. When *reinforcement* begins, responding increases over the first sessions, after which it remains at a fairly stable level. *Extinction* then gradually reduces responding to the former baseline level.

The bottom graph of Figure 5–1 shows changes in the rat's lever-pressing during and after punishment of lever-presses with electric shock. Because punishment reduces responding, some responding must exist to begin with or no decrease could be

FIGURE 5–1 Comparing effects of reinforcement and punishment on hypothetical lever-pressing of a food-deprived rat. The top graph shows unreinforced lever-pressing (baseline), the increase when lever-pressing produces food (reinforcement), and the return to earlier levels when reinforcement ends (extinction). The bottom graph shows responding maintained by reinforcement (baseline), the decrease when response-produced shock is superimposed on this performance (punishment), and the return to earlier high levels when punishment ends (recovery). The bottom graph uses responding maintained throughout by reinforcement as the baseline against which to illustrate effects of punishment because a decrease in responding is not easily seen against a baseline in which responding is already infrequent.

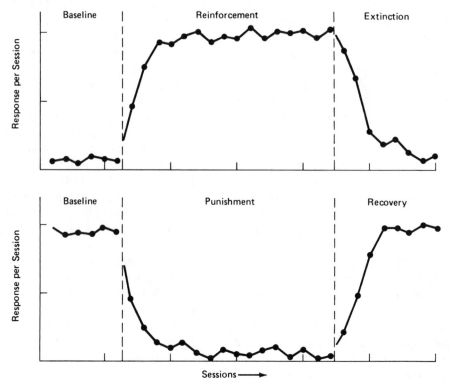

observed. In this example, responding is already maintained by food reinforcement, which continues throughout all sessions; the effects of punishment are then assessed by superimposing punishment on this baseline. The *baseline* shows the responding maintained before lever-pressing is punished. When *punishment* begins, lever-pressing decreases to a maintained low level. In *recovery*, punishment is discontinued and responding gradually returns to the former baseline level.

Reinforcement and punishment are symmetrical: The former increases responding whereas the latter decreases it, but their effects continue as long as the procedures are maintained and disappear after the procedures end (responding returns to earlier levels). Actual rather than hypothetical effects of punishment are shown in Figure 5–2 (Estes, 1944).

The effects in Figure 5–2 are clear. Nevertheless, the effectiveness of punishment

has long been a matter of controversy. Punishment was incorporated into Thorndike's early versions of his Law of Effect. Thorndike argued then that behavior could be stamped out by annoyers as well as stamped in by satisfiers. Statements of Thorndike's law that included the punishment component were called the *strong* Law of Effect. Later, Thorndike withdrew the punishment component, and the version that remained, which included only the stamping in of behavior, was called the *weak* Law of Effect. Thorndike based his conclusion on experiments on human verbal learning in which responses followed by saying "right" were enhanced whereas saying "wrong" had less effect than saying nothing. Thorndike accepted the finding as general evidence against the effectiveness of punishment.

Thorndike's conclusion had sufficient impact that even the data in Figure 5–2 were interpreted to mean that punishment

FIGURE 5–2 Cumulative record of the effect of punishment superimposed upon a reinforcement baseline. The response was a rat's lever-press. Food reinforcement continued throughout the session, and the punisher was shock. Responding decreased during punishment and recovered after punishment was discontinued. (From Estes, 1944, Figure 10).

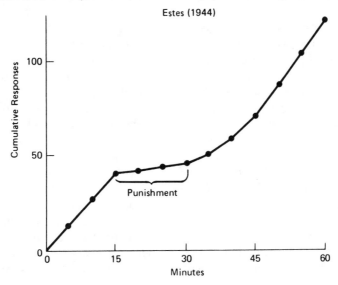

was an ineffective procedure. The argument, based on the recovery of responding after punishment, was that punishment was not to be taken seriously as a technique for changing behavior because it suppressed responding only temporarily. Yet on the basis of this criterion, reinforcement also would have to be judged ineffective. For some reason, different criteria were imposed for the effectiveness of punishment than for the effectiveness of reinforcement. Even though responding was reduced during punishment, investigators looked not at that reduction but rather at the recovered responding after punishment was discontinued. What follows provides sound reasons for endorsing the conclusion that punishment is undesirable for eliminating behavior and that alternative techniques should be used whenever possible. But if this conclusion remains correct, it is only because Thorndike and his successors were right for the wrong reasons.

In more recent times, investigators turned again to punishment and studied conditions that modify its effectiveness in suppressing behavior (e.g., Azrin & Holz, 1966; Church, 1963). The following conclusions are based on experiments with electric shock as a punisher of a pigeon's food-reinforced key-pecking: The more intense and immediate the punisher, the more effective it is; a punisher introduced at its maximum intensity suppresses responding more effectively than a punisher introduced at low intensity and gradually increased to maximum intensity; and the effectiveness of the punisher may change over extended periods of punishment, as when a punisher of low intensity gradually becomes ineffective after many presentations (cf. Azrin & Holz, 1966, pp. 426–427).

These experiments not only changed the criteria for the effectiveness of punishment, but also examined whether punishment had been judged adequately according to the old criteria. On occasion a single punisher or a few punishers, if sufficiently intense and if a consequence of a weakly maintained response, could make a response disappear for days or months or perhaps even the rest of the organism's life; thus, it was argued that punishment could have permanent effects after all. Such cases are exceptional, and we need not be concerned that recovery may sometimes be so slow that it is to all intents and purposes unobservable. Consider the analogous argument for reinforcement. We would not be surprised if someone who won a million-dollar lottery prize continued to buy occasional lottery tickets even if that behavior was never again reinforced. We would not reject the existence of extinction on those grounds; we therefore should not reject recovery after punishment because punishment sometimes has durable effects.

Some incidental features of punishment probably contributed to its unusual treatment. A reduction in responding can be studied only if some responding already exists: A response that is never emitted cannot be punished. Thus, experiments on punishment usually superimpose punishment on reinforced responding. But the effects of punishment may then depend on what maintains responding (Urcuioli, Mandell, & Nevin, 1976). For example, punishment by shock will probably reduce food-reinforced lever-pressing less if a rat is severely food-deprived than if it is only mildly food-deprived.

Another difficulty is that punishing stimuli are likely to have other effects that occur whether or not they are produced by responses. As in reinforcement, the punishment effect must depend on the *relation between responses and punishers* (contingency) and not simply on the *deliv-*

ery of punishers. For example, shock may decrease the rate at which a pigeon pecks a key even if shocks are delivered independently of key-pecks. It is necessary to show that the shocks have greater effect when produced by pecking than when they occur independently of pecking (cf. Azrin, 1956).

Prejudices against recognizing punishment were so strong that effective procedures were sometimes even given a different name, *passive avoidance.* For example, assume a rat is on a platform above an electrified grid. On stepping down onto the grid, the rat is shocked and so is less likely to step down in the future. Saying that stepping down was punished by shock was appropriate, but it was also possible to say that the organism was passively avoiding the punisher, by holding back from stepping down. This usage allowed effective punishment procedures to be discussed in the vocabulary of passive avoidance while other procedures that did not reduce responding were used to defend the claim that punishment was ineffective.

Punishment is a name for a relation between responding and consequences. The issue is mainly when it is appropriate to apply this name. Early in its evolution, the analysis of punishment emphasized the impermanence of its effects. For this reason, punishment long went unacknowledged as a fundamental behavioral operation. But the existence of consequences that reduce responding is no longer questioned. Except that the effects differ in sign, punishment parallels reinforcement: Reinforcement increases reinforced responding and punishment decreases punished responding. Both operations have temporary effects; when they are discontinued, responding returns to earlier levels. Because punishment can modify human behavior, questions inevitably will arise about the ethics of its application. But such questions are not likely to be resolved without an adequate analysis of its properties.

THE RELATIVITY OF PUNISHMENT

In experiments on punishment, punishers are usually chosen for their reliable effect on a variety of responses, because such stimuli reveal the effects of punishment most clearly. One such punisher is electric shock, which can be measured accurately and can be presented at levels that are effective and yet do not damage tissue. Such stimuli, however, are only extreme instances of punishers, and even stimuli that ordinarily serve as reinforcers can become punishers under appropriate conditions.

For example, food that is reinforcing at the beginning of a holiday feast may become aversive by the time the meal has ended. Other events that superficially seem aversive, such as falling from a height, may be reinforcing under certain circumstances (consider sky diving and ski jumping). Like reinforcers, punishers cannot be defined in absolute terms nor in terms of common physical properties. Rather, they must be assessed in terms of the relation between punished responses and the responses produced by the punisher.

The Premack principle of reinforcement (Chapter 4) stated that an opportunity to engage in more probable responses will reinforce a less probable response. The analysis has also been extended to punishment (Premack, 1971). Let us return to the apparatus that can control a rat's opportunities to run in a running wheel or to drink from a drinking tube. It has been modified by a motor that can either lock the running wheel in position, thereby preventing the rat from running, or rotate it at a fixed speed, thereby forcing the rat to run.

In this apparatus, depriving the rat of an opportunity to run while giving it free access to water makes running more probable than drinking; depriving it of water while giving it an opportunity to run makes drinking more probable than running (cf. the relative probabilities of running and drinking in the two parts of Figure 4–10). Rotation of the wheel can now be made a consequence of drinking: Each time the rat drinks, the wheel begins to turn and the rat is forced to run. When running is more probable than drinking, this operation increases drinking, and it is appropriate to say that drinking is reinforced by running. But when running is less probable than drinking, this operation has an opposite effect: Now drinking decreases when running is its consequence, and it is appropriate to say that drinking is punished by running. This example illustrates either reinforcement or punishment of one response (drinking) by another (enforced running), depending on their relative probabilities.

The stimuli and responses in typical experiments on reinforcement and punishment had been chosen to make those procedures work (e.g., with food-deprived rats, eating is far more probable than lever-pressing). They thereby obscured the potential reversibility of consequences as reinforcers and punishers. Responding can be raised or lowered by changing its consequences, and these effects are determined by the behavioral and not the physical properties of the consequences.

SIDE EFFECTS OF PUNISHMENT

As with reinforcers, punishers can have effects independent of their contingent relation to responses. If an organism is shocked or burned or pinched, some of its responses may have little to do with

whether these events were brought on by the organism's own behavior. Difficulties arise in analyzing punishment because such effects must be distinguished from those that depend on the relation between responses and their consequences. Some effects of shock may be primarily physiological, as when successive shocks systematically reduce a rat's skin resistance. Depending on the nature of the shock source, the effectiveness of later shocks may then vary with the rat's resistance. Other effects are primarily behavioral, as when the apparatus fails to prevent responses by which the organism can reduce its contact with the shock source (e.g., fur is an insulator, and rats have sometimes minimized effects of shock as a punisher by pressing the lever while lying on their furry backs; Azrin & Holz, 1966). In either case such side effects must be taken into account.

Eliciting Effects of Punishers

Figure 5–3 is from an experiment (Camp, Raymond, & Church, 1967) that compared effects of response-produced and response-independent shock. Lever-pressing was maintained by food reinforcement in three groups of rats. Measured against a no-shock control group, shock reduced responding in both groups, but it suppressed responding much more when it was response-produced than when it was response-independent (see also Church, 1969). This difference makes it appropriate to say that the response-produced shock was a punisher. Events affect behavior most when behavior can affect those events in turn (Rachlin, 1967, p. 87). Just as we must distinguish between effects of reinforcer deliveries and of the contingent relation between responses and reinforcers, so also must we distinguish between effects of punisher deliveries and of the

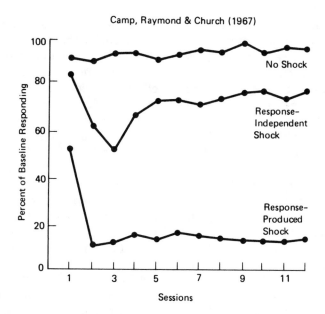

Camp, Raymond & Church (1967)

FIGURE 5–3 Effects of response-independent and response-produced shock on rats' lever-pressing maintained by food reinforcement. At the start of the experiment, rate of shock in the response-independent-shock group was matched to that in the response-produced-shock group. Response-produced shock reduced responding more than response-independent shock. (From Campbell, Raymond, & Church, 1987, Figure 5.)

contingent relation between responses and punishers.

The punishment of two classes of species-specific behavior in the Mongolian gerbil (Walters & Glazer, 1971; see also Shettleworth, 1978) provides another example. Sand digging, part of the gerbil's nesting behavior, consisted of scooping sand and kicking it backwards; alert posturing, a defense reaction occasioned by sudden or aversive stimuli, consisted of standing erect on the hindpaws with ears cocked. Delivering shock was difficult in the sandbox where the experiment was conducted, so a tone was established as an aversive stimulus by repeatedly pairing it with shock in a different setting. When the tone was contingent upon digging, it was an effective punisher. Digging decreased on producing tone and recovered after the

contingency was discontinued; while digging decreased, alert posturing increased. But when the tone was contingent on alert posturing, it was not effective. Alert posturing increased and did not return to earlier levels for several sessions after the contingency was discontinued; there was no appreciable change in digging. Presumably the eliciting effect of the tone on alert posturing was more powerful than its punishing effect. Thus, in punishment as in reinforcement it is important to acknowledge the separate effects of response-stimulus contingencies and stimulus deliveries.

As another example, consider a monkey in a restraining chair (Kelleher & Morse, 1968; Morse & Kelleher, 1977, pp. 193–198). Shock electrodes are placed on the monkey's tail. At 10-minute intervals, the monkey's lever-press will deliver shock to its own tail. A few minutes after it has been placed in the chair, it begins to press. Eventually 10 minutes elapse and its next press delivers a shock. The monkey briefly jumps and for a while stops pressing. But soon it starts pressing again, responding more and more rapidly until shocking itself once more at the end of the next 10-minute interval. It repeats this performance throughout daily sessions. When shock is discontinued, its lever-pressing virtually ceases; when shock is reinstated, lever-pressing returns. If shock level is raised, lever-pressing increases; if shock level is lowered, it decreases. Shocks depend completely on the monkey's behavior; it would receive no shocks if it did not press the lever. Why doesn't the monkey simply stop pressing?

The paradox is that the same shock that maintains responding when produced by the first lever-press after each 10-minute interval suppresses responding if produced instead by every lever-press; it can also be used to initiate and maintain escape and avoidance behavior (Barrett & Spealman, 1978; Barrett & Stanley, 1980). How then do we decide whether the language of punishment is appropriate? If every lever-press produces shock, we call the shock a punisher because this consequence reduces responding. But when lever-presses produce shock only at 10-minute intervals, should we call the shock a reinforcer because this consequence generates responding? (It would not help to yield to the temptation to call the monkey a masochist. Masochism is simply a name we use when a stimulus that we believe should be a punisher serves as a reinforcer. The term is not explanatory.)

As long as human behavior also includes the problem of self-injury, our concern with such phenomena is justified. Perhaps it is more appropriate to compare response-produced and response-inde-pendent shock rather than response-produced shock and no shock at all. Electric shock elicits manual responses such as lever-pressing in monkeys. These eliciting effects of shock may be strong enough to override the punishing effects, so that lever-pressing occurs in spite of and not because of the punishment contingency (cf. Bacotti, 1978; Malagodi, Gardner, Ward, & Magyar, 1981). If so, the case is analogous to that of the parent who tries to stop a child from crying by punishing the crying and has trouble because the punisher elicits the very response that the parent is trying to suppress.

Discriminative Effects of Punishers

Another side effect of punishment may come about because punishers can acquire discriminative properties, as when a response is reinforced only when it is also punished. Consider two alternating conditions (Holz & Azrin, 1961). In one, a pigeon's key-pecks had no consequences; in the other, every peck produced shock and some produced food reinforcers. Pecking was maintained at a low rate when pecks produced no shock, because then they never produced food either; but pecking increased once pecks began to produce shock, because only then did they occasionally produce food. Sample records with food reinforcement completely discontinued are shown for two pigeons in Figure 5–4. With no shock, the rate of pecking was low. When responses began to produce shock, the rate increased. When shock was discontinued, a brief increase in rate (arrows) was followed by a decrease to the earlier low levels.

Again we may ask whether the shocks can be called punishers. In fact, we should conclude from Figure 5–4 that shock was a reinforcer. The main difference here between the shock and other more familiar

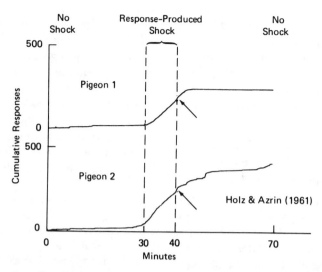

FIGURE 5–4 Discriminative effects of shock. Before the session shown, two conditions had alternated: The pigeons' pecks produced neither food nor shock, or the pecks always produced shock and occasionally produced food. In the sessions shown, no food was presented. For both pigeons, initially low response rates increased when responses began to produce shock and decreased to earlier levels when shock was discontinued. (From Holz & Azrin, 1961, Figure 3.)

reinforcers is that the shock acquired its power to reinforce through its relation to food; it would lose its power if that relation were discontinued. Perhaps these types of relations are relevant to human behavior. For example, a battered child might provoke a parent to the point of a beating because beatings are often followed by more attention from a then-remorseful parent than ever follows less traumatic parent-child interactions. A parent's attention can be a potent reinforcer and may sometimes override the effects of consequences that would otherwise serve as punishers. This illustrates how a behavioral analysis may even be relevant to such problems as child abuse.

SUMMARY

Punishment is the inverse of reinforcement; it is defined by decreases in consequential responding, whereas rein-

forcement is defined by increases. Its vocabulary parallels that of reinforcement: Punishers are stimuli and punishment is an operation or a process. Its effects are ordinarily temporary; responding usually recovers to earlier levels after punishment is discontinued. In studying punishment, baseline levels of responding must be high enough to make the reduction in responding easily visible; for that reason, experiments on punishment often superimpose it on a baseline of reinforced responding. The effectiveness of punishers, like that of reinforcers, is determined by the relative probabilities of the punished response and the responses occasioned by the punisher; punishment occurs when a more probable response forces the organism to engage in a less probable response. Punishment can be complicated by eliciting or discriminative effects of punishers. The task of an experimental analysis is to separate such side effects from the primary effects of the punisher. These effects occur because punishment necessarily includes both stimulus presentations and a contingency between responses and stimuli; the effects of the stimulus presentations must be distinguished from those of the contingency.

Section B   Negative Reinforcement: Escape and Avoidance

Organisms may get rid of as well as produce stimuli. For example, a rat does not ordinarily expose itself to shock, and if shock does occur the rat escapes from it if given the opportunity. Presenting an aversive stimulus can be the basis for punishment, but removing or preventing it can be the basis for reinforcement. When a response terminates or prevents an aversive stimulus and thereby becomes more probable, the stimulus is called a *negative reinforcer* and the operation is called *negative reinforcement*. Positive and negative reinforcement are distinguished by whether a response produces or removes a stimulus.

Later we will encounter some problems in the vocabulary of positive and negative reinforcement. Here we mainly acknowledge a vocabulary with substantial precedent. It is standard usage that *positive* and *negative*, as modifiers of the term *reinforcement*, refer to the consequence produced by responding (whether the response adds something to the environment or takes something away), and that *negative reinforcer* refers to the stimulus itself and not to its removal (if removal of shock reinforces a rat's lever-press, shock is the negative reinforcer and not the shock-free period that follows the response). This vocabulary was established gradually (at one time, negative reinforcement was defined as above in some textbooks but as equivalent to punishment in others). As indicated by

the etymologies introducing each chapter of this text, language evolves. Thus, the evolving language of reinforcement may eventually make the distinction between positive and negative reinforcement of marginal value (cf. Michael, 1975). Nevertheless, when we do invoke the vocabulary of positive and negative reinforcement and punishment, we will adhere to standard usage, summarized as follows:

A. *Reinforcement* makes the reinforced response *increase*.
B. *Punishment* makes the punished response *decrease*.
C. The modifier *positive* means that the consequence of responding is the *addition* of a stimulus to the organism's environment.
D. The modifier *negative* means that the consequence of responding is the *subtraction* of a stimulus from the organism's environment.
E. *Reinforcers* and *punishers* are stimuli and not the absence of stimuli (given that it is possible to make an unambiguous distinction).

The last item above is parenthetically qualified because the distinction is sometimes difficult. For example, is it more appropriate to think of a traffic ticket in terms of the piece of paper presented to you or your loss of money when you pay the fine? Similarly, is it more appropriate to think of an exam in terms of getting a high grade or avoiding a poor one?

ESCAPE

Escape procedures are the simplest examples of negative reinforcement: An organism's response *terminates* an aversive stimulus. They differ from avoidance procedures, in which the response prevents or delays an aversive stimulus. This vocabulary is consistent with everyday usage: We *escape* from aversive circumstances that already exist, but we *avoid* potential aversive circumstances that have not yet occurred.

For example, you might leave a party to escape from the company already there or to avoid someone expected to arrive later.

The conditions for escape can be arranged for a rat by constructing a compartment with an electrified grid floor. Movement from one place to another as the escape response is illustrated in Figure 5–5, from a shock-escape experiment with rats in a runway (Fowler & Trapold, 1962). Running speed was fastest when shock was terminated as soon as the rat reached the end of the runway. The longer the delay between reaching the end of the runway and terminating shock, the slower the rat ran. This is one of many examples of quantitative effects of reinforcement. For example, with both positive and negative reinforcement, immediate reinforcement is more effective than delayed reinforcement (*delay* parameter) and large reinforcers are more effective than small ones

(*magnitude* or *intensity* parameter; see *parameter* in the Glossary).

It is easy to make movement from one place to another an escape response, but more discrete responses such as lever-presses are often preferred. We can arrange that a rat's lever-press in the presence of shock turns off the shock, or in the presence of bright light turns off the light (e.g., F. S. Keller, 1941). If responding increases because of its consequences in either case, we say that the response has been reinforced. Let us therefore compare positive and negative reinforcement: In the absence of food, responding that produces food increases; in the presence of shock, responding that removes shock increases. The parallel is straightforward. Yet escape procedures receive less attention than more complex procedures. Research on negative reinforcement is dominated by avoidance, in which aversive stimuli are

FIGURE 5–5 Relative running speed as a function of delay of shock termination in runway escape responding of rats. The longer the delay between reaching the end of the runway and shock termination, the slower the rats ran. Each point is based on the last 4 of 28 escape trials. (From Fowler & Trapold, 1962, Figure 1)

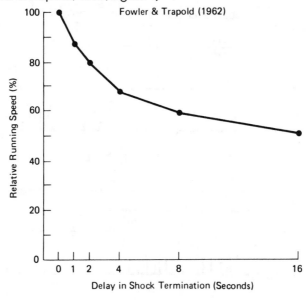

prevented or delayed by responses that occur in their absence.

Elicited Responding and Escape

The reason for the relative neglect of research on escape is that it is usually easy to raise the probability of a rat's lever-presses or a pigeon's key-pecks using positive reinforcement, but it is sometimes difficult to do so using negative reinforcement in escape procedures (e.g., Hoffman & Fleshler, 1959). This is at least in part because the temporal relations between the reinforced response and responses produced by the reinforcer differ in positive and negative reinforcement. The alternative conditions are diagrammed in Figure 5–6.

In positive reinforcement, the reinforcer is absent when the reinforced response is emitted. After the response, the reinforcer is presented and occasions other responses. For example, if a rat's lever-press is the reinforced response and food is the reinforcer, food is absent while the rat presses; eating does not occur until after the press, when food is presented. Lever-pressing and eating occur at different times and so do not compete directly with each other.

In negative reinforcement, however, the negative reinforcer is present while the reinforced response is to be emitted; only after the response is it removed. For example, if a rat's lever-press is the reinforced response and shock is the negative reinforcer, shock is present before lever-presses occur. Some of the responses it generates, such as elicited jumping or squealing or perhaps behavior that reduces contact with the shock source, may

FIGURE 5–6   Different temporal relations between reinforced responses and other responses produced by the reinforcer in positive reinforcement (top) and negative reinforcement (bottom). In food reinforcement, responses occasioned by food (chewing, etc.) follow reinforced lever-presses and so are less likely to compete with them than in shock escape, when responses occasioned by shock (jumping, etc.) precede reinforced lever-presses.

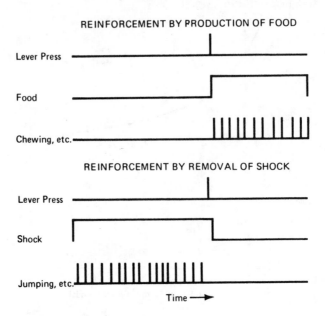

be incompatible with lever-pressing. As long as shock is present and produces these responses, they compete with lever-pressing. Once a lever-press turns off the shock, they decrease and no longer compete with lever-pressing. But now shock is absent, so further presses cannot have shock-terminating consequences.

Similarly, if the negative reinforcer is bright light from which the rat can escape by pressing a lever, the rat may reduce the effects of the light by closing its eyes and hiding its head in a corner. Any movement from that position is punished by greater exposure to the light, and so the rat is not likely to come out of the corner and press the lever. But escape from light by lever-pressing can be maintained if this escape response occurs and is reinforced before other competing responses have become well established (F. S. Keller, 1941).

The Ambiguity of Distinguishing Between Positive and Negative Reinforcement

An important criterion for distinguishing positive from negative reinforcement is whether responses generated by the reinforcer occur at times when they can interfere with reinforced responses. Thus, a distinction based merely on whether stimuli are presented or removed may be of limited utility. An experiment on escape from cold illustrates the point (Weiss & Laties, 1961). A rat was placed in a cold chamber in which its lever-presses were reinforced by the operation of a heat lamp. On the one hand, this procedure may be regarded as positive reinforcement; it involves adding energy to the environment in the form of heat when a lever-press occurs. On the other hand, relative to neutral temperatures, cold may function as a stimulus through its effects on temperature receptors in the rat's skin. Although

cold is the absence of heat, it is a significant event in the organism's environment and may be regarded as aversive. By this interpretation the procedure should be called negative reinforcement, because turning on the heat lamp after a response terminates the effects of cold.

In escape from cold, it is difficult to specify whether reinforcement involves presenting or removing a stimulus. It is easy to find ambiguities in other instances of reinforcement. For example, we could argue that water reinforcers terminate aversive stimuli generated by a dry mouth, or that food reinforcers terminate aversive stimuli generated by the depletion of nutrients in the bloodstream (cf. Hull, 1943). Why then did the distinction between positive and negative reinforcement take on behavioral significance?

Let us reconsider the rat in the cold. Before the reinforced lever-press occurred, the rat huddled in a corner and shivered. These responses reduced the likelihood that the rat would press the lever. Once a lever-press occurred, the heat lamp turned on and these competing responses became less likely, but the rat cannot escape from cold if it is no longer cold. Responses that competed with the reinforced response occurred before rather than after reinforcement, so this example seems more like escape from shock than production of food or water (cf. Figure 5–6). Thus, it is probably more appropriate to call it negative rather than positive reinforcement. But we have not eliminated the ambiguity. Reinforcement always involves changes in the organism's situation and inevitably leads to differences in responding before and after the change. At best, we can regard such changes as producing a continuum of effects, ranging from those in which other responses are highly likely to precede and compete with the reinforced response, to those in which they do not do so or perhaps even raise the likelihood of the reinforced response.

AVOIDANCE

In avoidance, the aversive stimulus is not present when the reinforced response occurs. The two major varieties of avoidance procedure are called *postponement* and *deletion*. Deletion procedures are analogous to swatting a mosquito before it gets to you: Once you have swatted it, you have permanently prevented that particular mosquito from biting you. Postponement procedures are analogous to putting coins in a parking meter: You postpone the violation flag as long as you put in coins and reset the meter, but once you stop putting in coins, the meter eventually runs out.

As an example of a deletion procedure, assume that a rat is placed in a chamber with a lever and a floor grid through which brief shocks may be delivered. Shocks are scheduled to be delivered once a minute, but if the rat presses the lever-before the next one is due, that shock is omitted. In this procedure, the rat can avoid shock completely by pressing at least once a minute. Deletion procedures are sometimes conducted in discrete trials. For example, a light comes on for 30 seconds. If the rat presses the lever during the trial, no shock is delivered when it ends; a shock is delivered only if it fails to do so. We examine these and related procedures in more detail later.

Let us now consider an example of a postponement procedure (Sidman, 1953). Two clocks control shock deliveries. Which clock runs depends on whether the last event was a shock or a lever- press. The first clock times the *shock-shock* or *SS interval*, the time between shocks if the rat does not press the lever. Whenever a shock is

delivered, this clock resets to zero and starts timing a new SS interval. Whenever the rat does press the lever, control shifts to the second clock. This clock times the *response-shock* or *RS interval*, the time by which each lever-press postpones the next possible shock. While this clock runs, each press resets it to zero and starts a new RS interval. In these circumstances, the rat can postpone the shock indefinitely by always pressing the lever before the current RS interval ends. If no response occurs and a shock is delivered at the end of an RS interval, control switches back to the SS-interval clock. With this procedure, called *Sidman avoidance,* or *continuous avoidance,* avoidance responding can be studied independently of escape responding; shock can be prevented by avoidance responses, but once delivered the shock is so brief that there is little if any opportunity to terminate it.

Data are illustrated for one rat's lever-pressing in Figure 5–7, which shows rate of responding as a function of RS interval with SS interval as a parameter. Across functions, the RS interval that produced the maximum rate of pressing depended on the SS interval. First consider an avoidance schedule with a 5-second RS interval and a 2-second SS interval. Any responding at all reduces shock, and a rate of one response every 4 seconds or so avoids shock completely. When the RS interval is shorter than the SS interval, however, some patterns of pressing increase rather than decrease shock. For example, consider a schedule with a 2-second RS interval and a 5-second SS interval. A rat that never presses receives a shock every 5 seconds, or 12 per minute. But if the rat presses every 3 seconds, a shock is delivered 2 seconds after each press and the rat receives 20 shocks per minute (strictly speaking, if this increase in shock rate reduces responding

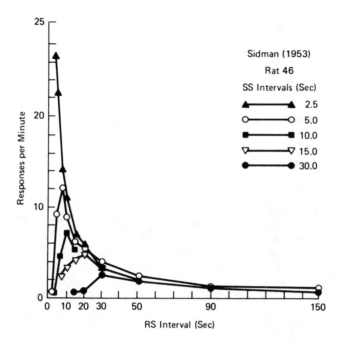

FIGURE 5–7   Rate of Rat 46's lever-pressing as a function of RS interval, with SS interval as a parameter. The SS interval is the time between shocks if no responding occurs between shocks. The RS interval is the time by which each press postpones the next possible shock. (From Sidman, 1953, Figure 1A)

it is appropriate to say that responding is punished). The rat can completely avoid shock by responding fast enough that 2 seconds never pass without a press, but the increase in shock produced by lower rates of pressing may prevent it from ever attaining such a performance.

Species-Specific Defense Reactions

The advantage of avoidance over escape procedures is that opportunities for the reinforced response occur in the absence of the aversive stimulus. Thus, other responses generated by the aversive stimulus need not continuously compete with avoidance responding. Nevertheless, just as it is easier to turn some responses into escape responses than others, it may be easier to turn some responses into avoidance responses than others. For example,

pigeons avoid shock more readily if they can do so by moving from one side of a chamber to another than if they can do so by pecking (e.g., Macphail, 1968). In avoidance procedures, it is more difficult to make the case that such differences depend on competition between the reinforced response and other responses generated by the aversive stimulus. It has been argued instead that the differences arise because organisms are variously equipped with defense responses that are species-specific. If so, success with avoidance procedures will depend upon whether the experimenter chooses a response that the organism is already prepared to emit in aversive situations (Bolles, 1970; Seligman, 1970).

Bolles summarizes the argument as follows:

What keeps animals alive in the wild is that they have very effective *innate* defensive reactions which occur when they encounter any kind of new or sudden stimulus....These defensive reactions are elicited by the appearance of the predator and by the sudden appearance of innocuous objects. These responses are always near threshold so that the animal will take flight, freeze, or threaten whenever any novel stimulus event occurs. It is not necessary that the stimulus event be paired with shock, or pain, or some other unconditioned stimulus. The mouse does not scamper away from the owl because it has learned to escape the painful claws of the enemy; it scampers away from anything happening in its environment, and it does so merely because it is a mouse. The gazelle does not flee from an approaching lion because it has been bitten by lions; it runs away from any large object that approaches it, and it does so because this is one of its species-specific defense reactions. Neither the mouse nor the gazelle can afford to *learn* to avoid; survival is too urgent, the opportunity to learn is too limited, and the parameters of the situation make the necessary learning impossible. (Bolles, 1970, p.33)

Avoidance, as the Bolles passage implies, has sometimes been a focus of controversy. Bolles's point concerns the extent to which avoidance behavior is learned. Without doubt, current behavior can be significantly determined by evolutionary variables (even the capacity for responding to be reinforced must have evolved in some way). It is generally accepted that species-specific behavior often limits what can be learned.

Consider, for example, the transition from elicited to emitted responding in a rat's acquisition of signaled avoidance (a deletion procedure). In this procedure, a warning stimulus such as a buzzer precedes shock. If the rat responds during the buzzer and before shock, the shock is omitted; if it responds after the shock has begun, the shock is removed. In other words, the rat avoids shock by responding

during the warning stimulus; if it fails to avoid and shock begins, it then escapes from shock by responding.

In such experiments, a frequent choice of response is some form of locomotion, such as jumping a hurdle or running from one side of the chamber to the other. Furthermore, the avoidance response is typically the same as the escape response. With rats such locomotor responses are likely to be elicited by aversive stimuli even in the absence of a response-shock contingency. Once they have been produced by shock, they may continue when shock is absent. Thus, the rat's first few avoidance responses may occur mainly because of their earlier elicitation by shock (cf. Chapter 3 and Azrin, Hutchinson, & Hake, 1967; Hutchinson, Renfrew, & Young, 1971). Once avoidance responding begins, it is an experimental question whether it continues because it prevents shock or because it is an instance of species-specific behavior that is easily generated by aversive situations.

Some differences may also depend on species-specific determinants of what is aversive. For example, demonstrations of escape from or avoidance of the sound of running water by beavers raise the intriguing possibility that the aversiveness of such sounds contributes to the building and maintenance of their dams and lodges (cf. Hartman, 1975).

The Nature of the Reinforcer in Avoidance

Another issue is specifying what reinforces avoidance responding. When a successful avoidance response occurs, its important consequence is that nothing happens to the organism. How can the absence of an event affect behavior? According to one view, avoidance responding is maintained because the organism is escaping from some properties of the situation that accompanied past aversive stimuli. This view evolved from earlier procedures in which a warning stimulus preceded shock and the organism prevented shock by responding in the presence of the warning stimulus. Avoidance was most easily acquired when the avoidance response terminated the warning stimulus as well as prevented shock. It was assumed that the aversiveness of the warning stimulus was established through its consistent relation to shock, and therefore that this immediate consequence, escape from the warning stimulus, was the effective reinforcer. In fact, one purpose of Sidman's avoidance schedule was to demonstrate avoidance without a warning stimulus.

This view, that the warning stimulus acquired its own aversive properties through its consistent relation to the aversive stimulus and that the termination of the warning stimulus therefore reinforced the avoidance response, was called a *two-process theory of avoidance* (Mowrer & Lamoreaux, 1946; Kamin, 1956). The main issue was the nature of the reinforcer. Some theorists were willing to accept the fact of avoidance without appealing to some reinforcing event occurring at the moment of the avoidance response. Others felt that it was necessary to specify such an event. When, as in Sidman avoidance, the event could not be located in some environmental warning stimulus that terminated with a response, these theorists instead located the event inside the organism. It was argued, for example, that the organism's state just after a response, when shock was not imminent, was reinforcing relative to its state long after a response, when shock might occur at any moment. The latter state acquired aversive properties through its relation to shock

and, like a warning stimulus, was terminated by a response. This change of state presumably occurred immediately with each avoidance response, so it was assumed that an account based on other temporally remote events was unnecessary.

Debates on the status of such avoidance theories have a complex history (e.g., Anger, 1963; Herrnstein & Hineline, 1966; Hineline, 1977), with some even changing sides (e.g., Schoenfeld, 1950, 1969). Gradually the issues shifted to experimental questions about the conditions under which avoidance responding can be maintained: Must the organism be able to reduce the total number of shocks in a session or is it sufficient for the organism to be able to postpone individual shocks even though the same number of shocks is eventually delivered? It turns out that either condition can maintain avoidance responding (Hineline, 1970, 1981b). Soon these questions became ones about the establishing operations that make negative reinforcers effective (Hineline, 1981b).

An establishing operation that makes positive reinforcers more effective is *deprivation*. The analogous operation for negative reinforcers is *presentation* (it would be called *satiation* if the stimulus were food instead of shock); it is the presentation of aversive stimuli that makes their removal reinforcing. Even more so than with positive reinforcement, these establishing effects must be distinguished from discriminative, eliciting, and other effects of stimuli. Furthermore, the relativity of reinforcement holds for negative as well as positive reinforcement. An avoidance procedure involves response-contingent transitions from one situation to another, and its effectiveness is determined by the situation that follows the avoidance response as well as the one that precedes it.

An example is provided by a case in which not every shock is avoidable. Can avoidance responding be maintained when responding reduces the likelihood of shock but, unlike Sidman avoidance, does not reliably postpone each one? Herrnstein and Hineline (1966) arranged an avoidance schedule in which a rat was shocked with some probability at the end of every 2 seconds. Shock occurred with one probability if no lever-press occurred and with a different probability if a lever-press did occur. For example, in one condition a starting shock probability of 0.3 was reduced to 0.2 by a lever-press; if the rat pressed at least once every 2 seconds, it reduced the shock rate from 9 to 6 shocks per minute. Lever-pressing was maintained by this procedure.

Now consider a case in which each lever-press raises the shock probability from 0.1 to 0.2: now, by pressing at least once every 2 seconds the rat increases the shock rate from 3 to 6 shocks per minute. Even though the consequence of lever-pressing is still a shock probability of 0.2, the rat stops pressing. Relative to a starting shock probability of 0.3, the transition to a shock probability of 0.2 reinforces responding; relative to one of 0.1, it punishes responding.

Shocks were delivered probabilistically in this procedure, so even with shock probabilities that maintained avoidance responding (e.g., 0.3 reduced to 0.1 by lever-pressing) some lever-presses were immediately followed by shock and some periods without presses passed without shock. Thus, no consistent temporal relation existed between individual responses and individual shocks. Nevertheless, the likelihood of shock increased more rapidly on the average as time elapsed without lever-pressing than as time elapsed after a lever-press. Thus, those who

sought an immediate consequence of responding found it possible to argue that the reduction in average aversiveness produced by a lever-press was sufficient to reinforce avoidance responding. And so the debate went.

These positions illustrate the difference between *molecular* and *molar* orientations toward the analysis of behavior. The first deals with behavior in terms of moment-to-moment sequences of events in a given setting; the second deals with properties that can be measured only over extended time periods. For example, a molecular approach to avoidance examines the individual time intervals that separate individual responses and individual shocks, whereas a molar view examines the more general relation between rate of responding and rate of shock over a large sample of responses and shocks (note that rate can be determined only by sampling events over an extended period of time).

The issues have not been and perhaps cannot be resolved. Either molecular or molar properties of behavior can be important in different settings. It is also reasonable to assume that evolution has equipped organisms with the capacity to respond differentially to many properties of the situations in which they find themselves. Situations can be created in which a rat postpones shocks within trials even though it does not reduce the overall shock rate, and in which it reduces the overall shock rate even though responding shortens the time to the next shock (Hineline, 1981b). Thus, there seems no a priori justification for assuming that an organism whose responding is determined by the molecular properties of one situation (e.g., the consistent temporal relations between responding and shocks created by the RS and SS intervals of Sidman avoidance) would be incapable of responding according to the molar properties of another (e.g., the consistent overall relations between response rate and shock rate created by a probabilistic avoidance schedule). If this is so, it is not a matter of choosing one or the other approach but rather of deciding which is more appropriate to the analysis of a given situation.

EXTINCTION

As with positive reinforcement and punishment, the effects of negative reinforcement are temporary. And as with these other operations, the effects of terminating contingencies between responses and aversive stimuli must be distinguished from the effects of simply terminating the aversive stimuli. In avoidance, turning off the shock source is sometimes considered an extinction operation. If avoidance responding is maintained at such a rate that shocks are rare, the absence of shocks will make little difference and responding will continue for a long time. In fact, one widely acknowledged property of avoidance responding is its persistence even after aversive stimuli are discontinued. (If instead the procedure is shock escape, turning off the shock eliminates responding simply because there is no occasion for escape in the absence of the aversive stimulus.)

Consider the alternatives. With food reinforcement, we can arrange extinction either by turning off the feeder or by breaking the connection between responses and the feeder. Both have the same effect: Food is no longer delivered. That is not so with shock escape or avoidance. Shock continues if responses can no longer remove or prevent it. In Sidman avoidance, for example, all shocks would be controlled by the SS-interval clock; responses would no longer operate the RS-

interval clock. This procedure would discontinue the response-shock contingency, but if responding had been keeping the frequency of shock low it would also increase the number of shocks. Thus, the effects of changing the shock rate would have to be separated from those of changing the contingency.

Discontinuing the aversive stimulus has been the more commonly used extinction procedure in avoidance, but presenting the aversive stimulus while discontinuing the consequences of responding is probably more appropriate. The time course of extinction depends on the nature of the extinction operation and the rate at which aversive stimuli occur before and after the onset of extinction (cf. Hineline, 1977, pp. 377–381). In any case, extinction after negative reinforcement shows that the effects of negative reinforcement are temporary.

POSITIVE AND NEGATIVE PUNISHMENT

The distinction between positive and negative reinforcement is easily extended to positive and negative punishment (though here, too, ambiguous cases are possible). Responses may be punished by some events, such as shock or forced running in a running wheel. Responses also may be punished by terminating events. For example, removing food contingent on a food-deprived rat's lever-presses is likely to reduce lever-pressing and therefore illustrates negative punishment. The problem is that punishment might be hard to demonstrate in this instance. If the rat is food-deprived with food available, it will probably be eating rather than pressing, so we will have few opportunities to punish lever-pressing by removing food (consider Figure 5–6 with food and shock reversed). For this reason, studies of negative punishment have not usually removed the positive reinforcer itself; they have instead removed a stimulus in the presence of which responses are reinforced. (This parallels the emphasis on avoidance rather than escape in research on negative reinforcement.)

For example, assume that two levers are available to a monkey and that presses on one lever produce food whenever a light is on. We can expect some pressing on the other lever, but it can be punished by making each one produce 2 minutes during which the light turns off and presses on the first lever no longer produce food. Such periods are called *timeout*, and the operation is sometimes called *punishment by timeout from positive reinforcement* (e.g., Ferster, 1958). Other instances of negative punishment in which the operation is signaled have been called *omission training* (e.g., Sheffield, 1965, see also Chapter 9).

THE LANGUAGE OF AVERSIVE CONTROL

The presentation or removal of stimuli can reinforce or punish behavior. The findings suggest that reinforcement is most effective if the reinforced response is compatible with or at least independent of the responding occasioned by the punisher. Thus, it may be easy to reinforce jumping with shock removal (escape) but difficult to punish it with shock presentation.

Stimuli that can reinforce by their presentation can also punish by their removal, and vice versa. We therefore spoke of *punishers, negative reinforcers,* and *aversive stimuli.* Each was introduced in a different context, but this was fitting because context determines the behavioral function of any stimulus. Thus, aversive stimuli were introduced in connection with elicitation; punishers entered with the discussion of consequences that reduced responding; and negative reinforcers joined these

terms during the treatment of consequences that increased responding. It would be convenient if we could assume that each term identified different aspects of a single category of events. We might then speak of shock interchangeably as an aversive stimulus, a punisher, or a negative reinforcer, depending on the situation.

For many stimuli much of the time, this assumption is probably correct. If we know a stimulus is effective as a punisher, we can reasonably expect it to be effective as a negative reinforcer; this consistency is part of our justification for calling it aversive. Consistencies are to be expected because these categories have their origins in relations among the probabilities of different responses in behavioral hierarchies. But these very probabilities should remind us of the relativity of reinforcers and punishers. We must beware of taking the assumption too much for granted. The fact that we may easily reinforce jumping with shock removal whereas we may not so effectively punish it with shock presentation shows that the symmetry of reinforcement and punishment is limited.

Failures of symmetry between reinforcement and punishment have perhaps encouraged attempts to reduce either one to a special case of the other. Some instances of punishment have been described in the language of *passive avoidance:* By not responding, the organism was passively avoiding the stimulus arranged as a punisher for responding. But then we might as well say that not responding (e.g., not stepping down from a platform onto an electrified grid) is a response that can be reinforced (cf. Dinsmoor, 1954). If the language works in this case, why not in any case of punishment?

Implicit in these accounts is the question of what counts as behavior. Whenever responding is punished, we could say that not-responding is reinforced, and whenever responding is reinforced, we could say that not-responding is punished. With such an extension of our vocabulary, the difference between reinforcement and punishment appears to vanish. Yet we usually can tell the difference between instances of reinforcement and instances of punishment. In fact, the differences are often of serious concern. For example, we must not be indifferent to whether a parent reinforces a child's cooperative behavior with praise, or punishes the failure to cooperate with beatings.

It is easier to speak in terms of discrete responses than in terms of their absence. When possible, therefore, direct descriptions in terms of recordable responses such as lever-presses or key-pecks are preferable to indirect ones. An organism exhibits more or less behavior at different times, and we need not assume that all failures to act are in themselves actions. We do not have to achieve absolute zero to acknowledge that temperature is a dimension that varies in quantity. Similarly, we do not have to produce a totally nonbehaving organism to acknowledge that an organism's behavior is a dimension that can change in quantity. The behavior called not-responding or other behavior, as a class that allows the totality of behavior to be constant and always to add up to unity, gives us one degree of freedom too many. The implication is that if we punish a response, we should know what happens to it before we go looking for an account in terms of other behavior, and we should know what else the organism is doing before we begin to speak of not-responding as behavior.

The Ethics of Aversive Control

The behavioral properties of aversive control have implications that are consistent with ethical arguments against aversive control. For example, it is important to point out that a parent who arranges aversive contingencies for a child's behavior may acquire aversive properties; to the extent that the child then learns to escape from or avoid the parent's company, contingencies other than those available to the parent are likely to begin to influence the child's behavior. But there are possible exceptions: If punishment seemed the only technique available to reduce the dangerous self-mutilating behavior of an autistic child, punishment might be a lesser evil than the permanent damage the child might self-inflict. To the extent that ethical precepts are concerned with acceptable and unacceptable outcomes of our actions, examining the consequences of responding cannot help but be relevant.

Skinner considers the status of our culture in the following quotation; his points are mainly directed to the differences between reinforcement and punishment, but they are easily extended to other areas of aversive control.

Civilized man has made some progress in turning from punishment to alternative forms of control. Avenging gods and hellfire have given way to an emphasis upon heaven and the positive consequences of the good life. In agriculture and industry, fair wages are recognized as an improvement over slavery. The birch rod has made way for the reinforcements naturally accorded the educated man. Even in politics and government the power to punish has been supplemented by a more positive support of the behavior which conforms to the interests of the governing agency. But we are still a long way from exploiting the alternatives, and we are not likely to make any real advance so long as our information about punishment and the alternatives to punishment remains at the level of casual observation. (Skinner, 1953, pp. 192–193)

Operants:
The Selection of Behavior

> Operant, *a class of responses, can be traced to the Latin* opus *(work), which is also a source of* operation *and* copy. Class *can be traced to the Latin* classus, *a division of Roman citizens eligible for military draft and perhaps thereby a summons or call. In* classify, *it is linked by the suffix, -fy, to the Latin* facere, *to do. Forms of* facere *appear in* fact, modify, difficult, *and* effect. *In* office, *from* opi- plus - ficere, *and thus the doing of work, it is connected to* operant. Work *itself has Greek origins, and is related to* organism *through the Greek* organon *(tool).*

We have seen how to change behavior by presenting stimuli and by arranging consequences for responding. One way to discuss the effects of these operations is in terms of the relative positions of responses in the behavioral hierarchy: The organism's behavior consists of a reper-tory of responses, each with a different probability. But if we restrict our attention only to these responses, we miss some of the most interesting features of those changes in behavior called *learning;* we miss the circumstances in which an organism comes to respond in new ways. In learning, an organism may emit responses it was unable to emit before learning began. We must therefore examine how new responses may be added to an organism's repertory. In this chapter we begin by considering *shaping,* a procedure for generating new responses. This will lead us to consider how classes of responses are defined as units of behavior, in the concept of the *operant.* This concept provides the basis for discussing the structure of behavior.

The rat's lever-press and the pigeon's key-peck have often served as our examples of responses. But if we simply place a rat in front of a lever or a pigeon in front of a key, we may not observe lever-presses or key-pecks. With some organisms, we will be fortunate and these responses will occur after not too long a wait; with others we may have to wait one or several hours; and an occasional organism may remain so long without responding that it exceeds our patience. Reinforcement cannot have any effect if the response to be reinforced is never emitted. Fortunately, an alternative is available. Instead of waiting for the response, we may generate a response by successively reinforcing other responses that more and more closely approximate it.

Section A **Shaping: The Differential Reinforcement of Successive Approximations**

Consider the pigeon's key-peck. Once the pigeon begins to eat whenever the feeder is operated, the experimenter operates it only when the pigeon turns toward the key. After reinforcing two or three movements toward the key, the experimenter then reinforces not just any movement toward the key, but only those that include forward motion of the pigeon's beak. By this time, the pigeon spends most of its time in front of the key, and the experimenter can shift attention from the pigeon's turning toward the key to its forward beak movements. These more closely approximate key-pecking than turns toward the key, and once their reinforcement has guaranteed that they will continue to occur, it is no longer necessary to reinforce turning toward the key. By this time, the pigeon's beak movements are full-fledged pecks and soon one strikes the key. At this point, the experimenter can withdraw, because the apparatus can be arranged so that further pecks operate the feeder automatically.

An experienced experimenter can usually shape a pigeon's key-peck within 10 or 15 reinforcements. Some aspects of skill in shaping can be stated explicitly. For example, reinforcing movements is more likely to shape responding efficiently than reinforcing postures. Other aspects cannot be formulated so readily. For example, shaping must ordinarily compromise between extremes of frequent and infrequent delivery of reinforcers. Frequent delivery leads to quicker satiation and may overly strengthen some responses that later will not be part of the response to be shaped. On the other hand, infrequent delivery may reduce responding in general, and once the organism becomes inactive the progress in shaping up to that point may be lost. The experimenter must work within the limits imposed by these extremes, but explicit rules for judging just where these limits lie for any particular organism do not exist (cf. Platt, 1973; Eckerman, Heinz, Stern, & Kowlowitz, 1980).

Furthermore, some features of shaping are fairly specific to the particular response and organism being studied, whereas others are relevant to shaping a variety of responses in a variety of organisms. For example, an experimenter who has worked often with pigeons knows that reinforcing a small beak movement aimed directly at the key will more effectively produce key-pecking than reinforcing a large sidewise beak movement that finishes in front of the key. On the other hand, whatever the response and the organism, an opportunity to reinforce a response should not be missed if it more closely approximates the response to be shaped than any other response that had been reinforced before.

The art of shaping may be applicable to such varied skills as gymnastics, lovemaking, playing a musical instrument, seduction, handwriting, and setting up someone as a victim of a con game. As these examples suggest, shaping can be put either to good use or bad, and many use it without even realizing they are doing so. When it is put to good use, it might as well be done effectively; when it is put to bad use, the best defense against it is knowing how it works.

Shaping is based upon *differential reinforcement*: At successive stages, some responses are reinforced and others are not. In addition, the criteria for differential reinforcement change as responding changes, in *successive approximations* to the response to be shaped. The property of behavior that makes shaping effective is that behavior is variable. No two responses are the same, and reinforcement of one response produces a spectrum of responses, each of which differs from the reinforced response along such dimensions as topography (form), force, magnitude, and direction. Of these responses, some are closer to the response to be shaped than others and may be selected to be reinforced next. Reinforcing these responses produces still others, some of which may come even closer to the response to be shaped. Thus, reinforcement can be used to change the spectrum of responses until the one to be shaped occurs.

This aspect of shaping is sometimes supplemented by another more general effect of reinforcers. Some reinforcers increase activity. For example, food delivery makes a food-deprived pigeon active (it is therefore difficult to use food to reinforce its holding of a posture; cf. Blough, 1958). Thus, a response more closely approximating the one to be shaped occasionally occurs simply because the delivery of some reinforcers makes an organism more active.

There is a paradox to shaping. Reinforcement is said to raise the probability of the reinforced response. But no response is ever repeated exactly. How then can we appeal to reinforcement as the basis for the shaped response when reinforcers are delivered after responses that only approximate it? In fact, if individual responses are never repeated how can we speak of reinforcement at all? We acknowledged this problem in Chapter 1 but did not resolve it. In what follows, we will see that we must treat not single responses but rather classes of responses.

Section B   Differentiation and Induction

If we watched a rat's lever-presses we might see the rat press the lever with either paw or both paws or by sitting on it or perhaps even by biting it. Each is a different response, and even if two presses were made with the same paw they would not be identical. Nevertheless, we call all of them lever-presses. On the other hand, if the rat made similar movements at the other end of its chamber, distant from the lever, we would not call those responses lever-presses no matter how closely they resembled the earlier ones that did operate the lever.

It is not sufficient to speak of behavior only in terms of individual responses. Individual responses are instances of behavior and each can occur only once; responses can have common properties but cannot be identical in all respects. Although later responses resemble the reinforced response more or less closely, the later responses cannot be exactly the same as the reinforced response. On the other hand, we cannot group all responses together without distinction, because we would be left with nothing to speak of but behavior in general. We must settle for an intermediate level of analysis, at which we speak neither of individual responses nor of behavior in general, but rather of *classes of responses* defined by common properties (Skinner, 1935a).

RESPONSE CLASSES

In experiments on the rat's lever-press, the lever is attached to a switch that closes whenever the rat moves the lever with sufficient force through a sufficient distance. The common property of all lever-presses is this consequence of the press: Each response that closes the switch qualifies. Defining response classes in terms of common environmental effects is the basis for both recording responses and arranging consequences for them. For example, an experimenter could record lever-presses by counting closures of the switch and arrange that all such responses are reinforced with food.

But this class produced by the experimenter has behavioral significance only if it is affected by the experimental operations imposed on it. The experimenter must ask a fundamental behavioral question: Can consequences modify the likelihood of responses in the class? If so, it can be called an *operant* class; an operant class is a class of responses affected by the way in which it operates upon or works on the environment. Lever-presses and key-pecks are convenient examples, but operant classes can include more extensive and complex cases.

Early in the psychology of learning, when operant behavior was called *instrumental* or *voluntary*, it was assumed that only responses of the skeletal musculature could enter into classes modifiable by their consequences. Other classes of responses called *autonomic*, such as those of glands and smooth muscles, had not been shown to be modifiable in this way. Such responses were typically elicited, and Pavlov's conditioning procedures (see Chapters 1 and 9) had shown how new stimuli could come to elicit them. At that time, evidence that these responses could be modified through reinforcement or punishment was negligible. Furthermore, it can be argued that such changes in autonomic responses are likely to be mediated by other kinds of behavior (as when exercise produces an elevation in heart rate).

Despite controversy (e.g., Dworkin & Miller, 1986), some autonomic responses seem to be modifiable by their consequences. Consider the salivary response. Salivation occurs spontaneously as well as when elicited by a stimulus such as food in the mouth (e.g., Zener & McCurdy, 1939; cf. Chapter 3 in this text). Consequences can be arranged for spontaneous or emitted salivation, as measured in drops of saliva. The consequence of salivation must not be food, however, because the effect of food as a reinforcer would be hard to distinguish from its effect as a elicitor of salivation. Thus water, which does not elicit salivation, was used to reinforce salivation in water-deprived dogs (N. E. Miller & Carmona, 1967). Salivation increased when it produced water (reinforcement) and decreased when it prevented the delivery of water (punishment). Responses in this autonomic class—salivation—were modified by their consequences; in other words, these autonomic responses could appropriately be called an operant class. (See also Harris & Turkkan, 1981, and Turkkan & Harris, 1981, on shaping of blood pressure elevation.)

An operant is a response class that can be modified by the consequences of the responses in it. This definition of a response class depends on behavioral properties of responding; it is independent of physiological properties such as the somatic-autonomic distinction. The behavioral properties of operant classes are based on the operation called *differential reinforcement*, the reinforcement only of responses that fall within a specified class. This operation makes subsequent responding conform more and more closely to the defining properties of the class. The essential feature of an operant is the correspondence between a class of responses defined by its consequences and the spectrum of responses generated by these consequences.

SOME EXAMPLES OF DIFFERENTIAL REINFORCEMENT

Let us place a food-deprived rat in a chamber with a horizontal slot 30 centimeters (about 12 inches) long in one wall (cf. Antonitis, 1951; Gollub, 1966). Photocells let us record where the rat pokes its nose through the slot. We label successive 2-centimeter segments along the slot as positions 1 through 15, reading from left to right. Food can be delivered into a cup in the wall opposite the slot. Food deliveries are accompanied by a distinctive noise, and the rat quickly comes to the cup and eats whenever food is delivered.

In the absence of reinforcement, the rat spends only a little time near the slot. Occasionally it sniffs at the slot and puts its nose in it as it moves about, but these responses are relatively infrequent and have no systematic relation to the positions along the slot. A frequency distribution of the rat's responses as a function of position is shown in *A* of Figure 6–1.

Now let us reinforce the poking of the rat's nose through the slot, but only if the nose-pokes occur at positions 9 through 12. The initial effect of reinforcement, in *B*, is to increase responding at all positions; it is not restricted only to those correlated with reinforcement. This phenomenon, the spread of the effect of reinforcement to other responses not included in the reinforced class, is called *induction* (an occasional synonym is *response generalization*). In the example, reinforcing responses at positions 9 through 12 affected responding not only there but also at other positions across the entire slot.

As we continue differential reinforcement, reinforcing responses at positions 9 through 12 but not elsewhere, responding gradually increases at positions correlated with reinforcement and decreases at the other positions. These effects are shown in

C, D, and *E.* Eventually, most responses are within the boundaries that determine whether a response is to be reinforced, as in *E,* and a point may be reached at which, even though some unreinforced responses still occur, the distribution of responses across positions does not change with continued differential reinforcement.

In the example, the distribution of emitted responses came to conform closely to the boundaries of the class of reinforced responses. This process is called *differentiation,* and responding produced in this way is said to be *differentiated.* Differential reinforcement created a response class defined by response position. Yet if the distribution of responses in *E* represents the maximum differentiation possible, what can be said about the responses that continue at positions 6, 7, and 8, or 13, 14, and 15? They are outside the boundaries of the class of responses correlated with reinforcement and, according to a strict interpretation of the defining properties of operants, cannot be counted as members of the operant class. They can at least be spoken of in terms of induction: These responses are so close to the class of reinforced responses that the effects of reinforcement have spread to them from the reinforced class. This view simply attributes responding within the boundaries of the reinforced class to differentiation, and responding outside these boundaries to induction. The same operation generates responding outside as well as inside these boundaries, and this responding can be represented as one continuous distribution.

The difficulty can be resolved by recognizing that the example actually involves two different classes. The first is the basis for reinforcement and is represented by dashed vertical lines in Figure 6–1; these lines show how consequences (food) de-

FIGURE 6–1 Hypothetical response distributions illustrating differential reinforcement of response location. A rat pokes its nose into a 30-centimeter horizontal slot in the chamber wall; photocells register this response at one of 15 positions reading from left to right. The distribution of response positions when no responses are reinforced is shown in *A*. In *B* through *E*, responses at positions 9 through 12 (bounded by dashed vertical lines) are reinforced with food; filled areas show reinforced responding. In *B*, the effects of reinforcement spread across the entire length of the slot; this spread is called *induction*. In *C* through *E*, responding becomes restricted more and more to the positions correlated with reinforcement; this concentration of the effects of reinforcement is called *differentiation*. With continued differential reinforcement, the distribution of responses becomes stable and corresponds fairly closely, as in *E*, to the class of responses correlated with reinforcement.

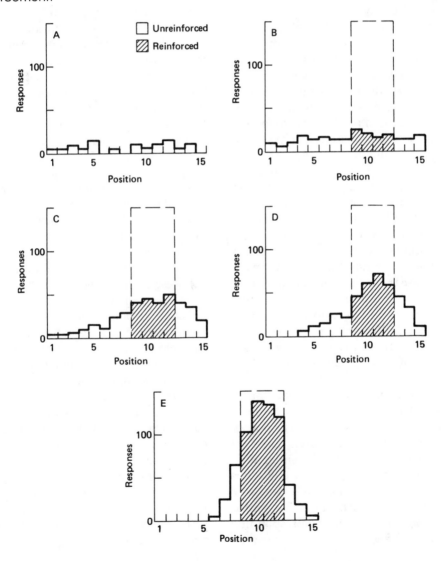

pend upon response position. The lines show the conditional probabilities of food given a response as a function of position; probability is 1.0 given responses in positions 9 through 12 and zero elsewhere. This distribution defines a class of responses in terms of the consequences of responses within that class. The second class of responses is given by the actual performance produced by reinforcement. At any time this class is represented by the current distribution of responses (e.g., early during differential reinforcement, as at *C*, or late, as at *E).* The two classes need not correspond exactly. In fact, the degree of correspondence between the behavior that is reinforced and the behavior generated by this reinforcement is a fundamental dimension of any class of reinforced responses.

Let us now consider another hypothetical example, illustrated in Figure 6–2 (cf. Herrick, 1964). Again we use photocells to record the positions at which the rat pokes its nose through a slot, but this time the slot is vertical rather than horizontal. The 15 positions are numbered consecutively reading from the bottom to the top. Before reinforcement begins, the rat occasionally puts its nose in the slot as it sniffs about the chamber, but these responses occur predominantly at the lower positions, as in *A* of Figure 6–2. Perhaps a response would eventually occur at position 15, at the top of the slot, if we were patient enough. But shaping is a preferable option.

First we arrange reinforcement for responses at position 7 or higher, as in *B.* Responding increases, but most responses continue at the lower positions. Later we raise the criterion for differential reinforcement to position 9, as in *C.* By this time, responding at the lower positions has decreased, the distribution has shifted toward higher positions, and responding has occurred for the first time at position

13. Responding becomes more concentrated in the region correlated with reinforcement in *D*, when the shaping criterion is raised to position 11. Finally, in *E*, the criterion is raised to position 13. Had this criterion been imposed on the initial performance, in *A*, no reinforceable responses might ever have occurred. With differential reinforcement of successive approximations, however, the distribution has shifted to higher levels, with maximum responding at position 12. Nevertheless, this maximum remains below the boundary separating reinforced from unreinforced responses, and more responses are unreinforced than reinforced in these circumstances. The basis for this outcome is simple: The rat can reach some positions more easily than others. But what implications does such an outcome have for defining response classes in terms of their consequences?

In this instance, the class of responses defined by consequences (responses at positions 13 and higher, which were reinforced) differed from the class generated by those consequences (responding up to position 15, but with the maximum at position 12). Responding was obviously modified by its consequences, but some of it was outside the boundaries of the reinforcement criterion. We cannot speak of either class alone; the operant class must be defined in terms of the relation between the environment (the consequences it arranges for responses) and behavior (the responding produced by these consequences). For convenience, we will occasionally speak of operants solely in terms of classes defined by consequences or solely in terms of the distributions generated by these consequences, but it is important to remember that they are more strictly defined in terms of the correspondences between the two classes (cf. Catania, 1973a).

FIGURE 6–2 Hypothetical response distributions illustrating the differential reinforcement of successive approximations to a response (shaping). The situation is similar to that in Figure 6–1, except that the slot is vertical instead of horizontal and the 15 positions are numbered from the bottom to the top of the slot. As in Figure 6–1, unfilled areas represent unreinforced responding, and filled areas represent reinforced responding. Before reinforcement, in *A,* more responding occurs at the lower than at the higher positions. In *B,* responses at position 7 or higher are reinforced; the lower boundary for reinforced responses is shown by the dashed vertical line. After this differential reinforcement has some effect, the criterion is moved up to position 9, in *C.* Later, it is moved to position 11, in *D,* and finally to position 13, in *E.* Shaping has produced some responses at position 15, the top of the slot, that had not been observed before reinforcement. At this point, the distribution of responding has its maximum at position 12, just below the minimum required for reinforcement.

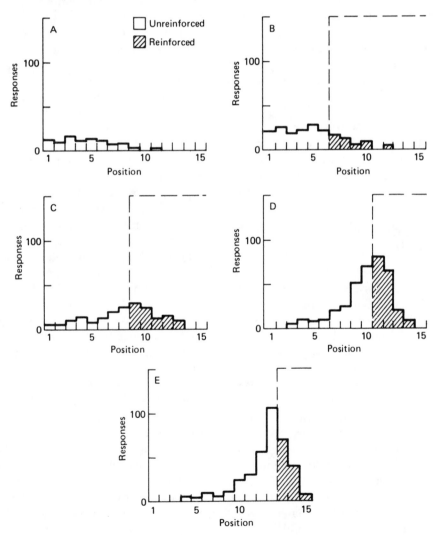

Reinforcement inevitably includes differentiation. Responses such as lever-presses and key-pecks must occur at a particular location and be of sufficient force or they will not produce the consequences arranged for them. We could repeat the examples of Figures 6–1 and 6–2 by substituting such dimensions as force of a lever-press or a key-peck. Responding can vary not only in its location or its force but also in its topography, or form; its duration; its direction; and so on. Differential reinforcement can be based on any dimension of responding, so any dimension might provide the defining properties of an operant class.

These examples illustrate the selection of behavior by its consequences. Within the lifetime of the individual organism, the selection of populations of responses is analogous to the selection of populations of organisms over evolutionary time. Both types of selection involve classes created by contingencies (cf. Chapters 2 and 16).

SCHEDULES OF DIFFERENTIAL REINFORCEMENT

Temporal properties of responding include latency, duration, and rhythm, any of which may provide the basis for differential reinforcement. For example, a procedure that differentially reinforces long latencies might reinforce a pigeon's peck on a lit key only if some minimum time has elapsed since the key light turned on. With criterion latencies shorter than 10 seconds, the pigeon's mean latency usually exceeds criterion, and more pecks are reinforced than unreinforced, but with a longer criterion fewer latencies are long enough to qualify for reinforcement and so fewer pecks are reinforced (the tendency for responding to exceed a short latency criterion and to fall below a long one is a

common feature of the differential reinforcement of temporal properties of behavior in human as well as nonhuman performances; Catania, 1970).

Differentiation of temporal properties of behavior is relevant to reinforcement schedules, treated in detail in Chapter 8. We will see that substantial quantities of behavior can be maintained even when only occasional responses produce a reinforcer. In reinforcement schedules, responses can be made eligible for reinforcement on the basis of the number of responses emitted, the time elapsed since some event, or some combination of these conditions. A property of particular interest is the separation of responses in time.

For example, you will successfully start a car with a flooded engine only if you wait long enough after your last attempt to start it; conversely, you will successfully inflate a bicycle tire using a pump with a leaky connection to the valve only if you pump rapidly enough. Analogously, reinforcement might be arranged for a pigeon's key-peck only if that peck has been preceded by 10 seconds of no pecking, or only if pecking has been emitted so rapidly that at least 20 pecks have occurred with the last 5 seconds. In the first case, pecking decreases; in the second, it increases. Yet to concentrate solely on the pecks might lead us to say that the first case was not an instance of reinforcement. In fact, the unit of responding reinforced in the first case was not a peck but rather a sequence including a pause plus a peck. To the extent that this combination becomes more likely (thereby demonstrating the effect of the reinforcers on the response class that produced them), the rate of pecking necessarily decreases.

The procedure in the first example, in which a response is reinforced only if preceded by a minimum time without a response, is called a *differential reinforcement of low rate* or *DRL* schedule (Ferster & Skinner, 1957). It is sometimes also called a schedule of *interresponse time* or *IRT* reinforcement (Malott & Cumming, 1964), because reinforcement is based on the spacing in time of individual responses rather than on the average rate generated by many responses occurring over an extended time. In general, the longer the interresponse time or IRT required for reinforcement, the lower the rate of responding (Staddon, 1965). In *DRL* performance, the rate of responding decreases because the likelihood of responses preceded by long pauses (long IRTs) increases. Thus, in DRL responding the IRT must be regarded as a component of a complex operant consisting of an IRT plus a response, in that order.

In the second example, in which reinforcement depends on 20 or more pecks within no more than 5 seconds, responding might increase, but only because the high rate of responding itself had been differentially reinforced. Such a schedule is called a *differential reinforcement of high rate* or *DRH* schedule. The DRH schedule has received less attention than the DRL schedule, mainly because it is harder to work with DRH than DRL schedules. Consider the pigeon whose pecking has been raised to a rate of more than 4 pecks per second by a DRH schedule requiring 20 pecks per 5 seconds. (In fact, a skillful experimenter can routinely produce rates in excess of 10 pecks per second in pigeons by gradually raising the criteria.) As long as the pigeon maintains this rate, pecks produce reinforcers frequently. But if for any reason the pigeon slows down, pecking meets the rate reinforcement criterion less often and thus produces fewer reinforcers. This in turn reduces the pigeon's rate of pecking further, which leads again to a decrease in reinforcers. This vicious circle may end in

a rate of pecking so low that the reinforcement criterion is never met, when the pigeon's pecking may cease completely. To reinstate responding, the experimenter would have to produce the high-rate performance again through shaping.

In the DRL schedule, however, an effect of reinforcers following pecks is that pecks occur more often. This higher rate of pecking means that pecks occur closer in time, and therefore fewer follow IRTs long enough to meet the reinforcement criterion. Thus, reinforcers decrease and the rate of pecking decreases in turn. But the decrease in rate simply makes it more likely that IRTs will be long enough to meet the criterion. Thus, pecking oscillates between increased rates accompanied by decreased reinforcement and decreased rates accompanied by increased reinforcement. Pecking is maintained over long periods of time by such contingencies, allowing differential reinforcement gradually to affect IRTs.

The significance of these examples is that we must be cautious about taking response rate as a fundamental measure of the effects of reinforcement. Response rate was once regarded as a measure of response strength (cf. reflex strength in Chapter 3; Nevin, 1974), but once it was recognized that rate was simply a property of behavior that could be differentiated like other properties such as force and topography, this view became less tenable. Although DRL responding occurs at a low rate, this responding is easily produced and maintained; and although DRH responding occurs at a high rate, this responding is hard to produce and fragile once produced.

Other classes of differential-reinforcement schedules exist, such as the *differential reinforcement of paced responding*, which sets both upper and lower limits on the IRTs that can precede reinforced responses and which tends to maintain a fairly constant response rate. The *differential reinforcement of other behavior,* or *of zero behavior* (usually abbreviated *DRO*) delivers a reinforcer if a specified time elapses without a response.

Consider, for example, a DRO schedule of 10 seconds arranged for a pigeon's pecks. This schedule reinforces the class of responses defined by 10 seconds without pecking. But if a reinforcer is delivered after every 10 seconds without pecking, then each peck must delay the reinforcer by at least 10 seconds. If pecks occur less often because they delay reinforcers, it would be appropriate to say they are negatively punished. In this case, as in distinguishing positive reinforcement of not-responding and negative punishment of responding, speaking in terms of specified responses may appear preferable to speaking in terms of their absence. But the DRO vocabulary is well established, and though potentially troublesome it defines a procedure rather than attributing functional properties to such events as not-responding.

COMPLEX BEHAVIOR: MAZE LEARNING

So far we have spoken mostly of relatively simple responses, such as the rat's lever press or the pigeon's key-peck. But complex sequences of responses can also be treated as operant classes (e.g., Schwartz, 1980). For example, a rat's negotiation of a maze might be regarded as a single but very complex response. Consider the simplest maze, the T-maze (Figure 4–2). If the left goalbox is empty and the right goalbox contains food, a response sequence that includes running from startbox to choice-point, turning right, and then running to the right goalbox will be reinforced. Sequences that include turning left will not be reinforced or (if the rat is allowed to

retrace its way from left to right goalbox) will at least not lead to the reinforcer as quickly. As the rat comes more and more frequently to choose the right path we may say that this T-maze performance has become differentiated.

But maze learning can involve more complex sequences. Consider the sequence of responses in the *double-alternation problem* (e.g., Hunter, 1928). At one end of a central runway, a choice-point offers a left turn (L) and a right turn (R), but both paths lead back to the other end of the runway. Without being removed from the apparatus the organism comes back up the central runway and again chooses left or right at the choice-point. If it makes a series of right and left turns in an appropriate order, food is presented to it as it returns to the central runway.

In such apparatuses, the experimental question was whether organisms could learn a double alternation sequence, either LLRR or RRLL. The sequence was learned with varying degrees of success by different species and by different organisms of the same species, but the more general issue was whether the organism's behavior at one time could determine its behavior at a later time (cf. Morgan & Nichols, 1979; we will later find that discrimination of features of one's own behavior is critical to some aspects of human language). An organism could not complete a double-alternation sequence successfully unless its behavior at the choice-point somehow took into account the turns it had made the preceding times around.

A major difference between this and the earlier examples of differentiation is in how the response class is specified. Linear position or force or duration are single dimensions along which particular responses can be located, but sequences of responses in double-alternation learning cannot be ordered unambiguously along a single dimension (e.g., the sequence LLLR contains only a single transition from L to R and the sequence LRLR contains as many L's as R's, but then which is more closely related to the reinforced sequence, LLRR?). An even more serious question is whether to treat a sequence of turns as a single unit of behavior or to subdivide it into smaller components. For example, in learning the LLRR sequence only R is followed immediately by a reinforcer; if more R's occur than L's, should individual turns or entire sequences be treated as units?)

As an organism learns response sequences in these and related tasks, differential reinforcement acts upon the behavior that the organism brings to the experiment. This behavior is often systematic. For example, a rat learning a maze at first might always take left turns, then later always right, then still later alternations between left and right, and so on until mastering the components of the maze. In a Lashley jumping stand with light and dark stimuli in which choices of the dark stimulus lead to food, a rat at first might mostly choose the light stimulus, then mostly the left one, then mostly the right one, until finally the rat begins consistently choosing only the dark one. Such systematic patterns were noted by Krechevsky (1932), who called them hypotheses and discussed their implications as follows:

> Almost every description of animal learning includes such phrases as *"random* exploratory movements"; "chance entrances"; "chance errors." It is either implicitly assumed or explicitly stated in most descriptions of learning that in the beginning of the process the animal is a "chance" animal. His responses are without purpose, without form, and without meaning. Helter-skelter trial and error seems to be the rule at first, and then, after such behavior has eventually

led the animal to experience the "correct" pattern, the various laws of learning step in to stamp in the correct responses and stamp out the incorrect. (Krechevsky, 1932, p. 157)

Krechevsky then contrasted this view with a different one, based upon his data:

> The animal...brings to each new situation a whole history of experiences. These experiences the animal is ready to apply. *From the very beginning*, perhaps, the animal goes about solving his problem in a straightforward, comprehensive manner wherein each response is...a meaningful part of his total behavior. The animal, in executing a series of movements which we call "perfect," "errorless," "learned," "integrated," is not doing something which has arisen from a series of "imperfect," "unintegrated," "chance" responses. He is now merely running through a different set of integrated responses, which series of integrated responses were *preceded by other just as integrated responses.* Such responses, "false solutions," "early systematic attempts," etc., we have dubbed with the dubious name of "hypotheses."...When the human individual *behaves* in the very same such and such way we must also say that he has an "hypothesis." However, we are primarily interested not in defending our terminology but in describing certain behavior. The term "hypothesis" has merely been chosen as a convenient tag for such behavior. (Krechevsky, 1932, pp. 528–529; cf. Levine, 1966)

RESPONSE SEQUENCES: CHAINING VS. TEMPORALLY EXTENDED UNITS

Once we break down a behavior sequence into components, we can treat the sequence as a succession of different operants, each defined by the reinforcing consequence of producing an opportunity to engage in the next until the sequence is terminated by a reinforcer. Such a sequence is called a response *chain*. An example was provided, in Chapter 4, by

Sidman's detailed analysis of a rat's lever-pressing reinforced by food. Rising up to the lever produced contact with the lever, which set the occasion for pressing the lever, which produced a seen food pellet, which set the occasion for moving to the food cup, and so on. Any given segment of the sequence serves the dual function of reinforcing the last response and producing the conditions that occasion the next one. A discriminative stimulus that serves such a reinforcing function is sometimes called a conditioned reinforcer; some experiments on conditioned reinforcement are treated in Chapter 8.

Some behavior sequences reasonably seem reducible to smaller units in this way, and an analysis into such components can be confirmed experimentally simply by seeing how independent the components are from each other (cf. Skinner, 1934). For example, if lever-pressing no longer produces food, lever-pressing may decrease, but we may also find, by delivering food independently of lever-pressing, that food continues to occasion movement to the food cup. This procedure demonstrates that the integrity of one component is not affected by altering the reinforcement contingencies for another.

Some sequences present different problems, however. For example, in one series of experiments (Straub, Seidenberg, Bever, & Terrace, 1979; Straub & Terrace, 1981), four keys in a pigeon chamber were lit green, white, red, and blue, with the location of each color varying from trial to trial. If the pigeon pecked the green, white, red, and blue keys in that order, the final peck on blue produced food; if it pecked them out of order, the trial was cancelled. The pigeon learned to peck white after green and red after white and blue after red even though the color locations changed from trial to trial and even though successive pecks in the sequence did not produce

stimulus changes. Furthermore, the pigeon's pecks were likely to conform to the reinforced sequence even with one of the colors absent (e.g., after pecking white, pecking blue rather than green if red was missing). As in the double-alternation problem from maze learning, the current response in the sequence must depend on the organism's past behavior. The same issue arises whenever an organism learns an arbitrary sequence of responses without accompanying stimulus changes (e.g., Boren & Devine, 1968); can the organism's own behavior function as a discriminative stimulus in occasioning future behavior?

But the critical question is not so much whether some behavior sequences are held together in this way; rather, it is whether this is the only basis for the development of behavior sequences. In the history of the psychology of learning, the positions taken on this issue were often symptomatic of serious divisions among researchers of different orientations, some holding that sequential behavior could always be interpreted in terms of the concatenation of components (variously called associations, chains, stimulus-response bonds, or conditioned reflexes), and others holding that sequential behavior could not be interpreted adequately in such terms. We will conclude that sequential behavior of both sorts is possible; the significant experimental question in any particular case is to determine the nature of the serial ordering.

Perhaps the most telling argument was made by Lashley (1951), who summarized earlier conceptions as follows:

...the only strictly physiological theory that has been explicitly formulated to account for temporal integration is that which postulates chains of reflexes, in which the performance of each element of the series provides excitation of the next. This conception underlay the "motor theories" of thinking which...sought to identify thought with inaudible movements of the vocal organs, linked together in associative chains. The...kinesthetic impulses from each movement serve as a unique stimulus for the next in the series. (Lashley, 1951, p. 114)

Lashley then described cases, including illustrations from both language and music, that made such accounts implausible. For example, in answer to the argument that each movement serves as a unique stimulus for the next, Lashley considered the complex sequence of movements required to pronounce the sounds of the word "right" in proper order. The order is not given by the sounds themselves, because the sounds can occur in a variety of orders and combinations (e.g., in the opposite order, as in "tire"). Thus, the sound sequence cannot be based solely on direct connections, but must depend on some larger organization. Lashley extended the case from sequences of sounds within words to sequences of words within sentences:

The word "right," for example, is a noun, adjective, adverb, and verb, and has four spellings and at least ten meanings. In such a sentence as "The millwright on my right thinks it right that some conventional rite should symbolize the right of every man to write as he pleases," word arrangement is obviously not due to any direct associations of the word "right" itself with other words, but to meanings which are determined by some broader relations. (Lashley, 1951, pp. 115–116)

And Lashley used music to point out that the sheer rapidity of some sequences constrained how the sequences might have been generated:

The finger strokes of a musician may reach sixteen per second in passages which call for a definite and changing order of successive finger movements. The succession of movements is too quick even for visual reaction time. In rapid sight reading it is impossible to read the individual notes of an arpeggio.

The notes must be seen in groups....Sensory control of movement seems to be ruled out in such acts. (Lashley, 1951, p. 123)

Lashley's argument, then, was that some sequential patterns of responding cannot be reduced to a succession of stimulus-response or S-R units. When a skilled typist rapidly types the letters *the*, these letters cannot be discriminative stimuli for the next stroke, first because the typist will be executing that next stroke even before the typed letters on the page can have any stimulus effects, and second because these letters cannot be unique discriminative stimuli if they can be followed by hitting the space bar or various other keys depending on whether the typist is typing the word *the* or *these* or *then* or *thermometer*.

The historical problem was probably that, in the face of such arguments, researchers felt a choice had been forced between assuming that sequential behavior depended upon stimulus-response sequences and assuming that it depended on temporally extended units of behavior not reducible to such sequences. The issue may instead be regarded as an experimental one. Clearly some sequences can be put together in such a way that each response produces stimulus conditions that set the occasion for the next one, whereas others must be integrated in such a way that the responses appear in the proper order without each depending on the consequences of the last. For any given behavior sequence the issue is deciding which type of sequence it is.

OPERANT CLASSES: FUNCTION VS. TOPOGRAPHY

We have seen how classes of behavior can be created through differential reinforcement, and how novel classes can be created through shaping, a variety of differential reinforcement that involves successive approximations to a new class of responses. The classes we have considered are defined by their functions and not by their topographical properties (what they look like). The significance of this distinction is illustrated by the problem of self-injurious behavior (*SIB*) in children with behavioral disabilities (cf. Iwata, Dorsey, Slifer, Bauman, & Richman, 1982; Iwata, Pace, Kalsher, Cowdery, & Cataldo, 1990; Wahler, 1975). Such behavior can include head-banging, biting one's own flesh until drawing blood, and a variety of other topographies.

Consider three male children who indulge in self-injurious behavior. They are housed in a treatment center, and each spends time in head-banging and in biting himself, so they cannot be distinguished on the basis of the topographies of their behavior. Yet we find that the first child increases this behavior mostly when people are around but not paying attention to him; the second child does so mostly when others ask him to complete some task (e.g., reading or simple arithmetic); and the third child engages in this behavior independently of its social context. For these three, the topographies of their self-injurious behavior are very similar but the functions are quite different. For the first child, the self-injurious behavior gets attention; for the second it avoids compliance with demands; and for the third the behavior does not seem to depend on any environmental contingencies.

This analysis recommends very different treatment programs for each child. The first child must be taught other and more effective ways of engaging the attention of others and must be brought into situations where he will be less deprived of attention. Tasks must be selected for the second child that are appropriate to his competence,

and his success at those tasks must be reinforced (his behavior suggests that it has been too often punished in the past). The source of the third child's self-injurious behavior is unknown, and the possibility that it has some organic source must be considered (perhaps the child was born to a drug-addicted mother and suffered prenatal damage to the developing brain).

The point is that it is more important to define behavior classes by their consequences than by their topographies. Even though the self-injurious behavior of all three children looks alike, the attention produced by that of the first child distinguishes it from the avoidance achieved by that of the second child; unfortunately, we have little to say about its consequences for the third child.

Let us now concentrate on the first child. Suppose we try to extinguish the self-injurious behavior by ignoring it. First of all we may have trouble doing so because we are unable to tolerate the damage the child may do to himself. We persevere nevertheless and discover that the self-injurious behavior does not decrease. One possibility is that we have not adequately identified the relevant class of behavior. Topography has again misled us. If the function of this behavior was to produce attention, it is probably part of a much larger class of behavior that includes shouting and acting up, hitting or otherwise abusing the caregivers in the treatment center, and any number of other responses that might function to get attention. This tells us how important attention is to this child, and it also reminds us that we cannot define response classes by what they look like. In this case, we must define a treatment program that uses attention to reinforce more effective and appropriate behavior. Both the child and his caregivers will benefit if the program is successful.

The self-injurious behavior was one class of behavior embedded in the larger and higher-order class we called attention-getting behavior. The larger class was held together by the common consequences of its members, just as the various topographies of lever-pressing (left or right paw, both paws, biting the lever, sitting on it) were held together by the common consequence of producing food. Common consequences are the glue that holds together higher-order classes of behavior (cf. Neuringer & Chung, 1967; Malone, 1990, p. 296). Furthermore, when a class of responses seems insensitive to its consequences, as when the first child's self-injurious behavior seemed not to extinguish, we must entertain the possibility that we have improperly defined the class and that it is part of a larger class the other members of which continue to have their former consequences.

OPERANT CLASSES AND NOVEL BEHAVIOR

The close correspondence between the class of responses with consequences and the class of responses generated by these consequences is the criterion for speaking of an operant class. As we have seen, these classes may be defined along single dimensions such as force or location or may have more complex properties. Our examples included differential-reinforcement schedules, mazes, integrated response sequences, and higher-order classes.

In each case, our major interest is with the dimensions along which responding conforms to the class of responses that is reinforced. The structure of behavior is such that we cannot always define such dimensions independently of reinforcement contingencies. For example, consider the reinforcement of novel responses in the porpoise (Pryor, Haag, & O'Reilly, 1969). These investigators shaped novel performances by reinforcing, in each session, some class of responses not reinforced in any previous session. After several sessions, the porpoise began to emit responses in each new session that the experimenters had never seen before. Response novelty had been differentiated, but how else is this operant class to be specified except by describing the criteria for reinforcement? The fact that we have difficulty measuring them does not rule out novelty or other complex dimensions of behavior as properties that may define operant classes. Novel behavior must be emitted before it can be incorporated into other behavior.

Even the variability of responding can be a basis for differential reinforcement (Neuringer, 1986; Page & Neuringer, 1985; Schoenfeld, Harris, & Farmer, 1966). But differential reinforcement with respect to novelty or variability raises questions. Reinforcers are produced by individual responses, and yet properties such as novelty and variability cannot be properties of individual responses. They can only be properties of responses in the context of other responses that have occurred earlier. A given response might be variable in the context of one sequence of past responses and stereotyped in the context of another. Thus, the fact that novelty and variability can be differentially reinforced means that organisms are sensitive to populations of responses and consequences over extended periods of time, and not merely to individual response-stimulus relations (cf. Chapter 5 on molar and molecular analyses).

We will return to the issue of behavioral classes later, especially in connection with verbal behavior, when we will treat the finding that some grammatical structures are more easily learned than others as similar in kind to the finding that rats learn single-alternation sequences (LRLR) more easily than double-alternation sequences (LLRR). In each case, the problem is to identify the dimensions along which responding may come to conform to the class of responses that has consequences. Perhaps these dimensions can sometimes be specified only by verbal description (e.g., the class of all responses not reinforced on earlier occasions, as in reinforcing the porpoise's novel responses).

Discriminated Operants: Stimulus Control

The Latin habere, *to have, and* capere, *to take or seize, are traceable to closely related Indo-European roots.* Habere *is an ancestor of* behavior, habit, *and* inhibit. Capere *led to* concept *and* perception, *words relevant to stimulus classes; thus, these words and behavior are distant relatives.*

There are no obvious ties among differentiation and induction, applied to response classes, and discrimination and generalization, applied to stimulus classes. Differentiation, from
the Latin dis-, apart, plus ferre, to carry, is related through the Indo-European bher-, to carry or bear, to birth, transfer, and metaphor (but not to interfere). Induction, from the Latin in-, in, plus ducere, to lead, is related through the Indo-European deuk, to drag or to lead, to duke, educate, and conduct. Discrimination, from the Latin dis-, plus crimen, judgment, is related through the Indo-European skeri-, to cut or separate, to crime, describe, and criterion. And generalization, from the Latin genere, to produce or cause, is related through the Indo-European gen-, to give birth or beget, to ingenious, kind, and nature.

Responses can be differentially reinforced not only with respect to response dimensions but also with respect to the dimensions of the stimuli in the presence of which they occur. For example, a rat's lever-presses in light are different from its presses in darkness, and reinforcement can be arranged for presses in the presence but not the absence of light. Similarly, a pigeon's key-pecks in green light are different from its pecks in red. If pecks are reinforced only in green, we say that reinforcement of pecks is correlated with green. A response class created by such differential reinforcement with respect to stimulus properties is called a *discriminated operant*.

Discriminated operants are a pervasive aspect of behavior. When driving, you proceed through an intersection if the traffic light is green but not if it is red. When speaking to someone, what you say is affected by such factors as what the other person just said, the other's posture and facial expression, and the setting of the conversation. Many earlier examples of reinforcement included discriminative control of responding. In discussing the rat's learning of a maze, we emphasized the increase in the choice of correct turns, but the rat that failed to discriminate the appropriate place at which to turn right or left would repeatedly bump the walls as it moved through the maze and could hardly master the maze as a whole.

Discriminative stimuli correspond to those colloquially called signals or cues. They do not elicit responses. Rather, they *set the occasion* on which responses have consequences and are said to *occasion* responses (cf. the concept of affordance; Gibson, 1979). An example of the development of stimulus control, control of responding by a discriminative stimulus, is shown in Figure 7–1 (Herrick, Myers, & Korotkin, 1959). Rats pressed a lever in the alternating presence and absence of light. When the light was on, lever-presses were occasionally reinforced with food. When it was off, presses were not reinforced. The notation for the stimulus correlated with reinforcement is S^D for *discriminative stimulus* or S^+ for positive stimulus; that for the one correlated with nonreinforcement or extinction is S^Δ, also for discriminative stimulus (Δ is delta, the Greek letter *d*), or S^- for negative stimulus (strictly, S^0 is more appropriate to denote the absence of a stimulus, but S^- is the more common usage).

In the procedure of Figure 7–1, light and dark alternated irregularly; when lit, the lamp remained on for periods ranging from 5 to 30 seconds. Lever-presses were reinforced according to a *variable-interval*, or VI, schedule of reinforcement: On the average, only one lever-press per 30 seconds was reinforced while the light was on.

The important features of this schedule are that it maintains a moderate and relatively constant response rate and that the varying times between successive reinforcers make time since the last reinforcer an unreliable predictor of when the next response will be reinforced. In these circumstances, if the rat presses more in the light than in the dark the light may be regarded as the controlling stimulus; such a rate difference could not have depended on the time between stimulus changes or the time between reinforcers because the temporal cycle of those events was unsystematic.

Over sessions, lever-pressing increased during light but decreased in its absence. Such increases often accompany such discriminations (behavioral contrast; see Chapter 8). Figure 7–1 also shows changes in a discrimination index, responding in light as a percentage of total responses. The index increased over sessions. To describe this outcome we can say that lever-pressing in the presence of light was a discriminated operant, that the light functioned as a discriminative stimulus for lever-pressing, or that lever-pressing was under the stimulus control of the light.

Section A   **The Nature of Discriminated Operants**

We can illustrate some properties of discriminated operants with a hypothetical example related to that of Figure 6–1. Again, a rat is in a chamber with a slot in one wall, but this time the rat cannot poke its nose into the slot. Instead, the slot is covered by a translucent plastic strip that can be lit by a series of 15 lamps behind it. In other words, the lamps provide a stimulus dimension analogous to the response dimension of Figure 6–1. A lever is centered beneath the slot and a feeder is on the

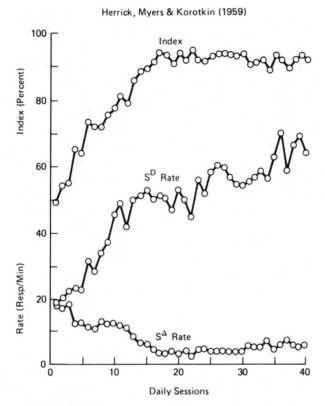

FIGURE 7-1   Rats' lever-pressing in the presence and absence of light. The light (S^D) was correlated with variable-interval reinforcement and its absence (S^Δ) with extinction. The discrimination index is the percent of total responses in the presence of light (100 times S^D rate divided by sum of S^D and S^Δ rates). The data are median rates from 8 rats. (From Herrick, Myers, & Korotkin, 1959, Figure 2)

opposite wall. Now we light the lamps behind the strip in irregular order and record the lever-pressing that occurs in the presence of each. If we do not reinforce lever-presses, pressing is infrequent and bears no systematic relation to the part of the strip that is lit. In fact, the data might be much like those in *A* of Figure 6–1, with the main difference that the *x*-axis represents stimulus position instead of response position.

At this point, we reinforce lever-presses only with the slit lit at positions 9, 10, 11, or 12; with light on anywhere else, presses are not reinforced. The initial effect of re-

inforcement is much like that in *B* of Figure 6–1: an increase in responding across all positions. The effect is not restricted to stimuli at the positions correlated with reinforcement; instead, it spreads to other positions. The spread of the effect of reinforcement in the presence of one stimulus to other stimuli not correlated with reinforcement is called *generalization*. In the example, reinforcing responding when lights 9 through 12 are lit affects responding in the presence of lights at all other positions. This example differs from the original one mainly in the dimension correlated with reinforcement: Chapter 6 dealt with a response dimension, but now we deal with a stimulus dimension.

Suppose we continue differential reinforcement with respect to stimulus location, reinforcing responses only when positions 9 through 12 are lit. Responding gradually increases during lights at these positions and decreases during lights elsewhere. Again, the effects are like those of Figure 6–1, in C, D, and E. Eventually most responses occur during lights at positions correlated with reinforcement, as in E, and a point may be reached at which, even though some responses still occur during lights at other positions, the distribution of responses does not change much with continued differential reinforcement.

In this example, the stimuli that occasioned responding came to conform closely to the class of stimuli correlated with reinforcement. This process is called *discrimination,* and responding controlled in this way by stimuli is said to be *discriminated.* Differential reinforcement with respect to stimuli created a response class defined by the stimuli in the presence of which responses occurred. But what about responses in the presence of stimuli outside the boundaries correlated with reinforcement (e.g., positions 6, 7, and 8, or 13, 14, and 15)? According to a strict interpretation, they do not count as members of the discriminated-operant class; they are spoken of in terms of generalization. Yet the operation of differential reinforcement generated responding both inside and outside these boundaries, so this responding is part of a continuous distribution.

The resolution is the same as in Chapter 6. We must recognize two classes of stimuli: One is the class correlated with a reinforcement contingency; the other is the class in the presence of which responding occurs. Our interest is not in either class alone but rather in the correspondence between them. The discussion closely parallels that of differentiation and induction in Chapter 6. This is fitting, because a stimulus in the presence of which a response occurs is another property of that response, like its force or its duration or its topography. Why then do we speak of differential reinforcement with respect to response properties in terms of differentiation and induction, whereas we speak of differential reinforcement with respect to stimulus properties in terms of discrimination and generalization?

One methodological factor may be crucial to the distinction. When we study differential reinforcement with respect to response properties, we record responses in different classes, but aside from arranging contingencies there is not much else we can do about them. If we see a rat about to poke its nose into position 7 along the slot, we cannot appropriately prevent the response even if the rat has responded many more times there than elsewhere. Suppose, however, that we were working with stimulus properties. We could present lights equally often at each position, or we could present lights at some positions but not others so that the rat would never have an opportunity to press the lever in the presence of some stimuli. Such cases justify saying that the stimuli in discrimination procedures set the occasion for responses: When a class of responses is defined by the presence of a stimulus, responses in the class cannot occur when the stimulus is absent.

Even this methodological distinction has exceptions. For example, consider the differential reinforcement of long inter-response times (the DRL schedule; Chapter 6). If a pigeon's peck is reinforced only after at least 5 seconds of no pecking, the pigeon may come to space its pecks about 5 seconds apart. We discussed this behavior in terms of the differentiation of a complex operant consisting of a pause plus a peck. We could instead treat the duration of the pause as a stimulus property and argue that the behavior should be dealt with as a discrimination based on time elapsed since the last peck. In this instance, in fact, the vocabularies are interchangeable. Whether we speak of differentiation and induction or of discrimination and generalization, the underlying operation is differential reinforcement. Both differentiation and discrimination involve correspondences between the dimensions upon which differential reinforcement is based and the dimensions of the resulting behavior. We will nevertheless maintain the established difference between the vocabularies of response properties and stimulus properties, because these vocabularies have an extensive and widely accepted historical foundation.

THE PROBLEM OF ATTENTION

In discussing the correspondence between the stimuli with which reinforcement contingencies are correlated and those to which the organism responds, we spoke in terms of the stimulus dimension selected by the experimenter. But stimuli have varied properties, and there are no guarantees that the organism will respond to just those properties selected. In differentiation, a rat's lever-presses might have fairly constant form even though only force is the basis for differential reinforcement. For example, the rat might reliably press the lever with its left paw even though this property is not critical to whether the response is reinforced. Similarly, in discrimination a rat might respond on the basis of the intensity of a visual stimulus even though differential reinforcement is based only on its shape. (Stimulus properties to

which an organism is likely to respond are sometimes called *salient*, but salience is not a property of a stimulus; it is a property of the organism's behavior with respect to the stimulus.)

The concept of *attention* arises from discriminated responding to properties of stimuli. Consider a pigeon whose key-pecks are occasionally reinforced with food. One of two stimulus combinations is presented on the key: a triangle on a red background or a circle on a green background. After 3 minutes of triangle-on-red, the next peck in the presence of this stimulus is reinforced; after 3 minutes of circle-on-green, the stimulus turns off without reinforcement. The arrangement during triangle-on-red is called a *fixed-interval* or FI schedule of reinforcement; the arrangement during circle-on-green is extinction. The fixed-interval schedule is examined in Chapter 8. For the present, it is enough to note that this schedule usually maintains responding that increases in rate as time passes in the interval and not the relatively constant response rate ordinarily maintained by a variable-interval schedule. If every peck during triangle-on-red produced a reinforcer, then the reinforcer deliveries themselves might acquire discriminative functions. We do not have to worry about such effects with FI reinforcement because no peck is reinforced until the interval ends.

Data for two pigeons are shown in Figure 7–2 (Reynolds, 1961a). The left graphs show rates of pecking during each stimulus compound after 18 hours of training. Both pigeons emitted more than 40 pecks per minute during triangle-on-red but pecked at relatively low rates during circle-on-green. In a test without reinforcement, the elements of each compound were presented separately. For Pigeon 105, almost all pecking occurred during the triangle;

PART III *Learning Without Words*

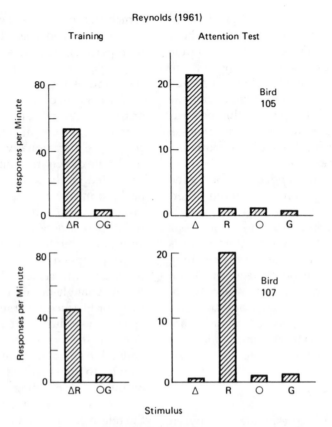

FIGURE 7–2 Key-pecking of two pigeons during reinforcement correlated with triangle-on-red and extinction correlated with circle-on-green (left: training), and during extinction tests with the stimulus elements presented separately (right: attention tests). Pigeon 105 was responding to form but not color; Pigeon 107 was responding to color but not form. (From Reynolds, 1961a, Figure 1)

red, the background color correlated with reinforcement, occasioned little more responding than either the circle or green, the elements previously correlated with extinction. For Pigeon 107, on the other hand, almost all pecking occurred during red; even though the triangle had been correlated with reinforcement during training, by itself it occasioned even less pecking than the circle or green. Pigeon 105 was attending to form and not color, and Pigeon 107 was attending to color and not form. During training, both form and color were correlated in the same way with reinforce-

ment. Only by separately examining the effects of the elements could we say what their discriminative functions were.

Attention is not merely an instance of generalization. For Pigeon 105, responding generalized from triangle-on-red to triangle without a background color but not to red without a triangle. We usually speak of attention not as a response to particular stimuli but rather as attention to *stimulus dimensions* (paying attention means listening to all of what is said and not just to some parts of it). We say that Pigeon 105 attended to form and not color because discriminated responding occurred with changes in form but not with changes in color. When stimuli are discriminated along one stimulus dimension but not another, we can say that the organism is attending to the first dimension but not the second.

Once an organism has attended to some stimulus properties in one situation, it is likely to attend to those properties in new situations (e.g., Lawrence, 1949). We can also change the likelihood that an organism will attend to stimulus properties simply by changing the way in which reinforcement is correlated with them (Johnson & Cumming, 1968). In the training phase of Figure 7–2, form and color were correlated equally well with reinforcement. For this reason, the experiment was particularly suitable for demonstrating some properties of attention. But if our major interest was form discrimination in the pigeon, we would make color irrelevant and only correlate some forms but not others with reinforcement.

Place-Learning vs. Response-Learning

The preceding issues are indirectly related to a long-standing controversy in psychology, on place-learning vs. response-learning (e.g., Restle, 1957). The response of moving from one place to another has had a privileged place in behavioral analyses (e.g., Olton, 1979). Going to food is not the same as producing food while remaining in place. One important difference between the two cases is that the environment changes more drastically when we move to a new location than when we introduce a new stimulus into our present one. Humans in particular have found ways to substitute other responses for ordinary locomotion: To go places, we step on gas pedals, turn steering wheels, press elevator buttons, and stand on escalators or moving walkways. Furthermore, move-

ment produces continuous changes in the environment, whereas sequences of other responses may produce no change until the sequence is completed. Beyond these differences, then, does it matter whether an organism moves to a new place or produces new stimuli where it is?

Such questions were implicit in the controversy over place-learning vs. response-learning. We can differentiate the right turns of a rat at the choice-point of a T-maze by reinforcing right but not left turns. We can then ask whether the rat's responding is based on response dimensions (movements to the right as opposed to movements to the left) or on stimulus dimensions (movements toward a particular place, without regard to the direction from which the rat approaches). For example, suppose the right arm of the T-maze points toward the brighter windowed east wall of a laboratory. The rat might learn right turns or it might learn to run toward the window. We could evaluate these alternatives by turning the T-maze around so that the right arm points west and the rat now approaches the choice-point from the north. If the rat turns right and therefore away from the window, it shows *response-learning*. If it turns left toward the window, it shows *place-learning*: It moves toward the same place, even though it does so by turning in a different direction. The question is whether the rat has learned right vs. left turns or east vs. west turns.

The rat's performance depends largely on the stimuli available both inside and outside the maze. The typical maze used to be topped by wire mesh or some other cover that allowed the experimenter to watch what the rat was doing. If an experimenter can look in, a rat can look out. Although it is nearsighted, the typical rat can discriminate the general direction of lights and other gross features of a room.

As long as stimuli are available outside the maze, they may become the basis for the rat's turning in a particular direction. But if those stimuli are eliminated by placing an opaque cover over the maze, the direction that the maze faces in the room becomes irrelevant and the rat cannot do anything but demonstrate response-learning. Place learning or response-learning therefore can depend on how the experimenter prepares the problem for the rat. By judiciously choosing conditions, an experimenter can make either outcome more likely than the other.

In natural environments, food at a given location is not necessarily replenished as it is in the goalbox of a laboratory maze. In foraging, an animal is more likely to move to a new location than to return to one where it has already consumed the available food. Again, the properties of the environment to which the organism attends may vary with constraints imposed by the experimenter (cf. Collier & Rovee-Collier, 1981; Lea, 1979). For example, when a rat is given daily sessions in an apparatus in which food is located at the ends of each of several alleys and the food is not replenished during the session, the rat learns not to repeat visits to alleys where it has already eaten (Olton & Samuelson, 1976). Spatial properties of environments are particularly important, but in appropriate circumstances a rat may learn other features of its environment (e.g., sequential patterns of reinforcer magnitudes; Hulse, 1977).

STIMULUS-CONTROL GRADIENTS

The methodology of discrimination procedures places a heavy burden on the experimenter. In differentiation procedures the organism determines the order of responses, but in discrimination procedures the experimenter must determine the order of stimuli. If an experimenter is interested in some stimulus continuum (i.e., some dimension along which stimuli can vary, such as intensity or position of a light), it might make a difference whether many or few stimuli are presented, or whether each is presented for a short or a long time, or whether they are correlated with both reinforcement and nonreinforcement or only with reinforcement. Different arrangements of stimuli are the basis for research on gradients of stimulus control.

Generalization Gradients

If responding is reinforced during some stimulus and a property of that stimulus is then varied, responding will depend on how much the stimulus has changed. For example, if a pigeon's key-pecks are reinforced when the key is lit yellow, the pigeon will continue to peck, though ordinarily at lower and lower rates, as the light is changed to orange and then red and then violet. This demonstrates generalization: the effects of reinforcement during yellow spreads to other colors.

Figure 7–3 presents data on generalization of pigeons' key-pecks to tones of different frequency after pecks were reinforced only during a tone of 1000 cycles per second (Jenkins & Harrison, 1960). In one procedure (no discrimination training), the tone was always present and pecks were reinforced according to a variable-interval or VI schedule. In a second procedure (presence-absence training), the tone was sometimes present and sometimes absent, and pecks were reinforced according to the VI schedule only during the tone. After training, reinforcement was discontinued and tones of other frequencies were presented for the first time, along with no tone and the original training tone; these stimuli were presented eight times each in mixed order.

For the three pigeons without discrimination training (Figure 7–3, top), neither

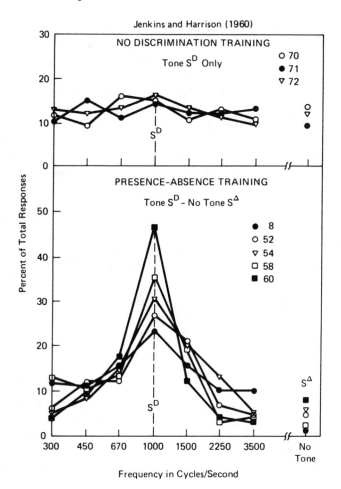

FIGURE 7–3 Generalization gradients as a function of tone frequency after reinforcement of key-pecks during a 1000-cycle-per-second tone (top: no discrimination training, 3 pigeons) or after reinforcement during the tone and extinction during its absence (bottom: presence-absence training, 5 pigeons). Without discrimination training, gradients were relatively flat; after presence-absence training, they were peaked at the reinforcement stimulus (S^D). (From Jenkins & Harrison, 1960, Figures 1 and 2)

the frequency of the tone nor its presence or absence had much effect on pecking. The generalization gradient was relatively flat or, in other words, the effect of reinforcement during the original tone spread uniformly to all the other stimuli. For the five pigeons given discrimination training (bottom), the original frequency produced higher rates of pecking than any other; in general, the closer to the original frequency, the higher the rate of pecking. It is not surprising that low rates of pecking occurred in the absence of the tone: Absence of tone was correlated with extinction. But for these pigeons response rate varied with frequency even though discriminated responding depended only on the presence or absence of the tone and not on its frequency. (The form of generalization gradients is also affected by other variables, such as level of deprivation or the reinforcement schedule during training; e.g., Hearst, Koresko, & Poppen, 1964.)

The peaked generalization gradient demonstrated that after but not before tone vs. no-tone training the pigeons attended to auditory stimuli. Attention is a name for this kind of phenomenon. A problem occurs when the term instead appears as an explanation. Attending to stimuli is something that organisms do. We decide whether we can say that an organism is attending to a stimulus on the basis of its behavior. We therefore should not use this term, derived from behavior, to explain the behavior that justified its use in the first place. (Similarly, if we say that one stimulus dimension is more salient than another because organisms are more likely to attend to it, we cannot then use this salience to explain their attention.)

Postdiscrimination Gradients

Stimulus-control gradients can also be obtained after discrimination between two or more stimuli along the dimension. Figure 7–4 compares such a postdiscrimination gradient with a generalization gradient (Hanson, 1959). For one group of pigeons (generalization), key-pecks during a single wavelength on the key were reinforced according to a VI schedule; the rate of pecking during this and other wavelengths was then determined in extinction. The gradient had its peak at the reinforcement stimulus; rate of pecking decreased as distance from this stimulus increased.

For a second group (postdiscrimination), key-pecks were reinforced according to a VI schedule during the same wavelength as the first group, but this wavelength alternated with another during

FIGURE 7–4 Stimulus-control gradients. The generalization gradient shows pigeons' key-pecking after reinforcement at a wavelength of 550 millimicrons (S^D). The postdiscrimination gradient shows key-pecking after reinforcement at 550 millimicrons (S^D) and extinction at 570 millimicrons (S^Δ). (The spectrum goes from violet and blue at short wavelengths to red at long wavelengths; the S^D and S^Δ were in the green-yellow region.) The generalization gradient peaks at the S^D. The postdiscrimination gradient shows a peak shift; maximum responding is shifted from the S^D in a direction away from the S^Δ. (From Hanson, 1959, Figure 1)

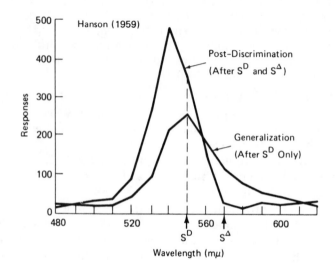

which pecks were not reinforced (extinction); as for the first group, the rate of pecking during this and other wavelengths was then determined in extinction. In this case, the peak of the gradient was displaced from the reinforcement stimulus in a direction away from the extinction stimulus (a peak shift). (Similar effects occur when the discrimination is based on a higher frequency of reinforcement during one stimulus than another; Guttman, 1959.)

One account of the form of the postdiscrimination gradient (Spence, 1937) assumed that reinforcement during a stimulus created a gradient of increased responding centered on that stimulus (excitatory gradient), that extinction during another stimulus produced a gradient of decreased responding centered on that second stimulus (inhibitory gradient), and that after discrimination training the responding produced by other stimuli could be predicted by subtracting the inhibitory from the excitatory gradient. Spence's theoretical gradient showed a peak shift: Its maximum was displaced from the reinforcement stimulus in a direction away from the extinction stimulus. But the new gradient, produced by subtraction, was everywhere lower than the original excitatory gradient; thus, it was consistent with the form but not the absolute value of postdiscrimination gradients (cf. Hearst, Besley, & Farthing, 1970).

Effects of discrimination training on the shape of gradients raised questions about the origins of the peaked generalization gradient. One suggestion was that the steepness of a gradient depended on the discriminability of stimuli at various points along the dimension. In the generalization gradient of Figure 7–4, for example, response rate decreased more steeply with wavelength below the reinforcement stimulus than above (e.g., the lower rate at 520 than 580 millimicrons). But when widths and steepnesses of generalization gradients around stimuli in different regions of the spectrum were compared with thresholds for changes in wavelength in these different regions, no simple relations between generalization and discriminability were found (Guttman & Kalish, 1956).

Another suggestion was that the peaked gradients depended on discrimination learning that occurred before the organism was brought into the experimental situation. For example, a pigeon presumably learns discriminations among the colors of the grains that it eats long before it sees yellows in a generalization test; its discriminations of color might then be sharpest in the yellow region of the spectrum simply because yellow predominates among the colors of these grains. We cannot be sure what color discriminations are acquired in natural environments, but we can create an environment in which color discriminations are not possible by raising an organism in monochromatic light, an environment lit by only a very narrow band of wavelengths such as the yellow light emitted by a sodium vapor lamp. To humans in such environments, objects have no color; everything appears in shades of gray. An organism reared in such an environment has no opportunity to learn color discriminations.

A suitable organism for monochromatic rearing is the duckling, which is capable of walking, pecking, eating, and drinking soon after it hatches; thus, reinforcement procedures can be started early. Generalization gradients across wavelengths from ducklings reared monochromatically have been sometimes flat (as in Figure 7–3, top; Peterson, 1962), and sometimes peaked (as in Figure 7–3, bottom; Rudolph, Honig, & Gerry, 1969; Tracy, 1970), suggesting that ducklings sometimes can attend to color even without color experience. When ducklings reared monochromatically were trained to discriminate between only two wavelengths, however, their postdiscrimination gradients were similar to those of normally reared ducklings, including peak shifts, even though the stimuli consisted mostly of wavelengths they had never seen before (Terrace, 1975). The implication is that the main effect of contingencies is on attention to color and not on consistencies of responding along the wavelength dimension (e.g., as when a duckling responds more to orange than to yellow after reinforcement during red).

Inhibitory Gradients

Once Spence's account was offered to handle the form of postdiscrimination gradients, interest arose in finding a way to record inhibitory gradients directly. The difficulties were both methodological and theoretical. To determine whether a stimulus reduced responding, there had to be some responding during the stimulus to start with. A procedure was needed that would separate the dimension along which the extinction gradient was determined from the one that was correlated with reinforcement (Jenkins, 1965; Hearst, Besley, & Farthing, 1970). Such a procedure is illustrated in Figure 7–5 (Honig, Boneau, Burstein, & Pennypacker, 1963). With one group of pigeons, the reinforcement stimulus was a vertical line on the key and the extinction stimulus was a lit key without a line; with a second group, these stimuli

FIGURE 7–5 Excitatory and inhibitory stimulus-control gradients after variable-interval reinforcement during one stimulus (S^D) and extinction during another (S^Δ). In two studies with pigeons (filled and unfilled symbols), a vertical line was correlated with reinforcement and its absence with extinction for one group; the stimuli were reversed for the other group. Responding during various line orientations and during absence of the line was determined during nonreinforcement. (From Honig, Boneau, Burstein, & Pennypacker, 1963, Figure 1)

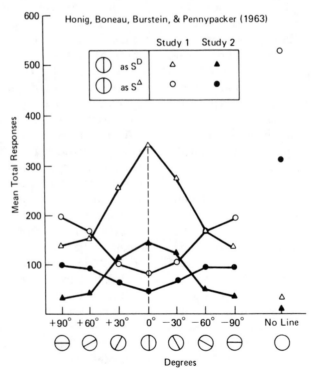

were reversed. For both groups, variable-interval (VI) schedules were used during training, and stimulus-control gradients along the dimension of line orientation were obtained during nonreinforcement.

Figure 7–5 shows data for two such groups from each of two studies. When vertical was correlated with reinforcement and its absence with extinction, the rate of pecking decreased with greater deviations from vertical (triangles); this is a reinforcement gradient like that of Figure 7–3 (bottom). When the absence of the line was correlated with reinforcement and the vertical line was correlated with extinction, however, the rate of pecking increased with greater deviations from vertical (circles). Changing the orientation of the line affected its distance from the vertical extinction stimulus but not its distance from the reinforcement stimulus, the absence of a line.

We can always raise questions about the stimulus dimensions to which an organism attends. For example, suppose the pigeon looks only at the upper edge of the key. As the line shifts from vertical, its top moves away from the upper edge and so the upper edge more closely resembles that of a key without a line. Such possibilities must be evaluated experimentally (e.g., by removing portions of the line and seeing whether this changes the pigeon's behavior; cf. Touchette, 1969). Another factor is that organisms are more likely to attend to properties of stimuli correlated with reinforcement (feature-positive discrimination) than to those correlated with extinction (Jenkins & Sainsbury, 1970; cf. Chapter 8 on observing responses).

FADING: STIMULUS CONTROL BY SUCCESSIVE APPROXIMATIONS

Just as the response properties that define an operant class can be changed gradually by shaping procedures, the stimulus properties that define a discriminated operant class can be changed gradually by analogous procedures called *fading*. Training does not have to start with difficult-to-discriminate stimuli. Instead, it can start with easy-to-discriminate stimuli and then move gradually to more difficult ones. For example, it is usually harder to teach a pigeon to discriminate between vertical and horizontal lines than between red and green. Once a discrimination between red and green exists, however, one between vertical and horizontal can be successively approximated by superimposing vertical on red and horizontal on green and then gradually fading out the colors (Terrace, 1963b).

Creating stimulus control through fading is often effective (e.g., Sidman & Rosenberger, 1967; Sidman & Stoddard, 1967), but as with shaping no simple rules exist to determine how rapidly stimuli should be faded in or out in particular situations. For example, if we superimposed vertical on red and horizontal on green and then partially faded out the colors, we might later find, after removing the colors completely, that the pigeon had learned to discriminate between vertical and horizontal. On the other hand, fading might be unsuccessful; if the organism attends only to the colors even when they became very faint, the discrimination may not transfer from color to line orientation. In this case, discriminated responding will probably disappear each time we dim the colors below certain threshold levels.

Just as shaping requires that some behavior is available to be shaped, fading requires that some discriminative responding is available to be shifted to a new stimulus dimension. For example, consider *errorless discrimination learning* (Terrace, 1963a). Soon after pigeons' pecks on a red key had been shaped with food reinforcement, reinforcement during red was continued according to a variable-interval schedule. Three-minute periods of red alternated with another stimulus, during which pecks were not reinforced. At first, this other stimulus was a dark key lasting 5 seconds. Over three sessions, its duration was gradually lengthened and it was changed from dark to dim and then to brighter and brighter green, until, to the human eye, its brightness matched that of the red key. By the end of these conditions, 3 minutes of red correlated with reinforcement alternated with 3 minutes of green correlated with extinction. Each pigeon in this group pecked the extinction key fewer than 10 times in the entire course of training; pecking occurred almost without exception on the red key rather than on the green key. For pigeons in other groups, for which this procedure was introduced later after initial training or for which green was abruptly introduced at full duration and intensity, the green extinction key was pecked hundreds and even thousands of times during equivalent periods of training.

The gradual fading in of green was in part effective because turning the red key dark early in training stopped the pigeon's pecking for a few seconds (any abrupt stimulus change might have had such an effect). Pecking was not likely to start again before the 5-second extinction stimulus ended. Thus, a difference in responding to the two stimuli occurred at the outset, and the gradual changes in the duration and intensity of the extinction stimulus built upon this difference. Once such discriminative responding had occurred, the faded-in extinction stimulus could be changed to a reinforcement stimulus and the pigeon might never respond during that stimulus and discover it. The sense in which such a performance is errorless is not obvious. We must be cautious about the language of

errors; the term *error* implies a judgment about the value of responding that may be inappropriate to a behavioral analysis. Nevertheless, the fading procedure is not solely of theoretical interest; it may have much practical significance because of its potential applications to education.

THE VOCABULARIES OF DIFFERENTIATION AND DISCRIMINATION

Both differentiation and discrimination involve differential reinforcement. The major difference is whether differential reinforcement is imposed on properties of responding or on properties of the stimuli during which responding occurs. The main implication of the difference is procedural: In studies of differentiation the experimenter must wait for the organism's responses, whereas in studies of discrimination the experimenter controls the order and duration of stimulus presentations. The vocabulary of differentiation and discrimination is summarized in the table on page 143.

Differential reinforcement can be based on simple dimensions of stimuli, such as intensity or location. The experimental question is whether responding conforms to the differential consequences, in that more responding occurs in the presence of the stimuli correlated with reinforcement than in the presence of those correlated with nonreinforcement.

Differential reinforcement may also be arranged for complex properties of stimuli that are not easily quantified. For example, children learning to read must be able to name the letters of the alphabet. But the properties important for distinguishing among some letters are different from those important in distinguishing among others (e.g., straight line vs. curve is important in distinguishing *U* and *V* but

DIFFERENTIAL REINFORCEMENT (OPERATION)	CONCENTRATION OF EFFECTS OF REINFORCEMENT (PROCESS)	SPREAD OF OF EFFECTS OF REINFORCEMENT (PROCESS)	DIFFERENTIAL REINFORCEMENT BY APPROXIMATIONS (OPERATION)
With respect to response properties	Differentiation	Induction	Shaping
With respect to stimulus properties	Discrimination	Generalization	Fading

not *V* and *N*), and different distinctions are important for lower-case than for upper-case letters (e.g., no pair of upper-case letters has the up-down or left-right reversals that must be mastered to read *b*, *p*, *d*, and *q*). The way in which a child learns to distinguish among letters of the alphabet depends on relations among such stimulus properties as symmetry, curvature, and closure. Those properties essential to discriminating among different letters are called *critical features* (e.g., Gibson, 1965).

It is not sufficient, however, to enumerate critical features. For some letters, the upper-case and lower-case forms differ more from each other than they differ from other letters (e.g., *e*, *E*, and *F*, or *h*, *n*, and *N*). Given the multitude of forms, what then defines the class of stimuli that occasions our saying *A* or *B* or *C*? This question is about the stimulus structure of the letters of the alphabet. The problem becomes even more complicated when different contexts are considered. For example, *O* could be either a letter or zero, and *I* could be either a letter or a roman numeral. The concept of an *X* or a *Y* or a *Z* is defined by the class of stimuli to which we respond with the corresponding letter name, but we will see that such classes are based on behavior rather than on common physical properties.

Section B   Animal Cognition

Discriminated operants are behavior classes defined by the stimuli that occasion responding. Such classes are often identified in our everyday vocabulary, as when we speak of stopping at a red traffic light or answering a telephone. The red light can vary in brightness and size and the telephone ring can vary in loudness and timbre, but responding is reasonably independent of variations along such dimensions, and so we speak in terms of these classes of events rather than in terms of particular instances.

In this text we often treat stimuli as if they were restricted to concrete objects or environmental events. But although we can learn to respond in consistent ways to objects or events in our environment, we also can discriminate features, sometimes called abstract or relational, that are independent of any particular object or event. The term *stimulus* may therefore function in a more general way, in the sense of some property of environmental events. For example, we might say that a chair had been placed to the right of a table. Although the chair and the table are concrete objects, being-to-the-right-of is not, and yet we can clearly discriminate this relation from being-to-the-left-of. In some discrimination experiments, therefore, re-lations among stimuli have been the dimensions of interest.

The field of animal cognition has been especially concerned with identifying the properties of environmental events that can be discriminated by different species. Their performances are of particular interest when they depend on discriminating complex relational properties of the environment. Studies of animal cognition have examined a variety of discriminative performances, including judgments of visual symmetry (e.g., Delius & Nowak, 1982); discriminations of numerousness (e.g., Davis & Pérusse, 1988); visual search (e.g., Blough, 1989); discriminative control by reinforcement contingencies or stimuli correlated with those contingencies (e.g., Killeen, 1981; Washburn, Hopkins, & Rumbaugh, 1991); the organization of behavior within a sequentially discriminated sequence (Terrace & Chen, 1991); temporal discriminations (e.g., Cheng & Roberts, 1989); and responding under the stimulus control of the organism's own behavior (e.g., Shimp, Sabulsky, & Childers, 1989), to mention only a few. Many examples of research on animal cognition are presented elsewhere in this text, so this section presents only a highly selective sample.

Consider a pigeon who watches a clock hand as it is projected on the center key of three pigeon keys (Neiworth & Rilling, 1987). The hand starts at vertical and rotates at a constant rate from vertical through 90°; then it disappears. A little later it reappears farther along, at 135° or 180°. The timing of its reappearance is either consistent or inconsistent with a constant rate of rotation while it was invisible. After a trial consistent with a constant rotation rate, left key-pecks are reinforced; after an inconsistent one, right key-pecks are rein-

forced. Pigeons learned to discriminate trials consistent with a constant rotation rate from those in which the constant rate was violated even though the rotating stimulus was absent some of the time; the discrimination also transferred to new locations of reappearance of the clock hand. This performance was not based on trial durations or specific locations of the clock hand, and it therefore demonstrates visual tracking even in the absence of the visual stimulus; such tracking is sometimes called imagery (see Chapter 15). Colloquially, we might say that the pigeon knew where the stimulus was even while it was invisible (a useful skill, as when an edible insect passes behind an obstruction and a bird awaits its emergence from the other side).

Studies of animal cognition are concerned with what an organism knows, and accounts are therefore often framed in terms of the structure of relevant stimuli (cf. Chapter 1 on structural and functional languages). For example, if an organism discriminates among stimuli on the basis of some critical feature, an animal cognitivist might say that the organism represents the stimuli to itself in terms of that feature (e.g., in the clock-hand example, that the pigeon represents or imagines its constant motion). The role of representations in biological theories was discussed in the context of natural selection in Chapter 2; the issue is taken up again in the context of cognitive and behavioral theories in Chapter 15, where we argue that imagery is best treated as a kind of behavior.

COGNITIVE MAPS

Whenever local environments have different properties it is advantageous for an organism to be able to find its way from one to another. An environment with a rich and stable supply of food is preferable to one with a poor and variable supply; an environment in which the food is easily accessible is preferable to one in which the same food exists but is less accessible; an environment with safe areas for breeding and for the rearing of offspring is preferable to one that is more dangerous; and so on. (The argument holds at least for many animal groups. It would take us too far afield to consider the phylogenic contingencies that operated in the evolution of plants, but it is appropriate to note that many plants disperse their seeds; animals are often involved in that dispersal, as when bees pollinate flowers.)

Once some kind of orientation has emerged, natural selection is likely to sharpen it over phylogenic time (cf. Chapter 2). It is therefore not surprising that many animal species readily find their way around in the world. Some of their navigation is learned and some is unlearned. Gallistel (1990) provides a detailed treatment that ranges from foraging in ants to echolocation by bats and choice of routes by chimpanzees, and ranging from orientations based on simple stimulus dimensions such as gradients of odor or light to varieties that are functionally equivalent to celestial navigation. Organisms that leave their nesting areas must be able to return to them; the more accurately they can do so, the more widely they can forage. Organisms that store food over the winter must be able to locate the food later; the more variable their sites and the more sites they can keep track of, the less likely they will be to lose what they have stored to their competitors (e.g., Balda, Kamil, & Grim, 1986). Organisms that are evading a predator must be able to locate escape routes; those that allow themselves to be pursued into blind alleys will not survive.

We considered some issues relevant to spatial orientation in discussing place-learning versus response-learning. The two kinds of behavior were distinguished mainly by whether stimuli outside the maze were available to the rat. If they were, the rat oriented itself within the larger stimulus complex, the room within which the maze was located; it learned places. If not, it mastered only specific turns within the maze; it learned responses. Additional complexities were introduced in other maze experiments (cf. Olton, 1979). For example, it was demonstrated that a rat sometimes chooses the shortest available route through a maze when another route preferred earlier is blocked, or that it sometimes takes appropriate shortcuts that have just been added to a maze even though it never traveled those shortcuts before. These outcomes provide the justification for speaking of *cognitive maps* (Tolman, 1948); the finding that organisms can locate an area even when approaching it from a new direction demonstrates that they learn spatial relations in addition to or perhaps even instead of specific paths.

The problems of determining the environmental features to which organisms attend as they move from one place to another emerge on a grander scale in animal homing and migration. Wasps return to their nests, bees to their hives, salmon to their rivers of origin, and birds to seasonal nesting grounds. Among the environmental features that may be important are landmarks, polarized light, chemical gradients, magnetic fields, and the location and movement of the sun and stars (e.g., Tinbergen, 1972; Walcott, Gould, & Kirshvink, 1979; von Frisch, 1953). In some of the cases in which organisms navigate to regions that they had never before visited in their lifetimes, they do so in isolation; in others, they do so in the company of other members of their species. Both cases must involve substantial phylogenic components, either with respect to important properties of environments or with respect to the contingencies that led to group migration (or both). With respect to long-distance migrations, the phylogenic contingencies may have involved the selection of those able to maintain orientation over gradually longer journeys as the continents very slowly drifted apart over geologic time (Skinner, 1975). A more detailed account of these phenomena is beyond the scope of this text, but they illustrate that an analysis of the stimulus properties that determine behavior is relevant to phylogeny as well as ontogeny.

NATURAL CONCEPTS AND PROBABILISTIC STIMULUS CLASSES

Concepts have been spoken of as generalization within a class of stimuli and discrimination between classes of stimuli (Keller & Schoenfeld, 1950). Thus, our concept of red must involve generalization among all stimuli we call red and discrimination between these stimuli and others we do not call red. Concepts are therefore to classes of stimuli what operants are to classes of responses. (Responding on the basis of some single property of stimuli is sometimes called *abstraction*, with the language of concepts restricted to responding on the basis of some combination of properties. We will not observe this distinction because of its potential for ambiguity. For example, being-to-the-left-of can be treated either as a single relational property or as a combination of properties necessarily including both a reference point and a stimulus to the left of that reference point.)

We already noted that it is often difficult to define discriminative stimuli by physical dimensions. For example, the proper-

ties that define the letter *A* vary according to whether it is upper-case or lower-case and whether it appears as type or as script. The capacity to discriminate among such stimuli exists in animals as well as humans (e.g., discriminations between various forms of the letter *A* and the digit 2 have been demonstrated in pigeons; Morgan, Fitch, Holman, & Lea, 1976). But the difficulty of defining stimuli in terms of measurable physical properties is not limited to arbitrary classes created by humans, such as letters and numbers. They exist also with everyday objects and events. What distinguishes dogs from other animals? On what basis do we generalize between a chihuahua and a husky by calling both of them dogs, while we discriminate between huskies and wolves or foxes?

Pigeons have been taught to discriminate between pictures that contain a human form and those that do not (e.g., Herrnstein & Loveland, 1975). Such discriminations have been called *natural concepts*. In one study (Herrnstein, Loveland, & Cable, 1976), slides were presented on a screen next to a pigeon's key and key-pecks were reinforced in the presence of some slides but not others. Some pigeons learned discriminations between pictures with and without trees; others learned discriminations between pictures with and without water; still others learned discriminations between pictures with and without particular people. After training with one set of slides (e.g., slides with and without trees), the pigeons discriminated among slides that had not been presented before. New slides were sometimes more accurately discriminated than slides used in training. The implications were that

> we cannot begin to draw up a list of common elements. To recognize a tree, the pigeons did not require that it be green, leafy, vertical, woody, branching, and so on (over-

looking the problem of common elements nested within terms like leafy, vertical, woody, and so on). Moreover, to be recognizable as a nontree, a picture did not have to omit greenness, woodiness, branchiness, verticality, and so on. Neither could we identify common elements in the other two experiments. If not common elements, what? No other theory is so easily characterized, though in crude terms an alternative suggests itself. Pigeons respond to clusters of features more or less isomorphic with the clusters we respond to ourselves. The green should be on the leaves, if either green or leaves are present. However, neither is necessary or sufficient. The vertical or branching parts should be the woody parts, although neither of these features is necessary or sufficient either. What we see as trees comprises a complex list of probabilistic conjunctions and disjunctions, the discovery of which would require far more effort than seems justified by any possible benefit. (Herrnstein, Loveland, & Cable, 1976, pp. 298–299).

Natural concepts are examples of *probabilistic stimulus classes*, classes in which each member contains some subset of features but none is common to all members. The number of features in the subset may vary from one class member to another. Such classes, sometimes called *fuzzy sets*, do not have well-defined boundaries, though class members may have family resemblances (cf. Rosch, 1973; Mervis & Rosch, 1981).

Some probabilistic stimulus classes are defined by reference to a *prototype*. A prototype is a typical member of a probabilistic class; it is derived from a weighted average of all of the features of all of the members of the class. For example, birds are a probabilistic stimulus class; most fly, but ostriches and penguins do not. In the production of a prototypical bird, feathers must be weighted more heavily than webbed feet because more birds have feathers than have webbed feet. Thus, a

robin is more prototypical than a duck because it shares more features with other birds than does a duck.

Other types of stimulus classes include polymorphous stimulus classes (Lea & Harrison, 1978; see Glossary) and equivalence classes (about which more later). In fact, the class of stimulus classes is itself a probabilistic stimulus class, in the sense that its definition changes as the boundaries of relevant research are expanded.

The problem of defining stimulus classes is a general one. It is not resolved by appealing to the procedures of physical measurement, because the reading of meters or other instruments is also discriminative behavior. Even the behavior of the scientist depends on discriminations learned in the laboratory. As we have already seen, distinctions among reinforcement, punishment, elicitation, and other behavioral processes are based upon such discriminations. Stimulus control is as fundamental with respect to our own scientific behavior as it is with respect to the behavior of the organisms that we study. Thus, any effective philosophy of science must take it into account.

Section C **Conditional Discriminations and Higher-Order Classes of Behavior**

Like contingencies, discriminations may be effective in some circumstances but not in others. For example, your response to a red traffic light depends on whether it is facing you or the traffic crossing the intersection. Such discriminations, in which the role of one stimulus is conditional upon other stimuli that are present, are called *conditional discriminations*. Consider the case of attention in the pigeon, illustrated in Figure 7–2. The available stimuli are triangles or circles on red or green backgrounds. If we add a lamp above the key, we can reinforce pecks in the presence of triangles when the lamp is lit and pecks in the presence of red when it is not. Under these circumstances, the pigeon will come to peck triangles but not circles, either on red or on green, when the lamp is on; and keys with red backgrounds but not green, either with triangles or circles, when it is off (cf. Reynolds, 1961a). In other words, whether the pigeon discriminates form or color is conditional on the status of the lamp.

We now consider several experimental procedures in which discriminative contingencies depend upon the context within which they are arranged. These include learning set, matching-to-sample, and the arbitrary matching procedures that pro-

duce equivalence classes. These procedures generate higher-order classes of behavior, in the sense that the classes are defined not by particular stimuli or responses, but rather by relations that include those stimuli and responses as special cases (cf. Chapter 6).

LEARNING SET

The learning of a new discrimination can be modified by the organism's history of discrimination learning. As illustrated by the phenomenon called *learning set* (Harlow, 1949), relations among stimulus properties may control responding independently of specific stimuli. Two different objects were presented to a food-deprived monkey in successive trials. Their positions varied

FIGURE 7–6 Learning set or learning-to-learn. Eight monkeys learned a variety of two-choice discrimination problems. Each set of points shows percent correct responses over the first six trials of each problem for blocks of successive problems (the y-axis starts at 50 percent, chance level). The rate of learning increased over successive problems. By the last block of problems, responding was almost 100 percent accurate by the second trial with each new problem. (Adapted from Harlow, 1949, Figure 2)

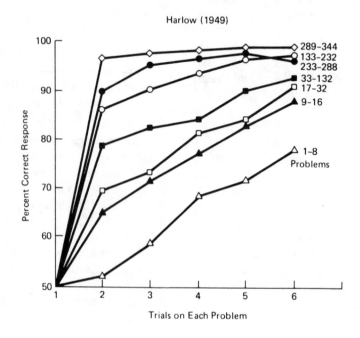

Harlow (1949)

from trial to trial. Food was under only one of the objects, and therefore the response of picking it up was differentially reinforced. After a number of trials, the monkey mastered the discrimination. Then, in a new problem, another pair of objects was presented, with differential reinforcement again arranged for picking up only one of them. Again, a discrimination emerged. A new problem with still another new pair was then presented, and later still another, and so on.

Data averaged across eight monkeys are shown in Figure 7–6. Each set of points shows the percent of correct responses over the first six trials across blocks of successive problems. Over the first eight problems (1–8), correct responses increased gradually over trials; by the sixth trial, they had not even reached 80 percent. In the next block of eight problems (9–16), correct responses increased more rapidly over trials. Over successive blocks, correct responding rose more and more rapidly over trials until, by the last block of trials (289–344), responding reached nearly 100 percent accuracy on the second trial of each new problem. In other words, the more problems the monkey had mastered, the more rapidly it mastered each new problem.

In this procedure, the discriminated operant cannot be described simply in terms of a stimulus pair. When successive discriminations are so rapidly acquired that monkeys consistently choose the stimulus correlated with reinforcement after a single trial with a new pair, performance depends on relations between stimuli and their correlated consequences over successive problems and not on the particular stimulus pairs that appear within single problems. Within each early problem, the monkey had to learn not only which stimulus was correlated with food but also many other aspects of the procedure (e.g., that food is correlated with just one of the

two stimuli rather than with position or other features of the setting; that this correlation does not change within a problem; that reaching simultaneously for both stimuli is not reinforced; and so on). During early problems, learning took place slowly because the monkey was learning these many things; eventually, when the monkey had learned these other things, all it had to learn in any new problem was which stimulus was correlated with food.

At this point, we may define the discriminated operant as follows: If the response to a stimulus is reinforced on the first trial of a new problem, responding to that stimulus continues on all subsequent trials; if it is not reinforced, responding switches to the other stimulus for all subsequent trials. In learning set, this is the performance that is reinforced and this is the performance that the organism's behavior approaches. Thus, the correspondence between the reinforcement contingencies and the behavior generated by these contingencies remains an appropriate criterion for this behavioral class. Learning set qualifies as a higher-order class because it is defined by these relations and not by the stimuli and responses of any particular problem.

A phenomenon that may be regarded as a variation on learning set is *learned helplessness* (Maier, Seligman, & Solomon, 1969). For example, rats that receive inescapable and unavoidable electric shock in one situation are sometimes less likely to learn avoidance responding when such responding becomes available in a new situation than rats not exposed to inescapable and unavoidable shock (cf. Maier, Albin, & Testa, 1973). Here again it is difficult to define the response class, except to note that the rats in the presence of inescapable and unavoidable shock apparently learned that their responses did not have important consequences; the behavior generated by these contingencies transferred to situations in which responding could have consequences. We might assume that, as a higher-order class, learned helplessness could be brought under the control of discriminative stimuli through differential contingencies.

Learning set not only illustrates the range and complexity of the stimulus and response classes that organisms can learn; it also shows that what happens when an experimentally naive organism is introduced into an experimental setting cannot be treated as a simple instance of learning (cf. Chapter 4 on the acquisition of behavior). To study learning, some investigators have therefore turned to the repeated acquisition of simple discriminations or simple response sequences. Paradoxically, they have come to study learning, defined by changes in performance, in the context of steady-state procedures, defined by stability in performance. For example, Boren and Devine (1968) arranged four groups of three levers each within a monkey's chamber. Within any session, only one particular sequence of presses was reinforced (e.g., left lever of group 1, right lever of group 2, middle lever of group 3, right lever of group 4), but the sequence changed from session to session. Once the monkey's rate of mastering a new problem each day became stable, these repeated acquisitions provided a baseline for studying a variety of phenomena: effects of different fading procedures; effects of drugs on learning; effects of different types of consequences for responses at various positions in the sequence; effects of creating the response sequence as a whole as opposed to building it up either from the beginning or from the end; and so on.

MATCHING-TO-SAMPLE

Many conditional discriminations involve arbitrary relations between the conditional discriminative stimulus and the discriminations for which it sets the occasion. Some cases in which those relations are not arbitrary are of special interest. For example, whether one stimulus in a set of stimuli matches one of the others or is an odd stimulus depends on, or is conditional on, the context of other stimuli within which it is presented. We now consider some properties of such conditional discriminations.

Matching-to-sample is illustrated as it might be arranged in a three-key pigeon chamber in Figure 7–7 (cf. Skinner, 1950;

FIGURE 7–7 Diagram of a matching-to-sample trial in a three-key pigeon chamber. After an intertrial interval of *t* seconds, a sample stimulus (green: *G*) appears on the center key. A peck on the center key turns on the two side keys. One comparison stimulus matches the sample; the other (red: *R*) does not. A peck on the matching comparison stimulus produces food and the intertrial interval for the next trial begins; a peck on the nonmatching comparison stimulus starts the next intertrial interval without food. The sample stimulus and the left-right locations of the matching comparison vary from trial to trial.

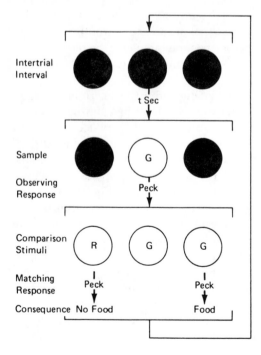

Ferster, 1960). During an intertrial interval, all the keys are dark. The trial begins with illumination of the center key, the *sample.* Typically a peck is then required on the center key; this peck guarantees that the pigeon looks at the sample stimulus (the peck is sometimes called an *observing response,* but the term also applies to other cases in which a response produces some discriminative stimulus; cf. Chapter 8). This response turns on *comparison* stimuli on the two side-keys. One matches the sample stimulus and the other does not. A peck on the matching side-key then produces a reinforcer followed by a new intertrial interval, whereas a peck on the nonmatching side-key is followed directly by the intertrial interval without a reinforcer (sometimes a nonmatching peck also extends the duration of the intertrial interval, on the assumption that such a consequence punishes nonmatching pecks).

The sample stimulus ordinarily changes from trial to trial (e.g., green on some trials and red on others); the position of the matching side-key also changes from trial to trial. A common feature of matching-to-sample is a correction procedure, which arranges a repetition of the same sample and comparison stimuli on the next trial if a trial ends with a peck on a nonmatching side-key. This procedure prevents the development of responding that is restricted to only one side-key or color. For example, suppose a pigeon pecked only the comparison stimulus on the left side-key. If the matching side-key nonetheless alternated irregularly between left and right, these pecks would be reinforced on half the trials (those with the matching stimulus on the left). Reinforcement on half the trials would probably be enough to maintain pecking on the left key indefinitely. On the other hand, with a correction procedure the pigeon would have to switch to the right key sooner or later, be-

cause a trial with a matching stimulus on the right would repeat itself until a right key-peck occurred and was reinforced. Similarly, if the pigeon always pecked red side-keys, these pecks would be reinforced on half the trials unless a correction procedure forced the pigeon to switch occasionally to green side-keys.

Suppose now that a pigeon is responding accurately in a matching-to-sample procedure with red (*R*) and green (*G*) stimuli. How should we describe this performance? Has the pigeon learned only to peck the left key in the presence of the configurations *RRG* and *GGR* and the right key in the presence of the configurations *GRR* and *RGG*? Or has it learned matching in general, the identity relation? We might present blue or yellow as new sample stimuli. If the pigeon matched these new colors we would feel more confident about speaking of generalized matching (in fact, matching in pigeons does not transfer easily to new colors, although the likelihood of such transfer depends on the details of training). But even if we saw matching with new colors, what if we failed to get matching with geometric stimuli as samples and comparison? We might simply say the pigeon has learned color but not form matching, noting that the human concept of matching seems not so limited by the specific dimensions of the matched stimuli. (Matching-to-sample has sometimes been called *identity matching,* but that term is best reserved for cases in which matching generalizes to novel sample and comparison stimuli, such as matching of forms after training with colors; with a limited stimulus set, what looks like matching on the basis of identity may instead be matching based on specific stimulus configurations.)

One approach is to modify the matching-to-sample procedure, in the hope of enhancing control by the sample and comparison stimuli. For example, the procedure can be changed so that production of the comparison stimuli depends on different patterns of responding for each sample stimulus (e.g., different response rates). Such procedures sometimes produce faster acquisition of matching, but unfortunately the enhanced stimulus control by the sample stimuli sometimes reduces that by the comparison stimuli (e.g., Urcuioli & Honig, 1980).

There are many variations on matching-to-sample. If reinforcement is arranged for pecks on the nonmatching rather than the matching side-key, the procedure becomes an instance of *oddity* responding, because this key is necessarily the odd one of the three keys (in other versions of oddity procedures, no sample is used; with pigeons in a three-key chamber, for example, each trial consists of lighting all three keys, with the odd key any one of them).

The relations among stimuli can also involve *arbitrary matching*. For example, we could train the pigeon to peck a green key given a square as a sample and a red key given a circle as a sample. We might then ask whether the pigeon might peck a square given a green sample and a circle given a red sample. We often expect such reversibility when we deal with words and objects, as when a child who has learned to point to a picture of a car on seeing the word *car* can also point to the word on seeing the picture. This reversibility, a property of *symbolic behavior,* is not to be taken for granted; for example, a child may show such reversibility without explicit training but a pigeon will not. Arbitrary matching can also be extended to cases in which the same matching response is trained with more than one comparison (e.g., pecking a green comparison key given either a circle or an ellipse as a sample, and pecking a red one given either a

square or a triangle; cf. Urcuioli, Zentall, Jackson-Smith, & Steirn, 1989, on many-to-one matching tasks).

SYMBOLIC BEHAVIOR: EQUIVALENCE CLASSES

If a pigeon's pecks are reinforced in the presence of green but not red, we would not be likely to speak of the pigeon's greening in the presence of pecks. Such a reversal makes no behavioral sense. This is not the case in matching, however. Both the sample stimulus and the matching comparison response are defined by the stimuli presented on the keys. We may therefore ask about a red response to a red stimulus, or about the reversibility of a vertical response to a diagonal stimulus, or about whether round responses to dim stimuli can be created by training round responses to large stimuli and then large responses to dim stimuli.

These cases illustrate the relations called *reflexivity, symmetry*, and *transitivity*. Reflexive relations are those that hold between a term and itself (e.g., $A = A$); symmetrical relations are those in which the order of terms is reversible (e.g., if $A = B$ then $B = A$); and transitive relations are those in which the common terms in two ordered pairs determine a third ordered pair (e.g., if $A = B$ and $B = C$ then $A = C$). Equivalences among classes of stimuli are defined by these relations (Sidman, Rauzin, Lazar, Cunningham, Tailby, & Carrigan, 1982; Sidman & Tailby, 1982), which are different from those between a discriminative stimulus and the responses it occasions. In other words, *equivalence classes* involve a type of stimulus control that is not encompassed by the three-term contingency.

Figure 7–8 illustrates how standard and arbitrary matching procedures can be used to demonstrate the relations of reflexivity,

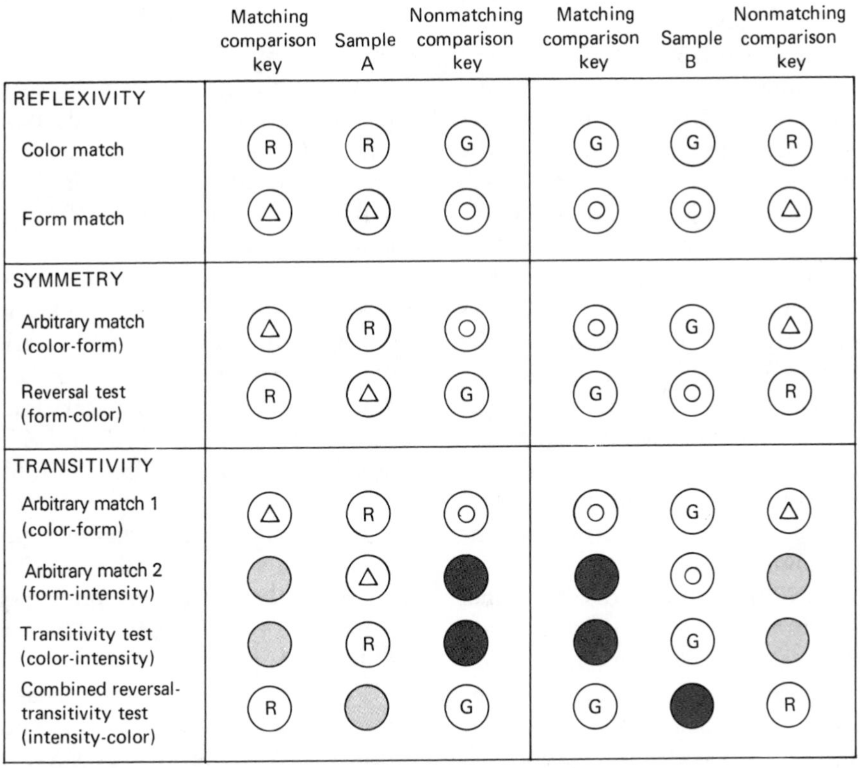

FIGURE 7–8 Matching procedures for studying three properties of equivalence relations: reflexivity (identity matching), symmetry (reversal of arbitrary matching), and transitivity (transfer across ordered pairs of arbitrary matches). Each three-key array is shown in only one of its two possible arrangements, with the matching comparison on the left. Symbols include red (*R*) and green (*G*), triangles and circles, and light and dark.

symmetry, and transitivity. Each procedure includes two sample stimuli, shown as *A* in the three-key array on the left, and as *B* in that on the right. For convenience, the matching comparison stimulus is always shown on the left in the three-key array, even though in practice the side positions of the comparison stimuli vary from trial to trial. As in Figure 7–8, a peck on the sample key produces the comparison stimuli, and a peck on the matching comparison key produces food whereas one on the nonmatching comparison key does not.

The top two rows of Figure 7–8 (reflexivity) illustrate standard matching proce- dures with color and with form. The next two rows (symmetry) illustrate first symbolic matching with color samples and form comparisons and then a reversal test. The bottom rows (transitivity) illustrate how the common stimuli in two symbolic matching procedures (color-form and form-intensity) can be combined in a test of transitivity (color-intensity). An alternative test, illustrated in the last row, combines reversal and transitivity tests (intensity-color); it is sometimes called an equivalence test, and the relation between the stimuli of the equivalence test is sometimes called an equivalence relation. The relations of the reversal and equivalence tests were never explicitly taught. If appropriate matching occurs in these tests, the new relations demonstrated by that behavior are called *emergent* relations, in the sense that they have emerged without explicit training (cf. Fields & Verhave, 1987).

We have already questioned whether the pigeon's standard matching performance depends on the identity relation in general or only on relations among particular stimulus pairs. It might be assumed that the identity relation between sample and comparison stimuli would make standard matching easier than arbitrary matching. For pigeons, however, the time it takes to produce matching depends more on the stimulus dimensions chosen for samples and comparisons than it does on whether the procedure is standard or arbitrary matching (e.g., Carter & Werner, 1978); for example, standard and arbitrary matching with red vs. green samples both develop more rapidly than either procedure with vertical vs. horizontal samples. Furthermore, with pigeons arbitrary matching produced with particular sample and comparison stimuli does not lead to matching when the sample and comparison stimuli are reversed (e.g., Holmes, 1979). Whatever the status of transitivity, the failure to demonstrate reflexivity and symmetry makes it inappropriate to speak of equivalences between sample and comparison stimuli in the pigeon's matching behavior.

In humans, however, equivalence relations are easily generated. For example, retarded youths who had already shown reflexivity (identity matching) first learned, given any one of 20 spoken picture words (*A*), to select the corresponding pictures (*B*) from a comparison set (e.g., car, dog, boy; Sidman & Cresson, 1973; Sidman, Cresson, & Willson-Morris, 1974). Then, given the same 20 spoken words,

they learned to select the corresponding printed words (*C*) from a set. For all 20 words, matching of spoken words to pictures (*AB*) and of spoken words to printed words (*AC*) also generated four other relations without additional training: two new relations through reversals (*BA*, given a picture naming it, and *CA*, given a printed word saying it), and two through transitivity (*BC*, given a picture selecting the corresponding printed word, and *CB*, given a printed word selecting the corresponding picture). Forty relations had been taught (20 each in *AB* and *AC*), and another 80 emerged indirectly (in *BA*, *CA*, *BC*, and *CB*). The reinforcement of arbitrary matching had created the beginnings of a reading repertory in these youths. The emergent relations justify calling their performances *symbolic matching* rather than arbitrary matching.

Each of the 20 equivalence classes consisted of a picture and the corresponding printed and spoken words. New classes could have been added with new pictures and corresponding words, and the number of equivalences could have been expanded by adding new relations (e.g., printed words and script words, pictures and actual objects). There are no obvious limits to the number of classes that can be created or the number of stimuli that can be included within each class. Such classes may be a special property of human behavior; whether they can be demonstrated with primates or other nonhuman organisms is a matter of controversy (e.g., see McIntire, Cleary, & Thompson, 1987, whose demonstration with macaque monkeys has been challenged on the grounds that some aspects of the performance were not emergent but instead were implicitly taught during training procedures; e.g., Saunders, 1989).

Any stimulus within an equivalence class can be regarded as a name for the other stimuli in the class. The possible relations between language and equivalence classes are of special interest (e.g., Catania, Matthews, & Shimoff, 1990; Devany, Hayes, & Nelson, 1986; Dugdale & Lowe, 1990). Are equivalence classes a prerequisite for naming, or is naming a prerequisite for equivalence classes? Perhaps neither alternative is appropriate: Language and equivalences may be two aspects of a single behavioral competence.

Equivalence classes are created within arbitrary matching procedures. To be functionally equivalent, the members of these classes must have the same functions not only within the matching procedures but also in other contexts. An example of functional equivalence is provided in an experiment by Vaughan (1988). A group of photographic slides of trees was divided into two arbitrary sets of 20 slides each. Pigeons' pecks were reinforced given slides from one set but not the other. Occasionally the correlation between the slide sets and reinforcement was reversed. After several reversals, the pigeons began to switch their responding from one set of slides to the other after only a few slides had been shown. In other words, the common contingencies arranged for the 20 slides in a set made them *functionally equivalent:* Once contingencies changed for just a few of the slides in the set, behavior changed appropriately for all of them. Note that this functional equivalence emerged because the same consequences were arranged for responses in the presence of all of the stimuli within a set; that is different from the emergence of equivalence relations in arbitrary matching. The slides in each set were functionally equivalent, but that does not mean that they were members of an equivalence class (cf. Sidman, Wynne, Maguire, & Barnes, 1989).

In other words, functional equivalence is not the same as membership in an equivalence class, and it must not be assumed that the logical properties of these classes are fully consistent with their behavioral ones. The functional equivalence of the members of an equivalence class must be tested experimentally. The question is whether some function acquired by one member of an equivalence class, such as a discriminative function, will transfer to the other members of that equivalence class.

The outcome is of considerable practical significance. Consider an example. A child has learned to obey a parent's words, *go* and *stop,* when crossing with a parent at a traffic intersection. In a separate setting, the child is taught that *go* and the green traffic light are equivalent and that *stop* and the red traffic light are equivalent (in other words, *go* and green become members of one equivalence class and *stop* and red become members of another). If the discriminative functions of the words *stop* and *go* transfer to the respective traffic lights, the child will obey the traffic lights without any additional instruction. An analogous type of transfer has been demonstrated with children: High and low rates of responding occasioned by one set of stimuli transferred to another set when the stimuli in the sets were made members of equivalence classes (Catania, Horne, & Lowe, 1989; see also DeRose, McIlvane, Dube, Galpin, & Stoddard, 1988). Earlier we discussed shaping and fading as procedures for producing new behavior; through transfer of function, equivalence classes provide one more way in which new behavior may emerge.

Equivalence classes demonstrated by reflexivity, symmetry, and transitivity are obviously relevant to the teaching of reading and to other important human applications. These classes are not reducible to classes of discriminative stimuli, because discriminative stimuli cannot be exchanged with the responses they occasion. Equivalence classes define symbolic behavior and will be important later in our analysis of language. We introduced one type of higher-order operant class in Chapter 6; that type was defined by the common consequences of its members. Equivalence classes provide another type defined by relations among stimuli. As yet, there is no standard taxonomy of higher-order classes of behavior, but if one is developed it may well define such classes in terms of the kinds of contingency relations that enter into them.

SUMMARY

We began this chapter by exploring parallels between differentiation and induction on the one hand and discrimination and generalization on the other. Both are outcomes of differential reinforcement; they differ mainly in whether this operation is arranged for stimulus properties or response properties. Functional aspects of stimulus control were treated in the context of experiments on attention, on stimulus-control gradients, and on fading procedures. In dealing with discriminable properties of the environment in the context of animal cognition, we then considered how complex relational features of the environment could serve as discriminative stimuli. Cognitive maps and natural concepts provided relevant examples.

Higher-order classes were introduced by a discussion of learning set. All of these cases emphasized stimuli, but we found it important to treat these stimuli in terms of their relations to responses and consequences. Discriminative control is based upon the three-term contingency: stimulus-response-consequence. None of these terms is significant in isolation. We may speak of differential reinforcement with respect to stimulus properties, or of the correlation of stimuli with contingencies, or of operant classes defined by the stimuli that set the occasion for responses in a class. These variations on the language of discrimination learning simply stress different aspects of the same three-term contingency.

But in the context of conditional discriminations and matching-to-sample, we arrived at another kind of stimulus-control relation not reducible to three-term contingencies. When reflexivity, symmetry, and transitivity are demonstrated for the samples and comparisons of standard and arbitrary matching procedures, we speak of such stimuli in terms of equivalence classes, and we distinguish them from discriminative stimulus classes. Equivalence classes are the defining property of symbolic behavior. New classes of behavior emerge when formal equivalence becomes functional equivalence.

Reinforcement Schedules

> Schedule *is derived from the Middle English* sedule, *a slip of parchment or paper, which is in turn derived from the Latin* scheda, *papyrus leaf, and the Greek* skhizein, *to split. The Indo-European root,* skei-, *to cut or split, links* schedule *to* schizo-, *as in* schizophrenia, *and to* science *and* conscious, *from the Latin* scire, *to know, in the sense of being able to separate one thing from another.*

Not all classes of responses have consistent consequences. The reinforcement of some responses but not others, sometimes called *intermittent* or *partial* reinforcement, is a general feature of behavior. You do not always win when you place a bet, you do not always find what you are looking for when you go to a store, and you do not always get a reply when you ask a question. Consider calling a friend on the telephone. Sometimes your call is reinforced by the opportunity to talk to your friend. At other times, your friend does not answer or the line is busy. *Continuous* or *regular* reinforcement, the reinforcement of every response within an operant class, is the exception rather than the rule. For this reason, we must examine the effects of *schedules of reinforcement*, arrangements that specify which responses within an operant class will be reinforced.

We have already considered some schedules (ratio schedules in Chapter 1; differential-reinforcement-of-low-rate schedules in Chapter 6; and interval schedules in Chapter 7). Schedules can arrange reinforcement on the basis of response number or time or the rate of responding. Number, time, and rate requirements can also be combined in diverse ways to produce more complex schedules. We will be concerned with the effects of reinforcement schedules not only as valuable experimental tools but also as ubiquitous properties of behavior in their own right (cf. Ferster & Skinner, 1957; Schoenfeld & Cole, 1972).

Section A **The Basic Schedules**

Let us return to the telephone example. Suppose you call your friend and get no answer. The likelihood of getting an answer later ordinarily depends on when and not on how many times you call. Your friend will be available and thus answer your call only if you call at a particular time. Similarly, suppose you call and get a busy signal. Calling again will not affect how long the busy signal lasts. Some variable time will elapse that depends only on how long your friend talks with someone else. Once your friend hangs up, your next call will produce a ring and an answer rather than a busy signal. You must call to get an answer, but only if you call at the right time.

These cases are everyday approximations to *variable-interval* or *VI* reinforcement schedules. The schedules reinforce a single response that occurs after a specified time has elapsed, and this time varies from one instance to the next; earlier responses have no effect. A VI schedule is designated by the average time to the availability of a reinforcer. Because the times when people are away from a phone are usually longer than the durations of their phone conversations, the situation in which a phone rings but is not answered could be described as a longer-valued VI schedule than that in which the call produces a busy signal.

Now consider a different situation. You have to make a call at a pay phone but have no change. You might ask passersby for change and your asking may be rein-

forced by getting the change you need. In this instance, the likelihood that the response will be reinforced does not depend on the passage of time. Instead, only some fraction of the people you ask are likely to be able and willing to make change for you. You have to keep asking until you encounter such a person. You might be successful after asking only a very few people or you might have to ask many. In other words, the availability of the reinforcer depends on number of responses rather than on the passage of time, and this number will vary from one reinforcer to the next. Such schedules are called *variable-ratio* or *VR* schedules. They are designated by the average number of responses required per reinforcer (i.e., the average ratio of responses to reinforcers).

It is important to specify responses and reinforcers when interpreting behavior in terms of schedules. For example, the behavior that leads up to calling, such as finding a pay phone or getting change for it, is different from the calling itself. The circumstances of the call, such as whether the last call resulted in no answer or a busy signal, are also relevant. Calling a friend who keeps an irregular schedule differs from calling a business that opens promptly at a given time. Calling after a busy signal to someone who usually leaves the line free after calls differs from calling an active number at which the line does not remain open very long.

In the following survey we will concentrate on simple responses such as pigeons' key-pecks and simple reinforcers such as food deliveries. It is important to remember, however, that accurately applying the language of reinforcement schedules to settings outside the laboratory demands that we carefully specify the responses and reinforcers that enter into these contingencies.

VARIABLE-INTERVAL
AND VARIABLE-RATIO SCHEDULES

In a variable-interval or VI schedule, the delivery of a reinforcer depends on the passage of a variable time and then the emission of a single response. In a variable-ratio or VR schedule, the delivery of a reinforcer depends on the emission of a variable number of responses without regard to the passage of time. Some properties of VI and VR schedules are illustrated by hypothetical cumulative records in Figure 8–1. Three records that might be generated by a 1-minute VI schedule (VI 1-min) are shown on the left (A, B, and C); three records that might be generated by a 100-response VR schedule (VR 100) are shown on the right (D, E, and F).

A VI schedule can be arranged by punching holes in a loop of tape that is driven past a switch at a constant speed by a motor and allowing a response to be reinforced each time one of the holes reaches the switch. A portion of such a tape is shown just above the time scale in Figure 8–1. Once the switch is operated, the tape usually stops until the reinforcer is delivered; at this point, the reinforcer is said to be *set up*, i.e., the next response is eligible to produce a reinforcer. An alternative method is to generate pulses at a fixed rate and randomly to select some proportion of them to set up a reinforcer for the next response. Schedules arranged in this way are sometimes called *random-interval* or *RI* schedules. In contemporary laboratories they are more often arranged by computers than by tape-drives (see *Interval schedule* in the Glossary for further details).

Records *A*, *B*, and *C* of Figure 8–1 illustrate an important property of VI schedules: Even though the three records differ considerably in rate, responding in each case produces the same number of

FIGURE 8–1 Hypothetical segments of cumulative records from performances maintained by a 1-minute variable-interval schedule (VI 1-min) and a 100-response variable-ratio schedule (VR 100). The horizontal strip above the VI time scale and the vertical strip next to the VR response scale represent portions of punched tapes that select responses for reinforcement. The three left records show that VI response rate affects responses per reinforcer but not reinforcement rate; the three right records show that VR response rate affects reinforcement rate but not responses per reinforcer.

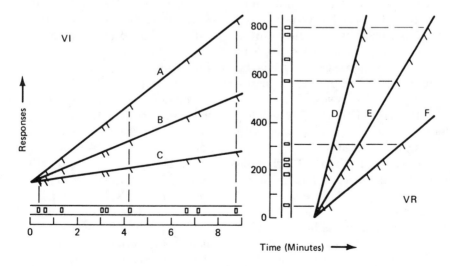

reinforcers. The VI schedule provides a relatively constant reinforcement rate over a substantial range of possible response rates. The response rate that produces all scheduled reinforcers does, of course, have a lower limit, because reinforcers are not delivered unless responses occur. Reinforcers will be produced less often than specified by the VI schedule if the time between responses becomes long relative to the time between scheduled reinforcers. In practice, rates of responses such as pigeons' key-pecks are usually high enough that this is no problem. This independence of reinforcement rate from response rate, coupled with the relatively constant response rate that it generates, makes VI reinforcement a preferred baseline schedule (e.g., see Chapter 7 on stimulus-control gradients).

Now consider a variable-ratio or VR schedule. In practice, a computer program randomly selects responses for reinforcement, but again the punched tape serves as an illustration. In this case, responses instead of time move the tape past the switch. A portion of a tape for a VR 100 schedule is shown vertically next to the response scale accompanying the VR records in Figure 8–1; on the average, one response is reinforced per 100 responses, but the number varies from one reinforcer to the next. Each response advances the tape a fixed distance relative to the switch and when the switch senses a hole in the tape the next response is reinforced. The highest response rate, D, produces reinforcers most rapidly; the lowest, F, produces them least rapidly. Unlike VI schedules, therefore, reinforcement rate does vary with response rate in VR schedules.

Like the VI schedule, the VR schedule generates roughly constant rates of responding between reinforcers, at least with moderate ratio sizes. When the ratio of responses to reinforcers becomes very large, VR responding may be interrupted frequently by pauses. A VR schedule that

randomly selects some fraction of responses for reinforcement is sometimes called a *random-ratio* or *RR* schedule.

Response rates maintained by VI and VR schedules are illustrated in Figures 8–2 and 8–3. Both figures show data obtained with pigeons' key-pecks reinforced with food. In Figure 8–2, rate of pecking is plotted as a function of the reinforcement rate provided by the VI schedule (e.g., VI 1-min provides a maximum of 60 reinforcers per hour). Rate of pecking increased as a function of reinforcement rate, but the function was negatively accelerated; the change in response rate produced by a given change in reinforcement rate became smaller as reinforcement rate increased.

In Figure 8–3, rate of pecking is plotted as a function of the ratio, responses per reinforcer, arranged by a VR schedule. At VR 1 (left-most point), every response was reinforced. Even with reinforcement duration excluded, responding only slightly exceeded 25 responses per minute. Response rate was substantially higher at VR 10 (second point), and reached its maximum, more than 200 responses per minute, at VR 50. Response rate then decreased gradually with increasing VR size.

The effects of VR and VI schedules vary with the conditions under which they are arranged. For example, it makes a difference whether the organism receives all of its food within experimental sessions or receives some outside the sessions (these two situations have been called *closed* and *open* economies: cf. Hursh, 1980). Nevertheless, VI and VR schedules differ considerably. For example, the different scales of the two figures show that, over most of the range of values for each schedule, VI response rates are lower than VR response rates.

The schedules also differ in the way responding is affected when reinforcement is reduced or discontinued. The idealized cumulative records of Figure 8–4

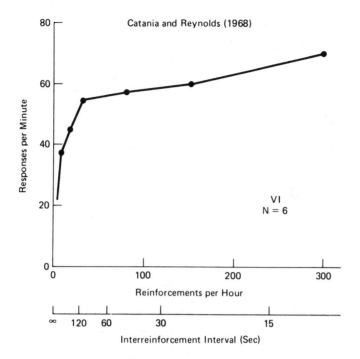

FIGURE 8–2 Rate of key-pecking as a function of rate of VI reinforcement, for six pigeons. The two scales at the bottom show the correspondence between rate of reinforcement and average interreinforcement intervals in VI schedules. (Adapted from Catania & Reynolds, 1968, Figure 1)

show responding maintained by VI and VR reinforcement and responding during extinction after VI and after VR reinforcement. A low rate of VI reinforcement produces less responding than a high rate of VI reinforcement, but in both cases responding is fairly uniformly distributed in time; in addition, the decrease in response rate during extinction is gradual after VI reinforcement. With VR reinforcement, on the other hand, the decrease in response rate with larger ratios comes about when responding begins to be interrupted by long pauses (the appearance of long pauses during ratio performance is sometimes called *ratio strain*); in addition, extinction after VR reinforcement usually produces abrupt transitions from high response rates to periods of no responding (a *break-and-run* pattern of responding).

What makes VI and VR schedules generate such different performances? It seems reasonable that VR schedules should generate higher response rates than VI schedules: Reinforcers are delivered more often when VR responding increases but not when VI responding increases. Yet how do these different relations between responding and reinforcers act on behavior? The separation between successive reinforcers is variable in both schedules. Would it matter, then, if several closely spaced reinforcers happened to be scheduled just as response rate decreased for some reason, or if a long period without reinforcement happened to be scheduled just as response rate increased?

Yoked Schedules

The *yoked-chamber* procedure (Ferster & Skinner, 1957) lets us study some variables

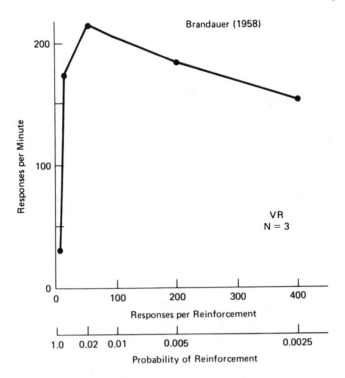

FIGURE 8–3 Rate of key-pecking as a function of VR schedule, for three pigeons. The two scales at the bottom show the correspondence between responses per reinforcement and probability of reinforcement. (Adapted from Brandauer, 1958, Table 2)

that operate within schedules. In yoked chambers, an organism's performance in one chamber determines the events that occur in a second organism's chamber. The procedure can equate reinforcement rates in VR and VI schedules: Each reinforcer produced by a VR schedule for one pigeon's key-pecks schedules a VI reinforcer for the next peck of a second pigeon. In other words, the second pigeon's pecks are maintained by a VI schedule in which successive interreinforcement intervals match those produced by the first pigeon's VR performance. In these circumstances, the two schedules differ in responses per reinforcer but not in time between successive reinforcers. Conversely, yoked schedules can equate responses per reinforcer for the two schedules by arranging that the re-

sponses emitted per VI reinforcer by one pigeon determine the ratios of a second pigeon's VR schedule. In this case, the second pigeon's pecks are maintained by a VR schedule in which successive ratios match those produced by the first pigeon's VI performance.

Cumulative records from both types of yoking are illustrated in Figure 8–5 (Catania, Matthews, Silverman, & Yohalem, 1977). For one group of pigeons, pairs were assigned to yoked schedules in which one pigeon's pecks per reinforcement in a VI 30-second schedule generated a second pigeon's VR schedule, as illustrated by Pigeons 402 and 410. For another group, pairs were assigned to yoked schedules in which one pigeon's interreinforcement intervals in a VR 25 schedule generated a

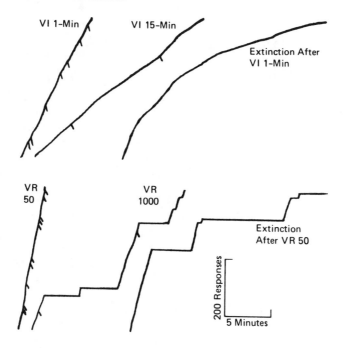

FIGURE 8–4 Patterns of responding during VI and VR reinforcement and during extinction after VI or VR reinforcement. These somewhat idealized cumulative records contrast the effects of the two types of schedules: with VI, a relatively constant response rate that decreases gradually during extinction, and with VR, a higher maintained response rate and, with large response requirements or during extinction, abrupt transitions between high rates and long pauses. Both schedules generate substantial amounts of responding in extinction.

second pigeon's VI schedule, as illustrated by Pigeons 414 and 406. Independent of whether VR is yoked to VI or VI is yoked to VR, VR schedules generate higher response rates than do VI schedules (see also Zuriff, 1970). These differences emerge rapidly: The records are from the last of only three 50-reinforcement sessions.

The yoking experiment shows that the rate difference between VR and VI schedules cannot be attributed to responses per reinforcer or to time per reinforcement, because the rate difference remains even when these are the same in both schedules. One other possibility is that, even with yoking, reinforcement rate on the average changes with response rate in VR but not

in VI schedules. It might be argued that the organism simply learns that in VR but not in VI schedules faster responding produces more frequent reinforcement.

Another alternative is the relation between interresponse times (IRTs) and probability of reinforcement (e.g., Anger, 1956; Kuch & Platt, 1976). An interresponse time or IRT is simply the time between two successive responses (cf. DRL schedules in Chapter 6). In VR schedules, the probability that a response will be reinforced depends only on the ratio; it does not vary with time elapsed since the last response. In VI schedules, on the other hand, the more time elapsed since the last response, the greater the chance that an

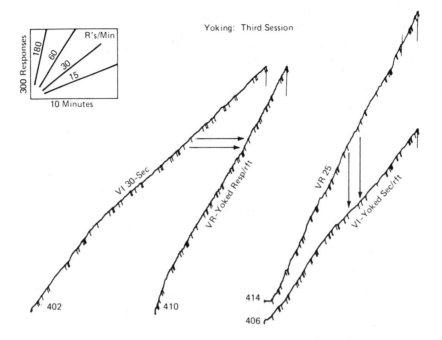

FIGURE 8–5 Cumulative records for the third session of yoking for two pairs of pigeons. Responses per reinforcement from Pigeon 402's VI performance generated a yoked VR schedule for Pigeon 410's pecks. Interreinforcement times from Pigeon 414's VR performance generated a yoked VI schedule for Pigeon 406's pecks. Horizontal arrows connecting the left records show correspondences of responses per reinforcement for that schedule pair; vertical arrows connecting the right show correspondences of interreinforcement intervals. In both cases, VR response rate was higher than VI response rate. (From Catania, Matthews, Silverman, & Yohalem, 1977, Figure 1)

interval has ended and therefore that the next response will be reinforced. In other words, a larger proportion of long than of short IRTs is reinforced in VI than in VR schedules; thus, relative to VR schedules, VI schedules differentially reinforce long IRTs. An increase in these long IRTs necessarily implies lower response rates. The differential reinforcement of IRTs may contribute to schedule performances but cannot be the whole story. For example, the rapid separation of yoked VR and VI response rates is not consistent with the relatively slow development of temporally spaced responding when the differential

reinforcement of IRTs is explicitly scheduled (see also Dews, 1962; Catania, 1971).

Limited Hold

One temporal contingency sometimes added to schedules is called the *limited hold* or *LH*. With a limited hold, a scheduled reinforcer remains available only for a limited time; if no response occurs within that time, the reinforcer is lost. For example, if one gets a busy signal when phoning into an overloaded switchboard, getting a ring and an answer may not become more likely as time passes, because the lines never remain open very long. If the lines at such a switchboard are busy again within only 5 seconds after someone hangs up, the schedule is a VI schedule with a 5-second limited hold. A caller is most likely to get through such a switchboard by hanging up immediately after a busy signal and dialing again within 5 seconds. In the laboratory, adding a limited hold to a schedule typically increases response rate (e.g., Hearst, 1958); in general, the shorter the limited hold the greater this increase, except that a very short limited hold may allow so few responses to be reinforced that the schedule fails to maintain responding. With a limited hold, reinforcement probability does not increase with increased time since the last response, because the limited hold may cancel the most recently available reinforcer before the next response occurs.

Reinforcement Schedules and Causation

The effects of reinforcers depend on the responses they follow, but reinforcers can follow responses both when produced by responses and when delivered independently of responses. Is responding affected in the same way when it produces a reinforcer as when it happens by accident to be followed by a reinforcer? We considered this question when we examined the phenomenon called superstition (Chapters 3 and 4). The possibility that organisms might be differently affected by causal and by coincidental temporal contiguities between responses and reinforcers has been discussed by Herrnstein (1966):

Is it possible that the accidental correlations in time among responses, stimuli, and reinforcers do not exert control over behavior?... One of the characteristics of accidental correlations between behavior and environmental events is *variability*. Every aspect of behavior may vary and yet be contiguous with a reinforcer that is independent of the behavior. In contrast, behavior that is instrumental must have at least one aspect that has a more or less fixed correlation with the reinforcer. Were animals sensitive to this difference, they could detect those events over which their behavior has no real control. (Herrnstein, 1966, pp. 42–43)

In an experiment by Lattal (1974), pigeons' key-pecks were reinforced according to a VI schedule. Once VI performance was stable, the schedule was changed: At the end of some intervals, the reinforcer was delivered immediately, without regard to responding. With decreasing percentages of response-produced reinforcers, response rate decreased. When the percentage of response-produced reinforcers was zero, so that food was completely independent of behavior, rates of responding approached zero. The decrease in response rate has interesting implications. For example, when a third of the reinforcers were response-produced, response rates were roughly half those when all reinforcers were response-produced, but even the pigeon with the lowest response rate responded at about 30 responses per minute, or a response every 2 seconds. This implies that response-independent reinforcers followed responses on the average by only about 1 second (because the reinforcer would occur on the average in the middle of a 2-second IRT). Given, therefore, that every reinforcer was likely to follow closely after some response, and that a third (the response-produced reinforcers) followed responses immediately, why didn't the accidental temporal relations between responses and reinforcers maintain responding at a rate close to that when all reinforcers were response-produced?

When reinforcers are delivered independently of responses, the time between the most recent response and the reinforcer is likely to vary from one reinforcer to the next. Lattal's data suggest that this variability counteracts superstitious responding. But what about cases in which the time between the most recent response and the reinforcer varies even though the reinforcer is response-produced? This occurs, for example, when delay of reinforcement is added to a schedule (see *Delay of reinforcement* in the Glossary, and cf. Dews, 1960).

A case is illustrated in the event records in Figure 8–6 (left). Vertical lines represent responses; arrows represent reinforcers. The top record shows a segment from a standard VI schedule: the interval ends at the dashed line and the next response, *a*, is followed immediately by the reinforcer. A segment from a VI schedule to which a 3-second delay of reinforcement has been added is shown in the middle record: the interval ends at the dashed line and the response *b* produces a reinforcer 3 seconds later; because other responses occur during this time, the time between the last response and the reinforcer (*c*) is shorter than the delay interval (*d*), and this time varies depending on the spacing of responses during the delay. The bottom record shows a segment from a variable-time (VT) or re-

sponse-independent schedule: At the dashed line, the reinforcer is delivered, and because it occurs independently of responses, the time between the last response and the reinforcer (*e*) varies.

The bar graph in Figure 8–6 shows data from three pigeons obtained with these schedules (Sizemore & Lattal, 1977; see also Williams, 1976). The rates of pecking maintained by VI with delay were between the moderate rates maintained by the VI schedule and the low rates maintained by the response-independent reinforcers of the VT schedule. We just concluded that the difference between VI and VT must depend in some way on the variable times between the last response and the reinforcer (*c* and *e*). Why then are the rates with delayed VI reinforcement higher than those with VT reinforcement?

These issues remain open to experimental analysis. Differential control by response-dependent and response-independent reinforcers must depend in some way on correlations among events integrated over time, but the complexity of that control is perhaps best illustrated by a human analogy (cf. Catania & Keller, 1981; see also Davis, Memmott, & Hurwitz, 1975). If a lobby eleva-

FIGURE 8–6 Hypothetical segments of event records from VI, VI with delay, and VT reinforcement schedules (left), and three pigeons' rates of key-pecking maintained by these schedules (right). (Adapted from Sizemore & Lattal, 1977, Table 1)

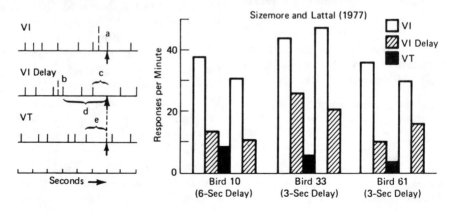

tor has no floor indicator, the only consequence of your pressing the elevator button might be the arrival of the elevator after a variable delay. But the elevator also might arrive because someone earlier pressed the button and then took the stairs instead, or because someone already in the elevator pressed the button for the lobby floor, or because this elevator always returns to the lobby after calls to other floors. One day the elevator door might open just as you reached out to press the button; on another it might arrive and leave and arrive again, even though you did not press the button in the interim. With these complications, you can never be sure that your button press caused the arrival of the elevator. Nevertheless, you will probably continue to press the button in the future. Your judgments about causation depend not on constant conjunctions of events but rather on a sampling of very complex contingencies.

Research on the effects of contingencies shows that organisms are very sensitive to the consequences of their own behavior. This sensitivity may depend on detailed or molecular relations between particular responses and reinforcers or on overall or molar properties of response and reinforcer rates (cf. Chapter 5). The distinction between events caused by behavior and events accidentally correlated with behavior is central to the concept of causation. For this reason, the study of reinforcement schedules is fundamental, and it is of practical as well as theoretical significance to demonstrate that humans may be similarly sensitive to the consequences of their own behavior (cf. Matthews, Shimoff, Catania, & Sagvolden, 1977). For example, in vigilance tasks such as monitoring a radar screen, the detection and report of a signal can be used to reinforce the behavior of looking at the screen. If an observer has a button that lights up a radar screen and button presses produce detectable sig-

nals according to a VR schedule, a high rate of observing is maintained; this observer will more accurately detect real targets not scheduled by the experimenter than will an observer sitting in front of a continuously lit radar screen without such a schedule in operation (Holland, 1958; but see also Chapter 11).

FIXED-INTERVAL AND FIXED-RATIO SCHEDULES

If the probability that a response will be reinforced is greater at some times than at others, the rate of responding is likely to be higher at those times than at the others (Catania & Reynolds, 1968). For example, suppose most intervals in a VI schedule are 10 seconds long, and the remaining intervals are between 50 and 100 seconds. Response rate will probably be high at about 10 seconds after reinforcement, and if a response is not reinforced then it might decrease over the next 20 or 30 seconds before increasing again later on. We have mostly considered VI and VR schedules designed to hold the probability of reinforcement roughly constant over time (in VI) or over number of responses (in VR). But schedules can be arranged in which the time to the availability of a reinforcer or number of responses per reinforcer is constant from one reinforcer to the next; such schedules are respectively called *fixed-interval* or *FI* schedules and *fixed-ratio* or *FR* schedules (in addition, schedules in which the time between response-independent reinforcers is constant are called *fixed-time* or *FT* schedules). The fixed schedules are of interest because they introduce discriminable periods during which no reinforcers occur.

Consider first the fixed-interval or FI schedule: A response is reinforced only after some constant time has elapsed since some environmental event; responses before this time have no effect. An example is looking at your watch as time passes during a lecture; in this case, the reinforcer is seeing that the time has come at which you can leave the classroom. Looking at the watch at earlier times does not make it run more rapidly. Responding maintained by FI schedules usually occurs at zero or low rates early in the interval and increases as the end of the interval approaches. We might similarly expect you to look at your watch more often as the end of the lecture approaches.

Sample cumulative records of FI performance are shown in *B* and *C* of Figure 4–6. Each record shows a sequence of fixed intervals. The concave-upward pattern of such records is sometimes called FI *scalloping*. Depending on the sessions of exposure to FI schedules and other variables, FI scallops may show relatively abrupt transitions from no responding to a roughly constant rate of responding, as in *B*, or gradually increasing rates after responding begins, as in *C*. The pattern of FI responding tends to be consistent over relative rather than over absolute time in the interval. For example, if responding reaches half its final or terminal rate 40 seconds into a 100-second fixed interval, it is likely to do so 20 seconds rather than 40 seconds into a 50-second fixed interval.

Treatments of FI performance must consider the finding that the FI scallop survives repeated interruptions. The phenomenon is illustrated in Figure 8–7 (Dews, 1962). Key-pecks of four pigeons were reinforced with food according to FI 500-second schedules. The left graph shows average rates of pecking in successive 50-second portions of the interval. In another procedure, the houselight was turned on and off in successive 50-second portions of the interval; after the last 50 seconds of the interval, it remained on until the peck at the end of the interval was reinforced. Pecking while the houselight was off decreased (dark bars in Figure 8–7). Nevertheless, when the houselight was on, the FI responding increased throughout the interval (shaded bars) just as it had when it was uninterrupted during the interval. Findings such as these have raised questions about whether the FI scallop represents a gradient of delayed reinforcement (in that

FIGURE 8–7   Rate of pecking in 50-second periods during a standard FI 500-second schedule of reinforcement (open bars, left), and during an FI 500-second schedule in which a light (shaded bars) and its absence (dark bars) alternated every 50 seconds (right), for four pigeons. Periods when the light was absent produced low response rates and therefore interrupted FI responding, but rate when the light was present increased in much the same way as in the standard FI. (Adapted from Dews, 1962, Figure 2)

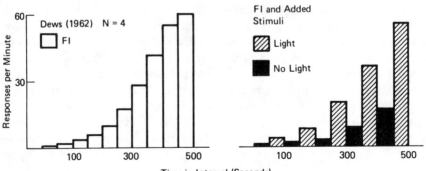

responses at various locations in the interval are consistently followed by the reinforcer at the end of the interval) or a gradient of temporal discrimination (in that the organism's different rates at different times in the interval imply discrimination of the elapsed time).

Let us now turn to fixed-ratio or FR schedules. In these schedules, the last of a fixed number of responses is reinforced. For example, winding up a spring-driven device such as a music box requires a fairly constant number of turns of the winding key. Reaching the point at which the key can no longer be turned is ordinarily a reinforcing consequence, because it sets the occasion for listening to the tune the music box plays. Each fixed ratio ends with a reinforcer; another reinforcer is delivered each time another ratio is completed. The first response after a reinforcer is never reinforced, so FR schedules typically generate postreinforcement pauses followed by high-rate responding. As FR size increases, the average duration of the postreinforcement pause increases (e.g., Felton & Lyon, 1966). Once responding begins after the postreinforcement pause, it typically occurs at a high rate and without interruption until the next reinforcer (another example of break-and-run responding; cf. VR schedules). The cohesiveness with which FR responding is maintained once it begins suggests that the FR sequence is not simply a succession of responses but is a behavioral unit in its own right.

Ordinarily the development of FR responding proceeds so rapidly that its details cannot easily be seen. Figure 8–8, however, shows FR responding developing gradually.

FIGURE 8–8 Development of FR 100 performance for a pigeon's food-reinforced keypecks. The typically rapid development of FR responding was slowed down by the concurrent operation of a VI schedule of reinforcement (not shown) for pecks on a second key. The cumulative record segments are from early portions of the numbered sessions of FR reinforcement.

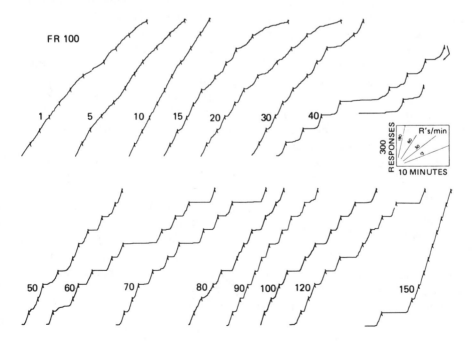

In a two-key pigeon chamber, the pigeon's pecks on one key were reinforced according to an FR 100 schedule while a VI schedule operated concurrently on the other key. The VI schedule on the other key retarded the development of the typical FR performance and in effect made it possible to examine it in slow motion; the change in temporal patterning that usually emerges in two or three sessions took place over 150 sessions. In early sessions, responding was fairly uniformly spaced between reinforcers. With continued exposure, lower response rates and eventually pauses began to follow reinforcers. The portion of the ratio consisting of uninterrupted high-rate responding gradually became longer, so that in later sessions responding continued with few if any interruptions after each postreinforcement pause. With successive sessions, the FR run appeared to build itself up backwards from the reinforcer.

The treatment of schedule performances as response units in their own right led to the development of higher-order schedules of reinforcement. For example, if reinforcement depends on completing a certain number of fixed intervals, the arrangement is a second-order schedule in which successive FI's are reinforced according to an FR schedule (e.g., Findley, 1962; Kelleher & Gollub, 1962; Bigelow, 1971). An analysis of the component performances in such schedules is concerned with the structure of behavior, and is analogous to examining the properties that define an operant class (cf. Chapter 6; Hawkes & Shimp, 1975; Shimp, 1976).

THE VOCABULARY OF REINFORCEMENT SCHEDULES

We have considered a variety of reinforcement schedules. Some of the vocabulary of these schedules is logical, but it also includes some admittedly idiosyncratic usages. For example, the names for FI and VI vs. FT and VT schedules are arbitrary (such names as fixed-duration and variable-duration, presumably abbreviated FD and VD, could have been justified just as easily). Nevertheless, the schedule differences must be noted. For example, FI, DRL, and FT schedules all require the passage of a constant time but they differ in response requirements. An FI schedule imposes no restriction on responding during the interval but one response must occur at its end; some time elapses during which few or many responses can occur, and then the next response is reinforced. A DRL schedule, however, requires a specified time without responses, and then the next response is reinforced; responses that occur too soon start the time over. Finally, in an FT schedule, the reinforcer is delivered at the end of the specified time whether or not responses have occurred. These schedule names emerged incidentally in the evolution of research on reinforcement schedules but have become well established.

Of several noteworthy attempts to classify reinforcement schedules more systematically (e.g., Schoenfeld, Cumming, & Hearst, 1956; Mechner, 1959; Dews, 1960; Snapper, Kadden, & Inglis, 1982; Schoenfeld & Cole, 1972), none has attained general usage. Table 8–1 summarizes major procedural distinctions among schedules. The schedule definitions apply whether reinforcers are arranged successively and without interruption or occur within separate trials (e.g., an FI is ordinarily timed from the last reinforcer, but if other events are arranged between successive intervals, timing can begin with the onset of some stimulus, such as a color presented on a pigeon key). Other schedule details are provided in the Glossary.

TABLE 8–1 Summary of Basic Reinforcement Schedules (T sec = time in seconds; N = number of responses)

NAME AND ABBREVIATION		CONTINGENCY	COMMENT
Variable interval (Random interval)	VI (RI)	T sec, then 1 response	T varies; with random intervals, responding rate is roughly constant
Fixed interval	FI	T sec, then 1 response	T constant; generates FI scallops
Variable ratio (Random ratio)	VR (RR)	N responses	N varies; high constant rates, but large N may produce ratio strain
Fixed ratio	FR	N responses	N constant; generates post-reinforcement pauses and high-rate runs
Variable time	VT	T sec	T varies; reinforcers are response-independent
Fixed time	FT	T sec	T constant; reinforcers are response-independent
Continuous reinforcement	(FR 1)	1 response	All responses reinforced; also abbreviated CRF
Extinction	EXT	—	As procedure, often used regardless of whether response had ever been reinforced
Limited hold	LH	Reinforcer cancelled if no reinforced response within T sec	T constant if not otherwise specified; LH, added to other schedules, cannot stand alone
Differential reinforcement of low rate (or long IRT)	DRL	T sec without response, then 1 response	Maintains responding easily; decreased responding increases reinforcement and thus prevents extinction
Differential reinforcement of high rate	DRH	1 response within T sec or less of last response	Alternatively, at least N responses within T sec; sometimes difficult to maintain, because decreased responding reduces reinforcement
Differential reinforcement of paced responding	DRP	1 response between T and T' sec of last response	Sets both upper and lower limits on reinforceable response rates
Differential reinforcement of other behavior	DRO	T sec without response	A negative-punishment or omission procedure; ordinarily decreases rate of designated response

The first two columns of Table 8–1 provide schedule names and their standard abbreviations. In practice, the abbreviations are usually accompanied by designations of time or number (e.g., VI 30-s, LH 5-s, DRL 10-s, FR 50; *s* is the standard abbreviation for seconds). The next column describes schedule contingencies, the conditions under which responses are eligible to produce reinforcers (cf. especially the relations between FI and FT and between DRL and DRO). The last column briefly comments on each schedule. The vocabulary of Table 8–1, in terms of reinforcement schedules, can also be extended to punishment schedules (e.g., Azrin, 1956; Deluty, 1976; Hendry & Hendry, 1963). The symmetry of reinforcement and punishment effects, illustrated in Figure 5–1, applies also to scheduling effects (e.g., superimposing an FI schedule of punishment on maintained responding produces an inverted scallop, a gradually decreasing response rate as the end of the interval approaches).

Section B **Schedule Combinations and Behavior Synthesis**

Schedules need not operate in isolation. New schedules can be created by combining the basic schedules. For example, reinforcers can be arranged for completing *either* of two schedule requirements (*alternative* schedules) or *both* of them (*conjunctive* schedules). In an alternative FI 30-second FR 50 schedule, either the first response after 30 seconds or the 50th response is reinforced, whichever comes first. In a conjunctive FI 100-second FR 20 schedule, a response is not reinforced until both 100 seconds have passed and 19 responses have already been emitted. *Adjusting* schedules vary as a function of some property of performance, as when a ratio varies in proportion to the last postreinforcement pause, or as when a

shock delivery changes the RS interval of an avoidance schedule. A schedule in which time and number requirements interact is an *interlocking* schedule. For example, an interlocking FR FI schedule might shorten the interval as a function of number of responses, or lengthen the ratio as a function of time (an instance of an interlocking schedule is winding a grandfather clock, in which the reinforcer is the tension of the fully wound spring; until the spring is completely run down, the number of turns required to wind it increases as time passes).

Schedules can alternate with each other, either with a correlated stimulus (*multiple* schedules) or without one (*mixed* schedules); the consequence of completing one schedule can be the onset of another schedule, either with a correlated stimulus (*chained* schedules) or without one (*tandem* schedules); schedules can operate at the same time, either for the same response (*conjoint* schedules) or for different responses (*concurrent* schedules); one schedule can be the unit of behavior upon which another schedule operates (*higher-order* schedules); and schedules operating concurrently can each produce other schedules (*concurrent-chain* schedules). These variables define several classes of schedule combinations defined in the Glossary. Some bear on problems of historical significance, such as discrimination learning (multiple schedules), conditioned reinforcement (chained and second-order schedules), and choice (concurrent and concurrent-chain schedules). We sample these schedules in a review of some specific research issues.

MULTIPLE SCHEDULES

We encountered multiple schedules as examples of stimulus control (e.g., multiple VI EXT in Figure 7–1). Two schedules alternate, each correlated with a different stimulus; we speak of stimulus control when the performance appropriate to each schedule occurs during the corresponding stimulus. For example, if an FI schedule operates for a pigeon's pecks in green and a VI schedule for its pecks in red, FI scallops in green may alternate with roughly constant VI response rates in red (reinforcement can alternate with extinction in multiple schedules, but in this example a different schedule is correlated with each stimulus).

Multiple schedules often serve as baselines in studies of variables that affect behavior. With multiple FI FR schedules, for example, drug effects on both FI and FR responding can be obtained with a single set of doses; drug effects often vary with the schedule that maintains responding. In *behavioral pharmacology* and *behavioral toxicology*, such baselines sometimes reveal large behavioral effects of substances such as pollutants at concentrations with only small physiological effects. Substances that act on behavior can be classified on the basis of such effects (e.g., Dews, 1970; Weiss & Laties, 1969).

Behavioral Contrast

Studies that use multiple schedules must take into account interactions between the component performances. Behavior in one component of a multiple schedule is often affected by what happens in the other. For example, if the schedule that maintains a pigeon's pecks during one stimulus changes from VI reinforcement to EXT (extinction) while VI reinforcement continues during a second stimulus, decreased key-pecking during the first stimulus is often accompanied by increased pecking during the second, even though the schedule that operates during the second is unchanged. The phenomenon, called *behavioral contrast*, is illustrated in Figure 8–9 (Reynolds,

FIGURE 8–9 Effects of extinction in one component of a multiple schedule on a pigeon's food-reinforced key-pecking maintained in the other. Schedules operated in alternate 3-minute periods of red and green. Over sessions, the schedule in green changed from VI 3-min to extinction and back to VI 3-min; a VI 3-min schedule was maintained in red. Behavioral contrast refers to the increased responding in the unchanged component (red) during decreased reinforcement in the other component (green). (After Reynolds, 1961b, as adapted by Terrace, 1966, Figure 10)

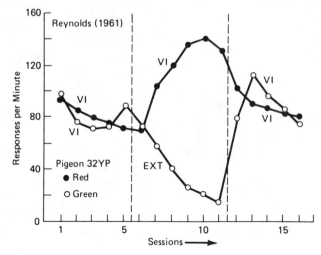

1961b). A multiple VI 3-minute VI 3-minute schedule operated for a pigeon's key-pecks in green and red. The schedule in green was changed from VI to EXT and then back to VI while VI reinforcement was maintained in red. Response rate in red increased during EXT in green even though the red VI schedule had not changed; both rates returned toward their earlier values when the green VI schedule was reinstated.

Contrast effects vary with responses, reinforcers, and organisms (e.g., Hemmes, 1973) and range from sustained increases to increases that last only a short time after a schedule change (e.g., Catania & Gill, 1964; Nevin & Shettleworth, 1966). One interpretation of behavioral contrast is that it is the summation of two types of pecking: pecking maintained by food reinforcers and pecking produced by a stimulus differentially correlated with their delivery (as when reinforcers are delivered during the VI stimulus but not the EXT stimulus of a multiple VI EXT schedule). The former pecks are operant, but the latter may be elicited responses. The two classes have been separated experimentally by their different durations and topographies (Keller, 1974; Schwartz, Hamilton, & Silberberg, 1975), and are treated further under the topic of autoshaping in Chapter 9.

Observing Responses

In any discrimination, the discriminative stimuli are effective only if the organism observes them. Procedures can ensure that a pigeon looks at discriminative stimuli by requiring it to peck a key to produce them. Consider extinction and VR reinforcement of a pigeon's pecks, alternating irregularly during a white key. In this mixed schedule (mix EXT VR), the pigeon usually pecks throughout both EXT and VR compo-

nents. But now we introduce an observing key, a second key on which pecks produce stimuli correlated with the component schedules: During EXT, pecks on this key turn the first key red for some time and during VR they turn it green. In effect, pecks on the observing key change the mixed schedule to a multiple schedule (mult EXT VR); when the multiple-schedule stimuli are present, the pigeon comes to peck at near-zero rates during red (EXT) and at high rates during green (VR).

Pecks on the observing key are maintained by such procedures (e.g., Kelleher, Riddle, & Cook, 1962). But what maintains this observing? One possibility is that the reinforcing effectiveness of the discriminative stimuli comes about through their relation to the food reinforcers arranged by their schedules; another is that they are observed because they permit the pigeon to behave more efficiently with respect to the component schedules. The question is sometimes posed as one of whether observing is maintained because discriminative stimuli are conditioned reinforcers or because they are informative (e.g., Hendry, 1969).

If information is involved, then the two discriminative stimuli should be equally informative even though one is correlated with extinction and the other with reinforcement. But observing behavior is not well maintained when it produces only the stimulus correlated with extinction (Dinsmoor, 1983). Similarly, stimuli correlated with differential punishment (reinforcement during one component and reinforcement plus punishment during the other) do not ordinarily maintain observing responses; the aversiveness of the multiple-schedule stimulus correlated with reinforcement plus punishment overrides its informative effects, even though a reduction in responding during that stimulus might reduce the rate of punishment below that during the mixed-schedule performance (Dinsmoor, 1983).

In other words, the reinforcing effectiveness of a discriminative stimulus depends not on informativeness but rather on the particular consequences with which it is correlated (similarly, the bearer of good news is welcome but not the bearer of bad news). Thus, a central problem in producing multiple-schedule performances may simply be that of getting the organism to observe the relevant stimuli (cf. H.M. Jenkins & Sainsbury, 1970, and Chapter 7 on feature-positive discriminations).

CHAINED AND SECOND-ORDER SCHEDULES

Chained schedules, introduced in Chapter 1 to illustrate some features of the analysis of behavior, have been used extensively to study *conditioned reinforcers*, reinforcers that acquire their capacity to reinforce through their relation to other stimuli already effective as reinforcers (Kelleher & Gollub, 1962). For example, the feeder light becomes a reinforcer only through its relation to food in the feeder. Because the opportunity to engage in highly probable responses reinforces less probable responses only if the opportunity is signaled, the concept of conditioned reinforcement is related to the discriminative functions of stimuli (cf. Fantino, 1977).

Conditioned Reinforcement

The example of chained schedules in Chapter 1 used chained ratio schedules. When successive components of the schedule each operated in the presence of a single stimulus (*tandem* schedules), responding was well maintained. The introduction of different stimuli in each component (*chained* schedules) substantially reduced

responding in the early components of the sequence. Similar effects occur with chained interval schedules (Catania, Yohalem, & Silverman, 1980).

The different stimuli in chained schedules reduce responding relative to that maintained with a single stimulus. How can we reconcile this finding with the assumption that the successive stimuli of the chain should become conditioned reinforcers through their relation to the food at the end of the sequence? The low rates in the early chained-schedule components represent the combined discriminative effects of each stimulus (responding is never reinforced with food during these stimuli) and the reinforcing effects of the onset of the next stimulus. With component durations matched, both chained and multiple schedules involve a sequence of stimuli ending with a reinforcer; they differ only in whether stimulus changes are response-produced (cf. chained FI FI FI with multiple EXT EXT FI; both end with a single reinforcer, but only the chained schedule requires responses at the end of the first two components). Everything else being equal, rates in the next-to-last component are typically somewhat higher in chained than in equivalent multiple schedules (Catania, Yohalem, & Silverman, 1980). In other words, the stimulus changes in chained schedules have some reinforcing effects, but they are mostly restricted to the late components, close to the food reinforcers.

This phenomenon is highly reliable (Kelleher, 1966; Gollub, 1977) and depends on a constant ordering of the chained stimuli; the long pauses are markedly reduced if the stimulus order changes from one reinforcer to the next (Kelleher & Fry, 1962). Analogous but inverse effects also hold for schedules of punishment; relative to tandem schedules, chained schedules of punishment reduce responding mostly in the final components of the chain (Silverman, 1971). An implication is that punishment after a deed is done may often have its greatest effect on the behavior that precedes getting caught and only minimal effects on the behavior leading up to the misdeed.

Brief Stimuli

The stimuli in chained schedules can become conditioned reinforcers, but they combine with discriminative effects in such a way that responding is reduced. Yet this outcome seems inconsistent with the effects of some stimuli that acquire their reinforcing properties. In human behavior, for example, money presumably becomes a reinforcer by virtue of the various commodities for which it can be exchanged (it is sometimes called a *generalized reinforcer*, because it does not depend on a specific primary reinforcer; cf. Ayllon & Azrin, 1968, on token economies).

Early experiments on the effects of conditioned reinforcers were conducted during extinction, after a history of consistent pairings with a primary reinforcer (e.g., making tone a conditioned reinforcer by following it with food and testing later with tone alone). Although this procedure countered the objection that responding might be maintained directly by the later primary reinforcer rather than by the conditioned reinforcer itself, it was also one in which the effectiveness of conditioned reinforcers diminished rapidly once the primary reinforcer was removed. Convincing demonstrations of conditioned reinforcers came only when reinforcement schedules were applied to their analysis: Schedules were arranged not only for the production of conditioned reinforcers by responses but also for the contingent relation between conditioned and primary reinforcers (e.g., Zimmerman, Hanford, & Brown,

1967). For example, if a tone becomes a conditioned reinforcer, it may maintain FI responding even if it is followed by food only one time in 20.

In second-order schedules, the completion of one schedule is a behavioral unit that is reinforced according to another schedule. For example, the second-order schedule FR 10 (DRL 5-sec) arranges a reinforcer for every tenth IRT that is longer than 5 seconds (this arrangement, with a brief stimulus at the completion of each first-order schedule, is one of several types of second-order schedules). Consider a schedule arranged for a pigeon's pecks in which the peck that completes each 60-second fixed interval produces a brief green light on the key and in which every tenth such interval is followed also by food; the notation for such schedules often includes the brief stimulus: FR 10 (FI 60-sec: green). Such schedules typically maintain FI scalloping within intervals, even though most intervals end without food.

In contrast to chained schedules, second-order schedules with brief stimuli can greatly amplify reinforced responding (e.g., Findley, 1962). For example, Findley and Brady (1965) reinforced a chimpanzee's push-button presses with food according to an FR 4000 schedule; postreinforcement pauses ranged from many minutes to hours. But when the light accompanying food delivery came on briefly after every 400 responses, responding increased and typical postreinforcement pauses decreased to 5 minutes or less. The light converted the simple FR 4000 schedule to a second-order schedule, FR 10 (FR 400: light), that amplified the amount of behavior maintained by the food reinforcers. Variables such as the component schedules and the relation between the brief stimuli and primary reinforcers determine the effectiveness of second-order schedules (Gollub, 1977). Both chained schedules and second-order schedules with brief stimuli involve conditioned reinforcers, but their opposite effects illustrate how critically schedule effects depend on the detailed relations among stimuli and responses and consequences (cf. Morse & Kelleher, 1977; see also Malone, 1990, pp. 294–296; Neuringer & Chung, 1967).

CONCURRENT SCHEDULES

Any reinforced response is likely to occur in a context of other behavior maintained by other consequences. We must therefore examine the effect on one response of reinforcement schedules operating for other responses. Concurrent schedules are schedules arranged simultaneously for two or more responses. Consider an FR 25 schedule of food reinforcement for a pigeon's pecks on one key and an FR 50 schedule operating concurrently for pecks on a second key. Alone, either schedule maintains responding, but when they operate concurrently, responding is likely to be maintained exclusively on the key with the FR 25 schedule. The outcome is not surprising. A reinforcer requires only 25 pecks on the first key but 50 on the second.

Now consider concurrent interval schedules, such as VI 30-second reinforcement of pecks on one key and VI 60-second reinforcement of pecks on the other. In this case, the pigeon produces 120 reinforcers per hour by pecking only the first key or 60 per hour by pecking only the second. By pecking both, however, it produces the reinforcers of both schedules, or 180 per hour. In this case, responding is likely to be maintained on both keys.

Although pigeons distribute their pecks to both keys with concurrent VI VI schedules, there is a complication. If pecks on one key are immediately followed by a reinforced peck on the other, the reinforcer may act on the sequence, so that the pecks on one key are maintained partly by reinforcers scheduled for the other (cf. Chapter 4 on superstition). For this reason, concurrent VI procedures often incorporate a *changeover delay*, which prevents either response from being reinforced immediately after a changeover from the other (Herrnstein, 1961). With a changeover delay, the pigeon distributes its responses to concurrent VI VI schedules roughly in proportion to the distribution of reinforcers they arrange (e.g., Herrnstein, 1961); in the example, the pigeon pecks the VI 30-second key about twice as often as the VI 60-second key.

Matching, Maximizing, and Choice

This phenomenon is sufficiently general that it has been proposed as a general law of behavior, called the *matching law* (Herrnstein, 1970; see also Catania, 1976b; Rachlin, 1971). It states that relative responding matches the relative reinforcement produced by that responding. The law even holds for concurrent ratio schedules, because exclusive responding on one schedule means that all the reinforcers will be delivered according to that schedule. Herrnstein's account has also been applied to the responding maintained by a single reinforcement schedule (e.g., Figure 8–2), on the assumption that other events besides the reinforcers arranged by the experimenter may have reinforcing effects, even though we cannot identify them.

The matching law effectively summarizes performances in a variety of schedules, but its status either as a convenient description or as a fundamental property of behavior rests on whether it can be derived from simpler processes. For example, consider how concurrent VI VI schedules operate when arranged for a pigeon's pecks on two keys. As the pigeon continues to peck one key, time passes during which the VI schedule for the other key may set up a reinforcer. Thus, a time will come when the reinforcement probability for changing over to the other key exceeds that for continuing to peck the same key. If the pigeon always emits the response with the highest current reinforcement probability and this response shifts from one key to the other as time passes, the pigeon will distribute its responses to both keys in concurrent VI VI schedules (Shimp, 1966; see also Hinson & Staddon, 1981; Silberberg, Hamilton, Ziriax, & Casey, 1978). This performance has been called *maximizing;* with several responses available, an organism that maximizes will emit the one with the maximum reinforcement probability. With unequal concurrent ratio schedules, this response is always the one with the smaller ratio, but with concurrent VI VI schedules the response with the maximum reinforcement probability changes from moment to moment; concurrent VI VI performance has therefore been called *momentary maximizing.*

Matching and maximizing seem contradictory alternatives, but they are measured in different ways. We cannot speak about matching unless we have some sample of responses and reinforcers from which to estimate relative frequencies, but we can speak about maximizing with a single response, simply by noting whether it was the one with the maximum reinforcement probability. To some extent, therefore, the issues involve the level of detail at which performances are analyzed (cf. Moore, 1982, and the molar-molecular distinction in Chapter 5). Furthermore, matching and maximizing do not exhaust the possibilities. For example, other analyses have ex-

amined whether concurrent performances can be described as *optimization* (the organism produces the highest possible overall reinforcement rate), *satisficing* (it meets some minimal requirement, such as a given amount of food intake), or *melioration* (it balances performance so as to produce equal reinforcement rates under different conditions); the quantitative details of these treatments are beyond the scope of the present account (cf. Mazur, 1991).

One feature of concurrent performances is that increases in the reinforcement of one response reduce the rate of other responses (e.g., Catania, 1969; Catania, Sagvolden, & Keller, 1988; Rachlin & Baum, 1972). If the response rate generated by a given rate of VI reinforcement is independent of how these reinforcers are distributed to the two keys, it follows that increasing the reinforcement of one response will reduce the rate of the other. The relation is illustrated in Figure 8–10, in which the curved line shows an idealized version of the function relating response rate to VI reinforcement rate (cf. Figure 8–2). The bar marked A shows response rate when response A alone is reinforced. Arranging an equal VI schedule for response B doubles the overall reinforcement rate (X to $2X$). According to the matching law, total responding will be equally distributed to the two keys, as shown by the bar at $2X$ marked A and B. The rate of A is now lower, concurrent with B, than when A was reinforced alone.

The relation between the two rates is similar to that in behavioral contrast, but whereas behavioral contrast in multiple schedules is best regarded as an increase produced during extinction, the interactions among concurrent schedules are best regarded as decreases produced by the reinforcement of other responses. Experiments that observe the effects on pigeons' pecking on one key while re-

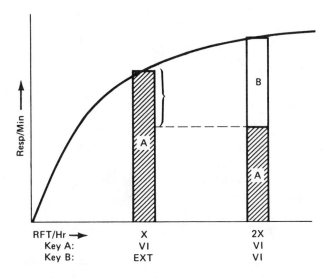

FIGURE 8–10 Combining the matching principle and the VI rate function (curved line; cf. Figure 8–2) to derive the reduction in the rate of one response (*A*) produced by reinforcing a concurrent response (*B*). The bracket shows how much reinforcement of *B* reduces *A*.

sponding and reinforcement are independently varied on a second key demonstrate that the interactions of response rate observed within concurrent VI schedules depend more on the reinforcers produced by each response than they do on competition between responses for available time (Catania, 1963b; but cf. Henton & Iversen, 1978). Although there are superficial similarities between multiple and concurrent schedules, it is risky to generalize from one to the other (cf. Killeen, 1972).

Variables with small effects in single-response schedules sometimes have large effects in concurrent schedules. Concurrent schedules are therefore often used to study reinforcement variables (e.g., reinforcement duration: Catania, 1963a; delay of reinforcement: Chung & Herrnstein, 1967). Furthermore, because concurrent schedules make different consequences simultaneously available, they provide

appropriate baseline procedures for the study of choice or preference.

CONCURRENT-CHAIN SCHEDULES

A common arrangement is the concurrent-chain procedure illustrated in Figure 8–11 (Herrnstein, 1964b). Two equal schedules operate in *initial links;* the consequence arranged for each is another schedule, a *terminal link.* This procedure separates the reinforcing effectiveness of the terminal link from the contingencies that maintain responding in that terminal link. For example, performances maintained by concurrent VR DRL schedules would not tell us whether a pigeon prefers VR to DRL schedules; these contingencies maintain high VR rates and low DRL rates but this does not imply a VR preference. Those rates need not be correlated with whether the pigeon will be more likely to produce opportunities to respond according to the

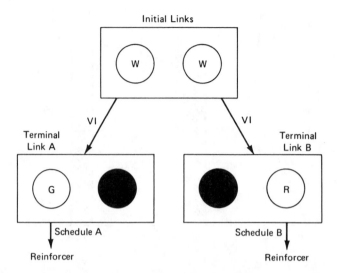

FIGURE 8–11 Schematic diagram of a concurrent-chain procedure as it might be arranged for a pigeon's key-pecks. In initial links, both keys are white (W) and equal but independent schedules (usually VI) operate for both keys. According to its schedule, pecks on the left key produce terminal link A, in which the left key is green (G) and the right key is dark; in terminal link A, pecks on green produce reinforcers according to schedule A. Similarly, according to its schedule, pecks on the right key produce terminal link B, in which the right key is red (R) and the left key is dark; in terminal link B, pecks on red produce reinforcers according to schedule B. The relative rates of pecking the two initial-link keys define preferences for the respective terminal links. For example, if a pigeon pecked the right white key more often that the left white key, it would be appropriate to say that the pigeon preferred schedule B to schedule A.

VR schedule than according to the DRL schedule. If instead the VR and DRL schedules were the respective terminal links in concurrent chains (e.g., schedules A and B in Figure 8–11), initial-link pecks producing the VR schedule might occur less often than those producing the DRL schedule. We judge preferences among situations not by how much behavior they produce but by the relative likelihoods with which an organism enters them.

Concurrent chains have shown that reinforcement rate is a more important determinant of preference than the number of responses per reinforcer (e.g., Neuringer & Schneider, 1968) and that variable schedules are preferred to fixed schedules (e.g., Herrnstein, 1964a). Studies of preferences among various parameters of rein-

forcement schedules can be technically complex, because they must control for differences in time or responses per reinforcer in terminal links and for occasional biases toward particular colors or toward one side or the other. For this reason, concurrent-chain procedures typically incorporate such features as reversals of the terminal-link conditions over sessions (cf. Cerutti & Catania, 1986); we will not attempt to treat such details here.

Natural Foraging and Behavior Synthesis

Beyond their use in studies of preference, concurrent-chains have also entered into the synthesis of complex behavior. Behavior analysis starts with complex behavior and breaks it down into its component parts. If the analysis is appropriate, it should be possible to synthesize the complex behavior by putting the parts back together again. Thus, if the interpretation of complex behavior in a natural habitat suggests that it consists of several simpler components, the interpretation can be tested by trying to assemble those components in a laboratory setting. A successful synthesis supports the interpretation; an unsuccessful one is likely to reveal inadequacies in the assumptions about what was going on in the natural setting.

In the field of *behavioral ecology*, this strategy is illustrated by studies of natural foraging (e.g., Fantino & Abarca, 1985; Kamil, Yoerg, & Clements, 1988). In their foraging, animals in the wild travel from one patch of food to another, staying or moving on to new ones depending on what they find. For example, a bird might fly to a bush in which the eggs of an edible insect have just hatched. As it eats, it gradually depletes its prey, and when it moves on depends on such factors as how much is left, how far it must go to find another bush, and what the chances are of finding other food there.

Some of these factors can be simulated within concurrent chains. For example, varying the schedules that operate in initial links is analogous to varying the time and effort involved in travelling from one bush to another, and varying the schedules in terminal links is analogous to varying the availability or depletion of different food sources at different sites. Concurrent-chain schedules that have synthesized performances in the laboratory simulating those in natural habitats have revealed some properties of foraging. For example, organisms are less selective in the food they accept if they must spend more travel time (more time in initial links) between potential food sources; and if one food is preferred over another, the availability of

the preferred food (the schedule that operates during the terminal link in which that food is the reinforcer) is a primary determinant of the choice of food patches (as shown by initial-link responding). In other words, natural foraging may be treated in terms of concurrent-chain schedules; properties of natural foraging, in turn, may suggest variables that are important in concurrent-chain performances.

Free-Choice Preference

We now consider another attempt to synthesize complex behavior using concurrent-chain schedules. Questions about freedom are questions about whether organisms prefer to have alternatives available. By making two keys available in one terminal link and only a single key in the other, we can ask whether pigeons prefer free choice to forced choice (Catania & Sagvolden, 1980). In free-choice terminal links, pecks on either of two keys produce a reinforcer at the end of a fixed interval; in forced-choice terminal links, the same FI schedule operates for pecks on a single key. Pigeons prefer free choice to forced choice in such schedules. These preferences do not depend on differences in the properties of terminal-link performances, such as responses per reinforcer, or on the distribution of responding to the two keys in free choice.

What, then, is the basis for the preference? Perhaps the pigeon has learned that different contingencies exist in free and forced choice. If one key fails during free choice, the other key is available as an alternative; if the single key fails during forced choice, no other key is available to fall back on. If the free-choice preference is learned, we should be able to reverse it, by making more reinforcers available during forced choice than during free choice. If we do so, the effects are only temporary; the free-choice preference returns when the reinforcers in the two terminal links become equal again. We cannot produce a durable forced-choice preference.

Perhaps the free-choice preference is an unlearned preference with a phylogenic basis. For example, given that food supplies sometimes are lost to competitors or disappear in other ways, an organism that chooses environments with two or more food sources will probably have advantages over one that chooses environments with only a single food source. If such preferences exist even in the behavior of pigeons, they cannot simply be the product of human cultures. They may occur because evolutionary contingencies have selected organisms that prefer free choice to forced choice. If so, we cannot eliminate this preference, even though we may be able to mask it temporarily (e.g., by punishing responding during free choice but not forced choice). This conclusion is based on data from pigeons, but it does not demean free-choice preference; it makes it more fundamental. Perhaps our human concept of freedom has biological roots.

A behavior synthesis may exhibit properties that were not accessible in the non-laboratory situations from which it was derived. In this example, the free-choice preference, once demonstrated, can be used in turn to define what qualifies as a free choice. For example, the pigeon prefers two FI keys to a single FI key, but it does not prefer an FI and an EXT key to an FI key alone. Thus, free choice does not consist of just the availability of two responses; they must each also be capable of producing a reinforcer.

Self-Control

Another example of behavior synthesis with concurrent-chain schedules is provided by the procedure illustrated in Figure 8–12 (Rachlin & Green, 1972). The initial links consisted of concurrent FR 25

FR 25 schedules (the usual VI initial links make terminal links available equally often, thereby equalizing the pigeon's exposure to each one; with FR schedules, the pigeon can enter one terminal link more often than the other). In terminal-link A, the keys were dark for T seconds and then lit red and green, respectively. A peck on red immediately produced 2 seconds of food; a peck on green produced 4 seconds of food after a 4-second delay. In terminal-link B, the keys also were dark for T seconds, but then only the green key was lit. As in the other terminal link, a peck on green produced the large reinforcer after a 4-second delay.

Confronted with both red and green in terminal-link A, the pigeon almost invariably pecks red, producing the small immediate reinforcer rather than the large delayed one (this has been called *impulsiveness*; Ainslie, 1974). Confronted with only green in terminal-link B, the pigeon necessarily produces the large delayed reinforcer. But what about the pigeon's preference for A versus B, given by its initial-link responding? The answer depends on T, the time from the start of the terminal link to the lighting of the terminal-link keys. When it is short (e.g., 1 second), the pigeon usually produces terminal-link A and then pecks red. When it is longer, the pigeon is more likely to produce terminal-link B; in that terminal link, only green is available. The relative rate of pecking the left initial-link key (left initial-link pecks divided by total initial-link pecks) is shown as a function of T in Figure 8–13. As T increased from 0.5 seconds to 16 seconds, the proportion of pecks producing terminal-link A decreased; the pigeon became more and more likely to enter terminal-link B and produce the larger reinforcer.

During initial links, the time to food equals T for the small reinforcer but T plus the 4-second delay for the large one. When

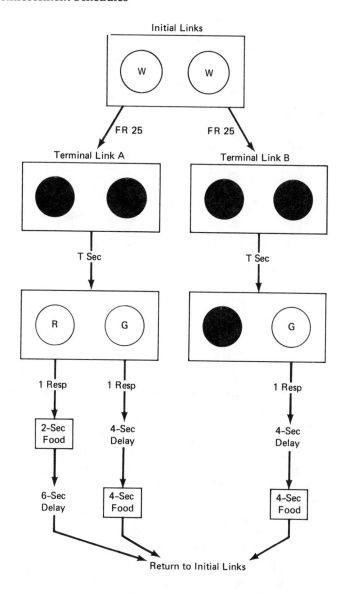

FIGURE 8-12   A concurrent-chain procedure that synthesizes some properties of impulsiveness, commitment, and self-control. According to FR 25 schedules, pecks on the white (W) initial-link keys are followed after *T* seconds by terminal links. In terminal-link *A*, red (R) and green (G) keys, respectively, make available an immediate small reinforcer or a delayed large one. In terminal-link *B*, the green key alone makes only the delayed large reinforcer available. (Adapted from Rachlin & Green, 1972)

T is short, this difference is relatively large (e.g., with a *T* of 1 second, the respective delays are 1 and 5 seconds) and the short delay outweighs the difference in rein-forcer magnitudes. When *T* is long, however, the difference becomes relatively small (e.g., with a *T* of 10 seconds, the respective delays are 10 and 14 seconds) and

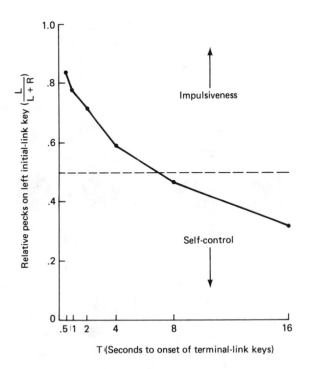

FIGURE 8–13 Relative initial-link pecks producing terminal-link *A* (left initial-link pecks divided by total initial-link pecks) as a function of *T*, the time to the onset of the terminal-link keys. (Cf. Figure 8–12; adapted from Rachlin & Green, 1972, Table 1)

the difference in reinforcer magnitudes becomes effective. By producing terminal-link *B* when *T* is long, the pigeon commits itself to the large reinforcer even though it would not do so at the onset of green if red were also present. For this reason, pecks that produce terminal-link *B* have been called *commitment responses:* They guarantee the large delayed reinforcer by making the small immediate one unavailable.

Human situations discussed in terms of self-control typically involve different consequences that are pitted against each other (Skinner, 1953; Rachlin, 1974). The pigeon example involved two reinforcers. Similarly, you might get something immediately by buying now, but saving the money might make something else affordable later. Other cases can involve aversive

events, as when an alcoholic refuses the immediate reinforcer of a drink and avoids the later aversive consequence of a hangover. Procedures like the one illustrated in Figure 8–12 bring such behavioral relations into the laboratory, by creating reinforcement schedules with analogous temporal properties.

With the concurrent-chain procedure we may examine impulsiveness and commitment with immediate and delayed reinforcers (e.g., Green & Snyderman, 1980) or immediate and delayed aversive stimuli (e.g., Deluty, 1978). We can also examine whether commitment is modifiable (e.g., Mazur & Logue, 1978) and whether the components of this synthesis of self-control involve variables comparable to those that operate in human behavior (e.g., Grosch &

Neuringer, 1981). Unlike the pigeon, humans sometimes do forego small and currently available reinforcers in favor of large delayed ones. Human instances of self-control presumably also involve verbal behavior (cf. Chapter 11). But if more complex processes operate in human self-control, they can only be identified by examining whether human cases are inconsistent with analyses in terms of reinforcer delays. For this reason, the behavior synthesis provides an essential reference performance for the analysis of self-control and illustrates the relevance of reinforcement schedules to human behavior.

SCHEDULE ANALYSIS AND BEHAVIOR SYNTHESIS

Reinforcement schedules bear on behavioral phenomena ranging from causal relations between behavior and environment to self-control and freedom of choice. Yet even so-called simple schedules are not simple; the complexity of schedule effects has made schedule analysis highly technical. We examined properties of variable and fixed ratio and interval schedules and briefly sampled other topics, including multiple, chained, second-order, concurrent, and concurrent-chain schedules. We often omitted procedural details. This is perhaps inevitable. Unlike most other areas in this text, reinforcement schedules did not even exist as a systematic subject matter until relatively recently (Skinner, 1938, 1956; Ferster & Skinner, 1957). One concern of this subject matter has been maintenance of behavior in the steady state (yet the change in behavior that accompanies any transition from one schedule to another is an instance of learning).

Once we have used schedules to explore the properties of complex behavior through a behavior analysis, we may be in a position to put the parts back together in a behavior synthesis. For example, we can test our interpretation of complex behavior in a natural habitat by trying to assemble its components in a laboratory setting. We cannot create a behavior synthesis without making explicit many of our assumptions about the properties of the behavior we are trying to synthesize. For that reason, we probably learn more from our failures than from our successes at synthesis.

The analysis of schedules forces us to recognize that response rate itself is a differentiable property of behavior along with topography, force, duration, and so on. Thus, an integration of the diverse phenomena of reinforcement schedules is likely to be based not on response rate and its derivatives as measures, but rather on more general properties of behavior that are independent of response rate, such as the resistance of behavior to change (Nevin, 1974).

CHAPTER **9**

Respondent Behavior: Conditioning

*The language of emotion includes a number of etymological clusters. For example, eager, anger, and anxiety share the same roots, as do choleric, melancholy, glad, and glee, and wrath and worry, and sad and satisfy (the last pair is also related to satiate). Fear, from the Indo-European per-, to try, to risk, to press forward or lead, has an extensive group of relatives that include experiment and apparatus, probability and opportunity, approach and depri-*vation, *and two contemporary synonyms for behavior,* comportment *and* performance.

In respondent conditioning, we encounter a topic that has dominated the psychology of learning so much that it has provided the opening chapters of many learning texts. In addition to *respondent conditioning,* it has gone by such names as *classical conditioning* and *Pavlovian conditioning,* and the language of conditioned reflexes has to some extent entered the everyday vocabulary (although in popular usage it is often confused with instances of learning in operant behavior).

The term conditioned, from the Russian phrase for conditioned reflexes, **условный рефлекс** (*uslovnyi refleks*), might better have been translated as *conditional,* because the name was applied to reflexes conditional upon relations among environmental stimuli. Respondent conditioning is an instance of stimulus control applied to stimulus-presentation operations rather than to the contingencies of consequential operations. In other words, instead of signaling the consequences of responding, a stimulus simply signals the presentation of some other stimulus. Pavlov's conditioned salivary reflexes are the prototype example: when a bell repeatedly signaled food in the mouth of a hungry dog, salivation began to be elicited by the signaling stimulus as well as by the food itself.

In discussing operant behavior, we spoke of classes of responses rather than individual instances because individual responses are never exactly repeated. Similar problems exist for elicited behavior. For example, successive elicitations of salivation by food may differ in latency, quantity, viscosity, and other properties. It is therefore appropriate to extend the language of classes to responses defined by the stimuli that produce them. These classes, called *respondents,* correspond to the behavior earlier called elicited or reflexive. Thus, salivation produced by food in the mouth is a respondent class; it must be distinguished from salivation produced by acid in the mouth, which is a different respondent class, and from spontaneous salivation, which is not a respondent class at all because it has no eliciting stimulus (spontaneous salivation is emitted rather than elicited; if we could identify an eliciting stimulus, we would not call it spontaneous).

In this chapter we first discuss the behavior generated by various types of Pavlovian or respondent conditioning. Then we consider how such behavior may interact with operant responding. We will find such interactions relevant to the topic of emotion. The chapter closes with a section on biological constraints on learning.

Section A   **Conditional Reflexes**

We produce respondent behavior by presenting stimuli, and we change respondent behavior by changing these stimuli. For example, by varying the concentration of acid in the mouth (e.g., dilutions of vinegar), we change the quality of saliva elicited. This means we are limited in the extent to which we can modify respondent

behavior. We can create new operants by shaping, but the properties of respondents are determined by their eliciting stimuli, so no equivalent procedure exists for respondent behavior. But we can alter the eliciting effects of stimuli. Let us examine Pavlov's (1927) procedure in more detail.

We begin with a dog in a harness with one of its salivary ducts connected to a system that records salivation. Two stimuli are used: the sound of a bell beside the dog, and food in a form that can be delivered directly into the dog's mouth. First we examine the effects of each stimulus separately. When the bell first rings, the dog pricks up its ears and turns its head toward it. This has been called an *orienting* response. With successive rings, it diminishes, perhaps even becoming undetectable; it can be reinstated by waiting a while before ringing the bell again (cf. habituation, Chapter 3). When food is placed in its mouth, the dog chews and salivates. These responses may diminish a little over food presentations, but their magnitude remains substantial over the course of a session.

Suppose now that the bell signals food by ringing 5 seconds before each food delivery. After a number of trials salivation sometimes begins in the 5-second period between bell and food, and sometimes the bell is followed by salivation even on an occasional trial when the food is omitted. In neither case can we attribute the salivation to food as an eliciting stimulus: In the first the salivation began before the food was presented, and in the second the food was not presented at all. To the extent that the bell has acquired the power to elicit salivation, we say that we have created a new respondent class, salivation elicited by the sound of the bell. We call the relation between bell and salivation a conditional reflex because it is conditional on the prior relation of bell and food.

The sequence of events is illustrated in Figure 9–1. The bell at first elicits orienting

responses, but these disappear with repeated presentations; at this point, the bell
is a *neutral stimulus.* In an unconditional
reflex, food elicits salivation; in this relation, the food is an *unconditional stimulus*
or *US* and the salivation is an *unconditional
response* or *UR.* Conditioning begins when
the bell reliably precedes food; at this
point, the bell still has no effect on salivation and can still be regarded as a neutral
stimulus. After a period of conditioning, a
conditional reflex has been created; the bell
elicits salivation before food is presented
(a), or the bell elicits salivation even when
food is omitted on an occasional trial (b).
The bell is now a *conditional stimulus* or *CS*
and salivation elicited by the bell is a *conditional response* or *CR.*

The difference between a conditional
stimulus and an unconditional stimulus is
not simply which comes first. If we reversed their order, the eliciting effects of
food followed by bell would not be much
different from those of food alone. In fact,

the relative effectiveness of stimuli as conditional and unconditional stimuli may be
predictable from the probabilities with
which the stimuli elicit their respective responses. For example, consider salivation
elicited by food in a dog's mouth and leg
flexion produced by shock to its leg. A mild
shock may become a conditional stimulus
eliciting salivation if reliably followed by
food, but a strong shock followed by food
is not likely to do so. On the other hand,
food may become a conditional stimulus
eliciting leg flexion if reliably followed by
a strong shock, but food followed by a
weak shock is not likely to do so. The
differences are consistent with the relative
probabilities with which food may elicit
salivation and mild or strong electric
shock may elicit leg flexion.

Differences between conditional and
unconditional responses are not solely
those of temporal order. For example, the
form or topography of a conditional leg
flexion typically differs from the uncondi-

FIGURE 9–1 Relations between stimuli and responses in respondent conditioning. An initially
neutral stimulus (BELL:NS) is followed by an unconditional stimulus (FOOD:US) that elicits
salivation. If the neutral stimulus begins to elicit responding like that elicited by the unconditional stimulus, the neutral stimulus is called a conditional stimulus (CS). OR, orienting
response; UR, unconditional response; CR, conditional response.

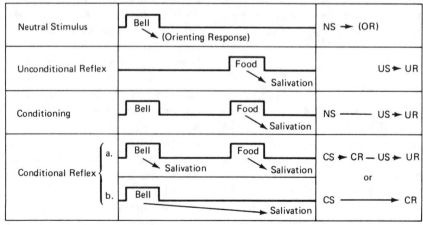

tional flexion elicited by electric shock. In general, a conditional response is not merely an unconditional response now elicited by a new stimulus; in other words, respondent conditioning cannot be interpreted as stimulus substitution; in Pavlov's classical case, for example, the bell does not become a substitute for food. Conditional stimuli can affect a broad range of responses in addition to those resembling the ones elicited by the unconditional stimulus.

Many different conditional reflexes have been created through respondent procedures (e.g., see Hull, 1934). Pavlov's salivary conditioning is probably the most familiar, but other studies demonstrated conditioning based on such unconditional reflex relations as the knee jerk elicited by a tap of the patellar tendon (Twitmyer, 1902) and limb withdrawal elicited by electric shock (Bechterev, 1933). Conditioning has worked with eyeblinks elicited by a puff of air to the eye (e.g., Gormezano, 1972), but conditioning of pupillary constriction elicited by light to the eye, once believed feasible, has not been successful (Young, 1958). The Russian literature includes a variety of conditioning demonstrations (e.g., Bykov, 1957). For example, for several days a dog was placed in a waiting area at neutral temperature before being moved into a heated room, and its metabolism and oxygen consumption began to decrease in the waiting area as well as in the heated room. Inversely, after waiting area stays were followed by being moved into a cool room, the dog's metabolism and oxygen consumption began to increase in the waiting area as well as in the cool room (Bykov, 1957, pp. 183–210).

Consider another example. The release of insulin by the pancreas is a UR produced by the US of sugar in the gut (Deutsch, 1974). This US is reliably preceded by the taste of sugar, which makes it likely that the taste will become a CS that releases insulin. Suppose now that you have just switched from soft drinks with sugar in them to sugar-free diet versions. As a CS, the sweet taste of the drink elicits the release of insulin, which is ordinarily used up as you digest the sugar. But now your drink has no sugar in it, so you can expect to feel weak or heady as the insulin produces a substantial drop in your blood sugar level (hypoglycemia). Similar conditioning effects have been demonstrated with a variety of physiological responses (e.g., reactions of the immune system: Ader & Cohen, 1985).

Respondent conditioning with some types of US's leads to CS's that elicit compensatory responses rather than responses similar to those elicited by the US. Such cases provide another kind of evidence that respondent conditioning is not merely stimulus substitution. One example occurs in respondent conditioning with opiates such as morphine or heroin (Siegel, 1975, 1977). Among the effects of these drugs is analgesia, an elevated pain threshold. With continued doses, events that lead up to administration of the drug (e.g., preparing the needle) are likely to become CS's that elicit a CR. But this CR does not enhance the analgesia and other drug effects; instead, it counteracts them (for example, it produces the opposite of analgesia—hyperalgesia, or a lowered pain threshold). As a result, it takes larger and larger doses to produce the original drug effect (these are some of the factors involved in the development of drug tolerance). To summarize: The US is the drug in the bloodstream and one component of the UR is analgesia; the CS is any event reliably preceding the drug administration and the CR is a physiological response that counteracts the analgesia and other effects of the drug.

Heroin addicts often take their drugs in the same place with the same company, using the same drug-taking ritual. Now consider the addict who for some reason takes the drug somewhere else and with different company. The dose is large but many of the CS's that usually precede it are absent, so a CR much smaller than usual is elicited. The drug effect occurs but this time it is not counteracted by the usual compensatory response. Under such circumstances, a drug dose that is ordinarily tolerated can instead be fatal (Siegel, Hinson, Krank, & McCully, 1982); hospital admissions and/or deaths from heroin overdose are especially likely when addicts take their drugs under unusual or unfamiliar circumstances.

TYPES OF CONDITIONING

The temporal relations between the two stimuli can be arranged in varied ways. Situations in which the onset of the conditional stimulus precedes that of the unconditional stimulus by no more than 5 seconds are sometimes arbitrarily grouped together as instances of *simultaneous conditioning*. This usage is perhaps based on two circumstances: The optimal interval between conditional and unconditional stimuli is roughly half a second (e.g., Kimble, 1947) and omissions of the unconditional stimulus sometimes reduce the reliability with which conditional responding is maintained. Short intervals like half a second provide little opportunity to observe conditional responding. The choice then was to omit the unconditional stimulus on some trials or to lengthen the interval between stimulus onsets. Because conditioning became less reliable with stimulus omissions, lengthening the interval be-

tween stimulus onsets became favored over occasionally omitting the unconditional stimulus, and the distinction between strict simultaneity and these relatively short delays was overlooked.

The effect of occasional omissions of the unconditional stimulus had theoretical ramifications. In a usage that is becoming rare, presentations of the unconditional stimulus in respondent conditioning were called reinforcement, and therefore the procedure in which this stimulus was omitted on occasional trials was called partial reinforcement. Distinctions between operant and respondent conditioning were then argued on the basis of the so-called partial reinforcement effect or *PRE*: Relative to reinforcement of every response, partial reinforcement generated substantial quantities of responding in operant behavior, as we saw in Chapter 8, whereas the analogous procedure in respondent conditioning seemed to reduce responding (but see Gibbon, Farrell, Locurto, Duncan, & Terrace, 1980). Now that the term reinforcement has become more restricted in its scope, the comparison no longer seems relevant. In its time, however, it provided one of the most persuasive grounds for distinguishing between the two types of conditioning.

Some arrangements of conditional and unconditional stimuli are contrasted with simultaneous conditioning in Figure 9–2. In both *trace conditioning* and *delay conditioning* a relatively long time elapses between the onset of the conditional stimulus and that of the unconditional stimulus; they are distinguished by whether the conditional stimulus turns off or remains present during that time. (The time from CS onset to US onset can vary independently of the temporal overlap of CS and US. For example, in delay conditioning the CS might end with US onset or end at the same time as the US; this feature of the timing of CS and US is not relevant to the procedural distinctions in Figure 9–2.) In both trace and delay conditioning, conditional responding at first occurs shortly after the onset of the conditional stimulus, but with successive trials it gradually moves closer to the time at which the unconditional stimulus is to be delivered. Trace conditioning acquired its name from the assumption that the conditional stimulus had to leave some trace in the organism's nervous system to be effective.

FIGURE 9–2 Schematic presentation of various respondent-conditioning procedures, showing bell as a CS and food as a US. In simultaneous conditioning, bell is followed within less than 5 seconds by food. Different time relations are illustrated in trace, delay, and temporal conditioning, and the stimulus order is reversed in backward conditioning. In differential conditioning, bell is followed by food but tone is not. CS, conditional stimulus; US, unconditional stimulus.

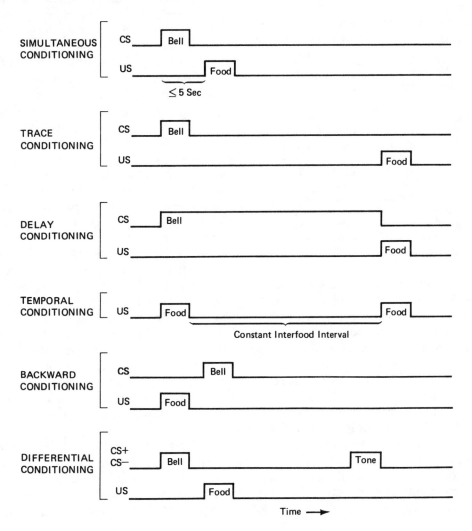

But successive presentations of the unconditional stimulus itself at regular intervals (e.g., every half-hour) also produce conditional responding; this procedure is called *temporal conditioning*, and responding has sometimes been spoken of as conditioned to time as a stimulus (temporal conditioning involves repeated presentation of a stimulus, and so is equivalent to some of the stimulus-presentation operations in Chapter 3).

The reversal of the order of the two stimuli is called *backward conditioning*. For theoretical reasons, it was long assumed ineffective in producing conditional responding. It is often less effective than other conditioning procedures, but it has occasionally been demonstrated, particularly with aversive CS's:

> ...common sense would lead one to expect animals to have the ability to respond defensively to a novel stimulus detected after a sudden aversive event. An animal that sighted an unfamiliar predator following an abortive attack surely would not submit to another attack (i.e., a forward pairing of the predator and pain) before reacting defensively. (Spetch, Wilkie, & Pinel, 1981, p. 163; cf. species-specific defense reactions in Chapter 5)

Finally, a procedure in which one stimulus becomes a conditional stimulus through its relation to the unconditional stimulus while a second stimulus does not do so because it never precedes the unconditional stimulus is called *differential conditioning*. The stimuli are sometimes called positive and negative conditional stimuli (CS+ and CS-).

In all of these cases, the CS must produce the CR because of its relation to the US, and not for other reasons. For example, if a visual stimulus and a traumatic shock occur together, a later startle to the visual stimulus might not mean it had become a CS. A startle response might be elicited by a variety of innocuous stimuli after a traumatic shock, even though these stimuli never occurred together with the shock. These are cases of *pseudoconditioning* (cf. sensitization, Chapter 3).

CONDITIONING AND CONTIGUITY

Some of the attention historically given to respondent conditioning may have depended on how easily it could be related to the concept of association, a principle of learning with substantial precedent in philosophy and psychology. Learning had been said to take place through the association of ideas, and conditional reflexes seemed to represent a primitive example of the formation of such associations. If ideas were associated, it was argued, then one would lead to the other. In a kind of mental chemistry, ideas were supposed to become associated through such properties as having common elements or occurring together in time. It remained then to suggest that ideas could be interpreted as responses generated by environmental events, so that remembering one event in the past would call up others it had occurred together with.

We need not dwell on the details. Even those parts of the contemporary psychology of learning that can still be called associationistic have evolved considerably from earlier formulations. We already noted that respondent conditioning cannot be interpreted simply as making one stimulus a substitute for another. For the present, the point is that respondent conditioning was regarded as a process at the root of all learning, and it was assumed to take place merely through the temporal contiguity of events, their occurrence together in time. Theoretical debates then revolved around the primacy of respondent conditioning and other processes, and particular attention was given to find-

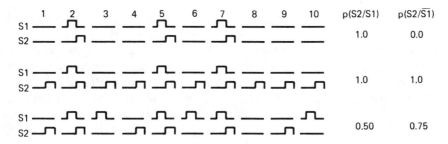

	p(S2/S1)	p(S2/$\overline{\text{S1}}$)
	1.0	0.0
	1.0	1.0
	0.50	0.75

FIGURE 9–3   Conditional relations between two stimuli, *S1* and *S2*. Rows represent samples of 10 trials from each of three conditioning procedures. Each involves exactly three pairings of *S1* and *S2* (in trials 2, 5, and 7), but *S1* predicts *S2* only in the first procedure. In the second, *S2* is equally likely given *S1* and not given *S1*, and in the third it is less likely given *S1* than not given *S1*. Probabilities of *S2* given *S1* and given no *S1* are shown at the right. (Cf. Rescorla, 1967)

ing ways of interpreting instrumental or operant behavior as an instance of behavior generated by respondent principles (for various sides of the argument, see Guthrie, 1935; Hull, 1943; Konorski, 1948; Mowrer, 1960; Schlosberg, 1937; Skinner, 1935b; Smith, 1954).

Part of the problem was that *contiguities* among stimuli were not adequately distinguished from stimulus-stimulus *contingencies*. Contiguity is defined by stimulus pairings, the number of times stimuli occur together. Even when the number of stimuli remains constant, however, contingency relations between conditional and unconditional stimuli can vary. For example, assume that bell (*S1*) and food (*S2*) are arranged within trials, and that we can ignore the stimuli that demarcate the trials. The rows in Figure 9–3 show samples of 10 trials from three conditioning procedures. In each, *S1* is paired with *S2* in trials 2, 5, and 7. In the top row, only those trials include *S2*, which is therefore perfectly correlated with *S1*: The probability of *S2* is 1.0 given *S1* but zero without it, and so *S1* perfectly predicts *S2*. In the middle row, *S2* occurs in every trial and so *S1* is irrelevant to whether *S2* occurs: The probability of *S2*

is 1.0 with or without *S1*. In the bottom row, *S1* occurs in 6 trials, but in only half of these is it followed by *S2*, whereas *S2* occurs in three-quarters of the trials in which *S1* is not presented: The probability of *S2* is lower with *S1* (0.50) than without it (0.75).

Figure 9–4 shows these three conditions within a contingency space for

FIGURE 9–4   A stimulus-stimulus contingency space. The unit square shows conditional probabilities of stimulus *S2* given stimulus *S1* or not given stimulus *S1*. The three lettered points correspond to the three procedures of Figure 9–3. (Cf. Figures 3–2 and 4–9)

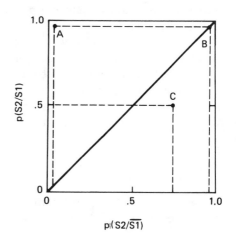

stimulus-stimulus relations. Only in the first procedure is *S1* likely to become an effective conditional stimulus; in the last procedure, *S1* might even reduce the likelihood of conditional responding elicited by the trial stimulus. The conditional relation between the two stimuli (contingency) rather than the number of pairings (contiguity) is the appropriate basis for classifying conditioning procedures (Rescorla, 1967, 1988).

STIMULUS COMBINATIONS IN CONDITIONING

Whether a stimulus becomes effective as a CS depends on the context of stimuli within which it appears (e.g., Kamin, 1969). Sometimes the context itself can become effective as a CS. For example, a rat may learn that a CS is followed by a US when it is in an experimental chamber but not when it is in its home chamber. The experimental chamber is, in effect, a stimulus in the presence of which the CS-US contingency operates (as a result, the rat may not respond to a CS presented in its home chamber). In the context of respondent conditioning, such stimuli have been called *occasion-setters*, in the sense that they set the occasions on which stimulus-stimulus contingencies operate (e.g., Rescorla, 1988). Such stimuli do not elicit responding; they modify the eliciting effects of other stimuli. Occasion-setting is one of many possible stimulus functions that may be produced by stimulus combinations in respondent conditioning. Let us now consider examples of a few others.

Overshadowing and Blocking

Suppose that loud tone and dim light presented together are followed by some US, such as a shock that elicits leg flexion. After conditional responding developed to this stimulus pair, we could present each stimulus separately and might find tone much more effective as a CS than light. (The concept of attention, as in operant discrimination, is relevant to respondent conditioning; we might say that the organism was attending more to tone than to light, or that tone was more salient than light; cf. Rescorla & Wagner, 1972.)

The tone-plus-light example assumed that the organism had no history of conditioning with either stimulus of the compound. The procedure is shown schematically as *overshadowing* in Figure 9–5. When the stimuli of a compound do not become equally effective CS's, the more effective stimulus is said to overshadow the less effective one. But such an effect may also occur when one of the two stimuli already has a history of conditioning. For example, suppose dim light became a CS by itself before it was presented together with tone. If simultaneous light and tone were then followed by shock until conditional flexions were observed, we might find when presenting the stimuli separately that light but not tone was effective as a CS, even though tone preceded the shock as reliably as did light. When a stimulus fails to become effective as a CS because it is presented together with some other already effective stimulus, we say that the stimulus with the prior history blocked conditioning to the new stimulus. This procedure is shown schematically as *blocking* in Figure 9–5. (Analogous phenomena can occur in operant discriminations and remind us that operant discrimination and respondent conditioning are both instances of stimulus control.)

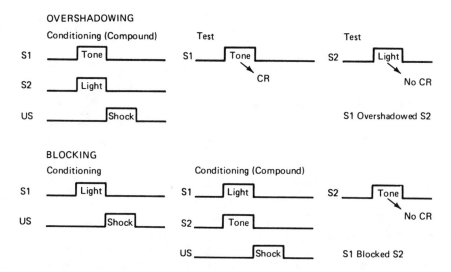

FIGURE 9–5 Schematic illustrations of overshadowing and blocking. In overshadowing, neither of the two stimuli of a compound had a prior history of conditioning but only one of them becomes effective as a CS (alternatively, one becomes more effective than the other). In blocking, one stimulus is made effective as a CS, and this history prevents the other from becoming effective when the two are presented together as a compound (alternatively, the first reduces the effectiveness of the second). *S1* and *S2*, stimuli; *US*, unconditional stimulus; *CR*, conditional response.

Inhibitory Stimuli in Compounds

Stimuli can signal omissions as well as presentations of other stimuli (cf. C in Figure 9–4). When they do so, they sometimes acquire the capacity to reduce the effectiveness of other CS's and are described as *inhibitory*. An example is shown in Figure 9–6, which illustrates a conditioning procedure involving food-elicited salivation in a dog. First, a bell is made a CS (CSA+). Once the bell reliably elicits salivation, a tone is presented either alone or together with a light on irregularly alternating trials. When tone (CSB+) is presented alone, it is followed by food. When it is presented with the light (CSx-), food is omitted. Eventually tone alone elicits conditional salivation but the pairing of tone and light does not. It might be assumed that the dog simply discriminates tone alone from the tone-plus-light

combination. But the inhibitory effect of the light is demonstrated when later presentations of the bell together with the light elicit less conditional salivation than the bell would have elicited if presented by itself.

In another procedure, we could follow the tone-light combination but neither of the stimuli alone by the US. In this case, we would eventually find that the combination but not the individual stimuli elicited the conditional response. In other words, as this demonstration shows, organisms can respond differentially not only to individual stimuli but also to relations among them.

Sensory Preconditioning and Second-Order Conditioning

We have considered cases of respondent conditioning based on US's that serve in

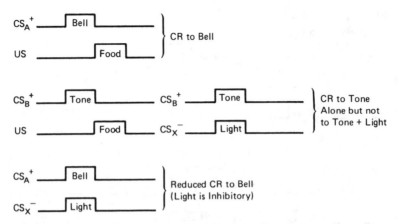

FIGURE 9–6 Schematic illustration of a procedure for demonstrating an inhibitory component of a stimulus compound. First, the succession of bell and food produces conditional salivation to the bell. Next, tone alone is followed by food but tone accompanied by light is not; conditional salivation occurs to tone alone but not to tone plus light. Finally, when light is presented together with bell, bell elicits less salivation than if it had been presented alone.

other situations as reinforcers (e.g., food) or punishers (e.g., shock). But does conditioning occur when relatively neutral stimuli such as lights or sounds serve as US's? The problem is that conditioning is difficult to assess when no elicited responses can easily be recorded. Two procedures concerned with effects of such stimuli, *sensory preconditioning* and *second-order conditioning*, are illustrated for conditional leg flexions in dogs in Figure 9–7.

First consider sensory preconditioning (Brogden, 1939). In the first phase, preconditioning, one stimulus signals a second stimulus. In the example of Figure 9–7, bell is consistently followed by tone. In the second phase, a conditional reflex is created in which the second stimulus becomes a CS. In the figure, tone is followed by shock. Once the conditional reflex is created, so that tone elicits leg flexion, the eliciting effects of the bell are tested. Leg flexion to the bell is then taken to mean that the bell became a CS relative to the tone during preconditioning. (For con-

venience, control groups used to counterbalance stimuli and to rule out sensitization and other effects have been omitted; cf. Chapter 3).

In second-order conditioning, the order of phases is reversed (cf. Rescorla, 1980). In the example in Figure 9–7, a conditional reflex in which tone elicits leg flexion is created first, by presenting tone and then shock. Later, bell is followed by tone. In this instance, the question is whether the CS created in the first phase can function as a US for another stimulus in the second phase. The difficulty is that the tone loses its effectiveness as a CS as it is repeatedly presented without shock in the second phase, but during just this time the bell must acquire its conditional properties. An alternative procedure, with bell followed by tone and then shock on all trials within a single phase, would be ambiguous; we would not know whether leg flexions elicited by the bell occurred because of the relation between bell and tone or bell and shock.

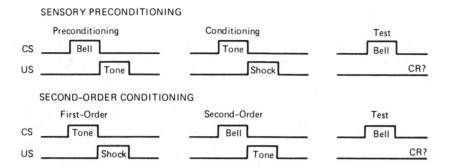

FIGURE 9-7 Schematic diagram of the phases of sensory preconditioning and second-order conditioning procedures, using bell and tone as CS's and shock-elicited leg flexions in a dog as the UR.

If the CS is presented alone after sensory preconditioning, thereby extinguishing the conditional reflex, the preconditioning stimulus also will no longer elicit a CR. In other words, in the example of Figure 9–7, presenting tone alone after the conditioning phase until the tone no longer elicits flexions will also make the bell lose its effectiveness as a CS. But the comparable procedure after second-order conditioning does not always extinguish the second-order conditional reflex (Rizley & Rescorla, 1972; but see also Holland & Ross, 1981; Nairne & Rescorla, 1981; Rescorla, 1979). In the example of Figure 9–7, presenting tone alone until it no longer elicits flexions may not eliminate the conditional flexions to the bell created during the second-order phase.

This outcome is paradoxical. Consider an analogous human case history. A young man sees blood in painful circumstances and the sight of blood becomes a CS that elicits those emotional responses we call fear. At a later time (equivalent to the second-order phase), he sees blood in an elevator and thereby acquires a fear of elevators. Then he goes into hospital work and in that context gradually gets over his fear of the sight of blood. According to Rizley and Rescorla's findings, this change will not reduce his fear of elevators even though the CR to blood had been the basis for the fear. This case is hypothetical and we must generalize cautiously from experimental to real-life situations. But these findings again demonstrate that respondent conditioning is not simply the substitution of one stimulus for another.

CONTIGUITY AND CONSEQUENCES

Instances of conditioning based on aversive stimuli such as electric shock were called *defensive conditioning*, on the assumption that the responses elicited by such stimuli occurred because they had some natural defensive function (cf. Chapter 5 on species-specific defense reactions). One frequently cited example is an experiment with an infant boy named Albert (Watson & Rayner, 1920). The aversive stimulus was the sound, just behind little Albert, of striking a suspended steel bar with a hammer. This sound produced startle or crying or withdrawal responses. When the sound followed presentations of a white rat, these responses began to occur in the presence of the rat and of other stimuli having properties in common with it, such as cotton wool. Watson and Rayner called these responses *conditioned emotional reactions*. Yet the details of the experimental procedure show that the initial clangs of the steel bar were not independent of behavior:

> 1. White rat suddenly taken from the basket and presented to Albert. He began to reach for the rat with left hand. Just as his hand touched the animal the bar was struck immediately behind his head. The infant jumped violently and fell forward, burying his face in the mattress. He did not cry, however.

> 2. Just as the right hand touched the rat the bar was again struck. Again the infant jumped violently, fell forward and began to whimper. In order not to disturb the child too seriously no further tests were given for one week. (Watson & Rayner, 1920, p. 4)

At least at the outset, therefore, Watson and Rayner's experiment used punishment of reaching toward the rat and not merely response-independent stimulus presentations. This was presumably important in getting Albert to attend to the white rat as a discriminative stimulus. Nonetheless, we cannot unambiguously attribute little Albert's responses to conditioning. We cannot even rule out the consequences of Albert's responses to the struck bar; after all, these responses led the experimenters to terminate the procedure for a week.

The problem, however, is not restricted to Watson and Rayner. Once we become alert to the possibility of response consequences in supposed conditioning procedures, we can often find them. For example, in early demonstrations of limb withdrawal elicited by shock, the method of attaching the electrodes was often a matter of indifference. Yet if both electrodes are attached to a dog's leg, a flexion cannot prevent shock delivery, whereas with either or both electrodes attached to

the floor on which the dog's paws rests, a flexion prevents or terminates shock delivery because once lifted from the electrodes the paw no longer completes the electrical circuit. In fact, the classic defensive reflex of Bechterev (1933) typically had both electrodes on a surface the organism touched, so that a response prevented or terminated the shock; Bechterev was therefore probably studying avoidance and escape behavior rather than respondent conditioning. Recognizing the different implications of the two methods of electrode placement was an important step in the evolution of the distinction between operant and respondent behavior (cf. Schlosberg, 1937; Skinner, 1935b; see also Kimmel, 1976).

Once consequences became implicated in a few cases of presumed respondent conditioning, it was tempting to seek them in all. For example, even with both electrodes attached to a dog's leg in defensive conditioning, might not the flexion have consequences? Suppose that a bell reliably precedes electric shock. How can we tell whether the shock is as aversive when it passes through a flexed rather than an unflexed limb? In defensive conditioning, the conditional flexion is ordinarily slower and different in magnitude than the unconditional flexion. Furthermore, if the dog's leg is already flexed when shock is delivered, less postural adjustment is required than if the dog stands on all fours and then shifts its weight to the remaining three legs when flexing the shocked leg (Wagner, Thomas, & Norton, 1967). Clearly salivation too has consequences; it affects taste and swallowing in the case of dry food and dilution of the solution in the case of acid on the tongue.

The introduction of respondent conditioning into learning theory began with attempts to reduce all instances of operant learning to special cases of respondent conditioning, but with such arguments the situation had been turned around. The case was made that all instances of respondent conditioning could be interpreted in terms of response consequences that were earlier unnoticed. The next step was to observe that autonomic responses such as salivation and constriction or dilation of blood vessels were often accompanied by somatic responses (i.e., action of the striate muscles, which produce skeletal movement). The position could then be taken that autonomic responses in respondent conditioning were artifacts, in that they incidentally accompanied behavior generated by operant or instrumental processes (Smith, 1954). The status of respondent conditioning therefore came to depend on demonstrations of conditioning that could not be interpreted in terms of the consequences of responding.

One approach was to see whether conditional responding could be modified by explicitly arranged consequences. If such consequences were ineffective, then the argument that the new reflex relation depended on other unidentified consequences would no longer be convincing. Sheffield (1965) therefore added consequences to the conditional salivation generated by the classical Pavlovian situation. Specifically, a conditional stimulus preceded food but food was omitted if the dog salivated on that trial. (The procedure is an example of negative punishment sometimes referred to as *omission training*). In other words, this arrangement converted the standard Pavlovian procedure to one in which the consequence of salivating was no food and the consequence of not salivating was food.

Salivation was not modified by its consequences in this procedure. Consider the performance of the dog Vicki. At the beginning of training, conditional salivation had not yet begun, and therefore tone was consistently followed by food. These circumstances produced conditional salivation, but in trials on which Vicki salivated, food was omitted and so conditional salivation decreased. Once conditional salivation decreased, the tone was again consistently followed by food and so conditional salivation reappeared. The cycle of conditional salivation, omitted food, decreased salivation, reinstatement of food, and return to conditional salivation was repeated, and for 40 days (800 trials) Vicki's cyclic conditional salivation remained fairly stable. Although Vicki could have received food on every trial by not salivating during the tone, Vicki did not learn to do so and received food on only some trials each day.

It would be premature to conclude that this settled the issue. A consequence effective as a reinforcer for one response may not be effective for another (Chapter 4). Food elicits salivation, so it is not surprising that salivating is ineffectively reinforced by food. Reductions of salivation have been shown when its consequence was the omission of a reinforcer, but the reinforcer was water, which does not itself elicit salivation (Miller & Carmona, 1967; cf. Chapter 6). Salivation, elicited in some circumstances, can be modified by its consequences in others. The issues are no longer those of reducing operant learning to respondent conditioning or vice versa, because too many lines of evidence distinguish between them (e.g., operant cases require responses but respondent conditioning may occur without responses, as when stimulus-stimulus contingencies arranged during paralysis by curare affect behavior after recovery from the paralysis; cf. Solomon & Turner, 1962).

AUTOSHAPING
AND AUTOMAINTENANCE

The cases of respondent conditioning so far have included both autonomic responses (e.g., salivation) and somatic or skeletal responses (e.g., leg flexion). Chapters 3 and 6 considered how these two classes contributed to theoretical distinctions between operant and respondent behavior. The demonstration that autonomic responses such as salivation could be modified by their consequences had substantial impact on these theories. That impact was paralleled by the demonstration that somatic or skeletal responses could be affected by respondent procedures. Both demonstrations implied that operant and respondent processes could not be distinguished by kinds of responses; the critical difference was instead in the respective response-stimulus and stimulus-stimulus contingencies.

We discussed earlier the ambiguity of experiments on conditional leg flexions to shock. The problem was that procedures could not be designed to guarantee that leg flexions would have no consequences. Perhaps partly for this reason, the demonstration of respondent conditioning of another skeletal response, the pigeon's key-peck, received special attention in a procedure called *autoshaping* (Brown & Jenkins, 1968; Schwartz & Gamzu, 1977). Because the key-peck was a common response for the study of consequential responding, it was important to determine the extent to which respondent processes might enter into those performances.

Autoshaping originated as a convenient alternative to shaping the key-peck by successive approximations (Chapter 6). It begins with a pigeon that eats reliably from the feeder but has not pecked the key. At intervals the key is lit and several seconds later the feeder is operated independently of the pigeon's behavior. Thus, the lit key becomes

a stimulus that signals food. The food occasions eating, which in the pigeon includes pecking. We therefore might say that food is a US and that pecking food is a UR. After a few presentations of lit key and then feeder, the pigeon begins to face and move toward the key when it lights. Within perhaps fewer than 10 and rarely more than 100 trials, the pigeon pecks the key whenever it is lit. After pecking is generated by autoshaping, the continuation of the procedure is called *automaintenance*. *Autoshaping* and *automaintenance* simply distinguish the changes in behavior leading up to the first peck from the maintained behavior following this peck.

In autoshaping and automaintenance, food deliveries occur independently of behavior. It is therefore difficult to attribute autoshaped pecking to its consequences. Nevertheless, once such pecking begins it is often followed by food. An argument based solely on the observation that no consequences of pecking are obvious may not be persuasive. Autoshaped pecks were therefore studied in omission procedures analogous to Sheffield's experiment with salivation: Food was delivered after the key light only on trials in which the pigeon did not peck the key (Williams & Williams, 1969). As with salivation, pecks often occurred in a substantial proportion of trials even though they caused the omission of food. The pecking presumably stabilized at a level at which enough trials occurred without pecks (and therefore with food) to maintain pecking in the other trials.

When food is repeatedly presented to a hungry pigeon, pecking becomes a dominant component of the behavior between food presentations (cf. Chapter 3 on interim and terminal behavior). Autoshaped key-pecking in the pigeon may therefore be interpreted as terminal behavior under the stimulus control of the key light: Pecks generated by repeated food presentations occur mainly during the key light, and come to be directed toward it so strongly that they strike the key and are recorded as key-pecks. Once autoshaped pecking begins, it may be maintained indefinitely by repeated presentations of key light and food even though it has no obvious consequences (in fact, relative to keeping its head in or near the feeder, the pigeon may delay its access to food by pecking the key).

Both the production and the maintenance of key-pecking in autoshaping and automaintenance have the critical features that define respondent conditioning, so the respondent vocabulary is appropriate. The key light is a CS. It acquires its capacity to elicit a CR, key-pecking, through its correlation with food. Food is the US and it elicits a UR, pecking. As in other cases, the contingent relation between key light and food, and not their pairing, determines whether autoshaped pecking occurs (e.g., Bilbrey & Winokur, 1973).

A distinctive feature of autoshaping is the directed nature of the conditional response: Pecks generated by the key light could occur anywhere in the chamber (in the air, at the wall, around the food hopper); instead, they are directed at the key. The inverse relation also holds: Pigeons tend to move away from stimuli correlated with the absence of food (Wasserman, Franklin, & Hearst, 1974). For example, if a green key precedes food but a red key does not, autoshaped pecking occurs during green but the pigeon moves to the opposite side of the chamber during red. The directed nature of autoshaped pecking has been called *sign-tracking* (Hearst & Jenkins, 1974). A response must be emitted before it can be reinforced, and it may sometimes be emitted because it was once elicited. Perhaps then the behavioral relations that occur in autoshaping are prototypes of the processes from which operant behavior evolves.

Chapter 8 considered behavioral contrast, the increase in response rate in an unchanged component of a multiple schedule when the reinforcement rate in the other component decreased. One account of behavioral contrast is that autoshaped pecks, generated by the differential correlation of the multiple-schedule stimuli with food, are added to operant pecks. Some experiments have distinguished two classes of key-pecks on the basis of duration and topography (e.g., Keller, 1974; Schwartz & Williams, 1972).

The topography of autoshaped pecks is affected more by the US than by contingencies (Jenkins & Moore, 1973). For example, the pigeon's peck at grain is briefer than and differs in form from the pigeon's drinking. Autoshaped pecks produced by key light and food resemble eating pecks whereas those produced by key light and water resemble drinking. When autoshaped pecks are based upon food, the pigeon looks as though it were eating the key, but when they are based upon water, the pigeon looks as though it were drinking the key. On the other hand, autoshaping can occur even when the US elicits behavior unrelated to pecking. For example, pigeons will come to peck a lighted key if the key light is reliably followed not by food but rather by access to a social area (Peele & Ferster, 1982).

SUMMARY

Our treatment of the basic components of respondent conditioning, CS's and US's and CR's and UR's, was followed by a brief survey of types of conditioning, including simultaneous, trace, delay, temporal, and backward conditioning. We distinguished between pairings and stimulus-stimulus contingencies defined by conditional probabilities. We also examined findings with various stimulus combinations in conditioning, including overshadowing and blocking, inhibitory stimuli in stimulus compounds, sensory preconditioning, and second-order conditioning. We concluded with an example of the conditioning of a skeletal response, the pigeon's peck, in autoshaping and automaintenance.

Section B   **Operant-Respondent Interactions: Emotion**

Operant and respondent processes can interact when respondent-conditioning procedures are combined with operant or consequential procedures. For example, a stimulus that reliably precedes or signals shock may not only elicit leg flexion; it may also interfere with behavior that has been maintained by its consequences, such as lever-pressing maintained by food rein-

forcement. We sometimes describe comparable behavior in humans in terms of fear or anxiety; procedures such as these are often regarded as relevant to emotion.

CONDITIONING AND EMOTION

Stimuli that signal the presentation of other stimuli can be superimposed on baselines of ongoing operant behavior. For example, suppose a rat's lever-pressing is maintained by an interval schedule of food reinforcement; from time to time a tone is presented; at the end of each tone, shock is delivered. In these circumstances, the tone typically reduces lever-pressing, especially as the time of shock delivery approaches. This phenomenon, originally demonstrated by Estes and Skinner (1941), has been given various names: *anxiety, conditioned suppression,* and *conditioned emotional response,* or *CER.* It is illustrated in Figure 9–8, which shows development of

FIGURE 9–8 Development of and recovery from suppression during a preaversive stimulus. A rat's lever-presses were maintained by a VI 2-min schedule of food reinforcement (reinforcers are not included in the cumulative records). The left records show the effects of superimposing a 3-minute tone followed by electric shock on baseline lever-pressing. The dashed vertical lines and downward displacements of the pen mark off periods of tone. By trial 27, lever-pressing was almost completely suppressed by the tone. The right records show recovery from suppression when the tone was no longer followed by shock. (Adapted from Geller, 1960, Figure 3)

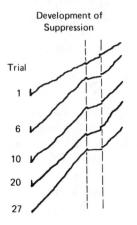
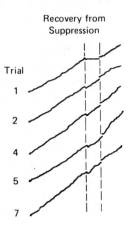

and then recovery from suppression (Geller, 1960). The rat's lever-presses were maintained by a VI 2-min schedule of food reinforcement; 3-minute presentations of tone were followed by shock. After the tone came to suppress responding, shock was discontinued and lever-pressing in tone recovered to earlier levels.

The procedure is an instance of respondent conditioning: One stimulus, tone, signals another stimulus, shock. (The shock is presumed to be aversive, so the tone is called a *preaversive* stimulus.) This is another case in which behavior produced by the CS differs from that produced by the US. The tone suppresses reinforced lever-pressing, but lever-pressing begins again soon after shock has been delivered.

If we looked more closely at the rat's behavior during the tone, we would find that these contingencies had affected many other classes of responses besides lever-pressing (i.e., heart rate, respiration; cf. Blackman, 1977; Rescorla & Solomon, 1967). We are most likely to invoke the language of emotion when an event has widespread effects across many different response classes, so we may be tempted to speak of the rat's fear or anxiety. If we do so, we must recognize that such terms do not explain the rat's behavior. It would not do to say later that the rat stopped pressing the lever during tone because it was afraid; the effect of the tone on the rat's lever-pressing led us to speak in terms of the rat's fear in the first place.

Our language of emotions is complex. We speak of emotions in others and in ourselves on the basis of both situations and the behavior that occurs in those situations (cf. Bem, 1967; Ortony & Turner, 1990). For example, we might speak of the behavior produced by preaversive stimuli in terms of fear or anxiety, but if we observed aggressive behavior directed to-

ward another we would be more likely to speak of anger. In either case, we must be clear that these are names for certain behavioral effects; they do not explain. Consider, for example, the question of why someone acts in a particular way. We might answer that the person is sad or depressed. If asked how we know, we might answer that we can tell from how the person acts. But what more have we said than that the person is acting that way because the person is acting that way? It would be more useful to know that the person is acting that way because of some specific event, such as the loss of a job or the breakup of a love affair.

A practical application of our understanding of preaversive stimuli is provided by the treatment of children under intensive care, as in hospital burn units (Cataldo, Bessman, Parker, Pearson, & Rogers, 1979). These children are subjected to unpredictable and uncontrollable aversive events at any time of the day or night: injections, changes of dressings, intravenous feedings, and so on. A typical outcome of their long-term care is that they become lethargic and withdrawn; they do not react to events around them (cf. learned helplessness in Chapter 7). For these children, the hospital setting has become one massive preaversive stimulus.

Some help can be provided by giving the children at least some control over part of the environment some of the time (e.g., in social interactions with visitors or ward staff, in choices of meals whenever possible, and so on), but constraints on care delivery may limit the feasibility of this approach. Another alternative is suggested by the analysis in terms of preaversive stimuli. If a red light turns on over the child's bed at least 10 minutes before any aversive procedure is started, the red light becomes a preaversive stimulus. Its onset will become aversive too, but the advantage of the procedure is that the absence of the red light becomes a safety signal, a time when the child is safe from aversive medical procedures (the safety may be relative, in that the child may still be in pain some of the time and emergencies may sometimes not allow time for use of the red light; in any case, relative safety is better than none at all). When such procedures are used, the absence of the light becomes a time when the child's physiological reactions to the conditions that signal aversive events can be relaxed and when behavior with reinforcing events as a consequence is more likely to be maintained; these outcomes may also facilitate the child's recovery.

PREAVERSIVE AND PREAPPETITIVE STIMULI

Although the language of emotion is important in our interactions with other people, it has not proved particularly useful in behavioral analyses of the effects of preaversive stimuli. Instead, the interactions between respondent conditioning and operant behavior, as when preaversive or preappetitive stimuli are superimposed on reinforced responding, have been analyzed more effectively in terms of experimental parameters, such as baseline reinforcement schedule, baseline response rate, and so on.

The finding that positively reinforced responding can be suppressed by preaversive stimuli (Estes & Skinner, 1941) was later supplemented by the finding that negatively reinforced responding (avoidance; see Chapter 5) can be enhanced by such stimuli (Sidman, Herrnstein, & Conrad, 1957). In other words, a rat whose lever-pressing avoids shock may increase rather than decrease its lever-pressing during a stimulus that precedes an unavoidable or inevitable shock. This enhanced responding has been called conditional or conditioned enhancement or facilitation or acceleration. Once such enhanced responding develops during negatively reinforced responding, it may continue with responding maintained by positive reinforcement. For example, rhesus monkeys' lever-pressing maintained by orange juice reinforcers was originally suppressed during a clicking noise that preceded shock, but after the monkeys acquired a history of lever-pressing that avoided shock and were returned to the initial procedure, lever-pressing during the preaversive stimulus was enhanced rather than suppressed (Herrnstein & Sidman, 1958).

The situations were then extended to superimposing preappetitive rather than preaversive stimuli on baseline operant behavior. For example, a key light that preceded response-independent food deliveries increased pigeons' key-pecking when superimposed on key-pecking maintained by DRL reinforcement (Herrnstein & Morse, 1957). By analogy to the labeling of suppression during preaversive stimuli as anxiety, it was tempting to speak of such enhancing effects of preappetitive stimuli in terms of joy. The enhancement of positively reinforced and suppression of negatively reinforced responding by preappetitive stimuli (e.g., Leitenberg, 1966; Rescorla & Solomon, 1967) seemed to parallel the suppression of positively reinforced and enhancement of negatively reinforced responding by preaversive stimuli. But the contingencies were complicated (e.g., they sometimes allowed autoshaped key-pecks to combine with the effects of preappetitive stimuli), and continued study of preaversive and preappetitive stimuli showed such an account to be oversimplified (e.g., Kelleher, Riddle, & Cook, 1963; Azrin & Hake, 1969; Blackman, 1977).

As an example, Figure 9–9 shows that shock level and baseline response rate jointly determine whether preaversive stimuli suppress or enhance a rat's lever-pressing reinforced with food (Blackman, 1968). During red light and noise, lever-presses were reinforced according to a DRL 15-second schedule with a limited hold of 5 seconds (i.e., a press was reinforced only if emitted within 15 to 20 seconds of the last press); during white light and no noise, an FI 20-second schedule operated with a 5-second limited hold. In these multiple DRL FI schedules, DRL components maintained lower response rates than did FI components. Later, occasional 1-minute tones that preceded brief shock were added and shock level was varied to determine the relation between shock magnitude and degree of suppression. Figure 9–9 (left) shows response rate during tone (the preaversive stimulus) as a function of shock level. In the

FI component, response rate consistently decreased with increasing shock level. In the DRL component, however, response rate increased at low shock levels and decreased only at higher levels. Figure 9–9 (right) shows the same data converted to a suppression ratio, the change in response rate expressed relative to baseline response rate.

The different effects for FI and DRL performance show how behavioral effects can vary as a function of baseline conditions. Superimposing preaversive stimuli on reinforced responding is a respondent-conditioning procedure, and it has opposite effects depending upon the baseline performance upon which it is superimposed. Similar types of interactions are critical to psychopharmacology, the analysis of the effects of drugs on behavior; there again, the effect of a drug may vary considerably depending on baseline performance.

FIGURE 9–9 Response rates (left) and suppression ratios (right) during a preaversive stimulus. Effects of the preaversive stimulus depended jointly on the level of shock that followed it and the schedule that maintained responding. The data are from a rat whose lever-pressing was maintained by multiple DRL FI schedules of food reinforcement. With FI responding, the preaversive stimulus suppressed responding at all shock levels; with DRL responding, it enhanced responding at low levels and suppressed it only at higher levels. (Adapted from Blackman, 1968, Figure 2)

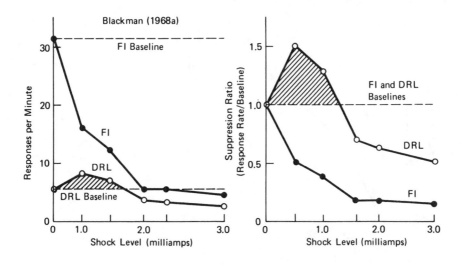

The effects of preaversive stimuli are determined not only by properties of baseline performance but also by properties of the schedule of stimulus presentation. For example, suppression varies jointly with the duration of a preaversive stimulus and its frequency of presentation. The degree of suppression also depends in part on how much the reduced response rate affects the rate of reinforcement: Less suppression occurs when the reduction in responding greatly reduces the reinforcers per session and more when the reduction only slightly affects reinforcers per session (Stein, Sidman, & Brady, 1958; Smith, 1974).

As with the other cases of respondent conditioning, the effects of preaversive and preappetitive stimuli on operant behavior depend not on pairings with aversive or appetitive stimuli but rather on stimulus-stimulus contingencies. The point is illustrated in Figure 9–10 (cf. Figure 9–3), which shows suppression of a

rat's reinforced lever-pressing produced by various combinations of shock probabilities in the presence and absence of preaversive stimuli (Rescorla, 1968; see also Davis & McIntire, 1969). For example, if 40 percent of the preaversive stimuli are paired with shock (probability of shock given CS = 0.40), a range of effects from complete suppression to no suppression at all can be obtained depending on the probability of shock when the preaversive stimulus is absent. (The different contingencies are sometimes spoken of in terms of predictive value: The preaversive stimulus is said to have predictive value when the probability of shock is different in its presence than in its absence and no predictive value when shock is equally probable in each condition; cf. the stimulus-stimulus contingency space of Figure 9–4 and Keller, Ayres, & Mahoney, 1977).

Responding in the presence of a signaling stimulus is affected by its relation to

FIGURE 9–10 Suppression during a preaversive stimulus (CS) as a function of different shock probabilities during its presence and absence. For example, with a shock probability during the preaversive stimulus of 0.4, or *p(SHOCK/CS)* = 0.4, the suppression of lever-pressing depended on shock probability in its absence, or *p(SHOCK/no CS)*. Effects ranged from complete suppression when the latter probability was zero to none when it equalled *p(SHOCK/CS)*. The same data are plotted in both halves of the figure; *p(SHOCK/CS)* is the parameter on the left and *p(SHOCK/no CS)* is that on the right. In this suppression ratio, baseline equals 0.5. (Adapted from Rescorla, 1968, Figure 3.)

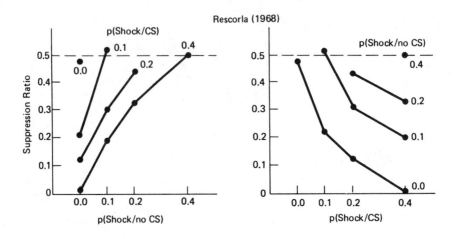

the stimulus that it signals. In the classical Pavlovian case of respondent conditioning, it seemed at first as though one stimulus substituted for the other, but with preaversive and preappetitive stimuli we have seen again that respondent phenomena cannot be treated as stimulus substitution. As usual, it is appropriate to recall that stimuli have multiple functions, and it seems especially likely that such functions would have to be taken into account in situations that combine operant and respondent procedures. We may recall that respondent phenomena were invoked in discussions of the maintenance of operant behavior (e.g., the two-factor theory of avoidance; see Chapter 5). If we demonstrate that the warning stimulus in an avoidance procedure becomes aversive as avoidance responding develops (e.g., Hoffman & Fleshler, 1962), we can conclude that its aversiveness came about through respondent processes, but this does not mean that its aversiveness was necessary for the acquisition of avoidance responding (cf. Chapter 5).

Section C   **Biological Constraints on Learning**

Chapter 2 examined the joint phylogenic and ontogenic sources of behavior and learning. The phylogenic origins of behavior can impose constraints not only on the stimuli and responses that enter into operant and respondent contingencies but also on the relations that can be established among the stimuli and responses. This section considers a few examples.

SENSORY CONSTRAINTS

With respect to stimuli, some of the most obvious constraints on learning depend on the organism's sensory systems. For example, a pigeon's behavior is more likely to be affected by visual stimuli than is a bat's, whereas a bat's behavior is more likely to be affected by auditory stimuli than is a pigeon's. If an organism's sensory capacities are not taken into account, results of learning experiments can be misleading. For example, rats have ears much smaller than ours, so the sound frequencies to which they are most sensitive are much higher than those for humans. The experimenter who arranges procedures using stimuli that are easily heard by rats may not be able to tell whether the stimuli are on or off, but the one who arranges procedures with auditory stimuli that are easily heard by humans may incorrectly conclude that the rat learns slowly and with difficulty.

Experimenters must be alert to the possibility that stimuli to which they are insensitive are important discriminative stimuli for the organism they are studying. For example, the results of early studies of maze learning must be interpreted with caution because of the rat's olfactory sensitivity. If the maze is not thoroughly cleaned between subjects, a rat's performance may depend on odor trails left by other rats rather than on what it had learned on its own earlier runs through the maze. Similarly, if the odor of a food US reaches a dog during the presentation of the CS in a respondent procedure, the dog's salivation after the CS may depend on the odor rather than on the CS-US contingency.

Constraints can involve stimulus configurations as well as single dimensions of stimuli. For example, in contagious yawning one person's yawn elicits yawns in others. The effectiveness of the yawn as an eliciting stimulus is determined by a complex combination of facial features that includes movements of the eyes as well as the mouth (Provine, 1989b). In humans, the properties of faces that are involved in yawns and smiles and frowns have be-come important over a long phylogenic history of social behavior (Provine & Fi-scher, 1989). If they need to be learned at all, they are more easily learned than are arbitrary geometric configurations.

MOTOR CONSTRAINTS

Anatomical constraints on responding pose no problem. We don't expect flight to be the same in pigeons and bats and bees (and we don't even ask about the possibil-ity of flight in the rat). Species differences in motor capacity are more likely to raise questions when they do not have a clear anatomical basis.

In a study of leg movements in infancy, Thelen and Fisher (1983) recorded the tim-ing and topography with which 3-month-old infants kicked at a mobile. The visual consequences of kicking varied: Some in-fants saw the mobile move when they kicked at it and others did not. These con-sequences affected the rate and vigor of kicking but not the temporal coordina-tions among the flexion and extension phases of the kick. In other words, some features of the kicks were modifiable but others were not. Similarly, contingencies may affect the direction in which you walk but not the detailed coordinations of mus-cles and joints by which you do so.

Locomotion has both phylogenic and ontogenic components, and the details of motor coordination do not arise from con-tingencies between responses and stimuli. Coordinations in walking involve rela-tions among the muscles within a given limb and among the limbs and other parts of the body (e.g., the relaxation of one mus-cle as an opposing muscle contracts). Many aspects of these coordinations oper-ate independently of the environment (cf. Gallistel, 1980; see also von Holst, 1939;

Gray, 1953); they are often called *motor programs*. The horse trainer does not have to shape the details of stepping or the order of leg movements as a horse speeds up from a walk to a trot to a canter to a gallop. A show horse might be taught spe-cial steps, such as the rack, but even in these cases the new topography modu-lates existing patterns.

Another example is flight in birds. How do the wings come to beat in synchrony? Must the bird fly to discover that it cannot stay in the air by flapping with only one wing or by bringing one wing down while raising the other? The relevant experiments deprived hatchling chicks of flapping and flight experience by wing restraint or other means and then tested their wing coordina-tion at various later stages (e.g., Provine, 1981). Flapping was synchronous from the start, demonstrating that this aspect of flight does not depend on environmental contingencies. Many aspects of flight coor-dination are "prewired"; they are built into bird behavior. Nevertheless, the environ-ment remains important in two ways: The evolution of flight in birds depended on the aerodynamic environments of their ances-tors; where and when a bird flies, though not the details of its flight coordination, are determined by its present environment.

Species differ in many ways, and con-straints on the topography of responses must not be confused with constraints on their functions. This point is illustrated by contrasting a cat stalking a mouse in a natural environment with a cow that is taught to stalk:

...given a prey which bears the same rela-tion to a cow, in speed and mutual stimula-tion, as a mouse does to a cat, it should not be too difficult to set up contingencies under which a cow will "stalk"—that is, approach slowly when at a distance in order not to alert the prey and then move quickly to

capture. The prey would have to be something like an animated bundle of corn. (Skinner, 1977, p. 1011)

Skinner then points out that this "stalking" by the cow, in speed and other characteristics, would look quite different from
the stalking by a cat. Nevertheless, the
functional properties of the behavior of
cow and cat are similar, even if they differ
considerably in structural details.

CONSTRAINTS ON CONSEQUENCES

We may extend our examples to the capacities of various stimuli to reinforce or to
serve as US's. Like sensory and motor capacities, these also differ across species. It
hardly needs to be said that the effectiveness of reinforcers has a phylogenic basis.
An organism for which neither food nor
water was ever effective as a reinforcer
would hardly be likely to live long enough
to pass its genes on to another generation.
But more subtle properties of environments
may also be important, such as the sensory
consequences that maintain exploratory behavior or the novel consequences that may
make an organism cautious in sampling an
unknown food or familiar food in an unknown place (cf. *neophobia*; e.g., Mitchell,
Scott, & Williams, 1973).

Before the relativity of reinforcement
was recognized, findings in which standard
reinforcers for a species failed to have their
characteristic effects were hard to deal with.
Breland and Breland (1961) used several
cases to argue against the generality of reinforcement as a behavioral process.

In one demonstration with raccoons,
food was delivered when a raccoon picked
up coins from the ground and deposited
them in a container. After some repetitions
of the procedure, the raccoon began persis-
tently to rub the coins together instead of

releasing them into the container. The
Brelands and others saw this outcome as
invalidating the principle of reinforcement.
But a relevant aspect of raccoon behavior is
that raccoons ordinarily rub and wash their
food before eating it. The coins apparently
provided a better opportunity for this behavior than the food that was supposed to
function as a reinforcer. In other words,
food was not effective as a reinforcer because rubbing had become sufficiently
more probable than eating. It is likely that
an opportunity for rubbing would have
been effective as a reinforcer for other responses, perhaps including eating.

Given that reinforcement relations are
based upon relative probabilities of responses, the different behavioral hierarchies of different species inevitably
constrain what they can learn. When an
experimental procedure is applied, there is
no guarantee that it will be effective. A
procedure that leads to learning with one
response or organism may not do so with
different responses or organisms, and a
response or an organism affected by one
procedure may be unaffected by others.
An essential part of the analysis of learning is to explore its limits.

PREPAREDNESS

Constraints may also involve the possible
relations between the stimuli and responses that enter into operant and respondent contingencies. Such relations
were implicit in the examples of constraints on consequences, because it was
necessary to treat them in terms of the
relative probabilities of the reinforced responses and the responses occasioned by
the reinforcers. We considered other examples in the treatment of species-specific
defense reactions in Chapter 5. For example, the ease with which avoidance

responding was acquired and maintained depended on species-specific relations between various avoidance responses and aversive stimuli.

Some relations between discriminative stimuli and responses may be easier to learn than others. For example, does it help if the stimuli and responses share common properties, as in responding on the left to a stimulus on the left and on the right to one on the right, instead of responding left to green and right to red? In the first case, locations are relevant properties of both the stimuli and the responses, but in the second stimulus qualities are correlated with response locations (e.g., Miller & Bowe, 1982). The shift from location to quality might be more important than a reversal of locations (recall Stratton's adaptation to inverting prisms; Chapter 4). Such relations may be crucial to the design of human-machine systems and in the mastery of motor skills (e.g., Bauer & Miller, 1982; Glencross, 1977; Mazur, 1986, Chapter 12).

We have considered cases involving relations between discriminative stimuli and responses, and between responses and reinforcers. Phylogenic contingencies may have prepared organisms to learn only some of the many possible relations among stimuli and responses in operant and respondent procedures. The concept of *preparedness* grew out of the observation that discrimination learning may be a function of the context of responses and reinforcers within which it occurs (cf. Seligman, 1970; Schwartz, 1974). Its significance was established through the analysis of a phenomenon called *bait-shyness* or *taste-aversion learning*, a variety of discrimination learning based upon differential punishment (but see also Rozin & Kalat, 1971).

In experiments on taste aversion, a rat stops eating a food if it later becomes sick (Revusky & Garcia, 1970). Nausea or other systemic consequences of eating can punish eating even though they follow eating only after a considerable delay. To study the role of discriminative stimuli, Garcia and Koelling (1966) let thirsty rats drink water sweetened by saccharin; their drinking was accompanied by clicks and flashes of light triggered electronically by their licks. In other words, the rats drank water that was bright and noisy as well as sweet. In one group, drinking was followed by X-irradiation that later produced sickness. In a second group, drinking was followed by shock. Later, the drinking of each group was measured when a sweet solution was presented and when drinking was accompanied by noise and light.

Figure 9–11 summarizes the results. Rats that had been X- irradiated drank less

FIGURE 9–11 Percent normal fluid intake of rats whose drinking of sweetened water was accompanied by clicks and lights. In one group, drinking was followed by X-irradiation; in a second, it was followed by electric shock. The discriminative stimulus that became effective in reducing drinking depended on the nature of the punisher. (From Garcia & Koelling, 1966, as presented by Revusky & Garcia, 1970, Figure 9)

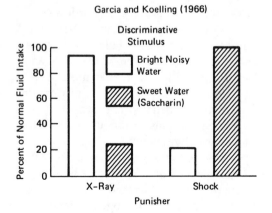

Garcia and Koelling (1966)

sweetened water, but their drinking was not affected by noise and light; those that had been shocked drank less when drinking was accompanied by noise and light, but their drinking was not affected by whether the water was sweetened. In other words, when the aversive stimulus was the delayed systemic consequence of X-irradiation, the rats learned only its relation to the taste of the water consumed earlier, but when the aversive stimulus was shock the rats learned only its relation to the external noise and light that preceded it. The delayed effects of X-irradiation punished the drinking of sweetened water, and the immediate effects of shock punished drinking accompanied by noise and light. It is not enough to say that the rats learned some stimuli or some responses more easily than others; they were predisposed to learn different relations among discriminative stimuli and contingencies in the different situations.

Revusky and Garcia (1970) discuss the implications of these findings in the context of a thought experiment in which you find $100 that has been left for you

by an insane billionaire experimenter because, two hours ago at lunch, you ate gooseberry pie for dessert instead of your usual apple pie. The experimenter wanted to increase the future probability that you would eat gooseberry pie. It is very unlikely that this experiment will be successful....Hundreds of events are bound to occur during the two hours between consumption of the gooseberry pie and the receipt of the $100. The odds are very great that you would have associated one of these intervening events with the $100....The results of our thought experiment are really shocking. We have selected an arbitrary reward of great potency and a response of which you probably were well aware...[and] we reached the conclusion

that the nature of the environment precluded association over a two-hour delay. (Revusky & Garcia, 1970, p. 20)

These investigators then suggest an alternative thought experiment: Instead of finding money, you get sick:

Since the gooseberry pie was new to you, you would probably conclude that the pie caused the illness. Here association over a two-hour delay agrees with our daily experience....But why has a change from a consequence of $100 to a consequence of sickness changed the situation?...There seems to be only one reasonable answer....The fact that infra-humans also can associate over long delays strongly suggests that there is an innate selective association of flavors with physiological aftereffects and, what is more important, a selective failure to associate irrelevant stimuli with toxicosis. (Revusky & Garcia, 1970, p. 21)

Such experiments are of course complicated by other differences between the two types of consequences. For example, electric shock has a more abrupt onset than do the gastric symptoms of X-irradiation. Furthermore, a case can be made that these experiments involve respondent relations rather than or in addition to operant ones. If respondent contingencies are arranged with taste as a trace CS and nausea as a US, the taste is likely to acquire its aversiveness as a result of its contingent relation to nausea even though the contingency operates over a delay.

The analysis of behavior is concerned with identifying the origins of particular instances of behavior. With both operant and respondent contingencies, our conclusions about what is learned must take both phylogeny and ontogeny into account.

CHAPTER **10**

Social Learning

The etymologies of the personal pronouns probably extend back to the very earliest of human languages. The histories of I *and its relatives (such as* ego *and* ich*) may be separate from those of* me *and* my *and* mine. *Some forms of* I *have a verblike quality, and pronouns are incorporated into verbs in some languages (e.g., as in the Latin* sum *and* es *for* I am *and* you are*). The distinctions among these and other personal pronouns, such as* you *and* she *and* they *and* he *and* us *and* it, *may be so fundamental as to be irreducible.*

   Self, *which is related to* sibling, separate, select, *and* ethnic, *carries an implication of possession (cf. the sense of its relative,* solitary, *as on one's own).* Other *has the etymological sense of the other one of two:* al- *(other) plus* ter *(two), as in* alternative. Community, *like* communicate, *implies a having in common.* Common *is a derivative of* con- *(with) and the Indo-European* mei- *(to go or*

move together with); some relatives are immune, mutate, migrate, *and* mean.

One variety of selection is the sort that operates on populations of organisms over successive generations. This was considered in Chapter 2, in the context of Darwin's treatment of evolution in terms of natural selection. Another variety is the sort that operates on populations of responses within the lifetime of the individual organism. Much of our discussion of the effects of consequences in subsequent chapters was concerned with this variety of selection. Organisms persist in doing some things and they stop doing others; the procedure of shaping provided an explicit example of the selection of behavior by its consequences.

   Chapter 2 also mentioned a third variety of selection. It too operated on behavior, but not simply on the behavior of the individual organism. Whatever behavior an organism acquires within its own lifetime, that behavior is eventually lost if the organism cannot pass it on to others. Once social learning becomes possible, however, behavior that has been learned can survive the death of the organism that learned it. The behavior then survives in what others do, perhaps not only in the behavior of descendants but even in the behavior of others who are genetically unrelated.

Section A   Kinds of Social Contingencies

Learning from others is particularly important in human behavior. A very substantial part of what any of us knows is what we have learned from others, and much has been explicitly taught, either in the informal context of interactions between family members or in the formal context of educational institutions. But the earliest types of social learning must have been much simpler. At what point did some organisms begin to learn to do things merely by watching what happened as other organisms did them?

We may think of observational learning as commonplace because it so often enters into human behavior. But it is not clear how much of it goes on even among nonhuman warm-blooded vertebrates (mammals and birds), and there is hardly any evidence at all for it in invertebrates (e.g., insects). Among primates, one widely cited example involved the feeding of sweet potatoes to macaque monkeys on a reserve in Japan that included a beach (Kawamura, 1963). The potatoes typically became sandy, but one juvenile monkey eventually originated the practice of removing the sand from the potatoes by rinsing them in the ocean. This practice then spread to other members of the colony.

Human cultures provide many examples of the social selection of behavior, the selection that occurs as behavior is passed on from one individual to another (cf. Harris, 1977; Skinner, 1981). Certain ways of raising children, of obtaining and preparing food, of building shelters, and of dealing with group members and with outsiders survive over successive generations. Some practices can spread to other groups who are not close genetic relatives of those who began them. In contemporary Western culture, for example, ethnic foods are prepared and eaten by many who are not members of the ethnic groups that originated them.

Some behavior that is socially transmitted survives because of its consequences. In early human history, the person who learned from someone else how to make a stone tool or fire or a garment was probably also more likely to survive long enough to pass the behavior on to someone else than a person who could not learn in that way (in every variety of selection, the selection operates at the level of the survival of individual members and not at the level of the survival of the group). The survival of other patterns of behavior may involve more complex contingencies.

Consider patterns of child rearing. Suppose that the children reared according to most patterns are as likely as adults to rear their own children according to one pattern as according to any other. But suppose also that a very few patterns work so that when the children become adults they are likely to rear their own children in the same way as their parents had reared them; these might be called self-replicating patterns of child rearing. In a large population, whenever one of the self-regulating patterns happens to be used by some parents it will be used again in the next generation, but the other patterns will come and go. Little by little, over many generations, the self-replicating patterns will displace the ones that are not self-replicating. Once traditional patterns of child rearing originate in this way, they are likely to survive for very long periods of time.

In earlier discussions of the first two varieties of selection, natural selection and operant selection, we noted that evolution and shaping depended upon variable populations on which selection could operate. Similar constraints exist at the level of cultural selection. For example, cultural practices that favor ethnic diversity may have advantages over ones that do not simply because they allow such variability.

LEARNING ABOUT OTHERS

In many situations, the discriminative stimuli provided by other organisms are more important than those provided by inanimate objects and events. For example, parental investment in offspring may be wasted if the parent cannot discriminate between its own offspring and the offspring of others; potential mates must be distinguished from potential competitors, and among the potential mates the receptive must be distinguished from the unreceptive; and so on. In many organisms, such properties are correlated with anatomical features (e.g., colorful plumage in birds), but often behavior is the crucial dimension.

The study of animal communication is concerned with the many ways in which organisms produce stimuli that affect the behavior of other organisms. "Examples of communication are numerous: song in birds, frogs, and crickets; tail-wagging and hackle-raising in dogs; 'grinning' in chimpanzees; human gestures and language" (Dawkins, 1976, p. 67; see also Dawkins & Krebs, 1978). It is more appropriate to speak of such stimuli in terms of their behavioral effects than in terms of the information they carry. Just as it may be misleading to speak of genes as carriers of information about phylogenic contingencies (Dawkins, 1982), it may be misleading to speak of social stimuli as carriers of information (see also Chapter 11).

Releasers and fixed-action patterns provide many examples of effects of social stimuli. In some cases, sometimes called *social facilitation*, the behavior that serves as a social stimulus and the behavior produced by that stimulus are topographically similar, as when one bird's takeoff triggers the flight of the other birds in a flock, or as when a few galloping steers set off a stampede. Such cases may superficially look like imitation, but they are limited to a narrow range of response classes and so must be distinguished from it (cf. Provine, 1989a; Meltzoff & Moore, 1977; Field, Woodson, Greenberg, & Cohen, 1982).

Discriminating the behavior of other organisms, whether of one's own or of other species, has clear selective advantages. Consider, for example, the relation between predator and prey. If just one antelope in a herd is limping a little, the lion that notices the limp may be more likely to make a capture. The antelope that can tell the difference between one lion that has not eaten for a while and another that has just finished a meal may be more likely to move away in the safest direction. A predator that can distinguish whether it has been noticed by its prey has a distinct advantage over one that has not; an advantage also accrues to a prey that can distinguish whether it has been noticed by its predator. Such discriminations presumably have an extensive phylogenic history. For example, attention to the behavior of prey may be one dimension upon which natural selection operates in the evolution of predators, just as attention to the behavior of predators may be one dimension upon which natural selection operates in the evolution of prey. Following from such selection, discriminations of social behavior may become so important that they override other types of discriminations.

Discriminations of the behavior of others are at the heart of our human concept of intentionality (cf. Dennett, 1987): We say we understand someone's intentions when our discriminations of the various properties of that person's past and current behavior enable us to act appropriately with respect to what that person will do in the future. In fact, if discriminating one's own behavior is a special case of discriminating the behavior of others (e.g., Bem, 1967), it can be argued that this topic encompasses all of the phenomena considered under the rubric of intentionality. Judgments of the intentions of others are, above all, social judgments, and it takes no special assumptions about the selective contingencies that must have operated on social behavior both within and across species to see that such contingencies could shape well-prepared capacities for social discriminations.

Social discriminations within species have many functions. They may operate within dominance hierarchies, or in the defense of territory, or as isolating mechanisms that maintain the integrity of a group against intrusions from outsiders, or in the distribution of limited resources among group members. Within species that live as social groups, such as most primates, individuals learn what sorts of behavior to expect of others with whom they have extended contact. The cooperative behavior that can emerge in such contexts (e.g., de Waal, 1989) requires social discriminations that may be the precursors of the behavior toward others that is called empathy (cf. Hoffman, 1975).

LEARNING FROM OTHERS

It is one thing to learn about other organisms. It is another to learn something from them (cf. Zentall & Galef, 1988). Sometimes the behavior of one organism allows another to act on the basis of stimuli that are available only to the first organism, as when a vocal call from one monkey allows another monkey to escape from a predator it had not seen. Warning calls are well-doc-

umented in bird behavior (e.g., Kroodsma & Miller, 1982). In monkeys, predator calls can vary with kinds of predator, and the response to the call can depend on who the caller is and who the listener is (e.g., Gouzoules, Gouzoules, & Marler, 1984; Seyfarth, Cheney, & Marler, 1980).

Observational Learning

Learning based on observing the behavior of another organism is called *observational learning* (e.g., Zentall & Levine, 1972; another occasional term is *vicarious learning*: Bandura, 1986). Sometimes what seems to be observational learning involves simpler processes. For example, food preferences in rats are learned in social contexts; it is hard to get rid of rats by poisoning because rats that did not ingest the poison may avoid it based on their interactions with other rats that did and became sick or died. When rats come together they sniff and lick at each other, so that by smell and taste one rat becomes familiar with some properties of the food that the other has recently eaten (Galef & Stein, 1985). If the food is novel and the other rat is healthy, the first rat will later prefer that novel food over other novel foods, but if the other rat is sick, the first rat will avoid that novel food (in other words, this is a socially mediated taste aversion; cf. Chapter 9). The learning will not occur without some kind of contact (e.g., mouth to mouth, mouth to fur) between the two rats. One rat has learned about some novel foods from another, but the effect is better regarded as one in which the combination of food stimuli with social stimuli makes some foods more or less effective as reinforcers or as aversive stimuli than as one in which one rat has learned on the basis of observing what happens to another rat.

Observational learning has been compellingly demonstrated with rhesus monkeys (Mineka, Davidson, Cook, & Keir, 1984; Mineka, Kier, & Price, 1980). Monkeys in the wild show fear of snakes (by screaming and other agitated behavior, and by avoidance of the snake). Even if their parents fear snakes, monkeys reared in the laboratory who have had no experience with snakes do not; for example, if food is on the other side of a container with a snake in it, they will reach across the container for the food. But if the laboratory-reared monkeys then briefly observe one of their parents behave fearfully toward snakes, they too become fearful. Their fear is intense and persistent; if tested 3 months later it is undiminished. What they have learned about snakes is based only on observing the parent's behavior toward a snake. There may be a phylogenic component, however, because such observational learning is more likely to occur with snakes or snakelike objects than with some other types of stimuli.

Imitation

The most important difference between observational learning and imitation is that in imitation the observer's behavior corresponds to that of the organism that has been observed. Imitation does not imply that the imitating organism has learned something about contingencies. Not all imitations are advantageous. A coyote that sees another coyote step into a trap would do well not to imitate that behavior. A hatchling bird that has not yet grown its flight feathers would do well not to try to follow its parents when they fly from its treetop nest.

Following may sometimes be imitative. In one experiment (Neuringer & Neuringer, 1974), food-deprived pigeons learned to eat from the experimenter's hand. When the hand then approached and pecked the key, producing food, the pigeons followed the hand and began to peck the key. The procedure often worked more rapidly than shaping of the keypeck. Under natural conditions, young animals may learn to behave like their parents simply by following parental sources of food. But not all following is imitative. For example, when one organism leads another to food, the proximity of that organism may acquire reinforcing properties. Following then emerges as behavior shaped by natural contingencies (cf. the duckling's following of an imprinted stimulus; Chapter 3).

We call responding *imitative* when one organism duplicates the behavior modeled by another organism. But imitation may be limited to the duplication only of specific instances that have been explicitly taught, or it may include correspondences between the behavior of model and observer even in novel instances, when it is called *generalized imitation;* in the latter case, imitative responding is a class of responses that may be differentially reinforced or, in other words, it is a higher-order class of behavior (e.g., Baer, Peterson, & Sherman, 1967; Gewirtz & Stingle, 1968; Poulson & Kymissis, 1988; Poulson, Kymissis, Reeve, Andreatos, & Reeve, 1991).

We do not know the pertinent physical dimensions of imitative behavior. The behavior of model and observer may look the same to us, but we must not assume that this is also true for the observer. For example, if touching the head is modeled in the game of *Simon says*, the leader's hand is seen but not felt by the child whereas the child's own hand is felt but not seen. There is no simple correspondence between someone else's seen hand and one's own felt hand, so how does the child learn to imitate?

One way an organism can learn correspondences between the seen and felt parts of its body is by behaving in front of a mirror. Humans and some primates seem to learn these correspondences without explicit training (e.g., Gallup, 1979). For example, if a chimpanzee experienced with mirrors has a spot painted on its eyebrow while it is asleep, it will touch the spot when it next sees its face in a mirror. Such responses to one's own body have sometimes been spoken of in terms of *self-awareness*. With other organisms, such as the pigeon, the correspondences have to be taught, by training discriminations among stimuli seen in a mirror (Epstein, Lanza, & Skinner, 1981). For example, first a pigeon's pecks at blue cardboard dots pasted at various places on its body were shaped. Next, discriminations among blue dots reflected in a mirror were taught by presenting the dots behind holes in one wall of a chamber only when the pigeon faced a mirror on the opposite wall; each dot was gone by the time the pigeon turned around, but only pecks at the hole where it had appeared were reinforced. When another blue dot was then attached to the pigeon's breast while it wore a short bib that allowed it to see the dot in the mirror but not by looking down, the pigeon pecked down toward the dot on its body even though it was seeing the dot only in the mirror.

The novel performance does not demonstrate a sense of self in pigeons, but it does illustrate a special class of stimulus-control relations in which stimuli and responses vary together along a dimension (*continuous repertoires*: e.g., Wildemann & Holland, 1972); continuous changes in one produce corresponding changes in the other. Discriminated behavior with respect to a mirror involves correspondences between continuous movements and the seen positions of one's body. Other instances include keeping a moving object framed in a camera, mixing paints to match a sample color, tuning a musical instrument, and steering a car along a winding road. In human behavior imitation is a particularly important example of this type of stimulus-control relation; for the individual who already has an established imitative repertoire, new behavior can often be generated more quickly and effectively this way than by shaping or other means.

The Social Origins of Language

Another way to learn from another organism is through verbal behavior: One can be told about contingencies instead of observing them. But verbal behavior cannot have originated in that way, because descriptions of contingencies require sentences and the earliest forms of language must have begun with single words. We will have more to say about verbal behavior in the next chapter, but here we deal briefly with its possible origins in human social contingencies.

The simplest and most obvious function of verbal behavior is instructional: It is a way in which one organism gets another to do something. By talking, we change each other's behavior. Verbal behavior allows one to do things via the mediation of another organism. Sometimes what gets done involves nonverbal effects, as when we ask someone to move something or to carry something to us; sometimes it involves verbal effects, as when we change what someone else has to say about something. If the primary function of language is that it is an efficient way in which one individual can change the behavior of another, it follows that this behavior is quintessentially social and can emerge only in organisms whose behavior is already sensitive to social contingencies.

Assume that the calls of a primate leader once determined the behavior of members of its band as reliably as a releaser elicits a fixed-action pattern. At first the vocabulary of releasers was limited to just a few calls, not yet qualifying as verbal behavior but with relatively simple effects corresponding to those of words such as *come* or *go* or *stop*. Over many generations, perhaps millennia, a more extensive repertory of more varied calls was differentiated. If the details of these calls were weakly determined phylogenically, this rudimentary vocal control could later be supplemented by variations produced by ontogenic contingencies. For example, a dominant speaker might learn to attack a listener who does not respond in the characteristic way, thereby punishing disobedience (as we will see in Chapter 11, many contemporary contingencies continue to maintain the effectiveness of verbal control by reinforcing the following of instructions and punishing deviations from it).

Once vocal behavior had expanded to an extensive repertory including arbitrary as well as phylogenically determined calls, idiosyncratic repertories developed by particular leaders would ordinarily be lost to later generations until some way of producing this behavior in the leaders' successors had evolved. Thus, the next step in this evolution, perhaps long in coming, was the repetition by the follower of the leader's verbal behavior (see also Jaynes, 1976, for an alternative scenario). Once some individuals begin repeating what others say, verbal behavior becomes a kind of behavior that can survive within the behavior of the group, as a candidate for the third type of selection that we discussed earlier, that of cultural transmission. The stage is then set for human verbal memory, for instruction and educational systems, and for the rapid and wide dissemination of cultural practices.

LEARNING ABOUT ONESELF

We discussed imitation in terms of the relation between one's own behavior and the behavior of others. Implicit in that discussion was the suggestion that we learn to discriminate properties of our own behavior in the context of learning about others. The case is even more obvious with verbal behavior, because we learn the language with which we describe our own behavior from others. It follows that what we know about ourselves is a social product. We do not see ourselves as others see us; instead, we see ourselves as we see others.

Let us begin with a human example from a verbal learning experiment (Vesonder & Voss, 1985). The experiment included three kinds of participants: learners who talked aloud while learning verbal items and then predicted how well they would remember the items on the next presentation; listeners who heard what the learner said and made similar predictions based on what they heard; and observers who made predictions based on how well learners did on past items without hearing what the learners said. The predictions of both the learners and the listeners were substantially better than those of the observers; the crucial point, however, was that the predictions of the learners and the listeners were essentially the same. The public behavior of the learner, to which the listener also had access, was good enough for the predictions; if the learner did know private things to which the listener had no access (e.g., levels of confidence), they did not make the learner's predictions any better. The findings are consistent with evidence suggesting that, just as we judge others on the basis of observations of their behavior, we judge ourselves on the basis of observations of our own behavior (e.g., Bem, 1967; Nisbett & Bellows, 1977).

Discriminating Properties of One's Own Behavior

The capacity to discriminate properties of one's own behavior is important in many types of human behavior. For example, the student who cannot tell the difference between a superficial and a thorough reading of a text may stop studying too soon. To the extent that the behavior of interest has environmental effects, it is sometimes difficult to distinguish between control of discriminated responding by the behavior itself and control by the stimuli produced by that behavior. For example, some students might judge their examination performances primarily on the basis of problems they encountered in answering particular questions, whereas others might judge them primarily on the basis of the consequences of their performances (e.g., the grades later posted).

The nonhuman synthesis of such discriminations is again of potential interest. In one procedure, a pigeon's pecks on a center key were followed by the lighting of two side-keys; pecks on the left side-key were reinforced if the pigeon had emitted 50 or fewer responses on the center key, and pecks on the right side-key were reinforced if the pigeon had emitted more than 50 (Pliskoff & Goldiamond, 1966). The pigeon's side-key pecks depended on the number of its center-key-pecks, and therefore may be interpreted as responses under the discriminative control of a property of the pigeon's own behavior. Stimulus control by number of responses and other properties of behavior such as the temporal patterning of responses have been demonstrated in a variety of experi-

ments (e.g., Reynolds, 1966; Shimp, 1982; Shimp, Sabulsky, & Childers, 1989; see also Capaldi & Davidson, 1979, on the discrimination of deprivation stimuli).

One technical problem in such procedures is that the organism's behavior is usually correlated with environmental stimuli. For example, the pigeon that has spent a longer time pecking has probably also spent more time in a position where it has been looking at the key. Is its discrimination then based on its behavior or on what it has been looking at?

In discriminating one's own behavior, stimuli are of course available from muscles, joints, and so on. These stimuli are called *proprioceptive* or *interoceptive*. The effects of *biofeedback* may depend on the ways in which such stimuli are augmented or supplemented (e.g., Hefferline, 1958). For example, if the reading on a meter or the loudness of a tone is made proportional to the electrical activity of a muscle, an individual may learn to control levels of muscle tension and relaxation. It seems plausible that biofeedback control should be correlated with discriminative capacity, but such relations between biofeedback control and discriminations of proprioceptive or interoceptive stimuli have yet to be demonstrated (e.g., Cott, Pavlovski, & Black, 1981; Lacroix & Gowen, 1981).

Consider one more nonhuman example, in which a pigeon is taught to report its own drug state (Lubinski & Thompson, 1987). The general procedure is illustrated in Figure 10–1. Two pigeons share an experimental chamber separated by a clear plastic divider. The pigeon on the left is the requester pigeon; it has been taught arbitrary matching and some responses that depend on the behavior of the other pigeon. The pigeon on the right is the reporter pigeon; it has been taught to peck one of three stimuli depending on the drug

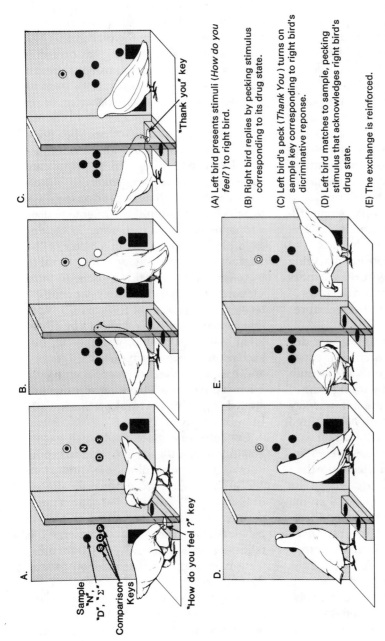

FIGURE 10–1 An interaction between two pigeons that is analogous to the reporting of an internal state. The five frames show the successive components of the procedure. The pigeon on the right in each frame has received a drug (stimulant, depressant, or control). In *A*, the requesting pigeon pecks its "How do you feel?" key. In *B*, the reporting pigeon has pecked one of its three keys, each of which is illuminated with a symbol corresponding to its three possible drug states. In *C*, the requesting pigeon reinforces that discriminative response by pecking its "Thank you" key, which turns on a flashing blue light above the reporting pigeon's keys. In *D*, the stimulus that the reporting pigeon had pecked appears as a sample stimulus on the requesting pigeon's keys; this pigeon has learned arbitrary matching to the three possible samples, and it pecks the letter corresponding to the drug that produced the reporting pigeon's drug state (Cocaine, Pentobarbital, or Saline). In *E*, the requesting pigeon has completed the arbitrary match; its contribution to the exchange is reinforced with food and that of the reporting pigeon is reinforced with water. (Adapted from Lubinski & Thompson, 1987, Figure 2)

(A) Left bird presents stimuli (*How do you feel?*) to right bird.

(B) Right bird replies by pecking stimulus corresponding to its drug state.

(C) Left bird's peck (*Thank You*) turns on sample key corresponding to right bird's dicriminative reponse.

(D) Left bird matches to sample, pecking stimulus that acknowledges right bird's drug state.

(E) The exchange is reinforced.

220

that it has been given. The sequence shown in the figure is roughly equivalent to a request by the first pigeon ("How do you feel?"), a report of its drug state as a reply by the second pigeon (a peck to the appropriate drug-state stimulus), and an acknowledgment by the first pigeon of the second pigeon's feelings (a peck on the drug-name key that matches the drug-state sample, followed by a "Thank you").

The pigeons' behavior is not, of course, verbal behavior. The point of this synthesis, however, is that it shows how public correlates of private events can be used to generate reports of those private events. The experimenters can reinforce the responses of the reporting pigeon on the basis of the drug that they administer to it. Once the reporting pigeon is discriminating its own drug state by pecking the appropriate key, a new drug can be administered and the pigeon's response can be interpreted as a report of the effect of the new drug in terms of the discriminative responding it learned with respect to the original drugs.

We will return to the issue of discriminating private events in Chapter 11. Their practical significance should be obvious; for example, the drinker who is a good judge of blood alcohol levels should know when to hand the car keys over to someone else. Another important feature of the pigeon simulation is that the reporting pigeon was taught the drug-state discrimination by the human experimenters. In human behavior, such discriminations may sometimes be incidentally learned, but we are most likely to learn them when they are taught to us by others. In other words, discriminations of our own behavior very often originate in the context of social behavior.

We have already mentioned other circumstances in which discriminations of one's own behavior are important (e.g., as in judging the adequacy with which one has studied course material). Such discriminations are also critical to a phenomenon once called *self-reinforcement* but now more properly referred to as *self-regulation* (e.g., Catania, 1975; Mahoney & Bandura, 1972). For example, a student who has made a commitment to watch television only after completing a study assignment might argue that the opportunity to watch television reinforces the studying. But any increase in studying that follows cannot be attributed to reinforcement; the student will only make the commitment to study if studying has already become important for other reasons. Whatever brings the student to make the commitment to "self-reinforce" studying in the first place will probably by itself make studying more likely.

Thus, when we speak of the standards that students set for fulfilling such commitments, it is inappropriate to say that they are reinforcing their own behavior; instead, the commitment is one basis for describing their discriminations between adequate and inadequate studying. The contingencies that generate these discriminations are complex and probably involve verbal behavior. The language of self-reinforcement does not clarify the phenomenon. In Chapter 8 we considered related issues in the topic of self-control; we will treat how discriminations of one's own behavior are relevant to language in Chapter 11, when we deal with the class of verbal responses called autoclitics.

Section B   Recapitulation

In this text so far, we have considered various behavioral procedures and findings: phenomena of elicitation, reinforcement, discrimination, and conditioning, among others. Before we apply these concepts to more complex types of behavior such as language, a review seems appropriate. We do so in the context of examples of social behavior involving parents and a child, some of which are related to topics that have been sampled in this chapter.

Beyond mere observation, the simplest of our behavioral operations was stimulus presentation (Chapter 3): No signal precedes the stimulus and no response need occur before it is presented. Suppose a nursing mother starts out by feeding her newborn infant independently of his behavior (let us assume that the child is male, not for sexist reasons but rather so we can distinguish easily between the mother and the infant as *she* and *he*). The mother's presentation of the nipple is an instance of stimulus presentation, and it may affect the infant's behavior. He is likely to turn toward her breast and begin to suckle. From the nursing mother's point of view, the suckling is also a stimulus, and it elicits the letting down of her milk. This glandular response moves the milk toward her nipples, where it becomes available to the suckling infant.

Assume now that the mother switches to demand feeding, and so feeds the infant only when he begins to cry. The feeding becomes a consequence of a response, crying. This relation is, of course, a response-stimulus contingency; we translate it as the effect of a response on the probability of a stimulus. In this instance, the infant is not fed unless he cries; without the crying the probability of a feeding is zero. This is of course only one example of a contingency. Responses can raise or lower stimulus probability (Chapters 4 and 5); they can turn things off as well as turn things on (they can also change other contingencies, but the present examples do not require such levels of complexity).

The contingency between crying and feeding is likely to affect the infant's behavior. We can expect an increase in his crying, but only after some time has passed since the last feeding, when milk has again become a reinforcing stimulus through the establishing operation of deprivation.

Let us now add stimulus control: We superimpose a discriminative stimulus on either of the other operations. First consider the mother's behavior. When she feeds the infant, the suckling produces the letting down of milk into her breasts. Once she begins feeding the infant whenever he cries, the crying becomes a reliable antecedent of the feeding and the mother discovers that she begins to let down her milk as soon as he begins to cry. The stimulus, crying, is followed by another stimulus, the infant's suckling at the mother's breast. This relation should be familiar as an example of Pavlov's respondent conditioning (Chapter 9). When Pavlov presented dogs with light and then food, the dogs began to salivate after light as well as after food, just as the mother lets down her milk during the crying as well as during the feeding.

But a discriminative stimulus can also be superimposed upon the consequential operations of reinforcement or punishment (Chapter 7). Now the infant has grown older and sleeps through the night. The mother begins the practice of feeding him when he begins to cry during the day but not when he does so during the night. These times are correlated with daylight and darkness, and soon the infant begins to discriminate between the two circumstances. Nighttime crying decreases relative to daytime crying, and later subtler discriminations allow the mother to begin to shape other kinds of behavior to replace the crying. Until then, during the daylight the infant is fed when he cries but during the dark he is not; in other words, light and dark become discriminative stimuli. During the light, crying raises the likelihood of a feeding, but during the dark it does not.

When we examine behavioral situations, it is often a useful exercise to describe them in terms of the appropriate operations; sometimes a proper description requires a combination of operations. For example, suppose that the mother has learned that when her infant begins to make fussy noises near bedtime, he is likely to fall asleep quickly if she picks him up and rocks him. His fussy noises set the occasion for rocking him and his subsequent falling asleep sets the occasion for tucking him into his crib. With regard to the mother's behavior, both parts of this sequence involve stimulus-control operations superimposed on consequential operations. The rocking produces a consequence, the sleeping infant, that is in turn a discriminative stimulus for the tucking in; a stimulus that is contingent on responding in one part of the situation serves as a discriminative stimulus in another (cf. chained schedules; Chapter 8).

These examples have involved interactions between the behavior of the infant and the behavior of the mother. In the context of such interactions, the infant learns to give special attention to social stimuli. These later become significant in many kinds of social behavior, such as attending to what others say, taking turns in conversation, and saying things that affect the behavior of others. As we shall see in the next chapter, verbal behavior is a very special kind of social behavior.

KINDS OF CONTINGENCIES AND CONTINGENT STIMULI

Let us call the stimuli involved in response-stimulus relations *contingent stimuli*. The preceding account used the

mother's milk and the infant's suckling as examples of contingent stimuli. But stimuli are of various sorts. We could replace those of the preceding examples with others that are aversive. The infant might be less fortunate, and the shouting of an abusive parent might occur independently of the child's behavior; or it might occur only after some response, such as crying; or it might occur only in the presence of some other stimulus, as when the child learns that his father shouts only when his mother is around; or it might be that if he cries his mother always quiets his shouting father, so that her presence is an occasion when he can avoid or escape from his father's shouting by crying. Each of these examples corresponds to contingencies involving aversive stimuli that have already been discussed.

It is sometimes convenient to distinguish among different types of contingent stimuli. Organisms work to produce or remain in the presence of some, called *appetitive, rewarding,* or *reinforcing:* food, entertaining company, money, among many others. They work to remove or stay away from others, sometimes called *aversive, noxious,* or *punishing:* noise, dull company, extremes of heat or cold, among many others. Some of these stimuli have obvious biological significance while others have acquired their significance during the organism's lifetime. It is difficult to classify any stimulus unambiguously as a reinforcer or a punisher (Chapters 4 and 5). And, having admitted appetitive and aversive stimuli as classes of contingent stimuli, we must also recognize that relatively neutral or insignificant stimuli may enter into contingencies. If the infant reaches out and touches his mother, for example, this movement is a response and contact is its consequence. Obviously, no stimulus is likely to be completely without significance; these classes represent points or regions in a continuous range of stimulus types rather than three discrete categories, and the designation of particular stimuli can change as a result of establishing operations.

A response may lower as well as raise the probability with which events occur. Suppose that the father finds the infant's cries aversive. If the infant is especially likely to start crying if his diaper has not been changed for some time, then the father can avoid the infant's crying by changing the diaper. The probability of crying increases as time passes without a diaper change, and it is reduced whenever a diaper change occurs. In other words, the diaper change is the father's avoidance response. A response-stimulus contingency is defined as the effect of a response on the probability of a stimulus, and we may distinguish among contingencies in terms of whether the effect is an increase or a decrease in probability. In the last case, in which the diaper change avoided the infant's crying, the stimulus was aversive and its probability was reduced by the father's response.

Now suppose that the infant has fallen asleep and while watching television the father accidentally awakens him by turning up the sound too loud. The infant begins to cry. The contingent stimulus, the crying, is again aversive, but this time a response, turning up the sound on the television, has raised its probability. The crying may punish the turning up of the sound, in that the father may now be less likely to do so while the infant is sleeping. Changes in probability are, of course, not limited to all-or-none cases. For example, the infant might not be fed every time he cries, and he might not awaken and cry every time the television sound is turned up (Chapter 8 on schedules).

In classifying contingent stimuli, we recognized relatively neutral or insignifi-

cant stimuli as well as appetitive or aversive stimuli. Contingencies also range from extremes in which responses raise or lower stimulus probability, and within this range is the special case in which a response has no effect on stimulus probability. This special case is equivalent to the stimulus-presentation operation. Stimulus presentations may involve the response-independent delivery of appetitive stimuli or aversive stimuli or relatively neutral or insignificant stimuli.

Kinds of contingencies and contingent stimuli are summarized in Table 10-1, in which they are shown combined with a discriminative stimulus. They are shown with some representative names in the psychology of learning applied to them. The procedures are not exhaustive, and the list is therefore incomplete. For any procedure in the psychology of learning, it is instructive to locate it or its various stages among the classes in Table 10-1.

Consider an example. The infant is older, and his mother has allowed him to crawl around and explore some of the rooms in his home. After he has done this a few times over several days, the mother takes him to a room in the corner of which is a new toy chest. She opens the chest and gives him a favorite toy. The next day she puts him down in another room and he immediately sets out for the room with the toy chest, getting there quickly and without making any wrong turns. His exploration of the room on the previous days involved behavior that produced relatively neutral consequences. But when a more significant consequence was introduced, the new chest with some of his toys in it, the child proved that he had learned the layout of the rooms. The example is analogous to an experiment on latent learning.

Consider one more example. The mother has often taken the infant to the doctor's office for routine exams. Time in

TABLE 10–1 Kinds of response-stimulus contingencies and contingent stimuli. Entries are representative classes of experimental procedures; those in parentheses illustrate cases in which a discriminative stimulus is superimposed on the contingency.

TYPE OF CONTINGENT STIMULUS	TYPE OF RESPONSE-STIMULUS CONTINGENCY		
	Response raises probability of stimulus	*Response does not affect probability of stimulus*	*Response lowers probability of stimulus*
Appetitive, rewarding, or reinforcing	Positive reinforcement (operant discrimination)	Stimulus presentation (respondent conditioning)	Negative punishment (omission training)
Relatively neutral, or insignificant	Sensory consequences (latent learning)	Stimulus presentation (sensory preconditioning)	Sensory consequences (latent learning)
Aversive, noxious, or punishing	Positive punishment (discriminated punishment)	Stimulus presentation (defensive conditioning)	Negative reinforcement (discriminated avoidance)

the waiting room has reliably been followed by seeing the doctor in the examining room. One evening the infant becomes ill and the mother takes him to a hospital urgent-care unit rather than to the doctor's office. There the doctor checks the infant's symptoms and then gives him an injection. The injection makes the infant cry. A few days later the mother takes the infant to the doctor's office for a follow-up exam. Even though the aversive injection had not been given to him in the examining room, the infant begins to cry as soon as he and his mother enter the waiting room. When the doctor's significance was changed by the injection, the crying in the waiting room proved that the infant had learned the contingent relation between the waiting room and seeing the doctor. The waiting room and seeing the doctor are analogous to the initially neutral stimuli of a sensory preconditioning experiment.

Constructing other examples that correspond to the various cells in Table 10–1 is a worthwhile exercise.

One way to judge the relative significance of events is to compare the probabilities of the responses they occasion. If we were interested in the child's responses of playing with toys and eating, we might see which he did when both the toys and food were freely available. When the child becomes older, an opportunity to play with friends might function to reinforce eating if he is reluctant to finish a meal, but if he has just encountered some cousins he has never met before at a family get-together and is reluctant to play with them, the opportunity to eat a favorite food may function to reinforce playing. In other words, the effect of a contingency may depend on the relation between the responses that produce and are occasioned by contingent stimuli (Chapter 4). In this context, establishing operations are concerned with the conditions that determine the effectiveness of contingent stimuli as reinforcers or as punishers.

We expressed experimental operations in terms of relations among stimuli and responses. Except for the mere observation of behavior, the presentation of stimuli is the simplest. But because responses can have environmental effects, we must also examine consequential operations, specified in terms of response-stimulus contingencies, the effects of responses on the probability of stimuli. (The special case of contingency in which the response has no effect on stimulus probability is equivalent to a stimulus-presentation operation.) Either stimulus-presentation operations or consequential operations can be signaled, or, in other words, can take place in the presence of particular stimuli. Thus, we must also be concerned with stimulus-control operations, whether they are superimposed on stimulus-presentation operations or on consequential operations. These operations can involve contingent stimuli that are appetitive, aversive, or relatively insignificant. Further, the contingencies into which they enter can involve increases in stimulus probability, decreases in stimulus probability, or no change in stimulus probability.

These classifications do not guarantee that any stimulus or any response will have only a single function; a stimulus in a contingent relation with one response may be in a discriminative relation with another, and a response elicited by one stimulus may be involved in contingencies with other stimuli. For example, the mother's presence may be a contingent stimulus, when she comes at the infant's cry, and a discriminative stimulus, when the infant learns that things happen in her presence that do not happen in her absence; the infant's cry may sometimes be elicited by events, such as painful stimuli, while at other times it may occur because such events as the mother's presence are its consequence. We come to understand behavioral situations by separating the various stimulus and response relations that enter into them. That is the business of an experimental analysis.

On close examination, some distinctions implied by the paradigm seem to diminish in importance. In the analysis of behavior, classifications of events often have fuzzy boundaries and distinctions may then become arbitrary. We noted such a case with respect to presenting or removing stimuli (e.g., is food effective as reinforcer by virtue of its presentation or because it terminates stomach contractions or other events correlated with hunger?). In the final analysis, we may completely discard the distinction between presenting and removing stimuli, recognizing that all consequential effects of responding can be characterized simply as environmental changes. We might then note that every procedure takes place in some environment, and so we might next get rid of discriminative stimuli, observing as we did that stimuli can be incorporated into the definition of the response. Thus, if a child's requests for candy are granted when his grandparents are present but not when they are absent, the response of this contingency can be defined to include only those requests made in the presence of his grandparents. If later our analysis shows us that we cannot even define response classes independently of contingencies, we might ultimately decide to dispense with that distinction. But such distinctions have been useful along the way. We can, so to speak, throw away the ladder after having climbed it.

PART IV *Learning With Words*

CHAPTER **11**

Verbal Behavior: Language Function

Our language words have diverse sources. Verbal, through Latin, and word, *through Old English, are derived from a common Indo-European root,* wer- *(to speak). The Germanic* spek- *or* sprek-, *from which comes the German* die Sprache *(speech or language), leads to the English* speak *and* speech. *The Greek* legein *(to speak) and* logos *(word) lead to* lexical, legible, *and such relatives as* logic *and* intelligent. Latin *provides* language *and* linguistics, *through* lingua *(tongue), and* vocal *and* vocabulary, *through* vox *(voice).*

Language is behavior. But our everyday vocabulary of language includes many assumptions that stand in the way of a behavioral account. For example, consider the common term *word*. When we speak of words, we seldom bother to distinguish spoken words from written ones. Yet speaking a word is not the same as writing it, and speaking and writing usually occur in different circumstances. Even worse, we often speak of *using* words, as if words were things instead of behavior.

We also speak of language as if it were directed toward environmental events or objects. We say that words or sentences refer to, deal with, speak of, call attention to, or are about things. The language of reference implicitly includes the direction from verbal behavior to environment. Everyday language does not include a vocabulary that emphasizes the opposite direction. We must therefore consider the possibility that everyday language has prejudiced the ways in which we analyze verbal behavior. Words are uttered or written in particular circumstances, but we hardly ever say that we utter nouns in the presence of relevant objects or that sentences are occasioned by relevant events. Instead, we say that words refer to objects or that sentences are about events. There is good reason for this usage; as we shall see, it is appropriate to the equivalences established within languages. But it may be misleading in an analysis of the behavior of speakers and listeners or readers and writers.

The language of meaning is another complication. Dictionaries do not contain meanings of defined words; they just contain other words. We speak metaphorically when we say that words contain meanings and that we convey these meanings to others through language (cf. Chapter 12). The metaphor of words as containers for meanings is well established, and yet the magnetic patterns that correspond to a tape-recorded voice or the patterns of pigment on a page that correspond to a handwritten message have no meaning unless someone listens to the recording or reads the note; the meaning is not waiting to be released from the tape or the paper. If anything is transmitted in language, it is verbal behavior itself: In listening and reading, our own behavior re-creates some features of the behavior of the speakers and the writers who constitute our verbal community. We share our verbal behavior; it is, above all, social behavior.

A primary task of the analysis of language is classifying verbal behavior. But the classification must be functional rather than structural or grammatical. A grammatical classification of words in a sentence does not tell us about the circumstances in which the sentence was produced or the consequences its production had for the one who produced it. Functional accounts of verbal behavior examine what verbal responses do. As with nonverbal behavior, structural and functional accounts of language complement each other. Unfortunately, verbal behavior has been controversial in the history of psychology, and structural and functional accounts have often been pitted against each other as if they were incompatible instead of complementary (cf. Titchener, 1898; Skinner, 1957; Chomsky, 1959; Catania, 1973b). This text attempts to deal consistently with both kinds of approaches.

Verbal responses are distinguished by the occasions on which they occur and the consequences they produce. They can be occasioned by either verbal or nonverbal stimuli, and they can have either verbal or nonverbal consequences. For example, a child might say "apple" in the presence of either the written word or an actual apple; as a consequence of saying "apple," the child might get either the verbal reply "right" or the apple.

First, we consider some relatively simple relations in which verbal behavior is reproduced in either the vocal or the written mode (as in echoing what someone has said or in taking dictation). These cases are followed by a treatment of how verbal behavior makes contact with the environment (as when we describe objects or events). We also explore some complex verbal processes (as in assertion and negation), to set the stage for discussing structural properties of verbal behavior in the next chapter. Then we deal with the behavior of speakers and listeners and with some of the consequences of verbal behavior. In particular, one individual can change the behavior of another by giving instructions; this may be the primary function of language. The properties of instructed behavior lead to a distinction between rule-governed behavior, determined by instructions, and contingency-shaped behavior, determined by consequences. We close by briefly comparing the distinctive features of human language with some examples of the nonhuman behavior that has been called animal language.

Section A   **The Units of Verbal Behavior**

Our verbal communities shape correspondences or equivalences between things and their names, between words and their definitions, between what we did and what we say we did, between what we promise and what we accomplish, and so on. The way in which such correspondences are learned and the conditions of their maintenance may determine how they function in verbal behavior (cf. Chapter 7 on equivalence relations). Our first examples consist of some formal verbal relations because the cases are familiar and the correspondences are well defined by our verbal community.

CORRESPONDENCES BETWEEN VOCAL AND WRITTEN CLASSES

The term *verbal* is a general one and applies to language in any modality; it must be distinguished from the term *vocal*, which is specific to spoken language. We could easily extend our account to other modalities (e.g., the gestural modality of sign language or the tactile modality of Braille), but we will restrict our attention to vocal and written verbal behavior.

Correspondences between verbal stimuli and verbal responses in formal verbal relations are implicit in the colloquial vocabulary: We say that words are the same whether they are heard, spoken, seen, or written, or, in other words, whether they are auditory or visual stimuli or responses. One elementary verbal function is the reproduction of verbal behavior: We repeat what others have said, or copy what others have written. Thus, our cases will include the various combinations of spoken or written stimuli and spoken or written responses.

Echoic Behavior

Imitation of some properties of vocal stimuli appears relatively early in human infants' acquisition of speech. This class of verbal relations is called *echoic*. When a parent says "mama" and the child repeats "mama," the child's response is echoic to the extent that it is occasioned by the parent's utterance and to the extent that the phonemes of the child's utterance have a one-to-one correspondence to those of the parent's. Even though the stimulus and the response have common properties, this verbal relation is not simple. The stimulus is a complex sound pattern. The response consists of articulations, the coordinated movements of lungs, vocal chords, tongue, lips, and so on. These produce sounds but are not themselves sounds. How does the child who hears "mama" or "dada" come to make precisely the articulations that produce sounds heard as equivalent by the parents (cf. the discussion of imitation in Chapter 10)?

Echoic behavior depends at least in part on the shaping of articulations by their vocal consequences. Even before their own vocalizations begin to be differentiated, infants have learned some discriminations among aspects of the speech of others (e.g., Eimas, Siqueland, Jusczyk, & Vigorito, 1971). Their initial babbling includes a range of human speech sounds, but native-language speech sounds are ordinarily retained in their spontaneous vocalizations whereas non-native-language speech sounds gradually disappear as the babbling evolves to self-repetitions (echolalic speech: e.g., "ma-ma-ma-ma-ma") and then to repetitions of the speech of others (echoic speech). They discriminate between sounds of their native language and sounds from an unfamiliar foreign language, but they do not readily discriminate between sounds from two unfamiliar foreign languages (Mehler, Jusczyk, Lambert, Halsted, Bertoncini, & Amiel-Tison, 1988). Discriminations of speech sounds that are easily learned at an early age may be difficult to learn later (e.g., Werker, 1989). For example, the distinction between spoken *r* and *l* in English does not exist in Japanese, and it is much more easily learned by a Japanese child than by an adult Japanese speaker.

Vocalizations can be reinforced (Bloom, 1984, Poulson, 1983, 1984). The vocalizations of infants are engendered and maintained by what the infants hear themselves saying; without these auditory consequences (as in cases of hearing impairment), the behavior does not develop. Perhaps native-language speech sounds become reinforcing relative to non-native-language sounds simply because they often accompany the activities of important care-givers in an infant's environment (cf. Trehub & Chang, 1977; DeCasper & Fifer, 1980). The articulation that produces something that sounds more or less like what mommy or daddy says may be reinforced automatically by this correspondence between the infant's and the parents' utterances; this is consistent with the demonstration of generalized vocal imitation in infants (Poulson, Kymissis, Reeve, Andreatos & Reeve, 1991).

The significant dimensions of *phonemes*—units of speech—are more easily defined by articulation (e.g., position of the tongue) than by acoustic properties (Lane, 1965; Liberman, 1982). The interactions of articulation and sound are complex; for example, many English consonants (e.g., *p, b, t, d*) cannot be produced unless accompanied by a vowel, and their acoustic properties vary as a function of their context (e.g., the sounds of *l* and *k* are different in *lick* from what they are in *kill*). Echoic behavior is not defined by acoustic correspondence; it is defined by correspondences of the phonetic units of a language.

Voices differ in many respects: An adult voice is deeper than that of a child, a woman's voice differs from that of a man, and people speak with varying regional dialects. If a young boy from a small town in New England repeats what a woman from Atlanta has just said, their utterances differ acoustically in many ways. But differences in vocal quality and regional dialect are irrelevant to whether the boy's behavior is echoic; the criterion for echoic behavior is the vocal correspondences of verbal units such as phonemes and words. Thus, the duplication of human sound patterns by parrots and other birds does not qualify as echoic behavior because their duplications are acoustic rather than phonetic (cf. Mowrer, 1950); they imitate passing trucks as well as human voices.

Echoic units can vary in size from individual speech sounds to extended phrases or sentences. A variety of verbal phenomena, such as speech errors (e.g., Fromkin, 1971), can help us to decide what these units are. The importance of the echoic production of individual sounds is demonstrated when we learn to pronounce words in an unfamiliar language or when we generate rhymes or alliteration in poetry (Smith, 1968; Skinner, 1972). For adult speakers, however, the units of echoic behavior are more typically whole words or phrases. The echoic production of extended phrases or sentences can be important in dramatics, as when an actor repeats the lines whispered by a prompter, or on ritual occasions, as when a bride and groom repeat the phrases of a marriage vow spoken by a member of the clergy. Echoic units are not defined by their size; they are defined by the correspondences into which they enter.

Echoic behavior does not simply accompany the acquisition of language and then vanish; it persists in the behavior of mature speakers. For example, you may repeat a telephone number just given to you or the name of someone you've just been introduced to. Nevertheless, echoic behavior does not imply that the speaker has understood what has been echoed; meaning does not enter into the definition of echoic behavior. As we will see later, problems of meaning in verbal behavior must be dealt with in other ways.

Transcription

Verbal stimuli and responses can also correspond when both are written. In such cases, the behavior is called *transcription*. For example, you might copy a number from a telephone book or copy an author and title in preparing a bibliography. Just as we distinguish vocal articulations and the sounds they produce in echoic behavior, we also distinguish the movements involved in producing words from the looks of the words in transcription. And just as echoic behavior depends on correspondences of verbal rather than acoustic properties, transcription depends on correspondences of verbal

rather than visual properties. A handwritten sentence may look very different from the print text from which it was transcribed (for example, the script letters run together but the printed ones do not). Nevertheless, writing the sentence qualifies as transcription if the script sentence matches the printed one in spelling, word order, and punctuation.

Units of echoic behavior can vary from individual phonemes to entire phrases or sentences; so also, units of transcription can vary from individual characters to extended passages, depending on the circumstances in which the behavior occurs. A child learns to copy single letters before learning to copy whole words. In doing so, the child learns the correspondences between arbitrary visual forms, such as the printed and script *a* in upper and lower case. There may be no visual property common to all forms of the letter *a* (cf. Gibson, 1965).

Transcription must be distinguished from copying in the pictorial sense (cf. Shahn, 1972, pp. 49, 244–245, 256). A skilled Asian calligrapher might produce an accurate copy of a printed alphabetic text even though unfamiliar with the European language in which the text is written, but such copying would not be verbal. The distinction is based on the behavioral units in the two kinds of copying. The critical features of the calligrapher's copying are the geometrical properties of the letters in the text and the marks produced by the calligrapher's strokes. The critical features of transcription, however, are the verbal units, such as letters, words, and phrases, in the original text and its copy. Visually, the calligrapher's copy might more closely resemble the original than a handwritten copy by a speaker of the language, but only the latter counts as transcription.

Except for their respective vocal and written modes, echoic behavior and transcription are formally similar. It is tempting to assume, perhaps because of the relative ease with which it is learned, that echoic behavior is simpler than transcription. Children ordinarily acquire echoic behavior early, even without specific instruction, but they do not ordinarily acquire transcription unless it is explicitly taught.

Pure transcription, in the sense of transcription unaccompanied by other responses (such as responses to the meaning of the text), probably occurs only rarely. A skilled typist, for example, may sometimes transcribe a text while not responding verbally to it in other ways (as when listening to a conversation elsewhere in the office); in such circumstances, the typist is unable to report the text content even though it was accurately transcribed. As with echoic behavior, meaning does not enter into the definition of transcription; it must be dealt with in other ways.

Textual Behavior

When a written verbal stimulus sets the occasion for a corresponding vocal verbal response, the behavior is *textual*. Thus, you might say aloud what is on a menu or read a bedtime story to a child. In textual behavior, the arbitrary correspondence between verbal stimuli and responses is more obvious than in either echoic behavior or transcription, because the stimuli and the responses are in different modes. A letter is a visual stimulus; it has no sound. A phoneme is an auditory stimulus; it has no shape. Yet these correspondences are so well established that we rarely note the arbitrary nature of these relations between shapes and sounds.

As with transcription, textual behavior is usually taught explicitly, and some controversies in its teaching are based on assumptions about the behavioral unit appropriate to various stages of instruction (e.g., whether, in teaching reading, the teacher should begin with individual letters, syllables, or entire words; cf. Gleitman & Rozin, 1973).

As with the other formal classes, textual behavior must be distinguished from other kinds of responses to written verbal stimuli. For example, if a sign says *STOP*, reading the word aloud is different from stopping; only the former is textual. In the mature reader, textual responses become less important than do other kinds of responses to written verbal stimuli. Vocal responses diminish in magnitude, become subvocal, and perhaps disappear completely as a child becomes a proficient reader. Reading is behavior, but textual responses, as defined here, are at best only one part of reading. For example, a father, while reading a bedtime story aloud to a child, might finish a page and suddenly realize that he does not know what just happened in the story; yet he might be able to tell from the child's reaction that he had read the page to the child without any serious errors or omissions.

This example, without understanding, is a pure case of textual behavior. The colloquial vocabulary does not distinguish between reading that is simply the saying of the words on a page and the kind of behavior we call reading for understanding (cf. Marcel, 1978; Shaffer & LaBerge, 1979; Fowler, Wolford, Slade, & Tassinary, 1981). Most of us have had the experience of finding ourselves in the middle of a page unable to say what we have just read. Such experiences are evidence for the importance of these distinctions (see also Kolers, 1985). Reading for understanding must include other behavior along with or instead of vocal or subvocal speech, so it is more than simply textual behavior.

Dictation-Taking

Just as a written stimulus can set the occasion for a vocal response, a vocal stimulus can set the occasion for a written response. This class of verbal behavior is called *dictation-taking* (we are concerned with the listener, who takes the dictation; for a discussion of the speaker, who dictates, see Gould, 1978). For example, you may write down a number given to you by a telephone operator, or you may take notes at a lecture. The units of dictation-taking are typically entire words or phrases, but individual letters may also serve (e.g., as when children are taught the written alphabet, or as when an unusual name is spelled out for a stenographer).

As with textual behavior, dictation-taking involves stimuli and responses in different modes. Some of its special properties follow from the relatively permanent record produced in the written text. In addition, occasions for dictation-taking are limited relative to textual behavior, because, unlike the vocal apparatus, writing implements are not parts of the human anatomy. Perhaps for this reason, we are not much tempted to pursue its possible covert manifestations; we are less likely to speak of submanual writing or typing than of subvocal reading (the motor theory of consciousness had argued that thought was merely vocal behavior that had been reduced in magnitude; Max, 1934). Nevertheless, textual behavior and dictation-taking are formally similar, and either can be accompanied by other kinds of verbal responses occasioned by verbal stimuli.

Relations Among the Classes

This account of formal verbal classes has been limited to vocal and written stimuli and responses. It could have been extended to other language modes (e.g., sending and receiving Morse code). The present classes distinguish verbal stimuli from verbal responses; the distinctions may be relevant to the acquisition of language. We speak of letters and words without regard to whether they are written or spoken, but the mode does matter in teaching. For example, a teacher who has only taught a child to name letters written on a chalkboard should not expect the child to be able to write the letters when they are spoken. The stimuli in the former task are responses in the latter, and vice versa. They are just one part of "knowing the alphabet."

To teach reading and writing is to teach equivalences between the vocal and the written modes of language. Perhaps these distinctions are obscured in the everyday vocabulary because such equivalences come easily to humans (cf. Chapter 7), or because language instruction is designed to eliminate them, or both. In any case, the relations are summarized in Figure 11–1.

FIGURE 11–1 Relations among the four formal classes (S, stimulus; R, response). Similar relations can be established for any other pair of verbal modes (e.g., vocal behavior and the gestures of American Sign Language).

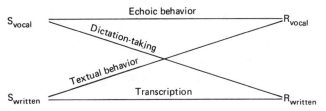

Each mode, vocal and written, has special characteristics. For example, spoken verbal behavior varies more freely in stress, rhythm, and intensity than does written verbal behavior, but it is also more transient. Some properties of verbal behavior are independent of mode. For example, for the immediate consequence of being able to dial a telephone number, it hardly matters whether you hear the number from a telephone operator or read it in a telephone book, or whether you repeat it aloud to yourself or write it down. Some consequences (e.g., the time it takes to get the number or the likelihood of retrieving it on another occasion) may affect how you look up a phone number next time, but those differences are not essentially verbal. Thus, once equivalences are established, it may be relatively unimportant to distinguish among the formal classes. But it may be useful to do so in studying language acquisition, as the formal classes successively develop, or in interpreting language pathologies, when the deficits may be characterized by the verbal classes affected (e.g., the language deficits called aphasias; cf. Sidman, 1971).

Thus far we have emphasized classes defined in terms of verbal modes, but other formal relations may be differentiated even within a mode. For example, if a student has learned only to translate from English to German, the student may have difficulty when asked to translate in the other direction, from German to English. Learning German responses to English stimulus words is different form learning English responses to German stimulus words. The problems are compounded when both spoken and written languages are involved. Language instruction usually recognizes these distinctions; a course in conversational French is expected to emphasize the vocal mode, whereas one in scientific Russian is expected to emphasize the written mode. (Bilingual verbal behavior might best be characterized in terms of the extent to which equivalence classes have been established that extend across both languages; cf. Kolers, 1966; Caramazza & Brones, 1980).

The formal classes illustrate the importance of distinguishing verbal stimuli from verbal responses. All the examples have been variations on that theme. Distinguishing between stimuli and responses presents little difficulty in the analysis of nonverbal behavior. For example, if a rat presses a lever only when a light is present, we call the light a stimulus and the lever-press a response; we are never tempted to reverse the terms. In verbal behavior, however, a speaker's response is a listener's stimulus and a writer's response is a reader's stimulus; furthermore, a speaker or writer at one time becomes a listener or reader at another.

INTRAVERBAL BEHAVIOR

The formal classes involve verbal responses occasioned by verbal stimuli. They are each characterized by one-to-one correspondences of verbal units; in transcription, for example, each word of a text has a unique equivalent in the transcribed version. But we learn many verbal relations that do not involve such formal correspondences. Such instances are called *intraverbal* (Skinner, 1957). We learn to recite the alphabet, to count, to give appropriate answers to arithmetic problems, to recite poems, to provide definitions for terms, and to state facts. The sequence of letters in the alphabet is no more orderly than that on a computer keyboard. Some similar letters of the alphabet are close together and others are widely separated (e.g., *M, N* but *D, T*), some voiced consonants precede and some follow the voiceless (e.g., *B, P* but *F, V*), and so on. Despite its arbitrary character, we learn the alphabet because so much is ordered according to it: dictionaries, telephone books, indexes. We are less able to recite the order of letters on a computer keyboard because we do not have to behave with respect to keyboards the way we do with respect to alphabetized lists.

The same points apply to chronologies, geographies, and much else of our everyday knowledge. No one now living ever saw Washington crossing the Delaware. You might argue that you saw the scene in a painting, but even if you had recognized Washington, could you have known that the setting was the Delaware River without a label on the painting that told you so? We do not ordinarily learn historical details by experiencing them. Instead, given names or dates, we learn to say when or in what order events occurred.

In intraverbal behavior, one verbal stimulus sets the occasion for another verbal response. The relation between stimulus and response is arbitrary; there are no systematic correspondences between them. Free association is an example (Galton, 1879). The immediate consequences of free associations are usually minimal, and any given verbal stimulus may set the occasion for a variety of different responses, so the procedure is assumed to tap verbal responses of relatively high probability in the speaker's verbal repertory. In his discussion of intraverbal behavior, Skinner (1957) treats free association as follows:

One verbal response supplies the stimulus for another in a long series. The net effect is revealed in the classical word-association experiment. Here the subject is simply asked to respond verbally to a verbal stimulus, or to report aloud any responses he may "think of"—that is, find himself making silently.

Echoic and textual responses are commonly produced but are either prevented by instruction or excluded from the results. Such an experiment, repeated on many subjects or on one subject many times, produces a fair sample of the responses under the control of a standard stimulus in a given verbal community....Many different responses are brought under the control of a given stimulus word, and many different stimulus words are placed in control of a single response. For example, educational reinforcement sets up many different intraverbal operants involving the cardinal numbers. *Four* is part of the occasion for *five* in learning to count, for *six* in learning to count by twos, for *one* in learning the value of π, and so on. On the other hand, many different verbal stimuli come to control the response *four*, e.g., *one, two, three*...or *two times two makes*....Many different connections between verbal responses and verbal stimuli are established when different passages are memorized and different "facts" acquired. The word-association experiment shows the results. (Skinner, 1957, pp. 73–74)

In its simplest forms, intraverbal behavior has been the focus of much research on human verbal learning, perhaps because of the relative ease with which verbal materials can be manipulated as stimuli. The classic experiments of Ebbinghaus (1885) were specifically concerned with the learning of arbitrary verbal combinations. Ebbinghaus created nonsense syllables for his experiments so that previous language experience would not contaminate learning. In current vocabulary, we would say that the experiments were designed to eliminate all possible verbal relations except intraverbal ones. Paired-associates learning (learning word pairs) and serial learning (learning ordered lists, as in learning to count) represent relatively pure cases of intraverbal behavior. Chapter 13 treats them in more detail.

Intraverbal relations are an important component of standard educational practice, as when a child who is mastering the multiplication table gives *42* as the response to 6 × 7. But the response is strictly intraverbal only if it does not depend on other intervening arithmetic behavior (e.g., adding six sevens, counting by sixes, or counting the boxes in a 6-by-7 rectangle). We will deal with cases in which the answer is derived rather than learned intraverbally when we have considered some environmental determinants of verbal behavior and some of its consequences.

Intraverbal behavior is involved only in cases in which successive parts of an utterance serve as discriminative stimuli for later parts. When extended utterances function as independent verbal units (cf. Chapter 6 on temporally extended units of behavior), it is inappropriate to say that the relations among their parts are intraverbal. Such maxims as *Haste makes waste* and *He who hesitates is lost* are reasonably regarded as verbal units in their own right. They must be analyzed in terms of their consistent sequential and relational properties (cf. Chapter 12) rather than in terms of intraverbal sequences.

THE CONTACT OF VERBAL BEHAVIOR WITH THE ENVIRONMENT

Verbal behavior would never have evolved had it made contact only with other verbal behavior. At some point it must make contact with events in the environment. We speak of this contact as *tacting;* a *tact* is a verbal response occasioned by a discriminative stimulus (cf. Skinner, 1957). For example, if a child learns to say "apple" in the presence of an apple, the child is said to be tacting the apple. The tact does not introduce any new process; it is merely a name for stimulus control as it enters into verbal behavior.

For the present purposes, the advantage of this vocabulary is that it is neutral with regard to whether the relevant stimuli are members of discriminative classes or equivalence classes; stimuli from both types of classes can occasion responses (cf. Chapter 7). Tacting has much in common with naming, but is distinguished from it by the presence of the tacted stimulus. We can name an object that is absent, but we cannot tact it (the major reason for the distinction is that, as we will see in Chapter 14 on remembering, our responses to past events are not determined directly by those events; rather, they are determined indirectly by our previous behavior with respect to them).

An unlimited number of tacts is available to the mature speaker. We tact objects (chairs and tables; pencils and books), living things (flowers and trees; birds and insects), weather conditions (rain and snow; sun and clouds), activities (walking and running; working and playing), and innumerable other features of the environment. Some tacts are general (e.g., *woman, man*) whereas others are restricted to relatively narrow circumstances (e.g., someone's name). The wealth of available tacts may be taken as a remarkable feature of human language, but this wealth should not obscure the simple relation that defines an instance of tacting.

It is useful to consider how tacts might be taught in a nonhuman organism; such examples force us to be explicit about the prerequisites for such behavior. Imagine a food-deprived pigeon in a chamber with a window on which different colors can be projected. Beneath the window are three keys. When the window is red, pecks on the left key produce food; when it is blue, pecks on the middle key do so; and when it is green, pecks on the right key do so. The pigeon will eventually peck the left key during red, the middle one during blue, and the right one during green. Is there any reason why the pigeon's performance should not be called the tacting of red, blue, and green? The stimuli are highly specific; the pigeon would not be expected to respond to red apples or shirts or sunsets as it does to the red light in the window. But the generality or specificity of the relevant stimuli is not a criterion for the tact relation. If we doubt the generality of the pigeon's response to red, we can just call the pigeon's left key-peck a tact of a red-lit window in this particular chamber.

What of the consequences of the pigeon's pecks? The pigeon would stop pecking if it were not food-deprived or if food were not a consequence. But even human tacting depends on its consequences. We do not move about tacting everything we see. Consequences are not criteria for tacting. An instance of tacting may have as its consequence approval, pay, an examination grade, or the help it gives to a listener; and, just as other responses are not always reinforced, tacts may sometimes produce no consequences at all.

Finally, we may object that the pigeon has no audience. Its pecks are appropriately occasioned by red and blue and green, but the pigeon is not speaking to anyone. This difficulty can easily be rectified, by arranging signs, *RED* and *BLUE* and *GREEN*, that respectively light after the pigeon pecks the left, middle, or right key. If our pigeon's performance was accurate and we could not look into the chamber, we could watch the signs and let the pigeon tell us which light was on.

But this arrangement is not relevant to the issue. We do not check to see whether someone was listening to decide whether or not we have named something. Audiences are important in creating and maintaining tacts, but they are not criteria for the tact relation. Tacting can be modified by audience variables and consequences, but these variables do not define tacting.

The pigeon's pecks in the presence of red and blue and green are relatively simple instances of stimulus control, but if the environment plays any role in determining what we say, stimulus control must be a component of verbal behavior. In other words, when we speak the language of tacts, we are simply speaking of stimulus control as it enters into verbal behavior.

Abstraction

We have emphasized the control of tacts by relatively simple environmental events. Strictly, we should say that tacts are controlled by properties of the environment rather than by particular stimuli or classes of stimuli. The property of color, for example, is the critical determinant of the verbal response *red*, whether that response is occasioned by red fire engines, traffic lights, or cheeks. Verbal discrimination based on a single property of a stimulus is called *abstraction*. The property is defined by the practices of the verbal community; it does not depend on whether we can provide an independent physical measure. For example, no range or distribution of wavelengths exists such that all visual stimuli within the range are called red whereas all those outside are not. We do not need to specify some measurable physical dimension of the stimulus to decide whether a particular verbal relation is a tact (in defining our terms, we start from behavior and not from physics; cf. Chapter 7 on concepts).

A concept formation experiment demonstrates the acquisition of tacts (Hull, 1920; cf. Chapter 7 on concepts). Learners mastered names for the members of sets of Chinese characters (three are shown in Figure 11–2). A name was consistently related to a radical that appeared in one character in each set, but the configuration within which it appeared varied from one set to another. Each set of 12 characters was

Radical   Characters in Lists

FIGURE 11-2 Radicals common to the Chinese characters used in six lists. Learners had to give the radical name to the character that contained it, but characters were not repeated in successive lists. Learners became able to name characters upon seeing them for the first time in new lists, and sometimes did so even when unable to define the common radical by sketching it. (From Hull, 1920, Figure 1)

presented until the learner gave the appropriate name for each and then a new set of 12 was presented. By the fifth set, learners named more than half the characters upon seeing them for the first time, and sometimes they gave the name even though they could not sketch the radical or describe the basis for their naming.

Tacting in this experiment differed from tacting in natural languages in that the basis for many of our tacts cannot be so explicitly defined. For example, we cannot say exactly what properties make an object a chair. A chair may have four legs or stand on a single pedestal, it may have a flat or a contoured seat or back, and it may be constructed from many different materials. We cannot even appeal to its function, because we call some objects chairs although they cannot be sat upon (e.g., a toy chair in a set of dollhouse furniture).

Extremely subtle properties can be tacted. They include relations among stimuli. For example, *above* and *below, near* and *far,* and *larger* and *smaller* tact properties of stimuli in relation to each other or to the speaker. Relational tacting occurs when you say that two objects are alike or are

different, or when you note that one item in a set is an odd item. Such terms rarely stand alone, and we will consider their joint dependence on relational properties of events and on other verbal responses when we consider the verbal relations called *autoclitic.* We also tact complex events extended in space or time, as when we identify a musical piece as one by Debussy or a painting as one by Monet. At another level of complexity, we might say that Debussy's music and Monet's paintings have something in common, even though it would be difficult to specify the common dimensions. Yet to call them both impressionist might be regarded as tacting common properties.

Sometimes the properties controlling a tact can be identified more with the speaker's own behavior than with any particular stimulus feature. For example, if a painting or a musical composition or a person occasions the word *marvelous,* this tact presumably depends on the responses generated in the speaker rather than on physical properties common to all of these stimuli. An interesting verbal case is the *tip-of-the-tongue* phenomenon. When you say a word is on the tip of your tongue, you are tacting the near-threshold availability of an appropriate verbal response in your own verbal behavior. Sometimes we can even report properties of an unrecalled word, such as its length or part of its spelling (Brown & McNeill, 1966).

The vocabulary of emotion is similarly based on complex relations involving situations and behavior. Tacts of love, hate, joy, and sorrow, whether in oneself or others, depend on overt manifestations such as laughter or tears and on the circumstances that generated the observed behavior. If this were not so, a verbal community could not maintain any consistency in this vocabulary; the variability of the language of emotions is itself evidence of the subtlety of the relations that are tacted.

Events and situations obviously have many properties that might be tacted. Whether any are tacted and which are tacted will depend on other variables acting upon the speaker. For example, we may tact the color of an apple in one circumstance and its smell in another. The situation presents no difficulties; verbal responses are determined in multiple ways.

Consider again the pigeon example. Now we alter the lights behind the chamber windows so that the colors appear bright, moderate, or dim. During a tone, left key-pecks produce food when the light is bright, middle key-pecks do so when it is moderate, and right key-pecks do so when it is dim, in each case regardless of color. Without the tone, everything is as it was before. If the pigeon's pecks become appropriate to intensity when the tone is present but remain appropriate to color when it is absent, we could say that the pigeon tacts intensity during the tone and color during its absence (cf. Chapter 7 on conditional discrimination).

Presence and absence of the tone in the pigeon example serve the same function as questions in human verbal behavior. A question, like the tone, is a conditional stimulus that sets the occasion for tacting some property of a stimulus (e.g., *What color is the apple?* or *What does it smell like?*). The audience, previous verbal behavior, and a variety of other factors may affect tacting. We do not tact indiscriminately. We tact some things in some circumstances and other things in other circumstances; we also learn that in some circumstances (e.g., remarking on someone's bad breath or dandruff), it may not be tactful to tact at all.

We also tact temporal dimensions of stimuli, as when we say that something lasted a long or a short time. Often we respond verbally to stimuli that are no longer present, but tacting only includes verbal responses that occur in the presence of or very shortly after the events that occasioned them (responses that occur long after require special treatment because they usually include other behavior besides tacting; cf. Chapter 14).

Sentences in different tenses can sometimes be regarded as classes of tacts controlled by temporal properties of the environment. Consider "It's raining," "It's beginning to rain," and "It just stopped raining." Each sentence is a response to rain, but they are distinguished by its different temporal properties. A past-tense verbal response such as "It rained" is likely to be determined by other kinds of stimuli, when it is not appropriate to call it a tact. For example, it might be uttered as an echoic or a textual response. If it is occasioned by present stimuli such as wet streets, it may be derived from other and more complex verbal behavior, such as "The streets are wet; therefore it must have rained."

The Extended Tact

The tact is a flexible relation. In some verbal communities, the stimulus properties controlling a tact are sharply defined. A student in a science laboratory, for example, is taught to be consistent in tacting apparatuses and materials and procedures. This precision is less common in everyday discourse. We often tact properties of the behavior of our acquaintances, but the conditions under which someone is said to be warm or reserved, energetic or lazy, interesting or dull, and so on, vary considerably from one speaker to another. The ways in which vocabularies have evolved over time are recognized in the etymologies or word histories introducing each chapter.

In the stimulus control of nonverbal behavior, we say a response has generalized if a response maintained during one stimulus occurs when some new stimulus is presented. For example, if our tacting pigeon pecked the left key when a novel amber light was presented, we would say that the response to red had generalized to amber. A similar generalization of verbal responses to new stimuli occurs in the extended tact. Simile and metaphor are familiar instances. We may say that someone is as busy as a bee or as sly as a fox (simile) or that someone is a hawk or a dove (metaphor). These extended tacts presumably originated through generalization across properties sometimes shared by humans and bees and foxes and birds. Language grows and changes through metaphor (cf. Esper, 1973; Jaynes, 1976; Skinner, 1989; see also Chapter 12).

Another type of extension of the tact occurs when new words are formed by combining existing ones (e.g., the words *dish* and *wash* predated the invention of dishwashers). Vocabularies change with environmental changes that are important

to the speakers of a language (but cf. Whorf, 1956). The ways in which tacts can be extended are so varied that a detailed account is not feasible. Stewart (1975) offers interesting examples in an account of the origins of place-names. For example, place-names are more likely to be based on unusual than on common features of a region. A valley in a forest of fir trees would not be named Fir Valley, but it might be named Oak Valley if a single oak tree stood there. Similarly, no stream is likely to be called Wolf Creek in an area where wolves are common, but a stream might be given that name in an area where wolves are rare if a pack of wolves was once sighted at the stream.

We have already noted the restriction that tacting must occur in the presence of or very shortly after the event tacted. What then of words that superficially seem to be tacts but cannot occur in the presence of what they name? When do we actually see governmental units like states or nations, subject matters like economics or politics, processes like creation or evolution, and so on? Such entities must enter into our verbal behavior in other ways; they do not exist in a form that can be tacted. The point is that tacting is not defined by parts of speech or other linguistic categories; rather, it is a type of behavior.

The Language of Private Events

Another important extension of the tact is to private events. Tacted stimuli are sometimes accessible only to the speaker, as when we say we have a headache. Such tacts depend on the verbal community for their origins and maintenance. The problem is how the verbal community can create and maintain these responses when it does not have access to the stimuli. A parent can teach a child color names because the parent can see the colors that the child sees and therefore can respond differentially to the child's correct and incorrect color naming. (So many different consequences follow from color naming that it ordinarily does not matter whether the parent teaches the color names through explicit instruction or simply allows the appropriate discriminations to become established through casual day-to-day interactions.)

With private events, the vocabulary can be taught only through extension from tacts based upon events to which the verbal community has access. For example, the child may learn to report pain because the parents have access to overt manifestations such as the event that caused an injury or the child's crying or facial expression; if the child has learned the names of body parts, the two kinds of verbal responses may be extended to the tact of pain in a particular place (cf. Skinner, 1945; Nisbett & Wilson, 1977).

A toothache is a discriminable event, but the person with the toothache has a different kind of access to it than does the dentist who is called upon to treat it. Both respond to the unsound tooth, but one does so by feeling the tooth and the other by looking at it and probing it with dental instruments. Their different contact with the tooth might be compared with the different ways a seeing and a sightless person make contact with a geometric solid if one is trying to teach its name to the other; the seeing person does so by sight and the sightless person by touch. One kind of contact is not necessarily more reliable than the other. For example, in the phenomenon of referred pain, a bad tooth in the lower jaw may be reported as a toothache in the upper jaw. In this case, the dentist is a better judge than the patient of where the pain really is.

We often think of private events such as our feelings and our thoughts as ones to which we have privileged access and therefore of which we have special knowledge. But we learned the relevant words from others, and all they had access to in teaching them to us were the public correlates of our private events. If we can be mistaken even about the location of a toothache, what assurance do we have that any of our other reports of our own private events are reliable?

Skinner (1963) makes the point by describing some students who had watched a pigeon in a classroom demonstration and then described what they saw in terms of the pigeon's expectations:

> They were describing what *they* would have expected, felt, and hoped for under similar circumstances. But they were able to do so only because a verbal community had brought relevant terms under the control of certain stimuli, and this had been done when the community had access only to the kinds of public information available to the students in the demonstration. Whatever the students knew about themselves which permitted them to infer comparable events in the pigeon must have been learned from a verbal community which saw no more of their behavior than they had seen of the pigeon's. (Skinner, 1963, p. 955)

Some verbal responses that superficially seem to tact private events may be determined instead by the situation within which our behavior occurs. For example, if upon sitting down to a meal you suddenly find yourself eating voraciously, you may say, "I must have been very hungry." You have not tacted some private hunger pang; you are saying of yourself what you would have said of someone else if you had observed that kind of eating in another.

Once we learn to tact properties of the public behavior of others, we may come to tact the same properties of our own behavior, whether it is public or not. If one person works hard at something with little compensation and another does so only with substantial compensation, we ordinarily say that the task was more important to the first person than to the second. But the same observations of our own behavior may lead us to say what is more or less important to us (Bem, 1967). Speaking of our beliefs or our understanding of the causes of our actions may follow more directly from our discriminations of our own public behavior than from anything private (e.g., Kiesler, Nisbett, & Zanna, 1969). This is not to deny private events. It is, instead, a cautionary note: The language of private events can easily distract us from the public causes of behavior.

Another problem with the language of private events is that the verbal community's control of these tacts is weak, because the verbal community has inconsistent access to the public correlates of these events. For example, when someone says "I have a headache" and leaves a social gathering, it is not clear whether the verbal response tacted a private stimulus or simply allowed the speaker to escape from unwanted company. Like the language of public events, the language of private events depends on the public practices of the verbal community. The implications have been explored in considerable detail by Skinner and by Wittgenstein (Day, 1969, discusses parallels between their treatments of private events). For our purposes, it is sufficient to note that verbal behavior does not ordinarily require that stimuli be simultaneously available to both speaker and listener. In fact, some of the important consequences of verbal behavior occur when the speaker tacts some event unavailable to the listener. Although the language of private events has its own particular difficulties, we need not invoke

any new categories of verbal responding to deal with it.

By themselves, tact relations are only one part of verbal behavior, but through them verbal behavior comes into contact with the environment. Without them there would be nothing of which we could speak. The question of truth is behavioral. Some of what we call truth depends on how verbal communities maintain correspondences between verbal behavior and environment. Those who lie do so because the consequences of lying differ from those of telling the truth, but lying can be effective only within verbal communities in which such correspondences are reasonably reliable ("Unless social interaction is to break down, the lie must always be the exception," Bolinger, 1973, p. 549; cf. Dawkins, 1976, pp. 82, 112).

THE CONSEQUENCES OF VERBAL OPERANTS

Verbal responses have consequences. They are operant classes. The consequences that serve as reinforcers for human verbal behavior are many and varied. Sometimes they are nonverbal (e.g., someone comes when called); sometimes they are verbal (someone answers a question). Sometimes they are fairly reliable (*Thank you* is often followed by *You're welcome*); sometimes they are not (only some questions produce answers). In addition, the tendency to speak may depend on some consequences while what is said may depend on others (one difficulty with experiments on verbal reinforcers was that they sometimes attempted to modify verbal behavior with the same consequences that were presumed to keep the speaker talking; e.g., Greenspoon, 1955; Rosenfeld & Baer, 1970).

One obvious kind of consequence for verbal behavior is illustrated when we are given something we ask for. If a child says *milk* and receives a glass of milk, we might say that the milk reinforces the verbal response. Verbal responses that specify their reinforcers have been called *mands* (Skinner, 1957); demands and commands, for example, specify behavior in which the listener must engage. The response need not occur in the presence of the reinforcer. For example, a child may ask for milk even if a glass of milk is not present.

An analogue from animal research may be helpful. Assume a rat in an experimental chamber with one lever that produces food and another that produces water. If the rat presses the first lever only when food-deprived and the second only when water-deprived, we could argue that the presses are, respectively, food requests and water requests. Although it would not be essential, we could make the analogy more convincing by arranging signs that lit up for the experimenter when either lever was pressed, saying *Please give me food* and *Please give me water*. The rat's vocabulary is limited to two levers, but the relations between the lever-presses and their consequences are similar to those between human verbal requests and their consequences.

Yet the account is not satisfactory. For example, imagine a child who sees a new toy, learns its name, and then asks for it even though asking for it could never have been reinforced in the past. As a category of verbal behavior, the mand cannot consist of many separate response classes corresponding to each of the many consequences that could be manded (cf. Schick, 1971); rather, it must be a single class of responses in which a reinforcer is specified by the verbal responses that in other circumstances tact it. No such class existed in the rat example.

Within the class of mands, some subclasses specify stimuli (*Please give me an apple*) and some specify the behavior of the listener (*Please wait for me*); others called questions specify the listener's verbal behavior (e.g., *Please tell me your name* or *What is this called?*). These classes may be further subdivided according to a variety of features. For example, we speak of a *prompt* when the appropriate verbal response is already known to the speaker (as in giving a hint to a child who is unable to solve a riddle) and a *probe* when it is not known (as in a police interrogation). In everyday discourse, we also distinguish mands by the consequences that may follow for the listener (pleas, requests, orders, etc.); for instance, a demand usually specifies an aversive consequence for a listener's noncompliance.

VERBAL BEHAVIOR CONDITIONAL UPON VERBAL BEHAVIOR

Verbal behavior, like any other event, can be tacted. No new kinds of relations are involved, but the complexities created when verbal behavior is built upon other verbal behavior need special comment. Verbal behavior that depends upon other verbal behavior and that modifies the effects of other verbal behavior is called *autoclitic.* It includes the complex orderings and arrangements of grammatical structure and verbal usages that modify the effect on the listener of other verbal behavior. *Relational autoclitics* involve verbal units that cannot stand alone because they must be coordinated with other verbal behavior; *descriptive autoclitics* involve discriminations of one's own verbal behavior. (Note that intraverbals also depend on other verbal behavior, but must be distinguished from autoclitics because they are limited to sequential verbal relations and do not require discriminations of one's own behavior.)

Relational Autoclitics: The Conjunction of Verbal Units

Some verbal responses can specify events only through their relations to other verbal responses. For example, words such as *above, before,* and *of* are not simply tacts of particular environmental circumstances. They occur in combination with other verbal responses and depend on these other verbal responses for their effects. Agreements of case and tense are also conditional upon properties of events tacted, so they too can be treated as autoclitics. A structural unit of verbal behavior, such as a sentence in passive voice and past tense, can be regarded as a complex of tacts of various relational and temporal properties of a set of events. "The dog ran" and "The birds fly" involve several discriminations: dog vs. bird, singular vs. plural, running vs. flying, past vs. present. Yet they all come together in these brief sentences.

A pigeon analogy again may be helpful. Suppose we add some new dimensions of stimulus control to the tacting of the earlier examples. We project a circle or square along with the colors in the window. We maintain left key-pecks during red, middle key-pecks during blue, and right key-pecks during green. But now we make food contingent upon fast pecking during circle and slow pecking during square. Next, we vary the size of the circles and squares, and we make reinforcement contingent upon the force of the pecks: strong pecks when the figure is large, and weak pecks when it is small. If the pigeon's pecks come under the combined control of these stimulus dimensions, we will observe fast strong pecking on the middle key during a small square on green. Just as a given set of events may occasion the separate words of a sentence in a particular grammatical order, the stimuli in the window may occasion respond-

ing that varies with their several properties. Incidental features of responding, such as the topography of successive pecks, may vary consistently with particular combinations of properties, just as stress patterns and other features of human verbal behavior may vary consistently across different grammatical forms (cf. Catania, 1980).

Performances based on such multiple determinants of responding have been produced with pigeons (Catania & Cerutti, 1986). Under thus far very limited circumstances, responding may emerge that is appropriate to novel combinations of stimulus properties (e.g., in the example, given training with respect to shape and size only during blue and green, pecking with appropriate rate and force on the left key during red; cf. Esper, 1973; see also Chapter 12 on productivity).

But the point is not to explore the pigeon's capacity for verbal behavior; rather, it is to illustrate the multiple dimensions of stimulus control over response properties in complex verbal behavior. When environmental properties occasion classes of verbal responses that are invariant even when they occur in combination with other response classes, we may treat such classes as verbal units (e.g., as when the present-tense, active-voice sentence structure remains invariant across a variety of different tacted events). Such units have complex structures, but only because they can be combined in novel ways can we generate novel verbal behavior under novel conditions; new events can be tacted only on the basis of verbal behavior available with respect to things already known. Even if you had never seen a purple cow, the separate tacts of purple and cowness would still allow you to say "Look at that purple cow" when you encountered one.

The new combinations that relational autoclitic processes can generate are important because our own verbal behavior often occasions later behavior (for example, you might act today on a reminder you wrote for yourself yesterday). Sometimes the later behavior is verbal: We reword sentences, draw conclusions, derive solutions. These manipulations are of special interest when, as in problem solving, they lead to behavior that was unavailable earlier. The power of verbal behavior resides in how it provides discriminative stimuli that occasion responding with important consequences (cf. Chapter 15 on problem solving).

Consider an example from mathematics, a convenient illustration because mathematical notation exactly prescribes the verbal responses appropriate to particular verbal stimuli. We judge the understanding of addition or multiplication by the number of ways in which someone can respond to relevant verbal stimuli. The person should be able to define the operations, to discriminate between cases to which they apply and cases to which they do not, to give answers to specific problems, and to derive each from simpler counting operations. Such behavior is verbal, and is necessary and sufficient for the statement that the person understands addition and multiplication.

The learning of arithmetic involves intraverbal and autoclitic processes. Its particular advantages come when it is combined with tacting of the numerosity of objects or events (cf. Ferster & Hammer, 1966). A child may calculate the number of objects in a rectangular array by multiplying the number of rows by the number of columns, or simply by counting all of the objects. Either operation is verbal, but the outcome is a verbal response that is appropriate to the quantity of objects in the array; it is a derived tact. The structure of arithmetic corresponds to the structure of the environment in such a way that new verbal responses generated arithmetically may then function effectively as tacts (*twelve* tacts the number of eggs in a full box of a dozen eggs; we do not have to count the eggs every time).

Much important verbal behavior is derived from other verbal behavior. We mentioned the problem of untactable entities such as subject matters (where and how could we tact philosophy or biology or psychology?). But we can progress from individuals and what they do and where we find them to groups of individuals and more general activities and broader areas, until we speak of academic institutions, governments, business organizations, religions, political parties, industries, branches of the military, and so on. We cannot point to these entities, but they are related to events we contact directly. Such derivations, however, are much less explicitly defined than those of mathematics or logic; we might therefore guess that the correspondences between the world and what we say about it become less reliable as our verbal behavior becomes further removed from its points of direct contact with the environment.

Such verbal behavior also permits us to respond to properties of the world that we cannot respond to in other ways. We cannot tact noon or Saturdays or February 3rd or the twenty-first century. These exist only by virtue of clocks and calendars; they cannot stand independently of verbal behavior (cf. Austin, 1962, on speech acts such as pronouncing a couple married or bestowing a title). The analogy between these cases and mathematical derivations does not explain verbal behavior, or explains it only in the sense of showing how verbal behavior works and how its properties differ from those of nonverbal behavior.

Descriptive Autoclitics: The Discrimination of One's Own Verbal Behavior

Many verbal responses tact the conditions under which other verbal behavior is emitted and thereby modify the responses of the listener. Consider the phrases *I doubt* and *I am sure* in "I doubt the coffee is ready" and "I am sure the coffee is ready." Each one modifies the way in which the listener is likely to act upon the statement that the coffee is ready. For the listener, *I doubt* and *I am sure* are analogous to the conditional stimuli of a conditional discrimination: In both cases the listener has heard *the coffee is ready,* but the listener is less likely to pour the coffee after *I doubt* than after *I am sure.*

Now consider the speaker. What has *I doubt* or *I am sure* tacted? It cannot be just the readiness of the coffee. It must be some property of the speaker's own tendency to say "The coffee is ready," and the relation of that statement to the actual state of the coffee. You cannot use *I doubt* or *I am sure* effectively unless you can discriminate your own behavior. In a situation in which you would like to be able to say "The coffee is ready," you must be able to tell whether it is appropriate to do so.

We do not tact everything we see, and conversely we sometimes respond as though tacting when the stimulus is absent. The qualifying autoclitic accompanying such verbal behavior is typically some form of the verbal response *no.* For example, we do not continuously say "The coffee is not ready" under conditions of unready coffee. Instead, this verbal response occurs when circumstances set the occasion for saying "The coffee is ready" (e.g., the smell of coffee, the question "Is the coffee ready?") even though that response would be inappropriate. If "The coffee is ready" does get said when coffee

is in fact not ready, inserting a *not* in it makes a big difference.

Assertion, like negation, is also autoclitic, but the verb *is* serves many functions. Sometimes it specifies that the verbal response it accompanies is a tact ("This is a book"), sometimes it prescribes equivalences between verbal responses ("A human is a featherless biped"), and sometimes it specifies temporal properties ("It is cold now"). The particular function of *is* often depends on other verbal responses or, in other words, on context. Not only does it function as a conditional stimulus with respect to the effect of other verbal behavior, but its function may in turn be conditional on other verbal behavior.

Autoclitics can have quantitative as well as qualitative effects. Examples are *few, some,* and *many,* and the plural forms of nouns and verbs. The effect of *often* in "This text is often misunderstood" can be paraphrased as a statement that it is often appropriate to say "This text is misunderstood." As we shall see in treating language structure (Chapter 12), we have no independent nonverbal means for characterizing these relations, but paraphrase is useful because it makes explicit the conditional relations among the components of the utterance. This is most obvious when autoclitics specify the listener's verbal behavior (e.g., *vice versa* is conditional upon preceding verbal behavior, and it may be interpreted as an instruction specifying that the listener generate a new verbal response reversing the order of components in the original verbal response).

Our verbal behavior would be impossible without autoclitic processes. In "I recall that it rained yesterday," "I read that it rained yesterday," and "I heard that it rained yesterday," the speaker specifies the source of the verbal response "It rained yesterday." Other descriptive autoclitics tact the speaker's reaction to current verbal behavior, as in "I am sorry to report that you missed the point" or "I am pleased to say that you did very well on the exam."

Descriptive autoclitics depend on discriminations of one's own verbal behavior, and the problems involved in cases of discriminating one's own nonverbal behavior (cf. Chapter 10) are duplicated in the verbal case. Such discriminations are characteristically human, and we know only a little about how they are learned or can be taught. We will not consider a pigeon analogue because it is not even clear how to construct one (cf. Catania, 1980, pp. 185–186). More important, descriptive autoclitics demonstrate that the analysis of verbal behavior is an issue of behavior and not of logic. Saying "This is so" or "That is probable" or "It cannot be" is verbal behavior with respect to other verbal behavior. To reduce such sentences to symbolic logic or the mathematics of probability may be useful in solving problems, but that reduction eliminates a central feature of human language. Discriminations of one's own behavior are prerequisites for what we call consciousness or self-awareness; descriptive autoclitics suggest that these phenomena are uniquely tied to the properties of human language (cf. Jaynes, 1976).

Section B   **Relations between Verbal and Nonverbal Behavior**

We have emphasized the stimuli that control verbal behavior, but we have also seen that verbal behavior has consequences. As with all operant behavior, these consequences affect subsequent verbal responding. In a speech episode such as a simple two-person conversation, each person provides an audience for the other. Audiences are varied in their properties; we speak into telephones, write messages, or address large groups of people. Often the consequences for the speaker are simply what a listener says later. It does not require a laboratory experiment to demonstrate that a listener's response can maintain a speaker's talk. We tend to stop speaking to people who do not react to what we say. To this extent, we may say that the listener's responses reinforce the speaker's verbal behavior (cf. Greenspoon, 1955; Rosenfeld & Baer, 1970, on *yes* or *uh-huh* as reinforcers of verbal classes such as plural nouns or the substantive content of conversations). One of the most general consequences of verbal behavior is that through it a speaker changes the behavior of a listener. Words are ways to get people to do things.

RULE-GOVERNED AND CONTINGENCY-SHAPED BEHAVIOR

Verbal behavior can have either verbal or nonverbal consequences, but in one way or another, the consequence is usually a change in the listener's behavior. For example, if you tell a friend who is about to go outdoors that it is going to rain, your friend may be more likely to take an umbrella. The verbal community maintains correspondences between verbal behavior and environmental events. The listener can act on the speaker's verbal behavior only if such correspondences are consistent. If the speaker's verbal behavior is occasioned by environmental events inaccessible to the listener, it may become a potent discriminative stimulus for the listener's behavior. For example, a listener's response to the tact *fire* may have important consequences even if only the speaker has seen the fire. Through the verbal behavior of others, we can respond indirectly to events that are distant from us in space or in time (but the tale of the boy who cried wolf illustrates how control by the speaker's verbal behavior may weaken if the speaker tacts unreliably).

Instructional Control

Sometimes what people do depends on what they are told to do; people often follow instructions. Such behavior, mainly determined by verbal antecedents, has been called *rule-governed* behavior; its properties differ from those of *contingency-governed* behavior, behavior that has been shaped by its consequences (Skinner, 1969; cf. Schlinger & Blakely, 1987). Some instructions affect nonverbal behavior ("Come here," "Sit down," "Go away"); others affect verbal behavior itself ("Tell me a story," "Say please," "Be quiet").

The most general function of language is instructional control; we tell each other what to do and what to say. Language is not an instrument of reason or a vehicle of truth; those properties are only corollaries of its primary function, to change behavior. Orders are given, advice is offered, laws are enacted, and so on; each case involves instructional control. This control is easiest to overlook when the instructed behavior is itself verbal. A script is a set of instructions to an actor and a text is a set of instructions to a reader. In both cases the instruction specifies verbal behavior— what is to be said. The instructor who defines a term, for example, specifies the circumstances in which the term and its definition will be appropriate in the student's future verbal behavior.

An important characteristic of instruction is that it substitutes verbal discriminative stimuli for natural contingencies, as when a parent tells a child "Don't touch the stove or you will burn yourself." This property of verbal instruction has far-reaching implications. Instructions can change the listener's behavior in situations in which the natural consequences by themselves are ineffective or are effective only slowly. If we invite friends for a visit, for example, we give them directions rather than letting them search for the place on their own.

Contingencies operate for the following of instructions. To the extent that instruction-following is characterized by the correspondence between the instruction and the listener's behavior and is therefore more than the following of particular instructions, it is another higher-order class of behavior. Sometimes the contingencies that maintain instruction-following are social ones, as when someone in the military follows orders because of the aversive consequences for not doing so, or as when someone grants a request to please someone else or to avoid hurting the other's feelings. Sometimes those contingencies depend on the relation between verbal formulations and nonverbal contingencies, as when someone successfully makes a repair by following a service manual, or as when someone avoids injury by acting on a warning. Zettle and Hayes (1982) have suggested the terms *pliance* for social contingencies on instruction-following and *tracking* for contingencies that involve correspondences between verbal behavior and environmental events.

Consider an example of rule-governed behavior. Without instructions someone types with the index fingers, one letter at a time, in the method called hunt-and-peck. This is faster for the novice typist than touch typing, in which each finger has a particular resting position at the keyboard. The immediate consequences of the two typing methods favor the former. But in learning touch typing, the long-term consequences of following instructions to place the fingers appropriately and to type each letter with a particular finger eventually outweigh the short-term advantages of the hunt-and-peck system. What is learned is not solely a particular method of typing. To follow instructions successfully, the learner must ignore natural consequences (in this instance, the text is at first produced more slowly by touch typing than by hunt-and-peck typing).

Because of the practical advantages of instruction, the verbal community shapes the behavior of following instructions across a substantial range of activities throughout a substantial portion of each individual's lifetime. This can happen only if the contingencies that maintain instruction-following are more potent than the natural contingencies against which they are pitted (we seldom bother to ask people to do things they would do on their own anyway). Thus, instructions may begin to override natural contingencies: People then do things when told to do them that they would never do if only the natural contingencies operated.

A major achievement of human verbal behavior is that it allows behavior to be controlled by descriptions of contingencies, in the verbal behavior of others, as well as by direct contact with the contingencies themselves. But the advantages of this unique property of verbal behavior are accompanied by special problems.

A history of following instructions may make individuals susceptible to verbal control by authority figures (e.g., Milgram, 1963). In addition to the abuses that can arise when people just follow orders, instructions can create problems in more subtle ways.

Insensitivity to Contingencies

Consider the simple task of pressing a telegraph key, with presses earning money according to various schedules of reinforcement. When key-pressing is established in humans by instructions instead

of by shaping, instructed performances are typically insensitive to the schedule contingencies, whereas shaped performances are often not (Matthews, Shimoff, Catania, & Sagvolden, 1977). Schedule effects observed with uninstructed responding in humans (e.g., higher rates maintained by ratio schedules than by yoked interval schedules; cf. Chapter 8) do not occur reliably when responding is instructed. Just telling a human in an experimental setting to "press the key" produces persistent responding that is insensitive to its consequences (cf. Lowe, 1980; Shimoff, Catania, & Matthews, 1981). Such insensitivities have been observed across a range of schedule contingencies (e.g., Wanchisen, Tatham & Hineline, 1988).

This property of instructed performances is relevant to those aspects of skill that we sometimes say cannot be taught. Skilled performances are those in which behavior is sensitive to its consequences from moment to moment, as when a woodcarver adjusts to the changing patterns of grain in a woodblock or a quarterback anticipates the movements of an opposing player or a ballet dancer accommodates to slight deviations in the steps of a partner. If rule-governed behavior is likely to be insensitive to its consequences, then skilled behavior must be contingency-shaped instead. We must learn by doing in such cases; instructions cannot substitute for the subtleties of direct contact with contingencies.

A related problem with rule-governed behavior is that we usually do not want others to do what we say simply because we say it. A parent or teacher who gives instructions to a child might prefer but cannot be confident that the natural contingencies will eventually control the relevant behavior and make instructions unnecessary. For example, a reason for telling a child to put overshoes on before going out to play in the snow is that the instruction may keep the child from coming home with cold and wet feet. If the child always obeys the instruction, the natural contingencies will never act on the child's behavior; if the child disobeys the instructions, the aversive consequences that follow from snow and unprotected feet may enhance the control by instructions on future occasions. Thus, if we try to teach by telling others what to do, we may reduce the likelihood that they will learn from the consequences of their own behavior. There is no easy solution to this dilemma. We must always choose between the immediacy and convenience of verbal instructions and their longer-term effects on the learner's sensitivity to the consequences of behavior.

Instructions have a role in a distinction between *intrinsic* and *extrinsic* reinforcers (e.g., Lepper & Greene, 1978). Some reinforcers are intrinsically effective whereas the effectiveness of others has to be established. For example, music is an intrinsic consequence of playing an instrument, but the music teacher's praise or grades are an extrinsic consequence. In one experiment (Lepper, Greene, & Nisbett, 1973), one group of children received gold stars for artwork; after the gold stars were discontinued, children in this group engaged in less artwork than those in a second group who never received gold stars. The gold stars, extrinsic reinforcers, were said to have undermined the intrinsic reinforcers, the natural consequences of drawing. But the children were told to earn the gold stars, and the experiment did not test their effectiveness as reinforcers. If they were reinforcers at all, they were reinforcers established by instructions. Thus, the results probably had nothing to do with a difference between intrinsic and extrinsic reinforcers; instead, they were probably a

demonstration of the insensitivity of instructed behavior to contingencies (Schwartz, 1982, provides another example of stereotypy determined by verbal behavior but attributed to reinforcers). To produce such effects, it may be sufficient merely to get the children talking about the relevant behavior and contingencies (cf. Wilson & Lassiter, 1982).

Cases of insensitivity to contingencies produced by verbal behavior can be found across a wide range of settings. For example, people learn the rules of an artificial language more effectively by working only with sample sentences than by working with the sentences plus statements of the grammatical rules (Reber, 1976); right-left confusions are less likely in spatial tasks that do not involve words than in those that do (e.g., Maki, 1979); individuals cannot ignore false labeling even if they did the labeling themselves (Rozin, Millman, & Nemeroff, 1986); remembering of faces and some other classes of stimuli that are difficult to put into words is impaired by naming of the stimuli (Schooler & Engstler-Schooler, 1990). It may be correct to conclude that some things are better left unsaid.

CORRESPONDENCES BETWEEN SAYING AND DOING

Verbal communities arrange correspondences between words and events. The correspondences operate in both directions, as in equivalence classes; we name things we see and locate things we name. Another correspondence important to the verbal community is that between what we say and what we do. Here also the correspondence can operate in both directions: If we do something we can then say we have done it, and if we say we will do something we can then do it (e.g., Risley &

Hart, 1968; Rogers-Warren & Baer, 1976; Paniagua & Baer, 1982). To the extent that the verbal community arranges contingencies for these correspondences, we can change behavior not only by instructing the behavior but also by shaping what is said about it. If both saying and the correspondence between saying and doing are reinforced, doing may follow. Through such contingencies, one's own verbal behavior may become effective as an instructional stimulus (e.g., Lovaas, 1964; Jaynes, 1976; but see also Baer, Detrich, & Weninger, 1988; Svartdal, 1989).

Shaping Verbal Behavior

In one experiment (Catania, Matthews, & Shimoff, 1982), students' presses on two buttons occasionally produced points exchangeable for money. When a blue light above the left button was lit, a variable-ratio (VR) schedule operated for presses on that button; when one above the right button was lit, a variable-interval (VI) schedule operated for its presses. Between alternations of the two schedules, the students filled out sentence-completion guess sheets (e.g., *The way to produce points with the left button is to…*). Their guesses were either shaped with differential points worth money or instructed. When the guess shaped for one button was *press quickly* and that for the other was *press slowly*, response rates on the two buttons changed in corresponding directions, without regard to schedule contingencies. Thus, shaping *press slowly* for the left button and *press quickly* for the right button produced relatively low VR rates and relatively high VI rates, opposite to those usually produced by these schedule contingencies (cf. Chapter 8).

When students were told what to guess, however, correspondences between the guesses and the response rates were incon-

sistent; sometimes guessing *press fast* was accompanied by fast pressing and guessing *press slow* by slow pressing, but sometimes these guesses were accompanied by equal response rates on the two buttons or by rates that differed in the opposite direction. Furthermore, the shaping of descriptions of the VR and VI schedule contingencies (e.g., the button works after a random number of presses or after a random time has passed) was also unreliably accompanied by corresponding rates. In other words, a description of what one does in an environment must be distinguished from a description of how that environment works; in correspondences between saying and doing, the vocabulary of behavior is more effective than the vocabulary of contingencies.

Correspondences between shaped verbal behavior and relevant nonverbal behavior begin early, and have been shown with children (Catania, Lowe, & Horne, 1990; cf. Bentall & Lowe, 1987; Bentall, Lowe, & Beasty, 1985). One possibility is that they come about because one's own behavior and the words that tact that behavior enter into equivalence classes. Procedures that affect one may then bring along the other (cf. Baer, Detrich, & Weninger, 1988; Matthews, Shimoff, & Catania, 1987).

One implication of these findings is that the shaping of verbal behavior is a potent technique for changing human behavior. Another is that the distinction between rule-governed and contingency-governed behavior is relevant to verbal as well as nonverbal behavior (Catania, Matthews, & Shimoff, 1990). Verbal behavior that is shaped or contingency-governed is, like nonverbal shaped behavior, sensitive to its consequences, but it is also accompanied by corresponding nonverbal behavior; if what we say is shaped, we do what we say.

On the other hand, verbal behavior that is instructed or rule-governed is, like non-verbal instructed behavior, relatively insensitive to its consequences, but it is less reliably accompanied by corresponding nonverbal behavior; if we are told what to say, what we do does not necessarily follow from what we say even if we reliably speak as we were told to.

The practical implication is that it may be easier to change human behavior by shaping what someone says than by shaping what someone does. Human nonverbal behavior is often rule-governed, but human verbal behavior is usually contingency-shaped (perhaps because we do not often talk about the variables that determine our own verbal behavior). Thus, the therapist may sometimes be effective simply by shaping a client's talk (Truax, 1966). In education, we sometimes teach by shaping what our students say through questions and discussion. More often we teach not by shaping but by instruction; in lectures, students are told what to say on examinations. If the courses include no direct contact with a subject matter, the former type of teaching may still be more likely than the latter to affect the student's interaction with the subject matter outside of the classroom.

THE LISTENER'S OR READER'S BEHAVIOR

Given that the speaker's verbal behavior provides discriminative stimuli for the listener, the listener's behavior is simply what is occasioned by these verbal stimuli. The listener's responses to verbal stimuli can be as varied as the responses to any other kinds of events. Many of the possible verbal responses have already been considered, in echoic, intraverbal, and other classes. Some nonverbal responses occasioned by verbal stimuli are also obvious enough that they do not require special consideration. Whether the critical stimulus is a red light, a traffic

officer's outstretched hand, the word *stop*, or a tree fallen across the road, the driver's stepping on the brakes illustrates stimulus control. As we move from watching an actual incident to watching the incident acted in a play or a film and then to reading the script for the actual incident and then to reading a description of the incident in a story, the common feature that holds these cases together must lie in consistencies of stimulus control over verbal and nonverbal behavior.

As with nonverbal stimuli, not all responses to verbal stimuli are operant. For example, if a spoken word is paired with a stimulus that elicits autonomic responses (e.g., shock), the word may come itself to elicit these responses. This phenomenon, sometimes called *semantic conditioning* (e.g., Riess, 1946), is a verbal equivalent to classical or respondent conditioning of nonverbal responses. Responding generated by these procedures generalizes across semantic as well as phonological dimensions of verbal stimuli. For example, if electric shock is paired with a farm word, such as *barn*, the conditioned galvanic skin response is more likely to generalize to other farm words, such as *cow*, than to words that simply have some letters in common with the original word, such as *burn*.

Yet if we say that a listener has understood something, it seems unlikely that we can provide an adequate account of the listener's response simply by appealing to pairings of words with words (as in the giving of definitions) or of words with events (as in the teaching of tacts). The problem of meaning must reside at least in part in properties of the listener's responses to verbal stimuli. One critical property may be the correspondence between the responses occasioned by a word or utterance and the responses occasioned by the nonverbal events that the word or utterance ordinarily tacts. Many studies of verbal behavior are concerned mainly with how verbal responses occasioned by events vary together in the verbal behavior of a speaker or have common effects on a listener (cf. Chapter 12 on semantics).

Whatever else is involved in the listener's behavior, the response to a tact must share some properties with the response to what is tacted. This is demonstrated when the properties of what is tacted interact with the properties of the relevant verbal behavior. For example, if words are printed in different colors, it is difficult to tact these colors rapidly if the words themselves are incompatible colornames (e.g., the word *red* printed in green; Stroop, 1935); we read words and do not ordinarily attend to physical properties such as the color in which they are printed. The relation between stimuli and the verbal responses they occasion clarifies some logical paradoxes of the language of reference. For example, consider the statement, *This statement is false.* If the statement is true, then it must be false; if it is false, then it must be true. Clearly it cannot be true and false at the same time. This is a paradox of logic but it is not a paradox of verbal behavior; a verbal response can be tacted by some other verbal response, but it cannot tact itself.

Meanings as Equivalence Classes

In dealing with the formal relations, we argued that the symmetry and reversibility of stimulus and response relations favored a vocabulary in terms of words rather than one in terms of specific vocal or written modalities. Similar correspondences exist in the relation between tacts and environmental events; these correspondences may be important when we speak of meaning, because the language of meaning is independent of whether words function as stimuli or as responses. This may be the most important way in which equivalence classes enter into verbal behavior. Consider, for example, rain as a stimulus, the word *rain*, and responses occasioned by rain, such as using an umbrella or putting on a raincoat. Both rain and the word *rain*, as stimuli, may occasion either a verbal response, the word *rain*, or a nonverbal response appropriate to rain. We may look out a window, see rain, and pick up an umbrella on the way out, but the latter response might also be occasioned by a verbal stimulus, as when a weather report predicts rain. On seeing rain, we may speak of the rain to someone else, who may then take an umbrella, but this speaking might also be occasioned by the weather report. The relations are summarized in Figure 11–3.

When a listener repeats what a speaker has said and we say that the listener has understood the speaker, we are not usually satisfied in calling the relation between *rain* as a verbal stimulus and *rain* as a verbal response echoic. Presumably then we judge understanding or meaning not by any single relation between stimuli and responses, but rather by the integrity

FIGURE 11–3 Relations among verbal and nonverbal responses occasioned by verbal and nonverbal stimuli (*S*, stimulus; *R*, response). Such consistencies establish equivalence classes and are essential to understanding and meaning. (Cf. Figure 11–1)

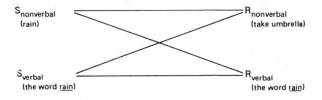

of the sorts of relations illustrated in Figure 11–3. We say that someone understands something that has been said when the individual repeats what has been said not because the other person else said it but for the same reasons that the other person said it (cf. Skinner, 1957). Such behavior implies the kinds of consistent relations among verbal and nonverbal responses illustrated in Figure 11–3, and therefore must be central to the concepts of meaning and understanding.

Section C   Verbal Behavior and Animal Language

We have considered some of the properties of verbal behavior: correspondences or equivalence classes, instructional control, and discriminations of one's own behavior in autoclitic processes. What we call language, then, involves complex interactions among a variety of different processes. Just as a taxonomy of processes is required for the analysis of nonverbal behavior (Chapters 1 through 10), we must develop a taxonomy of verbal behavior. That taxonomy includes classes different from those in the everyday vocabulary of language. Textual behavior is not equivalent to reading, although it may be its precursor. Transcription is not equivalent to pictorial copying, but depends on the establishment of units of written verbal behavior. Tacting is not equivalent to naming or referring, and yet as stimulus control of verbal behavior it is the point at which verbal behavior is anchored to environmental events. The effectiveness of verbal behavior depends on the coordination of these elementary components of verbal behavior with more complex processes. By themselves they are not even particularly verbal, but our verbal behavior is in many ways built upon them.

It is probably because verbal behavior involves so many different processes acting together that the issue of animal languages has typically engendered controversy. There certainly exist many cases in which the sounds or gestures of one animal influence the behavior of other members of that species; some were considered in Chapter 10. Birdsong, for example, has important effects in mating and the establishment of territories. The songs of birds often depend on the social context in which they sing (West & King, 1980); those of some birds have dialects, and birds who do not hear them at an early age do not sing them as adults (Marler & Peters, 1982). The dependence of birdsong on both genetic and environmental history has parallels in the development of human vocal behavior (as in the possibility of a critical period for learning), but the function and the structure of the two kinds of behavior differ in many important ways (e.g., in discriminations of melodies, absolute frequency is much more important for birds than for humans; Hulse, Cynx, & Humpal, 1984). Human language involves much more than vocal releasers or stimulus control based upon vocal stimuli (for that reason, discriminations based even on very subtle events, as by the horse, Clever Hans, have never counted as instances of verbal behavior; cf. Pfungst, 1911; Sebeok & Rosenthal, 1981).

Animal language has often referred broadly to any cases in which the behavior of one organism serves as either an eliciting or a discriminative stimulus for the behavior of another (e.g., Bright, 1985). Accounts of animal language have therefore been concerned with the full range of animal communication, ranging from the flashes of fireflies and the chirps of crickets to the territorial songs of birds and the coordinated songs of whales.

Many of these cases involve stimuli or responses of special interest, but their relevance to human verbal behavior is often limited.

As verbal classes, tacting involves stimulus control as it occurs in verbal behavior, manding involves consequences as they act in verbal behavior, and intraverbal responding involves chaining as it operates in verbal behavior. Those and other processes are important, and they have been studied with several species (e.g., tacting in the parrot; Pepperberg, 1983, 1987). Other research has been concerned with structural rather than functional aspects of human languages as they might enter into nonhuman behavior (e.g., discriminations of human phonetic categories by Japanese quail; Kluender, Diehl, & Killeen, 1987). Attention, however, has more often focused on aspects of human verbal behavior that are not obvious components of nonhuman behavior. For example, studies of the behavior of sea mammals such as dolphins and sea lions have shown that they are capable of sophisticated relational discriminations in both auditory and visual modes, but the sides taken on their verbal competence have depended on judgments of whether such complex properties as grammatical structure or equivalence relations have been demonstrated in their behavior (cf. Herman & Forestell, 1985; Schusterman, 1989).

In the search for animal language, investigators have most often turned to the primates (e.g., chimpanzees; cf. Savage-Rumbaugh, 1986). Early attempts to demonstrate language in chimpanzees were unsuccessful because they concentrated on language in the speech mode (Hayes & Hayes, 1951). But the chimpanzee's vocal apparatus restricts its capacity to produce differentiated vocal behavior, and the chimpanzee Viki learned to imitate only a few human utterances: *mama, papa, cup, up.*

Another question was whether the chimpanzee's capacity to remember transient and arbitrary stimuli was limited.

Researchers then switched to languages based on other modalities. The chimpanzee Washoe learned the gestures of American Sign Language (Gardner & Gardner, 1969); the chimpanzee Lana learned a language based on visual displays and keypresses at a computer console (Rumbaugh & Gill, 1976); and the chimpanzee Sarah learned a language based on arrangements of plastic chips of various shapes and colors on a magnetic board (Premack, 1970). In these projects, chimpanzees acquired large vocabularies and began to produce word combinations, but as some aspects of the chimpanzees' capacities for symbolic behavior were demonstrated, questions were raised about others. For example, after the chimpanzee Nim Chimpsky was taught some of the gestural vocabulary of American Sign Language, the structure of its word combinations was compared with that of the language of a human child (Terrace, Petitto, Sanders, & Bever, 1979; see also Thompson & Church, 1980). The sequential structure of Nim's word combinations was less orderly than a child's, and it was concluded that Nim's behavior could not be called language because it lacked adequate structure or syntax. Yet structure was deliberately avoided in the signing of Nim's teachers, so as not to impose it on Nim's signing, whereas a child's early verbal environment includes the structured speech of adults.

Other studies were concerned with such issues as the verbal implications of the chimpanzee's capacity to discriminate complex relational properties of the environment (e.g., Savage-Rumbaugh, Rumbaugh, Smith, & Lawson, 1980; Gillan, 1981; Gillan, Premack, & Woodruff, 1981; Braggio, Hall, Buchanan, & Nadler, 1982) and the emergence of instructional control from the language of tacting (especially in the interactions of the chimpanzees Austin and Sherman; Savage-Rumbaugh, Rumbaugh, & Boysen, 1978; cf. Epstein, Lanza, & Skinner, 1980). Some of these studies led in turn to syntheses of complex interactions (e.g., the reporting of private events; Lubinski & Thompson, 1987; cf. Chapter 10). Such demonstrations had special value because they forced all of the assumptions about what counted as verbal to be made explicit; you cannot tell a pigeon what to do in an experiment; instead, you have to shape every component that will be integrated into the final performance.

But once some features of human language had been demonstrated in the behavior of a chimpanzee or a pigeon or any other nonhuman organism, that feature could no longer be regarded as uniquely human; attention then turned to the definition of language rather than to the experimental analysis of its properties. The issue of grammatical structure, to be considered in Chapter 12, was the focus of much controversy. Given these debates, we cannot say whether chimpanzees are capable of language; the answer depends too much on how language is defined. We certainly can say, however, that their behavior includes some of the critical components of language (e.g., Savage-Rumbaugh, 1986). The horizons of research on nonhuman

language will open dramatically if symbolic behavior as characterized by equivalences classes can be demonstrated with nonhumans (cf. Chapter 8).

Just as we did not attempt definitions of learning and behavior, we will not try to define verbal behavior or language. We have seen that it includes many components: correspondences in the formal classes, stimulus control in intraverbals and in tacts, contingencies in instructional control, symbolic behavior in equivalence classes, and discriminations of one's own behavior in autoclitic processes. The list is certainly incomplete. To the extent that these processes are related to those of nonverbal behavior, they may hint at the origins and evolution of human language. The assumption that its primary function was to direct the behavior of others through instructional control suggests how such control might have emerged and been sharpened by the contingencies that operated within human social groups (cf. Jaynes, 1976; Skinner, 1981; Catania, 1985a, 1991b). Once the social selection of behavior began to operate on verbal behavior, the way was clear for the development of other functions as derivatives of its primary function. That is where we should seek the foundations of human concepts such as communication, computation, narrative, meaning, and truth.

CHAPTER 12
Psycholinguistics: Language Structure

Three primary terms in the analysis of language have been syntax, *the study of grammatical structure;* semantics, *the study of meaning; and* pragmatics, *the study of the functions of language.* Syntax *can be traced to the Greek* taxis, *arrangement;* semantics *to the Greek* sema, *a sign or thing seen; and* pragmatics *to the Greek* prassein, *to make happen or do. Pragmatics is a relative of* practice. Grammar, *through the Greek* graphein, *to scratch or write, and* gramma, *a picture or a writing, is closely related to* graph, program, *and* topography.

In this chapter we turn from the functions of verbal behavior to its structure. Language is organized. Words are ordered in

sentences and sentences are ordered in texts. We also speak of how words are related to each other, as when we say that words are similar or dissimilar in meaning. Psycholinguistics calls these topics *syntax* and *semantics. Syntax* deals with how words are organized in sentences; it is therefore concerned with the grammatical structure of language. In treating syntax, this chapter approaches language from the structural point of view of psycholinguistics, noting the relation of this vocabulary to the functional account of Chapter 11 when appropriate.

After syntax, we consider *semantics,* which deals with the problem of meaning. The introduction to verbal behavior questioned traditional concepts of meaning and reference. In this chapter we will see what can be said about these traditional concepts. In effect, we ask what properties of verbal behavior lead us to say that particular words are related in meaning. Psycholinguistics deals with a speaker's vocabulary in terms of the speaker's *lexicon,* the dictionary of words available in the speaker's verbal behavior. We must therefore examine the structure of the lexicon. These topics, often related, pave the way for our treatment of verbal learning and memory in later chapters. (Psycholinguistics has sometimes included a third topic, *pragmatics*, the uses of language; this corresponds most closely to the functions of language already considered in Chapter 11.)

A critical precursor of contemporary psycholinguistics was the effort to write programs for computer translation from one language to another. The history includes the evolution of computers in Allied efforts to break military codes during World War II (e.g., Hodges, 1985) and later applications of mathematics to problems of language structure during post-Sputnik efforts to translate Russian technical materials into English. Early attempts simply to substitute words in one language for their equivalents in another were not successful for a variety of reasons. For example, many words have multiple equivalents (e.g., should *bar* be translated as a noun, either a lever or a place to drink, or as a verb, to stop?), and grammatical distinctions in one language may be absent in another (e.g., given that Russian does not use articles, how does one decide whether the English translation of a Russian noun should be preceded by *a* or *the* or no article at all?).

One test for language translation programs is to translate a text from one language to another and then to translate the new text back to the original language: The sentence you get back should be the same as the one you put in. One illustration of the translation problem, probably apocryphal but often cited (with variations), is the translation to Russian and then back to English of *The spirit is willing but the flesh is weak;* it comes out as *Strong vodka, rotten meat.* Another is *Out of sight, out of mind.* It comes out as *Blind maniacs.* And if such a program generates *The lions leave by the end of summer,* its source sentence, though fitting, is not likely to be immediately evident (*Pride goeth before a fall*).

In general, the treatment that follows parallels some aspects of the evolution of computer programs in language transla-

tion. Such programs had to define explicit procedures for translation, including rules for substitution and transformation and ways to interpret ambiguous terms on the basis of the context provided by earlier text. Although these programs demonstrated some serious limitations on computer translation (e.g., Dreyfus, 1979; Winograd, 1980; cf. Chapter 15), they also led to a more thorough description of the complexities of syntax and semantics in human language. When the roles of various features of syntax and semantics were demonstrated in verbal behavior, these features were said to have *psychological reality;* we will explore several examples.

Section A   **Syntax: The Grammatical Structure of Language**

In what ways can we describe how words are organized in sentences? We can count or transcribe or classify words and we can analyze their arrangement in sentences. We can discriminate grammatical from ungrammatical examples of sentences. Among grammatical sentences, we can classify categories, such as active voice, passive voice, past tense, and so on. But how do we define the dimensions along which we make these distinctions? When we describe grammatical structure, sentences are our stimuli and their properties set the occasion for verbal responses, such as naming types of sentences. When we say one sentence is declarative (a statement) and another interrogative (a question), we are discriminating something about the sentences.

We could begin by trying to list all grammatical sentences. But that task would be neither feasible nor relevant. Most of what we say or write is novel. Sentences are only occasionally repeated, and a list of all possible sentences would be indefinitely large (if we placed no restrictions on length, it would be infinitely long). Even if we could produce such a list, our problem would not be solved, because we still would not know what made a sentence grammatical. Instead of sentence lists, we need an exhaustive description of kinds of sentences. In the language of psycholinguistics, we might speak of writing a grammar with a finite number of rules.

We will review three accounts of the structural regularities of grammatical sentences (Chomsky & Miller, 1963; Catania, 1972). The first is restricted to *sequential dependencies* between successive words or word sequences, corresponding to the chaining considered in Chapter 6. The second describes sentences and their grammatical structures in terms of their *constituents* or components. The third examines the *transformations* that show how one sentence or grammatical structure is related to others. For example, consider the saying, *He who hesitates is lost.* We examine sequential dependencies by presenting *He who hesitates* as a verbal stimulus and determining the likelihood with which *is lost* is given as a response. We consider constituents when we study how parts of the sentence come to be named subjects and predicates or pronouns and verbs. And we deal with grammatical transformations when we describe the relation between this saying and such paraphrases as *He is lost who hesitates.*

SEQUENTIAL ANALYSES

We have already treated some properties of sequential analysis in considering the verbal responses to verbal stimuli called word associations (intraverbal behavior in Chapter 11). These associations can be based on several words instead of single words as stimuli. Such sequences are the basis for constructing different *orders of*

approximation to English. For example, suppose you are asked to complete a sentence given its first three words. The first of the three words is then dropped, and the two remaining words plus the next word are presented to someone else, who now generates a sentence that continues those three words. Again the first word is dropped, and the next three remaining words are presented to still another participant, and so on. An example of a text produced in this way is

> the first list was posted on the bulletin he brought home a turkey will die on my rug is deep with snow and sleet are destructive and playful students always (Miller & Selfridge, 1950)

This is called a fourth-order approximation to English, because at each point a participant sees only the last three words and must add the new fourth word. According to this nomenclature, a zero-order approximation to English has words chosen randomly and a first-order approximation has words chosen randomly but in proportion to their frequencies in the language. Several orders of approximation to English and a passage of English text are illustrated by the following samples (from Miller & Selfridge, 1950):

Zero-order:	byway consequence handsomely financier bent flux cavalry swiftness weather-beaten extent
First-order:	abilities with that beside I for waltz you the sewing
Second-order:	was he went to the newspaper is in deep and
Third-order:	tall and thin boy is a biped is the beat
Fifth-order:	they saw the play Saturday and sat down beside him
Text:	the history of California is largely that of a railroad

Miller and Selfridge found that the more closely a text approximated English, the more accurately it was recalled. But if we simply add new words on the end of existing sequences, producing various approximations to English, we cannot guarantee that we will generate grammatical sequences. Common sequences of words can occur together in ungrammatical ways (*Haste makes waste not want not*) whereas rare sequences of words may be grammatical (*Sleeping green ideas dream furiously*). We do not determine the grammaticality of novel sentences on the basis of the likelihood of word sequences. It does not help much to examine sequential dependencies by recording the relative frequencies with which particular word sequences occur in some sample of sentences. In fact, we might judge some sequences ungrammatical even though they involve likely sequences of words, as in the saying, *The wages of sin is death.*

One reason sequential analyses cannot accommodate grammatical structure is that they cannot deal with relations between words that are separated by varying numbers of other words. For example, consider the sentences *The chimpanzee used sign language* and *The chimpanzee that was taught by the psychologist used sign language.* The words *chimpanzee* and *used* are adjacent in the first sentence but are separated by six other words in the second, and yet the two words are grammatically related in the same way in both sentences. We cannot represent that relation with a sequential analysis, because sequential probabilities when two words occur in immediate succession will necessarily differ from the probabilities when other words intervene.

Even if we could resolve that problem, we would soon encounter others. For instance, sequential analyses would not help us to deal with ambiguous sentences. An example is *Running experiments should be encouraged,* which might be read as recommending more support for research (*Encourage the running of experiments*) or more research on exercise (*Encourage experiments on running*). We cannot base our interpretation on a sequential analysis, because the same words occur in succession whichever way we read the sentence. The two interpretations cannot be distinguished by word sequences. The circumstances surrounding the sentence would be more relevant: It might help to know whether it was uttered in a psychology laboratory or at a track meet. But that is a matter of function rather than structure. This does not mean sequential processes cannot or do not operate in verbal behavior. What we say at one moment sometimes influences what we say in the next. We call such relations intraverbal. We learn verbal sequences along with, and sometimes independently of, grammatical structure (e.g., as when a child learns to recite the alphabet). But sequential dependencies are inadequate for defining grammatical structure (cf. Chapter 6).

CONSTITUENTS AND PHRASE STRUCTURE

One aspect of grammatical structure derives from the constituents or components of sentences or classes of sentences. We determine the constituents of a sentence by noting how its parts are related. Consider the sentence *A word to the wise is sufficient.* We can name its constituents: *word* is a noun, *is* a verb, *sufficient* an adjective, and so on. The relations are not defined by how close the words are to each other. For example, the word *is* is tied grammatically more to *word* than to *wise,* even though it is closer to the latter. The relations among words in sentences have been represented in various ways (e.g., Wundt, 1900; Chomsky & Miller, 1963). Three representations, sometimes called phrase-structure diagrams, are illustrated in Figure 12–1.

We could now discuss properties of noun phrases and verb phrases and so on. But the point is not to argue for one or another kind of description. Rather, it is to show the nature of an analysis of constituents. The illustrations in Figure 12–1 mainly involve naming them. How do we decide whether a word should be called one type of constituent or another? We distinguish among constituents not by the words alone, but by their relations to other words in the sentence. We cannot classify

constituents without also identifying the structure of the sentence.

Consider the following example: *He whose laughs last laughs last.* The word *laughs* appears twice, first as a plural noun and then as a verb; the word *last* also appears twice, first as a verb and then as an adverb. What we call *laughs* or *last* therefore depends on the relation of each to other words in the sentence. This poses a problem. We concluded earlier that we cannot identify the structure of a sentence without classifying its constituents, but this example demonstrates that neither

FIGURE 12–1   Three methods for representing the constituent structure of sentences. Each shows how a sentence can be analyzed into structural units ranging from individual words to phrases. Note that the sentences in the box diagram (I) and the bracketing diagram (III) have equivalent structures. In psycholinguistics, the tree diagram (II) has been the most common representation. Places where branches come together are called nodes; thus, *verb phrase* in the example is a node for *verb* and *noun phrase.*

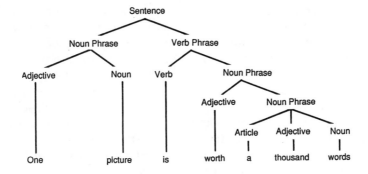

can we classify its constituents without identifying its structure. How then can we ever describe the structure of a sentence? To resolve this problem, we must identify consistencies of sentence structure. These consistencies are not in particular words or word sequences, but rather in various co-ordinations among words. We can classify words of a sentence as particular kinds of constituents because we have learned typical structures in our language (e.g., patterns of agreement between singular and plural nouns and verbs).

We may be tempted to look to the environment as a basis for deciding on sentence structure. But even if we show that certain kinds of sentences are likely to be uttered mainly in certain circumstances, we cannot appeal to them as a basis for naming constituents. This is because we can name the constituents even of some sentences partly made up of nonsense words. For example, compare the sentences *He who guffs merts* and *She merts his guffs*. Even though *guffs* and *merts* are not standard words, we would call each a verb in the first sentence whereas we would call *merts* a verb and *guffs* a plural noun in the second.

We must conclude that some grammatical classifications of words do not depend on the environment events of which we speak. They depend instead on the sentence structures within which words appear. Verbs, for example, are not defined as the class of words occasioned by activities; they are defined in terms of conjugation or other grammatical properties. Compare the activity word, *running*, in the sentences *The child is running* and *The child's running is fun to watch*. Only the first instance is classified as a verb. The case is even more obvious when the activity word changes form with a change in grammatical structure, as with *move* in *The chess player moved the knight* versus *The*

move surprised the other player, or with *examine* in *The jury examined the evidence* versus *Their examination was thorough*.

It would be incorrect to assume that the environment never determines our judgments of grammatical structure. For example, in treating sequential dependencies we considered ambiguous sentences. An instance is *Time flies*. Typically, as when this sentence is uttered at a reunion of old friends, we call *time* a noun and *flies* a verb. But if it is uttered in a biology laboratory as an instruction to record how long it takes these insects to get from one place to another, we might conclude instead that *time* is a verb and *flies* is a plural noun.

We are left with a paradox. On the one hand are sentences with structures that allow us to name their constituents without knowing the circumstances in which they were uttered (e.g., *He who guffs merts*); on the other hand are sentences with structures that do not allow us to name their constituents unless we know those circumstances (e.g., *Time flies*). (Such ambiguities can also be resolved by expanding the structure; consider *Time flies like an arrow* and *Fruit flies like a peach*.) In other words, any account of grammar that is either exclusively structural or exclusively functional is necessarily incomplete.

What have we accomplished so far? We have examined some ways of talking about the structure of sentences, but we have not explained how we discriminate among nouns, verbs, and other parts of speech. We have not even discussed the dimensions upon which such discriminations might be based. We have merely shown that we can name the constituents of sentences with some consistency (cf. Danks & Glucksberg, 1970). We have not identified any independent way to specify the properties of constituents and their relations to each other. But we faced the same problem in the treatment of abstraction. Verbal behavior and its properties are included among the events that we can learn to discriminate.

In any case, and perhaps more important, our response to a sentence is typically not a matter of naming its constituents or drawing a diagram of its phrase structure. If someone asks you a question, you don't have to say which words are nouns and which are verbs before answering. Children learn to speak and to understand sentences long before they are formally taught grammar and parts of speech. Our analysis of grammatical structure must be based on something more than our capacity to name constituents or to diagram structures. We must demonstrate the relation between these sentence properties and the speaker's or the listener's behavior. Experiments that seek to demonstrate such relations are said to be concerned with the *psychological*

reality of these dimensions of language (e.g., Fodor & Bever, 1965; Schane, Tranel, & Lane, 1975).

Figure 12–2 provides an example (Johnson, 1965). People were asked to memorize sentences with different phrase structures. When they were later asked to recall the sentences, the probability of errors was greatest at the major grammatical transitions. For example, errors were highly likely at the break between noun phrase and verb phrase in both types of sentences, even though this break occurred at word transition 3 in sentences of type I and at word transition 5 in sentences of type II. Sentences with different structures were matched for number of words and other properties, so position and other nongrammatical features were not the basis for the pattern of errors (cf. Jarvella, 1971, for a similar analysis at the level of phrase and sentence rather than word transitions).

FIGURE 12–2 Probability of an error in sentence recall as a function of word transitions in two different sentence types. Sentences of type I are illustrated by: (The1 tall2 boy)3 (saved4 the5 dying6 woman). In this type, error probability is highest at the break between noun phrase and verb phrase (transition **3**). Sentences of type II are illustrated by: ((The1 house)2 (across3 the4 street))5 (burned6 down). In this type, error probability is highest at the break within the noun phrase (transition **2**), and next highest at the break between noun phrase and verb phrase (transition **5**). In other words, errors are most likely at major breaks in phrase structure. (Adapted from Johnson, 1965, Table 2)

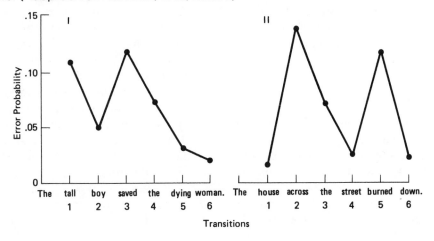

In other experiments (Fodor & Bever, 1965), listeners wearing earphones heard a sentence in one ear and a click in the other and were asked to locate where in the sentence the click occurred. When their judgments were wrong, they tended to displace the click in the direction of major sentence boundaries. This displacement did not depend on acoustic properties such as locations of pauses (Garrett, Bever, & Fodor, 1966). For example, the same tape recording produced all but the opening words in pairs of sentences like the following: (*In her hope of marrying*)$_X$ (*Anna$_Y$ was surely impractical*) and (*Your hope of marrying$_X$ Anna*)$_Y$ (*was surely impractical*). The major sentence boundaries were in parts of the recording that were acoustically identical. Nevertheless, a click in the middle of the word *Anna* was more likely to be heard displaced toward X than toward Y in the first sentence and toward Y than toward X in the second. These findings have been challenged on the basis of such factors as possible biases in listeners' reports of sentence locations (e.g., Dalrymple-Alford, 1976). But whether the results are interpreted as displacements in the heard locations of clicks or as systematic errors in the reports of the locations, they remain as demonstrations of the effects of sentence structure on behavior. This is the sense in which we are justified in saying that such structures have psychological reality.

TRANSFORMATIONS

In comparing sentences, we may note that some say different things while others say the same thing in different ways. In making such judgments, we are discriminating among relations between sentences. For example, consider the following three sentences: *He who hesitates laughs last*, *He who laughs last who hesitates*, and *He who laughs last hesitates*. The first two have something in common that neither has in common with the last. We say that the first two mean the same thing. Although they differ in word order, the structural relations among their constituents are the same (e.g., *who* is similarly related to *hesitates* in both sentences). We therefore call the second sentence a grammatical transformation of the first.

Transformations describe changes in sentence structure that preserve certain relations among the constituents. When we transform a sentence from active to passive voice (e.g., *The rat pressed the lever* and *The lever was pressed by the rat*), we preserve the subject-object relation among the nouns and the verb. When we speak of different sentences in terms of transformations that relate one to another, we are discriminating some structural features the sentences share.

Once we have described structural equivalences among sentences in terms of transformations, we can distinguish among kinds of sentence structures by how they can be transformed. For example, consider the sentences *He is hard to understand* and *He is last to understand*. They differ only in the adjectives *hard* and *last*. They seem similar in structure, but we can demonstrate a difference by examining how each may be transformed. We can transform the first to *To understand him is hard* but not to *He understands hard*. Conversely, we can change the second to *He understands last* but not to *To understand him is last*. The sentences appeared similar, but we distinguished between their structures by their different relations to other sentences. In the language of psycholinguistics, the sentences are called similar in *surface structure* (the particular order of constituents) but different in *deep structure* (the underlying structural features that distinguish them).

We sometimes judge how well a phrase or a sentence has been understood by whether it can be paraphrased appropriately (cf. Gleitman & Gleitman, 1970). For example, a grammatical transformation usually relates a question to its answer. If your question *Who bit the dog?* was answered by *The dog didn't bite anybody* instead of by *Nobody bit the dog*, you might assume your question had been misunderstood. Again, we cannot appeal to semantics for our classification. The classification of transformations does not specify the conditions under which any particular one occurs. Instead, it shows how different sentences may be related. Thus, we can transform or paraphrase sentences even if we substitute nonsense syllables for some constituents (e.g., given *The wizzle lerped the zorn*, we would identify *The zorn was lerped by the wizzle* but not *The wizzle was lerped by the zorn* as its passive equivalent).

Figure 12–3 illustrates relations among various transformations and combinations of transformations. The base sentence on which the transformations operate is *Haste makes waste*. This sentence provides the core material for the transformations and is called the *kernel* (in a stricter interpretation, even this present tense, active voice, positive, and declarative sentence is a transformation from the raw material that makes it up: subject noun *haste*, infinitive verb *to make*, and object noun *waste*). Possible transformations include present to past or future tense, active voice to passive voice, declarative to interrogative (question), positive (affirmative) to negative, or any combination. These transformations generate 24 unique sentences, and they are not exhaustive (e.g., consider changes from singular to plural, as in *The cat pauses* and *The cats pause*, or in

person, as in *I am bored, He or she is bored*, and *They are bored*). Furthermore, some transformations may be regarded either as simple transformations in their own right or as complex transformations based upon a combination of simpler ones (e.g., the question *Does haste make waste?* can be derived directly from the base sentence or indirectly from the intermediate emphatic transformation *Haste does make waste*).

What advantage does speaking in terms of transformations have over simply labeling sentences according to tense, case, and so on? With transformations, as with constituent structure, we again face the problem of the behavioral significance or psychological reality of these verbal properties. One interpretation is that the transformations correspond to something listeners or readers actually do in responding to spoken or written sentences. This is equivalent to saying that the transformation of a sentence from one grammatical form to another is a kind of behavior. Even though it cannot be observed directly, it may be possible to record its duration, its effects on other behavior, or how it is learned (e.g., Mehler, 1963; Miller, 1962; Baldie, 1976).

In one experiment (Savin & Perchonock, 1965), listeners were given sentences followed by sequences of eight words, as in the following: *The ball was hit by the boy. Grass, cat, truck, hour, desk, rain, shirt, blue.* The transformational complexity of the sentences and the list of words varied over presentations. The listeners were instructed to repeat the sentence after each presentation and then to recall as many of the eight words as possible. On the average, the number of words recalled decreased with increasing transformational complexity of the sentences. For example, the mean words recalled was 5.27 after kernel sentences, 4.67 after questions, 4.55

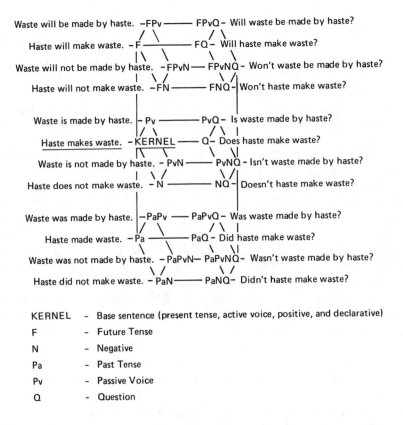

KERNEL – Base sentence (present tense, active voice, positive, and declarative)

F   – Future Tense

N   – Negative

Pa   – Past Tense

Pv   – Passive Voice

Q   – Question

FIGURE 12–3 Some transformations of the kernel sentence, "Haste makes waste." The middle block shows transformations from declarative to interrogative (statement to question, left-right), from active voice to passive voice (front-back), and from positive to negative (top-bottom). For each sentence type, the transformation to future tense is shown in the upper block and to past tense in the lower block. The closeness of the relation between two sentence types depends on the number of transformations that separate them (e.g., the future "Haste will make waste" is closer to the kernel "Haste makes waste" than to the past passive question "Was waste made by haste?").

after passive sentences, and 4.02 after passive questions. In other words, fewer words were recalled after sentences with two transformations (e.g., passive question) than after those with only one (e.g., passive), and fewer after those with only one than after those with none (kernel sentences). The finding is consistent with the assumption that the transformational complexity of the sentence limits the listener's capacity to recall words from the list.

But other factors complicate the interpretation (Glucksberg & Danks, 1969). Transformations are usually longer than kernel sentences (compare *The cat chased the mouse* with *The mouse was chased by the cat*). Even with sentences matched in number of words, listeners typically take less time to repeat kernel sentences than transformations of the kernel. Thus, the results may depend on the time that repetitions of the various transformations imposed between the end of the list and the opportunity to recall the words: The longer the time, the fewer the words correctly recalled.

Other research showed that kernel sentences can be memorized more quickly than can transformations (e.g., Mehler, 1963), and that grammatical structure affects the accuracy with which sentences are heard when they are masked by noise (e.g., Miller & Isard, 1963). A more direct study of transformations gave readers two lists of sentences (Miller, 1962). Each sentence in list 1 was related by some transformation to one in list 2. The reader matched list-1 sentences to corresponding list-2 sentences. For example, pairs such as *John warned the small boy* and *The small boy was warned by John* made up two lists that differed by a kernel-to-passive transformation. Time per transformation was estimated from the time per correct match for each pair of lists. By this analysis, kernel-to-negative, kernel-to-passive, and passive-to-passive-negative transformations took an average of 1.1 to 1.8 seconds, kernel-to-passive-negative took 2.7 seconds, and negative-to-passive took 3.5 seconds. The differences are consistent with the number of transformations by which pairs of lists differed: the first three pairs by a single transformation and the other three by two transformations. (The transformation from kernel to passive negative can be broken down into two parts—kernel to either passive or negative and then to passive negative; the transformation from negative to passive is assumed to be indirect, by way of negative to kernel and then kernel to passive.)

These findings suggest that transformations, like constituents, have psychological reality. We may recognize transformations as properties of verbal behavior, but they do not explain verbal behavior. We can describe some properties of combinations of transformations, as when we speak of a past-tense negative question in passive voice. We can note how transformations relate complex sentences to the simpler sentences from which they are derived (the psycholinguist speaks of the relation between a terminal sentence and its kernel or kernels). We might extend our account to more detailed features of grammatical structure (e.g., psycholinguists sometimes distinguish between obligatory and optional transformations, depending on whether general relations such as subject-predicate or other more variable properties of sentences are involved). Describing the structural properties of sentences is the point of grammar, but describing a sentence does not say how it was produced or understood nor does its production or understanding require a judgment about its grammaticality.

Hierarchical Organization

Transformations involve not only changes in the form of sentences but also ways in which sentences or sentence parts can combine with each other. For example, the sentences *The canary sang* and *The cat ate the canary* in combination can become *The canary that the cat ate sang* or *The cat ate the canary that sang*. These types of sentence structures are called *recursive*, because the addition of new segments can recur again and again. With the additional sentence, *The cat grinned*, the combination sentence could become *The canary that the cat that grinned ate sang* or *The cat that ate the canary that sang grinned*. Strictly speaking, these sentences are grammatical, even if they may not seem right. Sentences can be expanded by adding phrases at the beginning or at the end, when their structures are respectively called left-recursive and right-recursive, or by adding parts within or around the sentence, when their structures are respectively called self-embedding and self-enveloping. With the self-embedded sentence *The canary that the cat ate sang*, we can illustrate a self-enveloping structure by expanding it to *The music that the canary that the cat ate sang was off key.* Whether we regard the structure of this sentence as self-embedding or self-enveloping depends in large part on whether we started with *The music was off key* or with *The cat ate.*

In other words, we can describe a sentence as a hierarchical structure in which some features or components are necessarily subordinate to others. Whether a given component is higher or lower in such a description, however, may have nothing to do with the order in which components occurred when the sentence was produced or understood (cf. top-down vs. bottom-up processing; e.g., Danks & Glucksberg, 1980). For example, we might decide that one or the other of the above structures was an appropriate description depending on whether the sentence was part of a conversation that began with *I'm glad that the music stopped* or of one that began with *I'm glad that the cat ate.*

The analysis of hierarchical structure is a general problem in behavior, and was considered in our discussion of operant classes (Chapter 6). In verbal behavior, similarly, different units enter into different levels of analysis. Letters and phonemes combine in morphemes and words, which in turn form phrases and sentences, which in turn make up paragraphs and texts, and so on. Individual letters and phonemes can enter into a variety of different narratives, and a given narrative can be told in a variety of different words and sentences. We have been concerned here mainly with the structure of sentences, but such accounts can be extended from sentences to smaller units, such as the phonemes of speech (e.g., Liberman, 1982), or to larger units, such as story plots and other types of extended discourse (e.g., Bower, Black, & Turner, 1979).

There are other types of analyses of sentence structure. Some base syntactic structure on semantic considerations (e.g., case grammars; Fillmore, 1968). We move on to semantics in the next section. In our treatment of syntax, we have examined some features of the formal analysis of grammatical structure. Sentences are sequences of discrete units called words, but sequential dependencies cannot provide adequate structural descriptions because they cannot describe relations that are independent of the separation of words in a sentence. Sentence structure, however, can be described in terms of constituents and transformations. In our account of sentences, we classified words and their relations to each other and we examined how sentences can be related to other sentences that include the same or related words. The various methods of labeling or bracketing or diagramming sentence constituents allow us to describe structural relations within and among sentences (as when we distinguish among alternative structures of an ambiguous sentence).

The properties of sentences may also have behavioral significance; to the extent that transformations describe what we do when speaking or listening or reading or writing, they correspond to the autoclitic processes discussed in Chapter 11. Experiments concerned with the psychological reality of constituent and transformational structure illustrate how the behavioral effects of these dimensions of syntax can be studied.

Section B   Semantics: The Meaning of Verbal Units

To study semantics is to grapple with the problem of meaning. In everyday talk, we sometimes ask what people mean when they say things or whether one person has understood the meaning of another's words. Our treatment of verbal behavior made the point early that traditional vocabularies of meaning and reference can mislead. How can we reconcile the widespread appeal of the concept of meaning in everyday language with the ambiguities of that concept in a behavioral account?

Part of the problem is distinguishing between the production of verbal behavior by a speaker or writer and its comprehension by a listener or reader (meaning what you say is different from understanding what you mean when you say it). Correspondences between language production and language comprehension are ordinarily created in the course of language development, but we must not take them for granted. For example, a case report on an 8-year-old boy who understood spoken English but could not speak because of a congenital organic defect (Lenneberg, 1962) shows that comprehension can be independent of production (cf. Fraser, Bellugi, & Brown, 1963, on the developmental progression from imitation to comprehension to production). Behavioral accounts of language have tended to emphasize production whereas cognitive and psycholinguistic accounts have tended to emphasize comprehension. The treatment of semantics in this chapter therefore stresses comprehension: What happens when someone is said to understand a word or a sentence?

Let us begin with an experiment in which listeners heard a passage of text (e.g., an account of Galileo and the invention of the telescope), and then were asked whether a new sentence was one that had been in the passage (Sachs, 1967). The sentence was either identical to one in the passage (base sentence) or differed in any of three ways: a change in word order that did not affect grammatical structure (formal change); a change in grammatical voice (active-passive change); or a change in meaning (semantic change). The new sentence was presented either immediately after the original one from the passage or after 80 or 160 syllables of additional text. Examples of sentences used with the passage about Galileo are the following:

Base sentence:	He sent a letter about it to Galileo, the great Italian scientist.
Formal change:	He sent Galileo, the great Italian scientist, a letter about it.
Active to passive:	A letter about it was sent to Galileo, the great Italian scientist.
Semantic change:	Galileo, the great Italian scientist, sent him a letter about it.

The passages and base sentences were varied across different presentations and listeners.

When the new sentence immediately followed the original one, listeners identified it as identical or changed with better than 80 percent accuracy. When it was presented after 80 or 160 syllables of intervening text, accuracy decreased for all sentence types, but it stayed greater than 75 percent for semantically changed sentences whereas it dropped toward chance levels for the other sentence types. In other words, listeners were likely to recognize a sentence as different only if its meaning had changed; as long as the meaning remained the same, they did not notice formal and active-passive changes. Thus, the listeners were not remembering words or word orders. They were remembering something more fundamental: the *gist* of the sentence, or whatever it is that sentences have in common when we say they mean the same thing.

The finding that listeners are more likely to remember semantic structure than specific words or sentences is a general one (e.g., Bartlett, 1932; Fillenbaum, 1966). One study gave listeners related sentences such as *The ants were in the kitchen* and *The ants ate the sweet jelly* (Bransford & Franks, 1971). Later the listeners heard a mix of the original and new sentences and for each were asked to rate their confidence that it was one they had heard before. Some new ones combined original sentences, as in *The ants in the kitchen ate the sweet jelly.* The listeners were usually more confident that they had already heard the new combined sentences than that they had heard the simpler sentences that had actually been presented. They had learned something more abstract than particular words or sentences (but see also Katz & Gruenwald, 1974; Wang, 1977).

These findings should remind us of the intimate relation between semantics and syntax. When we examined transformations, we spoke of the psycholinguist's concept of deep structure; deep structure is the name for those properties of a sentence that remain constant over various transformations. What we hold constant when we change the syntactic structure of a sentence is its semantic structure.

THE MEASUREMENT OF MEANING

So far we have mainly considered sentences, but in semantics more attention has usually been given to individual words. What determines what a word means? In what ways can the meanings of different words be related? Word associations were the basis for some attempts to measure meaning (Galton, 1879; cf. Chapter 11). If listeners produced longer and more varied lists of words in response to one word than another, the first word was said to be more meaningful than the second. In addition, it was assumed that words closely related in meaning would occasion overlapping lists of associates. For example, common associations to both *infant* and *baby* might include *crib* and *bottle* but none of these might occur as a response to *guitar*. The different degrees of overlap among the lists of associates are consistent with what we already know: *Infant* and *baby* are closer in meaning than either is to *guitar.*

In word associations, concrete nouns like *wall* or *book* or *road* are likely to occasion more responses than prepositions like *of* or *to* or *at*. Given that responses may be occasioned even by nonsense words, associations can be used to assess the meaningfulness of such words relative to each other and to standard vocabulary words (e.g., Glaze, 1928). Word associations are not equivalent to meanings, but to the extent that we say that words are similar in meaning when we respond similarly to them, they are one appropriate measure of meaning.

Word associations can be ambiguous. For example, if *night* occasions *day, morning, sun,* and *moon,* are the later words responses to preceding ones or to the stimulus word itself? In this instance, we might guess that *sun* was probably occasioned more by *day* and *morning* than by *night,* but it is unclear whether *moon* was occasioned more by *night* or by *sun* or by *morning* (which shares three letters with it). We might want to see what each word occasions when it serves separately as a stimulus word.

The *semantic differential* was one attempt to measure meaning without such ambiguities (Osgood, Suci, & Tannenbaum, 1957; see also Hutchinson & Lockhead, 1977, and the orientation metaphors in Lakoff & Johnson, 1980). Words were rated along dimensions provided by word pairs, like *happy-sad, hard-soft*, and *slow-fast*. Similarities among ratings were then determined by a statistical procedure, factor analysis, which created a space within which words could be placed. Words that were close together in this space were said to be more alike in meaning than ones that were far apart. Words like *good, beautiful, clean*, and *pleasant* tended to cluster together, distant from other clusters such as *bad, foul, dirty*, and *ugly*.

The semantic differential was intended to deal with any word in the lexicon. More recent rating methods have concentrated on words in specific categories, such as colors or emotions (e.g., Fillenbaum & Rapoport, 1971; Reyna, 1981). Another technique, called *componential analysis* (Romney & D'Andrade, 1964), is based not on word ratings but on an analysis of the dimensions that distinguish words within particular word groups. For example, kinship terms in English are based upon gender (*mother-father, sister-brother*), generation (*grandmother-mother, son-grandson*), and line of descent (*mother-aunt, son-nephew*). The problem is that only groups with dimensions that can be specified lend themselves to such analyses (e.g., what are the dimensions of facial expressions?).

Each method describes semantic relations among words, so meaning could be defined merely as the relations measured by these methods, whatever their basis. This seems unsatisfactory, however, perhaps because such definitions leave us with little to say about the behavioral significance of meanings. Meanings are not properties of words themselves; they are properties of our responses to the words. For example, if you repeat a familiar word like your own name over and over, you may find that it loses its meaning; this implies that some response to it drops out after several repetitions. A red traffic light

means *stop* and a green one means *go*, but when you stop on red and go on green, you are responding to red and green and not to the meaning of red and the meaning of green. Written words in a language that no one understands have no meaning, and when a word is said to have many meanings (as in *bat* in a belfry and *bat* at a baseball game), it is the same word in each context; its meaning changes only in the sense that we respond differently to it.

If meaning is a feature of verbal behavior, we should be able to measure some of its properties. For example, we might see whether some types of semantic behavior take longer than others (cf. the analogous earlier treatment of syntactic structures; Miller, 1962). In one experiment with this rationale (Collins & Quillian, 1969), readers judged whether sentences were true or false by pressing one of two buttons. Sentences were constructed from an assumed semantic structure consisting of a hierarchy of categories defined by sets of relevant properties. An example is shown in Figure 12–4.

The assumption is that membership in each class is defined both by distinctive properties and by membership in the next higher class. For example, *canary* is defined by the properties *can sing* and *is yellow* and by membership in the class *bird*. The time taken to judge that a sentence is true should then depend on how far from the class a property is located in the hierarchical structure. Given the class *canary* and the three sentences *A canary can sing, A canary has feathers*, and *A canary breathes*, for example, judgment should be fastest for the first sentence and slowest for the last. In the first case, the property *can sing* is characteristic of canaries; in the second, *has feathers* is characteristic of being a bird, which in turn is a property of canaries; in the third, *breathes* is characteristic of being

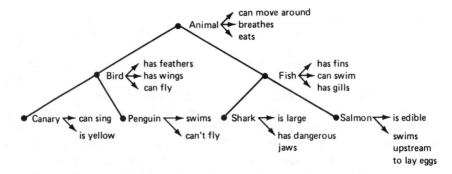

FIGURE 12-4 Hypothetical semantic structure with three levels. Each class is characterized by properties that define its members. Only a few sample properties are shown for each. (Adapted from Collins & Quillian, 1969, Figure 1)

an animal, which in turn is a property of being a bird, which in turn is a property of canaries. The structure allows for cases in which the property is incompatible with those that define the higher-level class; for example, *can't fly* is a property of penguins, so judging the truth of *Penguins can't fly* does not depend on first judging whether penguins are birds.

Judgment times of participants in the experiment were consistent with the types of hierarchical structure shown in Figure 12–4. Responding "true" took longer after sentences like *A canary eats* than after sentences like *A canary is yellow.* But hierarchical structure is not the only possible source of differences in judgment times, which may also be determined by such factors as the sizes of the different classes (e.g., Landauer & Meyer, 1972) and the frequencies of different word combinations in the language (e.g., *canary* and *sing* are more likely to occur together than *canary* and *breathe;* Conrad, 1972).

Semantics involves more than words themselves; it deals with words and their correspondences to classes of stimuli. When these classes do not have well-defined boundaries, they are examples of *probabilistic stimulus classes* (also called *fuzzy sets;* cf. natural concepts in Chapter 7). In such classes, each member contains some subset of features but none is common to all members; the number of features in the subset varies from one class member to another (cf. Rosch, 1973; Mervis & Rosch, 1981). Class members have family resemblances, and membership may be defined by reference to a *prototype,* a typical member of the class. A prototype is described by a weighted average of all the features of all the members of the class. For example, feathers are weighted more heavily than webbed feet among birds because more birds have feathers than have webbed feet. Thus, a robin is more prototypical than a duck because it shares more features with other birds than does a duck. As these examples show, the analysis of semantic structure does not explain probabilistic stimulus classes; it defines some of their properties.

METAPHOR

Metaphor demonstrates another aspect of semantic structure. In Chapter 11 it illustrated the extension of verbal behavior to new events. Once particular metaphors become effective within a verbal community, they are likely to evolve and interact and spread to a variety of situations. In Chapter 11 we noted an example in the case of language itself: Language is spoken of in the metaphor of communicating ideas. According to this metaphor, ideas and meanings are objects placed into words and then delivered to someone else (Lakoff & Johnson, 1980; Reddy, 1979). We *put our ideas into words;* we *have* ideas and *get them across to others;* our words *carry meaning* or are *empty;* our sentences *contain* or are *filled with* ideas; ideas can be *grasped* or *dropped* or *kicked around;* and so on. As we have seen, this metaphor is so well established that it is difficult to speak of language in other ways.

Other common systems of metaphors in our culture are those of time as money (e.g., we *spend* time or *save* it, and ask whether something is *worth* our time); of understanding as seeing (e.g., we *get the picture* or *look at things differently,* and describe arguments as *clear* or *opaque*); and of more as up and less as down (e.g., prices can *rise* or *fall,* and someone can be *under*age or *over*charged).

Systems of metaphors may also be coordinated with each other. For example, to say that a theoretical argument can be demolished by attacking its weak points is to combine the metaphor of discussion as war (arguments are *marshaled* or *undermined* or *shot down,* positions are *defended* or *given up,* and points are *won* or *lost*) with that of theory as a building (theories are *constructed,* rest on *solid* or *shaky foundations,* can be *supported* or *buttressed,* and may *stand* or *fall*).

On the other hand, systems of metaphors need not be consistent. For example, the metaphor of discussion as war may only occasionally make contact with that of discussion as exploration (issues are *gone over in depth* and *at different levels* and *from different approaches;* the *ground is covered;* the

speakers *map out their territories* and their arguments are *direct* or *roundabout*).

Metaphor is a pervasive property of language. Children learn it readily and adults cannot ignore it (e.g., Glucksberg, Gildea, & Bookin, 1982; Pollio & Smith, 1979; Winner, 1979). In semantic judgment tasks, reaction times are often shorter for metaphorical than for literal usages (Foss, 1988). Metaphor is not just the stuff of poetry; it is a fundamental aspect of verbal behavior. Much of our language about our own behavior has its origins in metaphorical usages (cf. Skinner, 1989).

The phenomenon of metaphor tempts us to talk about shared abstract properties captured by words, without reference to behavior. Yet the most important feature of metaphor is that it allows us to deal with the abstract in terms of the concrete. For example, the language of abstract dimensions like good-bad, happy-sad, and rational-emotional becomes that of a more accessible dimension, up-down. Hardly any dimension can be more abstract than time, but through metaphor it becomes a concrete spatial one: Tomorrow vs. yesterday becomes in-front-of vs. in-back-of. We are so used to saying our past is *behind us* and our future is *before us* that it is hard to imagine taking an about-face so that the future is in back and the past lies ahead; our time line turns with us.

The role of metaphor is also illustrated by the etymologies that introduce each chapter. Much of our technical vocabulary evolved metaphorically from concrete, everyday sources. These etymologies demonstrate some of the origins of our fundamental concepts. The creative aspect of metaphor, in other words, is to make the abstract substantial or, mixing the metaphor, to bring it down to earth.

We have not explicitly defined *meaning* or *metaphor.* As in other cases, our failure to do so does not imply that the terms are meaningless. Just as an independent specification of the stimulus is not essential to identifying discriminative relations, an independent specification of verbal classes is not essential to identifying the relations between words and events that we call meanings. We speak of classes of responses in terms of operants and of classes of stimuli in terms of concepts. But words can function either as responses or as stimuli (and thus can enter into equivalence relations); we therefore must speak of classes of words in other terms. It is probably appropriate to speak of them in terms of meanings.

Section C **Some Properties of Language**

Children who grow up in China speak Chinese, and children who grow up in France speak French. Clearly they each learn the specific grammars and vocabularies of their native languages. The question remains whether some general properties of human language that do not have to be learned underlie the details of particular languages. The extent to which the structural properties of human language are determined by biological constraints has been controversial (Lenneberg, 1967). The issues have been addressed in the search for universals of language, in studies of the variations in human languages that illustrate language relativity, and in the analysis of determinants of language development in children.

LANGUAGE UNIVERSALS

Properties assumed to be characteristic of all human languages have been called *language universals*. Various grammatical relations have been proposed as universals

(e.g., Greenberg, 1966). For example, it has been said that utterances in all human languages have subject-predicate structure, distinguish between singular and plural, are limited in the kinds of transformations that can operate on embedded structures, and have two classes of constituents called *open* (expandable classes with no limit on the number of possible members, such as nouns and verbs) and *closed* (fixed classes with a limited number of members, such as prepositions and conjunctions).

These properties may depend more on the conditions under which humans speak than on biological constraints on the kinds of sentences they can generate. The subject-predicate relation is one criterion for calling an utterance a sentence; it does not justify the omission of utterances without subject or predicate (e.g., *Hello, Ouch!, Oh?,* and *Aha!*). The difference between single objects and collections is presumably important in all human environments and to that extent determines the distinction between singular and plural; that distinction need not appear as a grammatical feature of a language (e.g., it does not do so in Japanese). Limits on the complexity of embedded phrases may depend on the limited span of immediate memory (see Chapter 14); they need not imply that there are constraints on syntactic structure. And some classes of words (e.g., nouns and verbs) are semantically related to an unlimited variety of events whereas others (e.g., prepositions and conjunctions) are syntactically related to a limited body of structural relations within sentences; thus, open and closed classes may be inevitable by-products of any hierarchical system qualifying as a language.

The universals of human language have yet to be specified. The most convincing case for such universals could be made by showing that humans cannot learn certain types of sentence structures, or at least that they can learn some types much more easily than others (cf. Bickerton, 1981). Such demonstrations would pose no problems for a behavioral account of language. In fact, to the extent that they involved limitations on language structure rather than on its functions, it might be most appropriate to regard them as spandrels (Gould & Lewontin, 1979; cf. Chapter 2).

Just as the anatomical features of birds and bees and bats determine the different ways in which each species flies, special characteristics of our species may determine the structure of human language and the way in which it develops. If we show that human verbal behavior always has certain structural properties or develops in certain ways, we have still to answer functional questions about the circumstances in which verbal behavior occurs. The anatomical analogy remains valid: An account of the different properties of flight in birds and bees and bats does not bear on where or when any of them takes off or lands; so also an account of language structure does not bear on what one speaks about or when one does so.

LANGUAGE RELATIVITY

The issue of language universals is concerned with what is constant across human languages; the issue of language relativity is concerned with what varies. All languages have unique characteristics, in phonetic structure, in vocabulary and in grammar. How do these features affect the ways in which people in different cultures interact with their environment? Do nonverbal discriminations depend on a speaker's lexicon? What are the implications of the varied words for types of snow in arctic cultures and the varied words for shades of green in tropical ones?

Nonverbal discriminations based on types of snow are more important than those based on shades of green in arctic environments, and vice versa in tropical ones. It therefore seems as plausible to argue that the nonverbal discriminations came first as to argue that they depended on vocabulary for their development. Verbal discriminations may parallel nonverbal ones, but such relations are not necessary ones: One response may be discriminated with respect to one stimulus while a second is independently discriminated with respect to another (cf. Catania, 1976a). This difference between *knowing how* and *knowing that* is similar. For example, one can know how to ride a bicycle without being able to say how one does it; conversely, one can say how the bicycle works without knowing how to ride it.

The case for the effects of language on nonverbal behavior is clearer, however, with respect to grammatical properties of language. For example, you cannot behave in the presence of past and future times but verbal behavior allows you to speak of them. Thus, the way you deal with time may depend on how past, present, and future tenses work in your language (Whorf, 1956). In other cases, languages in which nouns and verbs are exchangeable (thought vs. thinking, memory vs. remembering) may lead to different treatments of events and actions than those in which they are not (cf. Chase, 1938; see also the treatment of abstract nouns in Chapter 11).

Furthermore, the grammatical structure of a language may involve implicit logical relations that restrict what can be easily said. For example, Chinese grammar does not include convenient forms of the counterfactual conditional (If *A* had not occurred, then *B* would have) whereas English grammar does; on the other hand, English grammar does not include convenient forms of the exclusive and the non-exclusive *or* (A or B but not both vs. A or B or both) whereas Chinese grammar does. When passages involving the corresponding relations are presented to Chinese and English speakers, the Chinese speakers are more likely to have trouble interpreting the passages that involve the counterfactual conditional and the English speakers are more likely to have trouble with those that involve the two logical forms of *or* (Bloom, 1981; see also Braine & Rumain, 1981).

We should not be surprised that what one can do with a language varies from one language to another (the differences are obvious when they involve formal properties, as in the artificial languages of symbolic logic, calculus, and computer programming). To the extent that language is behavior, particular languages will inevitably have different functional properties. Language relativity is a reminder that we must deal with each language in the context of the environment within which it was shaped.

LANGUAGE DEVELOPMENT

Most children become fluent in their native language long before they begin formal education. Although there are many descriptions of the development of children's language with age, we have much to learn about the factors critical to that development (cf. Brown, 1973; Fletcher & Garman, 1986; Segal, 1975; de Villiers & de Villiers, 1978). The topic is extensive, and we can sample only a few aspects of it here.

Between the ages of 1 and 6 years, children increase their vocabularies at an average rate of five to eight words per day; by the age of 6, a child is likely to have a productive vocabulary of thousands of words (Wagner, 1985). Many function words (e.g., *more, bye-bye, allgone*) are included along with common nouns (e.g., *mama, milk, chair*) in the early vocabulary (e.g., Gopnik, 1981). During the same ages, the child's syntax progresses from single-word utterances to those of two words or more, sometimes described as roughly telegraphic (e.g., *stove hot, daddy go car*), and then to constructions that more and more closely approximate the syntax of adult speech. Problems of data collection range from those of recording and sampling children's speech at different ages to those of interpreting the speech phonetically, semantically, and syntactically (e.g., a young child's *more* probably has the sense of *give me* and not that of expressing a quantity; Moore & Frye, 1986).

Among the controversial issues is the extent to which consequences play a role in the child's acquisition of language. In appeals to the "poverty of the stimulus," some have argued that the child's verbal environment is not rich enough to support language acquisition, and therefore that some structural features of language are "prewired," in the sense that they will emerge even in the absence of relevant contingencies. Others have examined exchanges between parents and children, and have argued that contingencies do play an indispensable role (e.g., see Moerk, 1980, 1983; Whitehurst & Valdez-Menchaca, 1988).

The different positions sometimes follow from different views about the appropriate level of analysis for verbal classes. The child must learn not only individual phonemes and words and sentences but also larger units such as phonetic and semantic and syntactic structures. Furthermore, the consequences of verbal behavior are likely to be subtle and probably are not ones that need to be explicitly arranged. Contrived reinforcers such as praise or candies are less likely to be effective than such natural consequences of verbal behavior as hearing oneself say something similar to what one has heard others say, or getting something one has asked for, or hearing someone else say something relevant to something one has just said, and so on. With regard to the question of whether language is innate or learned, the reasonable conclusion is that both phylogeny and ontogeny contribute.

Deixis

One significant feature of the development of a child's language is the evolution of a *deictic* vocabulary; deictic terms are occasioned not by intrinsic properties of events or objects but rather by their relation to the speaker and listener (de Villiers & de Villiers, 1974; Wales, 1986). Examples are *here* vs. *there*, *this* vs. *that*, and *in front of* vs. *behind*. In each case, the appropriate term depends on where one is located; for example, when you are cooking, the kitchen is *this* room and the dining room is *that* room; but when you are eating the terms are reversed.

The acquisition of deixis follows closely upon that of other relational vocabularies (e.g., *big* and *little*, which involve relative rather than absolute size; the child is big relative to a pet frog but little relative to an adult). In combination with pronouns, the functions of deictic terms in language are analogous to those of variables in algebra; we can speak of things even if we cannot name them (*what is this?*, *who was there?*, *is that it?*: cf. Clark & Sengul, 1979; see also McKoon & Ratcliff, 1980, on anaphoric reference).

A special case of the deictic vocabulary is that of the personal pronouns (Charney, 1980; Cooley, 1908; Huxley, 1970). Children generally learn *it* before *me* and *you*, and the distinction between first and second person (*me-you*) emerges before distinctions within those classes (*I-me-my-mine* and *you-your-yours*). But *I* and *me* are not learned like one's name; one is called *you* rather than *I* or *me* when spoken to. How then do children come to say *I* and *me* appropriately when they become speakers instead of listeners?

It is hard to observe the conditions under which this feature of language develops. Personal pronouns are mastered by almost all children (but see Chiat, 1982). We can describe how the mastery evolves, but we do not know enough of its details to say what aspects of the child's verbal environment are crucial to that evolution. Given the great variability in the ways parents interact with their children, the properties that lead to deixis are probably common to human environments in general.

Personal pronouns and the deictic vocabulary involve discriminations among events as they are related to oneself, and so they are presumably related closely to the discriminations of one's own behavior that were discussed in the context of autoclitic processes and the concept of self-awareness (Damon & Hart, 1982; Kagan, 1981; see also Chapters 10 and 11). Such discriminations are often expressed in mental language, as in the various ways of describing the difference between having forgotten something and never having known it (cf. Skinner, 1945). We can describe how and when this language develops (e.g., Wellman & Johnson, 1979; Johnson & Wellman, 1980), but we still have little to say about how it can be effectively taught. These features of language development suggest, however, that human language and human self-awareness are inextricably related.

Productivity

Another important feature of language is its novelty; when we write a sentence, it is likely to differ from any other we have written before. This feature of language is called *productivity* (language shares this property with nonverbal behavior; cf. Chapter 11). We can deal with such novelty only in terms of the features that the new sentence shares with earlier ones; novel productions involve new combinations of already established syntactic and semantic classes (cf. Esper, 1973).

An illustration is provided by Berko (1958; cf. Catania, 1980). Children aged from 4 to 7 years read illustrated sequences of sentences that introduced a nonsense word; the last sentence was incomplete and prompted a different grammatical form of the nonsense word. For example, a sequence that prompted a plural was: *This is a wug. Now there is another one. There are two of them. There are two* _____. The regular plural in spoken English is formed by -z (as in *dogs*), by -s (as in *cats*), or by -es (as in *houses*), depending on the sound with which the spoken singular ends (e.g., -z after voiced endings such as *b, d, v*, and -s after voiceless endings such as *p, t, f*). The children usually produced standard plurals with -z and -s (e.g., most children responded *wugz* to the sample sequence above). But only about a third gave the -es plural to novel words like *tass* and *gutch* and *nizz* even though almost all of them gave *glasses* as the plural of *glass*. Thus, aspects of the standard plural usage in English develop successively. Children first learn specific words and word sequences, but then they begin to master larger units such as classes of plurals (cf. Palermo & Howe, 1970).

Other evidence that language acquisition is a progression from particular words to simple word groupings and then to syntactic and semantic structures of increasing complexity is in the usage of irregular verbs, such as *go, come,* and *break* (Kuczaj, 1977). Among young children, regular but nonstandard past-tense forms are common: *goed, comed, breaked*. Children do not always start with these regular forms, however. Often, the child first learns the standard but irregular forms as individual words: *went, came, broke*. After the child learns some standard regular past-tense forms, the irregular forms are displaced by the regular but nonstandard ones, even though the irregular forms had been part of the child's vocabulary for some time. Months or years later, the standard irregular forms reappear and become permanent components of the child's verbal behavior. The progression from standard irregular to nonstandard regular and back to standard irregular past-tense verb forms is consistent with a progression from the mastery of individual words through a stereotyped syntactic form to the varied structure of fluent language.

These examples have mainly involved syntactic structure, but the same points apply to the development of semantic structure. Events in a novel context can occasion novel grammatical utterances (as when a child gives the standard plural of a nonsense word), but utterances can also be semantically new (as when *drinkfruit* is coined as a name for a watermelon). We speak of such cases in terms of metaphor or analogy (cf. Esper, 1973; Jaynes, 1976). Metaphor is effective only to the extent that relations among events in the world correspond to the relations discussed here as examples of semantic structure. If grammar is a description of relations among syntactic structures, then metaphor is the grammar of semantics.

CHAPTER 13

Verbal Learning and Transfer

> *Verbal learning procedures include* serial *and*
> paired-associates *learning,* free recall, *and the*
> *special case of verbal discrimination called* ver-
> bal recognition. Verbal transfer *involves ways*
> *in which different verbal learning tasks affect*
> *each other. Most of these terms have been related*
> *to words considered elsewhere:* associates *to*
> consequence; recall *to* class; recognition *to*
> cognition; *and* transfer *to* differentiation. Se-
> rial, *through the Latin* serere, *to arrange or*
> *attach, is related to* series, sort, *and, perhaps as*
> *an arrangement of words,* sermon.

The area traditionally called verbal learning is concerned with what happens as we
learn word sequences, word combinations, and word contexts, and its literature
is extensive (e.g., Tulving & Madigan,

1970). This chapter examines four major
classes of verbal-learning procedures: serial learning, paired-associates learning,
free recall, and verbal discrimination. It
illustrates each class of procedures with a
sample of some characteristic findings
and some experimental and theoretical
issues it has generated. After this survey,
it examines some problems of the transfer
of learning: How does learning one set of
verbal materials affect the learning of
other materials? In positive transfer, the
learning of the first set enhances that of
the second; in negative transfer, the learning of the first set retards that of the
second.

Section A **Verbal Learning Procedures**

In a typical verbal learning procedure, we
present verbal stimuli to the learner and
then record verbal responses. Much is
taken for granted in such arrangements. If
we described them simply in terms of verbal discriminative stimuli and differentiated verbal responses, we would omit
significant features. For example, the
learner's performance is only rarely generated by differential consequences; instead,
it is usually generated by giving instructions. Furthermore, the consequences may
be hard to specify. The experimenter

designates responses as correct and incorrect or right and wrong. When the learner responds, the experimenter may say "right" or "wrong" or the learner may simply be shown the item designated as correct. These procedures are sometimes said to provide the learner with *feedback* or with *knowledge of results.* It is tempting to assume that telling or showing a learner that a response was correct is a reinforcing consequence, but such feedback can also be regarded as instruction (i.e., telling the learner that a response was correct is equivalent to saying, "Respond the same way next time"). Thus, it may be misleading to speak of the reinforcing properties of being correct and the punishing properties of being incorrect.

Other circumstances may influence the learner's behavior. For example, if the experiment ends as soon as a list is learned, the consequences of finishing early will differ for a learner satisfying a course requirement than for one whose pay depends on the total time spent learning the list. These and other features of the experimental setting that determine what the learner does are sometimes called *demand characteristics* (Orne, 1962). In verbal learning we will mainly deal with verbal stimuli and verbal responses; we will not much treat the consequences of verbal learning. Even if we cannot specify consequences, we can usually assume that they are fairly uniform throughout an experiment.

Verbal learning materials have ranged from such simple items as numbers and letters through nonsense syllables and words to such complex materials as sentences and extended texts. These materials are discussed in the context of specific experiments. Here we will only distinguish between *nominal stimuli* and *functional stimuli.* Nominal stimuli are the verbal items as defined by the experimenter; functional stimuli are the features of the

items that occasion the learner's response (cf. attention; Chapter 7). For example, if the stimulus items in a learning task are the three-letter sequences PDQ, TLC, and VIP but the learner attends only to the first letter of each, then the three-letter sequences are nominal stimuli and the first letters of each are functional stimuli.

Verbal learning experiments use verbal stimuli in both written and vocal modes, but written stimuli predominated in the early days of verbal learning research. The advantages of written stimuli are that they are uniform, easily described, and can be presented at well-defined rates and durations.

A popular device for presenting verbal stimuli was the memory drum, illustrated in Figure 13–1. Words were typed or printed on a paper loop or tape, and the roller advanced each item to the window at a controlled rate. In contemporary research, slide projectors and computer displays have displaced the memory drum. In early research, vocal verbal stimuli were less favored because their uniformity and rate of presentation were harder

FIGURE 13–1 A memory drum. Words on the paper tape are shown in the window for specified durations. For example, the items of a serial list might be presented repeatedly for 3 seconds each. The learner might be instructed to anticipate each item before it appears or to recite the list in its entirety at the end of each complete presentation.

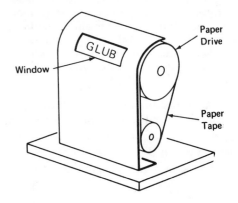

to control. For example, an experimenter who read a list to different learners might change the inflection or loudness of words over successive readings. Tape recording eliminated this problem, and contemporary research uses either written or vocal verbal stimuli, depending on the suitability of one or the other to a particular experiment. Similarly, the choice of written or vocal responses varies with experimental requirements. Learners can usually respond more quickly vocally than in writing, but the vocal response must be recorded whereas the written response is its own record.

Table 13–1 summarizes the major classes of verbal learning procedures. As its name implies, *serial learning* is the learning of a sequence of verbal items, as when a child learns to count or to recite the months. A sequence can be learned through *serial re-*

call or *serial anticipation*. For example, suppose a memory drum is used to teach the first 10 presidents of the United States through serial recall. Each name is shown briefly and the learner tries to recite the entire list in proper order only after all 10 have appeared; the list is repeated until the learner gives one or more correct repetitions. Alternatively, in serial anticipation, as each name appears the learner tries to say which will appear next (e.g., on seeing *Jefferson* saying "Madison," and then on seeing *Madison* saying "Monroe," and so on); this list also repeats until the learner gives some number of correct repetitions. Once the list is learned, the learner might be asked questions about the positions of names in the list, such as "Who was the ninth president?" (Harrison), "Which president was Tyler?" (tenth), or "Which president came before Van Buren?" (Jackson). A

TABLE 13–1   Classes of verbal learning procedures

NAME	DESCRIPTION	EXAMPLES
Serial learning	The items of a verbal sequence are learned in order.	Learning to recite the alphabet; learning a poem.
Paired-associates learning	Each of several verbal stimuli occasions a different verbal response; the order of stimulus-response pairs is unspecified.	Given a state name, naming the state capital; given words in another language, providing the English equivalent for each.
Free recall	The items in a list are named without regard to order.	Naming the members of the Supreme Court; naming the states.
Verbal discrimination	Responses are occasioned by the classes within which verbal stimuli fall; in other words, a discrimination in which the stimulus dimension is verbal.	Identifying the nouns in a paragraph of text; given names on index cards, sorting the cards into one stack of female names and another of male names.
Verbal recognition	A special case of verbal discrimination. The property that defines the discriminated class is whether the verbal item appeared in a specified earlier list or context.	Given a list of names, saying which were from one's high school graduating class; distinguishing between old and new technical terms while while reading a text.

well-learned serial list, the alphabet, illustrates the roles of context and position. We can all recite the alphabet and can probably quickly say which letter precedes or follows any other, but without counting how many can give the 11th letter or the numerical position of *S*?

Paired-associates learning generates correspondences between items on two lists, as in learning the dates of historical events or the equivalents in another language of English words. Each verbal stimulus sets the occasion for a verbal response. For example, if the pairs to be learned are book titles and authors, the sequence of items in a memory-drum window might be as follows:

> Don Quixote
> Don Quixote—Cervantes
> Candide
> Candide—Voltaire
> Moby Dick
> Moby Dick—Melville
> etc.

Each book title appears alone for several seconds. Whatever the learner's response, the title is then accompanied by the author. The full set of pairs is repeated, perhaps with the order of titles changed, until the learner correctly names each author before the name is presented. Questions can then be asked about the effects of changing response items or of reversing stimuli and responses. Paired-associates experiments, however, do not typically use familiar items and pairings; they are more likely to use nonsense syllables or arbitrary combinations of items.

In *free recall*, the learner is asked to name, in any order, items that had been presented earlier, as when you are asked to say what was on a misplaced shopping list or what questions had been on a test. In verbal learning studies, the list consists of

verbal items, but the procedure is like recall of nonverbal stimuli, as when a witness names those who were present at the scene of a crime; whether the stimuli are verbal or nonverbal, the responses in both cases are verbal.

Verbal discrimination is simply discrimination along some verbal dimension of stimuli, as when a child learns to distinguish vowels from consonants, or nouns from verbs, or grammatical sentences from ungrammatical sentences. Pairs of items are presented, and the learner chooses one item of each pair by naming it, pointing to it, or perhaps pressing a left or a right button. After each pair, the learner is informed which is correct. Two examples follow, with italics indicating correct items:

JEG-*VOB*	*JXF*-MCF
ZID-*FEP*	QMH-*DXJ*
BEW-DAX	FPW-*ZJC*
SEF-*PIB*	DHJ-ZGX
BUV-HIF	*JFM*-GZB

In the sequence on the left, the designation of correct items is arbitrary; on the right, the correct item of each pair is the one with the letter *J*. An alternative procedure is to present items one at a time, with the learner indicating whether each item is in the designated class (e.g., by "yes" or "no"). As with other verbal learning procedures, presentations continue until the learner meets some criterion.

One type of verbal discrimination is that between new and old items, as when a student in a language course distinguishes words already learned from new ones. This is called *verbal recognition*. The learner is given an initial list. Later, the learner is given another list with both new items and items from the initial one. The learner must identify (recognize) the items from the initial list. Except that it uses verbal materials, verbal recognition shares much with familiar instances of recognition (e.g., as in recognizing friends in a group of people, or in recognizing places one has visited). We now consider each type of verbal-learning procedure in more detail.

SERIAL LEARNING

Verbal-learning procedures experimentally realized the associationist principles developed by such philosophers as David Hume and James Mill. The associationists had advocated that human thought was based upon the association of ideas. Ideas were said to become connected or associated in various ways (e.g., through similarity, common elements, contrast), but especially through contiguity in space or time. Later, with the beginnings of modern chemistry, analogies were drawn between the formation of associations and the chemical combinations of atoms into molecules. Ebbinghaus (1885) saw the possibility of measuring the formation of arbitrary associations (cf. Stigler, 1978). He invented the nonsense syllable as an item that had not yet acquired verbal functions in the language and therefore would not be contaminated by associations that already existed (it was later shown that nonsense syllables did vary in meaningfulness, as measured by word-association procedures; Glaze, 1928).

The typical nonsense syllable was a three-letter consonant-vowel-consonant sequence (a *CVC trigram*). Ebbinghaus constructed many such trigrams, excluding those that were already words in the language, and then arbitrarily made up lists to be learned later. He learned these lists over a period of years, recording such data as the number of repetitions until he could reproduce a list without error. For a list of up to 7 trigrams, he required only a single reading for a correct reproduction; beyond that point, the repetitions required for a correct repetition increased with list

length, up to about 55 repetitions for a 36-trigram list. Later research showed that not only total learning time but also the learning time per item increased with list length. Another of Ebbinghaus's findings was that meaningful material could be learned more rapidly than nonsense syllables. In contrast to the 55 repetitions required for a 36-item list of nonsense syllables, Ebbinghaus learned 80-syllable stanzas of poetry (from Byron's *Don Juan* in English) in about 8 repetitions.

Together with other verbal-learning procedures, serial-learning provided a baseline for studying factors that influence human learning. For example, the finding that spaced practice is typically more effective than massed practice (e.g., Underwood, 1961) is often cited to support the superiority of distributing study evenly throughout a semester over cramming it all in at the end, just before examinations. The finding is so familiar that it is surprising to note that it was once regarded as counter-intuitive. It was argued that the massing of learning trials allowed less opportunity for the learner to forget items from one presentation to the next than if the trials were spaced in time. But this was not so, and the superiority of spaced over massed practice eventually contributed to accounts of verbal learning in terms of interference between items (the superiority of spaced over massed practice, however, is much more evident in motor-skill than in verbal leaning; Adams, 1954).

Other variables studied include meaningfulness (lists of words rated high in meaningfulness are learned more quickly than lists of words rated low); pronounceability (lists of easy-to-pronounce items are learned more quickly than lists of hard items); redundancy (organized lists are learned more quickly than random lists); similarity (lists of dissimilar items are learned more quickly than lists of similar items, where similarity is measured by common letters or other shared elements), and so on (e.g., McGeoch, 1942; G. A. Miller, 1958; Underwood & Schulz, 1960). A catalogue of factors that affect verbal learning (e.g., learning as a function of diet or of hours without sleep) can be expanded indefinitely, and the effects of any variable might depend critically on details of procedure.

One prominent feature of serial learning was the serial-position effect, illustrated in Figure 13–2 (Robinson & Brown, 1926). In a list, items at the beginning are usually learned most easily, followed by items at the end, and finally by items in the middle. The serial-position effect raised questions about the role of position in the list as opposed to that of preceding items. Serial learning had been regarded as a procedure in which each item was the stimulus that occasioned the next. But the learner can also answer questions about position (e.g., "What was the third item?" or "What was the next-to-last item?"). This finding led to attempts to define the functional stimuli in serial learning, those features of the list and the situation that occasioned correct responding (Woodward & Murdock, 1968). It is not obvious, however, how position can function as a stimulus.

The beginning and end of a list are usually marked by the pause that separates successive presentations. The pause is inevitable in serial recall, when the learner tries to reproduce the entire list after each presentation. In serial anticipation, on the other hand, the learner tries to name each item before it appears and the list can be repeated without interruption. Glanzer and Dolinsky (1965) taught two groups a

FIGURE 13–2 Serial-position curves (percent correct as a function of position of the item) after 1, 5, 9, 13, or 17 presentations of a serial list. The data are averages across 11 learners, each of whom learned 8 different 10-item lists of 3-digit numbers. At all stages of learning, percent correct was lower in the middle of the list than at its beginning or end. (Adapted from Robinson & Brown, 1926, Figure IX)

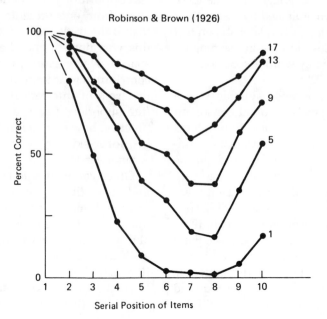

Robinson & Brown (1926)

repeating 10-item list by the method of serial anticipation (e.g., *A B C D E F G H I J A B C D E* ..., etc., where each letter represents a different item). The first group was given standard instructions, but the second group was told that because of a procedural error the list had started with item *A* even though item *F* was actually the beginning. The serial-position effect for the first group was appropriate to a list that began with item *A* (errors increased with items after *A* and then decreased toward the end of the list at *J*) whereas that for the second group was appropriate to a list that began with *F* (errors increased with items after F and then decreased toward the end of the list at *E*). Because the lists for the two groups were identical, position as a functional stimulus cannot be sought in the lists themselves; the data can be dealt with only in terms of the relation between the lists and the instructions.

We now return to Ebbinghaus. Other questions were raised by treating serial learning as the formation of associations among items. Could associations be formed only between successive items, or were remote associations possible (e.g., between every other item or every third item)? Were associations formed both forward and backward through the list? Ebbinghaus examined these issues by relearning lists of nonsense syllables one day after original learning with the order of items the same as or different from that of the original list. This was called the method of *savings*: The list was ordinarily learned more quickly on the second day than the first, and effects of changing the order of items were measured by the time saved on relearning. Ebbinghaus studied savings with 16-item lists in original, scrambled, and reverse orders, and with lists of every other, every third, every fourth, or every eighth item (e.g., in a list based on every third item, the order *A B C D E F G H* becomes *A D G B E H C F*). As shown in Figure 13–3, the greatest savings in relearn-

FIGURE 13–3 Original learning time (day 1) for 16-item lists of nonsense syllables and relearning time (day 2) after various reorderings of the lists: no change; reverse order; orders based on every second, third, fourth, or eighth item; and scrambled order. The data for each type of reordering are averages across at least 10 different lists learned on different occasions by Ebbinghaus. The shaded area shows savings as a function of the different types of reordering. (Adapted from Ebbinghaus, 1885, Chap. IX)

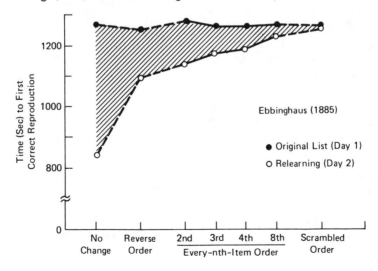

ing occurred with items in the original order and the least with items in the scrambled order. The reversed list produced more savings than any of the remaining ordered lists. From these data, Ebbinghaus concluded that both remote and backward associations had been formed during the original learning of each list.

If so many different kinds of associations can emerge within a serial list, serial learning might not be the way to study associations. It might be better to examine pairs of associates independently of a serial order. Serial learning could then be treated as a special case of paired-associates learning. For example, consider the following five-item serial list: NAJ, BEF, LUJ, PES, CED. In the presence of NAJ the learner must learn to say BEF; in the presence of BEF, LUJ; in the presence of LUJ, PES; and in the presence of PES, CED. The same relations could be created in a paired-associates list consisting of NAJ-BEF, BEF-LUJ, LUJ-PES, and PES-CED. The learner who mastered the original serial list would probably quickly learn this paired-associates list, and vice versa (Postman, 1968).

PAIRED-ASSOCIATES LEARNING

Despite the relation between paired-associates and serial learning just outlined, paired-associates procedures were apparently developed independently of Ebbinghaus's work on serial learning. The earliest experiments used colors rather than verbal items as stimuli; the response items were two- or three-digit numbers (Calkins, 1894). Verbal materials later became fairly standard for both stimuli and responses (Calkins, 1896), and paired-associates procedures, like serial-learning procedures, examined effects of a variety of verbal properties (e.g., meaningfulness of items).

The learner's task appears simpler with a paired-associates list than with a serial list: Each item occasions a unique response and the order of items is irrelevant. But even this relatively simpler task can be broken down into more fundamental components. Consider paired-associates learning as an instance of stimulus control. In contrast to stimulus control over a single response (e.g., as when a pigeon's key-pecks are reinforced in green but not red), paired-associates learning involves many stimuli and many responses. The several stimuli must be discriminated, the several responses must be differentiated, and each response must be occasioned by its particular stimulus. Discrimination among the items is usually taken for granted; discriminations among various letter and word sequences are well established in human learners. But before learning associations, the learner must learn which responses are appropriate. This component of paired-associates learning has been called *response integration* or *response availability* (Underwood & Schulz, 1960).

Consider the following two paired-associates lists:

DOG — 18	DOG — 3
ANT — 51	ANT — 1
CAT — 73	CAT — 4
FLY — 85	FLY — 2
BEE — 46	BEE — 5

Each list has only five pairs of items and therefore equal numbers of associations are to be learned. With the first list, the learner's responses will at first probably include numbers other than those on the response list (e.g., 72, 86, 45). Response integration is complete when the learner's responses include all the numbers in the response list and no others. This can occur even while the learner is still responding incorrectly to some of the stimulus items. The second list, however, requires minimal response integration. Once the learner discovers that the responses include only the digits 1 through 5, subsequent learning comprises only associations, the particular relations between stimulus and response items. Paired-associates learning will take much longer with the first than with the second list, but the difference is one of response integration and not association.

Even after being separated from response integration, the learning of associations remains complicated. Presented by itself, a single stimulus-response pair can be learned very quickly. To what extent, then, is the study of association complicated merely because many pairs are learned together at one time? (The circumstances resemble those in the history of maze learning, when mazes evolved through simpler and simpler forms, culminating in T-mazes and straight-alleys; cf. Chapter 4.) It became appropriate to study the learning of single associations rather than of many associations in a single setting (e.g., Estes, 1964). The issues rekindled a long-standing dispute in the psychology of learning, the *continuity-discontinuity* controversy. The question was whether the learning occurred gradually and continuously or took place discontinuously, in an all-or-none fashion. Were associations learned a little at a time or all at once?

In one experiment (Rock, 1957), a learner was shown eight CVC-trigram pairs and then was given an opportunity to respond to the eight stimulus items alone. The procedure was repeated until the learner responded correctly to all eight stimulus items. In one group of learners, only the order of pairs in the list was changed from one presentation to the next. In a second group, a pair was retained in the list only if the learner had responded

correctly to the stimulus item; otherwise that pair was dropped and a new pair was substituted. In other words, the only pairs retained over successive presentations of the list for the second group were those learned in just one presentation. The two groups learned their eight-pair lists at roughly equal rates; learning was as rapid with new pairs substituted as with old pairs repeated over successive presentations. Thus, trials on which a correct response had not yet occurred did not seem to contribute to learning.

Unfortunately, not all pairs of CVC trigrams are equally difficult to learn. For example, a nonsense syllable pair like CEN-TER forms a common word and so is more easily learned than a similar pair like NEC-RET that does not form a word. The problem with Rock's experiment was that the procedure for the second group was also a method for selecting a list of those pairs that were easiest to learn; pairs that could be learned on a single presentation were kept and more difficult pairs were dropped. When the experiment was repeated with CVC-trigram pairs that had been equated for difficulty, the group with a constant list learned more rapidly than did the group for which new pairs were substituted for unlearned old pairs (Underwood, Rehula, & Keppel, 1962).

No doubt associations can at least sometimes be learned on a single trial. It may be more important to ask about the properties of the association than to ask how quickly it can be formed. For example, is it symmetrical? In other words, once the stimulus item consistently occasions the response item, will the response item be equally effective in occasioning the stimulus item? (See Chapter 7 on equivalence classes.) The question is not simple, because failures to demonstrate symmetry may result from unavailability of the stimulus items as responses rather than from the reversibility of the association. For example, the naming of written letters is a paired-associates task with written stimuli and vocal responses; if a child who does not yet write learns to say "*A*" when presented with a written *A*, it would be no surprise if the child could not write an *A* in response to the spoken letter.

Even with such factors taken into account, associations are not necessarily symmetrical (e.g., Newman, 1972). The finding has practical implications. For example, in learning another language, to be able to give the equivalent English word in response to a word in the other language does not guarantee that one will be able to respond in that language when an English word is the stimulus item. The student is advised to learn the symmetry explicitly by studying the vocabulary in both directions (e.g., English-German and German-English). Such symmetries are the defining characteristics of bilingual skill (e.g., Kolers, 1966).

Other practical implications follow from studies of paired-associates learning. For example, what is the most effective order in which to present pairs of items? Should easy items be presented before difficult ones? Once a stimulus item occasions a correct response, how soon and how often should it be repeated? Experiments on such questions have led to methods of sequencing items that make paired-associates learning more effective than random sequencing or sequencing determined by the learner (Atkinson, 1972). Other issues relevant to the effects of some item pairs on the learning of others are considered in the section on transfer of learning later in the chapter.

By definition, an association has been learned when a verbal stimulus occasions its paired verbal response. Typically, such responding is produced by instructions rather than by differential reinforcement,

but that is not the only reason why paired-associates learning is seldom treated in the language of stimulus control. Another is that any human verbal learning that is not completely arbitrary will inevitably be more than the learning of associations.

FREE RECALL

One demonstration that a learner who has mastered a paired-associates list has learned more than associations is that the learner can usually name some items even if no stimulus item is presented. If the order of items is unimportant, this type of performance is called *free recall*. Recall experiments can be conducted with nonverbal stimuli. For example, we could present a collection of objects and then, after its removal, ask someone to name the objects in it. A commonplace example is when someone asks us to name the people we met at a party or other social gathering.

In experimental settings, however, free-recall procedures typically involve lists of verbal items. Free-recall procedures usually present a list of items once, followed by an opportunity for the learner to name the items without the list. Thus, free recall resembles the first trial of a serial-learning procedure, except that the learner is not instructed to name the items in their original order.

Given the similarity to serial-learning procedures, it is no surprise that serial-position effects occur in free recall also. Learners are most likely to recall items at the beginning and at the end of a list. These effects are often described in terms of two principles: primacy and recency. The principle of *primacy* states that the first items of a list are more likely to be recalled than later ones; the principle of *recency* states that the most recent items (i.e., those at the end of the list) are more likely to be recalled than earlier ones. It follows that items in the middle of the list are least likely to be recalled. But these principles do not explain serial-position effects in free recall; they merely summarize what learners do.

Primacy and recency can be demonstrated separately (Glanzer & Cunitz, 1966). Groups of learners recalled items from a list immediately after the list was presented, after 10 seconds of a counting task, or after 30 seconds of a counting task. A primacy effect (relatively higher probabilities of recall for early items) occurred in all three conditions; the recency effect (relatively higher probabilities for later items) was evident with no delay but was reduced or eliminated in the delay conditions. Imposing the delay prevented the end of the list from being the most recent event at the time of recall (cf. also the stimulus suffix effect; Baddeley & Hull, 1979; Crowder, 1976).

The position of an item in a list is only one of several factors influencing its likelihood of recall. Carefully read just once through the following 51-item list, starting at the left and going down each column. Immediately after finishing it, cover the page and then write down as many of the words in the list as you can:

DOG	PEEL	CHEYENNE
TICKET	APACHE	TIME
CAMEL	LEOPARD	SKIN
RUG	ELEPHANT	CAR
PLANE	CHIMES	BANANA
ORANGE	WIGWAM	CORN
MOHAWK	WOLF	TRACKS
DESTINY	*fate*	TIGER
TRUCK	TRAIN	BUS
APPLE	FOX	PUEBLO
SEAT	SEMINOLE	CLOCK
AIRPORT	HAND	HIDE
CABOOSE	GRAPE	LION
CHEROKEE	BEAR	PAPOOSE
WATCH	PIPE	PEACH
SQUAW	BISON	ENGINE
BOUNTY	FUTURE	MOCCASIN

Given the length of this list, if you are a typical unpracticed learner you probably recalled considerably less than half the items. You might or might not have recalled the earliest ones (DOG, TICKET), but you were more likely to recall them than the later ones. You probably recalled one or more items from the end (ENGINE, MOCCASIN) and the distinctive one in the middle (*fate*).

The greater likelihood of recall of unusual items in a list is called the von Restorff effect (von Restorff, 1933). It works with a variety of distinctive features, such as color (e.g., a word in red on a page of standard print) or size (e.g., a word in large type). Semantic novelty may also be effective (e.g., a common verb embedded in a list of animal names). But did you recall WOLF? Sometimes the effect is accompanied by a decrease in the likelihood of recall of neighboring items (Tulving, 1969).

A problem with explanations in terms of distinctiveness is that it is sometimes difficult to predict which items will be distinctive. Suppose that recall probability is much greater for one item on a list than for neighboring items. We might be tempted to say that the item must have been distinctive. But this does not explain anything; it simply demonstrates a condition in which we call an item distinctive.

The important dimensions of free recall are in the learner rather than in the list. The learner is not passive; the learner behaves with respect to the list. For example, in free recall, learners typically rehearse recent items by repeating them vocally or subvocally. In one procedure (Rundus, 1971; Rundus & Atkinson, 1970), words from 20-item lists were presented for 5 seconds each and learners were instructed to rehearse aloud. Their rehearsals were taped. Learners had more opportunities to rehearse early words than later ones (e.g., the fourth word could be rehearsed during presentations of any of the remaining 16, but the sixteenth could be rehearsed only during presentations of the last 4). As illustrated in Figure 13–4, higher recall probability of early words (primacy effect) was correlated with their more frequent rehearsal. The recency effect, however, was not correlated with rehearsal; recall probability increased for words at the end of the list, even though the opportunity to rehearse them was limited. What a learner recalls depends on what the learner does during and after the presentation of each item.

The difference between serial recall and free recall is in the instructions to the learner. In serial recall, the learner is instructed to name the items in their original order; in free recall, the learner is not told that order is important, or perhaps is specifically instructed to ignore order. But this does not mean that free-recall items are recalled in arbitrary orders. In fact, the order of recall of items often differs systematically from the original order in the list.

Consider the 51-item list presented earlier. Words in various semantic categories were distributed throughout it (e.g., native American words: MOHAWK, APACHE, WIGWAM, MOCCASIN, etc.; animal names: DOG, CAMEL, ELEPHANT, TIGER, etc.; travel words: TICKET, AIRPORT, TRACKS, BUS, etc.). At recall, the items within each category were likely to be named in clusters. The clusters depend on properties of the list, current circumstances, and the learner's verbal history. For example, the recall of BISON in a cluster of native American words might occasion some of the other animal names; ORANGE might be more likely to appear in a cluster of food words than separately as a color name; a learner who closely followed native American affairs would probably recall more items in this category than someone without such interests; and so on. Some items not on the list but semantically

FIGURE 13–4 Relation between rehearsal and probability of recall. Lists of 20 nouns were presented at a rate of 5 seconds per item. Learners were instructed to rehearse aloud, and were allowed 2 minutes of free recall after presentation of the list. (Adapted from Rundus & Atkinson, 1970, Figure 1)

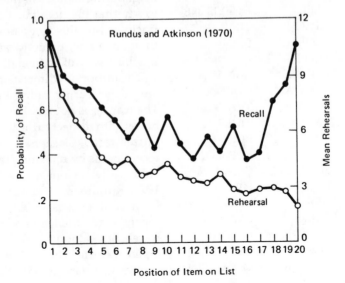

related to words in a cluster will probably be named; this type of error becomes more likely with longer lists and with delays between list presentation and recall (e.g., any of the following might appear in a recall list, even though only some were in the original list: NAVAJO, CAR, ENGINE, TEPEE, PANTHER, HIDE, TIGER, LOCO-MOTIVE, GIRAFFE, BUFFALO).

Clustering in free recall is most easily demonstrated with lists constructed to include semantic groupings (such clustering provides another method for studying semantic structure; cf. Chapter 12), but it occurs with varied lists and along various dimensions of verbal items (e.g., words that are common free-associates, or words related in spelling or pronunciation; cf. Bousfield, 1953; Brooks, 1968). Consistencies of structure cannot easily be demonstrated in the single recall of a list by one learner, so the quantification of clustering must develop techniques to cope with repeated recalls and with recall summarized over a group of learners (e.g., Tulving, 1962). In any case, the learner is not passive when given verbal lists. The clustering of the items in a list is one of several kinds of behavior the learner engages in during free recall.

VERBAL DISCRIMINATION

A common verbal discrimination procedure is simultaneous: Two verbal items are presented and the learner chooses one (by naming it, pointing, or pressing one of two buttons). The learner is then told whether the choice was correct. Unlike discriminations studied in animal laboratories (e.g., a rat's lever-pressing reinforced in light but not dark), the procedure usually includes many different stimulus items in both the correct and the incorrect class. Successive verbal discrimination procedures can also be arranged. For example, given verbal

items one at a time, the learner might be instructed to respond "yes" or "no" to each one; alternatively, the learner might be instructed to sort a deck of cards with verbal items printed on them into two or more piles. Still another type of verbal discrimination is *visual search*, as when someone is instructed to find items in a list or in a text (e.g., Healy, 1976). Examples are looking up a name in a telephone book, checking a word in a dictionary, and proofreading a manuscript for typographical errors. Research on visual search is usually more concerned with speed and accuracy than with the acquisition of discriminative control.

In simultaneous verbal discrimination, the procedure emphasized here, the items and their assignment by the experimenter to the correct or incorrect class are usually arbitrary (e.g., pairs of nonsense syllables, with the items to be correct chosen randomly). Such arbitrary discriminations may not be relevant to the verbal discriminations already part of our everyday language (e.g., discriminations among nouns, verbs, and other parts of speech, or along semantic dimensions, or along dimensions of alphabetical order or spelling). Some experiments have explored the acquisition of verbal discriminations in which some feature is always a property of the correct item. For example, the correct item might be defined as an item that includes a particular letter or letter combination, or an item that does not include a vowel, or an item that falls into some semantic class. Such procedures are verbal cases of experiments on concept formation (cf. Figure 11–2 and Chapter 7 on equivalence classes).

In still another type of arrangement, whether an item is correct is determined by its context. Consider the following verbal discrimination list, in which correct items are indicated by italics (in an experiment, the order of items in each pair would vary over presentations):

WOOD—*GLASS*
SPOON—STEEL
RUBBER—*KNIFE*
CEMENT—*NAPKIN*
FORK—GLASS

This list involves a conditional discrimination with respect to the item *GLASS*, which is correct in the first pair but not in the fifth. The discrimination is based upon semantic classes: The correct items are all parts of a table setting and the incorrect items are common materials. Because GLASS can be a member of either class, the learner's response must be based on the class membership of the other item. In this conditional discrimination, the relevant context is not only the item paired with GLASS but also the semantic structure of all of the pairs in the list.

A list with many conditional discriminations may be difficult to learn. Conditionality can also occur at the level of parts of an item. Consider the verbal discrimination lists that can be made from each of the following three sets of correct and incorrect items (correct items are marked by asterisks; cf. Chang & Shepard, 1964; Wickelgren, 1969):

FIT*	FIT*	FIT*
FIN*	FIN*	FAN*
FAT*	PAT*	PIN*
FAN*	PAN*	PAT*
PIT	FAT	FIN
PIN	FAN	FAT
PAT	PIT	PIT
PAN	PIN	PAN

From each set we could make up 32 pairs (each of the 4 correct items paired with each of the 4 incorrect items, and each of these 16 pairs with the correct item in the left or the right position). A verbal discrimination based on the first set would be

acquired quickly; the learner would soon choose the word beginning with *F* on every trial. In the second list, no single letter is consistently correct, but some letter combinations appear only in correct items (*FI-, PA-*) and others only in incorrect ones (*FA-, PI-*). Now note the properties of the third set. Every possible letter and pair of letters appear as often among correct as among incorrect items (e.g., *F—, -I-, —T; PA-, P-N, -AN*). In other words, given any part of an item, whether the item is correct is always conditional upon the rest of the item; only the item as a whole can consistently occasion correct responses. Such relations among the components of items are called *contingent associations;* lists constructed on such a basis can be exceedingly difficult to learn.

Verbal learning procedures usually repeat a list until the learner meets some criterion of correct responding. This is appropriate when the concern is with the relative difficulty of different types of lists. But when the concern is teaching, lists can be designed so that, through a progression of changes, they will efficiently produce particular verbal discriminations. In other words, verbal discriminations are well suited to fading procedures (cf. Chapter 7). The following progression of items is an illustration (the correct item of each pair is indicated by italics: adapted from Goldiamond, 1964):

A - B	DAISY MAE - *LI'L ABNER*
B - D	*ROBERT* - JULIA
B - V	ANNA - *BOB*
O - B	*BOY* - GIRL
FS - *BF*	*DANNY BOY* - BETTY ANN
JB - EL	*BYRON* - BETH
EAB - VOX	BETSY - *WILLIAM*
ABE - JANE	DOROTHY - *GEORGE*
MARY - *BERT*	*KENNETH* - ANTONIA
BILL - CONNIE	*JOHN* - ELIZABETH

Early in the list, the discrimination is based only on the letter *B*. At the transition from letters to words, the semantic difference, male-female, is introduced, with the male item always paired with the letter *B*. Later the *B* is included in both items, and in subsequent pairs the *B* is removed so that the correct item depends solely on gender. The gender discrimination in the final pair also includes a reversal of the letter discrimination that had been created at the beginning of the list. The fading from pictures to written items may be an effective method for teaching early reading skills (Gleitman & Rozin, 1973).

VERBAL RECOGNITION: A SPECIAL CASE OF VERBAL DISCRIMINATION

The discrimination between items in a list may be based upon which ones appeared in some earlier list. When this is so, we speak of the discrimination as verbal recognition. For example, only one item in each of the following pairs appeared in the 51-item list that illustrated free recall: CHIMES-WHEAT, WIGWAM-STATION, FUR-CORN, HIDE-BELL, ROOF-SEAT. If you correctly identify items from the original list you are said to recognize them. The response might be pointing at an item or naming it; in a less formal setting, it might be saying, "I recognize this as an item from the list." The response depends not simply on the stimulus but on the past circumstances in which the item had been presented (cf. Chapters 10 and 11 on discriminating one's own behavior).

The phenomenon of recognition is not restricted to verbal items. Discriminations based on whether people or places or objects are familiar or unfamiliar are examples of nonverbal recognition. One study (Shepard, 1967) compared recognition of words, sentences, and pictures. The procedure with words used a list equally divided between frequent words (e.g., *child, office*) and rare ones (e.g., *julep, wattled*). Immediately after inspecting a 540-word list, observers correctly identified 88 percent of the original words in test pairs made up of list words plus new words. Rare words were more likely to be identified correctly than frequent words. Immediately after inspecting a list of 612 sentences (e.g., "A dead dog is no use for hunting ducks"), observers correctly identified 89 percent of the original sentences in test pairs made up of original and new ones. The picture procedure examined recognition at different times after observers had inspected 612 pictures. After two hours, observers shown pairs made up of the original pictures and new ones correctly identified 99.7 percent of the original pictures. Correct identification decreased to 92 percent after 3 days, to 87 percent after 7 days, and to 58 percent after 120 days (50 percent is chance accuracy in this task).

The study, however, does not permit a conclusion about the superiority of recognition for nonverbal visual stimuli relative to verbal stimuli. With pairs of pictures, the observer was discriminating between pictures seen before (from the original series) and pictures probably never seen before; with words (especially frequent ones), the observer was discriminating between words both of which had been seen before in many contexts but only one of which had appeared on the original list.

Verbal recognition does not require discriminations between novel and familiar stimuli; instead, it is based on whether the verbal item occurred in some previous setting (i.e., a particular list). A common error in verbal recognition is recognition failure (i.e., an item from the original list is not identified as old). False recognition (i.e., an error in which an item not from the original list is identified as old) usually occurs less often and is most likely with new items semantically related to items on the list (e.g., Underwood & Freund, 1968).

Recognition may also depend on how new and old items are presented. When they are presented in pairs, the observer can respond correctly by identifying either the old item as old or the new item as new. This is not so if an old item is presented together with several new items (e.g., as in a multiple-choice test). In recognition studies, the new items are sometimes called distractor items. Recognition accuracy decreases as the proportion of new or distractor items increases (Kintsch, 1968). The probability of identifying correctly by guessing decreases with added distractor items (e.g., the probability is 50 percent when items are presented in pairs but only 25 percent when each old item is presented with three new ones); the adjustment for guessing, however, is too small to account for the decrease in recognition accuracy that accompanies an increase in distractor items.

It has often been assumed that recognition is involved in performances produced by other verbal learning procedures. For example, when a learner does not recognize a stimulus item from a paired-associates list, that item will usually not occasion the appropriate response item (e.g., Martin, 1967). It has therefore been suggested that recognition of items as stimulus items from the list is a necessary condition for paired-associates learning. The trouble is that the dependency may also work in the opposite direction. The learner may sometimes recognize a stimulus item from the list only because it has occasioned a response item.

Verbal recognition requires discriminative responding in the presence of items whereas free recall requires producing items that are absent. We can expect these two classes of behavior to have different properties. Nevertheless, many accounts of verbal learning have assumed that recognition and recall are closely related. One account (Anderson & Bower, 1972) suggests that recall occurs in two stages: First the learner generates items, and then the learner produces only those recognized as being from the list. Colloquially, we might say that the learner must think of the item first and must then decide whether it was on the list.

One deduction from such accounts is that recognition accuracy ought always to equal or exceed recall accuracy. In many studies, recognition is superior to recall even after guessing is taken into account (in recognition tests with paired new and old items, guesses are correct by chance half the time, but in recall of words or CVC trigrams, guesses are not likely to be correct by chance). Circumstances exist, however, in which recall accuracy is consistently superior to recognition accuracy (Tulving, 1974; Watkins & Tulving, 1975). For example, in one arrangement the learner was first given a paired-associates list (e.g., *glue-CHAIR*). Next, the learner was given free-association stimulus items likely to occasion response items from the paired-associates list (e.g., *table,* for which typical associates might be *CHAIR, CLOTH, DESK, DINNER*). Among the words produced in this free-association task, the learner was then asked to identify those that had appeared in the earlier paired-associates list (recognition). Finally, the stimulus items of the paired-associates list were presented (e.g., *glue-?*), and the learner's responses were recorded (recall). In procedures of this type, learners typically recognized fewer words from the original list than they were able to recall during the paired-associates condition.

This outcome not only makes untenable the model of recognition as a component of recall; it is also likely to surprise those who regard recognition as somehow simpler than recall. The important point perhaps is that the comparison may not be appropriate in the first place. Recognition and recall are different classes of responses occasioned by different classes of stimuli; these classes are measured in different ways and therefore their comparison may not be justified.

SUMMARY

We have examined the major classes of verbal-learning procedures: serial learning, paired-associates learning, free recall, verbal discrimination, and, as a special case of verbal discrimination, verbal recognition. In these procedures, performances are typically produced and maintained through instructions rather than through differential contingencies imposed on correct and incorrect responses. Although each procedure seems superficially simple, the human learner, while mastering any of these tasks, inevitably does much more besides. Thus, it is inappropriate to regard associations merely as verbal sequences; human verbal behavior has other structural properties besides the temporal ordering of events (e.g., clustering in free recall).

We have treated verbal learning procedures in the context of their historical development. Those procedures were designed in the service of accounts of verbal learning in terms of associations. Such accounts assumed that verbal learning produced stimulus-response relations in which particular verbal stimuli came to occasion particular verbal responses. But relations produced in verbal learning were not limited to one direction; verbal learning also produced equivalence relations among verbal items. We have already seen some implications of such treatments within psycholinguistics, and others will be considered in the chapter on remembering. But first we must turn to transfer of learning; once one verbal task has been mastered, we may ask how the mastery of others will be affected.

Section B   **Transfer**

Can the discipline of mathematics make one a more logical thinker? Will mastery of a classical language like Greek or Latin make it easier to learn economics or history or sociology? Does the mastery of music or art create skills that are useful in studying great works of literature? Research on transfer of learning or transfer of training began with simpler questions than these (Thorndike & Woodworth, 1901). A common assumption of earlier times was that traditional educational curricula were appropriate not simply because each subject matter might later be important to the student, but also because the disciplines "exercised the mind" or, in other words, taught general intellectual skills. Studies of how the learning of one task affected the learning of another were particularly relevant to this view. Yet each demonstration that transfer was specific to a particular learning task or that transfer was limited in some other way contradicted rather than supported the view. And the typical college curriculum gradually evolved from a fixed sequence of required courses to electives, distribution requirements, and other flexible course options.

Thorndike played a critical role in this history (Jonçich, 1968). His research interests gradually shifted from instrumental learning in animals to human learning in educational settings; this shift was accompanied by his increasing involvement in curricular matters such as course requirements for potential teachers. His findings on transfer probably influenced faculty committees responsible for establishing and reviewing course requirements and curricula. The transfer of learning from one subject matter to another is difficult to analyze. Some study skills probably generalize from one course to another. But examining how the mastery of a classical language influences a student's progress in mathematics or science or philosophy requires experimental procedures that are neither practical nor acceptable in the typical educational institution (e.g., random assignment of students to sequences of courses; matching groups according to previous academic achievement and other criteria; controlling for different instructors and teaching methods in different classes, etc.). Perhaps inevitably, research on transfer concentrated on simpler tasks, such as transfer from one paired-associates list to another (e.g., McGeoch, 1942).

POSITIVE AND NEGATIVE TRANSFER

A complication in studies of transfer is that they necessarily compare learners. To say whether learning task X affects the later learning of Y, we must know how Y would have been learned if X had not been learned first. Suppose that Y is learned rapidly and with few errors after the learning of X. With only that information, we cannot determine transfer from X to Y; perhaps Y was simply an easy task. Learning Y after X must be compared with learning Y alone. When learning Y after X is essentially equal to learning only Y, transfer is zero (in *zero transfer*, learning X does not affect learning Y). When learning Y after X is more rapid or occurs with fewer

errors than learning only Y, transfer is positive (in *positive transfer*, learning X makes Y easier to learn). When learning Y after X is slower or occurs with more errors than learning only Y, transfer is negative (in *negative transfer*, learning X makes Y harder to learn).

The history of research on transfer includes both verbal and nonverbal studies (e.g., transfer of motor skills from one hand to the other: cf. Woodworth, 1938). Specific cases of positive or negative transfer only permitted particular transfer effects to be catalogued, but paired-associates learning suggested an analysis from which general principles of transfer might emerge. Studies of transfer could be based on changes in stimulus items, changes in response items, or changes in their relations (Bruce, 1933). Table 13–2 illustrates several procedures in paired-associates transfer. The effect of learning one list on learning a second list can be examined when only stimulus items are changed, when only response items are changed, when both are changed, or when both remain the same but their pairing is changed.

Changing only stimulus items may produce positive transfer, especially if the first list included unfamiliar response items for which no additional response integration is now required (cf. paired-associates learning). Changing only response items, on the other hand, may produce negative transfer, because the stimulus items continue to occasion responses from the first list during learning of the second. Ideally, if relations among items are arbitrary, changing both stimulus and response items should produce no transfer; in practice, the procedure assesses *generalized* or *nonspecific* transfer in the learning of successive different lists (cf. Chapter 7 on learning set). Another variation on paired-

TABLE 13–2   Some transfer procedures with paired-associates lists. In each hyphenated letter pair, the first represents the list of stimulus items and the second represents the list of response items. Sample CVC items are shown for each procedure.

PROCEDURE	DESIGNATION		SAMPLE ITEMS	
	LIST 1	LIST 2	LIST 1	LIST 2
Stimulus change only	A-B	C-B	lan-qip	fis-qip
Response change only	A-B	A-C	req-kiv	req-zam
Stimulus and response change	A-B	C-D	xal-pom	cam-lup
Same lists, stimulus and response items re-paired	A-B	A-B$_r$	hab-lef guv-mot	hab-mot guv-lef

associates transfer is the re-pairing of unchanged lists of items. For example, the symmetry of associations can be studied by exchanging stimulus and response items (transfer from an *A-B* list to a *B-A* list). The roles of particular properties of items can also be studied by changing lists in various systematic ways (e.g., given *A* and *A'* as CVC lists differing only in vowels, transfer from an *A-B* list to an *A'-B* list, or given *B* and *B'* as word lists in which corresponding items in each list are synonyms, transfer from an *A-B* list to an *A-B'* list).

Whether transfer from one paired-associates list to another is positive or negative depends on the relations among the items in the two lists. These have been summarized on the basis of similarities between corresponding first-list and second-list items (Osgood, 1949). Positive transfer is maximal when stimulus items and response items in the two lists are identical (*A-B* to *A-B* transfer); negative transfer is maximal when stimulus items in the two lists are identical, and second-list response items are incompatible with first-list response items (*A-B* to *A-C* transfer; re-pairing, in *A-B* to *A-B$_r$* procedures, may also produce negative transfer). Transfer approaches zero as second-list

stimulus items become more different from first-list stimulus items (*A-B* to *C-B* or *A-B* to *C-D* transfer).

The significance of this summary of transfer, however, depends largely on the definition of similarity. Consider the learner who has learned *LOUD* as the response to a stimulus item. New lists might substitute new response items related to *LOUD* by spelling (*CLOUD*), as synonyms (*NOISY*), or as antonyms (*SOFT*). How can we judge the similarity between list-1 and list-2 response items? Are words with similar spellings but different meanings more or less alike than words with different spellings but similar meanings? Are antonyms antagonistic response items, or should antonyms and synonyms both be treated as semantically similar? Should we call these examples of *A-B* to *A-C* transfer, or are the relations close enough to justify speaking of *A-B* to *A-B'* transfer?

In fact, transfer would probably be positive in each case. Having learned *LOUD* in response to a stimulus item in the first list, the learner would readily learn *CLOUD* in response to the same item in a new list. But that would also be true for transfer from *LOUD* to *NOISY* or to *SOFT*. Transfer might even be greater with antonyms than with synonyms or spelling relations. This might lead us to say that antonyms are semantically more similar than synonyms and that similarity is better measured in semantic terms than in terms of spelling. But sooner or later we would encounter problems. For example, spelling might be more important in some verbal transfer procedures than in others. Such features of transfer data are probably best regarded as part of the definition of similarity. Similarity is not a stimulus property; rather, it is derived from behavior with respect to stimuli. It follows that doing the experiment remains the most appropriate way to judge the amount and direction of transfer from one task to another.

An understanding of transfer effects may be critical to the sequencing of tasks in instruction. For example, transfer may help produce some formal relations among spoken and written verbal stimuli and responses (Chapter 11). Consider the formal stimulus and response relations as a child learns the alphabet:

echoic behavior $S_{\text{vocal}}\,"a" \longrightarrow R_{\text{vocal}}\,"a"$

dictation-taking $S_{\text{vocal}}\,"a" \longrightarrow R_{\text{written}}\,A$

textual behavior $S_{\text{written}}\,A \longrightarrow R_{\text{vocal}}\,"a"$

transcription $S_{\text{written}}\,A \longrightarrow R_{\text{written}}\,A$

Ordinarily, echoic behavior is acquired long before a child learns to read and write. Thus, the transition to textual behavior might be regarded as A-B to C-B transfer (stimulus change only), and that to dictation-taking as A-B to A-C transfer (response change only). But we should not necessarily expect to observe the negative transfer and zero transfer predictable from the transfer relations summarized above. For example, if a child has never learned to write letters, there will not be much transfer from echoic behavior to dictation-

taking. If transcription had been learned, however, transfer to textual behavior might be easy. Thus, the order in which the classes are learned may be a critical aspect of the teaching of reading and writing; determining the most effective order is a problem of transfer. In the end, of course, we would be more interested in creating equivalence classes than particular stimulus-response relations.

PROACTION AND RETROACTION

We have seen how learning list 1 can affect learning list 2. This effect is called *proactive*, because the direction is from an earlier to a later task. But list-2 learning can also affect later list-1 performance. For example, after transfer from an A-B to an A-C list, the learner who had given B responses to A stimulus items may no longer be able to do so; the A stimulus items now produce C responses. This effect is called *retroactive*, because the direction is from a later to an earlier task. Most research on these effects has concentrated on cases in which learning one list interferes with rather than enhances performance on other lists (Müller & Pilzecker, 1900); such effects are called proactive and retroactive *inhibition*, or proactive and retroactive *interference*.

As with other instances of transfer, studies of proaction and retroaction compare performance on a succession of tasks with that on one task alone. The design of proaction studies is as follows:

	Learn	Learn	Test
Experimental Group	Task 1	Task 2	Task 2
Control Group	——	Learn Task 2	Test Task 2

Except that part of the task-2 performance is called a test phase, this procedure is equivalent to those discussed earlier. Task-2 learning is typically equated in some way for the two groups (e.g., number of trials or some criterion of correct responding), and some time usually separates task-2 learning and testing (on an immediate test, both groups would probably perform accurately and so there would be no difference to observe).

The design of retroaction studies is as follows:

	Learn	Learn	Test
Experimental Group	Learn Task 1	Learn Task 2	Test Task 1
Control Group	Learn Task 1	———	Test Task 1

For the experimental group, this procedure differs from the proaction procedure only in the task tested. For a sequence of two tasks, therefore, task 1 may have a proactive effect on task 2 at the same time that task 2 has a retroactive effect on task 1. The two effects, however, would have to be assessed in the two separate procedures. Proactive and retroactive effects across a variety of tasks can be studied with these procedures (e.g., Task-1 serial learning and Task-2 paired-associates learning, or Task-1 French vocabulary words and Task-2 Spanish vocabulary words). In a broader context, what is learned in one course may affect what is learned in a later course (proaction, as when preparation in algebra affects the mastery of calculus); conversely, what was learned in the earlier course may be affected by a later course (retroaction, as when technical vocabulary in an advanced science course affects the terminology learned in an introductory course).

EXTENSIONS TO NONVERBAL PROCEDURES

Instances of learning do not occur in isolation. Other learning preceded and is likely to follow. Every instance of learning may

be affected by what comes before and what follows, so proaction and retroaction, and transfer in general, are relevant to all learning. When a child learns the alphabet, the learning may be affected by earlier nonverbal discriminations among geometrical patterns (e.g., Gibson, 1965). Upper-case letters, unlike lower-case ones, do not include any up-down or left-right reversals (e.g., p vs. b; b vs. d); thus, transfer from upper-case to lower-case alphabets may depend on whether the child has already learned nonverbal up-down and left-right discriminations. Learning the verbal content of a laboratory manual may affect the ease with which a student later masters nonverbal laboratory skills. These examples are exceedingly complex. Even in more elementary cases, such as paired-associates learning, the study of transfer requires an analysis of the components of performance, such as association and response integration.

The simplest cases of transfer are those with a shift only from one discrimination to another. For example, reinforcement of a pigeon's pecks during green but not red might be followed later by reinforcement during blue but not yellow or during circles but not squares. Transfer from one color discrimination to another might be more rapid than from a color discrimination to a form discrimination. Similarly, reinforcement of a rat's jumps toward a left but not a right stimulus might be followed later by reinforcement of jumps toward light but not dark, or vice versa. Transfer from position to brightness might not be the same as transfer from brightness to position (failures of transfer have sometimes been called *fixations*).

Discrimination reversal may also be treated as a type of transfer procedure. For example, reinforcement of a rat's lever-presses in the presence but not the absence of tone might be followed by reinforce-ment in its absence but not its presence. Such reversals are often more rapid if the stimuli are switched after many sessions of the original discrimination than if they are switched after only a few sessions (the overlearning reversal effect, or ORE; e.g., Capaldi & Stevenson, 1957).

Related phenomena are *transposition* and *reversal* e.g., Honig, 1962). For exam-ple, suppose that two squares in a Lashley jumping stand are 2 and 4 centimeters wide and a rat learns to respond to the larger one. If a new pair with widths of 4 and 8 centimeters is presented, the rat will probably respond to the new larger square rather than the now smaller one it had responded to before. This transposition based on the relation between stimuli oc-curs only within certain absolute limits; if much larger sizes are presented (e.g., widths of 16 and 32 centimeters), the rat may show reversal by responding to the smaller square, closer in absolute size to the one it had responded to before. (An account of transposition and reversal has been offered in terms of excitatory and inhibitory generalization gradients; Spence, 1937; cf. Chapter 7).

Cases of transfer involving changes along the original stimulus dimension (e.g., from one color discrimination to an-other) are called *intradimensional shifts*. Re-versals are one type of intradimensional shift. Cases involving changes from one stimulus dimension to another (e.g., from color discrimination to form discrim-ination) are called *extradimensional shifts*. The effects of stimulus dimensions in transfer have been assessed by comparing intradimensional reversal shifts with extradimensional nonreversal shifts (Kendler & Kendler, 1962), as illustrated below; each task is represented by sample pairs of verbal-discrimination items in

which the italicized item of each pair is designated correct:

REVERSAL SHIFT		NONREVERSAL SHIFT	
Task 1	Task 2	Task 1	Task 2
XON-map	XON-*map*	XON-map	XON-map
nij-TOY	nij-*TOY*	*nij*-TOY	nij-*TOY*

In each list, item pairs are CVC trigrams that differ along two dimensions: non-sense syllable vs. common word and upper-case vs. lower-case. In both task-1 cases, the correct item is the nonsense syl-lable, whether in upper-case or lower-case. In task 2 after the reversal shift, the correct item is now the common word instead of the nonsense syllable; whether it is upper-case or lower-case remains ir-relevant. In task 2 after the nonreversal shift, however, the correct item is the one in upper-case; the nonsense-syllable vs. word dimension is no longer relevant. Analogous shifts can be arranged with nonverbal items (e.g., stimuli differing in both form and size). With adult humans, transfer usually occurs more rapidly with reversal than with nonreversal shifts, but the opposite is often the case with rats, monkeys, and very young children. These performances have been interpreted in terms of changes in attention to individ-ual stimuli and to stimulus dimensions (cf. Chapter 7).

SUMMARY

Transfer is assessed by comparing the learning of a single task with the learning of two or more tasks in succession. The learning of one task may enhance or inter-fere with the learning of others (positive and negative transfer), and it may affect the performance on tasks learned earlier or later (retroaction and proaction). Whether transfer is positive or negative depends on the detailed relations of the stimuli and responses in the two tasks. Stimulus similarity and response similarity have been used to classify transfer effects, but the nature of similarity limits the conclusions that can be drawn from such classifications. Similarity is not a physical property of stimuli; it is derived from behavior with respect to stimuli. Our examples of transfer were mostly from human verbal learning, but transfer is a general issue in learning and we also considered some nonverbal examples. We can sometimes make informed estimates of both verbal and nonverbal transfer, but the best way to find out about the direction and magnitude of transfer from one task to another is to do the experiment.

CHAPTER 14
Remembering

Memory *has its source in an Indo-European root* smer- *or* mer-, *to remember, through which it is related to* remember *and* mourn. *The root does not seem to be linked to the Indo-European* men-, *to think, which is the source of* mnemonic, *amnesia,* memento, reminiscence, automatic, *and, perhaps most interesting,* mind *and* mental. *For-*get *has a source in the Indo-European root* ghend-, *to seize or take. Through the Middle English* gessen, *to try to get, it is related to* guess, *and through the Latin* prehendere, *to hold before, it is related to* apprehend *and* comprehend.

The term *memory* is the popular name for the topics to be treated here, but this chapter is entitled "Remembering." Woodworth has outlined the rationale for preferring one usage over the other:

> Instead of "memory," we should say "remembering"; instead of "thought" we should say "thinking," instead of "sensation" we should say "seeing, hearing," etc. But, like other learned branches, psychology is prone to transform its verbs into nouns. Then what happens? We forget that our nouns are merely substitutes for verbs, and go hunting for the *things* denoted by the nouns; but there are no such things, there are only the activities that we started with, seeing, remembering, and so on.... It is a safe rule, then, on encountering any menacing psychological noun, to strip off its linguistic mask and see what manner of activity lies behind. (Woodworth, 1921, pp. 5–6)

The study of remembering is concerned with ways in which an organism's behavior now can be occasioned by events in the past, as when a delay is imposed between a stimulus and an opportunity to respond. Accounts of remembering often speak of what the organism does when the stimulus is presented as *memory storage*, of the intervening time as the period of *retention*, and of what the organism does when the response later occurs as *retrieval from memory*. Systematic relations between stimuli to be remembered and the responding occasioned by these stimuli are often discussed as *encoding;* for example, the learner who recites words aloud as they are presented visually is said to be encoding the visually presented words in a vocal mode.

Important events can occur during any of the three stages of a memory episode: the stimulus presentation, the imposed delay, and the opportunity for a response. *Short-term memory* and *long-term memory* are distinguished in part on the basis of whether the learner has had an opportunity to rehearse the to-be-remembered material immediately after it has been presented; if the learner does not have an opportunity to do so, the material may be quickly forgotten. Effects of events that occur during the delay between the stimulus and the opportunity for a response have been discussed in terms of *interference;* the learner may fail to remember because behavior has occurred during the delay that is incompatible with the responses appropriate to the to-be-remembered material. Finally, remembering may be affected by the conditions under which the learner is given an opportunity to respond; the study of *cue-dependent* or *state-dependent* learning shows that the closer the circumstances are to those in which the material was originally presented, the more likely it is that the learner will remember it.

Many theories of memory have been concerned with how memory works, but a dominant theme in experiments on memory is the study of what is remembered. Analyses of what is remembered, like analyses of the effects of reinforcement, tell us about important properties of behavior classes. Studies of memory usually deal with the human learning of verbal material. The structure of what is remembered is relevant to the distinction between different types of remembering, such as *semantic* memory and *autobiographical* or *episodic* memory; semantic memory involves remembering various properties of the learner's language, such as word meanings, whereas autobiographical memory involves remembering incidents in the learner's past.

A witness to an accident may later describe what happened. How do we deal with verbal responses that depend on stimuli no longer present? It would be helpful to know how much difference there is between describing the events while they occur and describing them later. (Recall that the presence of the stimulus at the time of the verbal response was a constraint in the definition of the tact; cf. Chapter 11.)

Let us start by using the pigeon again as an example. Our rudimentary example of tacting used a chamber in which a pigeon's pecks on a left or middle or right key were respectively reinforced during red or blue or green light in a window above the keys. In that example, the pecks occurred while the colors were present. Suppose now that each color appears only briefly and the keys on which the pigeon pecks become available only after the color is gone. (In one arrangement, a color appears in the window while the keys are dark; then the color disappears and the keys are lit white. Pecks on the keys are effective only after they are lit.)

If red appears for just a second and then the pigeon immediately pecks the left key, we can still say that the peck was occasioned by the brief red stimulus even though the stimulus was gone by the time the peck occurred. Now let us impose a 2-second delay between the brief presentation of red and the pigeon's opportunity to peck. If the pigeon still pecks the left key, we can still say that the peck is occasioned by the red stimulus. We might wonder how the pigeon can respond consistently to the different colors after various delays, but as yet we have no reason to assume that the behavior is different in kind from that when pecks occur in the presence of the colors. Imposing a delay between a stimulus and an opportunity for the response that it occasions does not necessarily alter the control of the response by that stimulus.

But, in fact, control of the pigeon's pecks by color is likely to diminish even with delays of 1 or 2 seconds, and responding will probably be near chance levels at a delay of 5 seconds (cf. Blough, 1959). We might be able to teach the pigeon to remember, however. We could shape different performances after red and blue and green, and then chain each performance to pecking on an appropriate key (e.g., once we get the pigeon to peck the left chamber wall after red, the next step is to get it to peck the left key if it is still pecking the left chamber wall when the keys become available; cf. *mediating behavior* in the Glossary). If each color occasioned pecking in a different location, the duration over which the pigeon could remember a color would depend only on how long it could maintain its pecking in that location during the imposed delay. Under such conditions, control by the colors could extend over delays of many seconds and perhaps even minutes. We could then study how the pigeon's remembering depended on the mediating behavior by interrupting that behavior during the delay (e.g., Jans & Catania, 1980).

It is tempting to say that we really should not call the pigeon's performance remembering if the temporal gap between stimulus and response is bridged by uninterrupted mediating behavior. Somehow it seems more appropriate to say that the pigeon's pecks are occasioned by its previous behavior rather than by the now-absent colors as stimuli. Yet we modify our remembering by keeping calendars and appointment books. Consider looking up a number in a telephone book and then reciting it over and over to yourself until you

have a chance to dial it. After you had dialed successfully, you would probably be willing to say that you had remembered the number even though the dialing depended more directly on your vocal repetitions than on the number as it appeared in print in the telephone book. Your vocal repetition illustrates behavior that is sometimes called *rehearsal*; it justifies the view that what is remembered is not so much stimuli as it is our own behavior toward those stimuli ("...what is reproduced on all occasions after the first is not the original but one's own reproduction of it"; Zangwill, 1972, p. 130; cf. Kolers, 1979; Raye, Johnson, & Taylor, 1980). The example shows that questions about what memory is can often be translated into questions about what it is that we remember.

Remembering is a complex subject matter with an extensive history. We discussed some of that history in the treatment of verbal learning (Chapter 13) and will consider it further only in passing. We began this chapter by examining the language of remembering in the context of a hypothetical pigeon experiment. Now we shift to contrasting examples, as we illustrate the complexity of human remembering in the context of the memory strategies called *mnemonic* systems. This treatment sets the stage for a more extensive survey of some research on human memory.

Section A　Mnemonics

Mnemonics are techniques for increasing the likelihood of remembering. Remembering may involve the persistence of behavior over time, as in rehearsal, but that is clearly only part of the story. If you remember an event that took place yesterday or last week or last year, we need not assume that you were somehow rehearsing it continuously from then until now.

The use of mnemonic systems makes the learner less dependent on rehearsal, which is the major component of memorizing material by rote. A simple example of a mnemonic technique is the conversion of a sequence of symbols into a sentence, as when a beginning student of music remembers the notes on the lines of the treble clef, *EGBDF,* as the sentence "*Every good boy does fine.*"

One well-established mnemonic technique is the *method of loci* (places). It is attributed to the Greek poet Simonides (Yates, 1966). Simonides is said to have left a banquet hall just before the roof collapsed and killed all the occupants. Although the bodies of the guests were unrecognizable, Simonides was able to identify them for their relatives by where they had been sitting at the banquet table. This demonstration that an orderly spatial arrangement contributed to accurate remembering is supposed to have led Simonides to invent the method of loci. The method became the basis for remembering the sequence of topics in speeches and was described by the Greek orator Quintilian:

> In order to form a series of places in memory, he says, a building is to be remembered, as spacious and varied a one as possible, the forecourt, the living room, bedrooms, and parlours, not omitting statues and other ornaments with which the rooms are decorated. The images by which the speech is to be remembered...are then placed in imagination on the places which have been memorized in the building. This done, as soon as the memory of the facts requires to be revived, all these places are visited in turn and the various deposits demanded of their custodians. We have to think of the ancient orator as moving in imagination through his memory building *whilst* he is making his speech, drawing from the memorised places the images he has placed on them. The method insures that the points are remembered in the right order, since the order is fixed by the sequence of places in the building. (Yates, 1966, p. 3)

For example, a student might imagine a systematic walk from one distinctive campus landmark to another: dormitories to dining hall to library to computer center to gymnasium and so on. To learn some ordered series, the student then imagines each item at each successive location. To recall the series, the student takes the imaginary walk again, remembering each item in its appropriate place. To learn a new sequence at a later time, the student repeats the imaginary walk in the same order, this time visualizing the new items in their places. The new series will be learned with relatively little interference from the first series (e.g., Bellezza, 1982), but the first series may no longer be well remembered. Thus, the method is useful mainly for series that need to be remembered only temporarily (e.g., shopping lists).

These mnemonic techniques work best with series of concrete items that are easily visualized or imagined. Unusual or bizarre items or combinations may have an advantage over common ones, but even more important is the spatial closeness or connection of the items and places. For example, in learning pairs of objects, learners remember the pairings more accurately if the objects stand in some relation to each other (e.g., one on top of the other) than if they are simply side by side (Wollen, Weber, & Lowry, 1972).

Various mnemonic devices were developed during Greek and Roman times, and in the Middle Ages they became methods for remembering religious doctrine (Yates, 1966). They gradually became the basis for ritualized forms of religious art, as when particular figures were used to represent the vices and the virtues. In the course of this evolution, the mnemonic origins of these art forms were gradually (and ironically) forgotten. Mnemonic techniques were given relatively little attention throughout much of the history of psychology, and interest in their significance for analyzing memory has developed only recently (e.g., Bower, 1970).

Some techniques are designed so that abstract items can be converted into concrete ones. The *peg-word* technique is a simple method for translating numbers into a sequence that can be visualized, as in *one is a bun, two is a shoe, three is a tree*, etc. An ordered list can then be learned by imagining each item together with the object corresponding to its numerical position in the list. These systems have an advantage over the method of loci, in that the learner can recall the item in any position without necessarily starting from the beginning of the list (e.g., to recall the third item, the learner has only to remember what was imagined with *tree*).

A more elaborate system provides a code for translating numbers into letters. This system has been a part of popular mnemonic techniques for roughly a century (e.g., Loisette, 1899). One version is the following:

Number	Consonants	Rationale
1	*t, d*	*t* has one downstroke.
2	*n*	*n* has two downstrokes.
3	*m*	*m* has three downstrokes.
4	*r*	*r* is the fourth letter of four.
5	*l*	*l* is the Roman numeral 50.
6	soft *g, j*	script *g* is an upside-down 6.
7	k, hard c	k can be combined with 7: $\mathbb{k}$
8	f, v	both 8 and script f have two loops.
9	p, b	backwards p or upside-down *b* is 9.
0	z, s	z is the first letter of zero.

With this code, any number can be converted into a word or a sequence of words in which consonant sounds correspond to successive digits. With a little practice, the learner can quickly translate numerical information, such as dates or telephone numbers, into a form that is easily remembered. The potential applications are limited only by the learner's ingenuity.

Consider an example. You are interested in the visual spectrum, but you sometimes forget which end is infrared and which is ultraviolet. Now you construct a colorful scene from early in the American Civil War. A union soldier, in his **blue** uniform and with his steel-**blue** *rifle* over his shoulder, is in a country kitchen taking leave of his sweetheart. Golden **yellow** *loaves* of fresh-baked bread are sitting on the counter as he *kisses* her on her **red** lips. *Rifle* translates to 485, roughly the wavelength of blue in millimicrons; *loaves* translates to 580, that of yellow; and *kisses* to 700, that of red. Infrared, then, is at the long wavelength end of the spectrum. It is also easy now to determine the approximate wavelengths of other colors (e.g., 530 or so is a good guess for green, because it is located between blue and yellow).

At this point, you may wish to try an exercise. First choose a sequence of a dozen familiar locations, as in an imaginary stroll through your neighborhood. The successive places should be distinctive ones that are encountered in definite order. For example, they might include a library, a playground, a school, a pharmacy, a parking lot, and so on. Next, construct an arbitrary sequence of 12 two-digit numbers (e.g., by consulting a random number table); for example, 66, 57, 28, 40, 87, etc. From the code above, you can now convert each number into a word. Each should include two and only two consonant sounds; ignore unsounded letters. For example, 66 can be coded as *judge*, because the *d* is silent. Concrete words are preferable to abstract ones (e.g., for 57, *lock* is preferable to *like*). Finally, as you derive each word, imagine it at the appropriate location (e.g., a giant *judge* sitting on the roof of the library, a pad*lock* attached to the playground swings, etc.). Later, you can use the successive locations to recall the words, and you can use the code to translate the words back to their respective numbers. On your first try, you may find it helpful to have the letter-to-number code on hand, but with practice you should find that you can learn an arbitrary sequence with relatively little effort. Remembering 50 or more numbers is not difficult for a skilled user of mnemonic techniques.

Such arbitrary feats of memory may be useful mainly to impress one's friends. More important is that they demonstrate the flexibility and capacity of human memory. Educational systems have tended to emphasize learning through understanding and have correspondingly de-emphasized or even discouraged memorization. It is unlikely, however, that a learner will be disadvantaged by learning in more than one way, and therefore mnemonic techniques can be an effective supplement to other methods of study. Mnemonic techniques, a far cry from the pigeon example discussed earlier, illustrate how varied the phenomena are that must be considered in the study of remembering. These mnemonic techniques are classes of behavior that can be learned. Even if we cannot say why humans are more likely to remember concrete items that are easily visualized than abstract items that cannot, we at least know that what the learner remembers depends on what the learner does.

Section B   The Metaphor of Storage and Retrieval

An episode of remembering is defined by three components: the initial learning of an item, the passage of time, and then an opportunity for recall of the item. In the research literature on memory, a metaphorical treatment of these three components has gradually evolved into a technical language. Initial learning is said to result in *storage* of the item, which determines how the item is retained over time; a period of *retention* is followed by the opportunity for recall; recall of the item is then called *retrieval* from storage. An item that has been stored is said to be *available*, but it is said to be *accessible* only if it can be retrieved. There exist other memory metaphors (cf. Roediger, 1980). For example, some theories have appealed to the metaphor of resonance, as when we say that something "rings a bell" when it reminds us of something else. The metaphor of storage and retrieval, however, has been most influential in determining the direction of memory research.

The stages of storage and retrieval are analogous to storing index cards in and then retrieving them from a file, or storing information in and then retrieving it from the memory banks of a computer. The important difference is that we cannot examine any place where remembered items are retained in the way we can examine the contents of a file drawer or the fine structure of a computer core. Even what is remembered remains unspecified. We can examine an index card or the electrical charges in a computer, but we cannot find a remembered item within a learner's head. Although the language of storage and retrieval is an effective analogy for what happens in remembering, we must recognize its metaphorical status. In fact, one objective of some research on memory is to explore the limits of the metaphor of storage and retrieval. One way to describe the functional properties of remembering is to determine the range of conditions over which the metaphor holds.

According to this metaphor, a remembered item is one that has been stored and retained and retrieved. The failure to remember an item may occur because the item was not stored in the first place, or because the item was stored and then lost from storage during retention, or because the item was not retrievable at the opportunity for recall (cf. Watkins, 1990). In this section we examine how remembering can be affected by events during these three phases.

STORAGE: ENCODING AND LEVELS OF PROCESSING

What a learner remembers is not so much the stimulus itself as the learner's response to it. That response inevitably differs from the stimulus, even when the two are in the same modality (as when a learner repeats a spoken verbal item aloud). Remembering, in other words, is not simply reproducing the stimulus. Even the immediate response to a stimulus cannot be interpreted in this way. The issue is long-standing. For example, the following from the Greek philosopher Theophrastus dates from about 300 B.C.:

> ...with regard to hearing, it is strange of him [Empedocles] to imagine that he has really explained how creatures hear, when he has ascribed the process to internal sounds and assumed that the ear produces a sound within, like a bell. By means of this internal sound we might hear sounds without, but how should we hear this internal sound itself? The old problem would still confront us. (Stratton, 1917, p. 85)

A more contemporary version of this point is the following:

> Suppose someone were to coat the occipital lobes of the brain with a special photographic emulsion which, when developed, yielded a reasonable copy of a current visual stimulus. In many quarters this would be

regarded as a triumph in the physiology of vision. Yet nothing could be more disastrous, for we should have to start all over again and ask how the organism sees a picture in its occipital cortex. (Skinner, 1963; see also Skinner, 1976, p. 74)

As in the analysis of stimulus control, the problem of remembering is not to be solved by trying to follow the stimulus into the organism; rather, we must discover how to characterize the ways in which the organism behaves with respect to the stimulus (cf. Craik, 1985, p. 200: "...it is not sensible to inquire about the characteristics of the memory trace when remembering is not occurring").

The learner's behavior with respect to the stimulus to be remembered has been called *encoding* (e.g., Melton & Martin, 1972). Consider the following experiment (Conrad, 1964). In one part, learners named spoken letters presented in background noise. In a second part, they saw a sequence of six letters and wrote them down in order. When learners erred in the first task, they did so along dimensions of common acoustic properties; for example, they were more likely to confuse *V* with rhyming letters such as *B* or *C* than with letters such as *N* or *X* that share visual properties with *V* (e.g., only *B* and *C* use curved lines; cf. Gibson, 1965). The second task used visually presented letters but produced the same types of errors as the first one; learners again erred more often along dimensions of common acoustic properties than of common visual properties. These errors must have occurred because the learners had encoded the stimuli acoustically rather than visually. We need not assume that the learners' responses were subvocal speech; that remains a reasonable possibility, but more important is that their remembering was based upon acoustic rather than visual properties of the stimulus letters.

Remembering depends on how the items to be remembered are encoded. For example, some tasks favor encoding based on semantic properties (defining technical terms); others favor encoding based on visual or phonological properties (learning spellings or pronunciations); still others favor encoding based on tonal or temporal properties (following the score of a musical composition). Properties that a learner might encode include the context in which an item appears; orders or spacings or durations of items; formal or semantic relations among items; and the instructions given to the learner. Encoding can vary from time to time and within or across tasks, and it can be based on combinations of properties as well as on single dimensions. It can be as simple as the repetition of the item (sometimes called *maintenance rehearsal*) or as complex as an extensive mnemonic system (sometimes called *coding rehearsal*). We will consider a few examples, in the context of two major classes of encoding called *substitution* and *elaboration*.

Simple substitution is the most straightforward encoding and corresponds to familiar examples of codes (as in Morse-code learning; cf. Keller, 1958). Consider learning a sequence of the binary digits, 0 and 1 (Miller, 1956). The sequence 010001101011101001 substantially exceeds the number of digits that can be remembered after a single presentation. Each group of three binary digits, however, can be replaced by a single octal digit, according to the following list:

000-0	100-4
001-1	101-5
010-2	110-6
011-3	111-7

The binary sequence then can be coded as the octal sequence 215351, which can be remembered after just one presentation. Reducing the number of items to be remembered by encoding groups of items is called *chunking* (note that chunks can be arbitrary; this is one factor that distinguishes chunking from clustering in free recall; cf. Chapter 13). The acoustic encoding of written letters can also be regarded as substitution, in that there is a unique correspondence between spoken and written letters.

A second type of encoding is called *elaborative* encoding, as when a CVC nonsense syllable or a sequence of consonants is transformed into a word or a phrase. For example, a learner might rehearse the nonsense syllable *BOH* as *BOTH without a T*, or the consonant sequence *QBF* as *Quick Brown Fox*. Another variety of elaborative encoding is visual imagery, already discussed in the context of mnemonics (cf. Paivio, 1971). Elaborative encoding does not guarantee the unique correspondence between items and the learner's responses that characterizes substitution, and thus an encoded item may be more likely to occasion an inappropriate response. For example, the learner using the method of loci who encodes the word *baggage* by imagining a tower of suitcases standing in a parking lot might instead say *luggage* at recall.

Encoding, whether by substitution or elaboration, is inevitably selective. Some stimulus properties are more likely to occasion responses than others. For example, written words are very likely to produce the kind of encoding called reading; it is not easy to look at a word without reading it. Can you disobey the instruction *Do not read this sentence*? (cf. Stroop, 1935 and Chapter 11). For written verbal stimuli, a reader's response is affected more by semantic properties of the text than by typeface or size. Such responding to verbal stimuli is called *semantic encoding* (cf. Chapter 12).

Simply naming something may qualify as encoding. Two experiments involved recognition tasks with rhesus monkeys and with humans (Cook, Wright, & Sands, 1991; Wright, Cook, Rivera, Shyan, Neiworth, & Jitsumori, 1990). The stimuli included kaleidoscope pictures or travel slides. Each stimulus was briefly presented on a screen; responses were the movement of a lever to the left or to the right. The monkey behavior was maintained by food reinforcers; the human behavior was maintained by a tone produced by correct responses (for convenience, we will treat it as a reinforcer, although instructions and feedback presumably were also important variables). For both monkeys and humans, the task involved successive presentations of six pictures at the top of the screen and then a single picture at the bottom. If the final picture was different from the previous six, a lever movement to the left was reinforced; if it was the same, a movement to the right was reinforced. In other words, a correct response to the right corresponded to recognizing the final picture as one that had appeared among the six.

The six pictures were presented at interstimulus intervals of 0.08, 1, or 4 seconds. With either the kaleidoscope or the travel pictures, the monkeys were most accurate at the shorter interstimulus intervals; the more slowly the pictures appeared, the more likely the monkeys to forget earlier ones. The human performances were similar with the kaleidoscope pictures, but with the travel pictures the humans became more rather than less accurate as the pictures were presented more slowly. One interpretation was that slower presentations allowed verbal encoding and rehearsal of the travel pictures

but were not helpful with the kaleidoscope pictures because they had no names (cf. Intraub, 1979). Thus, the next stage of the experiment with humans was to teach them arbitrary names for each of the kaleidoscope pictures. The recognition task with the kaleidoscope pictures was then repeated, and the human performances became similar to those with the travel slides: The slower the presentation rate, the more accurate they became. The implication is that the names allowed them to encode and rehearse the kaleidoscope pictures. The results are of interest both for the species difference they demonstrate and for their relevance to the role of naming in remembering. For the present purposes, the main point is that naming itself can function as a variety of encoding.

The several categories of encoding we have considered are neither exhaustive nor mutually exclusive. Mnemonic systems, for example, can combine substitution, as in the number-to-consonant code, with elaboration, as in visualizing objects according to the method of loci. We should not expect an exhaustive listing, because types of encoding are as unlimited as the different ways in which we can respond to events in the world. For the same reason, we should not expect any one type of encoding to be invariant across different learners or different tasks. Different learning histories and different contingencies upon remembering guarantee variability in the ways that we each encode stimuli.

Types of encoding differ not only in how likely they are to be used in different circumstances, but also in how likely it is that what is encoded will be remembered. Some kinds of encoding seem more superficial and therefore less memorable than others; this dimension of encoding has been called *level of processing* or *depth of processing* (Cermak & Craik, 1979). Fewer words from a list are recalled after tasks requiring responses to formal properties of words (e.g., crossing out vowels, counting the number of letters) than after tasks requiring semantic responses (e.g., assigning words to categories, discriminating among plant and animal names). The implication is that the deeper the level of processing, the more likely an item is to be remembered. We are certainly more likely to remember items to which we have responded in rich and novel ways (semantic structure and visual imagery are important sources of richness and novelty). As with so many other concepts we encountered, level of processing is descriptive and not explanatory. It describes relations between types of encoding and the likelihood of remembering; it does not explain the remembering. In other words, we speak of semantic encoding as deeper processing simply because we are more likely to remember a semantically encoded item than a structurally encoded one. The issue of how we remember again becomes one of what is remembered.

The topic of encoding reminds us that remembering is behavior and that the learner is active. The active role of the learner is captured by distinctions between intentional and incidental or implicit learning (e.g., Reber, Allen, & Regan, 1985) and between willful and nonwillful memory (Watkins, 1989).

RETENTION: THE QUESTION OF MEMORY REORGANIZATION

According to the metaphor of storage and retrieval, after an item has been encoded it may be stored. But how does it get stored, and what happens to it after it has been stored? At this point the metaphor of storage and retrieval does not help us much. Retention is implicit in the concept of stor-

age, and yet we have already noted that we cannot expect to find the to-be-remembered item inside the learner. We have not even specified what an item is: a word? a sentence or logical proposition? an association? a semantic or syntactic structure tagged with various markers corresponding to its temporal and relational origins? It is only because the item emerges at recall that we assume that it somehow existed throughout retention. That may be a bit like assuming that a pianist at a keyboard releases Beethoven's sonatas from their storage in the piano, or even, more simply, that the pianist releases sounds that have been stored in the strings; whoever searches for the sonatas or the sounds by disassembling the piano will be disappointed.

We cannot ask whether what is remembered changes during retention without resolving this point. Accounts of remembering that assume that what is remembered changes during retention have included theories of *consolidation*, which argue that what is learned becomes fixed or consolidated in memory over some time following learning, and theories of *incubation*, which argue that remembered events and relations are spontaneously reorganized over time (perhaps especially during sleep), sometimes so that their combination constitutes the solution to a long-standing problem (e.g., as in some examples of scientific creativity; Hadamard, 1949).

One study of memory change during retention used reproductions of remembered material over time (e.g., the successive retelling of stories; Bartlett, 1932). An example is provided in Figure 14–1 (Carmichael, Hogan, & Walter, 1932). With varied visual figures, the remembered figure changed over retention as a function of what it had been named. Gestalt psychology (Köhler, 1929) provided the most explicit theoretical case for these changes in

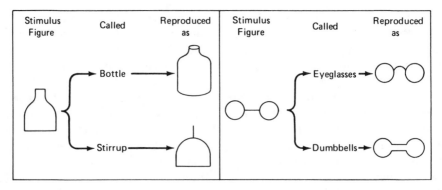

FIGURE 14-1 Examples of changes in remembered visual forms as a function of verbal labels. (Adapted from Carmichael, Hogan, & Walter, 1932, Figure 1)

memory during retention. The gestalt laws of perception (such as the law of closure, which stated that incomplete figures tend to be seen as completed) were assumed to operate on what is remembered as well as on what is seen. But changes during retention could not be distinguished from those that might have occurred during encoding and storage or at retrieval. If a visual stimulus is remembered as a word rather than a form because of verbal encoding, the learner who remembers the word at recall will draw the corresponding picture. The example suggests that there may be no need to postulate any gradual reorganization of visual memory traces.

Events that occur between storage and retrieval, however, can affect remembering. For example, consider the following simulation of eyewitness testimony in a courtroom (Loftus & Palmer, 1974). Observers who had viewed a film of an automobile accident were later asked to estimate the speed of the cars when they collided. In the wording for one group, the question was how fast the cars were going when they *hit* each other; for the other, it was how fast they were going when they *smashed into* each other. The wording made a difference. Speed estimates in the first group averaged about 8 miles per hour

whereas those in the second averaged more than 10. More important, when the observers were asked a week later whether there had been broken glass at the scene of the accident, those from the second group were more likely to say, incorrectly, that there was. Whether this distortion of memory depended directly on the difference between *hit* and *smashed into* or was instead mediated by the different estimates of speed, it is clear that events during retention affect the subsequent remembering.

The effects of the wording of questions on recall raise important questions about the reliability of eyewitness testimony. For example, everything else being equal, an eyewitness who is asked "Did you see the broken headlight?" is more likely to say yes than one who is asked "Did you see a broken headlight?" (Loftus & Zanni, 1975). The observer's verbal behavior under such questioning is rehearsal of sorts, but it has the disadvantage that it is initiated long after the event. Given that we can affect remembering by interrupting or otherwise interfering with rehearsal shortly after an event, we should not be surprised that we can also do so by distorting or interfering with it later on. The effects are sufficiently clear that we have little more to say about what happens during retention. Perhaps that is why we usually leave out retention when we speak of the metaphor of storage and retrieval.

RETRIEVAL: CUE-DEPENDENCY AND ACCESSIBILITY

We introduce retrieval with a quotation:

> In order to understand retrieval processes, some basic principles must first be accepted. One of the most important of these was formulated by St. Augustine more than 1500 years ago; we cannot seek in our memory for anything of which we have no sort of recollection; by seeking something in our memory, "we declare, by that very act, that we have not altogether forgotten it; we still hold of it, as it were, a part, and by this part, which we hold, we seek that which we do not hold." (Tulving & Madigan, 1970, p. 460)

In other words, we are not likely to remember an item or event in the absence of discriminative stimuli correlated with some properties of the item or event to be remembered. Sometimes these properties are specified by instructions, as when we are asked which of two items came earlier in a list, or whether we have met someone before, or where we were last year on the night of November 5. In these cases, the "parts we hold" are the items or a face or a date. At other times, circumstances define these properties, as when we cannot remember the article that we were supposed to buy at the store or where we put our keys. Here, the "parts" are our presence in the store or the activity that requires the keys.

An item that is stored is said to be *available* in memory. The item, however, may or may not be remembered. When it can be remembered, it is said to be *accessible*; when it cannot be remembered, it is said to be *inaccessible* (Tulving & Pearlstone, 1966). The trouble is that if an item is remembered we know that it was both avail-

able and accessible, but if it is not remembered we cannot tell whether it was unavailable or was available but inaccessible (cf. Watkins, 1990).

The accessibility of an item depends on the stimuli or cues present at the moment of recall. Their influence on remembering is called *cue-dependency*. For example, visualizing a place used in the method of loci reinstates one condition that existed when the item was encoded. Similarly, reciting the alphabet may help you to remember a forgotten name, because producing the person's initial reinstates one part of saying the name. When we use such techniques, we generate our own retrieval cues. The most critical feature of retrieval is producing conditions similar to those during encoding and storage.

Consider the experiment illustrated in Figure 14–2 (Tulving & Psotka, 1971). The recall of six 24-word lists was compared under three conditions. Each list included six semantic categories of four words each (e.g., military ranks: captain, corporal, sergeant, colonel; earth formations: cliff, river, hill, volcano); the categories differed from list to list. One condition was recall of each list immediately after it had been presented (original learning); another was recall after the presentation of all six lists (uncued recall); the third was recall after presentation of all six lists but with category names provided (cued recall). Uncued recall showed interference from intervening lists, but cued recall showed that the words had not been forgotten; when category names were provided, recall was roughly equivalent to that after original learning. In other words, according to the metaphor of storage and retrieval, the words were available but inaccessible during uncued recall; the category names in cued recall made them accessible.

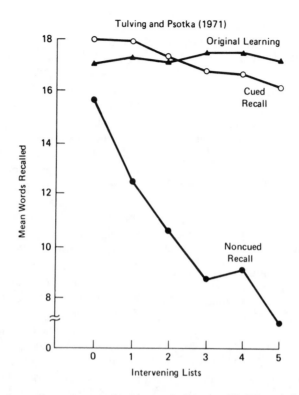

FIGURE 14–2 Number of words recalled from six 24-word lists in original learning, cued recall and noncued recall. Each list consisted of 4-word groups in six semantic categories (e.g., insects, metals, tools) and was shown three times at a rate of one word per second. Categories differed from one list to the next. Data from original learning show recall of each list immediately after its three presentations. Data from noncued recall, obtained after all six lists had been presented, show recall of each list as a function of the number of other lists that had intervened. Data from cued recall data were also obtained after all six lists had been presented, but the learners were given the names of the word categories in each list. Cued recall was roughly equivalent to recall after original learning. During noncued recall the words had been available but not accessible; they were made accessible by category names during cued recall. (Data from Tulving & Psotka, 1971, as presented in Tulving, 1974, Figure 2)

Chapter 13 illustrated a similar cue-dependency, in an experiment that made recall more likely than recognition. Recall is likely to be maximal when encoding and recall cues are based on common properties of the to-be-remembered item. Cue-dependency implies that much forgetting depends on differences between the conditions at storage and those at retrieval.

These conditions include not only the to-be-remembered stimuli and the learner's behavior with respect to them, but also the situation within which the learning took place. The special case of cue-dependency in which the condition of the learner at storage and retrieval affects recall has been called *state-dependent learning*. Cases studied include drugs and physiological states (e.g., electroconvulsive shock) as well as experimental settings (e.g., Bower, 1981; Overton, 1964). For example, what was learned while drunk may be more likely to be remembered if the learner is again drunk than if the learner is sober.

Cue-dependencies and state-dependencies may have important practical implications. But we may not wish to advise the student who is preparing for an examination to study in the room in which the examination will be held. For one thing, what has been learned will be useless after the course is over if the student cannot remember it anywhere else. More important, what is learned will be best remembered if many of the conditions for remembering arise out of the subject matter itself. A systematic subject matter is one in which each component prompts and is prompted by other components. To outline the subject matter, therefore, is to create an encoding that determines how well the various parts are remembered. The distinction between remembering something directly and deriving it from something else remembered is embodied in the distinction between *reproductive* and *reconstructive* processes in memory (e.g., Hasher & Griffin, 1978). For example, sometimes we may remember the solution to a particular mathematical problem; more often, however, and usually more effectively, we instead remember only the particular method of solving it (cf. Jacoby, 1978).

We have surveyed some memory research influenced by the metaphor of search. According to this metaphor, during retrieval the learner searches through the memory store for items having particular characteristics until the appropriate one is found. The store might be analogous to a stack of index cards in a cabinet or to the memory banks of a computer. But how does the metaphor deal with how rapidly

and accurately humans can discriminate between knowing something and not knowing it (Kolers & Palef, 1976; Glucksberg & McClosky, 1981). Why should search ever take longer when an appropriate item exists to be found than when such an item does not exist (and therefore when the search must examine every item in storage)?

Aside from the problem of how rapidly we can say that we do not know something, the metaphor is also strained by the vast capacity of human memory; if nothing else, a search through memory storage at every instance of remembering seems inefficient. Cue-dependency suggests a more restricted search limited by the conditions at recall. At this point, the extension of the metaphor demands that we distinguish among kinds of search. A random search through an unorganized list differs from a search for an item located in an ordered list (as in locating a word in an alphabetized index); both of these differ from a systematic search through categories that are organized hierarchically (as in locating an item in a department-store catalogue with sections devoted to different types of merchandise). As we shall see in Chapter 15, the types of search may be distinguished on the basis of their quantitative properties. An undifferentiated metaphor of search is not adequate for a general account of human memory, but particular differentiated versions may be relevant to some special classes of memory tasks.

Section C   Kinds of Remembering

Our example of the pigeon's remembering at the beginning of this chapter required continued behavior that bridged the temporal gap between the stimulus and the later response. The subsequent mnemonic examples did not include such uninterrupted intervening behavior. Clearly the cases are different. We would similarly distinguish between remembering an appointment after seeing it on one's calendar and remembering without consulting such a record. There are different varieties of remembering.

One criterion for organizing kinds of remembering is the period of time over which something is remembered; another is what is remembered. We will sample both types of classification. First we will treat the duration of remembering by examining three phenomena: the relatively brief persistence of the effects of a stimulus; the maintenance of responding occasioned by a stimulus, as in rehearsal; and responding after some time elapses without rehearsal. These categories have been respectively called *iconic memory, short-term memory,* and *long-term memory.* Then we will briefly treat categories of remembering defined by what is remembered, as in autobiographical and semantic memory.

ICONIC MEMORY: THE PERSISTING EFFECTS OF STIMULI

The effects of a stimulus may continue even after the stimulus presentation has ended. Persisting aftereffects of visual stimuli are called *icons,* and the topic of *iconic memory* is concerned with their time courses (an afterimage is one persisting effect of a visual stimulus; for a discussion of the relation between icons and visual afterimages, see Long, 1980). How is that time course to be measured? If an observer reports some letters that have been presented briefly, how is a report based on the sensory aftereffect to be distinguished from one based on the observer's continued rehearsal of the letters?

The problem can be solved by showing more items in the stimulus display than can

be included within the span of immediate memory and asking the observer for some sample of these items at various times after the display. We are limited in the number of items that we can rehearse or remember after a single brief presentation. This limit, typically within the range of 7 plus or minus 2 items (Miller, 1956), is called the *span of immediate memory.* For the present purposes, it serves as a tool for studying iconic memory. The range of the span of immediate memory is to some extent independent of the nature of the items. For example, you can remember roughly 5 to 9 words almost as easily as 5 to 9 letters, even though the words themselves include many more than 9 letters (cf. the earlier discussion of chunking in this chapter).

Just as an examination tests only part of the material that a student is supposed to have learned during a course and assumes that the score represents what proportion of the entire course has actually been learned, a sampling of what the observer reports at different times after the display assumes that the observer's responses represent the proportion of items that can be reported. The time course of iconic memory is measured over fractions of a second, but during this time the observer in effect can still read the items in the display even though the display is no longer there.

This experimental rationale was developed by Sperling (1960); data from one experiment are shown in Figure 14–3. A 4-by-3 matrix of letters and numbers was presented to observers for 50 milliseconds (0.05 sec). An example is the following:

$$
\begin{array}{cccc}
7 & I & V & F \\
X & L & 5 & 3 \\
B & 4 & W & 7
\end{array}
$$

Observers could not be expected to report all 12 items, so a tone of high or medium or low frequency served as an instruction to report the characters in the top or middle or bottom line of the matrix. The tone was sounded either before the display, at the moment the display ended, or at some time after the display (x-axis in Figure 14–3). The mean number of characters correctly reported from the single line was multiplied by three and taken as an estimate of the total reportable characters in the matrix (y-axis in Figure 14–3).

About 10 characters from the matrix could be reported when the instruction tone preceded the display or occurred as the display ended (delays of -0.10 and 0 seconds); when it followed the display with delays of 0.15 seconds or longer, the proportion of reportable characters decreased with increasing delay. When the instruction tone was delayed by 1 second,

the number of reportable characters was about equal to the span of immediate memory in this task (this span of about 4 to 5 items, at the extreme low end of the usual 5-to-9 item range, probably depends on the relative complexity of the observer's task, which includes a mix of letters and numbers and the matrix format). The region between the data points and the immediate-memory span (shaded area in Figure 14–3) is assumed to represent the persistence of the sensory effects of the display; this is the extent to which the observer can still read some of the matrix even though it is no longer present.

This experiment demonstrates that the sensory effects of a stimulus continue for a brief time after the stimulus has been presented. Similar effects have been demonstrated with auditory presentations of

FIGURE 14–3 Characters available from a 3-by-4 matrix of letters and numbers when the signal for reporting occurs at various times relative to the display. The signal was a tone of high, medium, or low frequency that instructed the observer to report the characters in the top, middle, or bottom row of the matrix. With increasing delays of the instruction tone, report accuracy approached the immediate-memory span for this task. Data are means across four observers. (Adapted from Sperling, 1960, Figure 7)

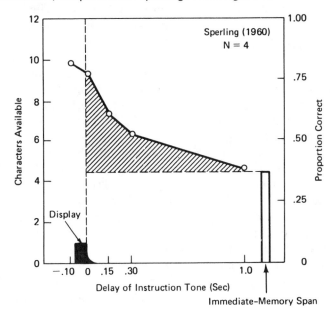

verbal stimuli, as in experiments in which different sequences of spoken letters were simultaneously presented in three auditory channels (left ear, right ear, and both ears; Darwin, Turvey, & Crowder, 1972). The effects of auditory stimuli appear to decrease more slowly, perhaps over several seconds, than do those of visual stimuli. The auditory case has been called *echoic memory* (but should not be confused with the echoic class of verbal behavior in Chapter 11; echoic memory involves the persisting effects of auditory stimuli without regard to the nature of the listener's response to those stimuli, whereas echoic verbal behavior is defined by the correspondence between the auditory stimulus and the listener's vocal response).

Obviously the finding that the sensory effects of a stimulus continue for a brief time after the stimulus ends has only a little to do with remembering over longer periods. Visual stimuli must be seen and auditory stimuli must be heard to be remembered, but remembering over minutes or days cannot be attributed to the persisting sensory effects of stimuli.

SHORT-TERM MEMORY: THE ROLE OF REHEARSAL

The recall of a human learner immediately after presentation of a verbal sequence, usually limited to about 5 to 9 items, is the span of immediate memory (Jacobs, 1887; Miller, 1956). For example, one can probably correctly repeat the sequence 706294 after a single hearing, but a correct repetition of the longer sequence 549628367102 is unlikely. The immediate memory span has been described as the limit of what can be held in consciousness. We sometimes report that we are seeing or hearing or remembering something by saying we are conscious of it.

The limit on the span of immediate memory provided the historical basis for studies of what has come to be called short-term memory (in some usages, primary memory, as in Waugh & Norman, 1965; cf. Daniels, 1895; Smith, 1895). A major question is whether the response is occasioned directly by prior stimuli or is instead occasioned indirectly by other intervening behavior, such as rehearsal. One way to address this question is with a task that prevents the learner from rehearsal between the presentation of items and the opportunity for their recall. The tasks used to measure the span of immediate memory incidentally create such conditions. If a long sequence of items is presented, the learner cannot simultaneously rehearse the early items and listen to the later ones. Some of the later items therefore interfere with or prevent the behavior upon which recall of earlier items depends.

Consider now the short-term memory experiment of Peterson and Peterson (1959; see also Brown, 1958). Vocal stimuli consisted of three consonants and then a three-digit number. The learner's instructions were to begin counting backwards by threes from the number and then, when a signal light flashed, to recall the consonants. A trial might start with the spoken items, CHJ 506; the learner then counted backwards, 506, 503, 500, 497, etc., until the signal light, which set the occasion for naming the consonants. The time from the consonants to the onset of the signal varied from 3 to 18 seconds. Under these conditions, recall accuracy decreased with delay until, at delays of 15 or 18 seconds, the proportion correct was less than 10 percent. In two other conditions, learners were allowed periods of vocal or silent rehearsal before they were given the number from which to count backwards. Figure 14–4 compares data from the original

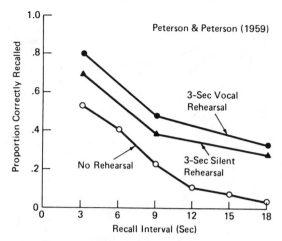

FIGURE 14–4 Proportion of 3-consonant items correctly recalled as a function of delay between presentation and opportunity for recall. In one condition (open circles), rehearsal was prevented by instructing the learner to count backwards by threes from a number that immediately followed each item. In two other conditions, the learner was allowed 3 seconds of silent rehearsal (filled triangles) or vocal rehearsal (filled circles) before starting to count backwards. (Adapted from Peterson & Peterson, 1959, Figure 3 and Table 1)

procedure (open circles) and data with 3 seconds of either silent rehearsal (filled triangles) or vocal rehearsal (filled circles) before the backwards-counting task. The way the learners responded to the consonants determined how well they were able to recall them. Recall is determined more by our behavior with respect to past stimuli than by the stimuli themselves.

These and related findings led to proposals of two distinct types of memory: short-term memory and long-term memory (e.g., Shiffrin & Atkinson, 1969). Items are said to be rapidly lost from short-term memory unless maintained there through rehearsal; by some means, perhaps through rehearsal itself, items in short-term memory are sometimes transferred to a more permanent long-term memory. Some accounts distinguish between two types of rehearsal (e.g., Craik & Lockhart, 1972; Rundus, 1977, 1980). In *maintenance* rehearsal, an item is simply repeated (as in

reciting a definition that one is memorizing); in *coding* rehearsal, the item is transformed or elaborated in some way (as in using a mnemonic system to convert numbers to words). Note that both types of rehearsal depend on encoding; as we saw earlier, even naming a stimulus can be regarded as a type of encoding.

Only a few items at a time can be held in short-term memory, but the capacity of long-term memory is virtually unlimited. More detailed analyses of data from short-term memory procedures complicated this view, however. Without rehearsal (Figure 14–4, open circles), the data at first seem to represent the gradual fading or decay of items to be remembered. But several lines of evidence suggest this is not so. Consider first the effects of varying the number of letters to be remembered, as in Figure 14–5 (Melton, 1963). A stimulus item containing 1, 2, 3, 4, or 5 consonants and then a 3-digit number were presented visually; the

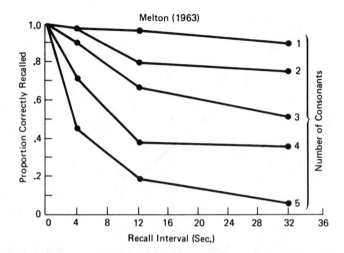

FIGURE 14–5 Proportion of consonants correctly recalled as a function of delay between presentation and recall, with number of consonants as a parameter. The consonants and a 3-digit number were presented visually; the learner read the consonants aloud and then began counting backwards by threes or fours until a visual signal for recall. (From Melton, 1963, Figure 2)

learner read the consonants aloud and then began counting backwards by threes or fours until a visual signal set the occasion for recall. When the item consisted of only a single consonant, recall accuracy remained high even over 32 seconds. The proportion of items recalled decreased more rapidly over time as the number of consonants increased. But now which set of data represents the time course of short-term memory? If recall of a single consonant is nearly perfect, then adding new consonants may simply interfere to some extent with recall of the old.

The two extreme possibilities in these procedures are perfect recall and no recall at all. Perhaps the backwards-counting task prevented rehearsal only partially, and intermediate outcomes occurred because learners had some opportunities for rehearsal even while engaging in that task. More rehearsal is presumably necessary for recall of more consonants, so recall accuracy at a given delay should

decrease with the number of consonants. Thus, the form of the short-term memory function may depend mainly on the learner's opportunity to respond to the stimulus items (cf. Crowder, 1976, p. 196). Perhaps it is relevant that the recall probability of three consonants was greater in Melton's experiment (Figure 14–5) than in Peterson and Peterson's (Figure 14–4): Melton's learners recited the consonants aloud and were therefore guaranteed at least one rehearsal before they began the backwards counting, whereas the Petersons did not do so. One experiment used visual stimuli and the other used vocal stimuli, but the opportunity for immediate responding was probably more important than the modality difference.

Once we recognize that each item can affect the recall of others, we can ask whether the numbers in the backwards-counting task prevent rehearsal or interfere with recall in some other way. If each number produced by the learner during backwards counting is an item, does recall vary with time or with number of items? This problem was addressed by surveying memory experiments in which delays between items and recall included various numbers and rates of intervening items (Waugh & Norman, 1965). Data from many studies indicated that the number of intervening items during the delay was more important than its duration. For example, learners were given numbers at rates of 1 or 4 per second and then were asked to name the number at a particular location in the sequence. Recall probability after 4 items in 1 second was about equal to that after 4 items in 4 seconds, even though the delay between the first item and recall was about 1 second in the former case and 4 seconds in the latter. On the other hand, recall probability was greater after a delay with 2 intervening items in 2 seconds than after one with 8 items in 2 seconds. If any rehearsal occurs while items are presented, items presented slowly should permit more rehearsal than items presented rapidly. It is difficult to reconcile this outcome with an account of short-term memory in terms of the effects of restricting rehearsal.

Still another problem is that recall probability changes over the first few trials of a short-term memory procedure (e.g., Keppel & Underwood, 1962). For example, recall of a 3-consonant item on the first trial of a short-term memory session is nearly perfect at a delay of either 3 or 18 seconds; over the next three to six trials, recall probability decreases, but the decrease is much greater when the delay is 18 seconds than when it is 3 seconds. In other words, the relation between recall probability and the delay imposed by an interpolated task, as in Figures 14–4 and 14–5, is absent at the beginning of sessions and builds up over

several trials. This is an example of proactive inhibition (cf. Chapter 13); learning the consonants on the first trial interferes with the recall of other consonants on later trials. We will have more to say about such proactive effects later.

Changes in stimulus items can temporarily eliminate the proactive effect in short-term memory. For example, recall probability increases substantially for a trial or more after the items to be remembered are changed from letters to numbers or vice versa. Similar effects also occur with words as stimulus items (e.g., with changes in semantic categories, as from food to furniture; Wickens, 1970). These procedures may be more relevant to defining verbal classes than to analyzing short-term memory.

Short-term memory procedures are usually designed to prevent rehearsal rather than to encourage it. It is therefore curious that rehearsal has played such a substantial role in their interpretation. There is no single short-term memory function. Furthermore, interference among items, both within and across trials, makes it inappropriate to speak of short-term memory as the passive decay of items. Nevertheless, the recall of an item after its uninterrupted rehearsal differs from its recall if there has been no rehearsal. This difference, together with the relatively limited span of immediate memory, justifies the distinction between short-term memory and other types of memory.

LONG-TERM MEMORY: INTERFERENCE AND FORGETTING

In studies of short-term memory, the time from item presentation to recall is usually a matter of seconds, whereas in studies of long-term memory it may be minutes, hours, days, or perhaps even years. It has been argued on the one hand that short-term and long-term memory are separate types of remembering with different properties, and on the other that short-term and long-term memory are merely extremes on a single continuum determined by variables that affect remembering (e.g., Melton, 1963; Tulving & Madigan, 1970). The account here will mainly elaborate on a simple procedural consequence of the existence of a span of immediate memory.

When the number of items in a list exceeds the span of immediate memory, a single presentation is not sufficient for the learner's recall, even if recall follows immediately after the list ends. The only way to study the remembering of such lists is to arrange repeated presentations of some or all of the items to be learned. The amount to be remembered determines whether repeated presentations are needed; it is therefore more important in distinguishing between short-term and long-term memory than the period of time over which remembering is measured. Long-term memory includes all cases in which

the items to be remembered exceed the immediate memory span. Such remembering does not allow uninterrupted rehearsal between presentation and recall; such remembering requires repeated presentations of the to-be-remembered items; thus, such remembering is likely to be studied over relatively longer time periods than those common to research on short-term memory.

Data from the classic study of long-term memory by Ebbinghaus (1885) are shown in Figure 14–6. The remembering of non-sense-syllable lists was assessed by the method of savings (cf. Chapter 13) at 20 minutes, 1 and 8.8 hours, and 1, 2, 6, and 31 days after original learning. The largest decrease in the proportion remembered (in other words, the most forgetting) occurred shortly after original learning. Even after 31 days, however, the savings on relearning exceeded 20 percent. Ebbinghaus entertained the alternative possibilities that memories deteriorated over time or that they remained intact but were gradually overlaid by or hidden beneath other

FIGURE 14–6 Ebbinghaus's forgetting curve. Ebbinghaus learned and relearned 13-syllable lists. At different times between original learning and relearning, he measured how much was saved from the original learning. Forgetting was substantial even soon after original learning (the first point is at 20 minutes), but after 31 days savings were still greater than 20%. (Adapted from Ebbinghaus, 1885, chap. VII)

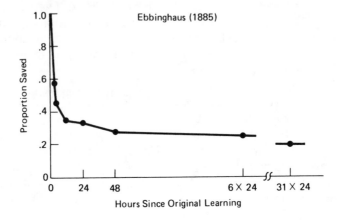

memories. (In more contemporary vocabulary, the distinction is sometimes expressed as one between decreasing *availability* of items with time, as items are lost from memory, and decreasing *accessibility* with unchanged availability, as items remain in memory but become harder and harder to retrieve).

These two views were the precursors of many theories of forgetting. Those based upon the passive decay of memories, sometimes called *trace* theories, often assumed correspondences between remembering and hypothetical processes in the nervous system. Those based upon competition among different memories, sometimes called *interference* theories, were more likely to rely upon environmental and behavioral variables. Nevertheless, the notion of memories as traces that fade or decay over time was implicit in many early generalizations (e.g., Jost's law: If two associations are of equal strength but different ages, the older will lose strength or be forgotten more slowly than the newer; Jost, 1897). The problem with such generalizations is that what is remembered varies with how remembering is measured. For example, forgetting as measured by savings on relearning a list differs from that measured by recall or recognition of the items. An easily learned list is not necessarily better remembered than a list learned with difficulty. Two lists that differ in difficulty or in the time to meet learning criteria may be forgotten at approximately equal rates if mastery of the items on the two lists is equated (Underwood, 1964).

The effects of sleep on memory provided one way to distinguish between accounts of memory in terms of decaying traces and those in terms of interference. There is no convincing evidence for learning during sleep, but less forgetting of what is learned while awake occurs during sleep than during an equal waking period (Jenkins & Dallenbach, 1924). One interpretation was that events during waking are more likely than events during sleep to interfere with what has been learned. Other accounts, however, grew out of theories such as memory *consolidation,* which argued that memory is relatively impermanent immediately after learning, and that a period of time was required after learning for memory to become fixed or consolidated. According to this theory, various events can disrupt the consolidation of memory, whereas sleep has no effect on or might even facilitate consolidation.

Consolidation theories were influenced by the phenomenon of *reminiscence* (Ballard, 1913; Kamin, 1957). Reminiscence, most likely to be observed with incompletely learned materials, is an increase in recall probability as time passes since the end of learning, perhaps followed later by the usual decrease in recall called forgetting. Reminiscence has been observed over minutes in some experiments and over successive daily sessions in others and depends on the details of learning and recall procedures. For example, increased recall with the passage of time is more likely with pictures than with verbal material (Erdelyi & Kleinhard, 1978). An important implication of reminiscence is that there is no such thing as a single function that describes remembering or forgetting; there even are circumstances in which recall becomes more rather than less likely over time.

In one form or another, accounts in terms of interference have dominated analyses of long-term memory. Early attempts to treat forgetting in terms of interference assumed that events between learning and recall were the major source of interference. The important events were assumed to act retroactively, so that recent events affected what was learned earlier. The critical finding for analyses in terms of interference was that interference worked the other way around: Earlier learning had substantial proactive effects, influencing the forgetting of more recently learned material (Underwood, 1957; Underwood & Postman, 1960). Figure 14–7 summarizes data from several experiments, and shows how the forgetting of a list varies as a function of the number of lists learned earlier (Underwood, 1957).

The demonstrations of proactive interference were significant because much data on human memory over more than half a century had been obtained from practiced learners who had served in experiments involving the learning of many lists. Ebbinghaus himself typified that circumstance, and even learners who did not participate in experiments with many different lists under many different conditions were ordinarily given practice lists before the experiment proper began. From those studies, the estimate of forgetting over 24 hours had been about 75 percent; Underwood's analysis showed that most of this forgetting is produced by proactive interference from the learning of earlier lists, and that without such interference forgetting is only about 25 percent (zero lists, Figure 14–7). In other words, a predominant cause of forgetting is that older learning interferes with remembering what has been learned more recently.

The remembering of one list learned in the laboratory varied with the prior learning of other lists in the laboratory. If a substantial amount of forgetting was produced by proactive interference from related material learned earlier in the laboratory, it was reasonable to ask how much of the forgetting that was left was produced by proactive interference from sources outside the laboratory (Underwood & Postman, 1960). Even someone in an experiment on verbal learning for the first time enters with an extensive history of

FIGURE 14–7 Recall of items on a list as a function of the number of lists previously learned. Each circle represents data from a different study. Forgetting was greater as the number of previous lists increased; in other words, forgetting depended on proactive interference from the learning of earlier lists. (Adapted from Underwood, 1957, Figure 3)

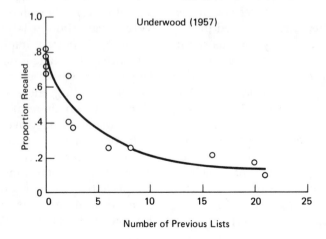

verbal behavior. If learning an earlier list in the laboratory can have some effect, then verbal learning outside of the laboratory should act in the same way. Transfer is also relevant: Depending on the relations among tasks, some kinds of prior learning might have larger proactive effects than others on the remembering of material learned later. The implications are tantalizing: Perhaps there would be little forgetting or no forgetting at all were it not for proactive interference (retroactive effects, however, can also contribute to forgetting). In any case, proactive interference does not explain forgetting; it is a name occasioned by the variables that affect forgetting (cf. Crowder, 1976, pp. 194–195).

THE STRUCTURE OF MEMORY: WHAT IS REMEMBERED?

We have considered various properties of memory. Many kinds of events and relations can be remembered. For example, the pigeon that pecks a key today because pecks yesterday occasionally produced food can be said to be remembering the past contingency between pecks and food. We have already questioned whether remembering of this sort is related in any simple way to remembering in human verbal learning. The vocabulary of memory may be occasioned by almost any situation in which current behavior is influenced by past events. We remember particular incidents, word definitions, contingencies, stimuli, language syntax, and our own behavior.

Procedural and Declarative Memory

Given this variety, we might expect properties of memory to vary with what is remembered (cf. Roediger & Craik, 1989). An example is motor memory (e.g., Baddeley, 1976). Two classes of motor memory have

been distinguished: discrete skills, such as typing or changing gear in a manual-shift car; and continuous skills, such as tracking a continuously moving target or steering a car. The distinction is important mainly because discrete skills can be forgotten whereas continuous skills rarely are (one does not forget how to swim or to ride a bicycle). The two skills seem closely related. Thus, if a memory difference can be observed even in this comparison, we must assume that other differences are likely over the range of different types of remembering. This section briefly surveys some memory classes distinguished by what is remembered.

The motor memory example is relevant to remembering operations or ways of doing things. Such remembering is sometimes called *procedural* memory, and is distinguished from *declarative* memory, which is verbal remembering or the remembering of facts (e.g., Tulving, 1985; cf. the distinction between knowing *how* and knowing *that* in Chapter 1).

Implicit and Explicit Memory

Procedural memory does not necessarily involve words. Some types of remembering cannot be assessed simply by asking what someone remembers. One may not know how much one knows. This is as true for the remembering of verbal material as for the remembering of ways of doing things, and it is the basis for distinguishing between *implicit* and *explicit* memory (e.g., Craik, 1983; Foss, 1988; Johnson & Hasher, 1987). These two types of remembering are usually well integrated in normal adults, but in those individuals with certain types of verbal deficits called *aphasias* they can be dissociated. For example, suppose an observer has the task of reporting tachistoscopically presented words (written words that are presented very briefly); one measure of the threshold for seeing the word is the duration at which the observer can reliably report it. This threshold can be reduced if a priming word—the same or a semantically related word—is shown at some time before the test word. With aphasic adults, thresholds can be reduced by priming words even though these aphasics cannot remember what the priming words were. In other words, verbal stimuli can have effects on later verbal behavior (they are implicitly remembered) even though they cannot be reported later (they are not explicitly remembered). Similar effects can occur in normal remembering (cf. the distinction between availability and accessibility; see also Skinner, 1957, on multiple causation in verbal behavior).

Autobiographical and Semantic Memory

When we speak of everyday remembering, we are usually concerned with particular incidents that occurred at certain times and places. This kind of remembering is called *autobiographical* or *episodic* memory, in that it involves the recall of episodes from our own life. One special case of autobiographical memory, sometimes called *flashbulb* memory (e.g., Bohannon, 1988; McCloskey, Wible, & Cohen, 1988), involves remembering the details of where one was at the time of a major and emotionally significant event. Even this type of remembering can be modified by the conditions under which the story is retold (flashbulb memory should not be confused with *eidetic* memory, the vivid recall of visual scenes; cf. Chapter 15 on imagery).

Autobiographical memory can be contrasted with *semantic* memory, which is our remembering of properties of language: word usages, idioms, and the functional aspects of grammar (Tulving, 1972, 1989; see also Miller, 1972, on lexical memory). You cannot understand a sentence if you cannot remember what the words mean. But there is a difference between remembering what a word means and remembering where you saw it last. Only the former is semantic memory. In serial learning, for example, the learner's task is to recall the items that appeared on a particular list in a particular setting. That list constituted an episode in the learner's life, and therefore the learner's recall is still an instance of autobiographical memory.

Such autobiographical remembering differs from that of remembering word meanings or mathematical relations, which are not recalled on the basis of a date or place of occurrence. The difference is implied by those cases of amnesia involving the forgetting of personal history without loss of language, but in many other respects autobiographical and semantic memory have similar functional properties (e.g., Anderson & Ross, 1980; McCloskey & Santee, 1981). The difficulty is that semantic properties of words were presumably learned in the context of particular episodes, and the distinction may therefore rest mainly with the frequency and recency of remembering.

In any case, the study of semantic memory usually deals with the structure of what is remembered rather than with the functional properties of remembering (cf. Anderson & Bower, 1973; Shimp, 1976). Relevant research was presented in Chapter 12, in the context of psycholinguistics. For example, a learner is more likely to remember semantic than syntactic properties of a sentence in a text (Sachs, 1967). Remembering a particular sentence that appeared in a particular text is autobiographical memory. But semantic structure is defined by how we generalize across syntactic transformations of sentences; one way we determine the nature of semantic and syntactic classes is by examining what is remembered. The correspondence between what is presented and what is remembered (recalled or recognized) defines structural classes in memory in the same way that the correspondence between the behavior that is reinforced and the behavior that is generated defines the structure of operant classes (cf. Chapter 6). In other words, using remembering to study the structure of verbal behavior is likely to be more profitable than using verbal behavior to study the nature of remembering.

A variety of experiments have examined the structure of what is remembered. Analyses of how stories and texts are remembered have led to accounts of the hierarchical structure of components of the story plot or text (e.g., Bower, Black, & Turner, 1979; Mandler & Johnson, 1977). Analyses of the remembering of words and texts in different languages have shown that the structure of the semantic classes of bilingual speakers extends across language boundaries, as when the learner's remembering of meaning is independent of the language in which items are presented (e.g., Kolers, 1966; MacLeod, 1976). Analyses of the implications that learners can derive from remembered and logically related sentences have shown how items of information can be organized into integrated structures (e.g., Moeser & Tarrant, 1977). Such studies inevitably combine autobiographical and semantic components of memory, because they include the remembering of both specific dated items and general structural relations.

Other Kinds of Remembering

We have not exhausted the list of kinds of remembering. For example, we have not considered *spatial* memory (remembering paths and things located on them), though such remembering was involved in the treatment of cognitive maps and in the mnemonic method of loci. Another memory distinction is that between *retrospective* and *prospective* memory, which is concerned with the difference between remembering tasks on the basis of past events or of what is to be done in the future (e.g., Urcuioli & Zentall, 1986; cf. Wixted, 1989). For example, you might arrive at a hardware store remembering what you wanted to repair or remembering the tool that you came there to buy.

Some accounts of kinds of remembering have attempted to organize them into a hierarchy of memory systems. Tulving (1985), for example, suggests that procedural memory comes first: It is shared by both verbal and nonverbal organisms. Semantic memory is then built upon procedural memory: Until a language exists, it is not possible to talk about remembered events. Finally comes autobiographical memory. It is implicit in such a hierarchy that discriminations relevant to one's own remembering emerge last. Such discriminations lead us to the final topic of this chapter, metamemory.

METAMEMORY

We have identified three memory classes: the persisting stimulus effects called iconic memory; the momentary recall, extendable through rehearsal but limited in capacity, called short-term memory; and the durable remembering called long-term memory. We have also considered some classifications of memory based on what is remembered.

Remembering is behavior (cf. Craik, 1983, p. 345), and remembering can be learned. Not only do we learn patterns of rehearsal that extend our short-term memory and mnemonic techniques that influence our long-term memory, but we also learn to judge the properties of our own remembering (e.g., Flavell, Friedrichs, & Hoyt, 1970). In other words, short-term and long-term memory are differentiated classes of remembering, and these classes are discriminated with respect to the circumstances in which they occur; how we remember will depend at least partly on past consequences of remembering. *Metamemory* can therefore be defined as the differentiation and discrimination of one's own remembering.

Running or Working Memory

Continually updating what is remembered by dropping some items and adding others is sometimes called *running memory* or *working memory*. Consider the short-order cook working on two eggs over easy and two scrambled, three orders of waffles, and a stack of pancakes. As each dish is handed out to be served and each new order is called in, some items can be forgotten while others must be remembered. Earlier breakfast orders over the course of the morning are potentially a major source of proactive interference. Nevertheless, this task is often performed with considerable skill. It cannot be done well simply through undifferentiated remembering. The number of orders that can be remembered and worked on at a given time is limited: The short-order cook must distinguish among orders that have been finished and can be forgotten, those in progress that must be watched, and

those not yet started that must be remembered. The updating of what can be forgotten and what must still be remembered is crucial to doing the job successfully (e.g., Bjork, 1978). Other examples are keeping track of cards played in a card game or following the changing statistics during an athletic event (most appropriately, running memory of races run, laps completed, relative positions of competitors, and other information at a track meet). In such circumstances, what can be forgotten is as important as what must be remembered.

Some studies have shown that learning some verbal items can be affected by instructing the learner to forget other items (e.g., Bjork, 1970). Interference by a given item is reduced by an instruction to forget that item. As might be expected, the reduction is greater when the instruction to forget precedes the presentation of the item than when it follows the item. But what sort of behavior occurs when the learner is instructed to forget? Are the items somehow deleted from memory, or do they remain while the learner comes to discriminate those to be remembered from those to be forgotten? One experiment (Waugh, 1972) examined free recall of a 40-item list of common one-syllable words. In one condition, some items included among the first 20 of the 40-item list were repeated among the last 20 items of that list. Even with the instruction to forget the first 20 items, the recall probability for these items was greater than that for new items. Whatever the learner did when instructed to forget did not cancel the effects of the items to be forgotten; the learner was more likely to recall those items when they appeared again in the second half of the list than to recall items that had not appeared before.

Discriminated Remembering

Not only can learners learn to remember and to forget differentially, as when they are more likely to remember unfinished than finished tasks (the Zeigarnik effect; Zeigarnik,. 1927), but they can also discriminate among various properties of their own remembering. The "tip-of-the-tongue" phenomenon (Brown & McNeill, 1966; cf. Chapter 11) is an example of a discrimination based upon the likelihood of remembering. We can sometimes say that we will be able to recognize a word even though we are unable to recall it at the moment. The accuracy of this discrimination can be assessed on the basis of partial reports of the word to be remembered. When a word is "on the tip of your tongue," you can often report such properties as its initial letter or number of syllables, and you are likely to recognize the word when you see it.

Both at storage and at retrieval, learners can estimate the likelihood of remembering; they can also usually discriminate between never having learned something and having learned and then forgotten it (Kolers & Palef, 1976; cf. Glucksberg & McClosky, 1981). Having remembered something, we often discriminate among the sources of that remembering. In recalling some incident, for example, you may be able to report that some facts are based on your own experience whereas you deduced others from the circumstances (e.g., Johnson & Raye, 1981). Another instance of discriminating your own remembering is when you describe your confidence or certainty about something you have recalled.

Our capacity to make such judgments changes over time (cf. Lachman, Lachman, & Thronesbery, 1979, on metamemory through the adult life span; Skinner, 1983, on intellectual self-manage-ment in old age). Such reports, closely related to the autoclitic processes of Chapter 11, though not themselves memory, may well be important components of remembering. For example, the student who cannot distinguish between having learned something well and having learned it inadequately is not likely to be able to study effectively or to ask appropriate questions (e.g., Bisanz, Vesonder, & Voss, 1978; Miyake & Norman, 1979). The topic of metamemory is important because it deals with the circumstances in which the learner engages in behavior relevant to remembering.

SUMMARY

We examined the phases of episodes of remembering in terms of the metaphor of storage and retrieval. We treated the major memory classes called iconic and short-term and long-term, based on the duration of remembering, and various memory classes, such as autobiographical and semantic and implicit memory, based on what is remembered. We considered the updating of running or working memory, and the differentiated and discriminated remembering called metamemory. It seems redundant to summarize these topics here in greater detail, because the essential vocabulary of memory has been included in the section headings of this chapter. These headings can be listed and remembered in a variety of ways: by rote rehearsal, by mnemonic techniques, or by reviewing the relations among particular experiments and concepts. Undoubtedly the reader who learns this material merely as a sequence of words will not remember it as well as the reader who has responded in other ways; we spoke of that difference as depth of processing. We have not explained memory for words, texts, specific events, structures, or our own behavior, but we have seen that what is remembered defines important units of behavior. Just as contingencies define functional response classes, what is remembered defines the structure of memory.

CHAPTER 15
Cognition and Problem Solving

Section A **Cognitive Processes**
Visual Imagery
Simulations
Processing Stages
Mental Representations

Section B **Problem Solving**
Functional Fixity
The Construction of Solutions

The Indo-European root gno- *is the source through Old English of* know *and* knowledge *and through Germanic of* cunning *and* can, *in the sense of being able to. Its Latin derivative is* gnoscere, *to know or to get acquainted with, and this is a root of* cognition, ignorant, *and* recognize. *Synonyms of* knowledge *are often related to sensory language. For example, the Indo-European* weid-, *to see, leads to* view *and* vision *through the Latin* videre, *to* idea *through the Greek* eidos, *and to* guide *and* wisdom *through various Old English and Germanic forms. The word* see *itself implies understanding, as in the phrase* I see, *and it has such relatives as the word* insight.

Early in this text, before embarking on our treatment of the effects of stimuli and contingencies, we distinguished between structural and functional problems in the analysis of behavior. Structural problems are those concerned with properties of response and stimuli classes; these classes are the fundamental units of behavior. We have now considered many response classes and stimulus classes, some defined by contingencies (rein-

forcers, operants, and discriminated operants) and others defined by what is occasioned or what is remembered (semantic and syntactic classes).

We indicated, in our initial discussions of function and structure, that concern with functional problems tends to be correlated with a behavioral vocabulary, whereas concern with structural problems tends to be correlated with a cognitive vocabulary. This text began by emphasizing the experiments and vocabulary that grew out of a behavioral tradition. That treatment was extended to verbal behavior, which began the transition to topics that are a primary concern of contemporary cognitive psychology. Those topics were examined in the context of psycholinguistics, verbal learning, and memory. This chapter further illustrates research methods and issues in cognitive psychology; it then proceeds to a brief treatment of problem solving, in which structural and functional analyses converge.

Section A Cognitive Processes

Most processes called cognitive (e.g., imagining or visualizing) are private events: We cannot see what someone else is thinking or imagining. But imagining, like walking or talking, is something we do. Some might argue that these private events should not be called behavior. Yet our treatment of behavior has not been limited to movements; operants, for example, are not defined by response topography. Certainly it is difficult to say just what a person does when imagining (cf. Chapter 11 on private events). Nevertheless, it is plausible to assume that such behavior shares something with the behavior of looking at things in the environment (we can discriminate our imagining from our seeing; when we fail to do so, we are said to have hallucinations; cf. Skinner, 1953; Paivio, 1975). The difficulty is that such behavior is relatively inaccessible to anyone but the one who engages in it. We may recall the recommendation to convert psychological nouns to verbs: Instead of "cognition and thought" we should say "knowing and thinking" (Woodworth, 1921; cf. Kolers & Roediger, 1984; Malcolm, 1971).

Consider the private event called paying attention. Chapter 7 treated attention as the control over responding by some stimulus features but not others. That treatment converted a word from the everyday vocabulary into a technical term, but the term remains part of our everyday language. *Attending* is a kind of response. The technical usage is not our present concern. Instead, the issue is what kind of a response attending is: How can we identify it and how can we measure its properties?

It is not enough simply to ask whether someone is attending. The problems of introspection, in which individuals report private events, have been amply demonstrated in the history of psychology. Introspection was not reliable. Different individuals, and even the same individual at different times, reported events in different ways. Attending presented particular difficulties: How does one attend to one's

attending? The difficulties were inevitable, because the language of private events must be based at some point upon what is publicly accessible to the verbal community (cf. Skinner, 1945, and Chapter 11). A private event is available only to the person behaving. This does not mean that private events are outside the boundaries of a behavioral analysis; it does imply, however, that reports of private events depend on consistencies across the vocabularies of public and private events. Imagining an object, for example, must have something in common with seeing the object.

The response of attending is not necessarily a movement. For visual stimuli, it may superficially seem like looking toward or even pointing at something. This kind of extension was implied when we gave pecks on a pigeon's key functions similar to those of attending and called those pecks observing responses (cf. Chapters 7 and 8). We can create contingencies for discrete responses such as pecks that are like those for other responses that we cannot so easily count. But we sometimes look without seeing, as when we daydream or are "lost in thought" (we then say we were not paying attention). If we treated attending and observing as merely equivalent to eye movements, we would make the mistake of regarding looking without seeing as equivalent to looking and seeing. The behavior called attending shares something with what we do when we say we are watching for or looking for something. Separate acts of looking at a given place may look the same even if what is looked for differs each time. For example, what we notice when we scan a page to find a name is not the same as when we scan to find a definition. In such contexts, attention has been called *perceptual set* or *readiness*.

When a response class does not involve movement, we may be able to record other properties such as duration or latency (cf. Chapter 12 and Posner, 1982). This rationale was extended to the response of attending by Sperling and Reeves (1980). Observers were instructed to look at a visual fixation point. Just to the left of this point, letters were presented in rapid sequence one at a time. Just to the right, a sequence of numerals was similarly presented. The observers could see both the letters and the numerals without moving their eyes. Their instructions were to attend to the letters until seeing a particular one (e.g., *B*), and then to shift attention to the numerals and report the one they saw. The observers were able to perform this task without eye movements and with rates of stimulus projection in excess of 20 per second. The time between the critical letter and each numeral was known, so it was possible to derive the time taken to switch attention from the letters to the numerals from the numeral that was reported. The observers could not report the one that appeared simultaneously with the critical letter; instead, they reported one that appeared some fraction of a second later. These durations provided latencies or reaction times for the shift of attention. Like the reaction times of more obvious responses, such as button-presses, these reaction times depended on task difficulty and other variables.

VISUAL IMAGERY

"Think of a cube, all six surfaces of which are painted red. Divide the cube into twenty-seven equal cubes by making two horizontal cuts and two sets of two vertical cuts each. How many of the resulting cubes will have three faces painted red, how many two, how many one, and how many none?" It is possible to solve this without seeing the cubes....

But the solution is easier if one can actually see the twenty-seven small cubes and count those of each kind. This is easiest in the presence of actual cubes, of course, and even a sketchy drawing will provide useful support, but many people solve the problem visually without visual stimulation. (Skinner, 1953, p. 273)

Even if attending is a response, what about more complex private events such as visualizing or imagining? We considered imagery in connection with mnemonic techniques in Chapter 14. The methods for measuring imagery are necessarily indirect, but experimental techniques have been developed to study it (Paivio, 1971). Here again, temporal measures have been particularly effective.

For example, observers were shown pictures of pairs of three-dimensional figures, with instructions to report whether the figures were the same (Shepard & Metzler, 1971). When they were the same, one was rotated relative to the other, as illustrated in Figure 15–1. For such figures, the latency of the report that they were the same was linearly related to the difference in orientation, in degrees of rotation. In other words, mental rotation, or rotation of an image, has some of the same properties as the rotation of an actual object: In both cases, the time taken to do the rotation is proportional to the distance through which the object is rotated. (The behavior of pigeons is different; when they are taught to discriminate same versus mirror-image rotated figures, their reaction times do not increase with the amount of rotation of one figure relative to the other; Hollard & Delius, 1982.)

By treating the image as a thing we must not be misled into using it to explain behavior; we should not set out to find a screen somewhere in the observer's head on which the image is projected. The

A.

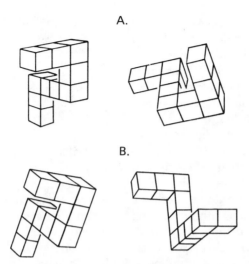

B.

FIGURE 15-1 Pairs of figures from a study of mental rotation in which observers were instructed to report whether two figures were the same. In *A*, they are the same but the right figure is rotated 80° from the left one in the picture plane. In *B*, they are different and cannot be matched by any rotation. (From Shepard & Metzler, 1971, Figure 1)

controversy over whether the image is pictorial or propositional (verbal) is probably less important than the recognition that the imagining of the object, like the rotation itself, is something the observer does (cf. Kolers & Smythe, 1979; Pylyshyn, 1979). The temporal properties of rotating real and imagined objects are similar because of the correspondence between what the observer does when seeing an object and what the observer does when imagining it. This correspondence has been discussed in terms of the functional equivalence of imagery and movement (Finke, 1979; Johnson, 1982). Imagining is visual behavior in the absence of the visual stimulus.

It has been suggested that Watson, the founder of behaviorism, denied the existence of images because he himself was incapable of visual imagery (Skinner, 1959). His denial, unfortunately, retarded the development of behavioral analyses of imagery. Whether the image has some physical status inside the observer's head

is beside the point. Saying that we imagine an object has an advantage over saying that we have an image of the object simply in its emphasis on what we do. What is at issue is not the status of images, but rather the role of such private events in accounts of behavior. Our primary concern must be to determine their properties rather than to base accounts of other kinds of behavior upon them. A behavioral account does not deny the existence of such events, but it limits the conditions under which they can properly serve as explanations of behavior; they should instead be regarded as instances of behavior in their own right (cf. Paivio, 1975, p. 287).

The example of mental rotation used visual stimuli. The response of visualizing also occurs in the absence of such stimuli, as we saw in the case of visual encoding as a mnemonic technique. In such cases, there is even more temptation to speak of the image as a thing seen rather than of imagining as behavior. In the "photographic" memory of someone with eidetic imagery, for example, reports of the details of past scenes are accompanied by eye movements similar to those when scanning a current visual scene (e.g., Haber, 1969). Yet to say that the reports or the eye movements are caused by the remembered image does not explain anything; an account of visualizing must be derived from the behavior of seeing and not from the stimulus properties of a private event.

Consider further research on visual imagery. In one experiment (Moyer, 1973; Moyer & Dumais, 1978), observers were given pairs of words (e.g., *mouse* and *elephant*) and were instructed to choose the larger. The greater the difference in size between the two named classes, the shorter the reaction time (e.g., the response to *truck-cat* was faster than that to *book-chair*). The words themselves did not differ systematically in size, and the relation between size difference and reaction time was similar to that with pictures rather than words as stimuli. These and related experiments (e.g., Paivio, 1975) suggest that the task involved imagery occasioned by words, presumably analogous to the visual encoding discussed in Chapter 14.

In another type of experiment, learners were given pairs of statements such as *A is taller than B* and *A is shorter than C*, or *X is to the left of Y* and *Z is to the right of Y*, and then were instructed to indicate whether such statements as *B is taller than C* or *Y is to the left of Z* were true or false (e.g., Brooks, 1968; Huttenlocher, 1968). Latency measures in this verbal task and in analogous visual tasks suggested that performance in the verbal task was better described as the visualizing of spatial relations than as verbal responding occasioned by the statements. The private construction of a spatial array in such a task seems to parallel the behavior of moving objects into various spatial arrangements. These experiments, therefore, identify visualizing as a behavior class and then demonstrate that this class enters into what the learner does.

Treating imagery as a kind of behavior as opposed to something that an observer "has" or "does not have" raises the possibility that visualizing can be taught (cf. the rehearsal of pictures; Graefe & Watkins, 1980). An artist presumably learns some of this behavior in progressing from sketching a live model to sketching without the model. Shaping of visualization might proceed by gradually dimming a scene as an observer describes it or sketches it and by gradually increasing the time between the presentation of the scene and the observer's description or sketch. There are few systematic studies of such phenomena.

SIMULATIONS

Our imagining is not limited to the visual mode. We not only visualize; we hold imaginary conversations, take imaginary journeys, and perform imaginary actions. These are all *simulations*, imitations in the absence of relevant stimulation of some parts of the behavior that might occur in various situations. Games have been used to simulate various properties of economic, political, and social situations. Just as war games played on game boards or in the actual field may demonstrate potential consequences of various strategies, so also our imaginings may bring us into contact with the possible consequences of our own actions. But just as military simulations may be imperfect because they fail to incorporate important variables in a combat situation, our imaginings may also often be fallible because they involve not real contingencies but only our own partial re-creations of them.

Dawkins (1976) makes the point by comparing computer simulations and human imagination. With respect to the computer simulation:

> The technique works like this. A model of some aspect of the world is set up in the computer. This does not mean that if you unscrewed the lid you would see a little miniature dummy inside with the same shape as the object simulated. In the chess-playing computer there is no "mental picture" inside the memory banks recognizable as a chess board with knights and pawns sitting on it. The chess board and its current position would be represented by lists of electronically coded numbers....But it does not matter how the computer actually holds its model of the world in its head, provided that it holds it in a form in which it can operate on it, manipulate it, do experiments with it, and report back to the human operators in terms which they can understand. Through the technique of simulation, model battles can be won or lost, simulated airliners fly or crash, economic policies lead to prosperity or to ruin. (Dawkins, 1976, p. 62)

In other words, the important properties of the computer program are not whether they generate or manipulate copies of the world but rather whether they operate in ways analogous to behavior with respect to features of the world (cf. Chapter 2 on blueprints versus recipes). Dawkins continues by discussing similar features of human behavior (he refers to organisms as survival machines that have been built by their genes):

> ...when you yourself have a difficult decision to make involving unknown quantities in the future, you do go in for a form of simulation. You *imagine* what would happen if you did each of the alternatives open to you...just as in the computer, the details of how your brain represents its model of the world are less important than the fact that it is able to use it to predict possible events. Survival machines which can simulate the future are one jump ahead of survival machines who can only learn on the basis of

overt trial and error. The trouble with overt trial is that it takes time and energy. The trouble with overt error is that it is often fatal. Simulation is both safer and faster. (Dawkins, 1976, pp. 62–63)

Organisms that have evolved with a capacity to simulate some of the consequences of their own behavior have some obvious advantages over those that have not. And once just a little bit of simulation has become possible, natural selection is likely to produce organisms that can more and more effectively simulate the environmental contingencies with which they come in contact (cf. Chapter 2 and Gallistel, 1990).

PROCESSING STAGES

As we have seen, temporal measures such as reaction times have been an important feature of the analysis of cognitive processes. Besides showing that private events take time, cognitive analyses have also been concerned with demonstrating other properties of these processes. For example, the distinction between *top-down* vs. *bottom-up* processing involves whether organisms begin with relatively gross discriminations and then master the finer details, or start with discriminations among the detailed parts and then build up the whole from those parts (e.g., Kinchla & Wolfe, 1979). Another distinction is that between *automatic* versus *controlled* processing. This distinction is occasionally ambiguous; it is sometimes analogous to that between unlearned and learned behavior and sometimes to that between respondent and operant behavior.

Still another concern, which we will now consider in some detail, is how cognitive tasks can be decomposed into their separate components or stages:

> One of the oldest ideas in experimental psychology is that the time between stimulus and

response is occupied by a train of processes or *stages*—some being mental operations—which are so arranged that one process does not begin until the preceding one has ended. This *stage theory* implies that the reaction-time (RT) is a *sum*, composed of the durations of the stages in the series, and suggests that if one could determine the component times that add together to make up the RT, one might then be able to answer interesting questions about mental operations to which they correspond. (Sternberg, 1969, p. 421)

Early treatments attempted to identify particular stages. For example, it was assumed that a discriminative stage could be derived by subtracting the simple reaction time to a single visual stimulus from the discriminated reaction time to one of two visual stimuli. At various times, stages such as stimulus registration, decision, and response initiation were postulated (cf. Sternberg, 1969; Posner, 1978).

Two problems complicated stage theories, however. One was that stage durations determined in different laboratories and even at different times in the same laboratory were highly variable, presumably because most tasks can be performed in varied ways. Second, and perhaps more important, stage durations were calculated by assuming that the presence or absence of one stage had no effect on the duration of other stages. This assumption might not be justified. For example, consider one task made up of stages *A-B-D* and another made up of stages *A-B-C-D*. If the duration of *D* depends on whether it follows *B* or follows *C*, the duration of *C* will not be equal to the difference between the time it takes to complete each task.

One solution is to devise a task in which one stage is repeated some number of times (e.g., *A-B-C-C-C-D*). In this case, the immediate contexts of stages *B* and *D* are unaltered by changing the repetitions of stage *C*. Thus, the increase in latency pro-

duced by an added repetition of *C* may be taken as equivalent to the duration of *C*. This was the rationale for experiments that explored memory search as a possible stage in remembering (Sternberg, 1966, 1969). An observer was first given a set of digits (e.g., 1, 3, 4, 9), called the positive set. Then, when digits from 0 through 9 were presented visually, the observer's instructions were to press one button if the digit was from the positive set and another if it was not.

Latencies from digit presentation to button-press were recorded over successive conditions that varied the number of digits in the positive set. Positive reaction times were those to digits that were in the positive set; negative reaction times were those to digits that were not. Reaction times were discarded when a response was incorrect.

To speak of search in this case is a metaphor, but what properties should such a metaphorical search have? The observer's response is determined by whether the presented digit matches a digit in the positive set. Thus, one stage of this task might consist of comparing the presented digit with the positive-set digits. Let us begin by assuming that the observer makes comparisons one at a time instead of all at once, or, in other words, that the observer engages in *serial search* instead of *parallel search*. Serial searches can vary in at least two different ways. First, the observer might complete all the comparisons before attending to matches or might stop comparing as soon as a match is found; these are *exhaustive* or *self-terminating* searches. Second, the observer might search the positive-set digits either in a random order or in a fixed order (e.g., beginning to end); these are *random-order* or *fixed-order* searches. Each type of search has different quantitative implications, as illustrated in Figure 15–2.

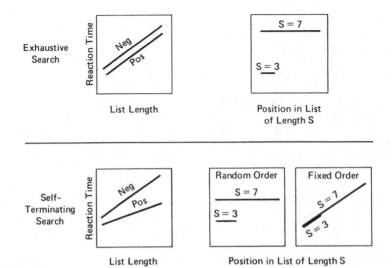

FIGURE 15–2 Quantitative implications of exhaustive and self-terminating patterns of serial search. In exhaustive search, reaction time as a function of list length has the same slope for positive as for negative items; in self-terminating search, the slope for positive items is half that for negative items. In exhaustive search, reaction time for positive items is independent of the positions of items in the list; in self-terminating search, reaction time as a function of position in the list depends on whether search is in random or fixed order. (From Sternberg, 1969, Figure 4)

Consider first the relation between reaction time and list length with exhaustive or self-terminating search. In exhaustive search the presented digit, whether in the positive set or not, is compared with all the positive-set digits. For example, if each comparison takes 50 milliseconds, each item added to the positive-set digits adds that much time to both positive and negative reaction times; thus, the slopes of these two functions are equal (the functions are parallel, but they might differ by a constant if positive and negative reaction times differ). With self-terminating search, however, on the average a match is found for positive digits after only half of the comparisons (any comparison from the first to the last might yield a match), whereas all comparisons are always made for negative digits because these digits have no match. In this case, each digit added to the positive set adds only 25 milliseconds on the average to positive reaction times but it adds 50 milliseconds to negative reaction times; the slope for positive items is therefore half that for negative items.

Next consider the relation between reaction time to a positive item and the position of that item in the positive set. If search is exhaustive, all comparisons are made and position in the list has no effect (in Figure 15–2, horizontal lines for list lengths of three and seven items). If the order of comparisons is random, self-terminating search also produces this independence between reaction time and position of the positive item in the list. But if the order is fixed, from the beginning of the list to the end, reaction times in self-terminating search vary with position; matches to items early in the list occur more quickly than those to items late in the list.

Figure 15–3 presents some data from this type of procedure. Positive and negative reaction times, averaged across eight observers, are shown as a function of number of digits in the positive set. Reaction times increased roughly linearly, at about 38 milliseconds per item, for both positive and negative items. These reaction times are consistent with the metaphor of search and imply that search in this task is exhaustive rather than self-terminating.

It may seem paradoxical that search should be exhaustive rather than self-terminating. Having found a match, why should the observer continue with comparisons through the end of the list? One possibility suggested by Sternberg is that comparing and then determining a match are themselves separate stages in the task;

if switching between them also takes time, then with relatively short lists exhaustive comparisons may be more efficient than individual comparisons each followed by the determination of a match.

This task is highly specific, and even changes in detail change the outcome (cf. Baddeley, 1976; Crowder, 1976). Some variations on these procedures, for example, produce reaction-time functions characteristic of self-terminating rather than exhaustive search; in addition, the functions relating reaction time to position of the item in the positive list are consistent with random-order search for some observers and fixed-order search for others (Sternberg, 1969; cf. Figure 15–2). The metaphor of search is strengthened by the quantitative detail of the data, but its range of

FIGURE 15–3 Mean reaction time for positive and negative items as a function of the number of items in the positive set, for eight observers. Errors (usually within 1 or 2 percent of total responses) were excluded from the data. Reaction time (*RT*) as a function of number of items (*N*) is roughly described by the equation: $RT = 400 + 38N$, where *RT* is in milliseconds. (From Sternberg, 1966, Figure 1)

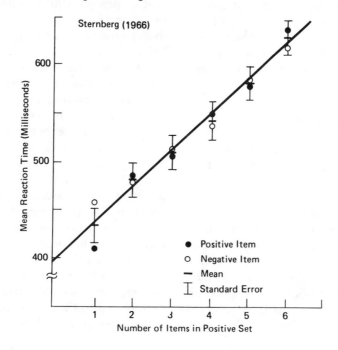

application is limited (e.g., the metaphor may not apply if the number of items in the positive set exceeds the span of immediate memory; cf. Chapter 14).

Furthermore, the metaphor is based on the assumption of serial rather than parallel search, in which items are compared simultaneously instead of successively. Parallel search might seem to imply that search should take a fixed amount of time regardless of the number of items in the positive set, but it is as reasonable to assume that comparisons in parallel search would become slower as the number of items increased. Thus, it is possible to develop accounts in terms of parallel search that are equivalent in outcome to those outlined for serial search (e.g., Townsend, 1971).

Despite these limitations, this type of approach has the advantage of a close adherence to the quantitative details of performance. An adequate description of the private events called processing stages will necessarily depend on combining studies that examine particular stages in isolation (as in the example of attending with which this section began) and those concerned with the dynamics of more complex tasks (as in the present example of search).

MENTAL REPRESENTATIONS

The temporal properties of attending and visualizing and searching help to define the structure of these private events. Other aspects of the structure of behavior are its sequential and hierarchical organization (cf. Butterfield, Slocum, & Nelson, 1991). For example, consider the sequential and hierarchical components of completing a college major. The major consists of individual courses, the order of which may be constrained by prerequisites; the courses may be decomposed into smaller units

consisting of assignments and examinations; these in turn may be further reduced to reading particular passages or answering certain questions, again perhaps in specified orders; and so on. The completion of the major corresponds in structure to the contingencies established by the educational environment. The development of cognitive structure can be regarded as the development of correspondences between the structure of the environment and the structure of behavior. Analyses of concept learning or of strategies in problem solving are sometimes based on the demonstration of such correspondences (e.g., Garner, 1974; Markman, Horton, & McLanahan, 1980).

The development of cognitive structure has been a central theme in the work of Piaget (e.g., Piaget & Inhelder, 1969; see also Fischer, 1980). Only a brief and inevitably oversimplified discussion is provided here. The several phases of child development in Piaget's system (sensorymotor, preoperational, concrete operational, and formal operational) correspond to a progression from relatively simple relations between motor responses and their consequences (as in reaching for and manipulating objects) to complex relations that depend both on correspondence between verbal and nonverbal behavior and on correspondences between environmental structure and behavior structure.

Piaget speaks of the development of such correspondences in terms of *accommodation* and *assimilation;* the child must accommodate to the constraints that environmental structures and contingencies impose upon her or his behavior, but these structures and contingencies are assimilated to the extent that they become incorporated into the child's behavior. What is assimilated, however, is sometimes said to be a structure, such as a mental representation. Cognitive development, therefore, is assumed to be the gradual enrichment of representations of the world; these representations then become the basis for behavior.

The phenomenon called *conservation* illustrates some aspects of cognitive structure dealt with in terms of representations. If the water in a short, wide beaker is poured into a tall, narrow beaker, a preschool child is likely to report that there is more water in the second beaker than there was in the first. This report is based on the higher level at which the water stands in the tall, narrow beaker. In Piaget's account of development, this type of response is characteristic of the preoperational phase; one property of this phase is that responding is based upon single properties of environmental events rather than upon relations among properties (but see Woodruff, Premack, & Kennel, 1978, on conservation in chimpanzees). Later, in the concrete operational phase, the child says that the amount of water is the same in one beaker as in the other. Such reports are restricted to specific instances, and it is only in the subsequent formal operational phase that the child begins to speak abstractly of these relations in terms of the conservation of matter.

One way to deal with this phenomenon is to attribute the increasing sophistication of the child's performance to successive refinements in the child's mental representations of events in the world. As the child moves from actually manipulating objects to imagining or talking about or thinking about manipulating those objects, the structure of the child's mental representations is said more and more closely to approximate the structure of the contingencies that operate for manipulating objects in the world. But the structure of these mental representations is derived from the

correspondence between behavior and environmental contingencies. It is therefore inappropriate to use those representations to explain the behavior. The representations exist in the child only in a metaphorical sense; their concrete existence is in our own discriminative behavior as we observe the child or, in other words, in the consistencies and correspondences that we observe in her or his behavior.

The issue is not different from one raised in the context of remembering, and it may be useful to extend an analogy that was introduced then. If you take a piano apart to find the music, you will be disappointed. You may have just listened to a performance of Beethoven's *Waldstein* Sonata, but when you are done you will have only pieces of wire and wood and felt and so on. You also will be disappointed if you try to find behavior inside the organism. The environment plays upon organisms as the pianist plays upon the piano. Just as it may take different virtuosi to bring out what is special about pianos and what is special about violins, what an environment brings out may depend on which organism it plays upon. Or, to take the analogy further, just as some musicians may bring out some music more skillfully from some instruments than from others, different environments may bring out some sorts of behavior more effectively from some organisms than from others.

But wait, you say, what about the player piano? In that case you can find a representation of the music: a roll of paper with holes punched into it. No matter that one can substitute, in more contemporary versions, a magnetic tape or a computer chip (we anticipated this feature of the analogy in choosing a piano rather than some instrument less compatible with representations, such as a violin or a trumpet). The holes in the paper are not music, and though one can be concerned with the way in which the holes are translated into the action of the keyboard, the account is incomplete unless one can say how the holes got punched in the first place. If we wish to deal with representations, we must start by putting them not inside the organism but inside the human observer who discovered the spatial or relational property of the environment to which the organism was responding. In other words, the issue is not so much whether representations exist as about which organism they belong in.

In any case, the development of conservation in children is not incompatible with properties of behavior that we have already considered. Several progressions must occur in parallel, and each is part of a hierarchy in which more complex classes of behavior are based upon simpler classes. At first, the child's discriminations are based upon a single dimension of objects (in this instance, height); discriminations based upon two or three dimensions (area and volume) come later. At the same time, the child's vocabulary becomes more finely differentiated (from *big-little* to *bigger-smaller* and then to *taller-shorter, fuller-emptier,* and so on; cf. Ward, 1980). Verbal behavior occasioned by specific instances becomes the foundation for the more general classes we call abstractions. Saying whether or not the quantity of water in one container equals that in another is not the same as choosing the contents of one or the other container or filling two containers to equal volumes, and none of these is equivalent to a statement of the principle of conservation of matter. On the one hand, it is important to recognize how very different these classes of behavior are; on the other, it is important to recognize that equivalences across these different classes are inevitable consequences of the way in which verbal and nonverbal behavior is related to events in the world.

The argument has been that organisms do not have to produce copies of stimuli before they can respond to them. But it is also important to note that not all representational accounts are copy theories. An organism that has responded to a stimulus is a changed organism. "Whether internal representations are copies or interpretations of images, something called 'seeing them' is still required. Notions such as 'convex edge,' 'concave edge,' and 'occluding edge' are a step in the right direction. They are the beginnings of an analysis of the stimulus rather than a replication" (Skinner, 1988, p. 337).

"Organisms are changed by contingencies of selection, they do not store them" (Skinner, 1988, p. 472). The issue raised by this statement is not whether a stimulus has produced some lasting effect (presumably in the nervous system, though that constraint is not necessary to the argument). The change is acknowledged, and the issue is about the form that it takes, and in particular whether it can be regarded as in some sense a copy of the stimulus. It might be argued that any physical manifestation of a stimulus as it persists in the organism is best regarded as a transformed copy of the stimulus, perhaps containing information about it. But cognitive processing does not require copies. For example, no copies are involved in the simulations of complex behavior that are created by the variety of computer programming called parallel distributed processing (Donahoe & Palmer, 1989; cf. Chapter 2 on copy theories in phylogenic selection).

Section B Problem Solving

We have examined only a few samples of research in cognition. Cognition is, after all, not learning; yet many issues in cognition are closely related to problems in learning. As the last experimental topic in this text, we turn to problem solving. Problem solving has sometimes been treated in the context of cognitive approaches, with emphasis on the structure of problems. An analysis of problem solving also raises functional questions, as when we are concerned with conditions that may make the solution of a problem more or less likely.

Let us begin with a structural approach to problem solving in the Hobbits-and-Orcs problem (Thomas, 1974; see also Greeno, 1974). Three hobbits and three orcs are traveling together. The orcs will not leave the hobbits behind, but they will overpower them if ever any hobbits are outnumbered by orcs. The group reaches a river that must be crossed and finds a boat that can hold only one or two creatures at a time. How do the hobbits organize the crossing so that no hobbits are ever outnumbered by orcs? An experiment presented this problem to solvers and explored the effects of feedback and other variables.

The problem allows only a few possible moves, and its solution can economically be presented as in Figure 15–4. Except for an alternative first move not shown and the two cases of branching moves at the beginning and end of the sequence, the only allowable alternatives to correct moves are ones that move backward through the sequence (this property of the problem was seldom recognized by solvers). For our purposes, it is sufficient to note that errors were more likely at some points in the sequence (states 321 and 110) than at others. These and other features of the data indicated that the problem-solver's performance did not consist simply of the separate moves. Instead, the solution was based on larger units consisting of sequences of moves that led to some intermediate arrangement of hobbits and orcs on the two sides of the river. Thus, the analysis

demonstrated correspondences between the structure of the problem and the structure of the problem-solver's solution.

Problems in which the steps are as explicit as this lend themselves well to computer solution (e.g., Newell, Shaw, & Simon, 1958). The computer can perform large numbers of calculations in short periods of time, and in problems involving well-defined alternatives the computer can select those branches leading to a solution more rapidly than a human can. Part of the field of *artificial intelligence*, or *AI*, is devoted to the design of computer programs for simulating such activities as problem solving. But computer programs are severely limited when those who write the programs cannot provide an exhaustive list of alternatives at some steps in the solution of a problem, or cannot define the terms entering into it, or cannot reduce it to a manageable size even for a computer (e.g., Dreyfus, 1979; see also Winograd, 1980). Each of these constraints was important in limiting the application of computer programs to language translation, as discussed in Chapter 12.

Computer programs designed to play chess are a case in point (Frey, 1977; Holding, 1985). Chess-playing programs have gradually evolved to play better chess. They compete with each other, and the best programs challenge human grandmasters. For the purposes of a computer program, chess is well-defined, in that all possible moves of each piece in any position on the chessboard are exactly specified by the rules of the game. Given 16 pieces on each side and a board of 64 squares, however, the possible moves and countermoves multiply so rapidly that even the most rapid programs on the largest computers are limited in the number of moves ahead that they can calculate (the quantities exceed in magnitude the number of atoms in the universe). If the computer

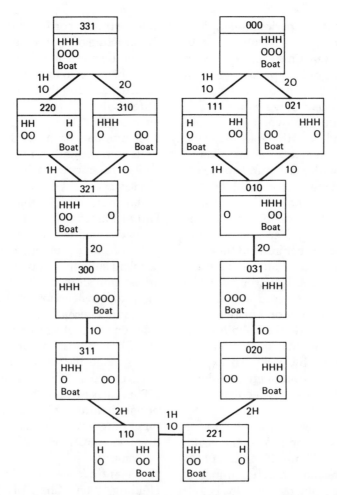

FIGURE 15–4 Successive states in the solution of the Hobbits-and-Orcs problem. Three hobbits and three orcs must cross a river. They have a single boat that can hold only one or two creatures, and under no circumstances may hobbits be outnumbered by orcs. Each state is represented by three digits: number of hobbits on starting side, number of orcs on starting side, and boat on starting side. In each state, the positions of the hobbits (*H*), the orcs (*O*) and the boat are shown below the digit code, and the creatures transported by the boat are shown in the transitions between states. Except for a transition to state 320 from the first state (crossing of one orc and the boat, not shown) no other moves are possible in which no hobbits are outnumbered by orcs. (Adapted from Thomas, 1974, Figure 1)

does not find a forced checkmate of its opponent in, say, the next 25 moves, how does it evaluate the relative strengths of all those possible future positions so as to select its best next move? More accurately, how does a human write a program that allows the computer to do that?

Some of the most spectacular chess games are those in which a checkmate is forced through the sacrifice of several pieces. If the computer evaluates positions on the basis of the relative number of pieces lost and if the mating move itself is beyond the limits of its calculations of future moves, it will never embark upon such a forced mate. The computer plays chess carefully; it does not make the mistakes of the amateur human player, such as exposing an unprotected piece to capture by the opponent. Nevertheless, chess-playing programs that now challenge human grandmasters do so mainly by brute force, in the sense that they include extensive libraries of many standard chess openings and they explore very many alternatives a great many moves ahead. They do not play chess like human grandmasters, who not only calculate the consequences of various moves and countermoves but also see various strengths and weaknesses to be exploited in the pattern of pieces on the board (e.g., Chase & Simon, 1973). The most successful future chess-playing programs will probably be those that most closely capture the structure of what the chessmaster sees in a form that can be used by the computer. The writers of such programs will presumably be expert in both chess and computer programming.

If chess grandmasters could describe what they did when analyzing a chess position, their descriptions could be used to design chess-playing computer programs. Playing a game of chess by following the instructions of such a program would be rule-governed rather than contingency-shaped chess playing (cf. Chapter 11). But grandmasters cannot describe what they do in a way that can be translated into a computer program. Grandmaster chess play is called intuitive, which is another way of saying that it is contingency-shaped rather than rule-governed. This kind of expert performance is not independent of verbal behavior, however, and it therefore suggests that there may be more than one variety of contingency-shaped behavior.

Dreyfus and Dreyfus (1986) made some observations about expert performance in the context of treating limits on the capacity of computers to simulate human judgments. Their examples included chess, medicine, and other areas. They noted that education in complex human skills often begins with rules; they suggest that proficiency develops when intuitive judgments begin to mix with rules, and that expertise involves performance that no longer depends on the rules. Their distinctions between the functions of rules and of intuitions are much like those between rule-governed and contingency-shaped behavior, but for them rule-governed behavior comes first, and intuitive or contingency-shaped behavior eventually grows out of it.

Their distinction is compatible with our earlier treatment of rule-governed behavior if we expand our taxonomy to include three classes of skilled behavior: contingency-shaped behavior that has never depended on verbal rules, corresponding to the variety of contingency-shaped behavior ordinarily treated in behavior analysis (as in nonhuman behavior); rule-governed behavior, in which verbal antecedents override the effects of nonverbal contingencies (as treated in Chapter 11); and, finally, expert performance, in which the continuing contact with the environment attenuates the control by verbal antecedents and allows behavior to become sensitive to subtle changes in contingencies (in what might be regarded as a second and different kind of contingency-shaped behavior that has yet to be explored in detail).

We cannot write out the rules of human expertise even in restricted domains such as chess. But that poses a serious problem, because we do not yet have a way to incorporate human expertise into the computer except by writing programs that tell the computer what to do. Unless and until new computer technologies (e.g., parallel distributed processing; Donahoe

& Palmer, 1989) allow computers to modify their own programs on the basis of contingencies, computer simulations of human expertise will inevitably be limited to rule-governed behavior.

The rules of chess are defined very explicitly. If the problems to be surmounted in writing expert computer programs are so formidable even in this limited domain, what about those domains in which the terms are less well-defined? Furthermore, once a computer program has been written to solve one problem, how can the structure of its solution be used to solve other problems? The question is relevant not only to computer programming but also to human problem solving, to which we now return. In the teaching of problem-solving skills within well-defined areas such as mathematics (e.g., Wertheimer, 1959), for example, analyses start with the solution of single problems and then move on to the transfer of solving strategies from one problem to another. Experiments on problem solving, therefore, have often dealt with the effects on problem solution of the problem-solver's history of solving problems.

FUNCTIONAL FIXITY

The Luchins' water-jar problem provides an example of such an experiment (Luchins, 1942; see also Luchins & Luchins, 1950). Given a water supply and three jars of different capacity, the problem is to produce a specified amount of water. For example, if jars *A*, *B*, and *C* have respective capacities of 21, 127, and 3, how does one arrive at exactly 100 units of water? In this instance, the solution is to fill *B* and then to pour out enough to fill *A* once and *C* twice. One group was given several successive problems that could be solved in this way while a second group was not. Later, both groups were tested on problems such as the following: How does one arrive at a quantity of 20 if jars *A*, *B*, and *C* have respective capacities of 23, 49, and 3? The first group solved the problem in the same old way, whereas the second group solved it more efficiently, by filling *A* and then pouring out enough to fill *C*.

We might call this an example of negative transfer or problem-solving rigidity, but it is more important that this is obviously a case in which the consequences of past behavior have affected current behavior. The literature on problem solving includes many variations on such situations (e.g., Duncker, 1945; Saugstad & Raaheim, 1960). For example, problem-solvers who were instructed to mount a candle on a wall were given either a box of candles and a box of matches and a box of tacks, or separate stacks of candles, matches, tacks, and boxes (Duncker, 1945). The solution was to tack a box to the wall so that it provided a flat surface on which a candle could be mounted. Those who received the candles and matches and tacks in boxes, however, were much slower to solve the problem than those who received the boxes separately; they received the boxes as containers and continued to treat them that way. Instances of failure to solve a problem that requires an unusual use of common tools or materials are sometimes described as cases of *functional fixity*; the commonplace items occasion responses appropriate to their everyday functions instead of the novel responses appropriate to the problem solution (cf. Chapter 11 on instructional control).

Another class of examples comes from experiments on probability judgment (cf. Estes, 1976, p. 53: "...the term *probability learning* characterizes a type of problem situation rather than a type of learning"). Decision theory is concerned with the finding that our estimates of the probabilities of events often differ substantially from the probabilities as calculated from actual event frequencies (e.g., Tversky & Kahneman, 1981, 1983).

Try an example. First guess how many 7-letter words in this chapter end in -*ing*. Then guess how many end in -_*n*_ , where the spaces can be any letter. There is a good chance that your answer demonstrates the *conjunction fallacy*, which occurs when people judge that the probability of several events occurring together is greater than the separate probabilities of each event. If your first number is bigger than your second, your answer is mathematically impossible. In the above example, there must be at least as many words ending in -_*n*_ as ending in -*ing*, because those ending in -_*n*_ include all those ending in -*ing*.

Consider a different kind of judgment in the context of an imaginary diagnostic situation in a psychiatric hospital. You are a staff member who has discovered a new clinical syndrome called narapoia. Narapoids are the opposite of paranoids; they are under the delusion that other people are plotting to do them good. You know that narapoids cannot possibly make up more than 1 percent of your clinical population and you have developed a test for narapoia that has only a 5 percent error rate. You give the test to someone who is being screened for admission to the hospital, and the person scores as a narapoid. Does the test score provide sufficient grounds for admission?

To make this question easier to answer, assume that you give the test to 1,000 patients in your hospital. No more than 1 percent are narapoids, so they total 10 or so; with your 5 percent error rate most or all of them will correctly score as narapoid. But of the 990 or so others, roughly 50 will be false alarms; they are not narapoid, but because of your 5 percent error rate they

will score so. In other words, you will get a total of about 60 narapoid scores, but given that only 10 or so are actually narapoid the chance that anyone with such a score has been correctly diagnosed is only 1 in 6. You cannot justify admission on the basis of the test alone; you need other diagnostic criteria (perhaps that is just as well, because you will be hard-pressed to devise an effective treatment; whenever you try to help your narapoid patients, you will only be confirming their delusions).

Narapoia is an imaginary syndrome, but the probability relations that it illustrates are of practical significance. For example, even with low error rates such judgments can lead to many false alarms in cases where false alarms can be very costly (as in lie detection or medical diagnoses). These types of biases in probability estimation are likely whenever there is some error as we sample for events that occur with low frequencies in large populations. Most of our everyday probability judgments are made in the context of more symmetrical distributions of event probabilities, and our histories of such judgments, as in functional fixity, transfer too easily to these sorts of extreme cases in which the familiar probability relations no longer hold. Teaching the mathematics of probability is one way to make such probability judgments more accurate; another is to provide experience with probability judgments over a range of situations that include these sorts of extremes (note that the former solution involves rule-governed behavior whereas the latter involves contingency-shaped behavior).

THE CONSTRUCTION OF SOLUTIONS

These experiments show how problem solving can be affected by discriminative stimuli and by contingencies. But what then constitutes problem solving? Consider an example from Skinner:

> You have been asked to pick up a friend's suitcase from an airport baggage claim. You have never seen the suitcase or heard it described; you have only a ticket with a number from which a match is to be found among the numbers on a collection of suitcases. To simplify the problem, let us say you find yourself alone before a large rotary display. A hundred suitcases move past you in a great ring. They are moving too fast to be inspected in order. You are committed to selecting suitcases essentially at random, checking one number at a time. How are you to find the suitcase? You may, of course, simply keep sampling. You will almost certainly check the same suitcase more than once, but eventually the matching ticket will turn up.... A much more effective strategy is to mark each case as it is checked—say, with a piece of chalk. No bag is then inspected twice, and the number of bags remaining to be examined is reduced as rapidly as possible. Simple as it seems, this method of solving the problem has some remarkable features.... It is the use of the chalk which introduces something new. Marking each suitcase as it is checked...is constructing a discriminative stimulus. (Skinner, 1969, pp. 136–137)

Problem solving, in other words, is behavior. The discriminative features of the situation define the problem, and the reinforcer is the solution of the problem. Often we solve problems by manipulating stimuli: looking something up, converting a verbal problem into a mathematical equation, and so on. It is important to recognize how we can affect our own behavior by modifying our environment. Consider, for example, a simple problem in multiplication. We might multiply 23 by 14 in this form:

$$
\begin{array}{r}
23 \\
\times\ 14 \\
\hline
92 \\
23 \\
\hline
322
\end{array}
$$

In the intermediate products, 92 and 23, we create discriminative stimuli that occasion the solution, 322. But what if we had to solve the problem and didn't have a pencil? Presumably the intermediate products would still enter into the solution, even if there was no written record of them. If we did not say them aloud, an observer might say we had engaged in "mental arithmetic" (cf. Ashcraft, 1982). But the role of the intermediate products is the same even if they are more public and more permanent in the first case than in the second. We still have much to learn about such processes, but we need not treat them as something other than behavior.

Now that we have seen how problem solutions can be affected by discriminative stimuli and contingencies, we have come nearly full circle. Let us return to the problem Köhler set for his apes, but with a different organism (Epstein, 1981). A pigeon is placed in a compartment with a movable box in a far corner and, hanging out of reach, a model banana (chosen, instead of a simple key, in deference to the work of Köhler). Earlier, the pigeon's pecks at the banana had been reinforced by access to food in a standard feeder. Also, the pigeon had been taught through shaping to move the box across the floor by pecking at it. Finally, the pigeon's feathers had been trimmed so that it could not fly, and its jumping and wing-flapping had already dropped to a low rate in the presence of the hanging banana. Under these circumstances, the pigeon looks from the banana to the box and back again. Soon it goes to the box and moves it under the banana. Once the box is there, the pigeon climbs it and pecks the banana, operating the feeder.

The pigeon's performance was novel. It solved the problem of getting to the banana by moving the box and then climbing it, even though it had never done so before. If the spontaneous combination of two classes of behavior is a component of insight, the pigeon's behavior certainly qualified. Presumably it was also important that the competing responses of jumping and wing-flapping had already been reduced in probability. But the primary difference between this demonstration and Köhler's experiment is in how much we know of each organism's history. The experimenter interested in problem solving might start simply by watching the behavior of the problem solver. Like Köhler in his study of insight in apes, the experimenter will discover what the problem-solver can already do. That is where our systematic treatment began, with the simplest behavioral operation: observation. But now we can see how much more was involved in the environments that Köhler constructed for his apes.

PART V *Conclusion*

Structure and Function
in Learning

The word psychology *comes from the Greek* psukhein, *to breathe, and* psukhe, *breath. Thus, when the psyche was said to leave the body of a mortally wounded warrior in the Homeric epics, the word may be understood to mean the warrior's breath and not his soul. A curious parallel exists between this word and* spirit, *from the Latin* spirare, *another word meaning to breathe. There is no evidence that these Greek and Latin words are etymologically linked. A similar relation between air and spirit exists in the Latin* anima, *originally a breath of air but later soul or spirit in such words as* animate *and* animosity, *and in the Greek* atmos, *vapor or air as it enters into the English* atmosphere *but breath or soul in the related Sanskrit* atman.

We have considered the varied phenomena of learning. We began with experimental operations. The first and simplest was the presentation of stimuli. Stimuli produce responses, but stimulus presentations can also have other effects; for example, they can modulate the way in which responses are distributed in time. Just as responses may follow stimuli, stimuli may follow responses. We therefore dealt also with the effects of contingencies, the consequences of responding, in treating the operations of

reinforcement and punishment. The effects of these operations led us to distinguish among positive reinforcement, positive punishment, negative reinforcement (or escape and avoidance), and negative punishment (or omission procedures). In exploring these procedures, we noted the importance of some consequences, less dramatic than such biologically significant stimuli as food and water, that affected an organism's orientation in its environment. In this context, we examined sensory-motor learning, visual fixation, latent learning, and other phenomena not usually classified according to the effects of reinforcers or punishers.

We distinguished between reinforcement and punishment by whether response consequences raised or lowered response probability, but we also recognized that distinguishing between the positive and negative cases was often arbitrary. As in reinforcement by a change in temperature, it was sometimes ambiguous whether some cases should be treated in terms of presenting or removing stimuli (e.g., presenting heat or removing cold). Instead, we treated these cases in terms of relations between the reinforced responses and the responses occasioned by their consequences. We noted that stimuli could have multiple effects, and that a stimulus that served as a reinforcer for a response might also have eliciting effects on that response or other responses. The task of an experimental analysis is to separate such different stimulus effects and to observe how elicitation and consequences can combine to determine the characteristics of a performance.

We also turned to the signaling effects of stimuli, in stimulus control. This operation can be superimposed either on the consequential operations of reinforcement and punishment, when we speak of discrimination learning, or on the operation of stimulus presentation, when we speak of respondent conditioning. Within these contexts, we explored a variety of behavioral phenomena and procedures: attention, stimulus-control gradients, reinforcement schedules, self-control, sensory preconditioning, and conditioned suppression, to mention only a few.

Having examined some relations among stimuli and responses produced by these operations, we shifted our concern to a different problem: characterizing the dimensions along which stimuli and responses vary. In discussing differentiation and discrimination, we saw that the relevant dimensions included not only relatively simple ones such as topography or intensity, but also complex ones involving the structure of stimuli and responses and the relations among them. The correspondence between the classes of responses with particular consequences and the classes of responses generated by those consequences was critical to defining behavioral classes; we distinguished between classes defined by response properties, called operants, and classes defined by stimulus properties, called discriminated operants.

In our examinations of concept formation and verbal behavior, we were forced to conclude that behavioral relations were primary, and that we could not appeal to physical measures to define such classes. Responses like attending, remembering, imagining, and thinking are not easily observed directly, but we decided early that it would be inappropriate to define behavior solely in terms of movement. Furthermore, in our analyses of symbolic matching we discovered relations among stimuli and responses that were not implicit in control by discriminative stimuli. The relations of reflexivity, symmetry, and transitivity can be demonstrated only within stimulus-control procedures that allow stimulus and response terms to be exchanged; they led us to define symbolic behavior in terms of equivalence classes. These classes later entered into our treatment of language.

Much of our account classified learning phenomena according to experimental operations. But there are no guarantees that imposing a particular procedure on a given organism's behavior will be effective. A procedure in which one organism learns may be one in which another does not, and an organism that learns under one procedure may not do so under another. Such findings do not invalidate our behavioral taxonomy, because the classifications are merely ways of naming phenomena and relating them to each other. That would not be so if we assumed that all learning was based on some one process or some small number of processes that act across all organisms and procedures.

TWO PSYCHOLOGIES OF LEARNING: A CAPSULE HISTORY

The psychology of learning evolved through examinations of the different experimental outcomes of a variety of procedures (cf. Catania, 1985b). As each procedure was considered in its historical turn, it was assigned an importance in proportion to its demonstrated effectiveness. At different times, the available experimental findings led to theoretical formulations dominated by laws of association or contiguity, rules of respondent conditioning, or principles of reinforcement and punishment. Sometimes this domination was so substantial that one or another process was presumed to be the fundamental and exclusive basis of all learning. Such formulations were inevitably open to challenge, because the phenomena of learning could not be accounted for exhaustively by any single process. Thus, the history of the psychology of learning, a tale of confusions and controversies, has been more often told in terms of theorists and their systems than in terms of the phenomena of learning.

Although the psychology of learning has at times been regarded as fundamental to experimental psychology, in the psychological laboratories of the late nineteenth century it was overshadowed by other issues, such as those of sensation and perception. By the turn of the century, research on animal behavior had been stimulated by the work of Darwin (1859) and a foundation for experiments on human memory and verbal learning had been provided by Ebbinghaus (1885). Both historical lines found homes within university laboratories, but despite their academic proximity they remained separate.

In the study of animal behavior, much early research was devoted to invertebrates (e.g., Jennings, 1906; Loeb, 1900; Lubbock, 1882), but attention gradually shifted to vertebrates. Instrumental learning had been introduced by the mazes of Small (1899–1900) and Yerkes (1907) and by the problem-boxes of Thorndike (1898). Thorndike soon moved from animal studies to analyses of human learning (e.g.,

Thorndike, 1921), but in so doing he was exceptional. Other students of animal learning were more likely to make the extension from animal to human behavior through theoretical statements than through experiments. Pavlov (1927; 1957, p. 285), for example, manifested an interest in human language in his theory of the second signal system, but his main impact was through his canine research. Once instrumental learning and respondent conditioning had been distinguished as phenomena in the early decades of the twentieth century, the stage was set for elaborations of discrimination learning, in the progression from jumping stands to rat chambers and pigeon boxes (Lashley, 1930; Skinner, 1930, 1938). The phenomena of reinforcement schedules were to follow later (Ferster & Skinner, 1957).

The systematic pronouncements of Watson (1919), strengthened by the parallel developments of logical positivism in philosophy (L. D. Smith, 1986) and of operationism in physics (Bridgman, 1927), made behaviorism a major orientation within psychology, and the 1930s and 1940s became a period of grand behavioral theories. Applications to human behavior and to language became an issue in the competition among the systems of Guthrie (1935), Skinner (1938), and Tolman (1948), among others, but attempts to integrate the processes of animal learning with the properties of language gradually lost influence as the fortunes of early behaviorist theories based on stimulus-response associations declined.

Meanwhile, the field of human learning and memory went its separate way. The precedence of Ebbinghaus dominated detailed studies of serial-position effects, massed- vs. spaced-practice, meaningfulness, backward associations, interference, and so on. Some controversies were long-lasting. For example, the plateaus in Morse-code learning at various stages of competence, demonstrated at the turn of the century (Bryan & Harter, 1899), remained a part of psychological lore until well into the 1950s, when the phantom phenomenon was at last put to rest (Keller, 1958). Thorndike and Woodworth (1901), inspired perhaps by questions about the educational value of such classical disciplines as Greek and Latin, had begun investigations of transfer of learning. Findings from these and other studies made the practical relevance of studies of human learning seem obvious, and the effects on verbal learning of such variables as sleep and distraction and motivation became the basis for advice on study habits. The theoretical underpinnings of these areas were the same as those of animal learning, but although laws of effect, contiguity, association, and generalization gave a superficial appearance of unity, the two experimental lines that had originated as separate entities remained so.

By the 1940s, the pattern was firmly entrenched and was most clearly illustrated by two textbooks of the time. *Conditioning and Learning,* by Hilgard and Marquis (1940), was devoted primarily to animal research; *The Psychology of Human Learning,* by McGeoch (1942), was concerned mainly with human learning and remembering. Each appeared later in revised editions (Kimble, 1961; McGeoch & Irion, 1952). Beyond the common appeal to theoretical principles such as association, there was little evidence in either the original or the revised editions that the two research traditions had substantially influenced each other.

It can reasonably be claimed that these two psychologies of learning remain separate in contemporary psychology. Having examined their histories we might ask

the point of treating these disparate subject matters together. Perhaps animal learning and conditioning and human learning and remembering are so little relevant to each other that they should go their separate ways. But here we have argued otherwise. Such a course would be a serious mistake for several reasons: Learning phenomena studied with animals also occur in human behavior; the nature of complex human learning is clarified by analyses in terms of more elementary processes; and perhaps most important, human behavior especially is characterized by the interplay between verbal and nonverbal responses, and we have yet to understand the origins of either.

We must determine not only which properties of our behavior are unique to humans but also which we hold in common with other organisms. Given the myriad properties of human language, we must assume that both the elementary phenomena of animal learning and conditioning and the complexities of human learning and remembering will enter into any effective account. Our treatments of such phenomena as equivalence classes, awareness, instructional control, and problem solving could not have proceeded without a prior analysis of stimulus control. To the extent that such important varieties of human behavior as autoclitics, self-control, deixis, and metamemory are based at least in part on verbal behavior that depends on discriminations of our own behavior, any analysis of them that fails to build upon the more elementary processes of stimulus control and contingencies is bound to be deficient. We must therefore conclude that the union of these two psychologies of learning is long overdue; we need a single psychology of learning that can encompass all of the varieties of animal and human learning.

STRUCTURE AND FUNCTION

Early in our account we distinguished between structural and functional analyses (cf. Titchener, 1898; Catania, 1972, 1973b). In a structural analysis, the relations among stimuli and responses are held constant while critical properties of one or the other are altered. We noted the properties of formal verbal units (as in phonemes and letters), hierarchical organizations in the structure of texts (as in relations among words, phrases, and sentences), and correspondences between stimulus structure and response structure (as in relations between text and speech). In a functional analysis, the stimuli and responses of interest are held constant while the relations among them are altered; the interactions between behavior and environment are studied in terms of contingency relations among discriminative stimuli, responses, and consequences.

Structural and functional problems are often interrelated. For example, the design of an illustrated reader for an elementary school class should consider both its structural features, in the details of text and pictures, and its functional features, in how the pictures are related to the sentences they illustrate. A problem of stimulus control exists if the pictures set the occasion for verbal descriptions that correspond so closely to the accompanying text that a teacher cannot tell whether a child is responding to the picture, reading the text, or doing both in some combination. The problem could be addressed by changing the relation between the pictures and the child's responses (e.g., making the pictures reinforcing consequences of, rather than discriminative stimuli for, reading). A systematic analysis might show that, as consequences, pictures maintain the picking up of books and the turning of pages, but as discriminative

stimuli they compete with the text in setting the occasion for verbal responses. This analysis might lead to a rationale for sequencing the relations among words and pictures to maximize both stimulus control by the words and reinforcing effects of the pictures. At the same time, a structural analysis of text and pictures could provide the basis for organizing the textual material, deciding on appropriate levels of complexity, and perhaps even determining how quickly pictures could be faded out (Harzem, Lee, & Miles, 1976).

Structure and function are complementary, not mutually exclusive. There is no reason why structural concerns should not enter into functional experiments, or vice versa. But in the evolution of psychology the distinction between structural and functional approaches became correlated with and eventually confused with another distinction, between the two languages of cognitive psychology and behaviorism. The cognitivist prefers to summarize the organization of the organism's behavior in terms of structures that the organism knows, for which the language of mind is convenient. The behaviorist prefers to anchor accounts of action to the details of functional relations among observable events, for which the language of stimuli and responses is appropriate. Yet relations between stimuli and responses must be implicit in the cognitive vocabulary, as it deals with relations between the structure of the environment and the structure of knowledge, just as structure is implicit in the behavioral vocabulary, as it deals with properties that define operants and discriminated operants (Butterfield, Slocum, & Nelson, 1991; Glaser & Bassok, 1989).

Biology also distinguished between structure and function, in anatomy and physiology, but an equivalent schism did not emerge within biology because the languages of anatomy and physiology did not diverge. For example, the debate over mechanism vs. vitalism, perhaps analogous to that between behaviorism and mentalism, remained reasonably independent of the distinction between anatomy and physiology (Hein, 1972; Catania, 1978). In psychology, the respective correlations of cognitive and behavioral languages with structural and functional problems made it difficult to recognize that the problems were different and therefore that these research areas might be complementary rather than mutually exclusive.

There is always a certain amount of ambiguity in the distinction between structure and function. But when the biologists of an earlier time debated the issues, their concerns were not so much with whether structural or anatomical problems could be distinguished from functional or physiological ones as they were with whether one or the other problem should be given priority. The arguments were based on assumptions about how, in the evolution of a species, the functions of an organ might determine its structure or how, in the development of an organism, the structure of an organ might determine its functions. The problem was resolved not with the domination of one or the other position, but rather with the recognition that structure and function are mutually determined by selection; the structural and functional properties of organisms within a species are each to be understood in terms of the evolution of that species.

Similar controversies over the primacy of structure or function exist in the history of the psychology of learning, although the issues were usually expressed differently. For example, consider latent learning: A hungry rat explores a maze with an empty goalbox; when later given food there, it demonstrates that it has learned the maze by negotiating it as rapidly and with as few blind-alley entries as a rat that has always found food in the goalbox. The rat's running, itself not learning, occurs because of its relation to the food in the goalbox; presumably it reflects what the rat learned. It was once important to distinguish between learning and performance, but the distinction was merely a basis for asserting the primacy of structure over function. What is structure here? It seems to be the particular sequence of turns. To say that the structure was learned, however, is not to say that it caused the learning. A theorist who wanted to reinstate the primacy of function over structure might then argue that the structure was learned because of the contingencies: Certain turns at certain choice-points led to certain new maze locations, and the rat learned these functional relations even without food in the maze. Even in negotiating the environment, the consequences of behavior matter. Then comes the argument that if contingencies define what is learned, they too cannot be a cause of learning. And so it goes.

The theorist arguing for the primacy of structure was probably a cognitivist, and the theorist arguing for the primacy of function was probably a behaviorist, and their different languages were not likely to help matters. Yet these structures and functions of behavior were both outcomes of learning. The problems can be resolved only by recognizing that behavioral structure and behavioral function are mutually determined by the relations between behavior and the environment. Both the structure and the function of behavior are to be understood in terms of their origins, and neither has primacy over the other.

Both structure and function have limits, and as learning theories evolved, they were necessarily accompanied by refinements and qualifications that restricted the range of phenomena to which they could be applied. Recognizing the boundary conditions for learning was implicit in these restrictions. Limits on learning pose no problems when they can be easily traced to an organism's sensory or motor capacities. For example, we are not surprised if certain stimuli are more likely to produce responses in some species than in others. We know that the visual and auditory systems of pigeons and bats make pigeons capable of visual discriminations impossible for bats and make bats capable of auditory discriminations impossible for pigeons. We are also not troubled by different capacities for responding. Pigeons and bats fly differently at least in part because the anatomical structures of their wings are different. Although the examples are obvious, they are not trivial. They illustrate how much we take the different sensory and motor capacities of different species for granted.

Like sensory and motor capacities, the effectiveness of different stimuli as reinforcers or punishers varies across species. Once we recognized the relativity of reinforcement, it was no longer adequate simply to identify which reinforcers or which punishers might be effective for a given species. These consequences can only be defined in relation to the responses that produce them. Within a single species, a reinforcer effective for one response may not be effective for others. As demonstrated by phenomena such as food aversion and acknowledged by the concept of preparedness, we cannot specify the limits on learning in terms of stimuli alone or responses alone. Instead, we must express these limits in terms of the types of relations that can be created between stimuli and responses in a given species. Organisms may be predisposed to learn different relations among stimuli and responses in different situations. We might regard these predispositions as limitations on the structure of behavior.

An organism's behavior in its current environment is determined by phylogeny as well as ontogeny. The relative contributions of nature and nurture have been a long-standing issue in psychology, and though the emphasis has often shifted in one direction or the other it remains clear that neither operates to the exclusion of the other. Some aspects of behavior are highly determined by evolutionary factors (e.g., the human vocal apparatus), and others by experience (e.g., the human language one speaks). Nature and nurture are extremes on a continuum, and we must therefore recognize that learning as well as evolutionary history can impose constraints on behavior.

Like nature and nurture, behavior too is best represented not by all-or-none categories but rather by various dimensions along which processes can be located. Reinforcement and punishment are extremes on a continuum of contingencies that range from those that increase responding, through those that do not affect responding, to those that decrease responding. Positive and negative reinforcement are extremes on a continuum of relations involving the relative temporal locations of the stimuli present when responses are reinforced. Differentiation and discrimination are extremes on continua that represent how much response properties and stimulus properties contribute to the criteria of differential reinforcement. Operant discrimination and respondent conditioning are extremes on a continuum that relate stimulus-control operations to contingencies, ranging from those in which responses change stimulus probability to those in which responses have no effect on stimulus probability. Syntax and semantics are extremes on a continuum that relates structural properties of verbal behavior to complex features of the verbal and nonverbal environment. Verbal recall and verbal recognition are extremes on a continuum of different sorts of activity entering into the classes of behavior that we call remembering. Behavioral and cognitive processes are extremes on a continuum that represents the relative accessibility or inaccessibility of things that organisms do.

The boundaries within which various experimental operations are effective in changing behavior do not alter the properties that define behavioral processes. It does not follow that we should begin to call a phenomenon by a different name if it turns out not to be as general as we once believed. If we argued that the sole principle of learning was demonstrated by one particular behavioral procedure or process, such as elicitation or reinforcement or stimulus control, then its generality would be challenged by the discovery of conditions that limited its applicability. Once we recognize that all of the various operations and processes may be important in their different ways, the discovery of the limitations of each becomes an integral part of our analysis rather than a challenge to it.

One crucial part of the distinction between behavioral and cognitive psychologies is the insistence by the former that its subject matter is behavior. The interpretation of cognitive processes such as remembering and imagining, for example, has been in terms of what organisms do. When some type of cognitive process, such as the processing of information, is expressed in terms that are not explicitly related to behavior, its status becomes similar to that of the tacting of private events (cf. Watkins, 1981). A consistent vocabulary can be developed for a cognitive process only if at some point it makes contact with the environment, just as the consistent tacting of a private event can be developed only if some correlate of that event is publicly available to the verbal community. That may be one reason why the status of representations as copies or as transformations of stimuli has been the basis for so much controversy.

Another source of controversy has been the relation between behavior and physiology. The assertion that behavior is a subject matter in its own right does not deny its intimate dependence on the organism's physiology. Consider again the evolutionary analogy. Natural selection overcame the challenges from orthogenesis and other alternatives and emerged as the primary account of evolution long before molecular biology had worked out the mechanisms of genetic transmission. The early geneticists had no biochemical evidence about genes; their conclusions were based only on the data of reproduction. Molecular biologists needed the findings of genetics and mutation and natural selection to know what to look for in the cell. They would have looked differently, and undoubtedly with less success, if they had started instead with orthogenetic or Lamarckian assumptions.

Similarly, those who are interested in the neurophysiology of learning need to know what happens in learning and behavior to know what they should be looking for in the nervous system. The neurophysiologist who thinks of learning mainly in terms of stimulus-response associations will look for very different things than the one who thinks of learning in terms of the selection of classes of responses by their consequences. B. F. Skinner has compared the relation between behavior analysis and neuroscience with that between genetics and biochemistry: "It is the function of the science of behavior at the present time to give neurologists their assignments, as it was the function of genetics prior to the discovery of DNA to give modern geneticists their assignment with respect to the gene" (Skinner, 1988, p. 60; see also p. 461).

Much progress has been made in our understanding of the neurophysiology of some relatively simple systems (e.g., Kandel & Schwartz, 1982), but neuroscience has yet to give its attention to mechanisms for ontogenic selection. Perhaps the accumulating evidence for growth and reorganization within the nervous system will turn out to be consistent with a selectionist account (e.g., Donahoe & Palmer, 1989; Yates, 1986).

LEARNING AND EVOLUTION

In discussing types of selection, we have argued that properties of learning parallel those of evolution, because the selection or survival of patterns of behavior in an organism's lifetime has much in common with the selection or survival of individuals in the evolution of a species (e.g., Skinner, 1966, 1975; Staddon & Simmelhag, 1971; Gilbert, 1972; Catania, 1978). Our discussion of social learning made a similar case for the selection of social and cultural practices (cf. Dawkins, 1976; Harris, 1977; Skinner, 1981). Each type of selection involves some kind of variation that provides the source materials upon which it operates, and each has some basis for selecting what survives.

The parallels between Darwinian natural selection and operant selection also extend to the problems of acceptance each has faced (see Chapter 2; cf. Catania, 1987). Like Galileo's displacement of the earth from the center of the universe to an orbit

around the sun, these accounts overturned traditional ways of thinking about the place of our species in nature. Some of the substantive challenges have also been similar. For example, artificial selection was familiar in Darwin's time; what was questioned was whether selection could operate naturally. The operant parallel is provided by shaping, which is also an artificial selection procedure, as when an experimenter shapes a pigeon's figure-eight turns or as when a behavior therapist shapes the vocalizations of a nonverbal institutionalized child. The effectiveness of shaping is self-evident; what is questioned is whether it operates naturally to produce some of the varied patterns of behavior that we see in everyday life.

It is not good enough to argue that in humans the effects of shaping are likely to be often masked by rule-governed behavior. It would be best to document cases in which the changes in contingencies are identified early and tracked. Typically, however, we only have outcomes, after the natural contingencies have already done their work. For example, we can assume that ontogenic selection was involved in shaping the skill with which grizzly bears catch salmon in the rivers of the Pacific Northwest, but we mainly see the differences between the inefficient performances of the young novices and the well-coordinated actions of the experienced adults; we do not see the shaping itself, because it continues over too long a time.

Furthermore, shaping can be hard to see if one does not know what to look for; someone who has actually done shaping is more apt to notice it when it happens naturally than someone who has only read about it. Thus, the parents who always wait a while before attending to a crying child may not notice that they have gradually shaped louder and more annoying cries. The attention reinforces the crying, and annoying cries are, by definition, the ones most likely to get attention. If one watches what a parent does when a child throws tantrums, it is often easy to guess where the tantrums came from.

Time is another factor in the acceptance of both types of selection. For Darwinian natural selection, the question was once whether the earth had existed long enough for such selection to have taken place; upward revisions of the age of the earth resolved the problem. The comparable problem is easier to deal with for operant selection. Even with rapid breeders like the fruit fly, genetic experiments take days. Shaping, however, can be demonstrated within minutes. If reinforcers can do so much to behavior when contingencies are deliberately arranged over relatively short periods of time, is it not reasonable to assume that they will also affect behavior when natural contingencies operate over substantial periods in an organism's lifetime? Many contingencies may take hold of behavior over the course of a year in the life of a young child. Compared to how long most artificial examples of shaping last, a year is an extremely long time. Some contingencies may be subtle, especially when we recognize the very broad range of events that can serve as reinforcers. Some may produce behavior that is desirable; others may do the opposite. Given what artificial contingencies can do in a short time, natural contingencies should be able to do a lot in a long time. It is certainly more appropriate to be alert for the effects of such contingencies than to assume that they do not exist.

In both natural and artificial environments, it is difficult to determine the boundaries of behavioral classes. Here again is a parallel between ontogenic and phylogenic selection. In each case, we must deal not with particular instances but rather with populations or classes of events. We speak of populations of organisms as species, and we speak of behavioral populations as response classes, such as operants, discriminated operants, and respondents (and in social learning we speak of populations of socially maintained response classes as cultural practices and as classes of verbal behavior).

It might be argued that our notions of response classes are much vaguer than the classes Darwin spoke of as species in his account of evolution (Darwin, 1859). Yet even though the word *species* is in Darwin's famous title, *On the Origin of Species*, Darwin knew that the term could not be given an unambiguous definition. In his book, he commented often on the problem of definition:

> I look at the term species, as one arbitrarily given for the sake of convenience to a set of individuals closely resembling each other [p. 52];...the amount of difference necessary to give two forms the rank of species is quite indefinite [p. 59]; [and]...we shall have to treat species in the same manner as those naturalists treat genera, who admit that genera are merely artificial combinations made for convenience. This may not be a cheering prospect; but we shall at least be freed from the vain search for the undiscovered and undiscoverable essence of the term species. (Darwin, 1859, p. 485)

In Darwin's account of evolution, the relations among populations of organisms could not be expressed adequately in terms of similar topographies (for example, males and females within some species differ more from each other in form than some pairs of organisms within completely unrelated species; the social insects in particular are striking instances).

For Darwin, the important basis for distinguishing among populations was descent. We define the relations among populations by looking at where they came from. Darwin's achievement, in fact, was more description than explanation. His account of evolution did not depend on any theory specifying the mechanics of evolution (his work predated genetics, and he even argued at times that acquired traits might be the source of variation on which evolution acted); rather, he had described the properties of evolution (Gould, 1975, p. 824). Darwin himself was skeptical about explanation: "It is so easy...to think that we give an explanation when we only restate a fact" (Darwin, 1859, pp. 481–482).

What has this to do with learning? The analogies between behavior and biology suggest that some solutions appropriate to biology will be appropriate to an analysis of behavior. We have seen the importance of descriptions of what happens in learning, and have given such descriptions priority over theories or mechanisms or models. For example, we found that the term *reinforcement*, which once served explanatory functions, now functions simply as a name for a particular behavioral phenomenon. Thus, we no longer ask whether reinforcement explains behavior. Instead, empirical questions about the generality of reinforcement are best regarded as questions about the range of circumstances to which this name can be applied. Similarly, the study of memory does not explain what is remembered; instead, what is remembered is the basis for determining behavioral structure, as in the analysis of the psychological reality of syntax and semantics. Theories and models come and go, but the descriptions of behavior remain (and it is fitting that we have sometimes found it appropriate to consider the results even of experiments conducted in an earlier century).

Darwin's treatment rejected the concept of immutable species in favor of classes defined by their descent or evolution. The psychology of learning has sometimes moved in the opposite direction. It sought to *explain* learning by inventing sources for responses (neural traces, associations, cognitive structures). But that was getting it backwards. We should use the development of behavior to define behavioral classes. We should define behavioral classes in terms of their descent: where they came from or how they were learned.

To some extent, we already do that, though seldom explicitly. We distinguish innate behavior from behavior acquired through experience. We speak of behavior produced by stimuli as elicited, and we speak of behavior occurring independently of stimuli as emitted. We say that responses engendered by stimulus presentations are respondent behavior, and responses engendered by consequences are operant behavior. We say that responses engendered by verbal antecedents are rule-governed, and responses engendered by consequences are contingency-shaped. Such distinctions constitute a behavioral taxonomy, a system for classifying kinds of behavior and kinds of behavioral processes (Catania, 1983).

In the analysis of behavior, we deal with populations of responses. These populations are sometimes not well-defined. The problem is not different from Darwin's. Darwin clearly recognized the arbitrary nature of the concept of species, but unambiguous definitions of species were no more critical to his account than unambiguous definitions of stimulus classes or response classes need be to a behavioral account (like natural classes of stimuli, these too are probabilistic stimulus classes). When we distinguish among words by the circumstances in which they are uttered (e.g., *fire* as a mand, a tact, an echoic, or a textual response; Chapter 11) we are simply distinguishing among classes of verbal responses on the basis of their origins. Ambiguous cases will necessarily occur because, just as organisms have many ancestors, responses have many origins. But there would be little need for an analysis if that were not the case.

BEHAVIOR ANALYSIS
AND BEHAVIOR SYNTHESIS

A behavior analysis begins with complex behavior and breaks it down into its components. These are the elements of our behavioral taxonomy. They can also be combined in various ways, when it may be appropriate to speak of behavior synthesis. For example, we can synthesize some kinds of sequential performances through chaining procedures. In a more complex instance, we may combine discriminative stimuli, reinforcement schedules, and delays of reinforcement in such a way that the resulting contingencies are analogous to those that occur when we speak of self-control (cf. Chapter 8). If our synthesis is successful, we may use it to clarify the behavioral properties of the performance; if it is unsuccessful, we may use it to identify components of the performance that were missed or taken for granted in preceding analyses (e.g., as when we study variables that affect the

likelihood of commitment responses in self-control procedures, or as when we discover, in designing an animal experiment analogous to some human performance, that verbal behavior had a role that was not allowed for). Because many important human problems involve creating new behavior (e.g., teaching developmentally delayed children), the applications of behavioral methods are often matters of behavior synthesis (cf. Catania & Brigham, 1978).

The term *learning* has receded into the background in all of this; perhaps it has outlived its usefulness. We can modify behavioral hierarchies, shape new responses, create higher-order classes, generate discriminations, form equivalence classes, and solve problems. Our understanding of these phenomena depends at least in part on whether we have developed a language that is consistent with them. We have often recognized the ambiguities of the present vocabulary of behavior, and we can assume that it will change as research progresses. Yet in emphasizing behavioral operations and processes, the vocabulary at least adheres closely to what is done and what is observed in experiments on behavior. The success of behavior analysis will be measured by its survival in the behavior of those who practice it and by the effectiveness of the behavior syntheses that follow from it.

Glossary

As the psychology of learning evolves, its terminology is progressively refined. This glossary defines some of that terminology. A set of definitions must be treated as a preliminary guide to the basic classifications and concepts in the relevant literature rather than as an inflexible set of rules. This glossary has been prepared in that spirit. A fuller and more technical glossary restricted to the experimental analysis of behavior is available in Catania (1991a); the evolution of some of the terminology can be examined by comparing current entries with those in an earlier version now out of print (Catania, 1968).

The present glossary attempts to acknowledge alternative definitions and to point out difficulties or potential ambiguities in existing usages. Nevertheless, sooner or later the reader must expect to encounter particular usages in the literature that disagree with the usages defined here.

Definitions are merely words that can substitute for other words, and the substitution is sometimes only an approximation. Because the framing or mastering of a definition is primarily verbal, it cannot be counted on to produce the discriminations upon which the development and evolution of that verbal behavior was based. For example, the student who has learned to define *reinforcement* may be able to offer a correct definition, but it does not follow that the student will then be able to discriminate reliably between actual instances of reinforcement and nonreinforcement in laboratory or real-world settings.

Glossaries are hardly ever exhaustive. This one is no exception. Over time old terms are modified or dropped and new ones are added. This glossary covers some of the major terminology of the psychology of learning as it appears in this volume and in the closely related literature. With some exceptions, it does not cover aspects of vocabulary consistent with everyday usage (e.g., technical terms that are nonetheless defined adequately in standard dictionaries), terms likely to be encountered in specialty areas or in other disciplines (e.g., drug classification in psychopharmacology), or specialized technical terms that appear only in passing in the text and can be located via the index. For a review of other glossaries in behavior analysis, psychology, and related disciplines, see Catania (1989); for a useful general dictionary of psychology, see Reber (1985).

In cross-references among definitions, *cf.* (as opposed to *see*) usually refers to useful contrasts and critical distinctions among related terms rather than to synonymous usages. Time is usually expressed in seconds; *t* and *n* indicate arbitrary quantities of time or number, where *t* and *n* are constants unless otherwise stated. Some matters of usage pertinent to the glossary as a whole are discussed under OPERATION.

A

Abstraction: discrimination based on a single property of stimuli, independent of other properties; thus, generalization among all stimuli with that property (e.g., all red stimuli as opposed to specific red objects). Cf. CONCEPT FORMATION.

Accessibility: in the metaphor of memory storage and retrieval, the retrievability of a stored item; an item that is stored but not retrievable is said to be *inaccessible*. Cf. AVAILABILITY.

Acquisition: the addition of new behavior to an organism's repertoire. The behavior may be a discriminated operant, a topographically complex operant, a conditional reflex relation, or the performance controlled by a schedule; thus, the term may refer to the change in performance caused by any change in contingencies. Cf. LEARNING, REPERTOIRE.

Adaptation: a reduction, usually during the prolonged presentation of a stimulus, in the behavior produced by that stimulus (e.g., adaptation to an experimental chamber). Cf. HABITUATION, POTENTIATION.

Adjunctive behavior: responding that reliably accompanies some other response that has been produced or occasioned by a stimulus, especially when the stimulus is presented according to a temporally defined schedule. Some usages emphasize the stimulus rather than the responding it engenders (e.g., in rats, food presentations typically produce eating reliably followed by drinking; the drinking is adjunctive and is sometimes said to be *induced* by the schedule of food presentation).

Adjusting (adj) schedule: a schedule varying as a function of some property of performance (e.g., an adjusting FR schedule in which the ratio increases or decreases depending on the duration of preceding postreinforcement pauses; an adjusting avoidance schedule in which schedule parameters change as a function of the frequency with which aversive stimuli occur).

Aggression: a side effect of presenting aversive stimuli or removing positive reinforcers, which may generate responses that injure other organisms (e.g., biting) and/or increase the effectiveness with which opportunities for such responses serve as reinforcers.

Alternative (alt) schedule: a schedule in which a response is reinforced when either of two (or more) schedule requirements is satisfied (e.g., in alternative FR 10 FI 60-s, the tenth response or the first response after 1 minute is reinforced, whichever comes first, and both schedule requirements then start over).

Analysis of behavior: see BEHAVIOR ANALYSIS.

Antecedent stimulus or **antecedent event:** a stimulus that precedes some event or contingency; typically, a discriminative stimulus in a three-term contingency.

Anticipation: see SERIAL LEARNING.

Anxiety: see EMOTIONAL BEHAVIOR, PREAVERSIVE STIMULUS.

Appetitive stimulus: usually, a positive reinforcer, especially one the effectiveness of which is modifiable by deprivation.

Arbitrary matching: see MATCHING-TO-SAMPLE.

Arousal: a state of readiness for behaving, metaphorically extended from arousal in the colloquial sense of awakening.

Artificial reinforcer: see CONTRIVED REINFORCER, EXTRINSIC REINFORCER.

Artificial selection: in the Darwinian account of evolution, the variety of selection practiced by humans, in selective breeding in horticulture, animal husbandry, etc. Cf. NATURAL SELECTION.

Association: see CONTIGUITY.

Attention: discriminative responding based on some stimulus or stimulus property. An organism is said to *attend to* a stimulus or stimulus property when variation of that stimulus or stimulus property changes behavior (e.g., a pigeon discriminating blue light from its absence is said to attend to color rather than brightness if variations in wavelength but not intensity change its performance). Cf. DISCRIMINATION, FUNCTIONAL STIMULUS.

Autobiographical memory: episodic memory. See REMEMBERING.

Autoclitic: a unit of verbal behavior that depends on other verbal behavior for its occurrence and that modifies the effects of that other verbal behavior on the listener. *Descriptive autoclitics* involve discriminations of one's own behavior, as when the word *not* depends on a mismatch between what one is inclined to say and the appropriateness of saying it; including *not* in the statement cancels some of its effects on the listener. *Relational autoclitics* involve verbal units that are coordinated with other units in such a way that they cannot stand alone, as when plurals depend on quantitative features of events or grammatical tenses depend on temporal features; novel verbal behavior is sometimes the product of novel combinations of such units occasioned by novel circumstances.

Automaintenance: the maintenance of autoshaped responding by continuing contingent stimulus-reinforcer relations. In *negative automaintenance*, the contingent stimulus-reinforcer relation operates on trials without responses, but the reinforcer is omitted on trials with responses. Cf. AUTOSHAPING.

Automatic reinforcer: a reinforcer related to a response in such a way that it is ordinarily produced automatically by the response (e.g., as in the relation between certain sexual activities and orgasm). Cf. CONTRIVED REINFORCER, INTRINSIC REINFORCER, PRIMARY REINFORCER.

Autoshaping: a respondent procedure that generates skeletal responses. In the most common example, a pigeon's pecks on a key are engendered by contingent presentations of a key light and a feeder; a fixed key-light duration is followed by food, which is not presented at other times. In some procedures, pecks on the key, once they occur, produce food immediately rather than at the offset of the key light. Cf. AUTOMAINTENANCE.

Availability: in the metaphor of memory storage and retrieval, the status of an item that has been stored; if it is stored, it is said to be available whether or not it can be retrieved. Any retrieved item is always both available and accessible; an unretrieved item might be either unavailable or available but inaccessible. Cf. ACCESSIBILITY.

Aversive control: see specific cases: ESCAPE, AVOIDANCE, PUNISHMENT, PREAVERSIVE STIMULUS.

Aversive stimulus: a stimulus effective as a *negative reinforcer* or as a *punisher*, or that suppresses positively reinforced operant behavior during another stimulus that precedes it (cf. PREAVERSIVE STIMULUS). A stimulus with any one of these effects is likely also to have the others, but it is not guaranteed to do so. Cf. NOXIOUS STIMULUS, PUNISHMENT, REINFORCEMENT.

Avoidance: the prevention of an aversive stimulus by a response. In *deletion* procedures, the response cancels presentations of the aversive stimulus; in *postponement* procedures, the response only delays presentations. In *discriminated, discrete-trials,* or *signaled avoidance,* an exteroceptive stimulus (sometimes called a *warning stimulus*) precedes the aversive stimulus; a response during this stimulus prevents the aversive stimulus on that trial. If no response occurs and the aversive stimulus is presented, escape from it typically depends on the same response that is effective for avoidance. In *continuous, free-operant,* or *Sidman avoidance,* no exteroceptive stimulus is arranged and, typically, there is no provision for escape. Each response postpones the aversive stimulus (usually, brief shock) for a fixed period called the *response-shock (RS) interval;* in the absence of responses, shocks are delivered regularly according to a *shock-shock (SS) interval.* Cf. NEGATIVE REINFORCEMENT.

B

Backward conditioning: respondent conditioning in which the CS follows rather than precedes the US. This procedure can be effective with aversive stimuli but is otherwise usually ineffective.

Bait-shyness: see TASTE AVERSION.

Bar: lever. See OPERANDUM.

Baseline: a stable and, usually, recoverable performance upon which effects of experimental variables are superimposed (e.g., a drug effect may be expressed as the change produced in baseline response rate by a dosage of the drug). The term is also used occasionally to refer to the horizontal starting position (zero responses) of a cumulative-recorder pen. Cf. STEADY STATE.

Behavior: anything an organism does. Although the definition is too inclusive as it stands, it cannot easily be restricted further (e.g., to activity of muscles or glands). For example, a shift of attention need not involve eye movements but qualifies as behavior. See also specific cases: COVERT BEHAVIOR, EMO-

TIONAL BEHAVIOR, SPECIES-SPECIFIC BEHAVIOR, OPERANT BEHAVIOR, OVERT BEHAVIOR, RESPONDENT BEHAVIOR.

Behavioral contrast: see CONTRAST.

Behavior analysis: breaking down complex behavior into its functional parts. A successful analysis should be able to produce the complex behavior by combining its parts in a behavior synthesis.

Bias: a systematic error in measurement (e.g., if a device cannot record all responses when they follow each other rapidly, data recorded with the device will be biased toward low response rates). For other usages, see also MATCHING LAW and PREFERENCE.

Biofeedback: feedback based upon physiological measures (e.g., blood pressure, heart rate, muscle tension). See FEEDBACK.

Blackout: a timeout arranged by turning off all lights in the chamber.

Blocking: an attenuation of respondent conditioning with one stimulus because of prior conditioning with another (e.g., if tone and bell together precede food after bell has become a CS, tone may remain ineffective as a CS even though it and bell have the same contingent relation to food). Cf. OVERSHADOWING.

Break: an abrupt transition from responding to no responding (cf. RATIO STRAIN).

Burst: a series of responses emitted at a high rate and bounded by lower-rate responding, especially after a stimulus.

C

Categories: see specific cases: ABSTRACTION, CONCEPT FORMATION, EQUIVALENCE CLASS, NATURAL CONCEPT, POLYMORPHOUS STIMULUS CLASS, PROBABILISTIC STIMULUS CLASS, PROTOTYPE.

CER: conditioned emotional response. See PREAVERSIVE STIMULUS.

Chain: a sequence of discriminated operants such that responses during one stimulus are followed by other stimuli that reinforce those responses and set the occasion for subsequent ones (see CHAINED SCHEDULE, CONDITIONED REINFORCER). Not all temporally integrated sequences are maintained through chaining; those that are not must be distinguished from those that are. Parts of a chain are variously called *components, links,* or *mem-*

bers. Procedures for creating chains often start with responses at the end of the sequence, closest to the reinforcer, and then work back (*backward chaining*); starting from the other end (*forward chaining*) is more difficult, because early responses may extinguish while later ones are being shaped. Chains with topographically similar responses are *homogeneous* (e.g., a pigeon's pecks in a chained schedule); those with topographically dissimilar responses are *heterogeneous* (e.g., a sequence consisting of alley-running, lever-pressing, and moving to a feeder).

Chained (chain) schedule: a compound schedule in which a reinforcer is produced by the successive completion of two or more component schedules, each operating during a different stimulus. The equivalent arrangement with the same stimulus during each component is a *tandem* schedule.

Chamber: a space designed to minimize interference from stimuli (e.g., laboratory noises) irrelevant to experimental conditions, and including devices for recording behavior (see OPERANDUM) and presenting stimuli. In typical chambers, stimulus sources include mechanisms for delivering reinforcers (e.g., food dispensers); discriminative-stimulus sources (e.g., speakers for presenting auditory stimuli; lamps or projectors for presenting visual stimuli); aversive-stimulus sources (e.g., see SHOCK); a houselight, which provides general illumination; feedback devices, which produce stimuli such as clicks after each response; and auditory sources that mask outside noises (often a fan that provides masking noise along with ventilation).

Changeover: the switching from one response to another, as when a pigeon in a two-key chamber moves from pecking the left key to pecking the right key. Cf. CONCURRENT OPERANT.

Changeover delay (COD): a feature sometimes incorporated into concurrent schedules to prevent sequences in which one response is closely followed by a reinforcer produced by a concurrent response. As usually arranged, the COD provides that no response can be reinforced within some time after a changeover has been completed (but CODs are occasionally timed from other events, such as the last response before the initiation of a changeover).

Changeover ratio (COR): a changeover contingency that provides that no response can be reinforced until some minimum number of responses has occurred since the last changeover. Cf. CHANGEOVER DELAY.

Chaos: a branch of mathematics dealing with nonlinear systems, which are drastically affected even by very small changes in their initial values (e.g., the flap of a butterfly's wings may be enough to affect the path of a storm system some weeks later). Like the weather, behavior is a nonlinear system. For measurement at any level of precision, the mathematics of chaos demonstrates that, although we can predict kinds of things that will happen, we cannot predict specific details (e.g., we can predict that a pigeon will peck a key, but not precisely when). This makes interpretation far more important, and in many behavioral applications it will be all that is feasible.

Choice: the emission of one of two or more alternative and, usually, incompatible responses. Cf. CONCURRENT OPERANTS, PREFERENCE.

Chunking: the arbitrary creation of larger verbal units, as when a mnemonic system is used to convert a sequence of digits to a single word.

Classical conditioning: see RESPONDENT CONDITIONING.

Closed economy: in operant contexts, the availability of appetitive stimuli only within the session, as reinforcers, with none provided independently of behavior on a supplementary basis outside of the session. Cf. OPEN ECONOMY.

Clustering: in free recall, the reorganization of items by the learner so that related ones are recalled together rather than in the order in which they appeared on the list.

COD: see CHANGEOVER DELAY.

Coding, coding response: an inferred variety of mediating behavior, as when humans remember visually presented letters on the basis of sound rather than geometric properties, perhaps as a result of saying or subvocally rehearsing them. Errors based on acoustic rather than visual similarity support the inference. Tacting may be one kind of coding. Cf. DECODING, ENCODING.

Cognition, cognitive processes: knowing, and the ways in which it takes place. Processes said to be cognitive are often varieties of behavior that need not be manifested as movements and therefore must be measured indirectly (e.g., doing mental arithmetic, shifting attention, imagining). Cf. BEHAVIOR, COVERT BEHAVIOR.

Cognitive map: a spatial schema or representation. In learning a coordinated set of spatial relations, an organism is sometimes said to be developing a cognitive map. The term is most likely to be invoked when the organism orients toward locations that it cannot see or otherwise respond to directly.

Collateral behavior: responding that, like mediating behavior, appears in a consistent sequential relation to reinforced behavior while not itself instrumental in producing the reinforcer. The term does not carry the implication that the responding mediates the reinforced behavior. Cf. MEDIATING BEHAVIOR.

Component: one of the schedules, or the stimulus associated with it, in a compound schedule. The term is usually restricted to cases in which the individual schedules making up the compound schedule operate successively rather than simultaneously.

Comparison stimulus: see MATCHING-TO-SAMPLE.

Compound schedule: a schedule in which two or more individual schedules are combined. The components may operate successively in alternation (MULTIPLE and MIXED) or as a sequence (CHAINED and TANDEM), or simultaneously (CONCURRENT and CONJOINT); they may also interact (ALTERNATIVE, CONJUNCTIVE, INTERLOCKING). See these and other specific cases: ADJUSTING, CONCURRENT-CHAIN, HIGHER-ORDER, PERCENTILE-REINFORCEMENT, PROGRESSIVE.

Concept formation: the formation of a discrimination based on a class of stimuli such that an organism generalizes among all stimuli within the class but discriminates them from those in other classes. Such classes play much the same role in analyses of discriminative stimuli as operants do in analyses of response classes. Cf. ABSTRACTION, DISCRIMINATION, GENERALIZATION, STIMULUS.

Concurrent-chain schedules: concurrent schedules in which the reinforcers are themselves schedules that operate separately and in the presence of different stimuli. For example, equal and independent concurrent VI VI schedules may operate for a pigeon's pecks on two white keys; according to the VI schedules, left pecks produce an FI schedule operating on a blue key and right pecks produce an FR schedule operating on a yellow key. The concurrent

VI VI schedules are called *initial links* and the separate schedules they produce are called *terminal links*. Preference for the conditions in the terminal links is given by relative response rates in the initial links. Cf. PREFERENCE.

Concurrent operants: two or more classes of alternative responses. Concurrent operants may be compatible (as when a rat simultaneously presses one lever with its left paw and another with its right) or incompatible (as when the pigeon, having only one beak, pecks only one of two keys at a time) as long as the organism can emit either or can change over from one to the other at any time (occasionally, responding and not responding are treated as concurrent operants). Discriminated operants also may be concurrent if at any time the organism has an opportunity to produce the stimuli that occasion them. For example, in a *changeover-key procedure*, a pigeon changes the stimuli and their associated schedules on one key (the *main key*) by pecking a second key (the *changeover key*). In this case, two concurrent schedules operate on one key, and changeovers are an explicit class of responses on the second key. See also CHANGEOVER, CONCURRENT SCHEDULES, PREFERENCE.

Concurrent (conc) schedules: two or more schedules operating simultaneously and independently, each for a different response, as when separate VI schedules are arranged for a pigeon's pecks on each of two keys. Cf. CONJOINT SCHEDULES.

Conditional: an often-preferred alternative to *conditioned*.

Conditional discrimination: a discrimination in which the reinforcement of responding during a stimulus depends on, or is conditional upon, other stimuli (e.g., matching-to-sample involves a conditional discrimination in the sense that whether a given comparison response is reinforced depends on the sample stimulus). Conditional-discrimination procedures involve four-term contingencies, in that they arrange stimuli in the presence of which different three-term contingencies operate.

Conditional probability: the probability of one event given some other event (e.g., if responses *A* and *B* occur equally often but *A* is followed by *A* 75 percent of the time and by *B* 25 percent of the time, the simple probability of *A* is 0.5, whereas its conditional probability given that the last response was *A* is .75). Cf. PROBABILITY; see INTERRESPONSE TIME for another example.

Conditioned: see CONDITIONAL.

Conditioned aversive stimulus: a stimulus that has acquired its aversive properties because it has reliably accompanied another aversive stimulus (e.g., in discriminated avoidance, the warning stimulus may become a conditioned aversive stimulus). Cf. PREAVERSIVE STIMULUS.

Conditioned emotional response (CER): see PREAVERSIVE STIMULUS.

Conditioned reflex or **conditional reflex:** a reflex produced by a contingent relation between stimuli (see CONTINGENCY). One stimulus, originally neutral, sets the occasion for presenting a second stimulus, the *unconditioned stimulus* (*US*). A conditioned reflex is created when the neutral stimulus becomes a *conditioned stimulus* (*CS*), eliciting a response by virtue of its contingent relation to the US. This response, a *conditioned response* (*CR*), is often related to but is not necessarily the same as the *unconditioned response* (*UR*) elicited by the US. Responses elicited by the CS before conditioning (e.g., orienting responses) tend to disappear as conditioning progresses (cf. HABITUATION).

The most typical respondent procedure, in which the CS is followed within no more than 5 seconds by the US, is ordinarily called *simultaneous conditioning* (brief delays were incorporated into most so-called simultaneous conditioning procedures because the CR cannot be measured independently of the UR if the CS and US are simultaneous, and strict simultaneity is actually less effective in conditioning than a brief delay between CS and US). Stimuli effective as US's in respondent conditioning are often effective as positive or negative reinforcers in operant selection, and an older usage of *reinforcement* to refer to presentations of the US still survives in some parts of the learning literature. See also BACKWARD CONDITIONING, DELAY CONDITIONING, HIGHER-ORDER CONDITIONING, TEMPORAL CONDITIONING, TRACE CONDITIONING. Also cf. UNCONDITIONED REFLEX and RESPONDENT.

Conditioned reinforcer or **conditional reinforcer:** a stimulus that functions as a reinforcer because of its contingent relation to another reinforcer. Such stimuli have also been called *secondary* reinforcers, but this designation is best reserved for cases in which the modifier specifies how many stimuli separate the conditioned reinforcer from a primary reinforcer (e.g., a secondary reinforcer is followed directly by a primary reinforcer, a tertiary by a secondary, etc.). In some cases, convenience dictates the assigned order (e.g., a feeder operation may be called a primary reinforcer even though the auditory and/or visual stimuli that accompany it are actually conditioned reinforcers that precede eating).

Conditioned response or **conditional response (CR)** or **stimulus (CS):** see CONDITIONED REFLEX.

Conditioned suppression: see PREAVERSIVE STIMULUS.

Conditioning: see RESPONDENT CONDITIONING. The term still appears occasionally in conjunction with *operant,* but *operant conditioning* has become a less common usage.

Conflict: a situation involving any of the following: a single response produces both a reinforcer and a punisher (*approach-avoidance* conflict); two or more incompatible responses each produce a different reinforcer (*approach-approach* conflict); or, each of two or more incompatible responses terminates or avoids only one of two or more different aversive stimuli (*avoidance-avoidance* conflict).

Conjoint (conjt) schedules: two or more component schedules, usually involving different reinforcers, operating for a single response (e.g., lever-presses simultaneously are reinforced according to an FR schedule and postpone shock according to an avoidance schedule). Cf. CONCURRENT SCHEDULES.

Conjugate reinforcement: reinforcement in which some property of a reinforcer varies systematically with some property of responding (e.g., as when the sharpness of focus of a reinforcing visual stimulus increases with the momentary rate of responding).

Conjunctive (conj) schedule: a schedule in which a response is reinforced when each of two (or more) schedule requirements is satisfied (e.g., in conj FR 10 FI 60-s, a response is reinforced only after at least 9 other responses have been emitted and at least 1 minute has elapsed since the last reinforcer).

Consequence: an event produced by some other event, especially, in operant contexts, an event produced by a response. It might include stimulus presentation or removal, a change in contingencies, or any other alteration of the environment. The term is particularly useful for referring to stimuli with an unknown status as reinforcers or punishers (presenting such events contingent upon responding has sometimes been called *consequation*).

Consolidation of memory: a theoretical process based on the assumption that something remembered is relatively impermanent immediately after learning, and takes some time to become fixed or consolidated.

Constituent grammars: phrase-structure grammars. See GRAMMARS.

Constructive memory: memory interpreted as a way of reconstructing rather than retrieving a copy of what is remembered. Remembering interpreted in this way is more like following a recipe than like reading a blueprint.

Consummatory response: behavior occasioned by a reinforcer. The term originated with reinforcers that were actually consumed (e.g., food and water) but has been extended to other reinforcers, perhaps to a point of limited usefulness (e.g., if the opportunity to run in a wheel is a reinforcer, wheel running is the consummatory response).

Context: the constant features of an experimental situation (e.g., the chamber within which an operant session occurs). Experimental contexts may acquire behavioral function, especially because they are embedded in the larger contexts that include the experimental session.

Contiguity: the juxtaposition of two or more events, especially in the case of their occurrence simultaneously or very closely together in time (e.g., the succession of a response and a reinforcer in a superstition procedure or the pairing of CS and US in a respondent procedure). Cf. CONTINGENCY.

Contingency: in the operant case, the conditions under which a response produces a consequence (e.g., in an FI, the reinforcer is said to be *contingent on* a response of a given force, topography, etc., as well as on the passage of time). An organism is said to *come into contact with a contingency* when its behavior produces some consequences of the contingency.

Studies of reinforcement schedules analyze contingencies and their effects (as when contingencies of reinforcement for various IRTs in VI and VR schedules are compared). In this most general usage, contingencies describe any relation, whether completely specified by experimental operations or an incidental and perhaps fortuitous consequence of them. In a more specific sense, contingencies are the conditional probabilities that relate some events (e.g., responses) to others (e.g., stimuli). The contingent relation that exists when responses produce reinforcers is defined by two conditional probabilities: the probability of the reinforcer given the response and its probability given no response. If both probabilities are not specified, contingent response-reinforcer relations cannot be distinguished from the incidental temporal *contiguities* that can result when responses and reinforcers occur independently over time. Response-reinforcer relations involve two terms, but they can be correlated with discriminative stimuli, thereby producing a *three-term contingency*. Conditional discriminations add a fourth term, and so on for other contingency relations of various orders of complexity.

The term *contingency* also applies to respondent cases, referring to the conditions under which some stimuli are followed by others. By analogy to the operant case, *stimulus-stimulus contingencies* expressed as conditional probabilities specify conditions more completely than descriptions in terms of pairings or temporal *contiguities*, distinguishing cases in which two stimuli always occur together from those in which they are frequently paired but also occur independently of each other; and stimuli correlated with stimulus-stimulus contingencies (sometimes called *occasion setters*) may enter into three-term or higher-order relations.

Contingency-governed behavior or **contingency-shaped behavior:** operant behavior. The terminology is ordinarily used to contrast responding that is not occasioned by verbal behavior with *rule-governed behavior*, behavior controlled by verbal antecedents (e.g., instructions).

Contingency space: any coordinate system within which contingencies expressed as conditional probabilities are plotted.

Contingent stimulus: a stimulus the presentation of which depends on a response-stimulus contingency.

Continuous avoidance: see AVOIDANCE.

Continuous repertoire or **continuous repertory:** behavior that tracks continuous changes in some property of the environment, as when a driver steers a car so as to keep it in its lane.

Continuous reinforcement (CRF): reinforcement of every response within the limits of an operant class.

Continuum: see STIMULUS CONTINUUM.

Contrast or **behavioral contrast:** a change in the rate of one response that occurs when either the rate of a second response or the reinforcement rate produced by that response is changed in the opposite direction, where the reinforcement rate maintaining the first response remains constant. For example, the rate of reinforced responding in one multiple-schedule component typically increases if reinforcement is reduced or discontinued in the other. The effect is most appropriately measured relative to a baseline performance in which responses in both components are maintained by the same reinforcement rate but has also been measured relative to rates in prior nonbaseline conditions. The term is usually restricted to responses in the presence of successive stimuli, as in multiple schedules, though similar phenomena occur within concurrent schedules. Cf. INDUCTION.

Contrived reinforcer: an artificial reinforcer. Cf. CONDITIONED REINFORCER, EXTRINSIC REINFORCER.

Control: the systematic modification or maintenance of behavior by manipulating relevant conditions. The manipulation of conditions distinguishes control from *prediction* and *interpretation*. If control is not possible because relevant conditions are not manipulable, adequate information about relevant variables may make prediction possible (e.g., as in the history of astronomy before space flight). Interpretation usually occurs after the fact. Given an outcome, a plausible account of the relevant variables can be offered, but it may be difficult to determine its adequacy. Nevertheless, such an analysis is often expected or demanded of students of behavior (as when a psychologist is asked to explain in a court of law why a defendant acted in some way). In its most common behavior analytic usage, the term appears in conjunction with some variable that has a demonstrable effect on behavior (e.g., *schedule control, stimulus control*). Cf. CHAOS.

Coordinate: the value of a point plotted on a graph. In a two-dimensional system, the value plotted along the x-axis is called the *abscissa* and that plotted along the y-axis is called the *ordinate*; the terms do not refer to the axes themselves.

COR: see CHANGEOVER RATIO.

Correction procedure: the repetition or continuation of experimental conditions and/or stimuli after given responses or after their absence (especially, in a discrete-trial simultaneous discrimination, after errors). For example, stimuli on one trial may be repeated on the next if an error occurred or if, in a trial of limited duration, no response occurred. In a free-operant case, a multiple VI extinction schedule may be arranged so that each response during the extinction component delays the onset of the VI component. The term can refer to any procedure that arranges continued or repeated opportunities for responses in alternative classes until a given response does (or does not) occur. Its colloquial origins imply procedures that eventually force an organism to emit a correct response (cf. ERROR), but the technical usage does not exclude procedures in which the alternative response classes cannot easily be categorized as correct responses and errors.

Correlated stimuli or **correlated reinforcers:** see CONJUGATE REINFORCEMENT.

Correlation: see STATISTICS. The term is often extended to procedures, especially stimulus-control procedures (e.g., as when a schedule operating in the presence but not in the absence of a stimulus is said to be *correlated with* that stimulus), and *molar* analyses often rely on correlations between overall measures of behavior (e.g., correlations between response rates and reinforcement rates).

Cost: see RESPONSE COST.

Covert behavior: behavior that is not observed or observable and is therefore only inferred. Alternatively, behavior inside an organism, but of such a sort or on such a small scale that it is not recordable or is recordable only with special equipment (e.g., thinking or counting to oneself, inferred from a human's verbal report, or muscle contractions too small to produce obvious movement).

CR: conditioned response. See CONDITIONED REFLEX.

CRF: see CONTINUOUS REINFORCEMENT.

Critical feature: a feature, perhaps one of several, upon which the discrimination among stimulus classes depends (e.g., critical features of letters of the alphabet include straight vs. curved, open vs. closed, etc.). Cf. FUNCTIONAL STIMULUS.

Critical period: the time during which a stimulus can become imprinted (cf. IMPRINTED STIMULUS). More generally, any time period to which the operation of some behavioral process is limited.

CS: conditioned stimulus. See CONDITIONED REFLEX.

Cue-dependent learning: see STATE-DEPENDENT LEARNING.

Cumulative record: a record in which total responses are plotted as a function of time, usually made by a marker or pen that moves a fixed distance with each response across a paper advancing at a constant speed. Thus, the faster the responding, the steeper the slope of the record. Moment-to-moment changes in slope show the details of changing response rates over time. Cumulative recorders typically include additional features; for example, the pen can be reset to its starting position (sometimes called the *baseline*) after a full excursion across the paper or after some event; it can be briefly displaced downward or to one side, producing a *pip*, to indicate a reinforcer or other brief event; it can be held in its downward position, producing a displaced line, to indicate stimuli or other extended conditions; and an event pen at the bottom of the record can be used to indicate when other events occur. Cf. RATE OF RESPONDING.

CVC trigram: in verbal learning procedures, an item made up of a consonant, a vowel and a consonant (often a nonsense syllable).

D

Data; datum: any recorded information, usually in numerical form. *Data* is plural; *datum* is singular.

Declarative memory: see REMEMBERING.

Decoding: the learner's behavior with respect to the item to be remembered at the time it is recalled. Cf. ENCODING.

Deep structure: the common structural features of sentences that are related to each other by grammatical transformations. Cf. SURFACE STRUCTURE.

Defensive conditioning: respondent conditioning in which the US is an aversive or noxious stimulus.

Deictic verbal behavior, deixis: verbal behavior in which the function of the terms is based on their relation to the speaker (e.g., personal pronouns, *here* vs. *there*; *this* vs. *that*). In its dependence on discriminations of the speaker's own behavior, deixis shares some properties with autoclitic behavior.

Delay conditioning: respondent conditioning in which the CS is presented for some fixed, extended time period (in most usages, no less than 5 seconds) before the US is presented.

Delay of reinforcement: the time from a response to a later reinforcer. Reinforcers usually lose effectiveness as delay increases, but properties of delay procedures complicate the determination of the delay-of-reinforcement function. In delay procedures that interpose a stimulus between the response and its delayed reinforcer (*signaled delay of reinforcement*), the stimulus probably functions as an immediate conditioned reinforcer. In procedures that interpose no stimulus, either the delay is extended by additional responses, thereby limiting response rate because a reinforcer is delivered only after a pause equal to the delay interval, or the delay is unaffected by additional responses, thereby allowing the delay to be effectively reduced to the shorter time between those responses and the reinforcer at the end of the delay.

Delayed matching-to-sample: see MATCHING-TO-SAMPLE and DELAYED RESPONSE.

Delayed response: a discriminative response that occurs some time after the removal of a discriminative stimulus, as when the sample in a matching-to-sample procedure is turned off several seconds before the comparison stimuli are presented (see MEDIATING BEHAVIOR for an example). Cf. REMEMBERING.

Deletion: see AVOIDANCE.

Density: a synonym for rate, as in reinforcement density or shock density. Cf. RATE OF REINFORCEMENT.

Dependency: roughly, a contingency completely specified by the experimenter or with a conditional probability very close to 1.0. Cf. CONTINGENCY.

Deprivation: an establishing operation, the reduction in the availability of a reinforcer, that increases the effectiveness of the reinforcer. With food reinforcers, two criteria for deprivation levels have been a fixed percentage of free-feeding body weight or a fixed period of deprivation after free feeding. Deprivation, also effective for such other reinforcers as a rat's

opportunity to run in a running wheel, may be a condition for making any positive reinforcer effective.

Descriptive autoclitic: see AUTOCLITIC.

Development of language: see LANGUAGE DEVELOPMENT.

Dictation-taking: A formal verbal class in which a vocal verbal stimulus occasions a corresponding written response. The correspondence is defined by the one-to-one relation of verbal units (e.g., letters or words). Cf. ECHOIC BEHAVIOR, TEXTUAL BEHAVIOR, TRANSCRIPTION.

Differential conditioning: usually, producing a discrimination in respondent conditioning. See RESPONDENT DISCRIMINATION.

Differential reinforcement: reinforcement of some responses but not others, depending on the intensive, temporal, topographical, or other properties of the responses (including the stimuli in the presence of which they are emitted; cf. DISCRIMINATED OPERANT); differential reinforcement defines operant classes (cf. OPERANT). When responding has come under the control of differential reinforcement, so that the proportion of responses falling within the limits of the operant class increases, responding is said to be *differentiated*. Cf. INDUCTION.

Differential-reinforcement schedules: schedules of differential reinforcement, especially when reinforcers depend on the temporal spacing of responses. Contingencies can be based on preceding interresponse times (IRTs), response rates during a preceding time, or periods of no responding either preceded by a response or without a required preceding response. They are usually arranged for free-operant responding, but also can be arranged within discrete trials.

In *differential-reinforcement-of-long-interresponse-times, differential-reinforcement-of-low-rate* (DRL) or *IRT > t* schedules, a response is reinforced only if at least *t* seconds has elapsed since the last response. An alternative and less common method, based on rates rather than IRTs, reinforces a response only if fewer than *n* responses were emitted during the last *t* seconds.

In *differential-reinforcement-of-high-rate* (DRH) or *IRT < t* schedules, a response is reinforced if at least *n* responses were emitted during the last *t* seconds. In this case, the alternative based on IRTs rather than rates is less common because reinforcing single short IRTs tends to produce short IRTs separated by frequent pauses rather than sustained high rates of responding.

A *paced-response* or *differential-reinforcement-of-pacing (DRP)* schedule arranges upper and lower limits on reinforced IRTs (e.g., an IRT between 5 and 10 seconds) or reinforced response rates (e.g., between 10 and 15 responses during the last 5 seconds). When the schedule is based on IRTs rather than rates, it is sometimes called *DRL with limited hold.*

Another type arranges delayed reinforcement after responses: A reinforcer is delivered if a response occurs and is followed by *t* seconds of no responding (see DELAY OF REINFORCEMENT). Still another does not require a response: A reinforcer is delivered after *t* seconds of no responding; this schedule has been called *differential reinforcement of zero behavior* or *other behavior (DRO)*. See also INTERRESPONSE TIME, RATE OF RESPONDING.

Differentiation: see DIFFERENTIAL REINFORCEMENT.

Discrete trials: see TRIAL.

Discriminated operant: an operant defined in terms of the stimuli during which it occurs as well as its environmental effect. This operant depends on the relations among three events (sometimes called the *three-term contingency*): a *stimulus* in the presence of which a *response* may be followed by *consequences*. In one sense, the stimulus sets the occasion on which the response may be reinforced; in another, it defines a property of the operant class and so sets the occasion for the response. In either sense, the joint dependence of the response on both stimulus and reinforcer distinguishes the relation from that of a reflex. See also OPERANT.

Discrimination: any difference in responding in the presence of different stimuli; in a more restricted usage, a difference resulting from differential consequences of responding in the presence of different stimuli. See also DISCRIMINATED OPERANT, GENERALIZATION, RESPONDENT DISCRIMINATION, SIMULTANEOUS DISCRIMINATION, STIMULUS, SUCCESSIVE DISCRIMINATION, VERBAL DISCRIMINATION. Usually the organism is said to discriminate among relevant stimuli. In some cases, however, it is useful to speak of responses as discriminating (e.g., if response rate varies with color whereas response location varies with form, rate discrim-

inates color while location discriminates form). Further, when discriminated responding is produced by differential contingencies in the presence of different stimuli, it is appropriate to say that the stimuli are discriminated but not that the contingencies are discriminated.

Discriminative stimulus: any stimulus with a discriminative function; according to an older usage, a stimulus correlated with reinforcement when another is correlated with extinction. The latter usage has become less common because it cannot easily be applied to stimuli correlated with different reinforcement schedules (e.g., multiple FI FR); it was the source of S^D ("S-dee": discriminative stimulus) and S^Δ ("S-delta": absence of discriminative stimulus) as abbreviations for the stimuli in a reinforcement-extinction discrimination. These abbreviations have lost ground to S^+ (positive stimulus) and $S-$ (negative stimulus). Strictly, S^0 ("S-zero") is more appropriate for the absence of reinforcement but $S-$ is typographically more convenient.

Displacement activity: an ethological term referring to a response (see FIXED ACTION PATTERN) occurring not in the presence of the stimulus that usually produces it (see RELEASER), but rather in the presence of one that usually produces some other response (cf. VACUUM ACTIVITY). Displacement activity and vacuum activity depend on deprivation of opportunities to complete the fixed action pattern, but displacement activity is likely to occur at lower levels of deprivation than vacuum activity.

Distributed practice: spacing periods of activity on a task. Cf. MASSED PRACTICE.

Distribution: a classification of events according to location along a continuum. For example, an IRT distribution classifies IRTs into several temporal categories (e.g., less than 1 second, 1 but less than 2 seconds, 2 but less than 3 seconds, and 3 or more seconds). *Frequency distributions* show the number of events per category; *relative frequency distributions* show the events per category as a proportion of the total. Each category is called a *class interval*, and class intervals are ordinarily of equal size. Distributions often include a category for all events falling beyond some point on the continuum (e.g., in the above example, 3 or more seconds) so that a category exists for any event no matter how extreme its value. Cf. INTERRESPONSE TIME, STATISTICS.

DMTS: delayed matching-to-sample. See DE-LAYED RESPONSE and MATCHING-TO-SAMPLE.

DRH: differential reinforcement of high rate. See DIFFERENTIAL-REINFORCEMENT SCHEDULES.

Drive operation: see ESTABLISHING OPERATION.

DRL: differential reinforcement of long inter-response times or low rate. See DIFFEREN-TIAL-REINFORCEMENT SCHEDULES.

DRO: differential reinforcement of zero behavior or other behavior. See DIFFERENTIAL-RE-INFORCEMENT SCHEDULES.

DRP: differential reinforcement of paced responding, or pacing. See DIFFERENTIAL-RE-INFORCEMENT SCHEDULES.

Duration of response: the time from the beginning to the end of a response (sometimes called *holding time*). Analyses of this property of responding depend heavily on procedural details. For example, if a reinforcer is delivered when a lever is pressed, response duration is short because the reinforcer occasions quick release, but if it is delivered upon lever release, then each member of the chain (press, hold, release) may be differently affected by the contingencies.

Duration of stimulus: see TEMPORAL DISCRIMINATION.

E

Echoic behavior: A formal verbal class in which a vocal verbal stimulus occasions a corresponding vocal verbal response. The correspondence is defined by the one-to-one relation of verbal units (e.g., phonemes or words), and not by acoustic similarity. Cf. DICTATION-TAKING, TEXTUAL BEHAVIOR, TRANSCRIPTION.

Echoic memory: see REMEMBERING.

Eidetic memory: sometimes called photographic memory, a rare type of remembering, usually in children, in which visual stimuli are described in detail, as if seen, long after they were presented.

Effect, Law of: see LAW OF EFFECT.

Elaborative rehearsal: see REHEARSAL.

Elicitation: the reliable production of a response by a stimulus in unconditioned or conditioned reflexes. Cf. RESPONDENT BEHAVIOR.

Emergent relation: conditional stimulus control that emerges as a by-product of other stimulus-control relations rather than through differential reinforcement. For example, if arbitrary matching has been arranged for pairs *AB* and *BC* (where the first letter of each pair corresponds to the sample and the second to the matching comparison) and testing shows that the transitive relation *AC* now also exists, then this relation is said to be emergent. Cf. EQUIV-ALENCE CLASS.

Emission: the occurrence of operant behavior. A response that occurs without an eliciting stimulus is said to be *emitted*. The term applies to responding occasioned by a discriminative stimulus as well as to undiscriminated responding. Cf. OPERANT BEHAVIOR.

Emotional behavior: correlated changes in a range of response classes (e.g., if a preaversive stimulus simultaneously alters heart rate, respiration, blood pressure, defecation, and operant behavior maintained by reinforcement, it may be said to produce emotional behavior). This and related terms evolved from an imprecise colloquial vocabulary, so types of emotional behavior cannot be defined unambiguously in terms of the response classes involved. They can be defined more consistently in terms of the operations that produce them (e.g., *fear, anxiety,* or, with another organism present, *anger,* produced by primary or conditioned aversive stimuli; *relief,* produced by the termination of aversive stimuli; *joy* or *hope,* produced by primary or conditioned reinforcers; and *sorrow,* produced by the termination of reinforcers). Different observers often disagree on defining characteristics of the various cases (e.g., stimulus magnitudes, the direction of change in different responses, etc.), so the terms have not acquired technical usages within the analysis of behavior. Cf. AGGRESSION, FRUSTRATION, PREAVERSIVE STIMULUS.

Encoding: the learner's behavior with respect to the item to be remembered at the time it is presented. Cf. DECODING, REHEARSAL.

Episodic memory: Autobiographical memory. See REMEMBERING.

Equivalence class: a stimulus class (usually produced through conditional discrimination in matching-to-sample) that includes all possible emergent relations among its members. The properties of an equivalence class are derived from the logical relations of reflexivity, symmetry, and transitivity. *Reflexivity* refers to the matching of a sample to itself, sometimes called identity matching (*AA, BB, CC;* in these examples, each letter pair represents a sample and its matching comparison stimulus). *Symmetry* refers to the reversibility of a relation (if *AB,* then *BA*). *Transitivity* refers to the transfer of the relation to new combinations through shared membership (if *AB* and *BC,* then *AC*). If these properties are characteristics of a matching-to-sample performance, then training *AB* and *BC* may produce *AC, BA, CA,* and *CB* as *emergent* relations (reflexivity provides the three other possible relations, *AA, BB,* and *CC*). Given *AB* and *BC,* for example, the combination of symmetry and transitivity implies the *CA* relation. The emergence of all possible stimulus relations after only *AB* and *BC* are trained through contingencies is the criterion for calling the three stimuli members of an equivalence class. The class can be extended by training new stimulus relations (e.g., if *CD* is learned, then *AD, DA, BD, DB,* and *DC* may be created as emergent relations). Stimuli that are members of an equivalence class are likely also to be *functionally equivalent.* It remains to be seen whether the logical properties of these classes are fully consistent with their behavioral ones. Cf. EQUIVALENCE RELATION.

Equivalence relation: a term with various usages, including functional equivalence (the relation between stimuli that have become members of a *functional class*) as well as the mathematical relations that define an *equivalence class* (especially the *CA* relation). The terminology of equivalence relations has often been interchanged with that of equivalences classes, but the class and relation terminologies should be distinguished because functionally equivalent stimuli are not necessarily members of an equivalence class. Cf. EQUIVALENCE CLASS.

Error: in a simultaneous discrimination, a response to a stimulus not correlated with reinforcement; in a successive discrimination, a response in the presence of a stimulus correlated with extinction. Because of its colloquial origins, the term often assumes an evaluative as well as a descriptive function. Cf. CORRECTION PROCEDURE.

Escape: the termination of an aversive stimulus by a response. A reduction in the magnitude of an aversive stimulus by a response is sometimes called partial or fractional escape. Cf. REINFORCEMENT.

Establishing operation: any operation that changes the status of a stimulus as a reinforcer or punisher: deprivation, satiation, procedures that establish formerly neutral stimuli as conditioned reinforcers or as conditioned aversive stimuli, and stimulus presentations that change the reinforcing or punishing status of other stimuli (e.g., as when an already available screwdriver becomes a reinforcer in the presence of a screw that needs tightening). Establishing operations are sometimes said to produce motivational or drive states within the organism.

Estes-Skinner procedure: see PREAVERSIVE STIMULUS.

Ethology: an area of biology concerned with the analysis of the behavior patterns that evolve in natural habitats, either in species or in individual organisms, with particular emphasis on those patterns that do not depend on, or are not known to depend on, prior operant selection or respondent conditioning. Cf. FIXED ACTION PATTERN, SPECIES-SPECIFIC BEHAVIOR, RELEASER.

Event recorder: a device that produces one or more time lines along which the timing of events is recorded (e.g., by displacement of a marker or pen that draws a line at a constant rate).

Evocation: the production of a response. A response is sometimes said to be *evoked* if it is unclear whether it is emitted or elicited.

Exercise, Law of: see LAW OF EXERCISE.

Excitation: roughly, the production of behavior or the variables that produce it, used especially in contrast with *inhibition.*

Expectancy: a colloquial term referring to behavior that precedes a predictable event. Expectancy depends on a history with respect to that event (it cannot depend on an event that has not yet occurred).

Exteroceptive stimulus: any stimulus presented at or outside of the organism's skin. Cf. INTEROCEPTIVE STIMULUS.

Extinction: in operant behavior, discontinuing the reinforcement of a response (or the reduction in responding that follows this operation). In negative reinforcement (escape and avoidance), extinction has often referred to the discontinuation of aversive stimuli, although the term applies more appropriately to discontinuing the consequences of responding: Aversive stimuli are presented but responses no longer prevent them. The discontinuation of punishment (see RECOVERY) is rarely referred to as a variety of extinction. In respondent conditioning, extinction is presenting the CS without, or no longer in a contingent relation to, the US (or the diminution in conditioned responding that follows this operation).

Extinction gradient: a gradient obtained after extinction, when the extinction stimulus is represented on the continuum along which the gradient is determined. In one type, responding is first reinforced during several stimuli along the continuum and is then extinguished during only one of them. In another, reinforcement is correlated with stimulus 1 and extinction with stimulus 2, but only stimulus 2 is represented on the continuum along which the gradient is determined (e.g., stimulus 1 is a form and stimulus 2 is a color, and the gradient is determined along the wavelength continuum). Cf. INHIBITORY GRADIENT.

Extrinsic reinforcer: a reinforcer that has an arbitrary relation to the responses that produce it (as when a musician plays for money rather than because the playing produces music). The term has also been applied to stimuli presumed to function as reinforcers because their function has been instructed (as when children are told that it is important to earn good grades); despite their label, such stimuli are often ineffective as reinforcers. Cf. INTRINSIC REINFORCER, CONDITIONED REINFORCER.

F

Facilitation: an occasional synonym for *potentiation.*

Fading: a procedure for transferring control of responding from one stimulus or set of stimuli to another by gradually removing one while the other is gradually introduced. Stimuli may be faded in or out (e.g., once a pigeon discriminates key colors, the discrimination may be transferred to line orientation by maintaining differential reinforcement while gradually decreasing color intensity and increasing line intensity). Cf. SHAPING.

Feature-positive stimulus: in a successive discrimination between one stimulus correlated with reinforcement and another correlated with extinction, a stimulus property present only during reinforcement components (e.g., as when, in discrete trials with pigeons, a star appears on a green key during reinforcement trials but the green key appears alone during extinction trials). Stimulus control is more eas-

ily produced when such stimuli are correlated with reinforcement (*feature positive*) than when they are correlated with extinction (*feature negative*). Cf. SIGN-TRACKING.

Feedback: roughly, a stimulus or stimulus property correlated with or produced by the organism's own behavior. The stimulus may in turn change the behavior, which again changes the stimulus, and so on. The mathematical relation between the behavior and the stimulus is called a *feedback function.*

FI: fixed interval. See INTERVAL SCHEDULE.

Fixed action pattern: an ethological term for a sequence of responses, usually but not necessarily produced by a releaser, the consistent patterning of which cannot be attributed to the operation of an operant chain. When the stimuli that elicit or set the occasion for a fixed action pattern are absent, their presentation, and thereby an opportunity to engage in the fixed action pattern, may serve as a reinforcer. Cf. RELEASER, DISPLACEMENT ACTIVITY, VACUUM ACTIVITY.

Fixed consecutive number (FCN): a two-operandum trial procedure in which trials are initiated by responses on one operandum and are terminated by a changeover to the other, and in which the changeover is reinforced if at least n responses preceded it (e.g., reinforcing a pigeon's left key-peck only if at least 10 right key-pecks preceded the changeover to the left key).

Fixed-interval schedule: see INTERVAL SCHEDULE.

Fixed-ratio schedule: see RATIO SCHEDULE.

Fixed-time schedule: see TIME SCHEDULE.

Fixity, functional: see FUNCTIONAL FIXITY.

Flashbulb memory: the detailed remembering of the context of a surprising and significant event in one's life (e.g., where one was on hearing the news of a major political assassination).

Foraging: searching for food. Foraging in natural habitats has been treated as a chain that includes search, prey identification, capture of prey, and handling and/or consumption of prey, with concurrent or concurrent-chain performances treated as analogous to parts of this chain (e.g., the foraging patterns according to which organisms switch from partially depleted patches of food to fresh ones can be characterized in terms of strategies examined within concurrent performances, such as *matching, momentary maximizing,* and *optimizing*).

Forced choice: see FREE CHOICE.

Formal verbal classes: see DICTATION-TAK-ING, ECHOIC BEHAVIOR, TEXTUAL BE-HAVIOR, TRANSCRIPTION.

FR: fixed ratio. See RATIO SCHEDULE.

Fractional escape: see ESCAPE.

Free choice: the availability of two or more concurrent operants even if one is consistently chosen over the other. The term is best re-stricted to cases in which each class is main-tained by reinforcement, but it has been extended to response classes correlated with extinction. With only one operant available, the choice is said to be *forced* (as when one of the two arms in a T-maze is blocked).

Free-feeding weight: the stable weight main-tained by a mature organism with unlimited access to food and water. A percentage of this weight (e.g., 80 percent) may serve as a criterion for a level of deprivation.

Free operant: see OPERANT.

Free recall: a verbal learning procedure in which the learner recalls the items of a list, usually after a single presentation, without re-gard to the original order of the items.

Frequency of reinforcement: total reinforcers, over a fixed time, over a session of variable duration, over a fixed number of responses or, in a trial procedure, over a fixed number of trials. With respect to reinforcement, frequency is most commonly a synonym of rate; the usage for responding is more likely to be variable. Cf. FREQUENCY OF RESPONDING, RATE OF REINFORCEMENT.

Frequency of responding: total responses, over a fixed time, over a session of variable duration or, in a trial procedure, over a fixed number of trials. Cf. FREQUENCY OF REINFORCE-MENT, RATE OF RESPONDING.

Frustration: any operation that reduces an organism's opportunities to emit highly proba-ble responses (or the consequences of such operations, especially emotional behavior, ag-gression, or escape from correlated stimuli). The term is most commonly applied to extinc-tion, which, with food reinforcers, eliminates an organism's opportunity to eat. Thus, in re-ferring to the behavioral consequences of an operation, the term is a label for some side effects of extinction.

FT: fixed time. See TIME SCHEDULE.

Functional analysis: an analysis in terms of behavioral functions (i.e., what effects re-sponses have); alternatively, an analysis in terms of functional relations, (e.g., the produc-tion of pupillary constriction by light might be discussed as a pupillary reflex, but a functional analysis deals with the phenomenon as a tran-sition from one point to another on a continu-ous mathematical function relating pupillary diameter to light intensity).

Functional class: a class the members of which have common behavioral functions, either pro-duced by similar histories or acquired through emergent relations. If two stimuli are members of a functional class, then the behavior occa-sioned by one will also be occasioned by the other; such stimuli are sometimes said to be *functionally equivalent*. Cf. EQUIVALENCE CLASS; see also EQUIVALENCE RELATION, OPERANT, STIMULUS.

Functional fixity: problem-solving behavior in which the common function of a tool, object, or material makes it less likely that the solver will use it effectively in a novel way.

Functional relation: a mathematical function appealed to by a functional analysis. Cf. FUNC-TIONAL ANALYSIS.

Functional stimulus: the properties of a stimu-lus that control behavior, as opposed to the properties of the *nominal stimulus* (e.g., for a pigeon attending to the color but not the form of a green circle, the functional stimulus is sim-ply green even though the nominal stimulus is a green circle). Cf. CRITICAL FEATURE.

Fuzzy set: see PROBABILISTIC STIMULUS CLASS.

G

Generalization: the spread of the effects of re-inforcement (or other operations such as extinc-tion or punishment) during one stimulus to other stimuli differing from the original along one or more dimensions. To the extent that responding is similar during two different stimuli, the organism is said to *generalize* be-tween them (the stimuli are said to be *general-ized*). If responding is identical during different stimuli, generalization between them is said to be complete (this outcome may also be de-scribed as the absence of discrimination or as the organism's failure to attend to the dimen-sion or dimensions along which they differ). Cf.

ATTENTION, DISCRIMINATION, INDUCTION, STIMULUS.

Generalization gradient: a gradient obtained after reinforcement correlated with a single stimulus (occasionally, in studies of the summation of gradients, two or more stimuli), when no discrimination has been trained between this and other stimuli on the continuum along which the gradient is determined.

Generalized imitation: see HIGHER-ORDER CLASS OF BEHAVIOR.

Generalized reinforcer: a conditioned reinforcer based on several primary reinforcers. Its effectiveness depends less on the establishing operations appropriate to any single primary reinforcer than does that of conditioned reinforcers based on only a single primary reinforcer. Money is often offered as an example of a generalized reinforcer of human behavior.

Goal gradient: systematic changes in responding that occur with changes in an organism's physical or temporal separation from a reinforcer (e.g., changes in running speed as a rat approaches the goalbox of a maze).

Go—no go discrimination: usually, a discrete-trials successive discrimination with reinforcement in the presence of one stimulus (*go*) and extinction in presence of the other (*no go*).

Gradient: a measure of responding in the presence of different stimuli as a function of their location along a continuum (cf. STIMULUS). Gradients are ordinarily determined by presenting the stimuli successively but in irregular order during extinction. The slope or steepness of a gradient is determined by how much change in responding occurs from one point on the continuum to another; the larger the change, the steeper the gradient. The case in which responding does not change is usually called a *flat* gradient, although it may also be called the absence of a gradient. See specific cases: EXTINCTION GRADIENT, GENERALIZATION GRADIENT, INHIBITORY GRADIENT, POST-DISCRIMINATION GRADIENT.

Grain: a reinforcer effective with food-deprived pigeons; also a characteristic of cumulative records (see RATE OF RESPONDING).

Grammars: descriptions of the structural or syntactic properties of verbal behavior. *Sequential* grammars appeal only to the discriminative effects of prior verbal stimuli (cf. INTRAVERBAL); they are inadequate for dealing with the most important structural features of verbal behavior and are largely obsolete. *Phrase-structure* grammars describe structures in terms of the relations among sentence *constituents* (e.g., noun phrases and verb phrases), whereas *transformational* grammars describe them in terms of relations among different sentences (e.g., active and passive voice); these two types of grammars, one intrasentence and the other intersentence, are complementary. (Other types of grammars, such as case grammars, explicitly appeal to semantic features in defining structural relations.)

H

Habituation: a reduction, over repeated presentations, in the respondent behavior elicited by a stimulus. Cf. ADAPTATION, POTENTIATION.

Helplessness, learned: see LEARNED HELPLESSNESS.

Hierarchy, of behavior or responses: a ranking of response classes on the basis of their relative probabilities. A more probable class is said to be higher in the response hierarchy.

Higher-order class of behavior: a class that includes within it other classes that can themselves function as operant classes, as when generalized imitation includes all the component imitations that could be separately reinforced. Higher-order classes may be a source of novel behavior (e.g., as in the generalized imitation of behavior that the imitator had not seen before). They also have the property that contingencies may operate differently on the higher-order class than on the classes that are its components. For example, if all instances are reinforced except imitations within one component class (e.g., jumping whenever the model jumps), that class may change with the higher-order class rather than with the contingencies arranged for it (i.e., imitations of jumping may not extinguish, even though no longer reinforced). Control by the contingencies arranged for the higher-order class rather than for component classes defines these classes; the component classes are sometimes said to be *insensitive* to the contingencies arranged for them. A higher-order class is sometimes called a *generalized* class, in that contingencies arranged for some component classes within it generalize to all the others. Generalized matching and rule-governed behavior are examples of higher-order classes.

Higher-order conditioning: respondent conditioning in which the stimulus that functions as the US in producing one conditioned reflex is itself the CS of another.

Higher-order schedule: a schedule that reinforces a complex operant consisting of completion of a schedule requirement (e.g., with FR 10 reinforced according to an FI schedule, every tenth response that occurs at least 50 seconds after the last reinforcer is reinforced; in this example, FR 10 is the first-order schedule and FI 50-s the second-order schedule). Such schedules often include a stimulus presented upon each completion of the first-order schedule, (e.g., adding a brief flash of light after every tenth response to the above example). The notation for such schedules includes the first-order schedule and the stimulus it produces in parentheses: FI 50-s (FR 10: stimulus). A *percentage-reinforcement* schedule is a higher-order schedule in which the second-order schedule is a VR.

History: conditions that an organism has been exposed to and its performances under them; often an abbreviation for *experimental history*, simply because experimental organisms are rarely observed continuously throughout their lives. History is particularly important when some conditions have irreversible or only slowly reversible effects.

Houselight: see CHAMBER.

I

Iconic memory: see REMEMBERING.

Identity matching: see MATCHING-TO-SAMPLE.

Imitation: behavior that duplicates some properties of the behavior of a model. Imitation need not involve the matching of stimulus features (e.g., when one child imitates the raised hand of another, the felt position of the child's own limb has different stimulus dimensions than the seen position of the other child's). Cf. HIGHER-ORDER CLASS OF BEHAVIOR.

Immediate memory: usually, short-term memory. See REMEMBERING.

Implicit learning: in human learning, contingency-shaped learning (as when one learns to speak grammatically even though one cannot state the grammatical rules).

Implicit memory: remembering demonstrated by the effect of an item on other behavior rather than by its recall (as when a priming stimulus enhances a learner's later recognition of a se-

mantically related word even though the learner cannot report what the priming stimulus was).

Imprinted stimulus: a stimulus that, by virtue of its presentation during some period in the lifetime of an organism, has become effective as a reinforcer. Imprinting is noted primarily in some bird species (e.g., ducks) and occurs within a few days of hatching.

Impulsiveness or **impulsivity:** see SELF-CONTROL.

Incentive: discriminative effects of reinforcing stimuli (as when the smell of food makes responses reinforced by food more likely); occasionally, a stimulus that changes the reinforcing or punishing status of other stimuli (see ESTABLISHING OPERATION).

Incidental chaining or **incidental reinforcement:** see SUPERSTITION.

Incidental learning: in human learning, learning that occurs in the absence of instructions or consequences, and usually contrasted with *intentional learning*.

Induction: the spread of the effects of reinforcement to responses outside the limits of an operant class (sometimes also called *response generalization*). This phenomenon is essential to shaping because through it responses more closely approximating some final form may be emitted and therefore reinforced (e.g., reinforcement of a 10-N key-peck may be followed by the first instance of a 15-N peck; cf. SHAPING). With discriminated operants, induction may refer to the spread of the effects of reinforcement to stimuli other than those defining the operant class (as when, after extinction during green and red, reinstating reinforcement during green produces both responding during green and a transient increase in responding during red; cf. GENERALIZATION).

Information: strictly, the reduction in uncertainly provided by a stimulus, usually quantified in *bits*, the number of binary decisions needed to specify the stimulus. One bit specifies 2 alternatives, two bits 4, three bits 8, and so on in increasing powers of 2. The term is often used in a colloquial rather than a technical sense (as in common applications of the phrase *information processing*).

Informative stimulus: a predictive stimulus; a discriminative stimulus, though not necessarily a conditioned reinforcer (e.g., a stimulus correlated with differential punishment that is superimposed on ongoing reinforced behavior is informative, but its onset does not ordinarily reinforce observing responses).

Inhibition: a process inferred from a response decrement. The term, extended to behavior by analogy to usage in physiology, is appropriate only when it can be demonstrated that the decrement is produced by an increment in something else (e.g., if reinforcing one response reduces the rate of another, the reinforcement may be said to inhibit the second response). The term is sometimes extended to accounts of the process of extinction, in part because extinction may be accompanied by increments in other responding (e.g., behavior characterized as emotional). Such accounts are often unsupported by demonstrations that the increments produce the extinction decrement rather than simply accompany it, and when they do not distinguish between conditions that reduce responding and those that fail to maintain it they may be misleading. See also PROACTION, RETROACTION.

Inhibitory gradient: an extinction gradient in which responding increases along the stimulus continuum as the distance from a stimulus previously correlated with extinction increases. This is taken to indicate that the extinction stimulus controls a low or zero rate of responding rather than fails to maintain responding. Cf. EXTINCTION GRADIENT, INHIBITION.

Inhomogeneous data: data derived from more than one type of performance and that, when summarized statistically, misrepresent the performances from which they were derived (as when an avoidance schedule produces both a moderate response rate and bursts of high-rate responding after shock, so that the average rate does not represent either contribution to overall rate).

Initial links: see CONCURRENT CHAIN SCHEDULES.

Innate behavior: see SPECIES-SPECIFIC BEHAVIOR.

Insensitivity to contingencies: see HIGHER-ORDER CLASS OF BEHAVIOR.

Insight: the sudden solution of a problem, especially in contrast to gradual "trial-and-error" learning. This now nontechnical term is mainly of historical interest.

Instinctive behavior: see SPECIES-SPECIFIC BEHAVIOR.

Instructional stimulus, instruction: typically, in nonverbal settings, a conditional discrimina-

tive stimulus (though a simple discriminative stimulus is sometimes also said to have instructional functions); in some usages, a rule (cf. RULE- GOVERNED BEHAVIOR).

Instrumental behavior: see OPERANT BEHAVIOR.

Intentional learning: the opposite of *incidental learning.*

Interdependent schedules: schedules in which the operation of one depends on some property of the other (e.g., in one version of interdependent concurrent VI VI schedules, each VI arranges setups only during runs of responding on the other).

Interdimensional: between or across dimensions.

Interference: see PROACTION, RETROACTION; cf. INHIBITION.

Interim behavior: varying responding that occurs, usually early or midway rather than late within interstimulus intervals, in superstition procedures or temporal conditioning. Cf. SUPERSTITION, TERMINAL BEHAVIOR.

Interlocking schedule: a schedule in which time, number, and/or IRT requirements vary together according to some function (e.g., in one schedule with interlocking intervals and ratios, the number of responses that will produce a reinforcer decreases linearly as time passes since the last reinforcer).

Intermittent reinforcement: reinforcing some but not all responses or, in other words, reinforcing according to any schedule except continuous reinforcement or extinction. See specific schedules.

Interoceptive stimulus: a stimulus inside the organism. The stimulus may be presented from outside, as when an experimenter passes electric current through an area of the brain, or it may be produced by the organism itself, as when responses produce proprioceptive stimulation on the basis of which the organism may discriminate among different movements. With self-produced stimulation, however, the stimuli and their discriminative functions are usually inferred rather than demonstrated.

Interpretation: see CONTROL.

Interresponse time (IRT): the time between two responses or, more strictly, from the beginning of one response to the beginning of the next. The time from a reinforcer to the next response is a latency and not an IRT, even if the reinforcer is response-produced. Reinforcing a response that ends an IRT is said to reinforce that IRT. An *IRT distribution* summarizes the temporal spacing of the responses making up a response rate (it does not show sequential patterning). In assessing probabilities of different classes of IRTs, calculating proportions of IRTs falling into an IRT class may be misleading because short IRTs reduce the organism's opportunity to emit responses at the end of longer ones. For this reason, conditional probabilities, *IRTs per opportunity (IRTs/Op)*, are often calculated: the probability of IRTs in a class interval, given that enough time had elapsed since the last response to permit an IRT to end in that class interval. For example, if 80 of 100 IRTs were less than 1 second, 10 were 1 but less than 2 seconds, and the remaining 10 were 2 or more seconds, then the organism had only 20 opportunities to complete the 10 IRTs of 1 but less than 2 seconds and the conditional probability for this class interval was 0.5 (10/20). Cf. CONDITIONAL PROBABILITY, RATE OF RESPONDING, DIFFERENTIAL-REINFORCEMENT SCHEDULES.

Intertrial interval (ITI): see TRIAL.

Interval schedule: a schedule in which some minimum time must elapse before a response is reinforced; early responses have no effect. The time is measured from some event, typically a stimulus onset or the last reinforcer (an alternate method times each interval from the end of the last one, without regard to the time from the end of the interval to the reinforced response). In *fixed-interval (FI)* schedules, the time is constant from one interval to the next, and performance is characterized by a pause after the reinforcer followed by a gradual or an abrupt transition to a moderate rate of responding. In *variable-interval (VI)* schedules, the time varies from one reinforcer to the next; compared with FI schedules, the rate of responding is relatively constant between reinforcers. Interval schedules are usually identified by average interval (e.g., FI 60-s and VI 60-s arrange one reinforcer per minute).

Historically, VI schedules used intervals selected in irregular order from a set of intervals, often described by a mathematical progression (e.g., arithmetic, geometric). Current practice favors schedules with a constant reinforcement probability over time within the interval (with probability measured by *reinforcers per opportunity* or *Rf/Op:* probability that a response will be reinforced at a given time in an interval,

given that the organism has reached that time). Such conditions are met by a type of VI schedule called *random interval (RI)*, which arranges a setup (makes the next response eligible to produce a reinforcer) with a fixed probability every *t* seconds. In RI schedules, the average interval equals *t* divided by the probability (e.g., arranging a setup once per second with a probability of 0.02 produces RI 50-s). In one version, the schedule stops operating after a setup until the scheduled reinforcer is produced, so that low response rates make the obtained reinforcement rate lower than what had been scheduled; in another, the schedule continues to operate and successive setups accumulate, so that obtained and scheduled reinforcement rates remain about equal even with low response rates.

Intradimensional: within a dimension.

Intraverbal: a verbal response occasioned by a verbal stimulus, where the relation between stimulus and response is an arbitrary one established by the verbal community. Intraverbal behavior is chaining as it occurs in verbal behavior; an example is reciting the alphabet. Either the speaker or someone else may provide the verbal stimulus (thus, intraverbals do not require discrimination of one's own behavior; they are not autoclitic).

Intrinsic reinforcer: a reinforcer that is naturally related to the responses that produce it (as when a musician plays not for money but because the playing produces music). Cf. EXTRINSIC REINFORCER.

IRT: see INTERRESPONSE TIME.

ITI: intertrial interval. See TRIAL.

J

Jumping stand: an apparatus used to study discrimination, especially with rats. The rat is forced to jump from platform to one of two doors on which stimuli are displayed. One door is unlocked, and by jumping to it the rat gains access to a reinforcer located behind it; if the rat jumps to the other door, which is locked, it falls into a net below the doors.

K

Key: see OPERANDUM.

Kinesis (plural: **kineses**): undirected movement that depends on stimulus magnitude (as when the random movements of an insect larva increase with light and stop when it reaches the dark).

Kinesthetic stimulus: see PROPRIOCEPTIVE STIMULUS.

Knowledge of results: A kind of feedback, usually verbal, given during human performance in various tasks (e.g., verbal learning, motor skills).

KOR: see KNOWLEDGE OF RESULTS.

L

Language: the features of the verbal behavior shared by the members of a verbal community, including their vocabulary and grammar. Cf. LINGUISTICS.

Language development: the emergence of language in the individual. Much of the controversy about language development revolves around assumptions about the respective phylogenic and ontogenic contributions to it.

Language relativity: the dependence of the behavior within a verbal community, both verbal and nonverbal, on the verbal discriminations incorporated within its language.

Language universals: the structural features common to all human languages, especially if they have phylogenic sources. If there are such features, what they are is controversial; furthermore, some may be spandrels.

Lashley jumping stand: see JUMPING STAND.

Latency: the time from an event, usually the onset of a stimulus, to a response.

Latent learning: see LEARNING.

Law of effect: Thorndike's classic statement of the principle of reinforcement and, in one version, punishment. Reinforcers and punishers were referred to as satisfying and annoying states of affairs that an organism tended respectively to maintain or renew and to put an end to or avoid. The *strong* law included both cases; the *weak* law deleted the effects of annoyers or punishers.

Law of exercise: the statement, in early accounts of learning, that repetition of a response contributes to its strength. The law has also been stated in terms of use and disuse. A more contemporary version states that the elicitation of a response may increase the likelihood of its emission.

Learned helplessness: a retardation in the acquisition of escape or avoidance responding

produced by a history in which responding during the relevant aversive stimuli has had no consequences.

Learning: roughly, acquisition, or the process by which behavior is added to an organism's repertoire; a relatively permanent change in behavior. The term has been used in so many different ways in both technical and colloquial vocabularies that it may be of limited usefulness. The decision about whether learning has occurred and what has been learned sometimes depends on what the experimenter looks at. Latent learning provides an example. A rat explores a maze, and the results of this exploration are assessed later when food reinforcers are available at the end of the rat's run through the maze. Latent learning is said to have occurred if the rat then negotiates the maze more rapidly and/or accurately than if it had not explored. The difficulty is that exploring the maze involves other contingencies (e.g., which turns lead where); these contingencies act on behavior but their effects are harder to get at than those involving the food reinforcers. Cf. ACQUISITION, PERFORMANCE.

Learning set or **learning-to-learn:** a case of transfer in which, on the basis of similar relations among stimuli in a sequence of discrimination problems, accuracy in later problems improves more rapidly over trials than in the earlier problems (perhaps to the point at which correct responses occur on the first presentations of a new problem). Cf. HIGHER-ORDER CLASS OF BEHAVIOR, TRANSFER.

Level of processing: the abstractness or richness of coding (e.g., encoding the number *2001* as a year or as the title of a film involves deeper levels of processing than encoding it as an arbitrary sequence of four digits).

Lever: see OPERANDUM.

LH: see LIMITED HOLD.

Limited hold (LH): termination of the availability of a reinforcer if the response to be reinforced does not occur soon enough (e.g., in FI 100-s with a 10-second limited hold, the first response between 100 and 110 seconds after the start of the interval is reinforced, but the interval ends without a reinforcer if no response occurs within that time).

Linguistics: the study of language, usually divided into the topics of *syntax* or grammatical structure, *semantics* or meaning, and *pragmatics* or the functions of language. *Psycholinguistics* is a branch of psychology concerned with demonstrating the psychological reality of linguistic categories and concepts. Cf. PSYCHOLOGICAL REALITY.

Link: a response in a chain or a component in a chained schedule.

Local rate: see RATE OF RESPONDING.

Long-term memory (LTM): see REMEMBERING.

LTM: long-term memory. See REMEMBERING.

M

Maintenance: continuation of the conditions that generated a performance. The analysis of maintained performance, as a subject matter, is different from but not incompatible with that of acquisition (e.g., many experiments concerned with effects of schedule parameters on performance do not really begin until acquisition has been completed). Cf. STEADY-STATE.

Maintenance rehearsal: see REHEARSAL.

Mand: a verbal response that specifies its reinforcer. In human verbal behavior, manding is usually a higher-order class, in the sense that a newly acquired tact can be incorporated into a novel mand (as when a child asks for a toy upon learning its name).

Manipulandum: see OPERANDUM.

Massed practice: uninterrupted activity on a task (as in cramming for an exam). In most tasks, massed practice is less effective than distributed practice.

Matching: in performances involving concurrent operants, distributing responses so that the relative response rate of each roughly matches its relative reinforcement rate. See MATCHING LAW and cf. MAXIMIZING, MELIORATION, OPTIMIZING.

Matching law: a quantitative formulation stating that the relative rates of different responses tend to equal the relative reinforcement rates they produce. The *generalized matching law* summarizes this relation in an equation in which relative response rate equals a constant multiplied by the relative reinforcement rate raised to a power. The constant takes into account units of measurement and includes *bias* (e.g., one response might call for a larger constant than another that is more effortful); the performance is described as *undermatching* when the exponent (the power to which the function is raised) is less than 1 and *overmatching* when it is greater than 1.

Matching-to-sample: a simultaneous conditional discrimination procedure, or the performance maintained by such a procedure. As it is typically arranged for pigeons, a *sample* stimulus is presented on the middle key of three keys. A peck on it turns on *comparison* stimuli on two side keys (see OBSERVING RESPONSE, SAMPLE-SPECIFIC BEHAVIOR). A peck on the matching side key is reinforced (perhaps according to some schedule); a peck on the other side key may produce a timeout or invoke a *correction procedure.* When the criterion for matching is physical correspondence (as when a pigeon must peck a green comparison given a green sample and a red comparison given a red one), the procedure is sometimes called *identity matching,* though accurate matching may be based on features other than the identity relation, such as stimulus configurations. When the matching is based on arbitrary sample-comparison relations (e.g., as when a pigeon must peck a circle given a green sample and a triangle given a red one), the procedure is sometimes called *arbitrary matching* (*symbolic matching,* an alternative terminology, has the disadvantage of suggesting that the sample and comparison stimuli have additional stimulus functions besides those in the matching-to-sample procedure). Cf. CONDITIONAL DISCRIMINATION, DELAYED RESPONSE, ODDITY PROCEDURE.

Maximizing: given two or more responses, emitting the one with the higher probability of reinforcement. If reinforcement probabilities change from moment to moment and responding follows the one currently highest, the maximizing is said to be *momentary maximizing.* Cf. MATCHING, OPTIMIZING, and note that matching requires a population of responses whereas maximizing can occur with a single response.

Maze: an apparatus through which an organism locomotes, usually from a startbox to a goalbox that contains some reinforcer such as food, and often including alternative paths that divide at *choice-points* and some of which end in a *blind alley* or *cul-de-sac.* Mazes come in a variety of configurations, including T-mazes or Y-mazes with a single choice-point; mazes with a single sequence of choices between blind alleys and a continuing path; and radial mazes with paths arranged like the spokes of a wheel.

Meaning: in verbal behavior, a response to verbal stimuli; or the defining properties of a class, usually including some verbal components, in which the members can serve either as stimuli or as responses.

Mediating behavior: behavior that occurs in a consistent relation to reinforced behavior and that, although reinforcers are not explicitly arranged for it, is maintained because it makes reinforcers more likely. For example, a stereotyped pattern of drinking is said to mediate spaced responding if, when the pattern is maintained, the next response is more likely to be late enough after the last response that it will be reinforced; or, two different postures held after one or another sample stimulus are said to mediate delayed matching-to-sample if a correct match is more likely when the organism has held the posture since the sample was presented (e.g., it leans to the right after a red but not a green sample and later is more likely to respond to red rather than green if still leaning to the right). Cf. COLLATERAL BEHAVIOR, SUPERSTITION.

Mediation: the contribution of intervening behavior to the relation between other events (as when coding mediates between the presentation of an item and its recall). For operant examples, see MEDIATING BEHAVIOR.

Melioration: allocating time to two or more response classes so all local reinforcement rates are equal. For example, assume a pigeon whose pecks in a changeover-key procedure are maintained by concurrent VI 20-s VI 60-s schedules. In an hour, the former provides about 180 reinforcers and the latter about 60, but if the pigeon allocates 45 minutes to the VI 20-s schedule and 15 minutes to the VI 60-s schedule both local reinforcement rates will equal about 4 per minute (180 in 45 minutes and 60 in 15 minutes). Cf. MATCHING, MAXIMIZING, OPTIMIZING.

Memory: see REMEMBERING.

Memory search: see SEARCH.

Memory span: the number of items that can be remembered after a single presentation, given that they are not coded or rehearsed.

Metacognition: differentiation and discrimination of one's own cognitive processes (as in shifting attention among tasks, or distinguishing between seeing something and just imagining it).

Metamemory: differentiation and discrimination of one's own remembering (as when keeping track of a constantly changing list of items in *running* or *working* memory, or judging whether some material just studied will be remembered).

Metaphor: the extension of concrete terms to complex and/or abstract events or relations for which relevant verbal responses are otherwise unavailable (as when pain is described not by how it feels but rather by the properties of objects that can produce it; e.g., pains can be sharp or stinging or dull).

Metastability: see STABILITY.

Metathetic stimuli: see STIMULUS CONTINUUM.

Microanalysis: see MOLAR AND MOLECULAR ANALYSES.

Misbehavior: a nontechnical term sometimes used to refer to the intrusion of behavior with phylogenic origins into ongoing operant behavior. For example, raccoons ordinarily rub and wash food before eating it; if food is used to reinforce their deposit into a container of objects they have picked up, they may begin to rub the objects together instead of releasing them into the container. The procedure raises the probability of rubbing, so the effect illustrates the relativity of reinforcers. Intrusions in the opposite direction (as when food-reinforced behavior intrudes into a fixed action pattern) are rarely referred to as misbehavior.

Mixed (mix) schedule: a compound schedule in which two or more component schedules operate in alternation, all during the same stimulus. Occasionally, a VI or VR schedule with a limited number of schedule values is referred to as a mixed schedule (e.g., a VR schedule arranged by randomly alternating between FR 10 and FR 20 may be called mixed FR 10 FR 20). Cf. MULTIPLE SCHEDULE.

Mnemonics: techniques for enhancing remembering.

Modeling: providing behavior to be imitated. Cf. IMITATION.

Molar and molecular analyses: analyses distinguished on the basis of the level of detail in the data they consider. Molar analyses generally consider overall measures such as average response rates over sessions, whereas molecular analyses break such measures down into components such as the distribution of IRTs that make up a particular response rate. Because many levels of analysis are possible, molar or molecular are sometimes defined relative to each other. Both rely on data sampled over some time and are therefore to be distinguished from *microanalysis,* which proceeds at the level of individual stimuli and responses.

Momentary maximizing: see MAXIMIZING.

Motivation: see ESTABLISHING OPERATION.

Motor programs: coordinations that do not depend on response feedback (e.g., in producing a phoneme, movements of lungs, vocal chords, tongue, and lips must be separately initiated at different times; thus, their coordination must be organized before the sound begins). Such coordinations cannot be based upon chaining.

Movement: cf. BEHAVIOR.

Multiple causation of behavior: the determination of behavior by two or more variables acting at the same time. Behavior is always controlled by multiple variables, although some may be more important than others. *Behavior analysis* involves procedures that allow the multiple factors controlling behavior to be examined one at a time.

Multiple (mult) schedule: a compound schedule in which two or more component schedules operate in alternation, each during a different stimulus. Alternation of the component schedules is typically arranged after reinforcers or after fixed or variable periods of time. The equivalent arrangement with the same stimulus during each component is a *mixed* schedule.

N

N: Newtons, a unit of force; **n:** usually, number.

Natural concept: a class of discriminative stimuli produced through presentations of complex natural stimuli (as when a pigeon discriminates between pictures with and pictures without trees in them). Cf. PROBABILISTIC STIMULUS CLASS.

Natural reinforcer: sometimes used in place of *primary reinforcer* or *intrinsic reinforcer*. The relativity of reinforcers limits the usefulness of this term; cf. REINFORCEMENT.

Natural selection: the Darwinian account of evolution in terms of the selection of members of a population over generations. Different features survive in a population as a result of interactions between the range of genetic variations available in the population and the properties of evolutionary environments.

Negative automaintenance: see AUTOMAINTENANCE.

Negative reinforcement: see REINFORCEMENT.

Negative stimulus: see DISCRIMINATIVE STIMULUS.

Negative transfer: see TRANSFER.

Neophobia: avoidance of novel stimuli, especially of new foods.

Nominal stimulus: see FUNCTIONAL STIMULUS.

Nonsense syllable: an arbitrary sequence of letters, usually a *CVC trigram*, that is not a word. Nevertheless, nonsense syllables can vary in meaningfulness (e.g., the close resemblance of LUQ to LUCK may make it more meaningful than QUL).

Noxious stimulus: often used as a synonym for aversive stimulus, but more strictly defined as a stimulus that affects pain receptors or produces tissue damage. In this strict sense, the term is useful for referring to an extensive class of stimuli without specifying behavioral consequences.

O

Observational learning: learning based on observing the responding of another organism (and/or its consequences). Observational learning need not involve imitation (e.g., organisms may come to avoid aversive stimuli upon seeing what happens when other organisms produce them).

Observing response: a response that produces or clarifies a discriminative stimulus and that may be maintained by the effectiveness of that stimulus as a conditioned reinforcer. Observing responses are sometimes only inferred (as when a pigeon's head movements are assumed to bring a visual stimulus into view or better focus), but conditions may be arranged to control them (e.g., in matching-to-sample the pigeon may be more likely to observe the sample if a peck on the sample key is required; in a more explicit arrangement, pigeon's pecks on one key may produce the stimuli correlated with the components of a multiple schedule on a second key).

Occasion: an opportunity for a response or some other event, or the circumstances under which a contingency operates, as when discriminative stimuli *set the occasion* on which responses have some consequence. When a stimulus is said to *occasion* a response, the term serves as a verb and distinguishes responses emitted in the presence of discriminative stimuli from those elicited by stimuli in a reflex relation.

Occasion setter: see CONTINGENCY.

Oddity procedure: a conditional discrimination procedure in which only one of three or more stimuli differs from the others in some property (e.g., color) and responses to the odd stimulus are reinforced. Versions of matching-to-sample in which responses to the comparison stimulus that does not match the sample are reinforced (mismatching) also qualify as oddity procedures. Cf. MATCHING-TO-SAMPLE.

Omission training: a version of differential reinforcement of zero behavior (see DIFFERENTIAL-REINFORCEMENT SCHEDULES); a reinforcer is delivered only if no response has occurred in a trial or within a given time. It is formally analogous to avoidance, with reinforcers substituted for aversive stimuli.

Ontogeny: the development or life history of an individual organism. Cf. PHYLOGENY.

Open economy: in operant contexts, the availability of appetitive stimuli not only as reinforcers within the session but also, independently of behavior, on a supplementary basis outside of the session (as when food is provided after a session of food-reinforced responding to maintain the organism at a standard percentage of free-feeding weight). Cf. CLOSED ECONOMY.

Operandum: any device that may be operated by an organism and that defines an operant class in terms of an environmental effect (*descriptive operant*; see OPERANT). Many operanda consist of switches (as in rats' lever-presses and pigeons' key-pecks, or as when a rat operates a switch by stepping off a platform). In the broadest sense, an operandum is any apparatus by means of which behavior is recorded. The term replaces an earlier one, *manipulandum,* which suggested a device that is handled. For other examples, see JUMPING STAND, WHEEL RUNNING.

Operant: a class of responses. Responses are assigned to classes because no two can be exactly the same. Special cases include the *free operant,* in which the completion of one response leaves the organism in a position to emit the next, and the discrete or constrained operant (see TRIAL). Classes defined descriptively (*descriptive operant*) are usually distinguished from those defined functionally (*functional operant*).

In the descriptive usage, usually for the purpose of recording responses, the class is defined in terms of its environmental effect (e.g., a lever-press defined by the operation of a switch; see OPERANDUM). To count as a member of an operant, a response must have a certain force, topography, and so on; another defining property may be the stimuli in the

presence of which it occurs (see DISCRIMINATED OPERANT). The effect that defines an operant in this usage may be different from the scheduled consequences of responses (e.g., in a schedule, every response in the class does not necessarily produce a reinforcer).

In the functional usage, an operant is a class modifiable by the consequences of responses in it. It is defined by the relation between consequences and subsequent responding. According to this definition, a response class is not an operant until its modifiability has been demonstrated. In most cases, operants defined descriptively and those defined functionally include roughly the same responses. If they do not, it may be appropriate either to change the method of recording or to search for variables that might limit the modifiability of the class. See also OPERANT BEHAVIOR.

Operant behavior: behavior that can be modified by its consequences. It has also been called *instrumental* and often corresponds closely to behavior colloquially called *voluntary* or *purposive.* Because of its relation to consequences, it is said to be *emitted* rather than elicited. Few responses, however, are either exclusively emitted or exclusively elicited. Many emitted responses (e.g., a pigeon's pecks) can also be made more probable by certain stimuli (e.g., spots on the pigeon's key); and many elicited responses can also occur in the absence of typical eliciting stimuli (e.g., spontaneous salivation). Operant and respondent classes are best regarded as extremes on a continuum along which the probability varies that a response will be produced by a stimulus. See also OPERANT.

Operant selection: the selection of behavior during the lifetime of an individual organism; the modification of operant behavior by its consequences (see especially DIFFERENTIAL REINFORCEMENT and SHAPING). This type of selection was once called operant or instrumental conditioning. Those who work in this research area are sometimes called *behavior analysts.*

Operant level: the baseline level of an operant, or the rate at which responses occur before they have been reinforced.

Operation: any experimental procedure or condition (e.g., presenting a stimulus, reinforcing a response, arranging a schedule, etc.). The behavioral vocabulary often fails to provide separate terms for operations and for their behavioral outcomes, or processes. For example, *a response was reinforced* may mean that the response produced a reinforcer or that it increased in rate as a result of producing a reinforcer; the correct reading is ordinarily given by context. This dual usage is common to a number of fundamental terms (e.g., conditioning, extinction, punishment). In this glossary, the process definitions of such terms are usually indicated parenthetically. Ambiguity can be avoided by restricting such terms to operations and describing outcomes directly in terms of changes in responding (e.g., *A response was reinforced and as a result its rate increased*).

Optimizing: responding so as to produce the maximum possible reinforcers over some extended time rather than from moment to moment, especially within concurrent or concurrent chain schedules. Contingencies can be designed under which optimizing requires a performance different from *matching, melioration,* or *momentary maximizing.*

Orienting response: in operant behavior, a response that puts an organism in a position to emit other responses or that allows it to attend to a discriminative stimulus (cf. OBSERVING RESPONSE). In respondent behavior, a response elicited by initial presentations of a stimulus (e.g., the first few times a bell is sounded or the first few times its sound is paired with food, a dog may prick up its ears and/or turn its head toward the bell; cf. CONDITIONED REFLEX).

Overall rate: see RATE OF RESPONDING.

Overmatching: see MATCHING LAW.

Overshadowing: an attenuation of respondent conditioning with one stimulus caused by the presence of another stimulus (e.g., if soft tone and loud bell together precede food, tone may remain ineffective as a CS even though it and bell have the same contingent relation to food). Cf. BLOCKING.

Overt behavior: behavior that is observed or observable, or that affects the organism's environment. Cf. COVERT BEHAVIOR.

P

Paced response; pacing: see DIFFERENTIAL-REINFORCEMENT SCHEDULES.

Paired associates learning: a verbal learning procedure in which each of several stimuli (usually verbal) sets the occasion for a different verbal response. The stimulus items are presented repeatedly in varied order until the learner meets some learning criterion.

Pairing: see CONTIGUITY and cf. CONTINGENCY.

Paradigm: a symbolic representation of relations. For example, a three-term contingency in which a response (R) produces a reinforcer (Rf) in the presence of a discriminative stimulus (S^D) might be written as: S^D:R→Rf. The term *paradigm* is often incorrectly used as a synonym for procedure.

Parameter: a variable that is held constant while some other variable changes. When different values of a parameter are examined, the parameter distinguishes different functions within a family of functions (e.g., a graph of avoidance behavior can show avoidance response rate as a function of either RS interval with SS interval as a parameter or SS interval with RS interval as a parameter).

Passive avoidance: a misnomer for punishment. To avoid passively is not to respond when responding has been punished. For example, a rat is placed on a platform above an electrified grid. Its failure to step down onto the grid has been called passive avoidance, in the sense that in doing so it is not shocked. But defining contingencies in terms of the absence of responses may be misleading, and it is more appropriate to say that stepping down is punished by shock.

Pause: a period of no responding, not necessarily bounded by responses. Cf. INTER-RESPONSE TIME, LATENCY, RATE OF RESPONDING.

Pavlovian conditioning: see RESPONDENT CONDITIONING.

Peak procedure: omitting some proportion of the reinforcers arranged by an FI schedule and thereby allowing responding to continue for some time after the usual end of the interval. Response rate typically passes through a maximum (the peak) and then decreases over time (the increasing and then decreasing rates are sometimes treated as the two sides of a temporal generalization gradient).

Peak shift: see POSTDISCRIMINATION GRADIENT.

Percentage reinforcement: the omission of a fixed proportion of the reinforcers arranged by a schedule. For example, in an FR 100 schedule with 50 percent reinforcement, only half of the completed ratios end with a reinforcer. A stimulus (e.g., a brief tone) is often substituted for the omitted reinforcer; without such a stimulus, the above schedule is the same as a VR 200 schedule in which the constituent ratios are all multiples of 100 responses.

Percentile-reinforcement schedule: a schedule in which the eligibility of a response to produce a reinforcer depends on its location within a response distribution (e.g., a schedule for long IRTs might reinforce any IRT in the top 25 percent of an IRT distribution taken over the last 100 responses). The schedule must specify both the percentile criterion for reinforcement and the source of the reference response distribution. Because its criteria for differential reinforcement are relative rather than absolute, it operates consistently over a range of changes in performance and therefore makes automated shaping possible.

Performance: behavior, usually over extended time periods. A subject matter in itself, performance has often been treated instead as an index of something else (e.g., learning, motivational states).

Phenomenon (plural: **phenomena**): an event; something that happens.

Phrase structure grammar: see GRAMMARS.

Phylogenic constraints: limitations on learning or differential capacities for learning that depend on phylogenic selection, including properties of the behavior classes that can be produced and limits on the contingencies that can modify behavior (e.g., it may be impossible to shape alternating as opposed to synchronized wing flapping in newly hatched birds). The terminology is rarely invoked when the limitations involve obvious anatomical features. See TASTE AVERSION for an example; cf. PREPAREDNESS.

Phylogeny: the development or evolutionary history of a species. Cf. ONTOGENY.

Place learning vs. response learning: the historical issue of whether organisms learned stimuli or movements (e.g., whether a rat in a maze learns a sequence oriented to stimuli outside the maze or just a particular sequence of turns; the outcome can go one way or the other depending on stimuli outside the maze).

Polydipsia: the schedule-induced enhancement of water intake. See ADJUNCTIVE BEHAVIOR.

Polymorphous stimulus class: a probabilistic stimulus class in which each member includes exactly N of M distinguishing features (as when a stimulus is a member of a class by virtue of containing exactly 2 of 3 critical features). In such cases, any feature may also appear in stimuli that are outside the class.

Positive reinforcement: see REINFORCEMENT.

Positive stimulus: see DISCRIMINATIVE STIMULUS.

Positive transfer: see TRANSFER.

Postdiscrimination gradient: a gradient obtained after a discrimination between one stimulus correlated with reinforcement and another correlated with extinction (occasionally, between two stimuli correlated with different reinforcement schedules), usually with both stimuli represented on the continuum along which the gradient is determined. It often includes a *peak shift*, a displacement of the point of maximum responding to one side of the reinforcement stimulus in a direction away from the extinction stimulus.

Postponement: see AVOIDANCE.

Postreinforcement pause: the period of no responding following a reinforcer, especially in an FR or an FI. In an FR, the pause is sometimes measured as the time to some response other than the first (e.g., the fifth response in FR 100), because pauses may separate the first few responses before the roughly constant rate of the FR run begins.

Potentiation: an increase, over repeated presentations, in the respondent behavior elicited by a stimulus (especially, an aversive stimulus). Cf. HABITUATION.

Pragmatics: see LINGUISTICS.

Preaversive stimulus: a stimulus that reliably precedes an aversive stimulus and thus may be a conditioned aversive stimulus. Such stimuli may reduce the responding maintained by positive reinforcers, an effect variously called *anxiety, conditioned emotional response* (CER), or *conditioned suppression*. In some contexts, the stimulus increases responding, as when presented during avoidance responding or during positively reinforced responding after a history of avoidance; this has been called *conditioned acceleration* or *conditioned facilitation*.

Prediction: see CONTROL.

Predictive stimulus: a discriminative stimulus. A stimulus predicts an event if the probability of the event given the stimulus differs from that without the stimulus. Cf. INFORMATIVE STIMULUS.

Preference: the probability of one of two or more alternative responses, derived from the relative frequencies of the responses over an extended sequence of choices. The term does not apply to cases in which the different probabilities of each response are produced by the different schedules according to which each response is reinforced. Preferences quantify the relative effectiveness of different consequences as reinforcers (cf. REIN-FORCEMENT); when each response produces a different consequence, the organism is said to prefer the consequence produced by the response that is most probable. If different probabilities of two or more responses cannot be accounted for, as when they occur despite identical consequences and schedules for each response, the preference is sometimes called a *bias*. Cf. CHOICE, CONCURRENT-CHAIN SCHEDULES, CONCURRENT OPERANTS.

Premack principle: the relativity of reinforcers and punishers. See REINFORCEMENT.

Preparedness: a capacity, presumably of phylogenic origin, to learn some response-stimulus or stimulus-stimulus contingencies more readily than others (e.g., organisms may learn relations between tastes and gastrointestinal consequences more easily than those between lights or sounds and such consequences). See TASTE AVERSION.

Primacy: see SERIAL-POSITION EFFECT.

Primary memory: an older term for short-term memory. See REMEMBERING.

Primary reinforcer: a reinforcer the effectiveness of which does not depend on its contingent relation to another reinforcer. Cf. CONDITIONED REINFORCER.

Priming: presenting a stimulus that affects behavior after the stimulus is removed (as when the brief presentation of one word lowers the recognition threshold of a semantically related word presented later).

Private events: in verbal behavior, events accessible only to the speaker (usually, events inside the skin). Private events have the same physical status as public events, but it is more difficult for the verbal community to shape tacts of private events.

Proaction: effects of learning at one time on other learning that occurs later. When the later learning is impaired, the effect is a variety of negative transfer called *proactive interference* or *proactive inhibition*. Cf. RETROACTION, TRANSFER.

Probabilistic stimulus class: a stimulus class in which each member contains some subset of features but none is common to all members. The number of features in the subset may vary from one class member to another (cf. POLYMORPHOUS STIMULUS CLASS). Such classes, sometimes called *fuzzy sets*, do not have well-defined boundaries, though class members may have family resemblances. Examples include *natural concepts* and classes defined by reference to a *prototype*.

Probability: a proportion or relative frequency, either scheduled or derived from data. The probability of an event is given by the number of times it occurs divided by the opportunities for it (how often it is possible). For example, if a stimulus is presented 50 times and on 40 of these a response occurs, response probability in the presence of that stimulus is 0.8 (40/50). Response probability can be based on response frequencies in the presence of a stimulus (as in the example), within successive short time periods, or relative to other responses. See also CONDITIONAL PROBABILITY.

Probe: a condition or stimulus introduced into a performance to clarify the variables controlling it (e.g., the interruption of FR responding by an occasional brief stimulus correlated with reinforcement of another response can be used to probe how strongly the FR responses are chained together).

Problem solving: constructing discriminative stimuli, either overtly or covertly, in situations involving novel contingencies; these stimuli may set the occasion for effective behavior (as when a verbal problem is converted into a familiar mathematical formula, or as when a listing of options clarifies complex contingencies). Cf. SIMULATION.

Procedural memory: see REMEMBERING.

Procedure: An experimental arrangement or operation. Cf. PARADIGM.

Process: the changes in behavior produced by an experimental operation. See OPERATION.

Processing: whatever goes on within an organism between the presentation of a stimulus and subsequent responding. Cf. COGNITIVE PROCESSES.

Processing, level of: see LEVEL OF PROCESSING.

Productivity: the generation of novel behavior through the recombination and reorganization of existing response classes.

Programming: arranging experimental conditions such as reinforcement schedules. In some usages, *programming* is restricted to arranging progressive changes in conditions (as in shaping or the transfer of stimulus control through fading) and is therefore distinguished from *scheduling,* arranging maintained conditions.

Progressive schedule: a schedule in which requirements change progressively with each reinforcer (e.g., in one progressive ratio schedule, the ratio increases by 5 responses after each reinforcer). The schedule sometimes allows the requirement to be reset to its initial value (e.g., by a response on a second operandum).

Proprioceptive stimulus: an interoceptive stimulus produced by the effects of movements and postures on receptors in muscles, tendons, or joints.

Prospective memory: see REMEMBERING.

Prothetic stimuli: see STIMULUS CONTINUUM.

Prototype: a typical member of a probabilistic class, described by a weighted average of all features of all members of the class (e.g., feathers are weighted more heavily than webbed feet among birds because more have feathers than have webbed feet; thus, a robin is more prototypical than a duck because it shares more features with other birds than does a duck). Cf. PROBABILISTIC STIMULUS CLASS.

Pseudoconditioning: the elicitation of responding by one stimulus as a result of its presentation in the same context as another, even though neither had been presented in a contingent relation to the other. See SENSITIZATION for an example.

Pseudotrial: a time period corresponding to that of a trial but within which no trial stimuli are presented. Pseudotrials are used to assess response probability in the absence of the trial stimuli over time periods corresponding to those of trials.

Psycholinguistics: see LINGUISTICS.

Psychological reality: the role of some class of events in behavior, especially in psycholinguistics (as when grammatical transformations are demonstrated as something that speakers do with sentences).

Psychophysics: an area of psychology that evolved out of the philosophical concern with the relation between mind and body. Psychophysics relates behavioral properties of stimuli to properties defined in physical terms. Studies of detection or discrimination examine *absolute thresholds,* or minimum effective stimulus intensities, and *difference thresholds,* or minimum effective differences between stimuli along

some continuum (see also SIGNAL DETECTION ANALYSIS). Studies of scaling relate the effects of changes in the properties of one stimulus to those of changes in the properties of another (e.g., if responding depends on auditory or visual stimulus intensity, determining how much one must be increased to equal the effect of doubling the other).

Punisher: see PUNISHMENT.

Punishment: the response-produced presentation of positive punishers or the termination of negative punishers (or, the response decrement or suppression that results). The terminology closely parallels that of reinforcement. *Punishers* are stimuli, *punishment* is an operation (or process), and responses rather than organisms are said to be punished. A stimulus is a *positive punisher* if its presentation reduces the likelihood of responses that produce it, or a *negative punisher* if its removal reduces the likelihood of responses that terminate it. Like reinforcers, punishers are relative and may be defined independently of their behavioral consequences (e.g., the probabilities of two responses can be assessed by forcing the organism to choose between engaging in one or the other, and if the more probable response then forces the organism to engage in the less probable one, the forced responding will punish the more probable response). These definitions parallel the definitions of reinforcers; punishers are equivalent except for the difference in sign. Cf. AVERSIVE STIMULUS, REINFORCEMENT.

R

R, r: usually, response.

Random control: a procedure for presenting two stimuli randomly in time, as a baseline against which to compare the effects of stimulus-stimulus contingencies. The random presentations are usually arranged in the context of a sequence of pseudotrials and therefore typically include incidental stimulus-stimulus contiguities as well as presentations of each stimulus alone.

Random-interval schedule: see INTERVAL SCHEDULE.

Randomness: variability generated by a process that produces events completely independent of one another, in the sense that none can be predicted from any of the others. It is a property of a distribution of events (or the process that generates the distribution); no single event can be random.

Random-ratio schedule: see RATIO SCHEDULE.

Rate dependency: changes in the magnitude and perhaps direction of effect of a variable that depend on baseline response rate, especially in reference to drug effects (e.g., as when some drug dose increases low response rates but decreases high ones).

Rate of reinforcement: reinforcers per unit time; sometimes used in preference to reinforcement frequency because frequency occasionally refers not to reinforcers per unit time but rather to reinforcers per response, per session, or per trial.

Rate of responding: responses per unit time. Several types have been distinguished: *overall* or *average rate*, determined over a substantial time such as an experimental session; *local, momentary*, or *moment-to-moment rate*, determined over a short time, particularly when it is relatively constant throughout that time; *running rate*, roughly equivalent to local rate, but sometimes with the provision that it is determined over a time bounded by pauses; and *terminal rate*, determined over a short time just before a reinforcer, especially in an FI. Criteria for distinguishing segments of performance, such as the response sequence over which a running rate is determined, may be based on informal criteria such as visual inspection, but they can be defined more explicitly (e.g., a period of no responding may be treated as a pause only if it is more than 5 s long).

Other terms distinguish changes in rate: *acceleration* or *positive acceleration* is a gradual increase, appearing as concave-upward curvature on a cumulative record; *deceleration* or *negative acceleration* is a gradual decrease, appearing as concave-downward curvature; cyclic changes are repeated increases and decreases, each completed over a roughly constant time; and compensation is a low rate immediately following an unusually high one, or a high one immediately following an unusually low one. The acceleration typically produced by an FI schedule is often called a *scallop*, especially in reference to its appearance in a cumulative record. The term has been extended to accelerations produced by other schedules but is ordinarily restricted to accelerations bounded by some event, such as a reinforcer. The curvature in an FI has been measured in terms of *quarter-life* (the time to complete one quarter of the responses within an interval) and *index of curvature* (a statistic based on the number of responses in successive fractions of an interval). Moment-to-moment changes in rate are often described in terms of *grain* (e.g., a relatively constant rate is said to have a finer grain than one that rapidly fluctuates), again, especially in reference to the appearance of a cumulative record. Cf. CUMULATIVE RECORD, INTERRESPONSE TIME.

Ratio schedule: a schedule in which the last of a specified number of responses is reinforced. In a *fixed-ratio* (*FR*) schedule, the number is constant from one reinforcer to the next; performance is characterized by pauses after the reinforcer followed by a relatively high and constant response rate. In a *variable-ratio* (*VR*) schedule, the number of responses varies from one reinforcer to the next; relative to FR schedules, the postreinforcement pause is ordinarily reduced or eliminated. A VR schedule is usually identified in terms of the average ratio, the average responses per reinforcer. In the variety of VR schedule called *random ratio* (*RR*), the ratio specifies the probability with which a response will be reinforced. For example, in RR 20 that probability is .05 (1/20) and is independent of the number of responses emitted since the last reinforcer. In some VR schedules, successive ratios are selected in irregular order from a set of ratios described by a mathematical progression, analogous to those used in VI schedules (see INTERVAL SCHEDULE).

Ratio strain: the appearance of pauses in VR responding, or in FR responding at times other than after a reinforcer (cf. POSTREINFORCEMENT PAUSE); a result of large ratio size and/or low reinforcement frequency.

Reaction time: usually equivalent to latency.

Reality, psychological: see PSYCHOLOGICAL REALITY.

Recall, verbal: see FREE RECALL.

Recency: see SERIAL-POSITION EFFECT.

Recognition, verbal: see VERBAL DISCRIMINATION.

Recovery: return to an earlier level of responding after responding has been reduced by an operation such as extinction or punishment. The vocabulary does not distinguish between recovery during maintained conditions and recovery after the conditions have been discontinued (e.g., *recovery during punishment* refers to a return of responding toward prepunishment levels while punishment continues, whereas *recovery after punishment* refers to a return toward those levels after punishment is discontinued).

Reflex: see UNCONDITIONED REFLEX, CONDITIONED REFLEX.

Reflexive relation or **reflexivity:** the identity relation. See EQUIVALENCE CLASS.

Regression: the reappearance of previously extinguished behavior during the extinction of more recently reinforced behavior.

Regular reinforcement: see CONTINUOUS REINFORCEMENT.

Rehearsal: behavior that occurs between storage and retrieval. In most usages, rehearsal includes encoding; occasionally it refers only to behavior that follows encoding. Some usages also distinguish among kinds of rehearsal: *maintenance rehearsal* involves repetitions of encoded items, and *elaborative rehearsal* involves further encoding and/or processing. See also REMEMBERING; cf. MEDIATING BEHAVIOR.

Reinforcer: see REINFORCEMENT.

Reinforcement: the response-produced presentation of positive reinforcers or termination of negative reinforcers (or the increase or maintenance of responding resulting from this operation). *Reinforcers* are stimuli (e.g., food); *reinforcement* is an operation (e.g., presentation of food) or a process. The operation reinforces responses, not organisms; organisms are sometimes said to be *rewarded*, but this term often implies effects of stimuli other than reinforcing effects. Earlier in its history, reinforcement was also applied to presentations of the US in respondent conditioning, but that usage is now unusual.

A stimulus is a *positive reinforcer* if its presentation increases the likelihood of responses that produce it, or a *negative reinforcer* if its removal increases the likelihood of responses that terminate or postpone it. The distinction is significant mainly when responses produced by the reinforcer can compete with the reinforced response (e.g., reinforcement by heat of a rat's lever-presses in the cold is more likely to be called negative reinforcement by removal of cold than positive reinforcement by presentation of heat because cold produces huddling and shivering that compete with lever-pressing).

Reinforcers can also be defined independently of their behavioral consequences. The effectiveness of a reinforcer depends on the relative probabilities of the responses it occasions and the responses to be reinforced; these can be altered by limiting the organism's opportunities to engage in one or the other response (*response deprivation:*

cf. ESTABLISHING OPERATION). If a less probable response produces a stimulus that occasions a more probable response, then the stimulus will reinforce the less probable response. This definition takes into account the *relativity of reinforcers;* the reinforcement relation is reversible (e.g., if water deprivation makes drinking more probable than wheel running, the opportunity to drink will reinforce running, but if limited access to the wheel makes running more probable than drinking, the opportunity to run will reinforce drinking). Cf. OPERANT, PUNISHMENT.

Relational autoclitic: see AUTOCLITIC.

Relational discrimination or **relational learning:** discrimination based on relational rather than absolute properties of stimuli (e.g., to the left of or to the right of; same or different; greater than or less than; see also MATCHING-TO-SAMPLE).

Relative rate: the rate of one event (especially a response or a reinforcer) as a proportion of the summed rates of that and other events (e.g., given the rates of A and of B, the relative rate of A is calculated as A divided by the sum of A and B).

Relativity (of language): see LANGUAGE RELATIVITY.

Relativity (of reinforcers): see REINFORCEMENT.

Releaser: an ethological term for a stimulus that elicits a stereotyped pattern of behavior (cf. FIXED ACTION PATTERN). Releasers are often US's provided by the behavior or the physical features of another organism. In some usages, releasers have some of the properties of discriminative stimuli that occasion operant behavior. The comparison is complicated because the functions of releasers are typically analyzed differently from those of CS's, US's and discriminative stimuli. For example, releasers are usually presented for extended time periods and may vary during those times (particularly when they depend on the behavior of another organism), whereas CS's and US's are more often presented briefly, in discrete trials. An artificial releaser that is more likely to produce a fixed action pattern than its natural counterpart is called a *supernormal* stimulus. Cf. DISPLACEMENT ACTIVITY, RESPONDENT BEHAVIOR, VACUUM ACTIVITY.

Remembering: a response occasioned by a stimulus no longer present, perhaps directly or perhaps through the mediation of other behavior with respect to that stimulus. Remembering is often discussed in terms of a metaphor of storage and retrieval, where *storage* occurs when the stimulus is presented, and *retrieval* occurs when it is recalled. The time between storage and retrieval is sometimes called the *retention* interval. See REHEARSAL, RETRIEVAL, STORAGE.

Types of remembering are sometimes distinguished by their time courses. *Iconic memory* and *echoic memory* refer, respectively, to the brief persistence of the effects of visual and auditory stimuli. *Short-term memory* (STM) is remembering based on a single presentation of items and without coding and/or rehearsal; it is of short duration (e.g., 10 to 20 s) and limited to roughly 5 to 9 items (historically, the span of immediate memory). *Long-term memory* (LTM) occurs after coding or rehearsal and/or multiple presentations of items, and is therefore of unlimited duration and capacity.

Remembering is also classified in terms of what is remembered. Examples include: *procedural memory* (remembering operations or ways of doing things), often contrasted with *declarative memory* (remembering facts); *autobiographical* or *episodic memory* (remembering specific events in one's life); *semantic memory* (remembering aspects of one's language); *spatial memory* (remembering paths and things located on them); and *retrospective memory* (remembering past events), often contrasted with *prospective memory* (remembering things one has to do in the future). See also METAMEMORY.

Reminiscence: an increase in recall probability as time passes since learning. Reminiscence is an occasional phenomenon that usually appears, if at all, shortly after learning.

Repeated acquisition: a procedure that examines acquisition as steady-state performance. For example, assume a monkey must emit a sequence of presses on four levers to produce a reinforcer and the required sequence changes each session. After many sessions, the monkey has had enough contact with correction procedures and other experimental details that all it has to learn within a session is the new sequence of presses. The repeated acquisition of new sequences may then be used as a baseline for studying how acquisition is affected by different variables (e.g., drugs). The consistent way in which the monkey masters each new sequence in steady-state performance may be called a *strategy*. Cf. HIGHER-ORDER CLASS OF BEHAVIOR, LEARNING SET.

Repertoire or **repertory:** the behavior an organism can emit, in the sense that the behavior exists at a nonzero level, has been shaped, or, if extinguished, may be rapidly reinstated. The organism need not be engaging in the behavior for it to be in its repertoire (e.g., a rat that has learned a maze has maze-running behavior in its repertoire even when not in the maze). To the extent that some responses in it are more likely than others, a repertoire consists of a hierarchy; operant procedures modify the relative positions of responses in the hierarchy.

Replicative memory: memory interpreted as the production of a copy of what is remembered. Cf. CONSTRUCTIVE MEMORY.

Representation: a transformation of stimuli occurring either when an organism responds to them or later (e.g., in remembering). In some accounts they are copies; in other accounts representations have arbitrary relations to stimuli, as when a visually presented letter is represented by its sound. Such representations are more like recipes than like copies, and they have behavioral dimensions. Cf. CODING, REMEMBERING.

Resistance to change: see STRENGTH.

Resistance to extinction: the responses emitted, the time elapsed, or the number of trials until performance has met some extinction criterion (e.g., the number of responses emitted before 10 minutes pass with no response). The measure must be specified, because one contingency or schedule may produce more resistance to extinction than another according to one measure but less according to a different one.

Respondent: a class of responses defined in terms of stimuli that reliably produce them (e.g., salivation elicited by food or acid in the mouth is a member of one respondent class, and salivation elicited by a CS is a member of another; spontaneous salivation, in the absence of identifiable stimuli, is not strictly a member of a respondent class, although it is sometimes loosely referred to as such). Cf. OPERANT.

Respondent behavior: behavior elicited by stimuli (cf. RESPONDENT, UNCONDITIONED REFLEX, CONDITIONED REFLEX). Respondent behavior was once considered primarily autonomic (e.g., responses of glands and smooth muscles), but the reflex relation defines respondent behavior regardless of the character of the response. Thus, skeletal responses may have respondent characteristics (see AUTOSHAPING; cf. OPER-ANT BEHAVIOR).

Respondent conditioning: the modification of respondent behavior by stimulus-stimulus contingencies, also referred to as *classical conditioning* or *Pavlovian conditioning*. Cf. CONDI-TIONED REFLEX.

Respondent discrimination: differential conditioning, a type of respondent conditioning in which one stimulus is followed by the US but a second is not (e.g,. food in the mouth follows bell but not tone). Discrimination has occurred when the CR is elicited by the first stimulus but not the second. The term does not refer to respondent conditioning in general, even though such conditioning entails discrimination between the presence and absence of the CS.

Response: a unit of behavior, a discrete and usually recurring segment of behavior. Cf. OPERANT, RESPONDENT, STRENGTH; see also specific properties: DURATION OF RESPONSE, RATE OF RESPONDING, TOPOGRAPHY OF RESPONSE.

Response competition: the reduction of one response by the time and/or effort involved in concurrent responding. The terminology distinguishes reductions directly caused by concurrent responding from those caused by the reinforcers produced by concurrent responding. Cf. INHIBITION.

Response cost: any property of responding or consequence of responding that may reduce or punish it. Examples include increases in response effort or force and response-contingent loss or reduction of reinforcers (especially, with humans, point loss superimposed on responding maintained by points; in such cases, however, the effectiveness of points as reinforcers is often assumed rather than confirmed experimentally).

Response deprivation: see ESTABLISHING OPERATION, REINFORCEMENT.

Response generalization: an alternative term for *induction*.

Response-independent reinforcer: the delivery of a reinforcer without reference to the organism's behavior. See TIME SCHEDULE.

Response induction: see INDUCTION.

Response rate: see RATE OF RESPONDING.

Response strength: see STRENGTH.

Resurgence: see REGRESSION.

Retention: the time between storage and retrieval in the storage-retrieval metaphor of memory.

Retrieval: in the memory metaphor of storage and retrieval, what the learner does at the time something is remembered. Retrieval is typically occasioned by a discriminative stimulus that sets the occasion for it (e.g., an instruction). Cf. DECODING, REMEMBERING.

Retroaction: effects of learning at one time on other learning that occurred earlier. When the earlier learning is impaired, the effect is a variety of negative transfer called *retroactive interference* or *retroactive inhibition*. Cf. PROACTION, TRANSFER.

Retrospective memory: see REMEMBERING.

Reversible effects: changes in performances that are eliminated, either immediately or over some time, when the operations that produced them are discontinued (e.g., if responding returns to earlier levels after punishment, the effects of punishment are reversible). Effects that are not completely eliminated are sometimes said to be partially reversible.

Reward: see REINFORCEMENT.

Rf: reinforcement or reinforcer. See REINFORCEMENT.

RI: random interval. See INTERVAL SCHEDULE.

RR: random ratio. See RATIO SCHEDULE.

RS interval: response-shock interval. See AVOIDANCE.

Rule-governed behavior: behavior, either verbal or nonverbal, under the control of verbal antecedents. In some usages, any verbal antecedent qualifies as a rule (as when one is told to do or say something). In others, rules are only those verbal antecedents that specify contingencies (as when one is told what will happen if one does or says something); such rules may alter the functions of other stimuli. Some rules are self-produced; the most effective verbal antecedents are those one generates oneself. Whether rule-following occurs in the presence of a rule is often ambiguous (one may repeat a rule to oneself at the time of following it); for that reason, rules do not necessarily qualify as discriminative stimuli even though they function as verbal antecedents. Cf. CONTINGENCY-GOVERNED BEHAVIOR, SPECIFICATION.

Run: a sequence of responses, bounded by pauses or by some event (e.g., an FR run is the response sequence within a single ratio).

Running memory: see METAMEMORY.

Running rate: see RATE OF RESPONDING.

S

S, s: usually, stimulus; also, seconds.

S +, S^D ("S-dee"): positive or discriminative stimulus; **S −, S^Δ** ("S-delta"): negative stimulus. See DISCRIMINATIVE STIMULUS.

Sample-specific behavior: in matching-to-sample, differential responding to each sample stimulus, usually introduced to ensure sample-stimulus control. For example, pigeon matching-to-sample may be arranged with a fixed-duration sample after which a peck on the sample-key turns on the comparison stimuli only if some differential criterion for such pecking is met (e.g., more than 5 pecks given green samples or fewer than 4 given red); the trial ends without comparison stimuli if sample-key responding does not meet the criterion. Sample-specific responding may guarantee attention to sample stimuli but does not necessarily do so for the sample-comparison relation.

Sample stimulus: see MATCHING-TO-SAMPLE.

Satiation: an establishing operation, continued presentation or availability of a reinforcer, that reduces its effectiveness as a reinforcer (or, as a process, the reduction in effectiveness produced by this operation). Satiation may occur as responses are reinforced, or it may be arranged independently of responses. One criterion for satiation with food reinforcers is prefeeding (presenting food for some fixed time or in some fixed amount before a session). Cf. DEPRIVATION.

Scallop: see RATE OF RESPONDING.

Schedule: a specification of the criteria by which responses become eligible to produce reinforcers. The term has also been extended to other operations (e.g., schedules of escape, avoidance or punishment). See specific cases: COMPOUND SCHEDULE, DIFFERENTIAL-REINFORCEMENT SCHEDULE, HIGHER-ORDER SCHEDULE, INTERVAL SCHEDULE, LIMITED HOLD, RATIO SCHEDULE, TIME SCHEDULE.

Schedule-induced behavior: see ADJUNCTIVE BEHAVIOR.

Schema: in cognition, an organized representation of events, especially in complex contexts (e.g., spatial schemas relating lengths, areas, and volumes, or social ones arranged in scripts, scenarios, and narratives). Cf. COGNITIVE MAP; REPRESENTATION.

Search: in the storage-retrieval metaphor of memory, search for a match to some target item. The search may be *exhaustive* (all items are checked) or *self-terminating* (the search ends when a match to the target is found).

Secondary reinforcer: see CONDITIONED REINFORCER.

Second-order: see HIGHER-ORDER CLASS OF BEHAVIOR; HIGHER-ORDER CONDITIONING; HIGHER-ORDER SCHEDULE.

Selection by consequences: operant selection or the ontogenic analogue of phylogenic or Darwinian selection, expressed as an abbreviated form of *the selection of behavior by its consequences*. In a more general sense, all varieties of selection involve consequences (e.g., the evolution of the eye depends on the consequences of more finely differentiated seeing). Phylogenic selection operates on populations of organisms over evolutionary time whereas operant selection operates on populations of responses within the lifetime of an individual organism. Cultural selection is a third kind of selection. It occurs when behavior is passed on from one member of a group to another (examples include imitated behavior and verbal behavior). See also ARTIFICIAL SELECTION, NATURAL SELECTION, SHAPING.

Self-control: a term derived from the colloquial vocabulary that applies to cases in which a relatively immediate small reinforcer is deferred in favor of a later large reinforcer or in favor of avoiding a later large aversive event, or in which a relatively immediate small aversive event is accepted when the acceptance leads to a later large reinforcer or avoids a later large aversive event. Examples include deferring a small purchase to save for a large one, refusing a drink to avoid a hangover, exercising to perform well in a later athletic event, and undergoing preventive dental procedures. The opposite of self-control is called *impulsiveness* or *impulsivity*.

Self-reinforcement: a misnomer for the delivery of a reinforcer to oneself based on one's own behavior. In so-called self-reinforcement, the contingencies and establishing operations that affect the behavior that is purportedly reinforced are confounded with those that affect the delivery of the reinforcer to oneself. The organism that appears to self-reinforce must be able to discriminate behavior that qualifies for the reinforcer from behavior that does not; this behavior is more appropriately described as an example of the discrimination of properties of one's own behavior.

Semantic memory: see REMEMBERING.

Semantics: see LINGUISTICS.

Sensitivity: in most behavioral usages, a measure of threshold (the organism's capacity to respond differentially to different stimuli or conditions; see PSYCHOPHYSICS).

Sensitivity to contingencies: see HIGHER-ORDER CLASS OF BEHAVIOR.

Sensitization: the lowering of a threshold, as when prior delivery of an aversive stimulus lowers the intensity at which a noise elicits a startle response.

Sensory preconditioning: in respondent conditioning, a type of higher-order conditioning in which a contingent relation between two stimuli precedes making one of them a CS. Sensory preconditioning is said to have occurred if the other stimulus elicits the CR solely by virtue of its relation to the first stimulus. Preconditioning procedures have also been extended to operant cases (e.g., correlating response-independent reinforcers with one stimulus that later will signal reinforcement but not with a second one that later will signal extinction sometimes facilitates acquisition of an operant discrimination between the stimuli).

Sequential dependencies: conditional probabilities of successive events (e.g., given concurrent responses *A* and *B*, the probabilities of *A* followed by *A*, *A* followed by *B*, *B* followed by *A*, and *B* followed by *B*).

Sequential grammar: see GRAMMARS.

Serial anticipation: see SERIAL LEARNING.

Serial learning: learning an ordered list of items. In *serial recall*, the learner has an opportunity for recall after the entire list is presented. In *serial anticipation*, items are presented one at a time and the learner has an opportunity to say which item comes next. In both cases, list presentations continue until the learner meets some criterion of learning.

Serial-position effect: differential recall of an item depending on its position in a list, especially in free recall. An early item is more likely to be recalled than a later one (*primacy*), and a very recent item is more likely to be recalled than an earlier one (*recency*). Thus, items at the beginning or end are more likely to be recalled than ones in the middle. The primacy effect is usually stronger than the recency effect.

Serial recall: see SERIAL LEARNING.

Set: loosely, a disposition to respond. The term may refer to stereotyped patterns of operant behavior (especially under stimulus control) or to effects of the conditional stimuli of a conditional discrimination. A common use of the term is provided by instructions at the start of an experiment, often said to produce in human subjects a set to attend to particular features of the subsequent experimental situation. Cf. ATTENTION.

Setup: in reinforcement schedules (especially interval schedules), an arrangement that makes a response eligible to produce a reinforcer.

Shaping: gradually modifying some property of responding (often but not necessarily topography) by differentially reinforcing successive approximations to a target operant class. Shaping is used to produce responses that, because of low operant levels and/or complexity, might not otherwise be emitted or might be emitted only after a considerable time. The variability of responses after one response has been reinforced usually provides an opportunity to reinforce a response that still more closely approximates the criteria that define the target operant class. Shaping is therefore a variety of operant selection.

Shock: a stimulus sometimes used as an aversive stimulus. Shock is usually delivered through a grid floor, parallel rods on which the organism stands and far enough apart that feces or urine cannot short-circuit them. A complication is that shock level may be altered by the organism's behavior (as when rats contact the shock source through either a furred or unfurred body area).

Short-term memory (STM): see REMEMBERING.

Side effect: any effect that accompanies the main effect with which an experimenter is concerned. The distinction is often arbitrary, because no stimulus has a single effect (e.g., a researcher interested in extinction-induced aggression may regard the decrease in previously reinforced responding during extinction as a side effect, whereas another researcher interested in operant extinction may regard the aggression as the side effect). Cf. MULTIPLE CAUSATION OF BEHAVIOR.

Sidman avoidance: see AVOIDANCE.

Signal: roughly, a discriminative stimulus or an occasion-setting stimulus; a stimulus that sets the occasion on which some contingency operates or on which some other stimulus may be presented. Cf. INFORMATIVE STIMULUS, PREDICTIVE STIMULUS.

Signal detection analysis: an analysis of stimulus detectability in terms of conditional probabilities of a response given a signal in noise or noise alone. A response to a signal in noise is a *correct detection,* or a *hit,* and one to noise alone is a *false alarm;* the absence of a response given a signal in noise is a *miss,* and to noise alone is a *correct rejection.* These measures change differently with changes in signal intensity than with changes in contingencies for responding or non-responding and therefore allow the effects of stimulus variables on detectability to be separated from those of contingencies.

Sign-tracking: responding directed toward some feature of a stimulus correlated with reinforcement. Cf. FEATURE-POSITIVE STIMULUS.

Simulation: imagining; especially, covert problem solving. Simulation that takes actual contingencies into account may mediate effective behavior in actual environments.

Simultaneous discrimination: a discrimination in which two or more discriminative stimuli are presented at the same time rather than successively (e.g., see JUMPING STAND) and which therefore involves two or more alternative responses. The locations of the stimuli are ordinarily at or close to those of the alternative responses (e.g., stimuli on each of two pigeon keys) and the organism is said to respond *to* one or the other stimulus. Cf. SUCCESSIVE DISCRIMINATION.

Skinner box: a term not in current usage. See CHAMBER.

Span, memory: see MEMORY SPAN.

Spandrel: an incidental by-product of selection.

Species-specific behavior: behavior observed in all or most members of a species (of only one or of both sexes, and perhaps only over limited times in each organism's life). Different usages may include: emitted behavior before its selection by consequences; unconditioned respondent behavior; and, in fairly consistent environments, stereotyped operant behavior maintained by species-specific primary reinforcers or conditioned reflexes that depend on species-specific unconditioned reflexes. See also specific examples: DISPLACEMENT ACTIVITY, FIXED ACTION PATTERN, RELEASER, VACUUM ACTIVITY.

Species-specific defense reaction (SSDR): avoidance or escape responding that has a phy-

logenic origin. Such behavior presumably evolved because natural environments do not allow organisms to learn certain types of avoidance or escape responses (e.g., a mouse that fails to avoid a predatory cat on its first encounter will probably never have another opportunity to do so).

Specification: the correspondence between a verbal response and what it tacts, when the verbal response occurs outside of the tact relation (as when a mand is said to specify its reinforcer even though the reinforcer is absent). The term is typically used in an informal rather than a technical sense, especially in reference to effects on a listener (as when the listener's response to a word is said to share properties with responses to what the word ordinarily tacts).

Spontaneous recovery: in operant or respondent extinction, an increment in responding at the beginning of one experimental session of extinction, relative to the level of responding at the end of the preceding session. Cf. WARM-UP.

SS interval: shock-shock interval. See AVOIDANCE.

Stability: session-to-session variability in performance (the lower the variability, the more stable the performance). A performance that can shift from one to another of two or more steady-state baselines maintained by the same conditions is said to be *metastable.* Cf. STEADY STATE.

State-dependent learning: learning that is most likely to be demonstrated when the learner is in the same context as in the original learning. The term is often reserved for learning under specific physiological conditions such as drug states (e.g., the learner who learned an item while drunk is more likely to remember it when drunk again than when sober).

Statistics: quantitative methods for summarizing data (descriptive statistics) or evaluating data (statistical inference). Descriptive statistics include measures of *central tendency,* or average value (e.g., mean, median, and mode); measures of *variability* or dispersion, or the spread of successive measures around an average value (e.g., range, standard deviation, variance); measures of *regression,* or the relation between two variables (e.g., the function best describing how two measures of responding vary together); and measures of *correlation,* or how well one variable predicts the value of another (e.g., the correlation coefficient, which is positive when two variables vary directly and negative when they vary inversely and the absolute value of which ranges from 1.0 when one variable is perfectly predicted by the other, to zero when one variable is completely independent of changes in the other). See also DISTRIBUTION, PROBABILITY.

Statistical inference estimates whether an experimental outcome is likely to have been produced by experimental operations or is better regarded as having occurred by chance. It compares an experimental outcome with a theoretical distribution of possible outcomes (e.g., normal, chi-square, or, in analyses of variance, F) based on the assumption that the outcome depended on chance. If the comparison shows that the outcome was highly unlikely on this basis (e.g., probability less than 0.05), the outcome is said to be *statistically significant*. Statistical and substantive significance are unrelated.

Steady state: performance maintained by a set of conditions after systematic session-to-session changes have become negligible (e.g., when the rate and pattern of responding within FI's does not vary systematically over sessions, the FI performance is said to have reached a steady rate). Steady-state performance is a preferred baseline for analyzing the effects of variables (if a baseline is unstable, it might be impossible to assess where it would have been had the variable not been introduced). The decision as to when a performance has reached a steady state depends on the criteria for stating that systematic changes have become negligible; such criteria have ranged from informal observation to stringent quantitative assessments.

Stereotyped response: a response with properties (especially topography) that are relatively invariant over successive occurrences.

Stimulus (plural: **stimuli**): any physical event, combination of events, or relation among events. The stimulus vocabulary classifies aspects of the environment in much the same way that the response vocabulary classifies aspects of behavior. Like responses, stimuli may be described in terms of physical or behavioral properties and, again like responses, they may be defined in terms of descriptive or functional classes (cf. OPERANT). The term may refer to any of the following: specific instances of physical events (e.g., the sound of a bell); combinations of events, sometimes also referred to as *compound stimuli* or *stimulus complexes* (e.g., feeder operations, with accompanying audi-

tory and visual components); the absence of events (e.g., a dark chamber as a stimulus); a relation among events (e.g., the matching relation as a stimulus in a matching-to-sample problem); specific physical properties of events (e.g., green referred to as a stimulus even though it is only one of several properties of a light); classes defined by physical properties (e.g., a stimulus class consisting of all lights within certain limits of intensity and wavelength); and classes defined in terms of behavioral functions (e.g., classes of effective discriminative stimuli or of stimuli effective as reinforcers or punishers).

When *stimulus* is used descriptively, the *continua* or dimensions along which stimuli vary (e.g., intensity, wavelength or frequency, spatial extent, duration) may be discussed in at least two distinct ways: A change in some stimulus property is said to produce a change in the stimulus, or it is said to change one stimulus to another. The usage is typically determined by convenience of exposition rather than convention (e.g., *the light was changed from green to blue* is equivalent to *the green light was replaced by blue*). When *stimulus* is used functionally, an event is not a stimulus unless it exerts control over behavior. Functional classes can often be characterized verbally even though their limits cannot be specified adequately in physical terms (e.g., red stimuli do not necessarily include wavelengths in the red region of the spectrum). See also ABSTRACTION, CONCEPT FORMATION, DISCRIMINATION, GENERALIZATION.

Stimulus continuum (plural: **continua**): a stimulus dimension. Stimulus continua that vary along intensive dimensions (e.g., brightness, loudness) are called *prothetic*; those that vary along nonintensive dimensions (e.g., color, pitch) are called *metathetic*. See also STIMULUS.

Stimulus control: the discriminative control of behavior (including control in respondent discrimination). See CONTROL, DISCRIMINATION, GENERALIZATION, STIMULUS.

Stimulus generalization: see GENERALIZATION.

Stimulus substitution: an account of respondent conditioning, no longer widely accepted, stating that the CS becomes a substitute for the US. But a CR is not simply a UR now elicited by a new stimulus; one of several problems is that CR's typically differ from UR's in many ways (e.g., chemical composition may distinguish the salivation elicited by a CS from that elicited by a US).

STM: short-term memory. See REMEMBERING.

Storage: in the memory metaphor of storage and retrieval, what the learner does when something to be remembered is presented. Some of the behavior relevant to the stimulus that occurs at or after storage has been called *rehearsal*. Cf. ENCODING, REHEARSAL, REMEMBERING.

Strain: see RATIO STRAIN.

Strategy: a higher-order discriminated operant characterized by relations among different stimuli, responses, and/or consequences occurring across trials and/or conditions, rather than by specific stimulus or response properties occurring within trials and/or conditions. Different strategies may be appropriate to different settings. For example, if the availability of reinforcers arranged by a VI schedule alternates between two levers, a *win-shift lose-stay* strategy (change levers after each reinforcer) will be effective, but a *win-stay lose-shift* strategy will not.

Strength: as a property of behavior, the resistance of behavior to change (e.g., resistance to extinction, to disruption by added stimuli, and/or to effects of reinforcing alternative responses). The term has also been used, in place of specific measures, to describe the general state of a response or reflex, on the assumption that the different measures vary together and reflect an underlying disposition to respond (e.g., if response latency decreases while magnitude, duration, and resistance to extinction increase, response strength is said to have increased). With operants, measures such as rate, latency, force, and duration have been used as indices of strength, but each is independently modifiable by differential reinforcement. For brevity without sacrificing generality, processes that might otherwise be described in terms of each of several different measures (especially rate, latency, and probability of response) are often described simply as increments or decrements in responding.

Stroop effect: a demonstration of competition between verbal and nonverbal responses to a verbal stimulus. It is difficult to name rapidly the different colors in which different color words are printed if the colors and the color words do not correspond.

Substitution: see STIMULUS SUBSTITUTION.

Successive discrimination: a discrimination in which two or more discriminative stimuli are presented one at a time rather than simultaneously and which therefore usually involves only a single response (e.g., as in a multiple schedule). In the most accurate usage, the organism is said to respond *in the presence of* each stimulus, but this usage is often abbreviated to responding *in, during,* or *to* each. Cf. SIMULTANEOUS DISCRIMINATION.

Summation: the accumulated effect of a repeated stimulus. A stimulus that does not elicit responding if presented only once may do so if presented repeatedly at a high enough rate.

Supernormal stimulus: see RELEASER.

Superstition: the modification or maintenance of behavior by *accidental* (also *adventitious, incidental,* or *spurious*) relations between responses and reinforcers, as opposed to those either explicitly or implicitly arranged (cf. CONTINGENCY). Classes of superstitions include: simple superstitions, in which responses are maintained, usually unstably, by reinforcers delivered independently of behavior; concurrent superstitions, in which one response is maintained by reinforcers produced by a different response; sensory superstitions, in which identical contingencies maintain different performances during different stimuli; and topographical superstitions, in which reinforcers produce and maintain a response topography that varies over a much narrower range than that specified by the limits of the operant class. Interpretations in terms of superstitious behavior must be drawn with caution, because it is inevitably variable either within or across organisms, and because performances that superficially appear to be superstitious can sometimes be shown to depend instead on subtle contingencies. Many human superstitions depend on rule-governed behavior rather than, or in addition to, accidental contingencies (e.g., to be superstitious about breaking mirrors, one need not first have seven years of bad luck after doing so).

Suppression: a reduction in responding directly or indirectly produced by an aversive stimulus (e.g., by punishment or by the presentation of a preaversive stimulus). The term is sometimes extended to any reduction of responding by a stimulus (e.g., an extinction stimulus), but such usages are not always accompanied by a demonstration that the stimulus reduced responding as opposed to having failed to maintain responding. Cf. INHIBITION.

Surface structure: the order of constituents in a particular sentence. Cf. DEEP STRUCTURE.

Symbolic behavior: in some usages, verbal behavior; in a fairly specialized usage, behavior the function of which has transferred from one stimulus to another by virtue of the membership of both stimuli in an *equivalence class.*

Symbolic matching: see MATCHING-TO-SAMPLE.

Symmetrical relation or **symmetry:** see EQUIVALENCE CLASS.

Syntax: see LINGUISTICS.

Synthesis: putting the parts obtained through analysis back together again. Cf. BEHAVIOR ANALYSIS.

T

T, t: usually, time.

Tact: a verbal discriminative response (as when the verbal response *apple* in the presence of an apple is said to *tact* the apple). The tact captures stimulus control as it enters into verbal behavior. The tact relation includes only responses in the presence of or shortly after a stimulus, and therefore is not equivalent to naming or reference.

Tandem (tand) schedule: a compound schedule in which a reinforcer is produced by the successive completion of two or more component schedules, all of which operate during a single stimulus. Cf. CHAINED SCHEDULE.

Taste aversion: rejection of substances with a given taste after their ingestion has been followed later by gastrointestinal distress or nausea (e.g., as produced by x-irradiation). It might be interpreted as operant behavior (punishment of ingestion of substances with this taste) or as respondent conditioning (where gastrointestinal distress is the US and taste becomes a CS). In either case, its special characteristic is the long delay (sometimes hours) between the taste and its aftermath. The procedure is ineffective over such delays if stimuli such as sounds or lights are substituted for taste. For this reason, taste aversion is often cited as an example of *preparedness.*

Taxis (plural: **taxes**): phylogenically determined movement or orientation toward or away from a stimulus (e.g., negative phototaxis is movement away from light). Cf. KINESIS.

Temporal conditioning: respondent conditioning in which a US is presented at regular intervals (e.g., every 10 minutes). Conditioning is said to have occurred when the CR tends to occur shortly before each US.

Temporal discrimination: discrimination based on temporal properties of stimuli (i.e., stimulus duration), often appealed to in accounts of spaced responding. For example, if a response is more likely to be emitted at 10 s than at 5 s since the last response, the two durations may be said to be discriminated. When changes in contingencies alter response rate, the temporal spacing of responses necessarily changes also. Thus, it is preferable to study temporal discrimination directly, as by reinforcing one response after one stimulus duration and a second after another. Duration as a discriminable property of stimuli has some unique features: A duration is not determined until time has passed, so a discriminative response cannot occur in its presence; and durations cannot change discontinuously, unlike other stimulus properties such as intensity.

Temporal integration: control of behavior by the distribution of events in time. Behavior can be affected by events extended over some time, and recent events may weigh more heavily than those further in the past. The way in which the events combine to affect current behavior is called temporal integration. When events are so far removed in time that they no longer contribute, they are said to be beyond the organism's *time horizon.*

Terminal behavior: stereotyped behavior that reliably occurs late in interstimulus intervals in superstition procedures or temporal conditioning, and usually related topographically to the behavior produced by the reinforcer or the CS (e.g., with pigeons, pecking given food presentations). Cf. INTERIM BEHAVIOR.

Terminal link: see CONCURRENT CHAIN SCHEDULES.

Terminal rate: see RATE OF RESPONDING.

Textual behavior: A formal verbal class in which a written stimulus occasions a corresponding vocal verbal response. The correspondence is defined by the one-to-one relation of verbal units (e.g., letters or words). Textual behavior is not equivalent to reading, because it does not include the additional behavior called understanding or reading for meaning. Cf. DICTATION-TAKING, ECHOIC BEHAVIOR, TRANSCRIPTION.

Three-term contingency: see CONTINGENCY.

Threshold: see PSYCHOPHYSICS.

Timeout (TO): a period of nonreinforcement arranged either by extinction during a stimulus or by removal of an opportunity to respond (e.g., with pigeons, which only rarely peck keys in darkness, by turning off all lights in the chamber). The term is occasionally extended to other cases (e.g., *timeout from avoidance,* during which no shocks are delivered) and so is more precisely specified as *timeout from positive reinforcement.*

Time schedule: a schedule of response-independent reinforcer deliveries. Aside from this difference, time schedules are classified like interval schedules. In *fixed-time (FT)* schedules, the time between reinforcers is constant (cf. TEMPORAL CONDITIONING); in *variable-time (VT)* schedules, it varies from one delivery to the next. A *random-time (RT)* schedule arranges a constant probability of reinforcer delivery at the end of constant recycling time periods. Cf. INTERVAL SCHEDULE.

Timing behavior: see MEDIATING BEHAVIOR, TEMPORAL DISCRIMINATION.

Titration schedule: a schedule in which one response changes a variable in one direction and either a second response or nonoccurrence of the first changes it in the other (e.g., one response increases stimulus intensity while another decreases it, or each response produces an increment while each 5-s period of no responding produces a decrement).

TO: see TIMEOUT.

Token reinforcer: a conditioned reinforcer (e.g., a coin) that the organism may accumulate and later exchange for other reinforcers.

Topographical drift: gradual changes over time in the topography of responses maintained by a superstition procedure.

Topographical tagging: the identification of different functional properties of responding by correlating each with a different topography, especially a different spatial location. For example, shock avoidance in rats often consists of moderate rates of lever-pressing interrupted by occasional high-rate bursts after shock. If an escape lever is added, so that presses on the original lever continue to avoid shock but the rat can terminate shock once it is delivered only by pressing the escape lever, the high-rate bursts move to that lever. Thus, the moderate rates that continue on the original lever are tagged by their location as depending on the avoidance contingency, whereas the high-rate bursts are tagged as depending on shock deliveries and the escape contingency.

Topography of response: spatial configuration or form (e.g., how an organism operates an operandum or moves from one place to another), sometimes also specifying location (e.g., the place on a key the pigeon's beak strikes). Topographies can be complex and are more often described verbally than quantitatively (e.g., specifying the limb with which a rat presses a lever).

Trace conditioning: respondent conditioning in which a brief CS presentation is followed by the US after some fixed, extended time period (according to general usage not less than 5 s, but usually considerably longer). Cf. TEMPORAL CONDITIONING.

Transcription: A formal verbal class in which a written stimulus occasions a corresponding written response. The correspondence is defined by the one-to-one relation of verbal units (e.g., letters or words) and not by similarity of visual features (e.g., a typed original may be transcribed in longhand). Cf. DICTATION-TAKING, ECHOIC BEHAVIOR, TEXTUAL BEHAVIOR.

Transfer: substituting one set of discriminative stimuli for another (or, as a process, the stimulus control maintained after such a substitution). Transfer may be based on common properties of two sets of stimuli or on similar correlations of the two sets of stimuli with differential contingencies. In verbal learning, transfer from one task to another is usually assessed with reference to a control group that did not learn the first task; it is positive if the first task enhances performance on the second and negative if it does the opposite. Cf. GENERALIZATION, LEARNING SET, PROACTION, RETROACTION, TRANSPOSITION.

Transformational grammar: see GRAMMARS.

Transitive relation or **transitivity:** see EQUIVALENCE CLASS.

Transposition: in transfer experiments, a reversal of stimulus function depending on control by relations among stimuli on a continuum rather than by their absolute values (e.g., a rat learns to choose the larger of two circles and the smaller one is then replaced by a new one larger than either of the others; transposition with respect to size is shown if the rat chooses the new larger circle rather than the circle, now smaller, it had previously chosen).

Trial: a discrete period, usually stimulus-correlated, during which an organism has an opportunity to respond. Trials are separated by intertrial intervals that may consist of any of the following: a stimulus condition (e.g., a dark chamber); removal of the operandum (or operanda); or removal of the organism from the chamber (especially when the organism, after emitting a response such as running an alley, is no longer in a position to respond again). Trials distinguish discrete-operant procedures from free-operant procedures. Cf. OPERANT, PSEUDO-TRIAL.

Two-factor theory: in general, any behavioral theory involving the interaction of operant and respondent processes; more specifically, an avoidance theory stating that avoidance responses are operants reinforced by termination of conditioned aversive stimuli established through a respondent process.

U

Unconditioned reflex or **unconditional reflex:** a relation between a stimulus and a response that does not depend on prior conditioning. A reflex is the reliable production of a response by a stimulus. The stimulus is an *unconditioned stimulus* (US), and the response is an *unconditioned response* (UR). The stimulus is said to elicit the response. Examples of unconditioned reflexes are the salivary reflex (salivation elicited by food or acid in the mouth) and the patellar reflex (a knee jerk elicited by a blow on the patellar tendon). In each case, the elicitation of the response by the stimulus, not the response alone or the stimulus alone, defines the reflex. Cf. RESPONDENT.

Unconditioned or **unconditional response (UR)** or **stimulus (US):** see UNCONDITIONED REFLEX.

Undermatching: see MATCHING LAW.

Universals of language: see LANGUAGE UNIVERSALS.

UR: unconditioned response. See UNCONDITIONED REFLEX.

US: unconditioned stimulus. See UNCONDITIONED REFLEX.

V

Vacuum activity: an ethological term referring to responding (see FIXED ACTION PATTERN) in the absence of the stimulus (see RELEASER)

that ordinarily produces it. Cf. DISPLACEMENT ACTIVITY.

Variability: see STATISTICS. Variability is the raw material upon which selection operates. It is also a property for which contingencies can be arranged, but no single response can have variability because variability can only be a property of a population of responses.

Variable-interval schedule: see INTERVAL SCHEDULE.

Variable-ratio schedule: see RATIO SCHEDULE.

Variable-time schedule: see TIME SCHEDULE.

Variation: see VARIABILITY; cf. SELECTION.

Verbal behavior: any behavior involving words, without regard to modality (e.g., spoken, written, gestural). The units that function as words are determined by the practices of a verbal community. Cf. LANGUAGE, VOCAL BEHAVIOR.

Verbal discrimination: any discrimination among verbal stimuli, as in discriminating among nouns and verbs in a sentence. Discrimination among items on the basis of whether they appeared in a given context, *verbal recognition,* is a special case of verbal discrimination.

Verbal learning: see FREE RECALL, PAIRED-ASSOCIATES LEARNING, SERIAL LEARNING, VERBAL DISCRIMINATION, VERBAL RECOGNITION.

Verbal recognition: see VERBAL DISCRIMINATION.

VI: variable interval. See INTERVAL SCHEDULE.

Vicarious learning: see OBSERVATIONAL LEARNING.

Vocal behavior: Behavior that produces sound. Vocal behavior is not necessarily verbal. Cf. VERBAL BEHAVIOR.

Von Restorff effect: the enhanced likelihood of recall of a distinctive item in a list.

VR: variable ratio. See RATIO SCHEDULE.

VT: variable time. See TIME SCHEDULE.

W

Warm-up: a low or zero response rate at the start of a session followed by an increase to the rate maintained later, especially in avoidance performances.

Warning stimulus: a stimulus that precedes an avoidable aversive stimulus. See AVOIDANCE.

Wheel-running: sometimes taken as an index of level of activity, especially in rats. The rat runs inside the wheel, which usually turns in only one direction to simplify recording of revolutions or distance run. Wheel running has a high baseline level and is relatively continuous compared to such discrete responses as lever-presses.

Win-shift lose-stay or **win-stay lose-shift:** see STRATEGY.

Working memory: see METAMEMORY.

Y

Yoking: connecting chambers so that the performance of an organism in one determines the stimuli and/or schedules for an organism in the other (e.g., equating VR and VI reinforcement rates by letting the times between reinforcers in one organism's VR performance determine the intervals of another organism's VI schedule). In within-organism yoking, an experimental condition is yoked to some property of the organism's own performance in an earlier condition.

Conclusions from yoking must be cautiously drawn. For example, assume two types of rats equally distributed among groups in a yoking experiment on the role of avoidance in shock-induced ulcers. Sensitive types are prone to ulcers when shocked; they also respond rapidly at low shock levels receiving few shocks, but sporadically at higher levels receiving many shocks. Insensitive types are resistant to ulcers when shocked; they also respond slowly at low shock levels receiving many shocks, but rapidly at higher levels receiving few shocks. For each shock received by an avoidance rat, an unavoidable shock is delivered to its yoked partner. At low shock levels, only yoked rats develop ulcers (only insensitive avoidance rats respond slowly and receive frequent shocks; they do not develop ulcers, but all their yoked partners also receive frequent shocks and half of those are sensitive). At higher levels, more avoidance rats develop ulcers than do their yoked partners (sensitive avoidance rats respond sporadically, thereby receiving frequent shocks and developing ulcers; all their yoked partners also receive frequent shocks but only half of those are sensitive and develop ulcers). Thus, a yoking experiment done at one shock level would yield a different conclusion about avoidance and shock-induced ulcers than one done at another level.

Z

Zeigarnik effect: the greater likelihood of remembering an unfinished than a finished task.

Acknowledgments

Thanks go to the sources below, as well as to the authors, for granting permission to use material from copyrighted works. Full citations appear in the References section.

Fig. 1–1, from Tinbergen and Perdeck (1950), published with permission of E. J. Brill Publishers. Fig. 1–3, from Lashley (1930), by permission of The Journal Press.

Fig. 3–3, from Staddon and Simmelhag (1971), copyright 1971 by the American Psychological Association; adapted by permission.

Fig. 4–12, from Tolman and Honzik (1930), published in 1930 by The Regents of the University of California; reprinted by permission of the University of California Press. Fig. 4–13, from Held and Hein (1963), copyright 1963 by the American Psychological Association; reprinted by permission.

Fig. 5–3, from Camp, Raymond, and Church (1967), copyright 1967 by the American Psychological Association; adapted by permission. Fig. 5–4, from Holz and Azrin (1961), copyright 1961 by the Society for the Experimental Analysis of Behavior, Inc.; published with permission of the Society. Fig. 5–5, from Fowler and Trapold (1962), copyright 1962 by the American Psychological Association; adapted by permission.

Fig. 7–2, from Reynolds (1961b), copyright 1961 by the Society for the Experimental Analysis of Behavior, Inc.; adapted with permission of the Society. Fig. 7–5, from Honig, Boneau, Burstein, and Pennypacker (1963), copyright 1963 by the American Psychological Association; reprinted by permission.

Fig. 8–2 from Catania and Reynolds (1968), copyright 1968 by the Society for the Experimental Analysis of Behavior, Inc.; adapted with permission of the Society. Fig. 8–5, from Catania, Matthews, Silverman, and Yohalem (1977), copyright 1977 by the Society for the Experimental Analysis of Behavior, Inc.; published with permission of the Society. Fig. 8–7, from Dews (1962), copyright 1962 by the Society for the Experimental Analysis of Behavior, Inc.; published with permission of the Society. Fig. 8–9, from Reynolds (1961b), copyright 1961 by the Society for the Experimental Analysis of Behavior, Inc.; adapted with permission of the Society.

Fig. 9–8, from Geller (1960), copyright 1960 by the Society for the Experimental Analysis of Behavior, Inc.; published with permission of the Society. Fig. 9–9, from Blackman (1968), copyright 1968 by the Society for the Experimental Analysis of Behavior, Inc.; adapted with permission of the Society. Fig. 9–10, from Rescorla (1968), copyright 1968 by the American Psychological Association; adapted by permission. Fig. 9–11, from Revusky and Garcia (1970), published with permission of Academic Press.

Fig. 10–1, from Lubinski and Thompson (1987), copyright 1987 by the Society for the Experimental Analysis of Behavior, Inc.; published with permission of the Society.

Fig. 12–2, from N. F. Johnson (1965), adapted with permission of Academic Press. Fig. 12–4, from Collins and Quillian (1969), adapted with permission of Academic Press.

Fig. 13–4, from Rundus and Atkinson (1970), adapted with permission of Academic Press.

Fig. 14–2, from Tulving (1974), published with permission of American Scientist. Fig. 14–3, from Sperling (1960), copyright 1960 by the American Psychological Association; adapted by permission. Fig. 14–5, from Mel-

ton (1963), published with permission of Academic Press.

Fig. 15–1, from Shepard and Metzler (1971), copyright 1971 by the American Association for the Advancement of Science. Fig. 15–2, from Sternberg (1969), by permission of the author. Fig. 15–3, from Sternberg (1966), copyright 1966 by the American Association for the Advancement of Science. Fig. 15–4, from Thomas (1974), adapted with permission of Academic Press.

References

[Bracketed numbers indicate the pages on which each reference is cited.]

Adams, J. A. (1954). Psychomotor performance as a function of intertrial rest interval. *Journal of Experimental Psychology, 48,* 131–133. [283]

Ader, R., & Cohen, N. (1985). CNS-immune system interactions: conditioning phenomena. *Behavioral and Brain Sciences, 8,* 379–394. [189]

Ainslie, G. W. (1974). Impulse control in pigeons. *Journal of the Experimental Analysis of Behavior, 21,* 485–489. [182]

Allison, J., Miller, M., & Wozny, M. (1979). Conservation in behavior. *Journal of Experimental Psychology: General, 108,* 4–34. [83]

Anderson, J. R., & Bower, G. H. (1972). Recognition and retrieval processes in free recall. *Psychological Review, 79,* 97–123. [294]

Anderson, J. R., & Bower, G. H. (1973). *Human associative memory.* Washington, DC: Winston. [326]

Anderson, J. R., & Ross, B. H. (1980). Evidence against a semantic-episodic distinction. *Journal of Experimental Psychology: Human Learning and Memory, 6,* 441–466. [326]

Anger, D. (1956). The dependence of interresponse times upon the relative reinforcement of different interresponse times. *Journal of Experimental Psychology, 52,* 145–161. [163]

Anger, D. (1963). The role of temporal discriminations in the reinforcement of Sidman avoidance behavior. *Journal of Experimental Psychology, 6,* 477–506. [107]

Antonitis, J. J. (1951). Response variability in the white rat during conditioning, extinction, and reconditioning. *Journal of Experimental Psychology, 42,* 273–281. [116]

Ashcraft, M. H. (1982). The development of mental arithmetic: a chronometric approach. *Developmental Review, 2,* 213–236. [348]

Atkinson, R. C. (1972). Optimizing the learning of a second-language vocabulary. *Journal of Experimental Psychology, 96,* 124–129. [288]

Austin, J. L. (1962). *How to do things with words.* Cambridge, MA: Harvard University Press. [245]

Ayllon, T., & Azrin, N. H. (1968). *The token economy.* New York: Appleton-Century-Crofts. [176]

Azrin, N. H. (1956). Some effects of two intermittent schedules of immediate and nonimmediate punishment. *Journal of Psychology, 42,* 3–21. [95, 172]

Azrin, N. H., & Hake, D. F. (1969). Positive conditioned suppression: conditioned suppression using positive reinforcers as the unconditioned stimuli. *Journal of the Experimental Analysis of Behavior, 12,* 167–173. [204]

Azrin, N. H., & Holz, W. C. (1966). Punishment. In W. K. Honig (Ed.), *Operant behavior: Areas of research and application.* New York: Appleton-Century-Crofts. [94, 96]

Azrin, N. H., Hutchinson, R. R., & Hake, D. F. (1966). Extinction-induced aggression. *Journal of the Experimental Analysis of Behavior, 9,* 191–204. [78]

Azrin, N. H., Hutchinson, R. R., & Hake, D. F. (1967). Attack, avoidance, and escape reactions to aversive shock. *Journal of the Experimental Analysis of Behavior*, **10**, 131–148. [106]

Azrin, N. H., Hutchinson, R. R., & McLaughlin, R. (1965). The opportunity for aggression as an operant reinforcer during aversive stimulation. *Journal of the Experimental Analysis of Behavior*, **8**, 171–180. [78]

Bacotti, A. V. (1978). Responding under schedules combining response-dependent and response-independent shock delivery. *Journal of the Experimental Analysis of Behavior*, **29**, 267–272. [98]

Baddeley, A. D. (1976). *The psychology of memory.* New York: Basic Books. [325, 339]

Baddeley, A., & Hull, A. (1979). Prefix and suffix effects: do they have a common basis? *Journal of Verbal Learning and Verbal Behavior*, **18**, 129–140. [289]

Badia, P., Suter, S., & Lewis, P. (1966). Rat vocalization to shock with and without a CS. *Psychonomic Science*, **4**, 117–118. [50]

Baer, D. M., Peterson, R. F., & Sherman, J. A. (1967). The development of imitation by reinforcing behavioral similarity to a model. *Journal of the Experimental Analysis of Behavior*, **10**, 405–416. [216]

Baer, R. A., Detrich, R., & Weninger, J. M. (1988). On the functional role of the verbalization in correspondence training procedures. *Journal of Applied Behavior Analysis*, **21**, 345–356. [251]

Balda, R. P., Kamil, A. C., & Grim, K. (1986). Revisits to empty cache sites by nutcrackers. *Animal Behaviour*, **34**, 1289–1298. [145]

Baldie, B. J. (1976). The acquisition of the passive voice. *Journal of Child Language*, **3**, 331–348. [265]

Ballard, P. B. (1913). Obliviscence and reminiscence. *British Journal of Psychology Monograph Supplements*, **1** (No. 2). [323]

Bandura, A. (1986). *Social foundations of thought and action.* Englewood Cliffs, NJ: Prentice-Hall. [215]

Barrett, J. E., & Spealman, R. D. (1978). Behavior simultaneously maintained by both presentation and termination of noxious stimuli. *Journal of the Experimental Analysis of Behavior*, **29**, 375–383. [98]

Barrett, J. E., & Stanley, J. A. (1980). Maintenance of responding by squirrel monkeys under a concurrent shock-postponement,

fixed-interval shock-presentation schedule. *Journal of the Experimental Analysis of Behavior*, **34**, 117–129. [98]

Bartlett, F. C. (1932). *Remembering.* Cambridge: Cambridge University Press. [270, 311]

Bauer, D. W., & Miller, J. (1982). Stimulus-response compatibility and the motor system. *Quarterly Journal of Experimental Psychology*, **34A**, 367–380. [210]

Baum, W. M. (1973). The correlation-based law of effect. *Journal of the Experimental Analysis of Behavior*, **20**, 137–153. [80]

Bechterev, V. M. (1933). *General principles of human reflexology* (trans. E. Murphy & W. Murphy). London: Jarrolds. [189, 198]

Bellezza, F. S. (1982). Updating memory using mnemonic devices. *Cognitive Psychology*, **14**, 301–327. [305]

Bem, D. J. (1967). Self perception: an alternative interpretation of cognitive dissonance phenomena. *Psychological Review*, **74**, 183–200. [203, 215, 219, 242]

Bentall, R. P., & Lowe, C. F. (1987). The role of verbal behavior in human learning: III. Instructional effects in children. *Journal of the Experimental Analysis of Behavior*, **47**, 177–190. [251]

Bentall, R. P., Lowe, C. F., & Beasty, A. (1985). The role of verbal behavior in human learning: II. Developmental differences. *Journal of the Experimental Analysis of Behavior*, **43**, 165–181. [251]

Berko, J. (1958). The child's learning of English morphology. *Word*, **14**, 150–177. [278]

Bernstein. D. J., & Ebbesen, E. B. (1978). Reinforcement and substitution in humans: a multiple-response analysis. *Journal of the Experimental Analysis of Behavior*, **30**, 243–253. [83]

Bickerton, D. (1981). *Roots of language.* Ann Arbor, MI: Karoma. [275]

Bigelow, G. (1971). Fixed-ratio reinforcement of spaced responding. *Journal of the Experimental Analysis of Behavior*, **16**, 23–30. [170]

Bilbrey, J., & Winokur, S. (1973). Controls for and constraints on auto-shaping. *Journal of the Experimental Analysis of Behavior*, **20**, 323–332. [201]

Bisanz, G. L., Vesonder, G. T., & Voss, J. F. (1978). Knowledge of one's own responding and the relation of such knowledge to learning. *Journal of Experimental Psychology*, **25**, 116–128. [329]

Bjork, R. A. (1970). Positive forgetting: the non-interference of items intentionally forgotten. *Journal of Verbal Learning and Verbal Behavior*, **9**, 225–268. [328]

Bjork, R. A. (1978). The updating of human memory. In G. H. Bower (Ed.), *The psychology of learning and motivation. Vol. 12*. New York: Academic Press. [328]

Blackman, D. E. (1968). Conditioned suppression or facilitation as a function of the behavioral baseline. *Journal of the Experimental Analysis of Behavior*, **11**, 53–61. [205]

Blackman, D. E. (1977). Conditioned suppression and the effects of classical conditioning on operant behavior. In W. K. Honig & J. E. R. Staddon (Eds.), *Handbook of operant behavior*. Englewood Cliffs, NJ: Prentice-Hall. [203, 204]

Blodgett, H. C. (1929). The effect of the introduction of reward upon the maze performance of rats. *University of California Publications in Psychology*, **4**, 113–134. [85]

Bloom, A. H. (1981). *The linguistic shaping of thought*. Hillsdale, NJ: Erlbaum. [276]

Bloom, K. (1984). Distinguishing between social reinforcement and social elicitation. *Journal of Experimental Child Psychology*, **38**, 93–102. [230]

Blough, D. S. (1958). New test for tranquillizers. *Science*, **127**, 586–587. [114]

Blough, D. S. (1959). Delayed matching in the pigeon. *Journal of the Experimental Analysis of Behavior*, **2**, 151–160. [304]

Blough, D. M. (1989). Odd-item search in pigeons: display size and transfer effects. *Journal of Experimental Psychology: Animal Behavior Processes*, **15**, 14–22. [144]

Boakes, R. A. (1973). Response decrements produced by extinction and by response-independent reinforcement. *Journal of the Experimental Analysis of Behavior*, **19**, 293–302. [80]

Bohannon, J. N., III (1988). Flashbulb memories for the space shuttle disaster: a tale of two theories. *Cognition*, **29**, 179–196. [326]

Bolinger, D. (1973). Truth is a linguistic question. *Language*, **49**, 539–550. [242]

Bolles, R. C. (1970). Species-specific defense reactions and avoidance learning. *Psychological Review*, **77**, 32–48. [105, 106]

Bolles, R. C. (1975). *Theory of motivation* (2nd ed.). New York: Harper & Row. [59, 81]

Boren, J. J., & Devine, D. D. (1968). The repeated acquisition of behavioral chains. *Journal of the Experimental Analysis of Behavior*, **11**, 651–660. [124, 150]

Bousfield, W. A. (1953). The occurrence of clustering in the recall of randomly arranged associates. *Journal of General Psychology*, **49**, 229–240. [291]

Bower, G. H. (1970). Analysis of a mnemonic device. *American Scientist*, **58**, 496–510. [306]

Bower, G. H. (1981). Mood and memory. *American Psychologist*, **36**, 129–148. [315]

Bower, G. H., Black, J. B., & Turner, T. J. (1979). Scripts in memory for text. *Cognitive Psychology*, **11**, 177–220. [268, 327]

Bowler, P. J. (1983). *The eclipse of Darwinism*. Baltimore: The Johns Hopkins University Press. [31]

Braggio, J. T., Hall, A. D., Buchanan, J. P., & Nadler, R. D. (1982). Logical and illogical errors made by apes and children on a cognitive task. *Journal of Human Evolution*, **11**, 159–169. [255]

Braine, M. D. S., & Rumain, B. (1981). Development of comprehension of "or": evidence for a sequence of competencies. *Journal of Experimental Child Psychology*, **31**, 46–70. [276]

Brandauer, C. (1958). *The effects of uniform probabilities of reinforcement on the response rate of the pigeon*. Unpublished doctoral dissertation, Columbia University. [162]

Bransford, J. D., & Franks, J. J. (1971). The abstraction of linguistic ideas. *Cognitive Psychology*, **2**, 331–350. [270]

Breland, K., & Breland, M. (1961). The misbehavior of organisms. *American Psychologist*, **16**, 681–684. [209]

Bridgman, P. W. (1927). *The logic of modern physics*. New York: Macmillan. [352]

Bright, M. (1985). *Animal language*. Ithaca, NY: Cornell University Press. [254]

Brogden, W. J. (1939). Sensory preconditioning. *Journal of Experimental Psychology*, **25**, 323–332. [196]

Brooks, L. R. (1968). Spatial and verbal components of the act of recall. *Canadian Journal of Psychology*, **22**, 349–368. [291, 335]

Brown, J. (1958). Some tests of the decay theory of immediate memory. *Quarterly Journal of Experimental Psychology*, **10**, 12–21. [318]

Brown, P. L., & Jenkins, H. M. (1968). Auto-shaping of the pigeon's key-peck. *Journal of the Experimental Analysis of Behavior*, **11**, 1–8. [200]

Brown, R. (1973). *A first language*. Cambridge, MA: Harvard University Press. [276]

Brown, R., & McNeill, D. (1966). The "tip of the tongue" phenomenon. *Journal of Verbal Learning and Verbal Behavior*, **5**, 325–337. [239, 329]

Bruce, R. W. (1933). Conditions of transfer of training. *Journal of Experimental Psychology*, **16**, 343–361. [296]

Bryan, W. L., & Harter, N. (1899). Studies on the telegraphic language: the acquisition of a hierarchy of habits. *Psychological Review*, **6**, 345–375. [353]

Butler, R. A. (1957). The effect of deprivation of visual incentives on visual exploration motivation in monkeys. *Journal of Comparative and Physiological Psychology*, **50**, 177–179. [87]

Butterfield, E. C., Slocum, T. A., & Nelson, G. D. (1991). Cognitive and behavioral analyses of teaching and transfer: Are they different? In R. J. Sternberg & D. K. Detterman (Eds.), *Transfer on trial*. Norwood, NJ: Ablex. [340, 354]

Bykov, K. M. (1957). *The cerebral cortex and the internal organs* (trans. W. H. Gantt). New York: Chemical Publishing. [189]

Calkins, M. W. (1894). Association. *Psychological Review*, **1**, 476–483. [286]

Calkins, M. W. (1896). Association. II. *Psychological Review*, **3**, 32–49. [286]

Camp, D. S., Raymond, G. A., & Church, R. M. (1967). Temporal relationship between response and punishment. *Journal of Experimental Psychology*, **74**, 114–123. [96, 97]

Capaldi, E. D., & Davidson, T. L. (1979). Control of instrumental behavior by deprivation stimuli. *Journal of Experimental Psychology: Animal Behavior Processes*, **5**, 355–367. [219]

Capaldi, E. J., & Stevenson, H. W. (1957). Response reversal following different amounts of training. *Journal of Comparative and Physiological Psychology*, **50**, 195–198. [300]

Caramazza, A., & Brones, I. (1980). Semantic classification by bilinguals. *Canadian Journal of Psychology*, **34**, 77–81. [234]

Carmichael, L. C., Hogan, H. P., & Walter, A. A. (1932). An experimental study of the effect of language on the reproduction of visually perceived form. *Journal of Experimental Psychology*, **15**, 73–86. [311, 312]

Carter, D. E., & Werner, T. J. (1978). Complex learning and information processing by pigeons: a critical analysis. *Journal of the Experimental Analysis of Behavior*, **29**, 565–601. [154]

Cataldo, M. F., Bessman, C. A., Parker, L. H., Pearson, J. E. R., & Rogers, M. C. (1979). Behavioral assessment for pediatric intensive care units. *Journal of Applied Behavior Analysis*, **12**, 83–97. [203]

Catania, A. C. (1963a). Concurrent performances: a baseline for the study of reinforcement magnitude. *Journal of the Experimental Analysis of Behavior*. **6**, 299–300. [179]

Catania, A. C. (1963b). Concurrent performances: reinforcement interaction and response independence. *Journal of the Experimental Analysis of Behavior*, **6**, 253–263. [179]

Catania, A. C. (1968). Glossary. In A. C. Catania (Ed.), *Contemporary research in operant behavior*. Glenview, IL: Scott, Foresman. [362]

Catania, A. C. (1969). Concurrent performances: inhibition of one response by reinforcement of another. *Journal of the Experimental Analysis of Behavior*, **12**, 731–744. [178]

Catania, A. C. (1970). Reinforcement schedules and psychophysical judgments: a study of some temporal properties of behavior. In W. N. Schoenfeld (Ed.), *The theory of reinforcement schedules*. New York: Appleton-Century-Crofts. [120]

Catania, A. C. (1971). Reinforcement schedules: the role of responses preceding the one that produces the reinforcer. *Journal of the Experimental Analysis of Behavior*, **15**, 271–287. [164]

Catania, A. C. (1972). Chomsky's formal analysis of natural languages: a behavioral translation. *Behaviorism*, **1**, 1–15. [259, 354]

Catania, A. C. (1973a). The concept of the operant in the analysis of behavior. *Behaviorism*, **1**, 103–116. [118]

Catania, A. C. (1973b). The psychologies of structure, function, and development. *American Psychologist*, **28**, 434–443. [228, 354]

Catania, A. C. (1975). The myth of self-reinforcement. *Behaviorism*, **3**, 192–199. [221]

Catania, A. C. (1976a). Concurrent performances: rate constancies without changeover delays. *Journal of the Experimental Analysis of Behavior, 25,* 377–387. [275]

Catania, A. C. (1976b). Drug effects and concurrent performances. *Pharmacological Reviews, 27,* 385–394. [177]

Catania, A. C. (1978). The psychology of learning: some lessons from the Darwinian revolution. *Annals of the New York Academy of Sciences, 309,* 18–28. [9, 38, 355, 358]

Catania, A. C. (1980). Autoclitic processes and the structure of behavior. *Behaviorism, 8,* 175–186. [244, 247, 278]

Catania, A. C. (1983). Behavior analysis and behavior synthesis in the extrapolation from animal to human behavior. In G. Davey (Ed.), *Animal models of human behavior.* Chichester: Wiley. [360]

Catania, A. C. (1985a). Rule-governed behaviour and the origins of language. In C. F. Lowe, M. Richelle, D. E. Blackman, & C. M. Bradshaw (Eds.), *Behaviour analysis and contemporary psychology.* Hillsdale, NJ: Erlbaum. [256]

Catania, A. C. (1985b). The two psychologies of learning: blind alleys and nonsense syllables. In S. Koch & D. E. O'Leary (Eds.), *A century of psychology as science.* New York: McGraw-Hill. [351]

Catania, A. C. (1987). Some Darwinian lessons for behavior analysis. A review of Peter J. Bowler's *The eclipse of Darwinism. Journal of the Experimental Analysis of Behavior, 47,* 249–257. [31, 358]

Catania, A. C. (1989). Speaking of behavior. *Journal of the Experimental Analysis of Behavior, 52,* 193–196. [362]

Catania, A. C. (1991a). Glossary. In I. H. Iversen & K. A. Lattal (Eds.), *Experimental analysis of behavior.* Amsterdam: Elsevier/North-Holland. [362]

Catania, A. C. (1991b). The phylogeny and ontogeny of behavior. In N. A. Krasnegor (Ed.), *Biobehavioral determinants of language development.* Hillsdale, NJ: Erlbaum. [256]

Catania, A. C., & Brigham, T. A. (Eds.) (1978). *Handbook of applied behavior analysis: social and instructional processes.* New York: Irvington. [361]

Catania, A. C. & Cerutti, D. (1986). Some nonverbal properties of verbal behavior. In T. Thompson & M. D. Zeiler (Eds.), *Analysis*

and integration of behavioral units. Hillsdale, NJ: Erlbaum. [244]

Catania, A. C., & Gill, C. A. (1964). Inhibition and behavioral contrast. *Psychonomic Science, 1,* 257–258. [174]

Catania, A. C., Horne, P., & Lowe, C. F. (1989). Transfer of function across members of an equivalence class. *Analysis of Verbal Behavior, 7,* 99–110. [155]

Catania, A. C., & Keller, K. J. (1981). Contingency, contiguity, correlation, and the concept of causation. In P. Harzem & M. D. Zeiler (Eds.), *Predictability, correlation, and contiguity.* New York: Wiley. [80, 166]

Catania, A. C., Lowe, C. F., & Horne, P. (1990). Nonverbal behavior correlated with the shaped verbal behavior of children. *Analysis of Verbal Behavior, 8,* 43–55. [251]

Catania, A. C., Matthews, B. A., & Shimoff, E. (1982). Instructed versus shaped human verbal behavior: interactions with nonverbal responding. *Journal of the Experimental Analysis of Behavior, 38,* 233–248. [251]

Catania, A. C., Matthews, B. A., & Shimoff, E. H. (1990). Properties of rule-governed behaviour and their implications. In D. E. Blackman & H. Lejeune (Eds.), *Behaviour analysis in theory and practice.* Hillsdale, NJ: Erlbaum. [155, 251]

Catania, A. C., Matthews, B. A., Silverman, P. J., & Yohalem, R. (1977). Yoked variable-ratio and variable-interval responding in pigeons. *Journal of the Experimental Analysis of Behavior, 28,* 155–161. [162, 164]

Catania, A. C., & Reynolds, G. S. (1968). A quantitative analysis of the responding maintained by interval schedules of reinforcement. *Journal of the Experimental Analysis of Behavior, 11,* 327–383. [161, 167]

Catania, A. C., & Sagvolden, T. (1980). Preference for free choice over forced choice in pigeons. *Journal of the Experimental Analysis of Behavior, 34,* 77–86. [181]

Catania, A. C., Sagvolden, T., & Keller, K. J. (1988). Reinforcement schedules: retroactive and proactive effects of reinforcers inserted into fixed-interval performances. *Journal of the Experimental Analysis of Behavior, 49,* 49–73. [178]

Catania, A. C., Yohalem, R., & Silverman, P. J. (1980). Contingency and stimulus change in chained schedules of reinforcement. *Journal of the Experimental Analysis of Behavior,* **33,** 213–219. [175]

Cermak, L. S., & Craik, F. I. M. (Eds.). (1979). *Levels of processing in human memory.* Hillsdale, NJ: Erlbaum. [310]

Cerutti, D., & Catania, A. C. (1986). Rapid determinations of preference in multiple concurrent-chain schedules. *Journal of the Experimental Analysis of Behavior,* **46,** 211–218. [180]

Chang, J.-J., & Shepard, R. N. (1964). Meaningfulness in classification learning with pronounceable trigrams. *Journal of Verbal Learning and Verbal Behavior,* **3,** 85–90. [292]

Charney, R. (1980). Speech roles and the development of personal pronouns. *Journal of Child Language,* **7,** 509–528. [277]

Chase, S. (1938). *The tyranny of words.* New York: Harcourt, Brace & World. [275]

Chase, W. G., & Simon, H. A. (1973). Perception in chess. *Cognitive Psychology,* **4,** 55–81. [345]

Cheng, K., & Roberts, W. A. (1989). Timing multimodal events in pigeons. *Journal of the Experimental Analysis of Behavior,* **52,** 363–376. [144]

Chiat, S. (1982). If I were you and you were me: the analysis of pronouns in a pronoun-reversing child. *Journal of Child Language,* **9,** 359–379. [277]

Chomsky, N. (1959). Review of B. F. Skinner's *Verbal behavior. Language,* **35,** 26–58. [228]

Chomsky, N., & Miller, G. A. (1963). Introduction to the formal analysis of natural languages. In R. D. Luce, R. R. Bush, & E. Galanter (Eds.), *Handbook of mathematical psychology. Vol. II.* New York: Wiley. [259, 260]

Chung, S.-H., & Herrnstein, R. J. (1967). Choice and delay of reinforcement. *Journal of the Experimental Analysis of Behavior,* **10,** 67–74. [179]

Church, R. M. (1963). The varied effects of punishment on behavior. *Psychological Review,* **70,** 369–402. [94]

Church, R. M. (1969). Response suppression. In B. A. Campbell & R. M. Church (Eds.), *Punishment and aversive behavior.* New York: Appleton-Century-Crofts. [96]

Clark, H. H., & Sengul, C. J. (1979). In search of referents for nouns and pronouns. *Memory and Cognition,* **7,** 35–41. [277]

Collier, G. H., & Rovee-Collier, C. K. (1981). A comparative analysis of optimal foraging behavior: laboratory simulations. In A. C. Kamil & T. D. Sargent (Eds.), *Foraging behavior.* New York: Garland. [136]

Collins, A. M., & Quillian, M. R. (1969). Retrieval time from semantic memory. *Journal of Verbal Learning and Verbal Behavior,* **8,** 240–247. [271, 272]

Conrad, C. (1972). Cognitive economy in semantic memory. *Journal of Experimental Psychology,* **92,** 149–154. [272]

Conrad, R. (1964). Acoustic confusions in immediate memory. *British Journal of Psychology,* **55,** 75–84. [308]

Cook, R. G., Wright, A. A., & Sands, S. F. (1991). Interstimulus interval and viewing time effects in monkey list memory. *Animal Learning and Behavior,* **19,** 153–163. [310]

Cooley, C. H. (1908). A study of the early use of self-words by a child. *Psychological Review,* **15,** 339–357. [277]

Cott, A., Pavlovski, R. P., & Black, A. H. (1981). Operant conditioning and discrimination of alpha: some methodological limitations inherent in response-discrimination experiments. *Journal of Experimental Psychology: General,* **110,** 398–414. [219]

Craik, F. I. M. (1983). On the transfer of information from temporary to permanent memory. *Philosophical Transactions of the Royal Society of London B,* **302,** 341–359. [325, 328]

Craik, F. I. M. (1985). Paradigms in human memory research. In L. Nilsson & T. Archer (Eds.), *Perspectives on learning and memory.* Hillsdale, NJ: Erlbaum. [308]

Craik, F. I. M., & Lockhart, R. S. (1972). Levels of processing: a framework for memory research. *Journal of Verbal Learning and Verbal Behavior,* **11,** 671–684. [319]

Crowder, R. G. (1976). *Principles of learning and memory.* Hillsdale, NJ: Erlbaum. [289, 320, 325, 339]

Dalrymple-Alford, E. C. (1976). Response bias and judgments of the location of clicks in sentences. *Perception and Psychophysics,* **19,** 303–308. [264]

Damon, W., & Hart, D. (1982). The development of self-understanding from infancy through adolescence. *Child Development,* **53,** 841–864. [277]

Daniels, A. H. (1895). The memory after-image and attention. *American Journal of Psychology*, **6**, 558–564. [318]

Danks, J. H., & Glucksberg, S. (1970). Psychological scaling of linguistic properties. *Language and Speech*, **13**, 118–140. [262]

Danks, J. H., & Glucksberg, S. (1980). Experimental psycholinguistics. *Annual Review of Psychology*, **31**, 391–417. [268]

Darwin, C. (1859). *On the origin of species*. London: John Murray (reprinted Cambridge, MA: Harvard University Press, 1966). [31, 36, 352, 358, 360]

Darwin, C. J., Turvey, M. T., & Crowder, R. G. (1972). An auditory analogue of the Sperling partial report procedure: evidence for brief auditory storage. *Cognitive Psychology*, **3**, 255–267. [318]

Davis, H., & McIntire, R. W. (1969). Conditioned suppression under positive, negative, and no contingency between conditioned and unconditioned stimuli. *Journal of the Experimental Analysis of Behavior*, **12**, 633–640. [206]

Davis, H., Memmott, J., & Hurwitz, H. M. B. (1975). Autocontingencies: a model for subtle behavioral control. *Journal of Experimental Psychology: General*, **104**, 169–188. [166]

Davis, H., & Pérusse, R. (1988). Numerical competence in animals: definitional issues, current evidence, and a new research agenda. *Behavioral and Brain Sciences*, **11**, 561–615. [144]

Dawkins, R. (1976). *The selfish gene*. New York: Oxford University Press. [31, 214, 242, 336, 358]

Dawkins, R. (1982). *The extended phenotype*. San Francisco: Freeman. [32, 35, 214]

Dawkins, R. (1986). *The blind watchmaker*. New York: Norton. [31, 32, 33, 36]

Dawkins, R., & Krebs, J. R. (1978). Animal signals: information or manipulation? In J. R. Krebs & N. B. Davies (Eds.), *Behavioral ecology*. Sunderland, MA: Sinauer. [214]

Day, W. F. (1969). On certain similarities between the philosophical investigations of Ludwig Wittgenstein and the operationism of B. F. Skinner. *Journal of the Experimental Analysis of Behavior*, **12**, 489–506. [242]

De Casper, A. J., & Fifer, W. P. (1980). Of human bonding: newborns prefer their mothers' voices. *Science*, **208**, 1174–1176. [230]

Delius, J. D., & Nowak, B. (1982). Visual symmetry recognition by pigeons. *Psychological Research*, **44**, 199–212. [144]

Deluty, M. Z. (1976). Choice and the rate of punishment in concurrent schedules. *Journal of the Experimental Analysis of Behavior*, **25**, 75–80. [172]

Deluty, M. Z. (1978). Self-control and impulsiveness involving aversive events. *Journal of Experimental Psychology: Animal Behavior Processes*, **4**, 250–266. [184]

Dennett, D. C. (1987). *The intentional stance*. Cambridge, MA: The MIT Press. [214]

DeRose, J. C., McIlvane, W. J., Dube, W. V., Galpin, V. C., & Stoddard, L. T. (1988). Emergent simple discrimination established by indirect relation to differential consequences. *Journal of the Experimental Analysis of Behavior*, **50**, 1–20. [155]

Deutsch, R. (1974). Conditioned hypoglycemia: a mechanism for saccharin-induced sensitivity to insulin in the rat. *Journal of Comparative and Physiological Psychology*, **86**, 350–358. [189]

Devany, J. M., Hayes, S. C., & Nelson, R. O. (1986). Equivalence class formation in language-able and language-disabled children. *Journal of the Experimental Analysis of Behavior*, **46**, 243–257. [155]

De Villiers, J. G., & De Villiers, P. A. (1978). *Language acquisition*. Cambridge, MA: Harvard University Press. [276]

De Villiers, P. A., & De Villiers, J. G. (1974). On this, that, and the other: nonegocentrism in very young children. *Journal of Experimental Child Psychology*, **18**, 438–447. [277]

de Waal, F. (1989). *Peacemaking among primates*. Cambridge, MA: Harvard University Press. [215]

Dews, P. B. (1960). Free-operant behavior under conditions of delayed reinforcement: I. CRF-type schedules. *Journal of the Experimental Analysis of Behavior*, **3**, 221–234. [166, 170]

Dews, P. B. (1962). The effect of multiple S$^\Delta$ periods on responding on a fixed-interval schedule. *Journal of the Experimental Analysis of Behavior*, **5**, 369–374. [164, 168]

Dews, P. B. (1970). Drugs in psychology. A commentary on T. Thompson & C. R. Schuster's *Behavioral Pharmacology*. *Journal of the Experimental Analysis of Behavior*, **13**, 395–406. [173]

Dill, L. M. (1974). The escape response of the zebra danio (*Brachydanio rerio*): II. The effect of experience. *Animal Behavior,* 22, 723–730. [56]

Dinsmoor, J. A. (1954). Punishment: I. The avoidance hypothesis. *Psychological Review,* 61, 34–46. [110]

Dinsmoor, J. A. (1983). Observing and conditioned reinforcement. *Behavioral and Brain Sciences,* 6, 693–728. [174, 175]

Donahoe, J. W., & Palmer, D. C. (1989). The interpretation of complex human behavior: some reactions to *Parallel Distributed Processing. Journal of the Experimental Analysis of Behavior,* 51, 399–416. [342, 346, 358]

Dreyfus, H. L. (1979). *What computers can't do* (rev. ed.). New York: Harper & Row. [258, 343]

Dreyfus, H. L., & Dreyfus, S. E. (1986). *Mind over machine.* New York: Macmillan. [345]

Dugdale, N., & Lowe, C. F. (1990). Naming and stimulus equivalence. In D. E. Blackman & H. Lejeune (Eds.), *Behaviour analysis in theory and practice.* Hillsdale, NJ: Erlbaum. [155]

Duncker, K. (1945). On problem solving. *Psychological Monographs,* 58, (5), Whole No. 270. [346]

Dunham, P. J. (1977). The nature of reinforcing stimuli. In W. K. Honig & J. E. R. Staddon (Eds.), *Handbook of operant behavior.* Englewood Cliffs, NJ: Prentice-Hall. [83]

Dworkin, B. R., & Miller, N. (1986). Failure to replicate visceral learning in the acute curarized rat preparation. *Behavioral Neuroscience,* 100, 299–314. [115]

Ebbinghaus, H. (1885). *Über das Gedächtnis.* Leipzig: Duncker & Humblot (*Memory,* trans. H. A. Ruger & C. E. Bussenius, New York: Teachers College, 1913; reprinted by Dover, 1964). [235, 283, 285, 322, 352]

Eckerman, D. A., Hienz, R. D., Stern, S., & Kowlowitz, V. (1980). Shaping the location of a pigeon's peck: effect of rate and size of shaping steps. *Journal of the Experimental Analysis of Behavior,* 33, 299–310. [113]

Eimas, P. D., Siqueland, E. R. Jusczyk, P., & Vigorito, J. (1971). Speech perception in early infancy. *Science,* 171, 303–306. [230]

Eisenberger, R., Karpman, M., & Trattner, T. (1967). What is the necessary and sufficient condition for reinforcement in the contin-gency situation? *Journal of Experimental Psychology,* 74, 342–350. [83]

Epstein, R. (1981). On pigeons and people: a preliminary look at the Columban Simulation Project. *Behavior Analyst,* 4, 43–55. [348]

Epstein, R., Lanza, R. P., & Skinner, B. F. (1980). Symbolic communication between two pigeons (*Columba livia domestica*). *Science,* 207, 543–545. [256]

Epstein, R., Lanza, R. P., & Skinner, B. F. (1981). "Self-awareness" in the pigeon. *Science,* 212, 695–696. [217]

Epstein, R., & Skinner, B. F. (1980). Resurgence of responding after the cessation of response-independent reinforcement. *Proceedings of the National Academy of Sciences,* 77, 6251–6253. [76]

Erdelyi, M. H., & Kleinbard, J. (1978). Has Ebbinghaus decayed with time?: the growth of recall (hypermnesia) over days. *Journal of Experimental Psychology: Human Learning and Memory,* 4, 275–289. [323]

Esper, E. A. (1973). *Analogy and association in linguistics and psychology.* Athens: University of Georgia Press. [240, 244, 278]

Estes, W. K. (1944). An experimental study of punishment. *Psychological Monographs,* 57, No. 263. [93]

Estes, W. K. (1964). All-or-none processes in learning and retention. *American Psychologist,* 19, 16–25. [287]

Estes, W. K. (1976). The cognitive side of probability learning. *Psychological Review,* 83, 37–64. [346]

Estes, W. K., & Skinner, B. F. (1941). Some quantitative properties of anxiety. *Journal of Experimental Psychology,* 29, 390–400. [202, 204]

Falk, J. L. (1971). The nature and determinants of adjunctive behavior. *Physiology and Behavior,* 6, 577–588. [52]

Falk, J. L. (1977). The origin and functions of adjunctive behavior. *Animal Learning and Behavior,* 5, 325–335. [52]

Fantino, E. (1977). Conditioned reinforcement: choice and information. In W. K. Honig & J. E. R. Staddon (Eds.), *Handbook of operant behavior.* Englewood Cliffs, NJ: Prentice-Hall. [175]

Fantino, E., & Abarca, N. (1985). Choice, optimal foraging, and the delay-reduction hypothesis. *Behavioral and Brain Sciences*, **8**, 315–330. [181]

Fearing, F. (1930). *Reflex action*. Baltimore: Williams & Wilkins. [42]

Felton, M., & Lyon, D. O. (1966). The post-reinforcement pause. *Journal of the Experimental Analysis of Behavior*, **9**, 131–134. [169]

Ferster, C. B. (1958). Control of behavior in chimpanzees and pigeons by time out from positive reinforcement. *Psychological Monographs*, **72**, (8, Whole No. 461). [110]

Ferster, C. B. (1960). Intermittent reinforcement of matching to sample in the pigeon. *Journal of the Experimental Analysis of Behavior*, **3**, 259–272. [151]

Ferster, C. B., & Hammer, C. E., Jr. (1966). Synthesizing the components of arithmetic behavior. In W. K. Honig (Ed.), *Operant behavior: areas of research and application*. New York: Appleton-Century-Crofts. [245]

Ferster, C. B., & Skinner, B. F. (1957). *Schedules of reinforcement*. New York: Appleton-Century-Crofts. [40, 72, 121, 158, 161, 185, 352]

Field, T. M., Woodson, R., Greenberg, R., & Cohen, D. (1982). Discrimination and imitation of facial expressions by neonates. *Science*, **218**, 179–181. [214]

Fields, L., & Verhave, T. (1987). The structure of equivalence classes. *Journal of the Experimental Analysis of Behavior*, **48**, 317–332. [154]

Fillenbaum, S. (1966). Memory for gist: some relevant variables. *Language and Speech*, **9**, 217–227. [270]

Fillenbaum, S., & Rapoport, A. (1971). *Structures in the subjective lexicon*. New York: Academic Press. [271]

Fillmore, C. J. (1968). The case for case. In E. Bach & R. T. Harms (Eds.), *Universals in linguistic theory*. New York: Holt, Rinehart & Winston. [268]

Findley, J. D. (1962). An experimental outline for building and exploring multioperant behavior repertoires. *Journal of the Experimental Analysis of Behavior*, **5**, 113–166. [170, 176]

Findley, J. D., & Brady, J. V. (1965). Facilitation of large ratio performance by use of conditioned reinforcement. *Journal of the Experimental Analysis of Behavior*, **8**, 125–129. [176]

Finke, R. A. (1979). The functional equivalence of mental images and errors of movement. *Cognitive Psychology*, **11**, 235–264. [334]

Fischer, K. W. (1980). A theory of cognitive development: the control and construction of hierarchies of skills. *Psychological Review*, **87**, 477–531. [340]

Flavell, J. H., Friedrichs, A. G., & Hoyt, J. D. (1970). Developmental changes in memorization processes. *Cognitive Psychology*, **1**, 324–340. [328]

Fletcher, P., & Garman, M. (Eds.) (1986). *Language acquisition* (2nd ed.). New York: Cambridge University Press. [276]

Fodor, J. A., & Bever, T. G. (1965). The psychological reality of linguistic segments. *Journal of Verbal Learning and Verbal Behavior*, **4**, 414–420. [263, 264]

Foss, D. J. (1988). Experimental psycholinguistics. *Annual Review of Psychology*, **39**, 301–348. [273, 325]

Fowler, C. A., Wolford, G., Slade, R., & Tassinary, L. (1981). Lexical access with and without awareness. *Journal of Experimental Psychology: General*, **110**, 341–362. [232]

Fowler, H., & Trapold, M. A. (1962). Escape performance as a function of delay of reinforcement. *Journal of Experimental Psychology*, **63**, 464–467. [101]

Fraenkel, G. S., & Gunn, D. L. (1961). *The orientation of animals*. New York: Dover. [37]

Fraser, C., Bellugi, U., & Brown, R. (1963). Control of grammar in imitation, comprehension and production. *Journal of Verbal Learning and Verbal Behavior*, **2**, 121–135. [269]

Frey, P. W. (Ed.). (1977). *Chess skill in man and machine*. New York: Springer-Verlag. [343]

Fromkin, V. A. (1971). The non-anomalous nature of anomalous utterances. *Language*, **47**, 27–52. [230]

Galef, B. G., Jr., & Stein, M. (1985). Demonstrator influence on observer diet preference: analysis of critical social interactions and olfactory signals. *Animal Learning and Behavior*, **13**, 31–38. [215]

Gallistel, C. R. (1980). *The organization of action*. Hillsdale, NJ: Erlbaum. [40, 43, 208]

Gallistel, C. R. (1990). *The organization of learning*. Cambridge, MA: The MIT Press. [87, 145, 336]

Gallup, G. G., Jr. (1979). Self-awareness in primates. *American Scientist*, **67**, 417–419. [217]

Galton, F. (1879). Psychometric experiments. *Brain*, **2**, 149–162. [235, 270]

Garcia, J., & Koelling, R. A. (1966). Relation of cue to consequence in avoidance learning. *Psychonomic Science*, **4**, 123–124. [210]

Gardner, R. A., & Gardner, B. T. (1969). Teaching sign language to a chimpanzee. *Science*, **165**, 664–672. [255]

Garner, W. R. (1974). *The processing of information and structure*. Hillsdale, NJ: Erlbaum. [340]

Garrett, M., Bever, T. G., & Fodor, J. (1966). The active use of grammar in speech perception. *Perception and Psychophysics*, **1**, 30–32. [264]

Geller, I. (1960). The acquisition and extinction of conditioned suppression as a function of the base-line reinforcer. *Journal of the Experimental Analysis of Behavior*, **3**, 235–240. [202, 203]

Gewirtz, J. L., & Stingle, K. G. (1968). Learning of generalized imitation as the basis for identification. *Psychological Review*, **75**, 374–397. [216]

Gibbon, J., Farrell, L., Locurto, C. M., Duncan, H. J., & Terrace, H. S. (1980). Partial reinforcement in autoshaping with pigeons. *Animal Learning and Behavior*, **8**, 45–59. [190]

Gibson, E. J. (1965). Learning to read. *Science*, **148**, 1066–1072. [143, 231, 299, 308]

Gibson, J. J. (1979). *The ecological approach to visual perception*. Boston: Houghton Mifflin. [10, 12, 130]

Gilbert, R. M. (1972). Variation and selection of behavior. In R. M. Gilbert & J. R. Millenson (Eds.), *Reinforcement: behavioral analyses*. New York: Academic Press. [358]

Gillan, D. J. (1981). Reasoning in the chimpanzee: II. Transitive inference. *Journal of Experimental Psychology: Animal Behavior Processes*, **7**, 150–164. [255]

Gillan, D. J., Premack, D., & Woodruff, G. (1981). Reasoning in the chimpanzee: I. Analogical reasoning. *Journal of Experimental Psychology: Animal Behavior Processes*, **7**, 1–17. [255]

Glanzer, M., & Cunitz, A. R. (1966). Two storage mechanisms in free recall. *Journal of Verbal Learning and Verbal Behavior*, **5**, 351–360. [289]

Glanzer, M., & Dolinsky, R. (1965). The anchor for the serial position curve. *Journal of Verbal Learning and Verbal Behavior*, **4**, 267–273. [284]

Glaser, R., & Bassok, M. (1989). Learning theory and the study of instruction. *Annual Review of Psychology*, **40**, 631–666. [354]

Glaze, J. A. (1928). The association value of non-sense syllables. *Journal of Genetic Psychology*, **35**, 255–267. [270, 283]

Gleick, J. (1987). *Chaos*. New York: Viking. [33]

Gleitman, L. R., & Gleitman, H. (1970). *Phrase and paraphrase*. New York: Norton. [265]

Gleitman, L. R., & Rozin, P. (1973). Teaching reading by use of a syllabary. *Reading Research Quarterly*, **8**, 447–483. [232, 293]

Glencross, D. J. (1977). Control of skilled movements. *Psychological Bulletin*, **84**, 14–29. [210]

Glucksberg, S., & Danks, J. H. (1969). Grammatical structure and recall: a function of the space in immediate memory or of recall delay? *Perception and Psychophysics*, **6**, 113–117. [266]

Glucksberg, S., Gildea, P., & Bookin, H. B. (1982). On understanding nonliteral speech: can people ignore metaphors? *Journal of Verbal Learning and Verbal Behavior*, **21**, 85–98. [273]

Glucksberg, S., & McCloskey, M. (1981). Decisions about ignorance: knowing that you don't know. *Journal of Experimental Psychology: Human Learning and Memory*, **7**, 311–325. [315, 329]

Goldiamond, I. (1964). A research and demonstration procedure in stimulus control, abstraction, and environmental programming. *Journal of the Experimental Analysis of Behavior*, **7**, 216. [292]

Gollub, L. R. (1966). Stimulus generalization of response-position in the rat. *Psychonomic Science*, **6**, 433–434. [116]

Gollub, L. R. (1977). Conditioned reinforcement: schedule effects. In W. K. Honig & J. E. R. Staddon (Eds.), *Handbook of operant behavior*. Englewood Cliffs, NJ: Prentice-Hall. [175, 177]

Gopnik, A. (1981). Development of non-nominal expressions in 1-2 year-olds: why the first words aren't about things. In P. Dale & D. Ingrams (Eds.), *Child language*. Baltimore: University Park Press. [276]

Gormezano, I. (1972). Investigations of defense and reward conditioning in the rabbit. In A. H. Black & W. F. Prokasy (Eds.), *Classical conditioning II*. New York: Appleton-Century-Crofts. [189]

Gould, J. D. (1978). How experts dictate. *Journal of Experimental Psychology: Human Perception and Performance, 4,* 648–661. [233]

Gould, S. J. (1975). Darwin's "Big Book." *Science, 188,* 824–827. [360]

Gould, S. J. (1977). *Ontogeny and phylogeny.* Cambridge, MA: Harvard University Press. [32]

Gould, S. J. (1989). *Wonderful life.* New York: Norton. [30]

Gould, S. J., & Lewontin, R. C. (1979). The spandrels of San Marco and the Panglossian paradigm: a critique of the adaptationist programme. *Proceedings of the Royal Society of London B, 205,* 581–598. [36, 37, 275]

Gouzoules, S., Gouzoules, H., & Marler, P. (1984). Rhesus monkey (*Macaca mulatta*) screams: representational signalling in the recruitment of agonistic aid. *Animal Behaviour, 32,* 182–193. [215]

Graefe, T. M., & Watkins, M. J. (1980). Picture rehearsal: an effect of selectively attending to pictures no longer in view. *Journal of Experimental Psychology: Human Learning and Memory, 6,* 156–162. [335]

Gray, J. (1953). *How animals move.* London: Cambridge University Press. [208]

Green, L., & Snyderman, M. (1980). Choice between rewards differing in amount and delay: toward a choice model of self-control. *Journal of the Experimental Analysis of Behavior, 34,* 135–147. [184]

Greenberg, J. H. (Ed.) (1966). *Universals of language.* Cambridge, MA: The MIT Press. [274]

Greeno, J. G. (1974). Hobbits and orcs: acquisition of a sequential concept. *Cognitive Psychology, 6,* 270–292. [343]

Greenspoon, J. (1955). The reinforcing effect of two spoken sounds on the frequency of two responses. *American Journal of Psychology, 68,* 409–416. [242, 247]

Grosch, J., & Neuringer, A. (1981). Self-control in pigeons under the Mischel paradigm. *Journal of the Experimental Analysis of Behavior, 35,* 3–21. [185]

Groves, P. M., & Thompson, R. F. (1970). Habituation: a dual-process theory. *Psychological Review, 77,* 419–450. [49]

Guthrie, E. R. (1935). *The psychology of learning.* New York: Harper. [193, 352]

Guthrie, E. R., & Horton, G. P. (1946). *Cats in a puzzle box.* New York: Rinehart. [79]

Guttman, N. (1959). Generalization gradients around stimuli associated with different reinforcement schedules. *Journal of Experimental Psychology, 58,* 335–340. [139]

Guttman, N., & Kalish, H. I. (1956). Discriminability and stimulus generalization. *Journal of Experimental Psychology, 51,* 79–88. [139]

Haber, R. N. (1969). Eidetic images. *Scientific American, 220,* 36–44. [335]

Hadamard, J. (1949). *The psychology of invention in the mathematical field.* Princeton, NJ: Princeton University Press. [311]

Hailman, J. P. (1969). How an instinct is learned. *Scientific American, 221* (6), 98–106. [19, 20]

Hall, W. G., & Oppenheim, R. W. (1987). - Developmental psychobiology: prenatal, perinatal, and early postnatal aspects of behavioral development. *Annual Review of Psychology, 38,* 91–128. [40]

Hanson, H. M. (1959). Effects of discrimination training on stimulus generalization. *Journal of Experimental Psychology, 58,* 321–334. [138]

Harlow, H. F. (1949). The formation of learning sets. *Psychological Review, 56,* 51–65. [148]

Harris, A. H., & Turkkan, J. S. (1981). Generalization of conditioned blood pressure elevations: schedule and stimulus control effects. *Physiology and Behavior, 26,* 935–940. [115]

Harris, C. S. (1965). Perceptual adaptation to inverted, reversed, and displaced vision. *Psychological Review, 72,* 419–444. [89]

Harris, M. (1977). *Cannibals and kings.* New York: Random House. [213, 358]

Hart, B. L. (1973). Reflexive behavior. In G. Bermant (Ed.), *Perspectives on animal behavior.* Glenview, IL: Scott, Foresman. [38]

Hart, B. M., Reynolds, N. J., Baer, D. M., Brawley, E. R., & Harris, F. R. (1968). Effect of contingent and non-contingent social reinforcement on the cooperative play of a preschool child. *Journal of Applied Behavior Analysis, 1,* 73–76. [78]

Hartman, A. M. (1975). Analysis of conditions leading to the regulation of water flow by a beaver. *Psychological Record, 25,* 427–431. [106]

Harzem, P., Lee, I., & Miles, T. R. (1976). The effects of pictures on learning to read. *British Journal of Educational Psychology, 46,* 318–322. [354]

Hasher, L., & Griffin, M. (1978). Reconstructive and reproductive processes in memory. *Journal of Experimental Psychology, 4,* 318–330. [315]

Hawkes, L., & Shimp, C. P. (1975). Reinforcement of behavioral patterns: shaping a scallop. *Journal of the Experimental Analysis of Behavior, 23,* 3–16. [170]

Hayes, K., & Hayes, C. (1951). The intellectual development of a home-raised chimpanzee. *Proceedings of the American Philosophical Society, 95,* 105–109. [255]

Healy, A. F. (1976). Detection errors on the word *the*: evidence for reading units larger than letters. *Journal of Experimental Psychology: Human Perception and Performance, 2,* 235–242. [291]

Hearst, E. (1958). The behavioral effects of some temporally defined schedules of reinforcement. *Journal of the Experimental Analysis of Behavior, 1,* 45–55. [165]

Hearst, E., Besley, S., & Farthing, G. W. (1970). Inhibition and the stimulus control of operant behavior. *Journal of the Experimental Analysis of Behavior, 14,* 373–409. [139, 140]

Hearst, E., & Jenkins, H. M. (1974). *Sign-tracking: the stimulus-reinforcer relation and directed action.* Austin, TX: Psychonomic Society. [201]

Hearst, E., Koresko, M. B., & Poppen, R. (1964). Stimulus generalization and the response-reinforcement contingency. *Journal of the Experimental Analysis of Behavior, 7,* 369–379. [138]

Hefferline, R. F. (1958). The role of proprioception in the control of behavior. *Transactions of the New York Academy of Sciences, 20,* 739–764. [219]

Hein, A., Vital-Durand, F., Salinger, W., & Diamond, R. (1979). Eye movements initiate visual-motor development in the cat. *Science, 22,* 1321–1322. [89]

Hein, H. (1972). The endurance of the mechanism-vitalism controversy. *Journal of the History of Biology, 5,* 159–188. [355]

Held, R., & Hein, A. (1963). Movement-produced stimulation in the development of visually guided behavior. *Journal of Comparative and Physiological Psychology, 56,* 872–876. [87, 88]

Hemmes, N. S. (1973). Behavioral contrast in pigeons depends upon the operant. *Journal of Comparative and Physiological Psychology, 85,* 171–178. [174]

Hendry, D. P. (1969). Reinforcing value of information: fixed-ratio schedules. In D. P. Hendry (Ed.), *Conditioned reinforcement.* Homewood, IL: Dorsey. [174]

Hendry, D. P., & Hendry, L. S. (1963). Partial negative reinforcement: fixed-ratio escape. *Journal of the Experimental Analysis of Behavior, 6,* 519–523. [172]

Henton, W. W., & Iversen, I. H. (1978). *Classical conditioning and operant conditioning.* New York: Springer-Verlag. [179]

Herman, L. M., & Forestell, P. H. (1985). Reporting presence or absence of named objects by a language-trained dolphin. *Neuroscience and Biobehavioral Reviews, 9,* 667–681. [255]

Herrick, R. M. (1964). The successive differentiation of a lever displacement response. *Journal of the Experimental Analysis of Behavior, 7,* 211–215. [118]

Herrick, R. M., Myers, J. L., & Korotkin, A. L. (1959). Changes in S^D and in S^Δ rates during the development of an operant discrimination. *Journal of Comparative and Physiological Psychology, 52,* 359–364. [130]

Herrnstein, R. J. (1961). Relative and absolute strength of response as a function of frequency of reinforcement. *Journal of the Experimental Analysis of Behavior, 4,* 267–272. [177]

Herrnstein, R. J. (1964a). Aperiodicity as a factor in choice. *Journal of the Experimental Analysis of Behavior, 7,* 179–182. [180]

Herrnstein, R. J. (1964b). Secondary reinforcement and rate of primary reinforcement. *Journal of the Experimental Analysis of Behavior, 7,* 27–36. [179]

Herrnstein, R. J. (1966). Superstition: a corollary of the principles of operant conditioning. In W. K. Honig (Ed.), *Operant behavior: areas of research and application.* New York: Appleton-Century-Crofts. [76, 165]

Herrnstein, R. J. (1970). On the law of effect. *Journal of the Experimental Analysis of Behavior, 13,* 243–266. [177]

Herrnstein, R. J., & Hineline, P. N. (1966). Negative reinforcement as shock-frequency reduction. *Journal of the Experimental Analysis of Behavior, 9,* 421–430. [107, 108]

Herrnstein, R. J., & Loveland, D. H. (1975). Maximizing and matching on concurrent ratio schedules. *Journal of the Experimental Analysis of Behavior, 24,* 107–116. [146]

Herrnstein, R. J., Loveland, D. H., & Cable, C. (1976). Natural concepts in pigeons. *Journal of Experimental Psychology: Animal Behavior Processes, 2,* 285–311. [146, 147]

Herrnstein, R. J., & Morse, W. H. (1957). Some effects of response-independent positive reinforcement on maintained operant behavior. *Journal of Comparative and Psychological Psychology, 50,* 461–467. [204]

Herrnstein, R. J., & Sidman, M. (1958). Avoidance conditioning as a factor in the effects of unavoidable shocks on food-reinforced behavior. *Journal of Comparative and Physiological Psychology, 51,* 380–385. [204]

Hess, E. H. (1973). *Imprinting.* New York: Van Nostrand Reinhold. [58]

Hilgard, E. R. (1951). Method and procedures in the study of learning. In S. S. Stevens (Ed.), *Handbook of experimental psychology.* New York: Wiley. [63]

Hilgard, E. R., & Marquis, D. G. (1940). *Conditioning and learning.* New York: Appleton-Century-Crofts. [353]

Hineline, P. N. (1970). Negative reinforcement without shock reduction. *Journal of the Experimental Analysis of Behavior, 14,* 259–268. [107]

Hineline, P. N. (1977). Negative reinforcement and avoidance. In W. K. Honig & J. E. R. Staddon (Eds.), *Handbook of operant behavior.* Englewood Cliffs, NJ: Prentice-Hall. [107, 109]

Hineline, P. N. (1981a). Constraints, competing behavior, and the principle of resonance. In C. M. Bradshaw, E. Szabadi, & C. F. Lowe (Eds.), *Quantification of steady-state operant behaviour.* Amsterdam: Elsevier/North-Holland. [52]

Hineline, P. N. (1981b). The several roles of stimuli in negative reinforcement. In P. Harzem & M. D. Zeiler (Eds.), *Predictability, correlation, and contiguity.* New York: Wiley. [107, 108]

Hinson, J. M., & Staddon, J. E. R. (1981). Maximizing on interval schedules. In C. M. Bradshaw, E. Szabadi, & C. F. Lowe (Eds.), *Quantification of steady-state operant behavior.* Amsterdam: Elsevier/North-Holland. [178]

Hodges, A. (1985). *Alan Turing: The enigma of intelligence.* London: Unwin. [258]

Hoffman, H. S., & Fleshler, M. (1959). Aversive control with the pigeon. *Journal of the Experimental Analysis of Behavior, 2,* 213–218. [102]

Hoffman, H. S., & Fleshler, M. (1962). The course of emotionality in the development of avoidance. *Journal of Experimental Psychology, 64,* 288–294. [207]

Hoffman, H. S., & Ratner, A. M. (1973). A reinforcement model of imprinting: implications for socializing in monkeys and men. *Psychological Review, 80,* 527–544. [47, 58]

Hoffman, H. S., & Solomon, R. L. (1974). An opponent-process theory of motivation: III. Some affective dynamics in imprinting. *Learning and Motivation, 5,* 149–164. [58]

Hoffman, M. L. (1975). Developmental synthesis of affect and cognition and its implications for altruistic motivation. *Developmental Psychology, 11,* 607–622. [215]

Hogan, J. A. (1971). The development of a hunger system in young chicks. *Behavior, 39,* 128–201. [56]

Holding, D. H. (1985). *The psychology of chess skill.* Hillsdale, NJ: Erlbaum. [343]

Holland, J. G. (1958). Human vigilance. *Science, 128,* 61–67. [167]

Holland, P. C., & Ross, R. T. (1981). Within compound associations in serial compound conditioning. *Journal of Experimental Psychology: Animal Behavior Processes, 7,* 228–241. [197]

Hollard, V. D., & Delius, J. D. (1982). Rotational invariance in visual pattern recognition by pigeons and humans. *Science, 218,* 804–806. [333]

Holmes, P. W. (1979). Transfer of matching performance with pigeons. *Journal of the Experimental Analysis of Behavior, 31,* 103–114. [154]

Holz, W. C., & Azrin, N. H. (1961). Discriminative properties of punishment. *Journal of the Experimental Analysis of Behavior, 4,* 225–232. [98, 99]

Honig, W. K. (1962). Prediction of preference, transposition, and transposition-reversal from the generalization gradient. *Journal of Experimental Psychology, 64,* 239–248. [300]

Honig, W. K., Boneau, C. A., Burstein, K. R., & Pennypacker, H. S. (1963). Positive and negative generalization gradients obtained after equivalent training conditions. *Journal of Comparative and Physiological Psychology,* **56,** 111–116. [140]

Hull, C. L. (1920). Quantitative aspects of the evolution of concepts: an experimental study. *Psychological Monographs,* **28,** No. 123. [237, 238]

Hull, C. L. (1934). The factor of the conditioned reflex. In C. Murchison (Ed.), *Handbook of general experimental psychology.* Worchester, MA: Clark University Press. [189]

Hull, C. L. (1943). *Principles of behavior.* New York: Appleton-Century-Crofts. [14, 103, 193]

Hulse, S. H. (1977). Structural complexity as a determinant of serial pattern learning. *Learning and Motivation,* **8,** 488–506. [136]

Hulse, S. H., Cynx, J., & Humpal, J. (1984). Cognitive processing of pitch and rhythm structures by birds. In H. L. Roitblat, T. G. Bever, & H. S. Terrace (Eds.), *Animal cognition.* Hillsdale, NJ: Erlbaum. [254]

Hunter, W. S. (1928). The behavior of raccoons in a double-alternation temporal maze. *Journal of Genetic Psychology,* **35,** 374–388. [122]

Hursh, S. R. (1980). Economic concepts for the analysis of behavior. *Journal of the Experimental Analysis of Behavior,* **34,** 219–238. [160]

Hutchinson, J. W., & Lockhead, G. R. (1977). Similarity as distance: a structural principle for semantic memory. *Journal of Experimental Psychology: Human Learning and Memory,* **3,** 660–678. [270]

Hutchinson, R. R., Renfrew, J. W., & Young, G. A. (1971). Effects of long-term shock and associated stimuli on aggressive and manual responses. *Journal of the Experimental Analysis of Behavior,* **15,** 141–166. [50, 53, 106]

Huttenlocher, J. (1968). Constructing spatial images: a strategy in reasoning. *Psychological Review,* **75,** 550–560. [335]

Huxley, R. (1970). The development of the correct use of subject personal pronouns in two children. In G. B. F. d'Arcais & W. J. M. Levelt (Eds.), *Advances in psycholinguistics.* Amsterdam: Elsevier/North-Holland. [277]

Intraub, H. (1979). The role of implicit naming in pictorial encoding. *Journal of Experimental Psychology: Human Learning and Memory,* **5,** 78–87. [310]

Ison, J. R., & Hoffman, H. S. (1983). Reflex modification in the domain of startle: II. The anomalous history of a robust and ubiquitous phenomenon. *Psychological Bulletin,* **94,** 3–17. [50]

Iwata, B. A., Dorsey, M. F., Slifer, K. J., Bauman, K. E., & Richman, G. S. (1982). Toward a functional analysis of self-injury. *Analysis and Intervention in Developmental Disabilities,* **2,** 3–20. [126]

Iwata, B. A., Pace, G. M., Kalsher, M. J., Cowdery, G. E., & Cataldo, M. F. (1990). Experimental analysis and extinction of self-injurious escape behavior. *Journal of Applied Behavior Analysis,* **23,** 11–27. [126]

Jacobs, J. (1887). Experiments on "prehension." *Mind,* **12,** 75–79. [318]

Jacoby, L. L. (1978). On interpreting the effects of repetition: solving a problem versus remembering a solution. *Journal of Verbal Learning and Verbal Behavior,* **17,** 649–667. [315]

Jans, J. E., & Catania, A. C. (1980). Short-term remembering of discriminative stimuli in pigeons. *Journal of the Experimental Analysis of Behavior,* **34,** 177–183. [304]

Jarvella, R. J. (1971). Syntactic processing of connected speech. *Journal of Verbal Learning and Verbal Behavior,* **10,** 409–416. [263]

Jaynes, J. (1976). *The origin of consciousness in the breakdown of the bicameral mind.* Boston: Houghton Mifflin. [218, 240, 247, 251, 256, 278]

Jenkins, H. M. (1965). Generalization gradients and the concept of inhibition. In D. I. Mostofsky (Ed.), *Stimulus generalization.* Stanford, CA: Stanford University Press. [140]

Jenkins, H. M., & Harrison, R. H. (1960). Effect of discrimination training on auditory generalization. *Journal of Experimental Psychology,* **59,** 246–253. [136]

Jenkins, H. M., & Moore, B. R. (1973). The form of the auto-shaped response with food or water reinforcers. *Journal of the Experimental Analysis of Behavior,* **20,** 163–181. [201]

Jenkins, H. M., & Sainsbury, R. S. (1970). Discrimination learning with the distinctive feature on positive or negative trials. In D. I. Mostofsky (Ed.), *Attention: contemporary theory and analysis.* New York: Appleton-Century-Crofts. [141, 175]

Jenkins, J. G., & Dallenbach, K. M. (1924). Obliviscence during sleep and waking.

American Journal of Psychology, **35**, 605–612. [323]

Jennings, H. S. (1906). *Behavior of the lower organisms.* New York: Macmillan. [352]

Johanson, I. B., & Hall, W. G. (1979). Appetitive learning in 1-day-old rat pups. *Science,* **205**, 419–421. [40]

Johnson, C. N., & Wellman, H. M. (1980). Children's developing understanding of mental verbs: remember, know, and guess. *Child Development,* **51**, 1095–1102. [277]

Johnson, D. F., & Cumming, W. W. (1968). Some determiners of attention. *Journal of the Experimental Analysis of Behavior,* **11**, 157–166. [135]

Johnson, M. K., & Hasher, L. (1987). Human learning and memory. *Annual Review of Psychology,* **38**, 631–668. [325]

Johnson, M. K., & Raye, C. L. (1981). Reality monitoring. *Psychological Review,* **88**, 67–85. [329]

Johnson, N. F. (1965). The psychological reality of phrase-structure rules. *Journal of Verbal Learning and Verbal Behavior,* **4**, 469–475. [263]

Johnson, P. (1982). The functional equivalence of imagery and movement. *Quarterly Journal of Experimental Psychology,* **34A**, 349–365. [334]

Jonçich, G. (1968). *The sane positivist. A biography of Edward L. Thorndike.* Middletown, CT: Wesleyan University Press. [295]

Jost, A. (1897). Die Associationsfestigkeit in ihrer Abhängigkeit von der Verteilung der Wiederholungen. *Zeitschrift für Psychologie,* **14**, 436–472. [323]

Kagan, J. (1981). *The second year.* Cambridge, MA: Harvard University Press. [277]

Kamil, A. C., Yoerg, S. I., & Clements, K. C. (1988). Rules to leave by: patch departure in foraging blue jays. *Animal Behaviour,* **36**, 843–853. [181]

Kamin, L. J. (1956). The effects of termination of the CS and avoidance of the US on avoidance learning. *Journal of Comparative and Physiological Psychology,* **49**, 420–424. [107]

Kamin, L. J. (1957). The retention of an incompletely learned avoidance response. *Journal of Comparative and Physiological Psychology,* **50**, 457–460. [323]

Kamin, L. J. (1969). Predictability, surprise, attention and conditioning. In B. A. Campbell & R. M. Church (Eds.), *Punishment and aver-*sive behavior. New York: Appleton-Century-Crofts. [194]

Kandel, E. R., & Schwartz, J. H. (1982). Molecular biology of learning: modulation of transmitter release. *Science,* **218**, 433–443. [358]

Katz, S., & Gruenwald, P. (1974). The abstraction of linguistic ideas in "meaningless" sentences. *Memory and Cognition,* **2**, 737–741. [270]

Kawamura, S. (1963). The problem of sub-cultural propagation among Japanese Macaques. In C. H. Southwick (Ed.) *Primate social behavior.* New York: D. Van Nostrand. [213]

Kelleher, R. T. (1966). Chaining and conditioned reinforcement. In W. K. Honig (Ed.), *Operant behavior: areas of research and application.* New York: Appleton-Century-Crofts. [175]

Kelleher, R. T., & Fry, W. T. (1962). Stimulus functions in chained fixed-interval schedules. *Journal of the Experimental Analysis of Behavior,* **5**, 167–173. [175]

Kelleher, R. T., & Gollub, L. R. (1962). A review of positive conditioned reinforcement. *Journal of the Experimental Analysis of Behavior,* **5**, 543–597. [170, 175]

Kelleher, R. T., & Morse, W. H. (1968). Schedules using noxious stimuli. III. Responding maintained with response-produced electric shocks. *Journal of the Experimental Analysis of Behavior,* **11**, 819–838. [97]

Kelleher, R. T., Riddle, W. C., & Cook, L. (1962). Observing responses in pigeons. *Journal of the Experimental Analysis of Behavior,* **5**, 3–13. [174]

Kelleher, R. T., Riddle, W. C., & Cook, L. (1963). Persistent behavior maintained by unavoidable shocks. *Journal of the Experimental Analysis of Behavior,* **6**, 507–517. [204]

Keller, F. S. (1941). Light aversion in the white rat. *Psychological Record,* **4**, 235–250. [101, 103]

Keller, F. S. (1958). The phantom plateau. *Journal of the Experimental Analysis of Behavior,* **1**, 1–13. [309, 353]

Keller, F. S., & Schoenfeld, W. N. (1950). *Principles of psychology.* New York: Appleton-Century-Crofts. [76, 146]

Keller, K. (1974). The role of elicited responding in behavioral contrast. *Journal of the Experimental Analysis of Behavior,* **21**, 249–257. [174, 201]

Keller, R. J., Ayres, J. J. B., & Mahoney, W. J. (1977). Brief versus extended exposure to truly random control procedures. *Journal of Experimental Psychology: Animal Behavior Processes, 3,* 53–65. [206]

Kendall, S. B. (1965). Spontaneous recovery after extinction with periodic time-outs. *Psychonomic Science, 2,* 117–118. [76]

Kendler, H. H., & Kendler, T. S. (1962). Vertical and horizontal processes in problem solving. *Psychological Review, 69,* 1–16. [300]

Keppel, G., & Underwood, B. J. (1962). Proactive inhibition in short-term retention of single items. *Journal of Verbal Learning and Verbal Behavior, 1,* 153–156. [321]

Kiesler, C. A., Nisbett, R. E., & Zanna, M. P. (1969). On inferring one's beliefs from one's behavior. *Journal of Personality and Social Psychology, 11,* 321–327. [242]

Killeen, P. (1972). A yoked-chamber comparison of concurrent and multiple schedules. *Journal of the Experimental Analysis of Behavior, 18,* 13–22. [179]

Killeen, P. R. (1981). Learning as causal inference. In M. L. Commons & J. A. Nevin (Eds.), *Quantitative analyses of behavior: Discriminative properties of reinforcement schedules.* New York: Pergamon. [144]

Killeen, P. R., & Amsel, A. (1987). The kinematics of locomotion toward a goal. *Journal of Experimental Psychology: Animal Behavior Processes, 13,* 92–101. [65]

Kimble, D. P., & Ray, R. S. (1965). Reflex habituation and potentiation in *Rana pipiens. Animal Behavior, 13,* 530–533. [50]

Kimble, G. A. (1947). Conditioning as a function of the time between conditioned and unconditioned stimuli. *Journal of Experimental Psychology, 37,* 1–15. [190]

Kimble, G. A. (1961). *Hilgard & Marquis' Conditioning and learning* (2nd ed.). New York: Appleton-Century-Crofts. [1, 76, 353]

Kimmel, H. D. (1976). Notes from "Pavlov's Wednesdays": Pavlov's law of effect. *American Journal of Psychology, 89,* 553–556. [198]

Kinchla, R. A., & Wolfe, J. M. (1979). The order of visual processing: "top-down," "bottom-up," or "middle-out." *Perception and Psychophysics, 25,* 225–231. [336]

Kintsch, W. (1968). An experimental analysis of single stimulus tests and multiple-choice tests of recognition memory. *Journal of Experimental Psychology, 76,* 1–6. [294]

Kish, G. B. (1966). Studies of sensory reinforcement. In W. K. Honig (Ed.), *Operant Behavior: Areas of research and application.* New York: Appleton-Century-Crofts. [87]

Kluender, K. R., Diehl, R. L., & Killeen, P. R. (1987). Japanese quail can learn phonetic categories. *Science, 237,* 1195–1197. [255]

Köhler, W. (1927). *The mentality of apes* (trans. E. Winter; 2nd rev. ed.). London: Routledge & Kegan Paul. [16, 17]

Köhler, W. (1929). *Gestalt psychology.* New York: Liveright. [311]

Kolers, P. A. (1966). Reading and talking bilingually. *American Journal of Psychology, 79,* 357–376. [234, 288, 327]

Kolers, P. A. (1979). Reading and knowing. *Canadian Journal of Psychology, 33,* 106–117. [304]

Kolers, P. A. (1985). Skill in reading and memory. *Canadian Journal of Psychology, 39,* 232–239. [232]

Kolers, P. A., & Palef, R. (1976). Knowing not. *Memory and Cognition, 4,* 553–558. [315, 329]

Kolers, P. A., & Roediger, H. L., III. (1984). Procedures of mind. *Journal of Verbal Learning and Verbal Behavior, 23,* 425–449. [332]

Kolers, P. A., & Smythe, W. E. (1979). Images, symbols, and skills. *Canadian Journal of Psychology, 33,* 158–184. [334]

Konorski, J. (1948). *Conditioned reflexes and neuron organization.* New York: Cambridge University Press. [193]

Krechevsky, I. (1932). Hypotheses' in rats. *Psychological Review, 39,* 516–532. [123]

Kroodsma, D. E., & Miller, E. H. (Eds.) (1982). *Acoustic communication in birds.* Vol. 2. New York: Academic Press. [215]

Kuch, D. O., & Platt, J. R. (1976). Reinforcement rate and interresponse time differentiation. *Journal of Verbal Learning and Verbal Behavior, 26,* 471–486. [163]

Kuczaj, S. A., III. (1977). The acquisition of regular and irregular past tense forms. *Journal of Verbal Learning and Verbal Behavior, 16,* 589–600. [278]

Lachman, J. L., Lachman, R., & Thronesbery, C. (1979). Metamemory through the adult life span. *Developmental Psychology, 15,* 543–551. [329]

Lacroix, J. M., & Gowen, A. H. (1981). The acquisition of autonomic control through biofeedback: some tests of discrimination theory. *Psychophysiology, 18,* 559–572. [219]

Lakoff, G., & Johnson, M. (1980). *Metaphors we live by.* Chicago: University of Chicago Press. [270, 273]

Landauer, T. K., & Meyer, D. E. (1972). Category size and semantic-memory retrieval. *Journal of Verbal Learning and Verbal Behavior, 11,* 539–549. [272]

Lane, H. (1965). The motor theory of speech perception: a critical review. *Psychological Review, 72,* 275–309. [230]

Lashley, K. S. (1930). The mechanism of vision: I. a method for rapid analysis of pattern vision in the rat. *Journal of Genetic Psychology, 37,* 453–460. [25, 352]

Lashley, K. S. (1951). The problem of serial order in behavior. In L. A. Jeffress (Ed.), *Cerebral mechanisms in behavior.* New York: Wiley. [124, 125]

Lattal, K. A. (1974). Combinations of response reinforcer dependence and independence. *Journal of the Experimental Analysis of Behavior, 22,* 357–362. [165]

Lawrence, D. H. (1949). Acquired distinctiveness of cues: transfer between discriminations on the basis of familiarity with the stimulus. *Journal of Experimental Psychology, 39,* 770–784. [135]

Lea, S. E. G. (1979). Foraging and reinforcement schedules in the pigeon: optimal and non-optimal aspects of choice. *Animal Behavior, 27,* 875–886. [136]

Lea, S. E. G., & Harrison, S. N. (1978). Discrimination of ploymorphous stimulus sets by pigeons. *Quarterly Journal of Experimental Psychology, 30,* 521–537. [147]

Leitenberg, H. (1966). Conditioned acceleration and conditioned suppression in pigeons. *Journal of the Experimental Analysis of Behavior, 9,* 205–212. [204]

Lenneberg, E. H. (1962). Understanding language without ability to speak: a case report. *Journal of Abnormal and Social Psychology, 65,* 419–425. [269]

Lenneberg, E. H. (1967). *Biological foundations of language.* New York: Wiley. [274]

Lepper, M. R., & Greene, D. (Eds.). (1978). *The hidden costs of reward.* Hillsdale, NJ: Erlbaum. [250]

Lepper, M. R., Greene, D., & Nisbett, R. E. (1973). Undermining children's intrinsic interest with extrinsic reward: a test of the "overjustification" hypothesis. *Journal of Personality and Social Psychology, 28,* 129–137. [250]

Levine, M. (1966). Hypothesis behavior by humans during discrimination learning. *Journal of Experimental Psychology, 71,* 331–338. [123]

Levitsky, D., & Collier, G. (1968). Schedule-induced wheel running. *Physiology and Behavior, 3,* 571–573. [53]

Ley, R. (1990). *A whisper of espionage.* Garden City Park, NY: Avery. [17]

Liberman, A. M. (1982). On finding that speech is special. *American Psychologist, 37,* 148–167. [230, 268]

Loeb, J. (1900). *Comparative physiology of the brain and comparative psychology.* New York: Putnam's. [352]

Loftus, E. F., & Palmer, J. C. (1974). Reconstruction of automobile destruction: an example of the interaction between language and memory. *Journal of Verbal Learning and Verbal Behavior, 13,* 585–589. [312]

Loftus, E. F., & Zanni, G. (1975). Eyewitness testimony: the influence of the wording of a question. *Bulletin of the Psychonomic Society, 5,* 86–88. [312]

Logan, F. A. (1960). *Incentive.* New Haven, CT: Yale University Press. [81]

Loisette, A. (1899). *Assimilative memory, or, How to attend and never forget.* New York: Funk & Wagnalls. [306]

Long, G. M. (1980). Iconic memory: a review and critique of the study of short-term visual storage. *Psychological Bulletin, 88,* 785–820. [316]

Lorenz, K. (1937). The companion in the bird's world. *Auk, 54,* 245–273. [58]

Lovaas, O. I. (1964). Cue properties of words: the control of operant responding by rate and content of verbal operants. *Child Development, 35,* 245–246. [251]

Lowe, C. F. (1980). Determinants of human operant behavior. In P. Harzem & M. D. Zeiler (Eds.), *Advances in the analysis of behavior. Vol. 1.* New York: Wiley. [249]

Lubbock, J. (1882). *Ants, bees, and wasps.* New York: D. Appleton. [352]

Lubinski, D., & Thompson, T. (1987). An animal model of the interpersonal communication of interoceptive (private) states. *Journal of the Experimental Analysis of Behavior, 48,* 1–15. [219, 220, 256]

Luchins, A. S. (1942). Mechanization in problem solving. *Psychological Monographs, 54* (6), Whole No. 248. [346]

Luchins, A. S., & Luchins, E. H. (1950). New experimental attempts at preventing mechanization in problem solving. *Journal of General Psychology, 42,* 279–297. [346]

MacLeod, C. M. (1976). Bilingual episodic memory: acquisition and forgetting. *Journal of Verbal Learning and Verbal Behavior, 15,* 347–364. [327]

MacPhail, E. M. (1968). Avoidance responding in pigeons. *Journal of the Experimental Analysis of Behavior, 11,* 629–632. [105]

Mahoney, M. J., & Bandura, A. (1972). Self-reinforcement in pigeons. *Learning and Motivation, 3,* 293–303. [221]

Maier, S. F., Albin, R. W., & Testa, T. J. (1973). Failure to learn to escape in rats previously exposed to inescapable shock depends on nature of escape response. *Journal of Comparative and Physiological Psychology, 85,* 581–592. [149]

Maier, S. F., Seligman, M. E. P., & Solomon, R. L. (1969). Pavlovian fear conditioning and learned helplessness: effects on escape and avoidance behavior of (a) the CS-US contingency and (b) the independence of the US and voluntary responding. In B. A. Campbell & R. M. Church (Eds.), *Punishment and aversive behavior.* New York: Appleton-Century-Crofts. [149]

Maki, R. H. (1979). Right-left and up-down are equally discriminable in the absence of directional words. *Bulletin of the Psychonomic Society, 14,* 181–184. [250]

Malagodi, E. F., Gardner, M. L., Ward, S. E., & Magyar, R. L. (1981). Responding maintained under intermittent schedules of electric shock presentation: "safety" or schedule effects? *Journal of the Experimental Analysis of Behavior, 36,* 171–190. [98]

Malcolm, N. (1971). The myth of cognitive processes and structures. In T. Mischel (Ed.), *Cognitive development and epistemology.* New York: Academic Press. [332]

Malone, J. C. (1990). *Theories of learning.* Belmont, CA: Wadsworth. [177]

Malott, R. W., & Cumming, W. W. (1964). Schedules of interresponse time reinforcement. *Psychological Record, 14,* 221–252. [121]

Mandler, J. M., & Johnson, N. S. (1977). Remembrance of things parsed: story structure and recall. *Cognitive Psychology, 9,* 111–151. [327]

Marcel, A. J. (1978). Unconscious reading. *Visible Language, 12,* 391–404. [232]

Markman, E. M., Horton, M. S., & McLanahan, A. G. (1980). Classes and collections: principles of organization in the learning of hierarchical relations. *Cognition, 8,* 227–241. [340]

Marler, P., & Peters, S. (1982). Long-term storage of learned birdsongs prior to production. *Animal Behaviour, 30,* 479–482. [254]

Martin, E. (1967). Relation between stimulus recognition and paired-associate learning. *Journal of Experimental Psychology, 74,* 500–505. [294]

Matthews, B. A., Shimoff, E. H., & Catania, A. C. (1987). Saying and doing: a contingency-space analysis. *Journal of Applied Behavior Analysis, 20,* 69–74. [251]

Matthews, B. A., Shimoff, E., Catania, A. C., & Sagvolden, T. (1977). Uninstructed human responding: sensitivity to ratio and interval contingencies. *Journal of the Experimental Analysis of Behavior, 27,* 453–467. [167, 249]

Max, L. W. (1934). An experimental study of the motor theory of consciousness. I. History and critique. *Journal of General Psychology, 11,* 112–125. [233]

Mayr, E. (1982). *The growth of biological thought.* Cambridge, MA: Harvard University Press. [33]

Mazur, J. E. (1986). *Learning and behavior.* Englewood Cliffs, NJ: Prentice-Hall. [210]

Mazur, J. E. (1991). Choice. In I. H. Iversen & K. A. Lattal (Eds.), *Experimental analysis of behavior.* Amsterdam: Elsevier/North-Holland. [178]

Mazur, J. E., & Logue, A. W. (1978). Choice in a "self-control" paradigm: effects of a fading procedure. *Journal of the Experimental Analysis of Behavior*, **30**, 11–17. [184]

McCloskey, M., & Santee, J. (1981). Are semantic memory and episodic memory distinct systems? *Journal of Experimental Psychology: Human Learning and Memory*, **7**, 66–71. [326]

McCloskey, M., Wible, C. G., & Cohen, N. J. (1988). Is there a special flashbulb memory mechanism? *Journal of Experimental Psychology: General*, **117**, 171–181. [326]

McGeoch, J. A. (1942). *The psychology of human learning*. New York: Longmans, Green. [284, 296, 353]

McGeoch, J. A., & Irion, A. L. (1952). *The psychology of human learning* (2nd ed.). New York: Longmans, Green. [353]

McGraw, M. B. (1945). *The neuromuscular maturation of the human infant*. New York: Columbia University Press. [57]

McIntire, K. D., Cleary, J., & Thompson, T. (1987). Conditional relations by monkeys: reflexivity, symmetry, and transitivity. *Journal of the Experimental Analysis of Behavior*, **47**, 279–285. [154]

McKoon, G., & Ratcliff, R. (1980). The comprehension processes and memory structures involved in anaphoric reference. *Journal of Verbal Learning and Verbal Behavior*, **19**, 668–682. [277]

Mechner, F. (1959). A notation system for the description of behavioral procedures. *Journal of the Experimental Analysis of Behavior*, **2**, 133–150. [170]

Meehl, P. E. (1950). On the circularity of the Law of Effect. *Psychological Bulletin*, **47**, 52–75. [72]

Mehler, J. (1963). Some effects of grammatical transformations on the recall of English sentences. *Journal of Verbal Learning and Verbal Behavior*, **2**, 346–351. [265, 267]

Mehler, J., Jusczyk, P., Lambert, G., Halsted, N., Bertoncini, J., & Amiel-Tison, C. (1988). A precursor of language acquisition in young infants. *Cognition*, **29**, 143–178. [230]

Meisch, R. A., & Thompson, T. (1971). Ethanol intake in the absence of concurrent food reinforcement. *Psychopharmacologia*, **22**, 72–79. [53]

Melton, A. W. (1963). Implications of short-term memory for a general theory of memory. *Journal of Verbal Learning and Verbal Behavior*, **2**, 1–21. [319, 320, 322]

Melton, A. W., & Martin, E. (Eds.), (1972). *Coding processes in human memory*. Washington, DC: Winston. [308]

Meltzoff, A. N., & Moore, M. K. (1977). Imitation of facial and manual gestures by human neonates. *Science*, **198**, 75–78. [214]

Mervis, C. B., & Rosch, E. (1981). Categorization of natural objects. *Annual Review of Psychology*, **32**, 89–115. [147, 272]

Michael, J. (1975). Positive and negative reinforcement, a distinction that is no longer necessary; or a better way to talk about bad things. *Behaviorism*, **3**, 33–44. [100]

Michael, J. (1982). Distinguishing between discriminative and motivational functions of stimuli. *Journal of the Experimental Analysis of Behavior*, **37**, 149–155. [27, 81]

Milgram, S. (1963). Behavioral study of obedience. *Journal of Abnormal and Social Psychology*, **67**, 371–378. [249]

Miller, G. A. (1956). The magical number seven plus or minus two: some limits on our capacity for processing information. *Psychological Review*, **63**, 81–97. [309, 316, 318]

Miller, G. A. (1958). Free recall of redundant strings of letters. *Journal of Experimental Psychology*, **56**, 485–491. [284]

Miller, G. A. (1962). Some psychological studies of grammar. *American Psychologist*, **17**, 748–762. [265, 267, 271]

Miller, G. A. (1972). Lexical memory. *Proceedings of the American Philosophical Society*, **116**, 140–144. [326]

Miller, G. A., & Isard, S. (1963). Some perceptual consequences of linguistic rules. *Journal of Verbal Learning and Verbal Behavior*, **2**, 217–228. [267]

Miller, G. A., & Selfridge, J. A. (1953). Verbal context and the recall of meaningful material. *American Journal of Psychology*, **63**, 176–185. [259]

Miller, J. D., & Bowe, C. A. (1982). Roles of the qualities and locations of stimuli and responses in simple associative learning. *Pavlovian Journal of Biological Science*, **17**, 129–139. [210]

Miller, N. E., & Carmona, A. (1967). Modification of a visceral response, salivation in thirsty dogs, by instrumental training with water reward. *Journal of Comparative and Physiological Psychology*, **63**, 1–6. [115, 199]

Mineka, S., Davidson, M., Cook, M., & Keir, R. (1984). Observational learning of snake fear in rhesus monkeys. *Journal of Abnormal Psychology*, **93**, 355–372. [216]

Mineka, S., Keir, R., & Price, V. (1980). Fear of snakes in wild- and laboratory-reared rhesus monkeys (*Macaca mulatta*). *Animal Learning and Behavior*, **8**, 653–663. [216]

Mitchell, D., Scott, D. W., & Williams, K. D. (1973). Container neophobia and the rat's preference for earned food. *Behaviorial Biology*, **9**, 613–624. [209]

Miyake, N., & Norman, D. A. (1979). To ask a question, one must know enough to know what is not known. *Journal of Verbal Learning and Verbal Behavior*, **18**, 357–364. [329]

Moerk, E. L. (1980). Relationships between parental input frequencies and children's language acquisition: a reanalysis of Brown's data. *Journal of Child Language*, **7**, 1–14. [276]

Moerk, E. L. (1983). A behavioral analysis of controversial topics in first language acquisition: reinforcements, corrections, modeling, input frequencies, and the three-term contingency pattern. *Journal of Psycholinguistic Research*, **12**, 129–155. [276]

Moeser, S. D., & Tarrant, B. L. (1977). Learning a network of comparisons. *Journal of Experimental Psychology: Human Learning and Memory*, **3**, 643–659. [327]

Moore, B. R., & Stuttard, S. (1979). Dr. Guthrie and *Felis domesticus* or: tripping over the cat. *Science*, **205**, 1031–1033. [79]

Moore, C., & Frye, D. (1986). Context, conservation and the meanings of *more*. *British Journal of Developmental Psychology*, **4**, 169–178. [276]

Moore, J. (1982). Choice and multiple reinforcers. *Journal of the Experimental Analysis of Behavior*, **37**, 115–122. [178]

Morgan, C. L. (1920). *Animal behaviour*. London: Edward Arnold. [16]

Morgan, M. J., Fitch, M. D., Holman, J. G., & Lea, S. E. G. (1976). Pigeons learn the concept of an "A." *Perception*, **5**, 57–66. [146]

Morgan, M. J., & Nichols, D. J. (1979). Discrimination between reinforced action patterns in the rat. *Learning and Motivation*, **10**, 1–22. [122]

Morse, W. H., & Kelleher, R. T. (1977). Determinants of reinforcement and punishment. In W. K. Honig & J. E. R. Staddon (Eds.), *Handbook of operant behavior*. Englewood Cliffs, NJ: Prentice-Hall. [97, 177]

Mowrer, O. H. (1950). On the psychology of "talking birds"—a contribution to language and personality theory. In O. H. Mowrer, *Learning theory and personality dynamics: selected papers*. New York: Ronald Press. [230]

Mowrer, O. H. (1960). *Learning theory and behavior*. New York: Wiley. [193]

Mowrer, O. H., & Jones, H. M. (1943). Extinction and behavior variability as a function of effortfulness of task. *Journal of Experimental Psychology*, **33**, 369–385. [78]

Mowrer, O. H., & Lamoreaux, R. R. (1946). Fear as an intervening variable in avoidance conditioning. *Journal of Comparative Psychology*, **39**, 29–50. [107]

Moyer, R. S. (1973). Comparing objects in memory: evidence suggesting an internal psychophysics. *Perception and Psychophysics*, **13**, 180–184. [335]

Moyer, R. S., & Dumais, S. T. (1978). Mental comparison. In G. H. Bower (Ed.), *The psychology of learning and motivation. Vol. 12*. New York: Academic Press. [335]

Müller, G. E., & Pilzecker, A. (1900). Experimentelle Beiträge zur Lehre vom Gedächtnis. *Zeitschrift für Psychologie*, Ergänzungsband 1. [298]

Nairne, J. S., & Rescorla, R. (1981). Second-order conditioning with diffuse auditory reinforcers in the pigeon. *Learning and Motivation*, **12**, 65–91. [197]

Neiworth, J. J., & Rilling, M. E. (1987). A method for studying imagery in animals. *Journal of Experimental Psychology: Animal Behavior Processes*, **13**, 203–214. [144]

Neuringer, A. J. (1969). Animals respond for food in the presence of free food. *Science*, **166**, 399–401. [82]

Neuringer, A. (1986). Can people behave randomly?: The role of feedback. *Journal of Experimental Psychology: General*, **115**, 62–75. [127]

Neuringer, A. J., & Chung, S.-H. (1967). Quasi-reinforcement: control of responding by a percentage reinforcement schedule. *Journal of the Experimental Analysis of Behavior*, **10**, 45–54. [177]

Neuringer, A. J., & Neuringer, M. (1974). Learning by following a food source. *Science*, **184**, 1005–1008. [216]

Neuringer, A. J., & Schneider, B. A. (1968). Separating the effects of interreinforcement time and number of interreinforcement responses. *Journal of the Experimental Analysis of Behavior, 11,* 661–667. [180]

Nevin, J. A. (1974). Response strength in multiple schedules. *Journal of the Experimental Analysis of Behavior, 21,* 389–408. [75, 121, 185]

Nevin, J. A., & Shettleworth, S. J. (1966). An analysis of contrast effects in multiple schedules. *Journal of the Experimental Analysis of Behavior, 9,* 305–315. [174]

Newell, A., Shaw, J. C., & Simon, H. A. (1958). Elements of a theory of human problem solving. *Psychological Review, 65,* 151–166. [343]

Newman, S. E. (1972). In search of associative symmetry. In C. P. Duncan, L. Sechrest, & A. W. Melton (Eds.), *Human memory.* New York: Appleton-Century-Crofts. [288]

Nisbett, R. E., & Bellows, N. (1977). Verbal reports about causal influences on social judgments: private access versus public theories. *Journal of Personality and Social Psychology, 35,* 613–624. [219]

Nisbett, R. E., & Wilson, T. D. (1977). Telling more than we can know: verbal reports on mental processes. *Psychological Review, 84,* 231–259. [241]

Olton, D. S. (1979). Mazes, maps, and memory. *American Psychologist, 34,* 583–596. [135, 145]

Olton, D. S., & Samuelson, R. J. (1976). Remembrance of places passed: spatial memory in rats. *Journal of Experimental Psychology: Animal Behavior Processes, 2,* 97–116. [136]

Orne, M. T. (1962). On the social psychology of the psychological experiment: with particular reference to demand characteristics and their implications. *American Psychologist, 17,* 776–783. [280]

Ortony, A., & Turner, J. (1990). What's basic about basic emotions? *Psychological Review, 97,* 315–331. [203]

Osgood, C. E. (1949). The similarity paradox in human learning: a resolution. *Psychological Review, 56,* 132–143. [297]

Osgood, C. E., Suci, G. J., & Tannenbaum, P. H. (1957). *The measurement of meaning.* Urbana: University of Illinois Press. [270]

Overton, D. A. (1964). State-dependent or "dissociated" learning produced with phenobarbital. *Journal of Comparative and Physiological Psychology, 57,* 3–12. [315]

Page, S., & Neuringer, A. (1985). Variability is an operant. *Journal of Experimental Psychology: Animal Behavior Processes, 11,* 429–452. [127]

Paivio, A. (1971). *Imagery and verbal processes.* New York: Holt, Rinehart & Winston. [309, 333]

Paivio, A. (1975). Neomentalism. *Canadian Journal of Psychology, 29,* 263–291. [332, 334, 335]

Palermo, D. S., & Howe, H. E., Jr. (1970). An experimental analogy to the learning of past tense inflection rules. *Journal of Verbal Learning and Verbal Behavior, 9,* 410–416. [278]

Paniagua, F. A., & Baer, D. M. (1982). The analysis of correspondence training as a chain reinforceable at any point. *Child Development, 53,* 786–798. [251]

Parsons, H. M. (1974). What happened at Hawthorne? *Science, 183,* 922–932. [79]

Parsons, H. M. (1978). What caused the Hawthorne effect?: a scientific detective story. *Administration and Society, 10,* 259–283. [79]

Pavlov, I. P. (1927). *Conditioned reflexes* (trans. G. V. Anrep). London: Oxford University Press. [22, 42, 187, 352]

Pavlov, I. P. (1957). *Experimental psychology and other essays.* New York: Philosophical Library. [352]

Peele, D. B., & Ferster, C. B. (1982). Autoshaped key pecking maintained by access to a social space. *Journal of the Experimental Analysis of Behavior, 38,* 181–189. [201]

Pepperberg, I. M. (1983). Cognition in the African grey parrot: Preliminary evidence for auditory/vocal comprehension of the class concept. *Animal Learning and Behavior, 11,* 179–185. [255]

Pepperberg, I. M. (1987). Evidence for conceptual quantitative abilities in the African grey parrot: Labeling of cardinal sets. *Ethology, 75,* 37–61. [255]

Peterson, L. R., & Peterson, M. J. (1959). Short-term retention of individual verbal items. *Journal of Experimental Psychology, 58,* 193–198. [318, 319]

Peterson, N. (1960). Control of behavior by presentation of an imprinted stimulus. *Science, 132,* 1395–1396. [58]

Peterson, N. (1962). Effect of monochromatic rearing on the control of responding by wavelength. *Science*, **136**, 774–775. [139]

Pfungst, O. (1911). *Clever Hans (the horse of Mr. Von Osten): A contribution to experimental animal and human psychology* (trans. C. L. Rahn). New York: Holt. [22, 23, 254]

Piaget, J., & Inhelder, B. (1969). *The psychology of the child* (trans. H. Weaver). New York: Basic Books. [340]

Platt, J. R. (1973). Percentile reinforcement: paradigms for experimental analysis of response shaping. In G. H. Bower (Ed.), *The psychology of learning and motivation. Vol. 7.* New York: Academic Press. [113]

Pliskoff, S. S., & Goldiamond, I. (1966). Some discriminative properties of fixed ratio performance in the pigeon. *Journal of the Experimental Analysis of Behavior*, **9**, 1–9. [219]

Pollio, H. R., & Smith, M. K. (1979). Sense and nonsense in thinking about anomaly and metaphor. *Bulletin of the Psychonomic Society*, **13**, 323–326. [273]

Posner, M. I. (1978). *Chronometric explorations of mind.* Hillsdale, NJ: Erlbaum. [337]

Posner, M. I. (1982). Cumulative development of attentional theory. *American Psychologist*, **37**, 168–179. [333]

Postman, L. (1968). Association and performance in the analysis of verbal learning. In T. R. Dixon & D. L. Horton (Eds.), *Verbal behavior and general behavior theory.* Englewood Cliffs, NJ: Prentice Hall. [286]

Poulson, C. L. (1983). Differential reinforcement of other-than-vocalization as a control procedure in the conditioning of infant vocalization rate. *Journal of Experimental Child Psychology*, **36**, 471–489. [73, 230]

Poulson, C. L. (1984). Operant theory and methodology in infant vocal conditioning. *Journal of Experimental Child Psychology*, **38**, 103–113. [73, 230]

Poulson, C. L., & Kymissis, E. (1988). Generalized imitation in infants. *Journal of Experimental Child Psychology*, **46**, 324–336. [216]

Poulson, C. L., Kymissis, E., Reeve, K. F., Andreatos, M., & Reeve, L. (1991). Generalized vocal imitation in infants. *Journal of Experimental Child Psychology*, **51**, 267–279. [216, 230]

Powers, R. B., & Osborne, J. G. (1976). *Fundamentals of behavior.* St. Paul, MN: West Publishing. [21]

Premack, D. (1959). Toward empirical behavior laws: I. Positive reinforcement. *Psychological Review*, **66**, 219–233. [82]

Premack, D. (1962). Reversibility of the reinforcement relation. *Science*, **136**, 255–257. [82]

Premack, D. (1970). A functional analysis of language, *Journal of the Experimental Analysis of Behavior*, **14**, 107–125. [255]

Premack, D. (1971). Catching up with common sense or two sides of a generalization: reinforcement and punishment. In R. Glaser (Ed.), *The nature of reinforcement.* New York: Academic Press. [82, 95]

Provine, R. R. (1976). Development of function in nerve nets. In J. Fentress (Ed.), *Simpler networks and behavior.* Sunderland, MA: Sinauer. [56]

Provine, R. R. (1981). Development of wing-flapping and flight in normal and flap-deprived domestic chicks. *Developmental Psychobiology*, **14**, 279–291. [208]

Provine, R. R. (1989a). Contagious yawning and infant imitation. *Bulletin of the Psychonomic Society*, **27**, 125–126. [214]

Provine, R. R. (1989b). Faces as releasers of contagious yawning: an approach to face detection using normal human subjects. *Bulletin of the Psychonomic Society*, **27**, 211–214. [207]

Provine, R. R., & Fischer, K. R. (1989). Laughing, smiling, and talking: relation to sleeping and social context in humans. *Ethology*, **83**, 295–305. [208]

Pryor, K. W., Haag, R., & O'Reilly, J. (1969). The creative porpoise: training for novel behavior. *Journal of the Experimental Analysis of Behavior*, **12**, 653–661. [127]

Pylyshyn, Z. W. (1979). The rate of "mental rotation" of images: a test of a holistic analogue hypothesis. *Memory and Cognition*, **7**, 19–28. [334]

Rachlin, H. (1967). The effect of shock intensity on concurrent and single-key responding in concurrent-chain schedules. *Journal of the Experimental Analysis of Behavior*, **10**, 87–93. [96]

Rachlin, H. (1971). On the tautology of the matching law. *Journal of the Experimental Analysis of Behavior*, **15**, 249–251. [177]

Rachlin, H. (1974). Self-control. *Behaviorism*, **2**, 94–107. [184]

Rachlin, H., & Baum, W. M. (1972). Effect of alternative reinforcement: does the source matter? *Journal of the Experimental Analysis of Behavior, 18*, 231–241. [178]

Rachlin, H., & Burkhard, B. (1978). The temporal triangle: response substitution in instrumental conditioning. *Psychological Review, 85*, 22–47. [83]

Rachlin, H., & Green, L. (1972). Commitment, choice and self-control. *Journal of the Experimental Analysis of Behavior, 17*, 15–22. [182, 183, 184]

Ratner, S. C. (1970). Habituation: research and theory. In J. H. Reynierse (Ed.), *Current issues in animal learning*. Lincoln: University of Nebraska Press. [50]

Raye, C. L., Johnson, M. K., & Taylor, T. H. (1980). Is there something special about memory for internally generated information? *Memory and Cognition, 8*, 141–148. [304]

Reber, A. S. (1976). Implicit learning of synthetic languages: the role of instructional set. *Journal of Experimental Psychology: Human Learning and Memory, 2*, 88–94. [250]

Reber, A. S. (1985). *The Penguin dictionary of psychology*. New York: Viking Penguin. [362]

Reber, A. S., Allen, R., & Regan, S. (1985). Syntactical learning and judgment, still unconscious and still abstract: comment on Dulany, Carlson, and Dewey. *Journal of Experimental Psychology: General, 114*, 17–24. [311]

Reddy, M. J. (1979). The conduit metaphor—a case of frame conflict in our language about language. In A. Ortony (Ed.), *Metaphor and thought*. New York: Cambridge University Press. [273]

Reid, A. K., & Staddon, J. E. R. (1982). Schedule-induced drinking: elicitation, anticipation, or behavior interaction? *Journal of the Experimental Analysis of Behavior, 38*, 1–18. [55]

Reid, R. L. (1958). The role of the reinforcer as a stimulus. *British Journal of Psychology, 49*, 202–209. [76]

Rescorla, R. A. (1967). Pavlovian conditioning and its proper control procedures. *Psychological Review, 74*, 71–80. [193, 194]

Rescorla, R. A. (1968). Probability of shock in the presence and absence of CS in fear conditioning. *Journal of Comparative and Physiological Psychology, 66*, 1–5 [206]

Rescorla, R. A. (1979). Aspects of the reinforcer learned in second-order Pavlovian conditioning. *Journal of Experimental Psychology: Animal Behavior Processes, 5*, 79–95. [197]

Rescorla, R. A. (1980). *Pavlovian second-order conditioning*. Hillside, NJ: Erlbaum. [196]

Rescorla, R. A. (1988). Pavlovian conditioning: it's not what you think it is. *American Psychologist, 43*, 151–160. [194]

Rescorla, R. A., & Skucy, J. C. (1969). Effect of response-independent reinforcers during extinction. *Journal of Comparative and Physiological Psychology, 67*, 381–389. [80]

Rescorla, R. A., & Solomon, R. L. (1967). Two-process learning theory: relationships between Pavlovian conditioning and instrumental learning. *Psychological Review, 74*, 151–182. [203, 204]

Rescorla, R. A., & Wagner, A. R. (1972). A theory of Pavlovian conditioning: variations in the effectiveness of reinforcement and nonreinforcement. In A. H. Black & W. F. Prokasy (Eds.), *Classical conditioning II*. New York: Appleton-Century-Crofts. [194]

Restle, F. (1957). Discrimination of cues in mazes: a resolution of the "place versus response" question. *Psychological Review, 64*, 217–228. [135]

Revusky, S. H., & Garcia, J. (1970). Learned associations over long delays. In G. H. Bower (Ed.), *The psychology of learning and motivation, Vol. 4*. New York: Academic Press. [210, 211]

Reyna, V. F. (1981). The language of possibility and probability: effects of negation on meaning. *Memory and Cognition, 9*, 642–650. [271]

Reynolds, G. S. (1961a). Attention in the pigeon. *Journal of the Experimental Analysis of Behavior, 4*, 203–208. [133, 148]

Reynolds, G. S. (1961b). Behavioral contrast. *Journal of the Experimental Analysis of Behavior, 4*, 57–71. [173, 174]

Reynolds, G. S. (1966). Discrimination and emission of temporal intervals by pigeons. *Journal of the Experimental Analysis of Behavior, 9*, 65–68. [219]

Richter, C. P. (1927). Animal behavior and internal drives. *Quarterly Review of Biology, 2*, 307–343. [80]

Riess, B. F. (1946). Genetic changes in semantic conditioning. *Journal of Experimental Psychology, 36*, 143–152. [252]

Risley, T. R., & Hart, B. (1968). Developing correspondence between the nonverbal and verbal behavior of preschool children. *Journal of Applied Behavior Analysis, 1,* 267–281. [251]

Rizley, R. C., & Rescorla, R. A. (1972). Associations in second-order conditioning and sensory preconditioning. *Journal of Comparative and Physiological Psychology, 81,* 1–11. [197]

Robinson, E. S., & Brown, M. A. (1926). Effect of serial position upon memorization. *American Journal of Psychology, 37,* 538–552. [284]

Rock, I. (1957). The role of repetition in association learning. *American Journal of Psychology, 70,* 186–193. [287]

Roediger, H. L., III. (1980). Memory metaphors in cognitive psychology. *Memory and Cognition, 8,* 231–246. [307]

Roediger, H. L., III, & Craik, F. I. M. (Eds.). (1989). *Varieties of memory and consciousness.* Hillsdale, NJ: Erlbaum. [325]

Rogers-Warren, A. R., & Baer, D. M. (1976). Correspondence between saying and doing: teaching children to share and praise. *Journal of Applied Behavior Analysis, 9,* 335–354. [251]

Romney, A. K., & D'Andrade, R. G. (1964). Cognitive aspects of English kin terms. *American Anthropologist, 66,* 146–170. [271]

Rosch, E. H. (1973). Natural categories. *Cognitive Psychology, 4,* 328–350. [147, 272]

Rosenfeld, H. M., & Baer, D. M. (1970). Unbiased and unnoticed verbal conditioning: the double agent robot procedure. *Journal of the Experimental Analysis of Behavior, 14,* 99–105. [242, 247]

Rozin, P., & Kalat, J. W. (1971). Specific hungers and poison avoidance as adaptive specializations of learning. *Psychological Review, 78,* 459–486. [210]

Rozin, P., Millman, L., & Nemeroff, C. (1986). Operation of the laws of sympathetic magic in disgust and other domains. *Journal of Personality and Social Psychology, 50,* 703–712. [250]

Rudolph, R. L., Honig, W. K., & Gerry, J. E. (1969). Effects of monochromatic rearing on the acquisition of stimulus control. *Journal of Comparative and Physiological Psychology, 67,* 50–57. [139]

Rudy, J. W., Vogt, M. B., & Hyson, R. L. (1984). A developmental analysis of the rat's learned reactions to gustatory and auditory stimulation. In R. Kail & N. E. Spear (Eds.), *Comparative perspectives on the development of memory.* Hillsdale, NJ: Erlbaum. [40]

Rumbaugh, D. M., & Gill, T. V. (1976). The mastery of language-type skills by the chimpanzee (*Pan*). *Annals of the New York Academy of Sciences, 280,* 562–578. [255]

Rundus, D. (1971). Analysis of rehearsal processes in free recall. *Journal of Experimental Psychology, 89,* 63–77. [289]

Rundus, D. (1977). Maintenance rehearsal and single-level processing. *Journal of Verbal Learning and Verbal Behavior, 16,* 665–681. [319]

Rundus, D. (1980). Maintenance rehearsal and long-term recency. *Memory and Cognition, 8,* 226–230. [319]

Rundus, D., & Atkinson, R. C. (1970). Rehearsal processes in free recall: a procedure for direct observation. *Journal of Verbal Learning and Verbal Behavior, 9,* 99–105. [289, 290]

Ryle, G. (1949). *The concept of mind.* New York: Barnes & Noble. [2]

Sachs, J. S. (1967). Recognition memory for syntactic and semantic aspects of connected discourse. *Perception and Psychophysics, 2,* 437–442. [269, 326]

Salapatek, P., & Kessen, W. (1966). Visual scanning of triangles by the human newborn. *Journal of Experimental Child Psychology, 3,* 155–167. [89]

Saugstad, P., & Raaheim, K. (1960). Problem solving, past experience and availability of functions. *British Journal of Psychology, 51,* 97–104. [346]

Saunders, K. J. (1989). Naming in conditional discrimination and stimulus equivalence. *Journal of the Experimental Analysis of Behavior, 47,* 379–384. [154]

Savage-Rumbaugh, E. S. (1986). *Ape language.* New York: Columbia University Press. [255, 256]

Savage-Rumbaugh, E. S., Rumbaugh, D. M., & Boysen, S. (1978). Symbolic communication between two chimpanzees (*Pan troglodytes*). *Science, 201,* 641–644. [256]

Savage-Rumbaugh, E. S., Rumbaugh, D. M., Smith, S. T., & Lawson, J. (1980). Reference: the linguistic essential. *Science, 210,* 922–925. [255]

Savin, H., & Perchonock, E. (1965). Grammatical structure and the immediate recall of

English sentences. *Journal of Verbal Learning and Verbal Behavior*, **4**, 348–353. [265]

Sawisch, L. P., & Denny, M. R. (1973). Reversing the reinforcement contingencies of eating and keypecking behaviors. *Animal Learning and Behavior*, **1**, 189–192. [82]

Schane, S. A., Tranel, B., & Lane, H. (1975). On the psychological reality of a natural rule of syllable structure. *Cognition*, **3**, 351–358. [263]

Schick, K. (1971). Operants. *Journal of the Experimental Analysis of Behavior*, **12**, 413–423. [243]

Schlinger, H., & Blakely, E. (1987). Function-altering effects of contingency-specifying stimuli. *The Behavior Analyst*, **10**, 41–45. [248]

Schlosberg, H. (1937). The relationship between success and the laws of conditioning. *Psychological Review*, **44**, 379–394. [193, 198]

Schoenfeld, W. N. (1950). An experimental approach to anxiety, escape and avoidance behavior. In P. H. Hoch (Ed.), *Anxiety*. New York: Grune & Stratton. [107]

Schoenfeld, W. N. (1966). Some old work for modern conditioning theory. *Conditional Reflex*, **1**, 219–223. [55]

Schoenfeld, W. N. (1969). "Avoidance" in behavior theory. *Journal of the Experimental Analysis of Behavior*, **12**, 669–674. [107]

Schoenfeld, W. N., & Cole, B. K. (1972). *Stimulus schedules: the t-τ systems*. New York: Harper & Row. [158, 170]

Schoenfeld, W. N., Cumming, W. W., & Hearst, E. (1956). On the classification of reinforcement schedules. *Proceedings of the National Academy of Sciences*, **42**, 563–570. [170]

Schoenfeld, W. N., Harris, A. H., & Farmer, J. (1966). Conditioning response variability. *Psychological Reports*, **19**, 551–557. [127]

Schooler, J. W., & Engstler-Schooler, T. Y. (1990). Verbal overshadowing of visual memories: some things are better left unsaid. *Cognitive Psychology*, **22**, 36–71. [250]

Schroeder, S. R., & Holland, J. G. (1968). Operant control of eye movements. *Journal of Applied Behavior Analysis*, **1**, 161–166. [89]

Schusterman, R. J. (1989). Please parse the sentence: Animal cognition in the procrustean bed of linguistics. *Psychological Record*, **39**, 3–18. [255]

Schwartz, B. (1974). On going back to nature: a review of Seligman and Hager's *Biological boundaries of learning*. *Journal of the Experimental Analysis of Behavior*, **21**, 183–198. [210]

Schwartz, B. (1980). Development of complex, stereotyped behavior in pigeons. *Journal of the Experimental Analysis of Behavior*, **33**, 153–166. [122]

Schwartz, B. (1982). Reinforcement-induced stereotypy: how not to teach people to discover rules. *Journal of Experimental Psychology: General*, **111**, 23–59. [250]

Schwartz, B., & Gamzu, E. (1977). Pavlovian control of operant behavior. In W. K. Honig & J. E. R. Staddon (Eds.), *Handbook of operant behavior*. Englewood Cliffs, NJ: Prentice-Hall. [200]

Schwartz, B., Hamilton, B., & Silberberg, A. (1975). Behavioral contrast in the pigeon: a study of the duration of key pecking maintained on multiple schedules of reinforcement. *Journal of the Experimental Analysis of Behavior*, **24**, 199–206. [174]

Schwartz, B., & Williams, D. R. (1972). Two different kinds of key peck in the pigeon: some properties of responses maintained by negative and positive response-reinforcer contingencies. *Journal of the Experimental Analysis of Behavior*, **18**, 201–216. [201]

Sebeok, T. A., & Rosenthal, R. (Eds.). (1981). *The Clever Hans phenomenon: communication with horses, whales, apes, and people*. New York: New York Academy of Sciences. [254]

Sechenov, I. M. (1863). *Reflexes of the brain* (trans. S. Belsky). Reprinted Cambridge, MA: The MIT Press, 1965. [44, 55, 57]

Segal, E. F. (1972). Induction and the provenance of operants. In R. M. Gilbert & J. R. Millenson (Eds.), *Reinforcement: Behavioral analyses*. New York: Academic Press. [55]

Segal, E. F. (1975). Psycholinguistics discovers the operant: a review of Roger Brown's *A first language: the early stages*. *Journal of the Experimental Analysis of Behavior*, **23**, 149–158. [276]

Seligman, M. E. P. (1970). On the generality of the laws of learning. *Psychological Review*, **77**, 406–418. [105, 210]

Seyfarth, R. M., Cheney, D. L., & Marler, P. (1980). Monkey responses to three different alarm calls: evidence for predator classification and semantic communication. *Science*, **210**, 801–803. [215]

Shaffer, W. O., & LaBerge, D. (1979). Automatic semantic processing of unattended words. *Journal of Verbal Learning and Verbal Behavior*, **18**, 413–426. [232]

Shahn, B. B. (1972). *Ben Shahn.* New York: Abrams. [231]

Sheffield, F. D. (1965). Relation between classical conditioning and instrumental learning. In W. F. Prokasy (Ed.), *Classical conditioning.* New York: Appleton-Century-Crofts. [110, 199]

Shepard, R. N. (1967). Recognition memory for words, sentences, and pictures. *Journal of Verbal Learning and Verbal Behavior,* **6**, 156–163. [293]

Shepard, R. N., & Metzler, J. (1971). Mental rotation of three-dimensional objects. *Science,* **171**, 701–703. [333, 334]

Sherrington, C. (1906). *The integrative action of the nervous system.* New York: Scribner's. [42]

Shettleworth, S. J. (1978). Reinforcement and the organization of behavior in golden hamsters: punishment of three action patterns. *Learning and Motivation,* **9**, 99–123. [97]

Shiffrin, R. M., & Atkinson, R. C. (1969). Storage and retrieval processes in long-term memory. *Psychological Review,* **76**, 179–193. [319]

Shimoff, E., Catania, A. C., & Matthews, B. A. (1981). Uninstructed human responding: sensitivity of low-rate performance to schedule contingencies. *Journal of the Experimental Analysis of Behavior,* **36**, 207–220. [249]

Shimp, C. P. (1966). Probabilistically reinforced choice behavior in pigeons. *Journal of the Experimental Analysis of Behavior,* **9**, 443–455. [178]

Shimp, C. P. (1976). Organization in memory and behavior. *Journal of the Experimental Analysis of Behavior,* **26**, 113–130. [170, 326]

Shimp, C. P. (1982). On metaknowledge in the pigeon: an organism's knowledge about its own behavior. *Animal Learning and Behavior,* **10**, 358–364. [219]

Shimp, C. P., Sabulsky, S. L., & Childers, L. J. (1989). Preference for starting and finishing behavior patterns. *Journal of the Experimental Analysis of Behavior,* **52**, 341–352. [144, 219]

Sidman, M. (1952). A note on functional relations obtained from group data. *Psychological Bulletin,* **49**, 263–269. [65]

Sidman, M. (1953). Two temporal parameters in the maintenance of avoidance behavior by the white rat. *Journal of Comparative and Physiological Psychology,* **46**, 253–261. [104, 105]

Sidman, M. (1960). *Tactics of scientific research.* New York: Basic Books. [84, 85]

Sidman, M. (1971). The behavioral analysis of aphasia. *Journal of Psychiatric Research,* **8**, 413–422. [234]

Sidman, M., & Cresson, O., Jr. (1973). Reading and crossmodal transfer of stimulus equivalences in severe retardation. *American Journal of Mental Deficiency,* **77**, 515–523. [154]

Sidman, M., Cresson, O., Jr., & Willson-Morris, M. (1974). Acquisition of matching to sample via mediated transfer. *Journal of the Experimental Analysis of Behavior,* **22**, 261–273. [154]

Sidman, M., Herrnstein, R. J., & Conrad, D. G. (1957). Maintenance of avoidance behavior by unavoidable shocks. *Journal of Comparative and Physiological Psychology,* **50**, 553–557. [204]

Sidman, M., Rauzin, R., Lazar, R., Cunningham, S., Tailby, W., & Carrigan, P. (1982). A search for symmetry in the conditional discrimination of rhesus monkeys, baboon, and children. *Journal of the Experimental Analysis of Behavior,* **37**, 23–44. [152]

Sidman, M., & Rosenberger, P. B. (1967). Several methods of teaching serial position sequences to monkeys. *Journal of the Experimental Analysis of Behavior,* **10**, 467–468. [141]

Sidman, M., & Stoddard, L. T. (1967). The effectiveness of fading in programming a simultaneous form discrimination for retarded children. *Journal of the Experimental Analysis of Behavior,* **10**, 3–15. [141]

Sidman, M., & Tailby, W. (1982). Conditioned discrimination versus matching to sample: an expansion of the testing paradigm. *Journal of the Experimental Analysis of Behavior,* **37**, 5–22. [152]

Sidman, M., Wynne, C. K., Maguire, R. W., & Barnes, T. (1989). Functional classes and equivalence relations. *Journal of the Experimental Analysis of Behavior,* **52**, 261–274. [155]

Siegel, S. (1975). Evidence from rats that morphine tolerance is a learned response. *Journal of Comparative and Physiological Psychology,* **89**, 498–506. [189]

Siegel, S. (1977). Morphine tolerance acquisition as an associative process. *Journal of Ex-*

perimental Psychology: Animal Behavior Processes, **3**, 1–13. [189]

Siegel, S., Hinson, R. E., Krank, M. D., & McCully, J. (1982). Heroin "overdose" death: the contribution of drug-associated environmental cues. *Science*, **216**, 436–437. [190]

Silberberg, A., Hamilton, B., Ziriax, J. M., & Casey, J. (1978). The structure of choice. *Journal of Experimental Psychology: Animal Behavior Processes*, **4**, 368–398. [178]

Silverman, P. J. (1971). Chained and tandem fixed-interval schedules of punishment. *Journal of the Experimental Analysis of Behavior*, **16**, 1–13. [176]

Simpson, G. G. (1951). *Horses*. New York: Oxford University Press. [34]

Sizemore, O. J., & Lattal, K. A. (1977). Dependency, temporal contiguity, and response-independent reinforcement. *Journal of the Experimental Analysis of Behavior*, **27**, 119–125. [166]

Skinner, B. F. (1930). On the conditions for elicitation of certain eating reflexes. *Proceedings of the National Academy of Sciences*, **16**, 433–438. [66, 352]

Skinner, B. F. (1931). The concept of the reflex in the description of behavior. *Journal of General Psychology*, **5**, 427–458. [11, 42]

Skinner, B. F. (1933). The rate of establishment of a discrimination. *Journal of General Psychology*, **9**, 302–350. [23]

Skinner, B. F. (1934). The extinction of chained reflexes. *Proceedings of the National Academy of Sciences*, **20**, 234–237. [124]

Skinner, B. F. (1935a). The generic nature of the concepts of stimulus and response. *Journal of General Psychology*, **12**, 40–65. [114]

Skinner, B. F. (1935b). Two types of conditioned reflex and a pseudotype. *Journal of General Psychology*, **12**, 66–77. [193, 198]

Skinner, B. F. (1938). *The behavior of organisms*. New York: Appleton-Century-Crofts. [24, 43, 66, 75, 185, 352]

Skinner, B. F. (1945). The operational analysis of psychological terms. *Psychological Review*, **52**, 270–277. [241, 277, 332]

Skinner, B. F. (1948). "Superstition" in the pigeon. *Journal of Experimental Psychology*, **38**, 168–172. [54, 79]

Skinner, B. F. (1950). Are theories of learning necessary? *Psychological Review*, **57**, 193–216. [66, 150]

Skinner, B. F. (1953). *Science and human behavior*. New York: Macmillan. [26, 111, 184, 332, 333]

Skinner, B. F. (1956). A case history in scientific method. *American Psychologist*, **11**, 221–233. [66, 185]

Skinner, B. F. (1957). *Verbal behavior*. New York: Appleton-Century-Crofts. [228, 234, 235, 236, 243, 254, 326]

Skinner, B. F. (1959). John Broadus Watson, behaviorist. *Science*, **129**, 197–198. [334]

Skinner, B. F. (1963). Behaviorism at fifty. *Science*, **140**, 951–958. [241, 308]

Skinner, B. F. (1966). The phylogeny and ontogeny of behavior. *Science*, **153**, 1204–1213. [39, 358]

Skinner, B. F. (1969). An operant analysis of problem solving. In B. F. Skinner, *Contingencies of reinforcement* (pp. 133–157). New York: Appleton-Century-Crofts. [248, 348]

Skinner, B. F. (1972). A lecture on "having" a poem. In B. F. Skinner, *Cumulative record* (3rd ed.). New York: Appleton-Century-Crofts. [231]

Skinner, B. F. (1975). The shaping of phylogenic behavior. *Journal of the Experimental Analysis of Behavior*, **24**, 117–120. [146, 358]

Skinner, B. F. (1976). *Particulars of my life*. New York: Alfred A. Knopf. [308]

Skinner, B. F. (1977). Herrnstein and the evolution of behaviorism. *American Psychologist*, **32**, 1006–1012. [209]

Skinner, B. F. (1981). Selection by consequences. *Science*, **213**, 501–504. [38, 213, 256, 358]

Skinner, B. F. (1983). Intellectual self-management in old age. *American Psychologist*, **38**, 239–244. [329]

Skinner, B. F. (1984). The evolution of behavior. *Journal of the Experimental Analysis of Behavior*, **41**, 217–221. [37]

Skinner, B. F. (1988). Replies to commentators. In A. C. Catania & S. Harnad (Eds.), *The selection of behavior*. New York: Cambridge University Press. [35, 342, 358]

Skinner, B. F. (1989). The origins of cognitive thought. *American Psychologist*, **44**, 13–18. [240, 273]

Small, W. S. (1899–1900). Experimental studies of the mental processes of the rat. *American Journal of Psychology*, **11**, 1–89. [64, 352]

Smith, B. H. (1968). *Poetic closure.* Chicago: Chicago University Press. [231]

Smith, J. B. (1974). Effects of response rate, reinforcement frequency, and the duration of a stimulus preceding response-independent food. *Journal of the Experimental Analysis of Behavior, 21,* 215–221. [206]

Smith, K. (1954). Conditioning as an artifact. *Psychological Review, 61,* 217–225. [193, 199]

Smith, L. D. (1986). *Behaviorism and logical positivism.* Stanford, CA: Stanford University Press. [352]

Smith, T. L. (1986). Biology as allegory: a review of Elliott Sober's *The nature of selection. Journal of the Experimental Analysis of Behavior, 46,* 105–112. [38]

Smith, W. G. (1895). The relation of attention to memory. *Mind, 4,* 47–73. [318]

Snapper, A. G., Kadden, R. M., & Inglis, G. B. (1982). State notation of behavioral procedures. *Behavior Research Methods and Instrumentation, 14,* 329–342. [170]

Solomon, R. L., & Corbit, J. D. (1974). An opponent-process theory of motivation: I. Temporal dynamics of affect. *Psychological Review, 81,* 119–145. [50, 59]

Solomon, R. L., & Turner, L. H. (1962). Discriminative classical conditioning in dogs paralyzed by curare can later control discriminative avoidance responses in the normal state. *Psychological Review, 69,* 202–219. [199]

Spalding, D. (1873/1954). Instinct with original observations on young animals. *Macmillan's Magazine, 27,* 282–293. Reprinted in *British Journal of Animal Behaviour, 2,* 2–11. [39]

Spence, K. W. (1937). The differential response in animals to stimuli varying within a single dimension. *Psychological Review, 44,* 430–444. [139, 300]

Spence, K. W., & Ross, L. E. (1959). A methodological study of the form and latency of eyelid responses in conditioning. *Journal of Experimental Psychology, 58,* 376–381. [46]

Sperling, G. (1960). The information available in brief visual presentations. *Psychological Monographs, 74,* (11, Whole No. 498). [316, 317]

Sperling, G., & Reeves, A. (1980). Measuring the reaction time of a shift of visual attention. In R. S. Nickerson (Ed.), *Attention and performance VIII.* Hillsdale, NJ: Erlbaum. [333]

Spetch, M. L., Wilkie, D. M., & Pinel, J. P. J. (1981). Backward conditioning: a reevaluation of the empirical evidence. *Psychological Bulletin, 89,* 163–175. [192]

Staddon, J. E. R. (1965). Some properties of spaced responding in pigeons. *Journal of the Experimental Analysis of Behavior, 8,* 19–27. [121]

Staddon, J. E. R., & Simmelhag, V. L. (1971). The "Superstition" experiment: a reexamination of its implications for the principle of adaptive behavior. *Psychological Review, 78,* 3–43. [53, 54, 79, 358]

Stein, L., Sidman, M., & Brady, J. V. (1958). Some effects of two temporal variables on conditioned suppression. *Journal of the Experimental Analysis of Behavior, 1,* 153–162. [206]

Sternberg, S. (1966). High-speed scanning in human memory. *Science, 153,* 652–654. [337, 339]

Sternberg, S. (1969). Memory-scanning: mental processes revealed by reaction time experiments. *American Scientist, 57,* 421–457. [337, 338, 339]

Stewart, G. R. (1975). *Names on the land.* New York: Oxford University Press. [240]

Stigler, S. M. (1978). Some forgotten work on memory. *Journal of Experimental Psychology: Human Learning and Memory, 4,* 1–4. [283]

Stokes, P. D., & Balsam, P. D. (1991). Effects of reinforcing preselected approximations on the topography of the rat's bar press. *Journal of the Experimental Analysis of Behavior, 55,* 213–231. [79]

Stratton, G. M. (1897). Vision without inversion of the retinal image. *Psychological Review, 4,* 341–360, 463–481. [88]

Stratton, G. M. (1917). *Theophrastus and the Greek physiological psychology before Aristotle.* New York: Macmillan. [308]

Straub, R. O., Seidenberg, M. S., Bever, T. G., & Terrace, H. S. (1979). Serial learning in the pigeon. *Journal of the Experimental Analysis of Behavior, 32,* 137–148. [124]

Straub, R. O., & Terrace, H. S. (1981). Generalization of serial learning in the pigeon. *Animal Learning and Behavior, 9,* 454–468. [124]

Stroop, J. R. (1935). Studies of interference in serial verbal reactions. *Journal of Experimental Psychology, 18,* 643–662. [253, 309]

Svartdal, F. (1989). Shaping of rule-governed behaviour. *Scandinavian Journal of Psychology*, 30, 304–314. [251]

Terhune, J. G. (1978). The relationship between momentary response probabilities and momentary reinforcement effects. *Animal Learning and Behavior*, 6, 187–192. [83]

Terrace, H. S. (1963a). Discrimination learning with and without "errors." *Journal of the Experimental Analysis of Behavior*, 6, 1–27. [141]

Terrace, H. S. (1963b). Errorless transfer of a discrimination across two continua. *Journal of the Experimental Analysis of Behavior*, 6, 223–232. [141]

Terrace, H. S. (1966). Stimulus control. In W. K. Honig (Ed.), *Operant behavior: Areas of research and application*. New York: Appleton-Century-Crofts. [173]

Terrace, H. S. (1975). Evidence of the innate basis of the hue dimension in the duckling. *Journal of the Experimental Analysis of Behavior*, 24, 79–87. [140]

Terrace, H. S., & Chen, S. (1991). Chunking during serial learning by a pigeon: III. What are the necessary conditions for establishing a chunk? *Journal of Experimental Psychology: Animal Behavior Processes*, 17, 107–118. [144]

Terrace, H. S., Petitto, L. A., Sanders, R. J., & Bever, T. G. (1979). Can an ape create a sentence? *Science*, 206, 891–902. [255]

Thelen, E., & Fisher, D. M. (1983). From spontaneous to instrumental behavior: kinematic analysis of movement changes during very early learning. *Child Development*, 54, 429–440. [208]

Thelen, E., Fisher, D. M., Ridley-Johnson, R., & Griffin, N. J. (1982). Effects of body build and arousal on newborn infant stepping. *Developmental Psychology*, 15, 447–453. [57]

Thistlethwaite, D. (1951). A critical review of latent learning and related experiments. *Psychological Bulletin*, 48, 97–129. [85]

Thomas, J. C., Jr. (1974). An analysis of behavior in the hobbits-orcs problem. *Cognitive Psychology*, 6, 257–269 [343, 344]

Thompson, C. R., & Church, R. M. (1980). An explanation of the language of a chimpanzee. *Science*, 208, 313–314. [255]

Thorndike, E. L. (1898). Animal intelligence: an experimental study of the associative processes in animals. *Psychological Review Monograph Supplements*, 2 (No. 4). [20, 63, 352]

Thorndike, E. L. (1921). *Educational psychology. Vol. II. The psychology of learning*. New York: Teachers College. [55, 352]

Thorndike, E. L., & Woodworth, R. S. (1901). The influence of improvement in one mental function upon the efficiency of other functions. *Psychological Review*, 8, 247–261. [295, 353]

Timberlake, W. (1980). A molar equilibrium theory of learned performance. In G. H. Bower (Ed.), *The psychology of learning and motivation. Vol. 14*. New York: Academic Press. [83]

Tinbergen, N. (1960). *The Herring Gull's world* (rev. ed.). New York: Basic Books. [18]

Tinbergen, N. (1972). *The animal in its world. Vol. 1. Field studies*. Cambridge, MA: Harvard University Press. [38, 145]

Tinbergen, N., & Perdeck, A. C. (1950). On the stimulus situation releasing the begging response in the newly hatched Herring Gull chick (*Larus a. argentatus Pontopp*). *Behavior*, 3, 1–38. [18]

Titchener, E. B. (1898). The postulates of a structural psychology. *Philosophical Review*, 7, 449–465. [228, 354]

Tolman, E. C. (1948). Cognitive maps in rats and men. *Psychological Review*, 55, 189–208. [85, 145, 352]

Tolman, E. C., & Honzik, C. H. (1930). Introduction and removal of reward, and maze performance in rats. *University of California Publications in Psychology*, 4, 257–275. [85]

Touchette, P. E. (1969). Tilted lines as complex stimuli. *Journal of the Experimental Analysis of Behavior*, 12, 211–214. [141]

Townsend, J. T. (1971). A note on the identifiability of parallel and serial processes. *Perception and Psychophysics*, 10, 161–163. [340]

Tracey, W. K. (1970). Wavelength generalization and preference in monochromatically reared ducklings. *Journal of the Experimental Analysis of Behavior*, 13, 163–178. [139]

Trehub, S. E., & Chang, H.-W. (1977). Speech as reinforcing stimulation for infants. *Developmental Psychology*, 13, 170–171. [230]

Truax, C. B. (1966). Reinforcement and nonreinforcement in Rogerian therapy. *Journal of Abnormal Psychology*, 71, 1–9. [252]

Tulving, E. (1962). Subjective organization in free recall of "unrelated" words. *Psychological Review*, 69, 344–354. [291]

Tulving, E. (1969). Retrograde amnesia in free recall. *Science,* **164,** 88–90. [289]

Tulving, E. (1972). Episodic and semantic memory. In E. Tulving & W. Donaldson (Eds.), *Organization of memory.* New York: Academic Press. [326]

Tulving, E. (1974). Cue-dependent forgetting. *American Scientist,* **62,** 74–82. [294, 314]

Tulving, E. (1985). How many memory systems are there? *American Psychologist,* **40,** 385–398. [325, 327]

Tulving, E. (1989). Remembering and knowing the past. *American Scientist,* **77,** 361–367. [326]

Tulving, E., & Madigan, S. A. (1970). Memory and verbal learning. *Annual Review of Psychology,* **21,** 437–484. [279, 313, 322]

Tulving, E., & Pearlstone, Z. (1966). Availability versus accessibility of information in memory for words. *Journal of Verbal Learning and Verbal Behavior,* **5,** 381–391. [313]

Tulving, E., & Psotka, J. (1971). Retroactive inhibition in free recall: inaccessibility of information available in the memory store. *Journal of Experimental Psychology,* **87,** 1–8. [313, 314]

Turkkan, J. S., & Harris, A. H. (1981). Shaping blood pressure elevations: an examination of acquisition. *Behaviour Analysis Letters,* **1,** 97–106. [115]

Tversky, A., & Kahneman, D. (1981). The framing of decisions and the psychology of choice. *Science,* **211,** 453–458. [347]

Tversky, A., & Kahneman, D. (1983). Extensional versus intuitive reasoning: the conjunction fallacy in probability judgment. *Psychological Review,* **90,** 293–315. [347]

Twitmyer, E. B. (1974). A study of the knee jerk (1902). *Journal of Experimental Psychology,* **103,** 1047–1066. [189]

Underwood, B. J. (1957). Interference and forgetting. *Psychological Review,* **64,** 49–60. [324]

Underwood, B. J. (1961). Ten years of massed practice on distributed practice. *Psychological Review,* **68,** 229–247. [283]

Underwood, B. J. (1964). Degree of learning and measurement of forgetting. *Journal of Verbal Learning and Verbal Behavior,* **3,** 112–129. [323]

Underwood, B. J., & Freund, J. S. (1968). Errors in recognition learning and retention. *Journal of Experimental Psychology,* **78,** 55–63. [294]

Underwood, B. J., & Postman, L. (1960). Extraexperimental sources of interference in forgetting. *Psychological Review,* **67,** 73–95. [324]

Underwood, B. J., Rehula, R., & Keppel, G. (1962). Item-selection in paired-associate learning. *American Journal of Psychology,* **75,** 353–371. [287]

Underwood, B. J., & Schulz, R. W. (1960). *Meaningfulness and verbal learning.* Philadelphia: Lippincott. [284, 286]

Urcuioli, P. J., & Honig, W. K. (1980). Control of choice in conditional discriminations by sample-specific behaviors. *Journal of Experimental Psychology: Animal Behavior Processes,* **6,** 251–277. [152]

Urcuioli, P., Mandell, C., & Nevin, J. A. (1976). Fixed-interval punishment of running in hamsters. *Learning and Motivation,* **7,** 290–295. [94]

Urcuioli, P. J., & Zentall, T. R. (1986). Retrospective coding in pigeons' delayed matching-to-sample. *Journal of Experimental Psychology: Animal Behavior Processes,* **12,** 69–77. [327]

Urcuioli, P. J., Zentall, T. R., Jackson-Smith, P., & Steirn, J. N. (1989). Evidence for common coding in many-to-one matching: retention, intertrial interference, and transfer. *Journal of Experimental Psychology: Animal Behavior Processes,* **15,** 264–273. [152]

Vaughan, W., Jr. (1988). Formation of equivalence sets in pigeons. *Journal of Experimental Psychology: Animal Behavior Processes,* **14,** 36–42. [155]

Verhave, T. (1967). Contributions to the history of psychology: IV. Joseph Buchanan (1785–1829) and the "law of exercise" (1812). *Psychological Reports,* **20,** 127–133. [55]

Vesonder, G. T., & Voss, J. F. (1985). On the ability to predict one's own responses while learning. *Journal of Memory and Language,* **24,** 363–376. [218]

Von Frisch, K. (1953). *The dancing bees.* New York: Harcourt, Brace. [145]

Von Holst, E. (1939). Die relative Koordination als Phänomen und als Methode zentralnervöser Funktionanalyse. Translated in von Holst, E. (1973) *The behavioural physiology of animals and man. Selected papers.* Coral Gables, FL: University of Miami Press. [40, 208]

Von Restorff, H. (1933). Über die Wirkung von Bereichsbildungen im Spurenfeld. *Psychologische Forschung, 18,* 299–342. [289]

Wagner, A. R., Thomas, E., & Norton, T. (1967). Conditioning with electrical stimulation of motor cortex: evidence of a possible source of motivation. *Journal of Comparative and Physiological Psychology, 64,* 191–199. [198]

Wagner, K. R. (1985). How much do children say in a day? *Journal of Child Language, 12,* 475–487. [276]

Wahler, R. G. (1975). Some structural aspects of deviant child behavior. *Journal of Applied Behavior Analysis, 8,* 27–42. [126]

Walcott, C., Gould, J. L., & Kirschvink, J. L. (1979). Pigeons have magnets. *Science, 205,* 1027–1029. [145]

Wales, R. (1986). Deixis. In P. Fletcher, & M. Garman, (Eds.), *Language acquisition* (2nd ed.). New York: Cambridge University Press. (pp. 401–428). [277]

Walters, G. C., & Glazer, R. D. (1971). Punishment of instinctive behavior in the Mongolian gerbil. *Journal of Comparative and Physiological Psychology, 75,* 331–340. [97]

Wanchisen, B. A., Tatham, T. A., & Hineline, P. N. (1988). Pigeons' choices in situations of diminishing returns: fixed- versus progressive-ratio schedules. *Journal of the Experimental Analysis of Behavior, 50,* 375–394. [249]

Wang, M. D. (1977). Frequency effects in the abstraction of linguistic ideas. *Bulletin of the Psychonomic Society, 9,* 303–306. [270]

Ward, T. B. (1980). Separable and integral responding by children and adults to the dimensions of length and density. *Child Development, 51,* 676–684. [342]

Washburn, D. A., Hopkins, W. D., & Rumbaugh, D. M. (1991). Perceived control in rhesus monkeys (*macaca mulatta*): enhanced video-task performance. *Journal of Experimental Psychology: Animal Behavior Processes, 17,* 123–129. [144]

Wasserman, E., Franklin, S., & Hearst, E. (1974). Pavlovian appetitive contingencies and approach vs. withdrawal to conditioned stimuli in pigeons. *Journal of Comparative and Physiological Psychology, 86,* 616–627. [201]

Watkins, M. J. (1981). Human memory and the information-processing metaphor. *Cognition, 10,* 331–336. [357]

Watkins, M. J. (1989). Willful and nonwillful determinants of memory. In H. L. Roediger, III, & F. I. M. Craik (Eds.), *Varieties of memory and consciousness.* Hillsdale, NJ: Erlbaum. [311]

Watkins, M. J. (1990). Mediationism and the obfuscation of memory. *American Psychologist, 45,* 328–335. [308, 313]

Watkins, M. J., & Tulving, E. (1975). Episodic memory: when recognition fails. *Journal of Experimental Psychology: General, 104,* 5–29. [294]

Watson, J. B. (1919). *Psychology from the standpoint of a behaviorist.* Philadelphia: Lippincott. [42, 352]

Watson, J. B., & Rayner, R. (1920). Conditioned emotional reactions. *Journal of Experimental Psychology, 3,* 1–14. [197, 198]

Waugh, N. C. (1972). Retention as an active process. *Journal of Verbal Learning and Verbal Behavior, 11,* 129–140. [328]

Waugh, N. C., & Norman, D. A. (1965). Primary memory. *Psychological Review, 72,* 89–104. [318, 321]

Weiss, B., & Laties, V. G. (1961). Behavioral thermoregulation. *Science, 133,* 1338–1344. [103]

Weiss, B., & Laties, V. G. (1969). Behavioral pharmacology and toxicology. *Annual Review of Pharmacology, 9,* 297–326. [173]

Wellman, H. M., & Johnson, C. N. (1979). Understanding of mental processes: a developmental study of "remember" and "forget." *Child Development, 50,* 79–88. [277]

Werker, J. F. (1989). Becoming a native listener. *American Scientist, 77,* 54–59. [230]

Wertheimer, M. (1959). *Productive thinking.* New York: Harper & Row. [346]

West, M. J., & King, A. P. (1980). Enriching cowbird song by social deprivation. *Journal of Comparative and Physiological Psychology, 94,* 263–270. [254]

Wetherington, C. L. (1982). Is adjunctive behavior a third class of behavior? *Neuroscience and Biobehavioral Reviews, 6,* 329–350. [52]

Whitehurst, G. J., & Valdez-Menchaca, M. C. (1988). What is the role of reinforcement in early language acquisition? *Child Development, 59,* 430–440. [276]

Whorf, B. L. (1956). *Language, thought, and reality.* Cambridge, MA: The MIT Press. [240, 275]

Wickelgren, W. A. (1969). Context-sensitive coding, associative memory, and serial order in (speech) behavior. *Psychological Review*, **76**, 1–15. [292]

Wickens, D. D. (1970). Encoding categories of words: an empirical approach to meaning. *Psychological Review*, **77**, 1–15. [321]

Wildemann, D. G., & Holland, J. G. (1972). Control of a continuous response dimension by a continuous stimulus dimension. *Journal of the Experimental Analysis of Behavior*, **18**, 419–434. [217]

Williams, B. A. (1976). The effects of unsignalled delayed reinforcement. *Journal of the Experimental Analysis of Behavior*, **26**, 441–449. [166]

Williams, D. R., & Williams, H. (1969). Automaintenance in the pigeon: sustained pecking despite contingent non-reinforcement. *Journal of the Experimental Analysis of Behavior*, **12**, 511–520. [200]

Wilson, D. M. (1959). Long-term facilitation in a swimming sea anemone. *Journal of Experimental Biology*, **36**, 526–531. [50]

Wilson, T. D., & Lassiter, G. D. (1982). Increasing intrinsic interest with superfluous extrinsic constraints. *Journal of Personality and Social Psychology*, **42**, 811–819. [250]

Winner, E. (1979). New names for old things: the emergence of metaphoric language. *Journal of Child Language*, **6**, 469–491. [273]

Winograd, T. (1980). What does it mean to understand language? *Cognitive Science*, **4**, 209–241. [258, 343]

Wixted, J. T. (1989). The vocabulary of remembering. A review of Kendrick, Rilling, and Denny's Theories of animal memory. *Journal of the Experimental Analysis of Behavior*, **52**, 441–450. [327]

Wollen, K. A., Weber, A., & Lowry, D. (1972). Bizarreness versus interaction of mental images as determinants of learning. *Cognitive Psychology*, **3**, 518–523. [305]

Woodruff, G., Premack, D., & Kennel, K. (1978). Conservation of liquid and solid quantity by the chimpanzee. *Science*, **202**, 991–994. [341]

Woodward, A., Jr., & Murdock, B. B., Jr. (1968). Positional and sequential probes in serial learning. *Canadian Journal of Psychology*, **22**, 131–138. [284]

Woodworth, R. S. (1921). *Psychology* (rev. ed.). New York: Holt. [302, 332]

Woodworth, R. S. (1938). *Experimental Psychology*. New York: Holt. [296]

Wright, A. A., Cook, R. G., Rivera, J. J., Shyan, M. R., Neiworth, J. J., & Jitsumori, M. (1990). Naming, rehearsal, and interstimulus interval effects in memory processing. *Journal of Experimental Psychology: Learning, Memory, and Cognition*, **16**, 1043–1059. [310]

Wundt, W. (1900). *Die Sprache*. Leipzig: Engelmann. [260]

Yates, F. A. (1966). *The art of memory*. Chicago: University of Chicago Press. [305]

Yates, F. E. (1986). *Self-organizing systems*. New York: Plenum. [358]

Yerkes, R. M. (1907). *The dancing mouse*. New York: Macmillan. [352]

Yerkes, R. M., & Watson, J. B. (1911). Methods of studying vision in animals. *Behavior Monographs*, **1** (no. 2). [24]

Young, F. A. (1958). Studies of pupillary conditioning. *Journal of Experimental Psychology*, **55**, 97–110. [189]

Zangwill, O. L. (1972). Remembering revisited. *Quarterly Journal of Experimental Psychology*, **24**, 123–138. [304]

Zeigarnik, B. (1927). Das Behalten erledigter und unerledigter Handlungen. *Psychologische Forschung*, **9**, 1–85. [329]

Zelazo, P. R., Zelazo, N. A., & Kolb, S. (1972). "Walking" in the newborn. *Science*, **176**, 314–315. [57]

Zener, K., & McCurdy, H. G. (1939). Analysis of motivation factors in conditioned behavior: I. Differential effect of change in hunger upon conditioned, unconditioned and spontaneous salivary secretion. *Journal of Psychology*, **8**, 321–350. [56, 115]

Zentall, T. R., & Galef, B. G., Jr. (1988). *Social learning*. Hillsdale, NJ: Erlbaum. [215]

Zentall, T. R., & Levine, J. M. (1972). Observational learning and social facilitation in the rat. *Science*, **178**, 1220–1221. [215]

Zettle, R. D., & Hayes, S. C. (1982). Rule-governed behavior: a potential theoretical framework for cognitive-behavioral therapy. *Advances in cognitive-behavioral research and therapy. Vol. I*. New York: Academic Press. [248]

Zimmerman, J., Hanford, P. H., & Brown, W. (1967). Effects of conditioned reinforcement frequency in an intermittent free-feeding situation. *Journal of the Experimental Analysis of Behavior*, **10**, 331–340. [176]

Zuriff, G. E. (1970). A comparison of variable-ratio and variable-interval schedules of reinforcement. *Journal of the Experimental Analysis of Behavior*, **13**, 369–374. [163]

Index